Ashish Choudhury · Arpita Patra

Fault-Tolerant Distributed Consensus in Synchronous Networks

Springer

Ashish Choudhury
Electronics City Phase 1
International Institute of Information Technology
Bengaluru, Karnataka, India

Arpita Patra
Indian Institute of Science
Bengaluru, Karnataka, India

ISSN 1619-7100 ISSN 2197-845X (electronic)
Information Security and Cryptography
ISBN 978-3-031-80459-5 ISBN 978-3-031-80460-1 (eBook)
https://doi.org/10.1007/978-3-031-80460-1

This Springer imprint is published by the registered company Springer Nature Switzerland AG
The registered company address is: Gewerbestrasse 11, 6330 Cham, Switzerland

Information Security and Cryptography

Information Security – protecting information in potentially hostile environments – is a crucial factor in the growth of information-based processes in industry, business, and administration. Cryptography is a key technology for achieving information security in communications, computer systems, electronic commerce, and in the emerging information society.

Springer's Information Security & Cryptography (IS&C) book series covers all relevant topics, ranging from theory to advanced applications. The intended audience includes students, researchers and practitioners.

Foreword

Not long ago, the term computer referred to a human who carried out calculations, and the term computing conjured up an image of a massive number-crunching act. The "digital" computers have changed all this in several unexpected ways and on an unimaginable scale in the past six to seven decades. Over the years, the notion of computing has gradually become more and more sophisticated progressing through the notions of data processing, information processing, knowledge processing and currently at an exciting phase covering computational intelligence and machine learning. The evolution of computing from simple sequential computing via various paradigms such as parallel computing, VLSI computing, real-time computing, secure computing, dependable computing, cloud computing and quantum computing is mind-boggling. All along this progression, the rapid growth in technologies and the convergence of communication and computational technologies resulted in one of the finest intellectual human creations of the modern age — distributed computing.

While evolving technologies strongly drive distributed computing, it has its own set of intellectually challenging and philosophically profound "holy grail" questions and problems. Distributed computing is carried out in a variety of network-based environments. Fault tolerance and security are among the core concerns in distributed computing. This is because some of the components of a distributed system may fail arbitrarily, and some of the system participants may behave arbitrarily. Thus, the major challenge is to design distributed algorithms that work correctly even in the presence of faults and adversaries in the system. One can easily imagine the massive chaos resulting in a network-based environment when faults disrupt communication and adversaries corrupt the communicated information. This is the primary reason why the most important holy grail problem of distributed computing is centred around the notion of consensus.

At some point in this exciting progression, Ashish and Arpita joined the research community and, in a short period, significantly impacted secure distributed computing. Their stellar research at IIT Madras, India and an aggressive continuation in their academic careers at IIIT and IISc Bangalore, India, have sown the seed for this monogram. It all started with their curiosity about finding the right analogue in distributed algorithms to the philosophically deep fundamental question in sequential computing. The "holy grail" question in sequential computing is what can be computed and, if so, how well it can be computed. The search for the analogue in distributed computing is significantly non-trivial because the notion of computing itself has various parameters or dimensions associated with it. Consider questions such as: can it be computed correctly when the current system has over 33% of malicious participants? Can it be computed correctly when 25% of the components are malfunctioning? These kinds of questions show the various forms the core question takes in the context of distributed computing in a network-based environment. Thus, the computability and related algorithmic questions arise in various forms. It is imperative that we first identify the various parameters or "dimensions" that would define the space of distributed computing. This taxonomy is fundamental to obtaining precise and formal descriptions of the problems and framing the fundamental questions in distributed computing.

Arpita and Ashish successfully introduced and formally described parameters that would specify the taxonomy in a complete and comprehensive manner. This taxonomy allows us to treat the entire problem domain in a unified manner. Various results obtained at various times and under different assumptions and models can all be viewed as a part of one simple, unified big picture. I believe this is a fundamental contribution to this monogram, which has everlasting value. The researchers and readers get to feel the continuity among various results, logically organise the existing results across various parameters and identify the major gaps and future directions for research in this area.

If you want to pick up one problem in distributed computing that would naturally qualify to frame the fundamental questions, it is the consensus problem. This monogram introduces a taxonomy for distributed consensus and discusses the algorithms for the consensus problem in a unified manner. There are so many great and delightful ideas in the literature of distributed consensus. Still, they are available in a scattered manner in several publications generated over a long period of time. A book presenting all great ideas and techniques in a unified manner will be a great asset to the current and future research community. Such a book would greatly enhance the understanding of the whole research area. One could see the research gaps and challenges naturally if the learning is done in a unified manner under a powerful and comprehensive taxonomy. The monogram by Arpita and Ashish fulfils this major need impressively. I am quite confident that this book, the follow-up monogram, and future expanded editions will profoundly impact the growth of fundamental research in distributed computing in the years to come.

Bangalore, September 2024 *C. Pandu Rangan*

Preface

Ever since its inception, fault-tolerant distributed consensus has been one of the widely studied topics in secure distributed computing. The topic has received renewed interest from the community, thanks to the advent of blockchain technology. There are two major categories of consensus protocols: (a) protocols in the synchronous communication model and (b) protocols in the asynchronous communication model. We strongly believe that the literature in each model is vast and important enough to demand a separate monogram. Since, very often, protocols and the techniques for the synchronous communication model serve as the basis for protocols in the asynchronous model, we choose to dedicate our first monogram to the former model.

This monogram aims to focus *only* on the synchronous communication model and present all the seminal possibility and feasibility results in this model since the inception of distributed consensus protocols. We present protocols both against computationally bounded and computationally unbounded adversaries. Detailed security proofs are provided for the seminal protocols. For a better understanding of the underlying concepts, pictorial illustrations are provided. We also present state-of-the-art efficiency improvement techniques for synchronous consensus protocols. In summary, this monogram intends to provide a comprehensive explanation of all the important concepts and techniques in this domain, and to unfold the evolution of this topic from its inception to till date.

This monogram is self-contained and can be read by those with familiarity with Discrete Mathematics and Algorithms. We assume *no* background in cryptography or distributed computing. The authors have used a large part of the material in this monogram for teaching graduate-level courses at their respective institutes. A set of companion video lectures for some of the topics in the monogram is freely available in the NPTEL course series at `https://archive.nptel.ac.in/courses/106/108/106108237/`.

Feedback and Errata

Our primary aim in this monogram is to provide a detailed introduction to the important topic of fault-tolerant synchronous distributed consensus, and we hope that we will succeed in our mission. We will be happy to receive feedback on this monogram, especially constructive comments about how to further improve it. We tried to ensure that there were no typos and errors. However, if you do find any, then we will be very obliged if you can kindly let us know by emailing at arpita@iisc.ac.in and ashish.choudhury@iiitb.ac.in. We plan to later maintain a dedicated homepage for this monogram with a complete list of known errata.

Bangalore,
September 2024

Ashish Choudhury
Arpita Patra

Acknowledgements

Ashish Choudhury

I would like to thank all my beloved teachers at IIT Madras for teaching me, especially Prof. Kamala Krithivasn, Prof. C. Pandu Rangan, and Prof. C. A. Choudum for teaching wonderful courses related to theoretical computer science, which sparked my love and interest in theoretical computer science. Special thanks to my PhD supervisor, Prof. C. Pandu Rangan, for being a great advisor, a great teacher, a great critic, a great friend and overall, a great philosopher. I would also like to thank Prof. Palash Sarkar and Prof. Nigel Smart, for being wonderful hosts and advisors during my post-doctoral research. I am also thankful to all my past and present thesis students for all the wonderful discussions related to distributed consensus, which greatly enhanced my knowledge about this topic. I am grateful to my wonderful co-author of this book, Arpita, who has always been a role model for me and several aspiring young researchers in India in the domain of secure distributed computing. Lastly, I would like to give a special thanks to my daughter Aparajita and to the all-mighty for whatever I am today.

Arpita Patra

First, I would like to thank my wonderful co-author of this book, Ashish, for being my constant companion in research since my Ph.D. days. He has been my continuous source of support in both academics and life. This monogram would not be possible without his sheer persuasion. It is he who felt that we must share and spread our excitement about distributed consensus, a topic we both love, cherish and relish in secure distributed computing. The love-factor apart, fault-tolerant distributed consensus has hugely advanced the theory of computation. Towards the goal of spreading the joy of distributed consensus, he has offered online courses on some of the topics, with the support of NPTEL, a great online platform for learning in India. While we are blessed to have some great books on distributed computing, the same is not true for fault-tolerant distributed consensus. An accessible book on this topic for curious students who are about to graduate or have just completed their graduation seemed like the next apt step. This monogram will surely serve as a stepping stone to the vibrant and beautiful world of distributed consensus. I am thankful that he convinced me about the need and offered to jointly write the book.

I would like to thank my PhD advisor, Prof. C. Pandu Rangan, for introducing me to the area of secure distributed computing and for creating the most conducive environment for learning during my PhD days.

I had the pleasure of working with many talented and hyper-active researchers who enriched my knowledge and deepened my understanding of cryptography and secure distributed computing over the years. Special mention goes to Benny Applebaum, Yuval Ishai, Ivan Damgaard, Eliran Kachlon, Gilad Asharov, Carmit Hazay, Yehuda Lindell, Nigel Smart, Ittai Abraham and Akshayaram Srinivasan.

I am grateful to all my past and current students for the dynamic and vibrant research ambience in which we grew and continue to grow together. They helped me widen my knowledge of the theory and practice of secure distributed computing. I would like to thank Divya Ravi, Ajith Suresh, Swati Singla, Megha Byali, Varsha Bhat, Nishat Koti, Shravani Patil, Protik Paul, Bhavish Raj Gopal, Shyam Murthy, Banashri Karmakar, and Ridhiman Dutta Roy for productive discussions over a multitude of topics and memorable time.

My parents, Sima and Ahibhushan Patra are my pillars of support. Thank you for always being there for me! Even today, they are the ones I look up to in times of distress and moments of joy.

Lastly, I would like to thank my daughter Aparajita and my better half Ashish. I owe them all that I am or hope to be. Without you, life has no meaning. Thank you for being part of my life!

Contents

Chapter 1
Introduction

There are a variety of real-life *distributed systems* where several computing devices communicate with each other to achieve certain “functionality" (goals). Examples of such systems include but are not limited to telecommunication systems, distributed information processing systems, VLSI chips, shared memory multiprocessors, banking systems, airline reservation systems, weather prediction systems, aircraft control systems and nuclear plant control systems [74, 13]. The algorithms running on these systems are often referred to as *distributed algorithms*. These algorithms are supposed to work “correctly" and achieve the desired goals, even if the individual computing devices have different operating speeds or even if some of the computing devices become “faulty" and do not follow the steps of the prescribed algorithm.

One of the important problems which arise in distributed systems is the so-called *coordination problem*, which requires the computing devices to *agree* on a common course of “action". For example, consider a distributed database system where the database is replicated and maintained across multiple servers which might be geographically isolated. Then, given a transaction, the servers need to agree on whether to commit the transaction or abort it. Similarly, consider an aircraft control system where different components might want to agree on the height of the aeroplane, based on the individual readings. Alternatively, they may want to agree on whether to classify a system component as faulty based on the outcome of separate diagnostic tests performed by different components.

In all the application scenarios that we discussed above, the goal is to reach *consensus* in a distributed system. If there are *no* faulty components, then achieving consensus is trivial and can be achieved by simply exchanging the respective inputs of the devices/systems/components with each other. However, faults are a very natural occurrence in any system or component. For example, there might be some occasional problems with the hardware of the components due to which they may no longer execute the steps of the prescribed algorithm. Or some of the components may be “controlled" by an adversarial entity that can dictate the behaviour of such components. Hence, what is desired is a mechanism to achieve consensus in a distributed system even if some of the components become faulty and start behaving in an arbitrary and erroneous fashion. *Fault-tolerant distributed consensus*

A. Choudhury and A. Patra, *Fault-Tolerant Distributed Consensus in Synchronous Networks*, Information Security and Cryptography,
https://doi.org/10.1007/978-3-031-80460-1_1

protocols offer such mechanisms. In the past, companies like Google and Facebook have deployed such consensus protocols to replicate mission-critical services such as Google Wallet and Facebook Credit [84]. The advent of Bitcoin [76] and subsequent cryptocurrencies have revolutionized and revived interest in this topic. Bitcoin and blockchain technology demonstrated that it is feasible to achieve consensus in a completely decentralized and permissionless environment, where anyone is allowed to participate.

1.1 Fault-Tolerant Distributed Consensus: A Powerful Abstraction

All the application scenarios discussed in the previous section can be abstracted as follows. There is a set of n mutually-distrusting entities, often called as *parties* and denoted by $\mathcal{P} = \{P_1, \ldots, P_n\}$, where $n \geq 2$. Each party P_i has some input. The distrust in the system is modelled by a centralized entity, called *adversary*, who can "control" a subset of the parties in a variety of ways, during the execution of any protocol. The parties not under the control of the adversary are called as *honest* parties, while the parties under the adversary's control are called *corrupt* parties. The honest parties *may not* know the identities of the corrupt parties. The goal is to design a protocol according to which the parties exchange messages and then compute an output, such that the output of the honest parties is the *same*, even if they start the protocol with different inputs.[1] There is also a *validity* condition, which describes the output values for each pattern of permissible input values of the honest parties.

It is not hard to see that the above abstraction captures all the real-world applications discussed in the previous section. Hence, a solution for the above abstract problem will imply a solution for all the applications discussed. Due to its powerful abstraction, distributed consensus holds central importance, both in the regime of cryptography as well as distributed computing. The problem has been widely studied over the last three decades, and several fundamental results have been achieved, both in the theoretical and applied regimes.

There are *two* variants of distributed consensus which have been widely studied in the literature. The first variant is called *Byzantine agreement* (BA), where the validity condition demands that if all honest participants start the protocol with a common input, then they should get it as the output at the end of the protocol. The second variant is called *Byzantine broadcast* (BB) (often referred to as the Byzantine generals' problem), where *only one* of the designated parties among $\mathcal{P}$ called *sender* has an input m. The consensus requirement is that all honest parties should have a common output at the end protocol, and the validity requirement is that the common output should be m, in case the sender is *honest*. As we will later

[1] We *do not* care about the output of the corrupt parties since we have no control over what the corrupt parties output.

show in the monogram, both these variants of distributed consensus are "equivalent" under certain "conditions" in the sense that given a BB protocol, one can design a BA protocol using the BB protocol as a black box and vice-versa.[2]

1.2 Various Dimensions to Study Distributed Consensus

The distributed consensus problem (both the BA as well as BB variant) has been studied in varieties of dimensions. Here, we discuss some of them.

Dimension 1 – Type of Communication Network.

In any consensus protocol, the parties need to exchange messages (computed as per the protocol instructions) over an underlying communication network. Depending upon the level of synchronization in the underlying network, consensus protocols can be primarily categorized as *synchronous* or *asynchronous*. In the synchronous protocols, it is assumed that the parties are synchronized through a global clock, and there is a strict (publicly-known) upper bound, say Δ, on the message delays. Consequently, any expected message which *does not* arrive within time Δ can be attributed to a *corrupt* sender party. Even though the synchronous communication model is simple to design and analyze protocols, it is difficult to ensure strict timeouts on message delays in real-world networks like the Internet, which is predominantly asynchronous and where the messages can be arbitrarily delayed. The security of any synchronous consensus protocol completely breaks down even if a single expected message from an honest party gets delayed beyond the Δ time bound.

In the asynchronous communication model, the parties are *not* synchronized, and the messages can be arbitrarily (but finitely) delayed. The only guarantee is that every sent message will be *eventually delivered*. Moreover, to model the worst-case scenario, the adversary is given the control of message scheduling. This models the behaviour of real-world networks like the Internet, where the underlying communication protocol (e.g. TCP/IP) repeatedly tries to deliver every sent message until it is delivered. Designing consensus protocols in the asynchronous communication model is practically motivated since the security of the protocol *does not* depend on any timing assumptions. Asynchronous protocols also have the advantage of running

[2] As mentioned in [74], the term *Byzantine* was coined in the landmark paper [70] and refers to *arbitrary* behaviour by potentially corrupt parties during the execution of any protocol, where the corrupt parties may deviate arbitrarily from the underlying protocol instructions. They introduced the BB problem as a Byzantine generals' problem, where there is a group of generals under the supervision of a master general who wait for instruction from the master general on whether to carry out an attack or not. The challenge here is for the generals to exchange messages with each other and come to an agreement on a common decision, even if a subset of the generals behave traitorously, possibly including the master general. The term Byzantine was used as a pun, since in their problem description, the battle scenario takes place in ancient Byzantium and the behaviour of the traitorous generals was described as "Byzantine" behaviour.

at the “actual speed" of the underlying network. More specifically, for a synchronous protocol, the participants have to pessimistically set the global delay Δ to a large value to ensure that the messages sent by every party reach their destination within the Δ time. But if the actual network delay δ is such that $\delta << \Delta$, then the protocol fails to take advantage of the faster network, and its running time will be proportional to Δ.

The major challenge in designing protocols in the asynchronous model is that a receiving party cannot distinguish between a *slow* but an honest sender party whose messages are delayed and a *corrupt* sender party who does not send messages at all. Due to this inherent phenomenon, asynchronous consensus protocols are more involved than their synchronous counterparts. In fact, the well-known FLP impossibility result *rules out* the possibility of any deterministic asynchronous BA protocol even in the presence of a single fault [50].

There is another category of consensus protocols designed in *partially-synchronous* networks [47]. The partially-synchronous model aims to find a “middle ground" between the synchronous and asynchronous communication models. Namely, the underlying network is assumed to behave asynchronously till a special event, which is known as *global stabilization time* (GST), after which the network starts behaving synchronously. The adversary can delay the GST event by any finite yet unknown amount of time, and the protocol participants *cannot* detect that GST has occurred. The advantage of the partially-synchronous model is that one can bypass the FLP impossibility result in this model.

A recent line of work [25, 40, 10, 39] design consensus protocols in the *network-agnostic* setting, where the parties *need not* know the behaviour of the underlying network. The network can behave either in a completely synchronous fashion or in a completely asynchronous fashion, and accordingly, the (network-agnostic) protocol provides the appropriate security guarantees.

Dimension 2 — With Setup or Without Setup.

In any consensus protocol, the *basic* setting is that of the *pairwise authentic* channels, where it is assumed that every party has a provision to send messages to every other party. This is abstracted by assuming that the underlying communication network is a *complete graph* of n nodes, where each node represents a party and each party has a link/edge with every other party. Moreover, the channels are *authentic*, meaning that for every edge, the parties publicly know the identity of the parties connected by that edge. This implies that during the execution of a protocol, any party, upon receiving a message, will know the identity of the corresponding sender party who sent that message. This basic model of pairwise authentic channels itself suffices to design consensus protocols. However, one can design protocols with better fault-tolerance (capable of tolerating more number of faults) and better efficiency, if the parties are provided with additional setup, like the setup for a signature scheme (which allows the parties to sign messages and verify signed messages).

Dimension 3 — Corruption Capacity of the Adversary.

Under this dimension, we have two categories of protocols. The more popular *threshold* protocols assume that the number of corrupt parties is bounded by a publicly-known threshold, say t and the protocols are secure, as long as at most t parties are corrupt during the protocol execution. The threshold model fits well in a scenario where all the n parties are equally "hard" to corrupt, and the adversary has the "resources" to corrupt any t of them. However, in reality, this *need not* be true as some of the parties may be better "guarded" than others. Hence, a more realistic model might be to consider an adversary who can corrupt a small number of well-protected parties or a large number of "poorly protected" parties. Unfortunately, the threshold model *does not* allow for such expressibility. Another limitation of the threshold model is that it seems quite restrictive to assume that *any* subset of t parties might collaborate to cheat others. Instead, the collusion may, in reality, depend on the composition of the set of parties and their relation to each other, rather than on the size of the subsets.

The *non-threshold* adversary model [61, 54, 9, 36] tries to get rid of the above restrictions. Here, the corruption capability of the adversary is specified by a publicly-known *adversary structure*, which is a collection of potentially corrupt subset of parties. During the execution of a protocol, the adversary can choose any one subset from the collection for corruption. It is easy to see that a threshold adversary is a *special* type of non-threshold adversary, where the adversary structure consists of all subsets of $\mathcal{P}$ of size at most t.

Dimension 4 – Corruption Power of the Adversary.

Under this dimension, we have *unconditionally-secure* and *conditionally-secure* protocols. The former category of protocols can tolerate *computationally-unbounded* adversaries, where there is *no* restriction on the computing resources of the adversary. The latter category of protocols can tolerate only *computationally-bounded* adversaries, where the computational power of the adversary is polynomial-time bounded. Consequently, cryptographic tools can be deployed in these protocols, whose security is based on various computational hardness assumptions. This is why the latter category of protocols are also termed as *cryptographically-secure* protocols.

Unconditionally-secure protocols can be further categorized as *perfectly-secure* where all security guarantees are achieved in an *error-free* fashion, or *statistically-secure* where a negligible (but non-zero) error is permitted in the protocol outcomes. Unconditionally-secure protocols are computationally very fast and provide everlasting security, since their security is *not* based on any computational-hardness assumptions. This, for instance, guarantees that these protocols remain secure even if quantum computers become a reality. The downside is that these protocols have relatively poor fault tolerance and require more interaction among the parties, compared to cryptographically-secure protocols.

Dimension 5 – Type of Corruption.

During the execution of any consensus protocol, the adversary can "control" the corrupt parties in different ways. The simplest form of corruption is the *fail-stop* corruption (also called as *crash-failures*), where a corrupt party can stop functioning at any time during the execution of a protocol and then remain "inactive" for the rest of the protocol execution. However, as long as the corrupt party is functioning, it follows the protocol instruction, with its entire state being monitored by the adversary. A more powerful form of corruption is the *Byzantine* corruption (also known as the *malicious* or *active* corruption), where the adversary can influence the corrupt parties to deviate from the prescribed protocol instructions in any arbitrary fashion.

Dimension 6 — Timing of Corruption.

Under this dimension, there are two categories of protocols. The first category of protocols is secure against a *static* adversary, who decides the set of corrupt parties at the onset of the protocol execution. The other category of protocols is secure against a more powerful *adaptive* adversary who can corrupt parties during the run time of the protocol [86, 3, 4].

Dimension 7 — Number of Times Consensus is Needed.

Under this dimension, we have *two* types of protocols. The first class is that of *single-shot* consensus protocols, where the parties need to reach consensus *only once*. The second class is that of *multi-shot* consensus protocols, where the parties need to reach consensus repeatedly over time. For example in modern cryptocurrency systems such as Bitcoin, the parties need to maintain and agree on an ever-growing public ledger which records the sequence of all the transactions that have taken place so far. The modern name for the second class of protocols is the *blockchain* protocol, thanks to the popularity of Bitcoin.[3]

Dimension 8 — Type of Participation.

Under this dimension, we have *two* categories of protocols. The classical consensus protocols are executed in a *permissioned* environment, where the number of protocol participants is fixed and their identity is known to all apriori. Consequently, in these protocols, the communication happens over authenticated channels. Modern consensus protocols are designed in a *permissionless* environment, where anyone can join or leave the consensus protocol at any time. Since there is no apriori knowledge of the identities of the protocol participants, communication happens

[3] Earlier, the blockchain (or the multi-shot consensus protocols) were called *state machine replication* (SMR) protocol.

over unauthenticated channels. The biggest challenge to design consensus protocols in the permissionless environment is where a single (corrupt) party can impersonate any number of parties to outnumber the honest parties and prevent consensus.[4] In fact, one can show that all classical consensus protocols which are designed for the permissioned setting turn insecure when executed in a permissionless environment.

Summary.

We summarize the various dimensions of studying distributed consensus in Table 1.1. A setting for distributed consensus can be obtained by picking one attribute from each column.

Network	Setup	Corruption Capacity	Corruption Power	Corruption Type	Timing of Corruption	# Consensus Needed	Participation
Synchronous	No	Threshold	Polynomial time	Crash	Static	Single-shot	Permissioned
Asynchronous	Yes	Non-threshold	Unbounded	Byzantine	Adaptive	Multi-shot	Permissionless
Network-agnostic							

Table 1.1: The taxonomy for studying distributed consensus in various dimensions

Irrespective of the setting considered for studying the consensus problem, the following three inherent questions are fundamental.

- *Possibility*: What are the necessary and sufficient condition(s) for the existence of any consensus protocol in a given setting?
- *Feasibility*: Does there exist an efficient consensus protocol in a given setting (given that a protocol is already proven to be possible)?
- *Optimality*: What are the inherent lower bounds on the “resources" needed for a consensus protocol in a given setting? How can we design protocols that make "optimal" use of the resources? The common resources that are considered are:
  - *Communication complexity*: It is the number of bits to be communicated by the *honest* parties in the protocol.[5]
  - *Time complexity*: It is the maximum time required in the protocol for the *honest* parties to compute their output.
  - *Computation complexity*: It is the measure of the amount of computation done by the *honest* parties in the protocol.

Interestingly, the answer to these questions changes from one setting to another. For instance, if no setup is available to the parties apart from the pair-wise point-to-point channels, then any BB/BA protocol can tolerate only up to $t < \frac{n}{3}$ Byzantine faults (see Chapter 5). On the other hand, if an additional setup for signatures is available, then one can design BA and BB protocol tolerating $t < \frac{n}{2}$ and $t < n$ Byzantine corruptions respectively (see Chapter 9). Similarly, it can be shown that any *deterministic* consensus protocol will need $t+1$ rounds of communication, where

[4] In blockchain protocols, this is often called the *Sybil* attack.

[5] We do not focus on the amount of communication done by the *corrupt* parties, since they may not follow the protocol instructions and end up doing arbitrary communications.

t is the number of corruptions (see Chapter 7). On the other hand, if one opts for randomization, then one can design randomized consensus protocols with a constant expected number of communication rounds, *independent* of the number of faults in the system (see Chapters 8 and Chapter 14).

1.3 Our Setting and Book Organization

In this book, we focus on *single-shot synchronous* consensus protocols in the *permissioned* setting, tolerating *threshold static* adversaries. We present protocols for both with and without setup and consider both polynomial-time and computationally-unbounded corruptions. Moreover, we consider *Byzantine* corruptions throughout this monogram. In Table 1.2, we highlight the various dimensions covered in this monogram, out of all the possible dimensions as discussed in Table 1.1.

Network	Setup	Corruption Capacity	Corruption Power	Corruption Type	Timing of Corruption	# Consensus Needed	Participation
Synchronous	**No**	**Threshold**	**Polynomial time**	Crash	**Static**	**Single-shot**	**Permissioned**
Asynchronous	**Yes**	Non-threshold	**Unbounded**	**Byzantine**	Adaptive	Multi-shot	Permissionless
Network-agnostic							

Table 1.2: The various dimensions out of the possible dimensions covered in this monogram

Even though the synchronous corruption model may seem weaker, designing consensus protocols in this model is non-trivial and demands sophisticated techniques. Moreover, often synchronous protocols serve as the basis for protocols in the asynchronous network.

The monogram is divided into *two* parts. The first part is dedicated to the consensus protocols *without* any setup. Consensus protocols with setup assumptions are discussed in the second part of the monogram. In the sequel, we present a very high-level overview of the contents covered in each part.

Part I: Distributed Consensus Without Any SetUp.

In the first part of the monogram, we will focus on distributed consensus *without* any kind of setup assumptions. Historically, this is the most widely studied setting considered in the literature for studying distributed consensus protocols. In this setting, the only assumption is that pairwise point-to-point channels connect the parties. We will consider both the pairwise-authentic channel setting as well as the pairwise-secure channel setting. All the results discussed in this part will consider *computationally-unbounded* adversaries and hence will achieve *unconditional-security*. Moreover, we will be focussing on *perfectly-secure* protocols. Such protocols provide *ever-lasting* security guarantees since the security is *not* based on any computational-hardness assumptions. Moreover, all security guarantees are achieved in an error-free fashion. We next give a brief outline of the various chapters that appear in the first part.

In Chapter 3, we will present the classic *exponential information gathering* (EIG) protocol, which is the *first* known distributed consensus protocol in the literature. Even though the protocol is *inefficient* (as the name suggests), there are several reasons for presenting the protocol, the foremost being its historical importance. The protocol also serves as a warmup to understand some of the central ideas and proofs in this domain.

In Chapter 4, we will present *efficient* consensus protocols, based on the well-known *phase-king* paradigm. We will present *two* protocols, one with *non-optimal* resilience but with *lesser* number of rounds and another one with the *optimal* resilience but with *more* number of rounds.

In Chapter 5, we derive the lower bound on the *resilience* of any distributed consensus protocol without any set-up. We first derive the lower bound for the protocols with a *single* corruption (i.e. $t = 1$), using the well-known *hexagon* argument. We then generalize it for protocols with *any* t corruptions by introducing another proof mechanism called *player partitioning*.

The protocols discussed in Chapter 3 and Chapter 4 are primarily for bit-BA and bit-BB, where the input of the parties is a *single* bit. In Chapter 6, we shift our attention to *multi-bit* distributed consensus protocols, where the input of the parties consists of L bits, where $L \geq 1$. A naive approach for designing consensus protocols in this setting would be to run L instances of any bit-BA/BB protocol in parallel. A better solution is to use *domain extension* for consensus protocols, where the number of instances of bit-BA/BB is *independent* of L. We will present *two* approaches for the domain extension, the first being the classical Turpin-Coan approach and the second one based on the properties of error-correcting codes over a finite field. En route, we also derive the lower bound on the communication complexity of *any* domain extension protocol.

The focus of Chapter 7 will be to derive the lower bound on another important complexity measure of distributed consensus protocols, namely the *round complexity*. We derive the lower bound on the number of rounds required for any *deterministic* distributed consensus protocol. For proving the bound, we will present the *bivalency* argument, another classical gem in the domain of distributed consensus protocols.

Since the number of communication rounds is a crucial complexity parameter for any distributed consensus protocol, an obvious goal will be to design consensus protocols with a *constant* number of rounds, *independent* of the number of parties and the number of corruptions. Unfortunately, this is *impossible* to achieve through any *deterministic* protocol, as implied by the lower bound presented in Chapter 7. An alternate and powerful approach used in the literature of distributed algorithms is to embrace *randomness* and hope to get a randomized consensus protocol with a constant number of rounds in *expectation*. The focus of Chapter 8 is to discuss the classical paradigm of designing randomized consensus protocols. En route, we will present several important building blocks of independent interest and present instantiation of these building blocks, such as *common coin* (CC), *verifiable secret sharing* (VSS) and *moderated* VSS (MVSS). Chapter 8 also marks our end of the journey of distributed consensus protocols *without* any setup, and we bid adieu to the first part of the monogram and move to the second part of the monogram.

Part II: Distributed Consensus With SetUp.

All the protocols discussed in the first part are *without* any setup assumption. Consequently, these protocols could tolerate upto t corrupt parties out of n parties where $t < \frac{n}{3}$. A natural question is whether one can improve the resilience of consensus protocols if the parties are provided with an additional (trusted) setup. This is precisely the main focus of the second part of the monogram, where we work and design such protocols.

We start the second part of the monogram by presenting the classic Dolev-Strong protocol for distributed consensus in Chapter 9. We present both the BB and BA variants of the protocol. Both the variants achieve the *optimal* resilience of $t < n$ and $t < \frac{n}{2}$ respectively. Additionally, both variants enjoy having the *optimal* number of communication rounds, namely $t + 1$, required by any *deterministic* consensus protocol.

Once the existence of BA with a *strict honest majority* (namely $t < \frac{n}{2}$) is established, the next two chapters (Chapter 10 and Chapter 11) are devoted to exploring whether one can do domain extension for BA with a strict honest majority. While Chapter 10 does this for BA with *statistical security*, in Chapter 11, we will see a much more efficient domain extension for BA if one is willing to settle with *cryptographic security*.

Since BB is possible with a *dishonest majority* (namely with $t < n$) in the presence of a setup, a natural question is whether one can do domain extension for BB with the condition $t < n$. Chapter 12 and Chapter 13 answer this question affirmatively. While Chapter 12 considers domain extension for BB in the dishonest majority setting with *statistical* security, the focus of Chapter 13 is cryptographic security.

The last chapter of the second part (Chapter 14) is devoted to BA protocols in the honest majority setting (i.e. with $t < \frac{n}{2}$) and a *constant* expected number of rounds. For this, we show how to design a *common coin* (CC) protocol from scratch. We will see a CC protocol with unconditional security based on VSS and a CC protocol with cryptographic security based on threshold signatures.

The contents of Part I and Part II are almost disjoint from each other, and one can easily read any part independently of the other. The dependency among the various chapters is illustrated in the dependency chart in Fig 1.1.

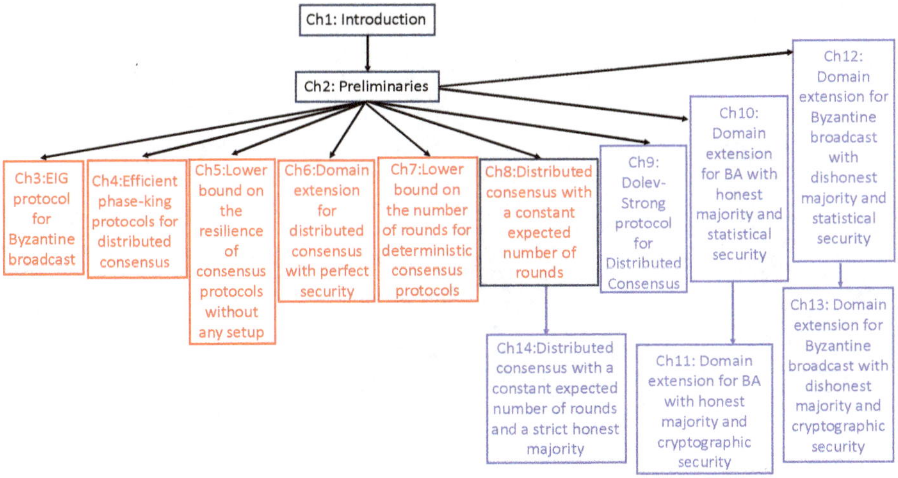

Fig. 1.1: Dependency among the various chapters of the monogram. The chapters marked red and blue belong to Part I and Part II respectively

Chapter 2
Preliminaries

In this chapter, we discuss the various cryptographic primitives and associated terminologies used in this monogram. We then formally define the various communication models which will be used in the monogram. We will formally define the BB and BA problems, and discuss the trivial necessary conditions required to solve these problems in *any* communication model, and then see the relationship between these two problems. Lastly, we will introduce a "weaker" variant of consensus called *graded* consensus, which will be used very often in this monogram as a stepping stone towards building consensus protocols.

2.1 Various Cryptographic Primitives

In this section, we give a high-level overview of the various cryptographic primitives that will be used in our protocols. We refer the readers to any standard text in cryptography such as [67] for a comprehensive treatment of these primitives.

The two cryptographic primitives used in this monogram are digital signatures and collision-resistant hash function (CRHF). We require that the "security" of these primitives should hold with a "high" probability or analogously, the probability that an attacker can "break" the security of these primitives should be "very small". The security is typically defined as a function of some customizable *security parameter* κ, which is typically the length of the cryptographic keys or the output size of the hash function, depending upon the context. Intuitively we desire that the larger the value of the security parameter κ, the more difficult it is for the adversary to break the security of the underlying primitive. Typically we require that the chances that an adversary can violate the specified security conditions of the underlying cryptographic primitive should be a *negligible* function of κ. Informally, a negligible function is one that "drops off" faster than any inverse-polynomial function.

Definition 2.1 ((Negligible Function [67])) A function $f(\kappa)$ is a *negligible* function of κ, if for every constant $c > 0$, there exists some κ_0, such that for all $\kappa > \kappa_0$ it holds that $f(\kappa) < \frac{1}{\kappa^c}$.

A. Choudhury and A. Patra, *Fault-Tolerant Distributed Consensus in Synchronous Networks*, Information Security and Cryptography,
https://doi.org/10.1007/978-3-031-80460-1_2

We will denote an arbitrary negligible function by $\mathsf{negl}(\kappa)$.

Examples of negligible functions include $\kappa^{-\log \kappa}, 2^{-\kappa}$, etc. Typically a quantity is shown to be negligible by showing it to be exponentially small in the parameter κ. An interesting property of negligible functions is that if $f(\kappa)$ is a negligible function and if $\mathsf{poly}(\kappa)$ is a polynomial function, then $f(\kappa) \cdot \mathsf{poly}(\kappa)$ is a negligible function.

Typically the security of any cryptographic primitive could be computational or unconditional. *Computational* security (also referred to as *cryptographic* or *conditional* security) means that the security of the primitive holds against an adversary, who is bounded to perform only probabilistic polynomial time computations (such an adversary is also referred to as a *probabilistic polynomial time* (PPT) adversary). *Unconditional* security means that even a computationally-unbounded adversary cannot violate the security requirements of the underlying cryptographic primitive.

2.1.1 Collision Resistant Hash Functions (CRHF)

Informally, a CRHF is used to compress *arbitrary* length binary strings to *fixed* length binary strings in a *deterministic* way. Since the domain size is larger than the codomain size, "collisions" are obviously present in the function; i.e. there always exist two *different* inputs which have the same hash output. The main security property required from a CRHF is that it should be "computationally difficult" to find such a collision. A CRHF's security could be conditional or unconditional. In this monogram, we will use both types of CRHF. We first discuss conditionally secure CRHF.

2.1.1.1 Conditionally-Secure CRHF

A conditionally (cryptographically) secure hash function $H : \{0,1\}^\ell \rightarrow \{0,1\}^\kappa$ is a *deterministic* function, which takes input an ℓ-bit string and generates a κ-bit string as output, satisfying all the following properties.

- **Compression**: The condition $\ell > \kappa$ holds.
- **Easy to compute**: Given any $x \in \{0,1\}^\ell$, computing $H(x)$ requires $\mathsf{poly}(\ell, \kappa)$ amount of time, where $\mathsf{poly}(\ell, \kappa)$ denotes a polynomial function in κ and ℓ.
- **Collision-resistance**: For any PPT algorithm B whose running time is some polynomial function in κ, the probability that B can output a collision for H is upper bounded by some negligible function of κ. That is, for every PPT algorithm B, the following holds.

$$\Pr\Big[H(x) = H(x') | x \neq x' \ \wedge \ x, x' \leftarrow B(1^\kappa)\Big] \leq \mathsf{negl}(\kappa).$$

Here $B(1^\kappa)$ denotes that the running time of B is some polynomial function in κ and $\mathsf{negl}(\kappa)$ denotes a negligible function in κ.

The variable κ above is the security parameter, which in practice is typically the output length of the hash function. For practical hash functions like SHA-256, the value of κ is at least 256.

2.1.1.2 Unconditionally-Secure CRHF

Unconditionally-secure CRHF can be based on universal hash functions [28], which are keyed hash functions. The function takes as input a key and a string that needs to be compressed and generates a compressed output, which is a function of the key and the input string. The collision-resistance property here is that for a *randomly* chosen key, the probability that two different input strings produce the same output is negligible. In more detail, an unconditionally-secure CRHF $U : \{0,1\}^\kappa \times \{0,1\}^\ell \rightarrow \{0,1\}^\kappa$ is a deterministic function, which takes input a κ-bit key and an ℓ-bit string and generates a κ-bit output, satisfying all the following properties.

- **Compression**: The condition $\ell > \kappa$ holds.
- **Easy to compute**: Given any $k \in \{0,1\}^\kappa$ and any $x \in \{0,1\}^\ell$, computing $U(k,x)$ requires $\mathsf{poly}(\kappa)$ amount of time, where $\mathsf{poly}(\kappa)$ denotes a polynomial function in κ.
- **Collision-resistance**: For every pair of inputs $m, m' \in \{0,1\}^\ell$ where $m \neq m'$, the following holds for any *randomly* chosen key $k \in \{0,1\}^\kappa$.[1]

$$Pr\Big[U(k,m) = U(k,m')\Big] \leq 2^{-\kappa}\ell$$

One can easily instantiate an unconditionally-secure CRHF over Galois field $\mathrm{GF}(2^\kappa)$ as follows. The key $k \in \{0,1\}^\kappa$ is interpreted as an element of $\mathrm{GF}(2^\kappa)$. The input $m \in \{0,1\}^\ell$ to be compressed is also interpreted as a polynomial f_m over $\mathrm{GF}(2^\kappa)$ of degree $\frac{\ell}{\kappa}$. For this, m is divided into blocks of κ-bits, and each block is interpreted as an element of $\mathrm{GF}(2^\kappa)$. The coefficients of f_m then consist of these elements over $\mathrm{GF}(2^\kappa)$. The hash output is then defined as $U(k,m) \stackrel{def}{=} f_m(k)$, which is a κ-bit output. It is easy to see that given a pair of *distinct* inputs m, m', the probability that $U(k,m) = U(k,m')$ holds for a *randomly* chosen key k is same as the probability that $f_m(k) = f_{m'}(k)$ holds. Two *different* polynomials of degree $\frac{\ell}{\kappa}$ can have at most $\frac{\ell}{\kappa}$ common values. The probability of a randomly selected k over $\mathrm{GF}(2^\kappa)$ being one of them is $2^{-\kappa} \cdot \frac{\ell}{\kappa}$. So, the probability that $f_m(k) = f_{m'}(k)$ holds is at most $2^{-\kappa} \cdot \frac{\ell}{\kappa}$.

In the rest of the monogram, we will use the notation $U_k(m)$ to denote the value $U(k,m)$.

[1] We stress that the condition holds only for a *randomly* chosen key from the key-space.

2.1.2 Digital Signatures

Digital signatures are digital analogue of physical signatures and are used for authenticating data. Informally, a digital signature scheme operates with a *pair* of keys, a *secret* key that allows to sign (authenticate) messages and a *public* key that allows to verify the authenticity of a signature. The secret signing key is available *only* with a designated *signer* party, who can use it to sign messages. The verification key is available publicly and can be used to verify any signed message.

The key security requirement from a secure signature scheme is *unforgeability*, which demands that it should *not* be possible for an adversary to forge the signature of an honest signer party, *without* knowing the signer's secret signing key. Moreover, this should hold even if the adversary has previously seen several signed messages of the signer, generated using the same signing key. Another key feature of digital signatures is *transferability*, meaning that they can be transferred between parties without losing their conclusiveness.

Signature schemes can provide both conditional as well as unconditional security. We next discuss conditionally-secure signatures.

2.1.2.1 Conditionally-Secure Signatures

A conditionally (cryptographically) secure signature scheme is a triplet of algorithms $(\mathsf{KeyGen}, \mathsf{Sign}, \mathsf{Verify})$. The *key-generation* algorithm KeyGen is a PPT algorithm, whose running time is polynomial in κ and which outputs a pair of keys $(\mathsf{sk}, \mathsf{pk})$ where $\mathsf{sk}, \mathsf{pk} \in \{0, 1\}^\kappa$. The key sk is called the *secret* key or *signing* key, while pk is called the *public* key or *verification* key. Syntactically, we denote the algorithm as $\mathsf{KeyGen}(1^\kappa) \rightarrow (\mathsf{sk}, \mathsf{pk})$.

The *signing* algorithm Sign takes input the message m to be signed along with the signing key sk and possibly some "randomness" r and generates a signature $\sigma^{(m)} \in \{0, 1\}^\kappa$ on the message m. Note that it is *not* necessary for the signing algorithm to be randomized, and for simplicity, we consider *deterministic* signing algorithms in this monogram. The running time of the algorithm should be polynomial in κ and the size of m and we denote the algorithm as $\sigma^{(m)} := \mathsf{Sign}_{\mathsf{sk}}(m)$.

The *verification* algorithm Verify is a *deterministic* algorithm which takes input a message-signature pair $(m, \sigma^{(m)})$ for verification along with the verification key pk. The algorithm outputs 1 if the pair is a *valid* message-signature pair, otherwise, the algorithm outputs 0. Syntactically, we denote the algorithm as

$$\mathsf{Verify}_{\mathsf{pk}}(m, \sigma^{(m)}) = \begin{cases} 1, & \text{if } \sigma^{(m)} := \mathsf{Sign}_{\mathsf{sk}}(m) \text{ and } (\mathsf{pk}, \mathsf{sk}) \leftarrow \mathsf{KeyGen}(1^\kappa) \\ 0, & \text{otherwise} \end{cases}$$

The main security property required here is that of *unforgeability*, meaning that given *only* a public key pk, no PPT adversary can compute valid signatures *without* knowing the corresponding signing key sk, except with a negligible probability. This requirement can be formalized rigorously through a challenge-response game and we refer the interested readers to [67] for the same.

There are several well-known instantiations of cryptographically-secure signature schemes; see, for example, [42, 82, 83].

2.1.2.2 Unconditionally-Secure Signatures (Pseudo-Signatures)

Unconditionally-secure signatures, also known as *pseudo-signatures* [31, 79] are secure even against computationally-unbounded adversaries; i.e. even if the adversary is computationally-unbounded, it will fail to forge a signature without knowing the signing key (except with a negligible probability). However *unlike* the conditionally-secure signatures which are arbitrarily transferable between the parties, pseudo-signatures support only a *restricted* number of transferability, and that too for the case when the set of potential verifiers is known in advance (which will be the case for our protocols which use pseudo-signatures).

In more detail, apart from the usual key-generation, signing and verification algorithms, there is an *additional* parameter λ, which denotes the *transferability* of the pseudo-signatures. The parameter λ denotes the number of times a pseudo-signature can be transferred among the parties and get verified, without letting the adversary break the unforgeability property.

For notational compatibility between conditionally and unconditionally-secure signatures, we use the *same* notations and terminologies for both types of signature schemes. We refer the interested readers to [51] for more details.

2.2 Various Communication Models

Throughout this monogram, we will design protocols in different communication settings. The basic communication model is that of a *complete synchronous* network of n parties, modelled as a complete *undirected* graph of n nodes, where each node corresponds to a party and where each party has a link/edge with every other party. Moreover, the channels are *authentic*, meaning that for every edge, the parties publicly know the identity of the parties connected by that edge. This implies that during the execution of a protocol, any party, upon receiving a message, will know the identity of the corresponding sender party. That is, for any edge (P_i, P_j) in the graph, if P_i (resp. P_j) receives a message over the edge, then P_i (resp. P_j) is guaranteed that the message has been sent by P_j (resp. P_i). In particular, this means that if both P_i and P_j are *honest* and if P_i (resp. P_j) sends a message m to P_j (resp. P_i), then an adversary *cannot* replace m with m'. The local clocks of the parties in this model are assumed to be synchronized, and there exists a *publicly-known* upper bound, say Δ, within which every sent message is guaranteed to be delivered. The protocols in this model can be conveniently described as a sequence of communication *rounds*, where for every $r \in \mathbb{N}$ with $r \geq 1$, any message received in the time slot $[r\Delta, (r+1)\Delta]$ as per the local clock of the receiving party is regarded as a round-r message. Moreover, if a message is received *outside* of the time allocated for a certain round (as per the local clock of the receiving party), then it is *ignored* by the corresponding receiving party. In every round, each party computes the messages to be sent to other parties in this round based on the messages sent and received till now, sends those messages to the respective parties, followed by receiving the messages sent by the other parties during the current round, in this order. In the rest of the book, we will refer to this model as $\mathcal{M}_{\mathsf{auth}}$.

The next communication setting is the *pairwise secure channel* setting, denoted as $\mathcal{M}_{\mathsf{secure}}$. Here apart from the channels being authentic, we assume them to be *private*. That means that any communication between *honest* P_i and *honest* P_j over the channel (P_i, P_j) will be known only to them. There could be several ways to realize such pairwise private channels. For instance, every pair of parties can use an instance of symmetric-key encryption [67], where the encryption scheme could be either conditionally-secure or unconditionally-secure, depending upon whether the underlying adversary is a PPT adversary or computationally-unbounded. Alternatively, the parties could use *secure message transmission* (SMT) protocols [44, 34] to realize pairwise virtual secure channels over an incomplete network. We do not go into the exact details of how such secure channels are realizable and instead abstract the underlying communication network as a complete graph of n nodes, with a secure channel existing between every pair of nodes. The *first* part of the book is devoted to the protocols in the $\mathcal{M}_{\mathsf{auth}}$ and $\mathcal{M}_{\mathsf{secure}}$ models.

In the *second* part of the book, we will also consider protocols where apart from the point-to-point authentic/secure channels, some "auxiliary" information will be *already* available to the parties, which is assumed to be distributed as a part of some *trusted* setup. While there can be different kinds of auxiliary information available to the parties, we will mainly focus on the case where a *public-key infrastructure* (PKI) setup is made available to the parties. As a part of this setup, we assume that for each party P_i, there exists a pair of keys $(\mathsf{sk}_i, \mathsf{pk}_i)$ for a signature scheme, with the *signing key* sk_i held by P_i and the *verification key* pk_i being *publicly* available. The PKI setup could be either for a conditionally-secure *digital signature* scheme secure against a computationally-bounded adversary or for an unconditionally-secure signature scheme (namely *pseudo-signatures*) secure against computationally-unbounded adversaries. We will use the following notations to refer to this model.

- $\mathcal{M}_{\mathsf{auth}}^{\mathsf{pki}}$: this will denote the pairwise authentic channel model $\mathcal{M}_{\mathsf{auth}}$, augmented with a PKI setup.
- $\mathcal{M}_{\mathsf{secure}}^{\mathsf{pki}}$: this will denote the pairwise secure channel model $\mathcal{M}_{\mathsf{secure}}$, augmented with a PKI setup.

Note that we do *not* specify whether the PKI setup is cryptographically or unconditionally-secure in the above notations. Looking ahead, we will explicitly specify the type of PKI setup when we design protocols in the above models. In the rest of the book, we will use the notation $\mathcal{M}$ to refer to an arbitrary communication model where $\mathcal{M} \in \{\mathcal{M}_{\mathsf{auth}}, \mathcal{M}_{\mathsf{secure}}, \mathcal{M}_{\mathsf{auth}}^{\mathsf{pki}}, \mathcal{M}_{\mathsf{secure}}^{\mathsf{pki}}\}$.

2.3 Variants of Distributed Consensus

We will consider two variants of the distributed consensus problem, *Byzantine Broadcast* (BB) and *Byzantine Agreement* (BA). In the literature, often both these problems are referred to as distributed consensus. However, there is a subtle difference between the two. In the former, there is a "special" designated sender party where only the sender party has some input, and the goal is to let each (honest) party get this input "consistently". On the other hand, in the latter, each party has some input, and the goal is to reach an agreement on a common output, even if the parties have different inputs. We now formally define these two problems.

Definition 2.2 (Byzantine Broadcast (BB)) Let Π be a protocol for the parties in $\mathcal{P}$ in the model $\mathcal{M} \in \{\mathcal{M}_{\mathsf{auth}}, \mathcal{M}_{\mathsf{secure}}, \mathcal{M}^{\mathsf{pki}}_{\mathsf{auth}}, \mathcal{M}^{\mathsf{pki}}_{\mathsf{secure}}\}$, where there is a designated *sender* party $\mathsf{S} \in \mathcal{P}$ with input $m \in \{0, 1\}^L$ and where each party has an output from the set $\{0, 1\}^L$, such that $L \geq 1$ and known publicly. Moreover, let t be the maximum number of parties that may be corrupted in a Byzantine fashion during the execution of Π, possibly including S.

- t**-liveness**: We say that Π has t*-liveness*, if all honest parties terminate the protocol Π.
- t**-validity**: We say that Π has t*-validity*, if the following holds.
  - If S is *honest*, then all honest parties output m.
- t**-consistency**: We say that Π has t*-consistency*, if all honest parties have the same output.

We say that Π is a t*-secure* BB protocol in model $\mathcal{M}$, if it has t*-liveness*, t*-validity* and t*-consistency*.

Note that the validity and consistency are "orthogonal" requirements. Namely, validity can be easily achieved by a single-round protocol where S sends its input to all the parties, who output the value received from S. However, this protocol will clearly *violate* the consistency property, since a *corrupt* S may send different inputs to the parties. On the other hand, consistency can be trivially achieved by the parties outputting a default value from $\{0, 1\}^L$, say 0^L. However, this protocol will *violate* the validity property since S might have a different input.

Definition 2.3 (Byzantine Agreement (BA)) Let Π be a protocol for the parties in $\mathcal{P}$ in the model $\mathcal{M} \in \{\mathcal{M}_{\mathsf{auth}}, \mathcal{M}_{\mathsf{secure}}, \mathcal{M}^{\mathsf{pki}}_{\mathsf{auth}}, \mathcal{M}^{\mathsf{pki}}_{\mathsf{secure}}\}$, where each party P_i has an input $u_i \in \{0, 1\}^L$ and an output $v_i \in \{0, 1\}^L$, such that $L \geq 1$ and known publcly. Moreover, let t be the maximum number of parties that may be corrupted in a Byzantine fashion during the execution of Π.

- t**-liveness**: We say that Π has t*-liveness*, if all honest parties terminate the protocol Π.
- t**-validity**: We say that Π has t*-validity*, if the following holds.
  - If all honest parties have input $u \in \{0, 1\}^L$, then all honest parties output u.
- t**-consistency**: We say that Π has t*-consistency*, if all honest parties have the same output.

We say that Π is a t*-secure* BA protocol in model $\mathcal{M}$, if it has t*-liveness*, t*-validity* and t*-consistency*.

In this monogram, we will consider *two* different categories of consensus protocols, depending upon the computational power of the adversary.

- **Unconditionally-secure Protocols**: These protocols provide all the security guarantees against a computationally-unbounded adversary. Such protocols provide *ever-lasting* security guarantees since the security is *not* based on any computational-hardness assumptions. The protocols under this category can be further categorized into two sub-categories.
  - **Perfectly-secure**: These protocols achieve all the security properties *without* any error.
  - **Statistically-secure**: These protocols achieve all the security properties except with some negligible error probability.
- **Cryptographically-secure Protocols**: The protocols under this category provide all the security guarantees against a computationally-bounded adversary.

We will use the notations $\mathsf{PerSec}, \mathsf{StatSec}$ and $\mathsf{CryptoSec}$ to refer to perfectly-secure, statistically-secure and cryptographically-secure protocols respectively. We will also use the notation Sec to refer to an arbitrary security notion from the set $\{\mathsf{PerSec}, \mathsf{StatSec}, \mathsf{CryptoSec}\}$.

While the *first* part of the monogram will be devoted to perfectly-secure protocols, statistically-secure and cryptographically-secure protocols will be considered in the *second* part of the monogram. This is because the former category of protocols is designed in the model $\mathcal{M} \in \{\mathcal{M}_{\mathsf{auth}}, \mathcal{M}_{\mathsf{secure}}\}$ discussed in the first part of the book. The latter category of protocols is designed in the model $\mathcal{M} \in \{\mathcal{M}^{\mathsf{pki}}_{\mathsf{auth}}, \mathcal{M}^{\mathsf{pki}}_{\mathsf{secure}}\}$ discussed in the second part of the monogram.

We next define the various measures associated with a consensus protocol.

2.3.1 Resilience, Round Complexity and Communication Complexity

The "quality" of any consensus protocol is judged based on the following three parameters.

- **Resilience**: It is the maximum number of corruptions t, which can be tolerated by the protocol.
- **Round Complexity**: It is the maximum number of rounds of communication required by the honest parties in the protocol.
- **Communication Complexity**: It is the maximum number of bits needed to be sent by the honest parties in the worst case during the execution of the protocol.[2]

A related complexity measure is the *message complexity*, which is the maximum number of messages that need to be sent by the honest parties in the worst case during the protocol execution. If the size of each message sent in the protocol is the same, then communication complexity can be easily derived by multiplying the message complexity by the size of each message. We will be interested in the communication complexity of the protocols.

[2] We do not measure the number of bits sent by the *corrupt* parties since we *cannot* prevent corrupt parties from sending arbitrary-size messages during the protocol execution.

We will often use the notation $\mathcal{BC}(L)$ to denote the communication complexity of a BB protocol where the input of the sender is of size L bits. Similarly, we will use the notation $\mathcal{BA}(L)$ to denote the communication complexity of a BA protocol where the input of the parties is of size L bits.

2.3.2 Trivial Necessary Conditions for BA and BB

From the definition of BA, it follows that an obvious necessary condition for BA (in any model and for any level of security) is that $t < \frac{n}{2}$ should hold. Otherwise, the corrupt parties, being the majority in number, would be able to "dictate" the outcome of the protocol, irrespective of the input of the honest parties. We now formalize this intuition.

Theorem 2.1 *Any t-secure BA protocol in the model* $\mathcal{M} \in \{\mathcal{M}_{\mathsf{auth}}, \mathcal{M}_{\mathsf{secure}}, \mathcal{M}^{\mathsf{pki}}_{\mathsf{auth}}, \mathcal{M}^{\mathsf{pki}}_{\mathsf{secure}}\}$ *and security level* $\mathsf{Sec} \in \{\mathsf{PerSec}, \mathsf{StatSec}, \mathsf{CryptoSec}\}$ *is possible only if* $t < \frac{n}{2}$ *holds.*

Proof We borrow the proof of the theorem from [51]. The proof is by a contradiction. So assume that there exists an arbitrary *t-secure* BA protocol Π in the model $\mathcal{M}$ with security type Sec with $t \geq \frac{n}{2}$, where $\mathcal{M} \in \{\mathcal{M}_{\mathsf{auth}}, \mathcal{M}_{\mathsf{secure}}, \mathcal{M}^{\mathsf{pki}}_{\mathsf{auth}}, \mathcal{M}^{\mathsf{pki}}_{\mathsf{secure}}\}$ and $\mathsf{Sec} \in \{\mathsf{PerSec}, \mathsf{StatSec}, \mathsf{CryptoSec}\}$. Moreover, for simplicity and without loss of generality, let the protocol be a bit-BA protocol where each party's input is a single bit; i.e., $L = 1$. Then consider a partition $\mathcal{P}_0$ and $\mathcal{P}_1$ of the set of parties $\mathcal{P}$, where $|\mathcal{P}_0| = n - t$ and $|\mathcal{P}_1| = t$. Since $t \geq \frac{n}{2}$, it follows that $t \geq n - t$ and hence during any execution of Π, the adversary can corrupt either $\mathcal{P}_0$ or $\mathcal{P}_1$. Now let us consider the following three possible executions of the protocol Π.

- **Execution** E: In this execution, all the parties in $\mathcal{P}_0$ participate in Π with input 0, while all the parties in $\mathcal{P}_1$ participate in Π with input 1. Moreover, the adversary decides *not* to corrupt any party.
- **Execution** E_0: In this execution, all the parties in $\mathcal{P}_0$ participate in Π with input 0, while all the parties in $\mathcal{P}_1$ participate in Π with input 1. The adversary decides to corrupt the parties in the set $\mathcal{P}_1$ in a *passive* fashion; i.e. the corrupt parties *do not* deviate from the protocol instructions.
- **Execution** E_1: In this execution, all the parties in $\mathcal{P}_0$ participate in Π with input 0, while all the parties in $\mathcal{P}_1$ participate in Π with input 1. The adversary decides to corrupt the parties in the set $\mathcal{P}_0$ in a *passive* fashion; i.e. the corrupt parties *do not* deviate from the protocol instructions. □

Let us now analyze the outcome of the above three executions. Consider the executions E and E_0. In both these executions, the parties in $\mathcal{P}_0$ are honest and not under the adversary's control and from the point of view of the parties in $\mathcal{P}_0$, these two executions are *indistinguishable*. On the other hand, consider the executions E and E_1. In both these executions, the parties in $\mathcal{P}_1$ are honest and not under the adversary's control and from the point of view of the parties in $\mathcal{P}_1$, these two executions are *indistinguishable*. From the *t-liveness* of Π, it follows that the honest parties will terminate and compute some output in all three executions. What can we say about these outputs?

In execution E, the parties in $\mathcal{P}_0$ as well as $\mathcal{P}_1$ are honest. From the *t-consistency* of Π, these parties should have a common output from the set $\{0, 1\}$ during the execution E. If the output is 0, then the parties in $\mathcal{P}_1$ will also output 0 in the execution E_1. This is because, as argued above, the executions E and E_1 are indistinguishable from the point of view of the parties in $\mathcal{P}_1$. So if the parties in $\mathcal{P}_1$ output 0 during execution E, then they should output 0 even during the execution E_1. However, the *t-validity* of Π demands that the parties in $\mathcal{P}_1$ should output 1 during the execution E_1. This is because the parties in $\mathcal{P}_1$ are honest in E_1 and have input 1. Hence, we get a contradiction.

Similarly, if the output of the parties in $\mathcal{P}_0$ and $\mathcal{P}_1$ is 1 in execution E, then the parties in $\mathcal{P}_0$ should also output 1 in the execution E_0. This is because, as argued above, the executions E and E_0 are indistinguishable from the point of view of the parties in $\mathcal{P}_0$. So if the parties in $\mathcal{P}_0$ output 1 during execution E, then they will output 1 even during the execution E_0. However, the *t-validity* of Π demands that the parties in $\mathcal{P}_0$ should output 0 during the execution E_0. This is because the parties in $\mathcal{P}_0$ are honest in E_0 and have input 0. Hence, we get a contradiction.

We have thus shown that it is *not* possible for Π to simultaneously achieve the validity and consistency properties, and hence Π does not exist. For a pictorial illustration of the above argument, see Fig 2.1.

We note that the proof of Theorem 2.1 will *not* work if $t < \frac{n}{2}$. Under this condition, the adversary *does not* have the capacity to corrupt *both* $\mathcal{P}_0$ and $\mathcal{P}_1$. We also note that the condition $t < \frac{n}{2}$ is *not* necessary for solving the BB problem. Intuitively this is because the validity is demanded only for a *single* honest party, namely the designated sender S. Hence the BB problem is well defined for $t < n$. Looking ahead, in the second part of the monogram, we will see *t-secure* BB protocols with the condition $t < n$ in the model $\mathcal{M}_{\mathsf{auth}}^{\mathsf{pki}}$.

Even though the requirements of BB and BA are slightly different, it turns out that they are "equivalent" as long as *majority* of the parties are *honest*. Namely, a protocol for BB will imply a protocol for BA and vice-versa. In the next couple of sections, we formally establish this equivalence.

2.3.3 BA Implies BB

We first show that BA always implies BB. Namely, let $\Pi_{\mathsf{BA}}^{(n,t)}$ be a *t-secure* BA protocol. Then one can easily design a *t-secure* BB protocol as follows: during the *first* round, the sender sends its input to all the parties over the point-to-point channels. While an *honest* sender will send the same input to everyone, a potentially *corrupt* sender may send different inputs to different parties. Then the parties run an instance of the BA protocol $\Pi_{\mathsf{BA}}^{(n,t)}$, where the input of the respective parties for the

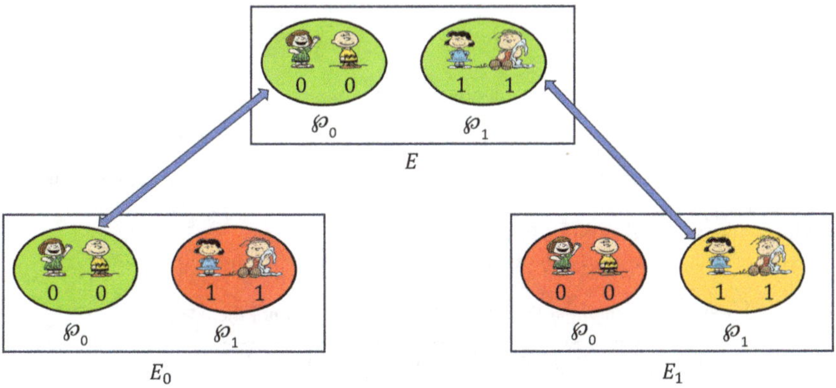

Fig. 2.1: Pictorial illustration of the executions E, E_0 and E_1 in the proof of Theorem 2.1. In all these executions, $\mathcal{P}_0$ and $\mathcal{P}_1$ constitute a partition of the set of parties $\mathcal{P}$ of size $n - t$ and t respectively. In all these executions, the inputs of the parties in $\mathcal{P}_0$ and $\mathcal{P}_1$ are 0 and 1 respectively. In execution E, no party is under the adversary's control as indicated by green sets, while in E_0 and E_1, the parties in $\mathcal{P}_0$ and $\mathcal{P}_1$ are honest, respectively (indicated by green sets). The corrupt parties do not deviate from the protocol instructions in executions E_0 and E_1. Executions E and E_0 are indistinguishable from the point of view of the parties in $\mathcal{P}_0$, while executions E and E_1 are indistinguishable from the point of view of the parties in $\mathcal{P}_1$. If the parties in $\mathcal{P}_0$ output 1 in execution E, then validity is violated in execution E_0. If the parties in $\mathcal{P}_1$ output 0 in execution E, then validity is violated in execution E_1

BA is the sender's input received at the end of the first round.[3] The output of the respective parties is the output that they get in the BA protocol.

It is easy to see that the termination, validity, and consistency of the BB follow from the termination, validity, and consistency of the BA, respectively. Note that the resilience of the resultant BB protocol is the *same* as that of the underlying BA protocol. We also note that the above reduction from BA to BB works *irrespective* of the communication model and the type of security achieved by the BA protocol. The formal steps of the resultant BB protocol are presented in Fig 2.2.

Protocol Π

Public Knowledge: A t-*secure* BA protocol $\Pi_{\mathsf{BA}}^{(n,t)}$ in the model $\mathcal{M} \in \{\mathcal{M}_{\mathsf{auth}}, \mathcal{M}_{\mathsf{secure}}, \mathcal{M}_{\mathsf{auth}}^{\mathsf{pki}}, \mathcal{M}_{\mathsf{secure}}^{\mathsf{pki}}\}$ with security level $\mathsf{Sec} \in \{\mathsf{PerSec}, \mathsf{StatSec}, \mathsf{CryptoSec}\}$, requiring r rounds of communication.

[3] If a party *does not* receive any input from the sender, then it takes some *default* input on the behalf of sender.

- **Round 1: Sender sending its input to all**
  - S on having the input $m \in \{0,1\}^L$, sends m to all the parties in $\mathcal{P}$, including itself.
  - For $i = 1, \ldots, n$, let $m_i \in \{0,1\}^L$ be the value received by P_i from S during this round.[a]
- **Rounds 2 to $r+1$: running the instance of BA**
  - The parties in $\mathcal{P}$ participate in an instance of $\Pi_{\mathsf{BA}}^{(n,t)}$ where for $i = 1, \ldots, n$, the input of party P_i is m_i.
  - For $i = 1, \ldots, n$, let $M_i \in \{0,1\}^L$ be the output computed by P_i during the instance of $\Pi_{\mathsf{BA}}^{(n,t)}$.
- **Output computation and termination**
  - For $i = 1, \ldots, n$, party P_i outputs M_i and terminate.

[a] If P_i does not receive any input from S by the end of this round, then it sets $m_i = 0^L$.

Fig. 2.2: Reduction from BA to BB

We now proceed to prove the prove the properties of the protocol Π.

Theorem 2.2 *Let $\Pi_{\mathsf{BA}}^{(n,t)}$ be a t-secure BA protocol in the model $\mathcal{M} \in \{\mathcal{M}_{\mathsf{auth}}, \mathcal{M}_{\mathsf{secure}}, \mathcal{M}_{\mathsf{auth}}^{\mathsf{pki}}, \mathcal{M}_{\mathsf{secure}}^{\mathsf{pki}}\}$ where the security is $\mathsf{Sec} \in \{\mathsf{PerSec}, \mathsf{StatSec}, \mathsf{CryptoSec}\}$. Moreover, let $\Pi_{\mathsf{BA}}^{(n,t)}$ require r rounds of communication over the point-to-point channels and incur a communication complexity of $\mathcal{BA}(L)$ bits if the inputs of the parties is of size L bits. Then protocol Π presented in Fig 2.2 is a t-secure BB protocol in the model $\mathcal{M}$ where the security is Sec. The protocol requires $r+1$ rounds of communication over the point-to-point channels and incurs a communication complexity of $\mathcal{BC}(L)$ bits where $\mathcal{BC}(L) = \mathcal{O}(nL) + \mathcal{BA}(L)$.*

Proof The number of communication rounds and the communication complexity follow trivially from the protocol description. The *t-liveness* follows from the *t-liveness* of $\Pi_{\mathsf{BA}}^{(n,t)}$ and the fact that the honest parties compute their output after $r+1$ rounds.

For *validity*, we have to consider an *honest* S. An honest S will send its input m identically to all honest parties during the first round. Consequently, $m_i = m$ will hold for each honest party P_i. This implies that all honest parties will participate with input m during the instance of $\Pi_{\mathsf{BA}}^{(n,t)}$. From the *t-validity* of $\Pi_{\mathsf{BA}}^{(n,t)}$ it follows that each honest P_i will output $M_i = m$ during the instance of $\Pi_{\mathsf{BA}}^{(n,t)}$. Consequently, all honest parties will output m in Π, thus proving the *t-validity*.

For *consistency*, we have to consider a *corrupt* S. From the protocol steps, it follows that every honest party will participate with some input from the set $\{0,1\}^L$ during the instance of $\Pi_{\mathsf{BA}}^{(n,t)}$. From the *t-consistency* of $\Pi_{\mathsf{BA}}^{(n,t)}$, it follows that every honest party will get a common output from the set $\{0,1\}^L$ during the instance of $\Pi_{\mathsf{BA}}^{(n,t)}$. Consequently, all honest parties will have a common output for Π, thus proving the *t-consistency*. □

2.3.4 BB Implies BA in the Honest-Majority Setting

We next show that BB also implies BA. Namely, let $\Pi_{\mathsf{BB}}^{(n,t)}$ be a *t-secure* BB protocol. If $t < \frac{n}{2}$, then one can design a *t-secure* BA protocol as follows: each party broadcasts its input (for the BA) through an instance of $\Pi_{\mathsf{BB}}^{(n,t)}$ by acting as a sender. The parties then output the majority of the outputs obtained from the BB instances if it exists. If a majority value does not exist, then they output some predetermined default value.

The *liveness* of $\Pi_{\mathsf{BB}}^{(n,t)}$ guarantees that all honest parties get some output. The *validity* of $\Pi_{\mathsf{BB}}^{(n,t)}$ will imply that if all honest parties have the same input, say u, then the majority of the BB outputs will be u since $t < \frac{n}{2}$ holds. Consequently, all honest parties will output u. The *consistency* of $\Pi_{\mathsf{BB}}^{(n,t)}$ will imply that all honest parties will have a *common* output from each BB instance, even if the designated sender of that instance is corrupt. Consequently, all honest parties will have a common output. The formal steps of the resultant BA protocol are presented in Fig 2.3.

Protocol Π

Public Knowledge: A *t-secure* BB protocol $\Pi_{\mathsf{BB}}^{(n,t)}$ in the model $\mathcal{M} \in \{\mathcal{M}_{\mathsf{auth}}, \mathcal{M}_{\mathsf{secure}}, \mathcal{M}_{\mathsf{auth}}^{\mathsf{pki}}, \mathcal{M}_{\mathsf{secure}}^{\mathsf{pki}}\}$ with security $\mathsf{Sec} \in \{\mathsf{PerSec}, \mathsf{StatSec}, \mathsf{CryptoSec}\}$, requiring R rounds of communication.

- **Rounds 1 to R: Broadcasting the inputs** — Each party $P_i \in \mathcal{P}$ does the following.
  - On having the input $u_i \in \{0,1\}^L$, act as a sender and invoke an instance of $\Pi_{\mathsf{BB}}^{(n,t)}$ with input u_i.
  - For $j = 1, \ldots, n$, participate in the instance of $\Pi_{\mathsf{BB}}^{(n,t)}$ invoked by P_j as a sender and let $u_{j,i} \in \{0,1\}^L$ be the output, computed during this instance of $\Pi_{\mathsf{BB}}^{(n,t)}$.
- **Output computation and termination** — Each party $P_i \in \mathcal{P}$ does the following.
  - If there exists some value which occurs more than $\frac{n}{2}$ times in the vector of values $(u_{1,i}, \ldots, u_{n,i})$, then output that value and terminate.
  - Else output $\{0,1\}^L$ and terminate.

Fig. 2.3: Reduction from BB to BA

We now proceed to prove the properties of the protocol.

Theorem 2.3 *Let* $\Pi_{\mathsf{BB}}^{(n,t)}$ *be a t-secure BB protocol in the model* $\mathcal{M} \in \{\mathcal{M}_{\mathsf{auth}}, \mathcal{M}_{\mathsf{secure}}, \mathcal{M}_{\mathsf{auth}}^{\mathsf{pki}}, \mathcal{M}_{\mathsf{secure}}^{\mathsf{pki}}\}$ *where the security is* $\mathsf{Sec} \in \{\mathsf{PerSec}, \mathsf{StatSec}, \mathsf{CryptoSec}\}$. *Moreover, let* $\Pi_{\mathsf{BB}}^{(n,t)}$ *require R rounds of communication over the point-to-point channels and incur a communication complexity of* $\mathcal{BC}(L)$ *bits if the input of the sender party is of size L bits. Then protocol* Π *presented in Fig 2.3 is a t-secure BA protocol in the model* $\mathcal{M}$ *where the security is* Sec *provided* $t < \frac{n}{2}$. *The protocol requires R rounds of communication over the point-to-point channels and incurs a communication of complexity of* $\mathcal{BA}(L)$ *bits where* $\mathcal{BA}(L) = n \cdot \mathcal{BC}(L)$.

Proof The communication complexity follows from the fact that there are n instances of $\Pi_{\mathsf{BB}}^{(n,t)}$ executed in the protocol, while round complexity follows from the fact that all these n instances can be executed in parallel.

The *t-liveness* of $\Pi_{\text{BB}}^{(n,t)}$ guarantees that each honest party will compute an output during each of the n instances of $\Pi_{\text{BB}}^{(n,t)}$ and terminate. Consequently, each honest party will compute an output during the protocol Π and terminate, thus guaranteeing *t-liveness* for Π.

Let each honest party P_i participate with input $u \in \{0,1\}^L$ in Π. From the *t-validity* of $\Pi_{\text{BB}}^{(n,t)}$ it follows that each honest party will compute the output u during the instance of $\Pi_{\text{BB}}^{(n,t)}$ executed by P_i as a sender. There can be at most t instances of $\Pi_{\text{BB}}^{(n,t)}$ executed by the *corrupt* sender parties, where the honest parties compute an output *different* from u. Since $t < \frac{n}{2}$, it follows that u will be the output from more than $\frac{n}{2}$ instances of $\Pi_{\text{BB}}^{(n,t)}$ and hence each honest party will compute the output u in Π, thus proving *t-validity* for Π.

Let the honest parties participate in the protocol Π will *different* inputs. Consider an *arbitrary* pair of *honest* parties P_j and P_k. We wish to show that both P_j and P_k compute the same output during Π. For this consider an *arbitrary* party P_i. If P_i is *honest*, then the *t-validity* of $\Pi_{\text{BB}}^{(n,t)}$ guarantees that $u_{i,j} = u_{i,k}$ holds, where $u_{i,j}$ and $u_{i,k}$ denote the output computed by P_j and P_k respectively during the instance of $\Pi_{\text{BB}}^{(n,t)}$ where P_i is the sender. On the other hand, even if P_i is *corrupt*, the *t-consistency* of $\Pi_{\text{BB}}^{(n,t)}$ guarantees that $u_{i,j} = u_{i,k}$ holds. This implies that the vector of outputs $(u_{1,j}, \ldots, u_{n,j})$ is the *same* as $(u_{1,k}, \ldots, u_{n,k})$. Since both P_j and P_k compute their respective output for Π as a *deterministic* function of the vectors $(u_{1,j}, \ldots, u_{n,j})$ and $(u_{1,k}, \ldots, u_{n,k})$ respectively (namely the majority function), it follows that both P_j and P_k will compute the same output in Π, thus proving *t-consistency* for Π. □

We finally conclude this chapter with two "weaker" variants of the consensus problem, which we will encounter several times in this monogram. The reason for considering these weaker variants is multifold. First, designing these primitives is relatively easy compared to full-fledged consensus protocols. Second, these primitives often serve as the stepping stone for designing full-fledged consensus protocols.

2.4 Graded Consensus

Graded consensus is a variant of distributed consensus, where each party associates a grade with its output, which is an indicator of the confidence level of the party in its output. The candidate grades are 2, 1 and 0, which are interpreted as *high, low* and *no* confidence, respectively. Graded consensus introduced in [48] is a weaker form of consensus, where consistency *may not* be achieved. That is, honest parties may have *different* outputs. However, the validity is guaranteed. Even though the primitive does not guarantee consistency, it does support a weaker form of consistency, which is called the *knowledge-of-agreement*. Namely, if any (honest) party gets an output with the highest grade (namely grade 2), then it is sure that every other honest party also has the same output, either with grade 2 or grade 1. That is, it is *not* possible for two different honest parties to obtain different outputs with the highest grade. As it turns out, this weaker form of consensus suffices as a building block for designing full-fledged consensus protocols. Similar to the distributed consensus, we have both the agreement as well as the broadcast variants of the graded consensus problem. We start with the broadcast variant first which is called *gradecast* (GC).

Informally, in a GC protocol, there is a designated *sender* $\mathsf{S} \in \mathcal{P}$ with input $m \in \{0,1\}^L$ and each party has an output from $\{0,1\}^L$, *along* with a grade from the set $\{0,1,2\}$. The goal of the primitive is to enable S to send its input to all the parties, such that depending upon the grade of the output, a party can conclude "something" about the output of the other parties and whether S has sent its input "consistently" to all the parties. If S is *honest*, then we require all honest parties to output the sender's value with the *highest* grade. Moreover, if any (honest) party gets an output with the *highest* grade, then it has the assurance that every other honest party will also have the same output, either with the grade 2 or 1. Formally, we have the following definition.

Definition 2.4 (Gradecast (GC)) Let Π be a protocol for the parties in $\mathcal{P} = \{P_1, \ldots, P_n\}$ in the model $\mathcal{M} \in \{\mathcal{M}_{\mathsf{auth}}, \mathcal{M}_{\mathsf{secure}}, \mathcal{M}^{\mathsf{pki}}_{\mathsf{auth}}, \mathcal{M}^{\mathsf{pki}}_{\mathsf{secure}}\}$, where there exists a designated *sender* party $\mathsf{S} \in \mathcal{P}$ with input $m \in \{0,1\}^L$ and where each party $P_i \in \mathcal{P}$ has an output (M_i, g_i) where $M_i \in \{0,1\}^L$ and $g_i \in \{0,1,2\}$, such that $L \geq 1$ and known publicly. Moreover, let t be the maximum number of parties which can get corrupt in a Byzantine fashion during any execution of Π, possibly including S.

- t**-liveness**: We say that Π has t*-liveness* if all honest parties terminate the protocol.
- t**-validity**: We say that Π has t*-validity* if the following holds.
  - If S is *honest*, then each honest party outputs $(m, 2)$.
- t**-knowledge-of-agreement**: We say that Π has t*-knowledge-of-agreement* if the following holds.
  - If any honest party P_i outputs $(M, 2)$, then every other honest party outputs either $(M, 2)$ or $(M, 1)$.

We say that Π is a t*-secure* GC protocol in the model $\mathcal{M}$, if it achieves t*-liveness*, t*-validity* and t*-knowledge-of-agreement*.

We next define the agreement version of graded consensus, which is called *graded agreement* (GA). Informally in a GA protocol, each party has some input and an output, along with a grade from the set $\{0,1,2\}$. The goal of the primitive is to find out if all *honest* parties have the same input, such that depending upon the grade of the output, a party can conclude "something" about the output of the other parties. Informally, if all honest parties have the same input, then all honest parties should have this output with a grade 2. Moreover, if any (honest) party gets an output with grade 2, then it is assured that every other honest party will also have the same output, either with grade 2 or 1. Formally, we have the following definition.

Definition 2.5 (Graded Agreement (GA)) Let Π be a protocol for the parties in $\mathcal{P} = \{P_1, \ldots, P_n\}$ in the model $\mathcal{M} \in \{\mathcal{M}_{\mathsf{auth}}, \mathcal{M}_{\mathsf{secure}}, \mathcal{M}^{\mathsf{pki}}_{\mathsf{auth}}, \mathcal{M}^{\mathsf{pki}}_{\mathsf{secure}}\}$, where each $P_i \in \mathcal{P}$ has an input $v_i \in \{0,1\}^L$ and output (w_i, g_i) where $w_i \in \{0,1\}^L$ and $g_i \in \{0,1,2\}$, such that $L \geq 1$ and known publicly. Moreover, let t be the maximum number of parties which can be corrupted by the adversary in a Byzantine fashion during any execution of Π.

- t**-liveness**: We say that Π has *t-liveness*, if all honest parties terminate the protocol.
- t**-validity**: We say that Π has *t-validity*, if the following holds.
  - If $v_i = v$ for every honest party P_i, then each honest party outputs $(v, 2)$.
- t**-knowledge-of-agreement**: We say that Π has *t-knowledge-of-agreement*, if the following holds.
  - If any honest party P_i outputs $(v, 2)$, then every other honest party outputs either $(v, 2)$ or $(v, 1)$.

We say that Π is a *t-secure* GA protocol in the model $\mathcal{M}$, if it achieves *t-liveness*, *t-validity* and *t-knowledge-of-agreement*.

Similar to BB and BA, depending upon whether the adversary is computationally bounded or unbounded, the security of a GC/GA protocol is either *unconditional* or *conditional* (*cryptographic*). Moreover, GC/GA protocols with unconditional security can be further categorized as *perfectly-secure* and *statistically-secure*, depending upon whether the properties are achieved *without* any error or with a *negligible* error. We will use the notation $\mathcal{GC}(L)$ to denote the communication complexity of any GC protocol where the input of the designated sender is of size L bits. Similarly, the notation $\mathcal{GA}(L)$ will denote the communication complexity of any GA protocol where the inputs of the parties are of size L bits.

We have seen earlier that BB and BA are equivalent if we are in the honest majority setting. Interestingly, the equivalence holds even for the two variants of the graded consensus problem.

2.4.1 GA Implies GC

In this section, we show that given an instantiation of GA, one can easily design a GC protocol. The idea used for getting a BC protocol from a BA protocol is reused here. Let $\Pi_{\mathsf{GA}}^{(n,t)}$ be a *t-secure* GA protocol, requiring r rounds of communication. We then show how to get a *t-secure* GC protocol with $r+1$ rounds of communication. During the *first* round, the sender distributes its input to all the parties over the point-to-point channels. Then, for the next r rounds, the parties run an instance of the GA protocol, where the input of each party is the message that it has received from the sender during the first round. The output from the instance of GA is then set as the output of the GC protocol. The protocol is formally presented in Fig 2.4.

Protocol Π

Public Knowledge: A *t-secure* GA protocol $\Pi_{\mathsf{GA}}^{(n,t)}$ in the model $\mathcal{M} \in \{\mathcal{M}_{\mathsf{auth}}, \mathcal{M}_{\mathsf{secure}}, \mathcal{M}_{\mathsf{auth}}^{\mathsf{pki}}, \mathcal{M}_{\mathsf{secure}}^{\mathsf{pki}}\}$ with security $\mathsf{Sec} \in \{\mathsf{PerSec}, \mathsf{StatSec}, \mathsf{CryptoSec}\}$, requiring r rounds of communication.

- **Round 1: Sender sending its input to all**
  - S on having the input $m \in \{0, 1\}^L$, sends m to all the parties in $\mathcal{P}$, including itself.

- For $i = 1, \ldots, n$, let $m_i \in \{0,1\}^L$ be the value received by P_i from S during this round.[a]

- **Rounds** 2 **to** $r+1$: running the instance of GA.
  - The parties in $\mathcal{P}$ participate in an instance of $\Pi_{\mathsf{GA}}^{(n,t)}$ where for $i = 1, \ldots, n$, the input of party P_i is m_i.
  - For $i = 1, \ldots, n$, let (M_i, g_i) be the output computed by P_i during the instance of $\Pi_{\mathsf{GA}}^{(n,t)}$, where $M_i \in \{0,1\}^L$ and $g_i \in \{0,1,2\}$.
- **Output computation and termination**
  - For $i = 1, \ldots, n$, party P_i outputs (M_i, g_i) and terminate.

[a] If P_i does not receive any input from S by the end of this round, then it sets $m_i = 0^L$.

Fig. 2.4: Reduction from GA to GC

The properties of the protocol Π stated in Theorem 2.4 simply follow from the properties of the protocol $\Pi_{\mathsf{GA}}^{(n,t)}$.

Theorem 2.4 *Let* $\Pi_{\mathsf{GA}}^{(n,t)}$ *be a t-secure GA protocol in the model* $\mathcal{M} \in \{\mathcal{M}_{\mathsf{auth}}, \mathcal{M}_{\mathsf{secure}}, \mathcal{M}_{\mathsf{auth}}^{\mathsf{pki}}, \mathcal{M}_{\mathsf{secure}}^{\mathsf{pki}}\}$ *with security* $\mathsf{Sec} \in \{\mathsf{PerSec}, \mathsf{StatSec}, \mathsf{CryptoSec}\}$. *Moreover, let* $\Pi_{\mathsf{GA}}^{(n,t)}$ *require r rounds of communication over the point-to-point channels and incur a communication complexity of* $\mathcal{GA}(L)$ *bits, if the inputs of the parties are of size L bits. Then protocol Π presented in Fig 2.4 is a t-secure GC protocol in the model* $\mathcal{M}$ *with security* Sec. *The protocol requires $r+1$ rounds of communication over the point-to-point channels and incurs a communication complexity of* $\mathcal{GC}(L)$ *bits where* $\mathcal{GC}(L) = \mathcal{O}(nL) + \mathcal{GA}(L)$.

Proof The *t-liveness* follows from the *t-liveness* of $\Pi_{\mathsf{GA}}^{(n,t)}$. The communication and round complexity follow from the protocol inspection. For *t-validity*, consider an *honest* S. During the first round, S will send its input *m identically* to *all* the parties. Consequently, all honest parties will participate in the instance of $\Pi_{\mathsf{GA}}^{(n,t)}$ with input m. Hence, from the *t-validity* of $\Pi_{\mathsf{GA}}^{(n,t)}$, it follows that all honest parties will compute the output $(m, 2)$ during the instance of $\Pi_{\mathsf{GA}}^{(n,t)}$ and then output $(m, 2)$ for Π.

For *t-knowledge-of-agreement*, let P_i be an *honest* party who outputs $(M, 2)$ during Π. This implies that P_i computes the output $(M, 2)$ during the instance of $\Pi_{\mathsf{GA}}^{(n,t)}$. Then, from the *t-knowledge-of-agreement* property of $\Pi_{\mathsf{GA}}^{(n,t)}$, it follows that every other honest party will compute the output $(M, 2)$ or $(M, 1)$ during the instance of $\Pi_{\mathsf{GA}}^{(n,t)}$. Hence, every honest party will output either $(M, 2)$ or $(M, 1)$ for Π. □

We next show that GC implies GA as well if we are in the honest-majority setting.

2.4.2 GC Implies GA in the Honest Majority Setting

In this section, we show that given an instantiation of GC, one can design a GA protocol, provided $t < \frac{n}{2}$. The idea is similar to the one used to get a BA protocol from a BB protocol, with special care taken to determine the output. Let $\Pi_{\mathsf{GC}}^{(n,t)}$ be a *t-secure* GC protocol, requiring R rounds of communication. We then show how to get a *t-secure* GA protocol with R rounds of communication.

In the protocol, each party broadcasts its input (for the GA) through an instance of $\Pi_{\mathsf{GC}}^{(n,t)}$ by acting as a sender. The parties then check if there exists some value which has occurred as output with the highest grade (namely grade 2) during the majority of the GC instances and take it as the output for GA with grade 2. Else they check if there exists some value which has occurred as output with the medium or highest grade (namely grade 1 or grade 2) during the majority of the GC instances and take it as the output for GA with grade 1. Otherwise, the parties output their respective inputs with grade 0.

The *liveness* of $\Pi_{\mathsf{GC}}^{(n,t)}$ guarantees that all honest parties terminate the protocol. The *validity* of $\Pi_{\mathsf{GC}}^{(n,t)}$ will imply that if all honest parties have the same input, say v, then the majority of the GC outputs will be $(v, 2)$ since $t < \frac{n}{2}$ holds. Consequently, all honest parties will output $(v, 2)$. If any honest party outputs a value w with grade 2, then it implies that the majority of GC outputs for that honest party are $(w, 2)$. The *knowledge-of-agreement* of $\Pi_{\mathsf{GC}}^{(n,t)}$ then guarantees that these GC instances output either $(w, 2)$ or $(w, 1)$ for every other honest party. Consequently, every other honest party will either output $(w, 2)$ or $(w, 1)$. The formal steps of the resultant GA protocol are presented in Fig 2.5.

Protocol Π

Public Knowledge: A *t-secure* GC protocol $\Pi_{\mathsf{GC}}^{(n,t)}$ in the model $\mathcal{M} \in \{\mathcal{M}_{\mathsf{auth}}, \mathcal{M}_{\mathsf{secure}}, \mathcal{M}_{\mathsf{auth}}^{\mathsf{pki}}, \mathcal{M}_{\mathsf{secure}}^{\mathsf{pki}}\}$ with security $\mathsf{Sec} \in \{\mathsf{PerSec}, \mathsf{StatSec}, \mathsf{CryptoSec}\}$, requiring R rounds of communication.

- **Rounds** 1 **to** R**: Broadcasting the inputs** — Each party $P_i \in \mathcal{P}$ does the following.
  - On having the input $v_i \in \{0, 1\}^L$, act as a sender and invoke an instance of $\Pi_{\mathsf{GC}}^{(n,t)}$ with input v_i.
  - For $j = 1, \ldots, n$, participate in the instance of $\Pi_{\mathsf{GC}}^{(n,t)}$ invoked by P_j as a sender and let $(u_{j,i}, g_{j,i})$ be the output, computed during this instance of $\Pi_{\mathsf{BB}}^{(n,t)}$ where $u_{j,i} \in \{0, 1\}^L$ and $g_{j,i} \in \{0, 1, 2\}$.
- **Output computation and termination** — Each party $P_i \in \mathcal{P}$ does the following.
  - If there exists some value $u \in \{0, 1\}^L$ such that the pair $(u, 2)$ occurs more than $\frac{n}{2}$ times in the vector of pairs of outputs $((u_{1,i}, g_{1,i}) \ldots, (u_{n,i}, g_{n,i}))$, then output $(u, 2)$ and terminate.
  - Else if there exists some value $u \in \{0, 1\}^L$ such that the pair $(u, 2)$ occurs N_1 times and the pair $(u, 1)$ occurs N_2 times in the vector of pairs of outputs $((u_{1,i}, g_{1,i}) \ldots, (u_{n,i}, g_{n,i}))$ where $N_1, N_2 \geq 1$ and $N_1 + N_2 > \frac{n}{2}$, then output $(u, 1)$ and terminate.
  - Else output $(v_i, 0)$ and terminate.

Fig. 2.5: Reduction from GC to GA

We now proceed to prove the properties of the protocol.

Theorem 2.5 *Let* $\Pi_{\mathsf{GC}}^{(n,t)}$ *be a t-secure GC protocol in the model* $\mathcal{M} \in \{\mathcal{M}_{\mathsf{auth}}, \mathcal{M}_{\mathsf{secure}}, \mathcal{M}_{\mathsf{auth}}^{\mathsf{pki}}, \mathcal{M}_{\mathsf{secure}}^{\mathsf{pki}}\}$ *where the security is* $\mathsf{Sec} \in \{\mathsf{PerSec}, \mathsf{StatSec}, \mathsf{CryptoSec}\}$. *Moreover, let* $\Pi_{\mathsf{GC}}^{(n,t)}$ *require R rounds of communication over the point-to-point channels* *and incur a communication complexity of $\mathcal{GC}(L)$ bits if the input of the sender party is of size L bits. Then protocol Π presented in Fig 2.5 is a t-secure GA protocol in the model $\mathcal{M}$ where the security is* Sec *provided $t < \frac{n}{2}$. The protocol requires R rounds of communication over the point-to-point channels and incurs a communication of complexity of $\mathcal{GA}(L)$ bits where $\mathcal{GA}(L) = n \cdot \mathcal{GC}(L)$.*

Proof The communication complexity follows from the fact that there are n instances of $\Pi_{\mathsf{GC}}^{(n,t)}$ executed in the protocol, while round complexity follows from the fact that all these n instances can be executed in parallel.

The *t-liveness* of $\Pi_{\mathsf{GC}}^{(n,t)}$ guarantees that each honest party will compute an output during each of the n instances of $\Pi_{\mathsf{GC}}^{(n,t)}$ and terminate. Consequently, each honest party will compute an output during the protocol Π and terminate, thus guaranteeing *t-liveness* for Π.

Let each honest party P_i participate with input $v \in \{0,1\}^L$ in Π. We wish to show that all honest parties will output $(v, 2)$ in Π. From the *t-validity* of $\Pi_{\mathsf{GC}}^{(n,t)}$ it follows that each honest party will compute the output $(v, 2)$ during the instance of $\Pi_{\mathsf{GC}}^{(n,t)}$ executed by P_i as a sender. There can be at most t instances of $\Pi_{\mathsf{GC}}^{(n,t)}$ executed by the *corrupt* sender parties, where the honest parties compute an output *different* from v. Since $t < \frac{n}{2}$, it follows that $(v, 2)$ will be the output from more than $\frac{n}{2}$ instances of $\Pi_{\mathsf{GC}}^{(n,t)}$ and hence each honest party will compute the output $(v, 2)$ in Π, thus proving *t-validity* for Π.

Let P_i be an honest party who outputs $(w, 2)$ during Π. It implies that there exists a subset of parties $\mathcal{A}$ where $|\mathcal{A}| > \frac{n}{2}$ such that P_i computes the output $(w, 2)$ during the instances of $\Pi_{\mathsf{GC}}^{(n,t)}$, executed by each sender party in the set $\mathcal{A}$. For proving the *t-knowledge-of-agreement* for Π, we need to show that every other honest party will output $(w, 2)$ or $(w, 1)$ in Π. So consider an arbitrary honest party P_j different from P_i. From the *t-knowledge-of-agreement* it follows that P_j will either compute the output $(w, 2)$ or $(w, 1)$ during the instances of $\Pi_{\mathsf{GC}}^{(n,t)}$, executed by each sender party in the set $\mathcal{A}$. There can be at most t instances of $\Pi_{\mathsf{GC}}^{(n,t)}$ executed by the sender parties *not* in $\mathcal{A}$, where the honest parties compute an output *different* from w. Since $t < \frac{n}{2}$, it follows that $(w, 2)$ or $(w, 1)$ will be the output for P_j from more than $\frac{n}{2}$ instances of $\Pi_{\mathsf{GC}}^{(n,t)}$. Consequently, P_j will output either $(w, 2)$ or $(w, 1)$, thus proving *t-knowledge-of-agreement* for Π. □

Chapter 3
EIG Protocol for Byzantine Broadcast

In this chapter, we present the classical *exponential information gathering* (EIG) protocol for Byzantine broadcast (BB) due to [78]. The protocol is *inefficient* and may require an *exponential* amount of computation and communication (as indicated in its name). Despite these, it is of great historical importance, since it is the *first* protocol for BB. The protocol is *perfectly-secure*. Furthermore, it enjoys the characteristics of having *optimal resilience* as well as *optimal* number of communication *rounds*, required for *any* BB protocol *without* any setup. Both these lower bounds will be proven in the subsequent chapters. While we present the BB-variant of the protocol, one can easily obtain a BA protocol from it, *without* affecting its resilience and number of communication rounds. As a warm-up, we first present the EIG protocol for a simplistic setting involving a *fixed* number of parties. The goal of the warm-up protocol is to introduce the EIG data structure and the way it is populated, which constitute the cruxes of the EIG protocol. This will be followed by the generalization of the protocol for *arbitrary* number of parties.

3.1 Network Model and Adversary Setting

We consider the pairwise-authentic channel setting in this chapter, namely the model $\mathcal{M}_{\mathsf{auth}}$, where the parties in $\mathcal{P}$ are connected by pairwise-authentic channels. We assume a *computationally-unbounded* adversary Adv who can corrupt any t parties in a Byzantine fashion where $t < \frac{n}{3}$. For convenience, we use the following convention in our protocols: if any party P_i is expecting some message from an underlying domain from some sender party P_j during any round r and if either *no* message or a syntactically *incorrect* message comes from P_j, then P_i *substitutes* some *default* message from the corresponding domain on the behalf of P_j and process it as per the protocol.[1] Hence, we will *not* make our protocols complicated unnecessarily and

[1] Clearly, if this happens then P_j is a *corrupt* party. Consequently, the underlying protocol should still achieve the desired properties, as it should be the case if, during some execution, the *corrupt* P_j would have sent the default message to P_i.

A. Choudhury and A. Patra, *Fault-Tolerant Distributed Consensus in Synchronous Networks*, Information Security and Cryptography,
https://doi.org/10.1007/978-3-031-80460-1_3

add instructions for the case when no message or syntactically incorrect messages are delivered. Also, for simplicity, we will assume that the input of the sender party is a *single* bit. However, we stress that all the protocols presented in this chapter will work even if the input of the sender is from the set $\{0, 1\}^L$ where $L \geq 1$.

3.2 Warmup: EIG Protocol with $t = 1$ and $n = 4$

In this section, we present the EIG protocol assuming that the set of parties $\mathcal{P} = \{A, B, C, D\}$ and Adv can corrupt any *one* party among $\{A, B, C, D\}$; i.e. $t = 1$ and $n = 4$. Notice that this satisfies the condition $t < \frac{n}{3}$. Moreover, for simplicity and without loss of generality, we assume that A is the designated *sender* for the protocol, with input $m \in \{0, 1\}$.

The idea behind the protocol is very simple: during the first round, A sends m to every party and terminates. To check whether a potentially *corrupt* A has sent different inputs to different parties, they check the "consistency" of the input as received from A, by exchanging the message as received from A during the second round and outputs the *majority* of these values. The idea here is that since $t = 1$, either the sender A could be corrupt or one of the parties among $\{B, C, D\}$ could be corrupt. If A is *honest*, then it would send the *same* message m to everyone and hence every *honest* party among $\{B, C, D\}$ will output m, since it will constitute the majority (this guarantees the *validity*). On the other hand, if A behaves *maliciously* by sending different messages to the parties in $\{B, C, D\}$, still they will output a *common* output since all of them will know the different versions of the message sent by A during the first round (this guarantees the *consistency*).

From the above description of the protocol, it follows that during the protocol, each party has a value that it received *directly* from the sender during the *first* round and the values that the other two parties report to have received from the sender during the *second* round. And finally, based on this information, each party computes its final output. We will re-interpret the whole process as if each party maintains the information received during the two rounds in a special data structure called *EIG-tree* and based on the values in its EIG-tree, each party makes a final decision. Re-interpreting the computation in terms of EIG-tree will be useful when we generalize the protocol for *any* $t < \frac{n}{3}$.

Re-interpreting the protocol in terms of EIG-tree.

Each party (other than the sender) maintains a local copy of EIG-tree. The tree consists of *two* levels, corresponding to the two communication rounds in the protocol and stores whatever information a party receives throughout the protocol during those two rounds. The root of the tree is labelled A, and the value assigned to this node is denoted by $V(A)$. Every party assigns $V(A)$ the value it receives from A during the first round. The root has 3 children, labelled AB, AC and AD and the value assigned to these nodes is denoted by $V(AB)$, $V(AC)$ and $V(AD)$ respectively. Each party assigns $V(AB)$, $V(AC)$ and $V(AD)$ the values which B, C and D respectively sent during the second round, saying it received that value from A. Each party then computes the majority of the values stored in the leaf nodes of its EIG-tree, and this is taken as the final output (see Fig 3.1).

We call the above protocol $\Pi_{\text{EIG}}^{(4,1)}$ and formally present it in Fig 3.2. Since every party will be maintaining a *local* copy of the EIG-tree in the protocol, we denote the copy of the tree for party $i \in \{B, C, D\}$ as $T_i^{(4,1)}$. Similarly, $V_i(\sigma)$ will denote the value assigned by party $i \in \{B, C, D\}$ to the node labelled σ in the tree $T_i^{(4,1)}$.

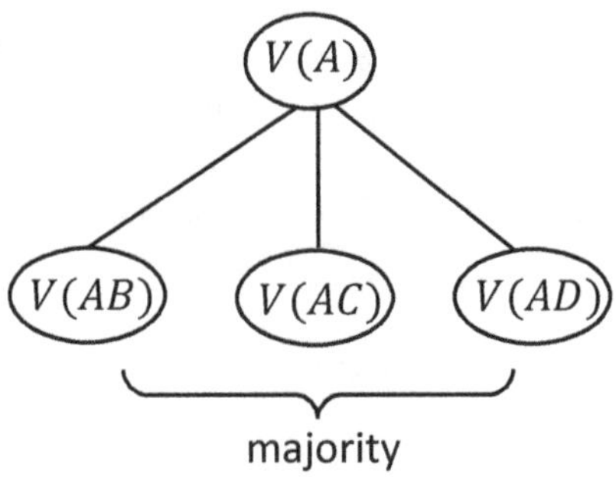

Fig. 3.1: Information gathering tree for $t = 1$ and $n = 4$

Protocol $\Pi_{\text{EIG}}^{(4,1)}$

Initialization: Initialize the tree $T_i^{(4,1)}$ by setting the value of all the nodes in $T_i^{(4,1)}$ to $\perp$.

- **Round 1: Sender distributing its input**
  - Party A on having the input m, sends m to all the parties in the set $\{B, C, D\}$, outputs m and terminates.
  - Let $m^{(i)}$ denote the message received from A. Set $V_i(A) = m^{(i)}$ in the EIG-tree $T_i^{(4,1)}$.
- **Round 2: Parties exchanging the inputs received from the sender**
  - Send $m^{(i)}$ to *all* the parties in $\{B, C, D\}$.[a]
  - Let $m^{(ji)}$ denote the message received from party $j \in \{B, C, D\}$. Set $V_i(Aj) = m^{(ji)}$ in the EIG-tree $T_i^{(4,1)}$.
- **Output Computation:** Let $O_i \stackrel{def}{=} \text{majority}(V_i(AB), V_i(AC), V_i(AD))$. Output O_i and terminate.

[a] Note that node i *implicitly* sends $m^{(i)}$ to itself.

Fig. 3.2: The information gathering protocol for the parties $\{A, B, C, D\}$, where A is the designated sender. The above steps are executed by each $i \in \{B, C, D\}$

We next formally prove that protocol $\Pi_{\mathsf{EIG}}^{(4,1)}$ satisfies the properties of BB. The liveness property is trivial, since all honest parties terminate the protocol at the end of the second round. We start with the proof of the *validity* property.

Lemma 3.1 *Protocol* $\Pi_{\mathsf{EIG}}^{(4,1)}$ *achieves* 1*-validity.*

Proof For validity, we have to consider the case when the sender, namely the node A, is *honest*. This implies that Adv can corrupt one of the nodes in the set $\{B, C, D\}$. For simplicity and without loss of generality, let B be the corrupt node. Since A is *honest*, it sends m to all the parties during the first round and consequently $V_C(A) = V_D(A) = m$ holds, since $m^{(C)} = m^{(D)} = m$ will hold. Since C and D are honest, they will send m to all the parties during the second round and hence $V_C(CA) = V_C(DA) = V_D(CA) = V_D(DA) = m$ holds, since $m^{(CC)} = m^{(DC)} = m^{(CD)} = m^{(DD)} = m$ will hold. Node B may send incorrect values during the second round, and consequently, $V_C(AB) \neq V_D(AB)$ may hold. However, irrespective of the value of the node labelled AB, the majority of the children of the root will have value m, in both $T_C^{(4,1)}$ as well as $T_D^{(4,1)}$. Consequently, $O_C = O_D = m$ holds and hence both C and D will output m. For a pictorial depiction of the above argument, see Fig 3.3.

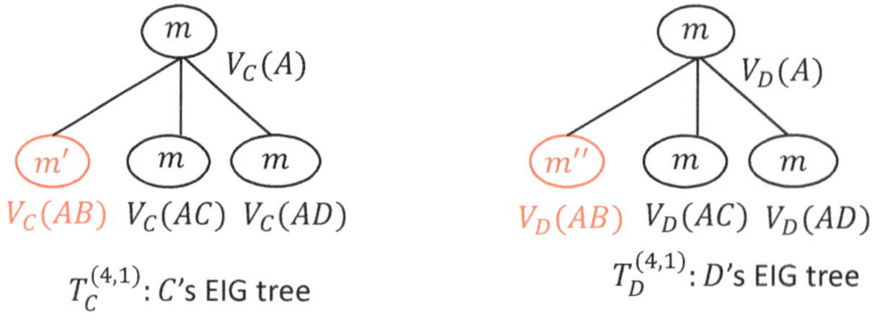

Fig. 3.3: Pictorial depiction of the validity property for the protocol $\Pi_{\mathsf{EIG}}^{(4,1)}$, assuming that the node B behaves maliciously. A corrupt B can report different values being received from the sender A to C and D, due to which the value of the node labelled AB might be different in C's and D's EIG-tree, as shown in red colour. However, still the majority of the children of the root node will have the value m in both the trees and hence m will be the final output

We next prove the *consistency* property.

Lemma 3.2 *Protocol* $\Pi_{\mathsf{EIG}}^{(4,1)}$ *achieves* 1-*consistency.*

Proof For consistency, we have to consider the case when the sender, namely the node A behaves *maliciously* and sends different messages to different parties. Consequently, $m^{(B)} \neq m^{(C)} \neq m^{(D)}$ and hence $V_B(A) \neq V_C(A) \neq V_D(A)$ will hold at the end the first round. However, since B, C and D are all *honest*, they will correctly report the value received from A during the second round. Consequently, the following will hold.

- $V_B(AB) = V_C(AB) = V_D(AB) = m^{(B)}$;
- $V_B(AC) = V_C(AC) = V_D(AC) = m^{(C)}$;
- $V_B(AD) = V_C(AD) = V_D(AD) = m^{(D)}$. □

Since $O_i = \text{majority}(V_i(AB), V_i(AC), V_i(AD))$ for every party $i \in \{B, C, D\}$, due to the above conditions $O_B = O_C = O_D$ will hold and all the honest parties will output a common value. For a pictorial depiction of the above argument, see Fig 3.4.

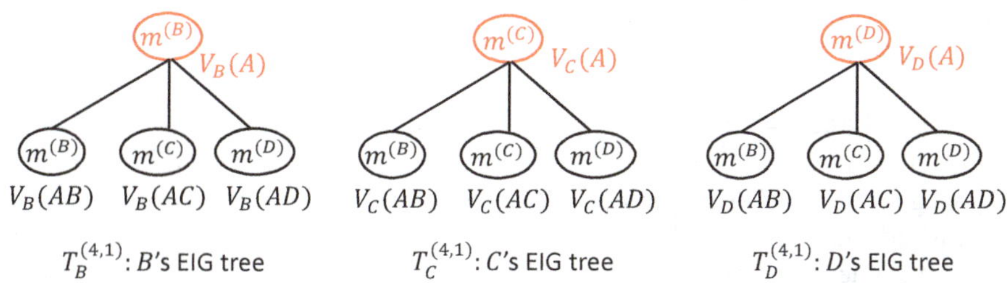

Fig. 3.4: Pictorial depiction of the consistency property for the protocol $\Pi_{\mathsf{EIG}}^{(4,1)}$, assuming that the sender A behaves maliciously. A corrupt sender can send different values during the first round, due to which the value of the node labelled A (root node) might be different in the EIG-tree of all honest parties, as shown in red colour. However, during the second round, all honest parties will correctly report the value received from the sender to each other, due to which the value of children of the root node will be the same in the EIG-trees of all honest parties. Consequently, all honest parties will have a common output

3.2.1 More Discussion on the Protocol $\Pi_{\mathsf{EIG}}^{(4,1)}$

Before proceeding further, we discuss a few important aspects of the protocol $\Pi_{\mathsf{EIG}}^{(4,1)}$. Especially, we discuss the importance of the number of rounds in the protocol and what goes wrong if the adversary corrupts more than one party in the protocol.

Why 2 rounds?

One may wonder what goes wrong if the protocol $\Pi_{\mathsf{EIG}}^{(4,1)}$ is executed *only* for one round. We first note that in the protocol, during the first round, only the sender sends messages to the other parties. If we run the protocol $\Pi_{\mathsf{EIG}}^{(4,1)}$ for *only* one round, then the parties have to output whatever message they receive from the sender. This is because if there are any messages exchanged among the parties during the first round, then they will be *independent* of the sender's input and hence *cannot* be considered for determining the final output.

The modified protocol will still *achieve* validity. This is because if the sender is *honest*, then it will send the *same* input to everyone. However, the *consistency* may be *violated*. This is because a potentially *corrupt* sender may send *different* inputs to different parties and there will be *no* follow up rounds, to check for any *inconsistency* among the messages distributed by the sender.

Why $n = 4$ and $t = 1$?

What goes wrong if in the protocol $\Pi_{\mathsf{EIG}}^{(4,1)}$, the adversary corrupts *more than* 1 party? Let us consider *validity*. The validity will *no longer* hold because even though an *honest* sender will send the same message to all the parties in round one, during the second round, the corrupt parties may report receiving different inputs from the sender in such a way that the incorrectly reported inputs constitute the majority, leading to the honest parties computing an output, which is *different* from the sender's input.

To demonstrate the above attack, consider the case when $t = 2$ and the adversary corrupts the parties B and C. Let the input of A be $m = 0$, which it sends to every party during the first round. During the second round, party D (which is an honest party) will report receiving 0 from the sender during the previous round. However, both B and C report receiving input 1 from the sender in the previous round. Consequently, as shown in Fig 3.5, party D ends up computing the output 1, which is *different* from the input of the sender and hence the *validity* property is *violated*.

From the above discussion, it follows that the protocol $\Pi_{\mathsf{EIG}}^{(4,1)}$ are *optimal* in terms of the number of rounds, as well as the number of maximum corruptions which it can tolerate (namely resilience). Later in the subsequent chapters, we will formally show that in the setting considered in the protocol $\Pi_{\mathsf{EIG}}^{(4,1)}$, *any* BB protocol can tolerate *only* up to one corrupt party and will require at least two communication rounds.

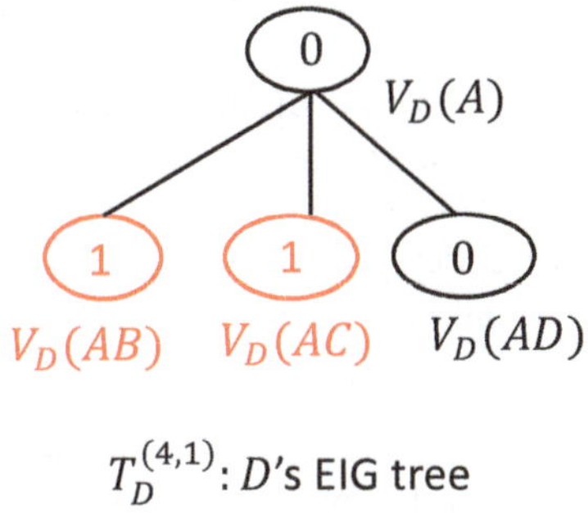

Fig. 3.5: Pictorial depiction of the violation of the validity property in the protocol $\Pi_{\text{EIG}}^{(4,1)}$, if adversary corrupts two parties, namely the parties B and C. While the value of the root node will be assigned the value of the sender's input in D's tree, the majority of its children will be assigned a different value, since the corrupt B and corrupt C reports receiving the bit-complement of the sender's actual input. Consequently, the honest D outputs a value, different from the sender's input.

3.3 Generalizing the EIG Protocol for any $t < \frac{n}{3}$

In this section, we will try to extend and generalize the protocol $\Pi_{\text{EIG}}^{(4,1)}$, for *any* n and t, satisfying the condition $t < \frac{n}{3}$. We first try a naive extension and show that the resultant protocol *fails* to achieve any security guarantees.

3.3.1 Naive Extension of the Protocol $\Pi_{\text{EIG}}^{(4,1)}$

Consider a pair of values (n, t), where $t < \frac{n}{3}$. What happens if we simply run the protocol $\Pi_{\text{EIG}}^{(4,1)}$ *as it is*, where the parties exchange messages for two rounds, populate their respective copies of EIG-tree and make a final decision? Will the resultant protocol achieve validity and consistency?

Let us first consider the validity property. As it turns out, the t-validity will be achieved. Intuitively this is because if the sender is *honest*, it will send the *same* input, say m, to *all* the parties during the first round. Now even if we exclude the sender, the *majority* of the remaining parties will be honest and will report m to have been received from the sender, to each other during the second round. Consequently, all honest parties will output m (we leave the formal details as an exercise). Next, consider the *consistency* property. As it turns out, consistency is *not* guaranteed. Namely, a corrupt sender can distribute *different* messages to different parties during the first round. Later, during the second round, when the parties try to check the consistency of the received message, the adversary can report in such a way that different honest parties may end up computing different outputs.

To make the argument more formal, let $n = 3t + 1$, which is the *smallest* value of n, satisfying the condition $t < \frac{n}{3}$. Let $\mathcal{P} = \{P_1, \ldots, P_{3t+1}\}$ and without loss of generality, let P_1 be the sender. Moreover, for simplicity and without loss of generality, let $\{P_1, \ldots P_t\}$ be the set of t parties under the control of the adversary during the protocol. Hence the set of honest parties is $\{P_{t+1}, \ldots, P_{3t+1}\}$. Let $\mathcal{H}_0 \stackrel{def}{=} \{P_{t+1}, \ldots, P_{2t}\}$ and $\mathcal{H}_1 \stackrel{def}{=} \{P_{2t+1}, \ldots, P_{3t+1}\}$ be a disjoint partition of the set of honest parties. Then consider the following strategy by the adversary. During the first round, P_1 as a sender sends 0 and 1 as its input to all the parties in the set $\mathcal{H}_0$ and $\mathcal{H}_1$, respectively. During the second round, the parties in $\mathcal{H}_0$ and $\mathcal{H}_1$ will report 0 and 1, respectively, as the input received from the sender. Parties $P_2, \ldots, P_t$ report 0 as the input received from the sender to the parties in $\mathcal{H}_0$. On the other hand, they report 1 as the input received from the sender to the parties in $\mathcal{H}_1$. Consequently, at the end of the second round, for the parties in $\mathcal{H}_0$, the number of parties who have reported receiving 0 as the input from the sender turns out to be $(t - 1) + t = 2t - 1$, while the number of parties who have reported to receiving 1 as the input from the sender turns out to be $t + 1$. Hence for any $t \geq 3$, the number of parties reporting 0 as the sender's input turns out to outnumber the number of parties who report 1 as the sender's input, since $2t - 1 > t + 1$. As a result, the parties in $\mathcal{H}_0$ will output 0. On the other hand, for the parties in $\mathcal{H}_1$, the number of parties who have reported receiving 1 as the input from the sender turns out to be $(t - 1) + t + 1 = 2t$, while the number of parties who have reported to receiving 0 as the input from the sender turns out to be t. Hence for any $t \geq 1$, the number of parties reporting 1 as the sender's input turns out to outnumber the number of parties who report 0 as the sender's input, since $2t > t$. As a result, the parties in $\mathcal{H}_1$ will output 1. This is a clear violation of the *consistency* property.

For a pictorial depiction of the above attack, see Fig 3.6. We demonstrate the attack assuming $t = 3, n = 10$ and where $\mathcal{P} = \{A, \ldots, J\}$, with party A being the sender. Moreover, we assume that the adversary controls the subset of parties $\{A, B, C\}$. In the demonstration, the set $\mathcal{H}_0 = \{D, E, F\}$ and $\mathcal{H}_1 = \{G, H, I, J\}$.

3.3.2 An Incorrect Modification to the Naive Extension of $\Pi_{\mathsf{EIG}}^{(4,1)}$

If we look closely into the attack against the naive extension of the protocol $\Pi_{\mathsf{EIG}}^{(4,1)}$, as demonstrated in Fig 3.6, it turns out that the reason behind the violation of the consistency property is that the *corrupt* parties may report different inputs being received from the sender to different honest parties during the second round. For

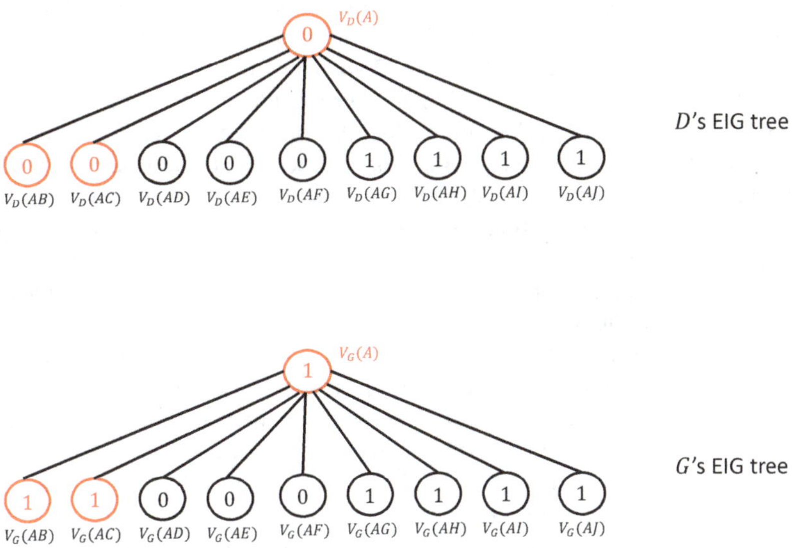

Fig. 3.6: Pictorial depiction of the violation of the consistency property in the naive extension of the protocol $\Pi_{\mathsf{EIG}}^{(4,1)}$ for $t = 3$ and $n = 10$. The set of parties is $\{A, \ldots, J\}$, with A being the designated sender and where the adversary corrupts the subset of parties $\{A, B, C\}$. The set of honest parties consists of two disjoint partitions $\mathcal{H}_0 = \{D, E, F\}$ and $\mathcal{H}_1 = \{G, H, I, J\}$. The picture shows how consistency is violated for the honest parties D and G. During the first round, the adversary sends 0 as its input to the parties in $\mathcal{H}_0$ and 1 as its input to the parties in $\mathcal{H}_1$. Due to this, the root node of the EIG-tree of the parties in $\mathcal{H}_0$ will have the value 0, while the root node of the EIG-tree of the parties in $\mathcal{H}_1$ will have the value 1 (shown in red colour for the EIG-trees of D and G). During the second round, the corrupt parties in the set $\{B, C\}$ report 0 and 1 as the value being received from the sender to the parties in $\mathcal{H}_0$ and $\mathcal{H}_1$ respectively. Due to this, the nodes with labels AB and AC will have values 0 and 1, respectively, in the EIG-tree of the parties in $\mathcal{H}_0$ and $\mathcal{H}_1$ respectively (shown in red colour for the EIG-trees of D and G). Consequently, the majority of the children of the root node will have value 0 in the EIG-trees of the parties in $\mathcal{H}_0$, while the majority of the children of the root node will have value 1 in the EIG-trees of the parties in $\mathcal{H}_1$. As a result, the parties in $\mathcal{H}_0$ and $\mathcal{H}_1$ will output 0 and 1 respectively

example, the corrupt parties B and C report different inputs being received from the sender A to the parties in $\mathcal{H}_0$ and $\mathcal{H}_1$, due to which the nodes with labels AB and AC (namely the ones whose labels end with the identity of *corrupt* parties) take *different* values, in the EIG-trees of different honest parties. To achieve consistency, we somehow need to ensure that this should *not* happen.

What happens if we add an *additional third* round of communication, where we now ask each party to further relay whatever information it received during the *second* round to all the parties, ensuring that no "redundant" information is relayed. For example, consider the node labelled AB. Then, during the *third* round, we ask each party $i \in \{C, \dots, J\}$ to relay what B reported to i about A's input during the second round. Namely, we ask each party $i \in \{C, \dots, J\}$ to relay the value it assigned to the node labelled AB, namely the value $V_i(AB)$, in its EIG-tree. The idea here is that at the end of the *third* round, every party will know what was the value that B reported about A's input to the different parties during the *second* round. And then by taking the *majority* of these reported values, the parties decide a *new value* that one should consider on behalf of B, about the value that B received during the first round from the sender, hoping that it ensures that the node with label AB takes the same *new value* in the EIG-tree of all the honest parties. Notice that during the third round, we *do not* ask the party B to relay the value of the node labelled AB in its EIG-tree, because we want the parties to know what the "others" have to tell about what B reported about A's input. Similarly, to have a "uniform" value for the node labelled AC across the EIG-tree of all the honest parties, we ask every party $i \in \{B, D, \dots, J\}$ to report the value $V_i(AC)$ to everybody during the third round and then take a majority of these values, to decide the *new value* for the node labelled AC. In general, during the third round, every party $i \in \{B, \dots, J\}$ reports the value $V_i(\sigma)$ of all the nodes with label σ at height 1 in its EIG-tree to all the parties, such that i *does not* occur in σ.[2] To represent the different values of the node labelled σ reported by different values, we *extend* the EIG-tree by introducing a new *level*, by introducing children for the nodes labelled σ, where the children are assigned labels σj, corresponding to every distinct party $j \in \{B, \dots, J\}$, which *does not* occur in σ.[3] Upon receiving the value $v = V_j(\sigma)$ from party j during the *third* round, party i assigns the value v to the node labelled σj; i.e. i sets $V_i(\sigma j) = v$. Then based on the different "versions" of the value of the node labelled σ received from different parties, each party i assigns a *new value* for the node labelled σ, denoted by $NV_i(\sigma)$, by taking the *majority* of the received values; i.e. $NV_i(\sigma)$ is set to the *majority* of the assigned values $V_i(\sigma j)$. Before proceeding further, we note that the principle behind the third round is *similar* to that behind the second round, namely "gossiping" with each other and relaying whatever the parties heard in the previous round and then, based on the "majority" decision, trying to find a "consistent" view for the previous round of communication.

Now let us analyze the effect of the *newly introduced* third round. Let us first consider the nodes labelled σ, *ending* with the label of an *honest* party. Such nodes already enjoy the luxury of having the same value across the EIG-tree of all honest

[2] We follow the convention, where the root is considered at height 0 in the EIG-tree.

[3] Remember that we are *not* asking party j to report about the value it assigned to the node labelled σ if j is already *present* in σ.

parties, even *without* introducing the third round; i.e. $V_i(\sigma)$ takes the same value across the EIG-trees of all honest parties i at the end of the second round, for such nodes. Interestingly, the *new value* for such nodes will be the *same* in the EIG-tree of all honest parties. That is, $NV_i(\sigma)$ will be the same across the EIG-tree of all honest parties i. More interestingly, the new value will be the *same* as the "old" value; i.e. $NV_i(\sigma) = V_i(\sigma)$ will hold. And hence, the third round *does not* "disturb" the *common* value, that had been *already* assigned to such nodes at the end of the second round. Intuitively, this is because the *majority* of nodes will report the *same* value for the node labelled σ during the *third* round, which will be then considered as the new value for the node labelled σ (see Fig 3.7 for an illustration).

Unfortunately, the problem that was illustrated in Fig 3.6 still persists for the nodes labelled σ, which ends with the label of a *corrupt* party. This is because, as illustrated in Fig 3.6, the value of such nodes was already *different* at the end of the second round in the EIG-trees of different honest parties. And now, during the third round, corrupt party(ies) may report the value of these nodes differently to different honest parties, leading to a scenario that even at the end of the third round, different honest parties may end up assigning *different* new values to the node labelled σ in their respective EIG-trees. For an illustration, see Fig 3.8.

3.3.3 Further Modification to the Protocol $\Pi_{\text{EIG}}^{(4,1)}$

As discussed in the previous section, adding the third round of communication to the protocol $\Pi_{\text{EIG}}^{(4,1)}$ *fails* to ensure the *consistency* property. Specifically, as illustrated in Fig 3.8, the (new) value of the nodes ending with the label of a corrupt party may still take *different* values in the EIG-trees of different honest parties. What if we include an *additional* fourth round of communication, where each party sends the values it assigned to the different nodes at the end of the third round to every party (with the same "restrictions" being enforced as used for the third round). And then based on the majority rule, the parties compute new values for the different nodes at level 2 in their respective EIG-trees.

Interestingly, now irrespective of the behaviour of the corrupt parties, at the end of the *fourth* round, the new value of *any* node labelled σ at level 2 will be the same in the EIG-tree of all honest parties, *irrespective* of whether σ ends with the label of an honest or a corrupt party (we will see a formal proof for this later). For instance, consider the node labelled ABC in Fig 3.8, which acquired *different* values in the EIG-trees of party D and J. Now due to the newly introduced *fourth* round, the new value of the node labelled ABC will be the same in the EIG-tree of all honest parties. This is because now, during the fourth round, *only* the parties $D, \ldots, J$ are allowed to report the value of the node labelled ABC in their respective EIG-trees.[4] Since all these parties are honest, they will report the values correctly and consequently, all

[4] Party B and C are *not* allowed to report the value of the node labelled ABC in their respective EIG-trees, since the labels B and C occur in the label ABC.

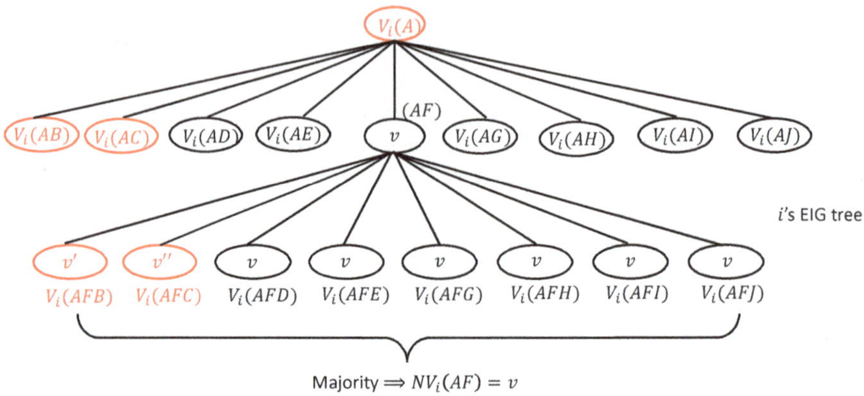

Fig. 3.7: Pictorial depiction of the newly introduced third round in the naive extension of the protocol $\Pi_{\mathsf{EIG}}^{(4,1)}$ for $t = 3$ and $n = 10$. The set of parties is $\{A, \ldots, J\}$, with A being the designated sender and where the adversary corrupts the subset of parties $\{A, B, C\}$. The picture illustrates the computation of the new value for the node labelled AF, in the EIG-tree of any honest party $i \in \{D, \ldots, J\}$. During the first round, the sender A may send different inputs to different honest parties, which causes the root node to have different values in the EIG-tree of different honest parties, as shown in the red colour. Let v be the input received by party F during the first round, which it reports to all the parties in the second round. As a result, the value stored in the node labelled AF will be v in the EIG-tree of all honest parties $i \in \{D, \ldots, J\}$. During the third round, the honest parties D, E, G, H, I and J will send v as the value of node labelled AF to all the parties, while corrupt parties B and C may report arbitrary values. Note that party F is not allowed to report the value of the node labelled AF in its EIG-tree, since the label F occurs in the label AF. The majority of the children of the node labelled AF will have labels ending with the label of an honest party. And each honest party will assign the value v to these nodes, while the children ending with the labels of corrupt parties can take any arbitrary values (as shown in red colour), depending upon what the corrupt parties B and C report about the value of the node labelled AF in their EIG trees. Based on the majority rule, each honest party will assign v as the new value for the node labelled AF

the honest parties will make the *same* decision regarding the new value of the node labelled ABC.

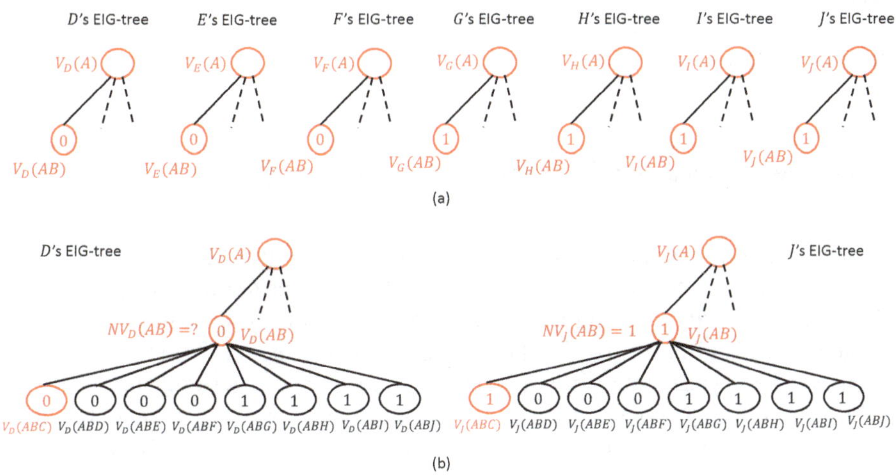

Fig. 3.8: Pictorial depiction of the newly introduced third round in the naive extension of the protocol $\Pi_{\mathsf{EIG}}^{(4,1)}$ for $t = 3$ and $n = 10$. The set of parties is $\{A, \ldots, J\}$, with A being the designated sender and where the adversary corrupts the subset of parties $\{A, B, C\}$. The picture illustrates the computation of the new value for the node labelled AB, in the EIG-trees of the honest parties D and G. During the first round, the sender A sends different inputs to different honest parties, due to which the root node takes different values in the EIG-tree of different honest parties, as shown in the red colour in Figure (a). During the second round, the corrupt party B reports different input being received from A in the previous round to different honest parties; to D, E and F it reports receiving 0 from A and to G, H, I and J, it reports receiving 1 from A. Due to this, the value of the node labelled AB will be 0 in the EIG-tree of D, E and F, while it takes the value 1 in the EIG-tree of G, H, I and J, as shown in Figure (a); we do not show the rest of the nodes in the EIG-trees of different parties. During the third round, the honest parties $D, \ldots, J$ correctly report the value of the node labelled AB in their respective EIG trees. However, the *corrupt* party C reports *different* versions of the node labelled AB to different honest parties. Namely, to D, party C reports 0 as the value of the node labelled AB in C's EIG-tree, while to party J, it reports 1 as the value of the node labelled AB. Consequently, as shown in Figure (b), party J will set 1 as the new value for the node labelled AB in its EIG-tree, but the new value for the node labelled AB in D's EIG-tree will be uncertain, since there is *no* majority among the values assigned to the children of the node labelled AB

Once the new value for *every* node at level 2 is computed, the parties can go one level *up* in the tree and compute the new values of every node at level 1 (based on the majority of the new values computed for the children of the nodes at level 1). And then by applying the same logic at the root level, the parties compute the new value of the root node, which is taken as the final output. One can now show that irrespective of the behaviour of the corrupt parties, the new value of the root will be the *same* across the EIG-trees of all honest parties (we will prove this formally in the next section).

3.3.4 The Generalized EIG Protocol for any $t < \frac{n}{3}$

Based on the discussion till now, we present the generalized EIG protocol $\Pi_{\mathsf{EIG}}^{(n,t)}$ for any n and t, satisfying the condition $t < \frac{n}{3}$. We consider a set of parties $\mathcal{P} = \{P_1, \ldots, P_n\}$, with P_1 being the designated sender having input $m \in \{0, 1\}$. The protocol consists of $t + 1$ rounds of communication. During the first round, P_1 sends its input to everyone. And in the remaining t rounds, the parties exchange messages with each other, to consistently decide upon a *common* value, which should be considered as the final output, such that the output should be m, if P_1 is *honest*. In general, during each round $r \in \{2, \ldots, t+1\}$, every party (*except* the sender) sends whatever information it has received from the other parties at the end of the previous round, with certain restrictions (to ensure that redundant information is not relayed).

Each party maintains a *local copy* of the EIG-tree, denoted by $T_i^{(n,t)}$ which is a labelled tree with $t + 1$ levels, corresponding to the $t + 1$ rounds in the protocol, with the root being assigned the level 0. The label of any node will be *identical* across all the copies of the tree and follows the following labelling mechanism.

- The root of the tree is assigned the label 1, namely the index of the sender party.
- Each node at level $r \in \{1, \ldots, t\}$ is assigned a label σ of size $r + 1$, consisting of the index of $r + 1$ *distinct* parties from $\{P_1, \ldots, P_n\}$, with the *first* index being *always* 1 (namely the index of the *sender* party). That is, σ is of the form $1 j_1 j_2 \ldots, j_r$, where $j_1, \ldots, j_r$ are *distinct* indices from the set $\{2, \ldots, n\}$.
- Each node labelled σ at level r, will have a child, corresponding to *each* party P_j, whose label *does not* appear in σ and the child will have label $\sigma' = \sigma j$. Consequently, each node at level r will have $n - (r + 1)$ children. We will say that the node labelled σj, *corresponds* to the party P_j

For an illustration of the labelling used in the EIG-tree and the various terminologies associated with EIG-trees, see Fig 3.9.

Let us now understand how values are assigned to the various nodes in the EIG-tree in the protocol. The information obtained by each party P_i in every round is stored in the P_i's copy of the EIG-tree. We will denote the value that P_i assigns to the node labelled σ by $V_i(\sigma)$. The value that P_i receives from the sender during the *first* round is stored in the root of the EIG-tree. Then during each round $r \in \{2, \ldots, t+1\}$, each party P_i (*except* the Sender) sends the *most-recently-filled* level of its EIG-tree to all. Namely, for each node labelled σ at level $r - 2$ which has been assigned a value by P_i at the end of round $r - 1$, party P_i sends the value $V_i(\sigma)$ assigned to the node σ, to all the parties, provided i *does not* occur in the label σ.[5]

[5] This is to *prevent* unnecessarily sending "redundant" piece of information in the protocol, as will be cleared in the sequel.

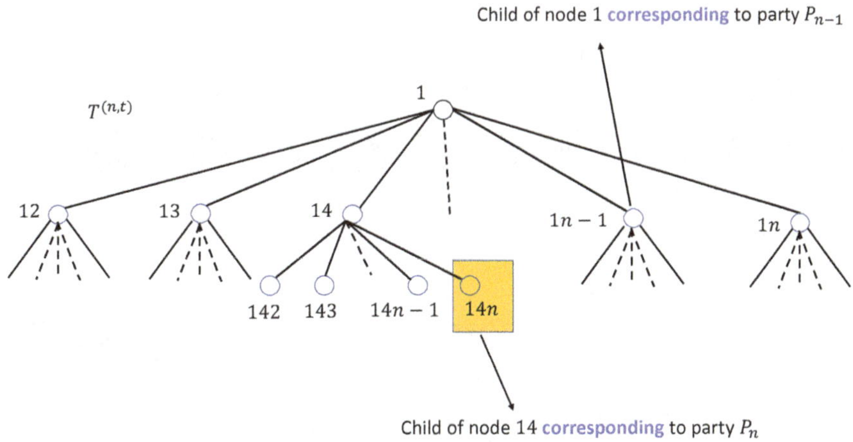

Fig. 3.9: Pictorial depiction of the labelling of the nodes used in the EIG-tree and the various terminologies associated with the EIG-trees.

Upon receiving the information exchanged during the round r, every party assigns value to the nodes in the *next* level of its EIG-tree. In more detail, party P_i, upon receiving the value $v = V_j(\sigma)$ from P_j, assigns the value v to the child labelled σj in its EIG-tree; i.e. $V_i(\sigma j)$ is set to v. Note that there *will* be a child of node labelled σ with label σj, since corresponding to each party P_j where j *does not* occur in the label σ, there will be a child of the node labelled σ with label σj.

The interpretation of setting $V_i(\sigma j) = v$ is that during round r, party P_j has reported to P_i, that during round $r - 1$, party P_j has assigned the value v to the node labelled σ in P_j's EIG-tree.[6] For a pictorial illustration of how the EIG-tree is populated in the protocol, see Fig 3.10.

After $t + 1$ rounds, the parties start computing *new values* for each node in their respective EIG-trees, using the "majority" rule, in a *bottom-up* fashion, starting with the leaf nodes. Since leaf nodes *do not* have any children, the values assigned to these nodes at the end of $t + 1^{th}$ round is *retained* as their new value. On the other hand, the new value of any internal node is set to the majority of the new values of all its children node (if there is no majority, then the new value is set to a default value, say 0). Finally, once the new value for the root node is computed, it is taken as the final output. Protocol $\Pi_{\mathsf{EIG}}^{(n,t)}$ is formally presented in Fig 3.11.

---

[6] It is precisely for this reason that any party P_j where j *appears* in σ is *not* asked to communicate the value $V_j(\sigma)$ of the node labelled σ in P_j's EIG-tree to any party. This is because there will be *no* child of σ to store this piece of information.

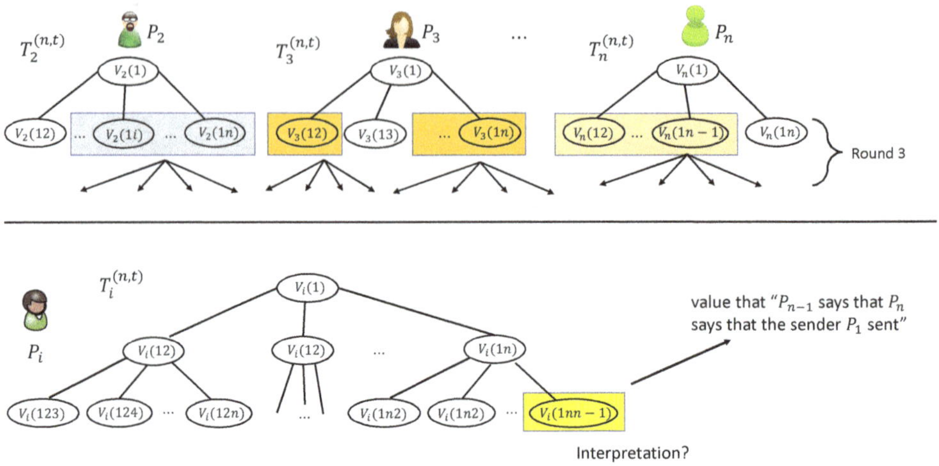

Fig. 3.10: Pictorial depiction of how the parties populate their respective copies of EIG-trees based on the communication happening during various rounds. The top picture illustrates the third round. Every party except the sender sends the values of the highlighted nodes at level 1 in their respective EIG-trees to every party. For instance, party P_3 sends the values of all the nodes except the node labelled 13 to all the parties (since 13 contains the label 3). The bottom picture shows which nodes are assigned values by party P_i in its EIG-tree at the end of the third round. For instance the node labelled $1nn-1$ is assigned value v, provided P_{n-1} sends v as the value for $V_{n-1}(1n)$, namely the node labelled $1n$ in P_{n-1}'s EIG-tree. Note that P_{n-1} is supposed to set $V_{n-1}(1n)$ to v at the end of the second round, provided P_n has reported to P_{n-1} during the second round that it had received v from P_1 during the first round. Hence the interpretation of P_i setting $V_i(1nn-1) = v$ at the end of the third round is that "P_{n-1} says that P_n says that the sender P_1 sent the input v

Protocol $\Pi_{\text{EIG}}^{(n,t)}$

Initialization: Initialize the tree $T_i^{(n,t)}$ by setting the value of all the nodes in $T_i^{(n,t)}$ to $\bot$.

- **Round 1: (sender distributing its input)**
  - Party P_1 on having the input m, sends m to all the parties in the set $\{P_2, \ldots, P_n\}$, outputs m and terminates.
  - Let m_i denote the message received from P_1.[a] Set $V_i(1) := m_i$ in the EIG-tree $T_i^{(n,t)}$.
- **Round $r \in \{2, \ldots, t+1\}$: parties exchanging previous-round information**
  - For each node labelled σ at level $r-2$ in $T_i^{(n,t)}$, send the value $V_i(\sigma)$ to all the parties in $\{P_2, \ldots, P_n\}$, provided i *does not* occur in the label σ.
  - Upon receiving the value $v_{ji}^{(\gamma)}$ from P_j for the node labelled γ at level $r-2$ where j does not occur in γ, set $V_i(\gamma j) := v_{ji}^{(\gamma)}$, where γj is the child of the node labelled γ ending with label j in $T_i^{(n,t)}$.[b]

- **(Computation of new values):** For each node labeled σ in $T_i^{(n,t)}$, compute its new value $NV_i(\sigma)$ as follows, starting with the leaf nodes.
  - If σ is the label of a leaf node, then set $NV_i(\sigma) := V_i(\sigma)$.
  - Else, set $NV_i(\sigma)$ to the majority of the new values of the children of the node labelled σ. That is, set $NV_i(\sigma) := \text{majority}\{NV_i(\sigma j)\}_{j \in \{2,\dots,n\} \text{ and } j \text{ does not occur in } \sigma}$. If there is no majority, then set $NV_i(\sigma) := 0$.
- **(Output computation and termination):** Output $NV_i(1)$ and terminate.

[a] If no value is received from P_1 by the end of the first round then set $m_i := 0$.
[b] If no value for the node labelled γ is received from P_j by the end of round r then set $v_{ji}^{(\gamma)} := 0$.

Fig. 3.11: The EIG protocol for the parties $\{P_1, \dots, P_n\}$, where P_1 is the designated sender, tolerating up to t corruptions. The above steps are executed by each $P_i \in \{P_2, \dots, P_n\}$

We now proceed to prove the properties of the protocol $\Pi_{\text{EIG}}^{(n,t)}$. We first provide a couple of useful facts about the EIG tree. The first fact is that for every *internal* node, the *majority* of its children will correspond to an *honest* party.

Claim 3.1 If $t < \frac{n}{3}$ then for any node in the EIG-tree labelled σ at level $r \in \{0, \dots, t-1\}$, the majority of the children of the node will have labels which end with the indexl of an honest party.

Proof Consider an *arbitrary* node with label σ at an *arbitrary* level r where $r \in \{0, \dots, t-1\}$. Then the label σ is of size $r+1$ and consists of $r+1$ *distinct* indices from the set $\{1, \dots, n\}$, with the *first* index being 1. From the construction of the EIG-tree, it follows that the node labelled σ will have a child with label σj, corresponding to each party $P_j \in \{P_2, \dots, P_n\}$, such that j *does not* occur in σ. Since indices of $r+1$ distinct parties are already present in σ, it follows that there will be $n-(r+1)$ children of the node labelled σ. Now among these children, in the worst case, there might be t children corresponding to *corrupt* parties and have label σj, where P_j is a *corrupt* party. Hence there will be at least $n-(r+1+t)$ children, corresponding to the *honest* parties and have label σj where P_j is an *honest* party. Now $n-(r+1+t) \geq t+1$ holds as $t < \frac{n}{3}$ and hence it follows that the label of the majority of the children of the node labelled σ will end with the index of an *honest* party and hence correspond to an *honest* party. □

The second useful fact about the EIG-tree is that *any* path from the root to *any* leaf contains at least one node, corresponding to an honest party.

Claim 3.2 If $t < n$, then in the EIG-tree, *any* path from the root to *any* leaf contains at least one node corresponding to an honest party.

Proof Consider an *arbitrary* path p from the root labelled 1 to a leaf node. The length of p will be $t+1$ and there will be $t+1$ nodes along the path, where for any $r \in \{0, \dots, t\}$, the label of the node in p at level r will consist of $r+1$ *distinct* indices from the set $\{1, \dots, n\}$. Let us consider the set $\{1, i_1, \dots, i_t\}$ of the *last* indices in the labels of all the nodes that are encountered in the path p. From the properties of the EIG-tree, each of the indices in the set $\{1, i_1, \dots, i_t\}$ are distinct. We also note that at most t indices in the set$\{1, i_1, \dots, i_t\}$ may correspond to *corrupt* parties. Hence from the pigeonhole principle, it follows that at least one of the indices $i_j \in \{1, i_1, \ldots, i_t\}$ is that of an *honest* party. Consequently, the node along the path p whose label σ ends with i_j corresponds to an honest party. □

We now start proving the properties of the protocol $\Pi_{\mathsf{EIG}}^{(n,t)}$. We first consider the scenario when the sender is *honest* and prove the *validity* property. To prove the validity, we need to show that each honest party will set m (the input of the sender) as the new value of the root node in its EIG-tree. For this, we provide a couple of helming claims. We first show that any node that *corresponds* to an *honest* party will be assigned the same value in the EIG-tree of every *honest* party.

Claim 3.3 In protocol $\Pi_{\mathsf{EIG}}^{(n,t)}$ for every node that corresponds to an honest party, the value of that node will be the same in the EIG tree of all honest parties.

Proof Consider an *arbitrary* node with label σ that corresponds to an *honest* party. That is, $\sigma = \sigma' k$, where P_k is an *honest* party. Moreover, let the node occur at level r, where $r \in \{0, \ldots, t\}$. Furthermore, consider an *arbitrary* pair of *honest* parties P_i and P_j. We wish to show that $V_i(\sigma) = V_j(\sigma)$ holds. Let $V_k(\sigma') = v$. Since P_k is *honest*, it will send the value $V_k(\sigma') = v$ to *all* honest parties during round $r + 1$ and each honest party will receive it at the end of round $r + 1$. It then follows from the protocol steps that both P_i and P_j will assign the value v to the child of the node labelled σ', with label $\sigma' k$. Hence $V_i(\sigma) = V_j(\sigma)$ will hold. □

The second claim is that for every node that corresponds to an *honest* party, the new value of that node will be the same in the EIG-tree of all honest parties. Moreover, the new value will be the same as the old value.

Claim 3.4 If $t < \frac{n}{3}$ then in the protocol $\Pi_{\mathsf{EIG}}^{(n,t)}$ for every node labelled σ that corresponds to an honest party, $V_i(\sigma) = V_j(\sigma) = NV_i(\sigma) = NV_j(\sigma)$ holds for every pair of honest parties P_i and P_j.

Proof Consider an *arbitrary* node labelled σ, corresponding to an *honest* party, occurring at level r where $r \in \{0, \ldots, t\}$. That is, $\sigma = \sigma' \ell$, where P_ℓ is an *honest* party. Moreover, consider any *arbitrary* pair of honest parties P_i and P_j. We prove the claim by using a *backward-induction* on the level r of the node labelled σ.

Base case: The base case is when $r = t$, implying that the node labelled σ is a *leaf* node. Since the node labelled σ is a leaf node, from the protocol steps, it follows that $NV_i(\sigma) = V_i(\sigma)$ and $NV_j(\sigma) = V_j(\sigma)$ holds. Moreover, from Claim 3.3, the condition $V_i(\sigma) = V_j(\sigma)$ holds. Hence, it follows that $V_i(\sigma) = V_j(\sigma) = NV_i(\sigma) = NV_j(\sigma)$ holds.

Inductive Hypothesis: Let the claim be true for any level $r \in \{t, t-1, \ldots, k\}$, where $0 < k$. We next proceed to prove the inductive step, where the level r of the node labelled σ is $k - 1$.

Inductive Step: Let $r = k - 1$. Let $\mathcal{H}$ be the set of *honest* parties in the set $\{P_2, \ldots, P_n\}$. From Claim 3.3, it follows that $V_i(\sigma) = V_j(\sigma)$ holds for every

$P_i, P_j \in \mathcal{H}$. Let $V_i(\sigma) = V_j(\sigma) = v$. Let $\mathcal{H}_\sigma$ be the set of honest parties from $\mathcal{H}$, whose index *does not* occur in σ. Then in the protocol, every party $P_i \in \mathcal{H}_\sigma$ sends v as the value for $V_i(\sigma)$ during round k, which is received by all the parties in $\mathcal{H}$ at the end of Round k.[7] Consequently, corresponding to *every* $P_m \in \mathcal{H}_\sigma$, *every* party $P_i \in \mathcal{H}$ will set $V_i(\sigma m) = v$, where σm denotes the labelled child of the node labelled σ corresponding to P_m. Since the nodes labelled σm occur at level k, from the inductive hypothesis, it follows that $NV_i(\sigma m) = v$ holds as well for every $P_i \in \mathcal{H}$ and every $P_m \in \mathcal{H}_\sigma$. Moreover, since $t < \frac{n}{3}$, from Claim 3.1 it follows that $|\mathcal{H}_\sigma| \geq t + 1$ and hence *majority* of the children of the node labelled σ will correspond to an honest party. Furthermore, since the new value of all such children is v, it follows that every party $P_i \in \mathcal{H}$ will set $NV_i(\sigma) = v$, thus proving the inductive step. □

The validity property now follows from Claim 3.4 and the fact that if the sender is *honest*, then it will send the same input to all the parties during the first round.

Lemma 3.3 *If $t < \frac{n}{3}$, then protocol $\Pi_{\mathsf{EIG}}^{(n,t)}$ achieves t-validity.*

Proof Let P_1 (the sender) be *honest*. Then during the first round, it will send m to all the parties. Consequently, every *honest* party P_i will set $V_i(1) = m$ in its EIG-tree $T_i^{(n,t)}$. Moreover, since P_1 is *honest*, it implies that the root node of the EIG-tree corresponds to an *honest* party. Consequently, from Claim 3.4, it follows that every *honest* P_i will set $NV_i(1) = m$. Since P_i outputs the value $NV_i(1)$ in the protocol, it follows that each honest party outputs m. □

We next consider the case when P_1 (namely the sender) may be *corrupt* and send *different* inputs to different honest parties during the first round. We wish to show that even in this case, the output of all honest parties will be the *same*. Note that Claim 3.4 will *not* be useful to prove the consistency. This is because if P_1 is *corrupt*, then the root of the EIG-tree *no longer* corresponds to an *honest* party. Consequently, we need to prove a different set of properties for the EIG-tree. Specifically, we now show that for any node labelled σ in the EIG-tree, if every path from that node to every leaf node encounters at least one node corresponding to an *honest* party, then the new value of the node labelled σ will be the same across the EIG-trees of all *honest* parties. Since we have already shown in Claim 3.2 that every path from the *root* node to every leaf node encounters at least one node corresponding to an *honest* party, this implies that even if the sender behaves maliciously, all *honest* parties will assign the *same* new value to the root node in their respective EIG-trees. And this further implies that all honest parties will output the same value.

Claim 3.5 If $t < \frac{n}{3}$ then in the protocol $\Pi_{\mathsf{EIG}}^{(n,t)}$, for every node labelled σ for which every path from the node labelled σ to any leaf contains at least one node corresponding to an honest party, the condition $NV_i(\sigma) = NV_j(\sigma)$ holds for every pair of honest parties P_i, P_j.

[7] Recall that in the protocol a party P_i is allowed to send the value of $V_i(\sigma)$ during Round k, *only if* $i \notin \sigma$.

Proof Consider an *arbitrary* node labelled σ, occurring at level r where $r \in \{0, \ldots, t\}$, such that every path from the node labelled σ to any leaf node contains at least one node corresponding to an *honest* party. Moreover, consider any *arbitrary* pair of *honest* parties P_i and P_j. We prove the claim by using a *backward-induction* on the level r of the node labelled σ.

Base case: The base case is when $r = t$, implying that the node labelled σ is a *leaf* node. In this case, any path from the node labelled σ to any leaf node consists of *only one* node, namely the node labelled σ. Moreover, from the premise of the claim, it follows that the node labelled σ corresponds to an *honest* party. In this case, it follows from Claim 3.4 that $NV_i(\sigma) = NV_j(\sigma)$ holds, thus proving the claim for the base case.

Inductive Hypothesis: Let the claim be true for any level $r \in \{t, t-1, \ldots, k\}$, where $0 < k$. We next proceed to prove the inductive step, where the level r of the node labelled σ is $k - 1$.

Inductive Step: Let $r = k - 1$. Now there are two possible cases for the node labelled σ, depending upon whether it corresponds to an *honest* or a *corrupt* party.

- **Case I: Node labelled σ corresponds to an honest party.** In this case, we can again use Claim 3.4 and conclude that $NV_i(\sigma) = NV_j(\sigma)$ holds.
- **Case II: Node labelled σ corresponds to a corrupt party.** In this case, consider any *arbitrary* child of the node labelled σ, with label $\sigma' = \sigma j$. It follows that *every* path from the node labelled σ' to *every* leaf node will encounter at least one node, corresponding to an *honest* party. If not, then let p be a path from the node labelled σ' to some *leaf* node, say with label γ, such that p *does not* have any node corresponding to an *honest* party. Then consider the path p', from the node labelled σ to the leaf labelled γ, via the node labelled σ' and the nodes along the path p. Clearly p' *does not* have any node corresponding to any *honest* party. However, this is a *contradiction*, since as per the premise of the claim, the path p' *must contain* at least one node, corresponding to an *honest* party.

  Note that the node labelled σ' occurs at level k. Since we have shown that *every* path from the node labelled σ' to *every* leaf node will encounter at least one node, corresponding to an *honest* party, it follows from the *inductive hypothesis* that $NV_i(\sigma') = NV_j(\sigma')$ holds. From the protocol steps, the new value for the node labelled σ is set to the *majority* of the new value of its children. Now since for every child labelled σ' of the node labelled σ all honest parties set the same new value, it follows that after applying the majority rule, all honest parties will set the *same* new value for the node labelled σ. Consequently, $NV_i(\sigma) = NV_j(\sigma)$ will hold, thus proving the inductive step. □

The *consistency* property of $\Pi_{\mathsf{EIG}}^{(n,t)}$ now follows from Claim 3.5 and Claim 3.2.

Lemma 3.4 *If $t < \frac{n}{3}$, then protocol $\Pi_{\mathsf{EIG}}^{(n,t)}$ achieves t-consistency.*

Proof From Claim 3.2, each path from the root node labelled 1 to any leaf node in the EIG-tree will encounter at least one node, corresponding to an *honest* party.

Hence from Claim 3.5, the condition $NV_i(1) = NV_j(1)$ will hold, for every pair of *honest* parties P_i, P_j. As a result, all honest parties will output the same value. □

We next derive the complexity of the protocol.

Lemma 3.5 *Protocol* $\Pi_{\mathsf{EIG}}^{(n,t)}$ *incurs a communication of* $O(n^t)$ *bits and requires* $t+1$ *communication rounds.*

Proof From the construction of the EIG-tree, it follows that there are $O(n^t)$ leaf nodes in *total*, across the EIG-trees of *all* honest parties. These leaf nodes are assigned values based on the messages exchanged by the parties. Consequently, the communication complexity of the protocol is $O(n^{(t)})$ bits. The number of communication rounds follows from the protocol inspection. □

From Lemma 3.5 it follows that the communication complexity of the protocol $\Pi_{\mathsf{EIG}}^{(n,t)}$ is *exponential* (in t). It is not difficult to see that even the computation complexity (namely, the amount of computation performed by the honest parties) of the protocol is also exponential (in t). It is precisely for this reason that the protocol is also called *exponential information gathering* protocol. Theorem 3.1 now follows from Lemma 3.3, Lemma 3.4 and Lemma 3.5. The *t-liveness* follows from the fact that all honest parties terminate the protocol after $t + 1$ rounds.

Theorem 3.1 *If* $t < \frac{n}{3}$ *then protocol* $\Pi_{\mathsf{EIG}}^{(n,t)}$ *is a t-secure BB protocol with perfect security in the model* $\mathcal{M}_{\mathsf{auth}}$ *where the input of the sender party is a single bit. The protocol requires* $t + 1$ *rounds of communication over the point-to-point channels and incurs a communication complexity of* $\mathcal{BC}(1)$ *bits where* $\mathcal{BC}(1) = O(n^t)$.

3.3.5 Protocol $\Pi_{\mathsf{EIG}}^{(n,t)}$: Further Discussion

We now discuss about two important features of the protocol $\Pi_{\mathsf{EIG}}^{(n,t)}$, namely it *resilience* (fault-tolerance) and the *round complexity* (namely the number of communication rounds).

The resilience of the protocol $\Pi_{\mathsf{EIG}}^{(n,t)}$.

Protocol $\Pi_{\mathsf{EIG}}^{(n,t)}$ can tolerate up to t corruptions where $t < \frac{n}{3}$. One may wonder what goes *wrong* if $t \geq \frac{n}{3}$? It follows that if $t \geq \frac{n}{3}$, then Claim 3.1 is *no longer* true. Namely, for the nodes at level $t-1$, the number of child nodes corresponding to *honest* parties *may not* be in majority. Consequently, Claim 3.4 will no longer hold as well, thus nullifying the proof of validity (see the proof of Lemma 3.3). Consequently, if $t \geq \frac{n}{3}$, then protocol $\Pi_{\mathsf{EIG}}^{(n,t)}$ may *no* longer satisfy the t-validity. Hence protocol $\Pi_{\mathsf{EIG}}^{(n,t)}$ is "best" in terms of the resilience, which *cannot* be further improved.[8] In fact, one can also show that if $t \geq \frac{n}{3}$, then the protocol *does not* achieve *t-consistency* as well. We leave it as an exercise for the reader to come up with concrete adversarial strategies when $t \geq \frac{n}{3}$ and show how t-consistency and t-validity properties are *violated* in the protocol $\Pi_{\mathsf{EIG}}^{(n,t)}$.

The round-complexity of the protocol $\Pi_{\mathsf{EIG}}^{(n,t)}$.

In protocol $\Pi_{\mathsf{EIG}}^{(n,t)}$, the parties exchange messages for $t+1$ communication rounds. One may wonder what goes *wrong* if the protocol is executed only for t rounds instead. The t-validity property will *still* hold, since Claim 3.1 and hence Lemma 3.3 will *still* hold (we leave it as an exercise for the reader to verify this). What about the t-consistency property? It turns out that the t-consistency *may not* be guaranteed. This is because Claim 3.2 *may not* be true and there *might* be paths from the root node to leaf nodes, where one *may not* encounter any node corresponding to an *honest* party. As a result, Claim 3.5 may *no longer* be true and hence there might be nodes corresponding to *corrupt* parties, whose new value may be *different* in the EIG-trees of different honest parties. This will further affect the t-consistency property. Hence protocol $\Pi_{\mathsf{EIG}}^{(n,t)}$ is "best" in terms of the number of communication rounds, which *cannot* be further improved.[9] We leave it as an exercise for the reader to come up with concrete adversarial strategies when the protocol $\Pi_{\mathsf{EIG}}^{(n,t)}$ is executed *only* for t rounds and show how t-consistency is *violated*.

From the above discussion, it follows that protocol $\Pi_{\mathsf{EIG}}^{(n,t)}$ offers *optimal* resilience and *optimal* round complexity, guaranteed by *any deterministic* BB protocol in the model $\mathcal{M}_{\mathsf{auth}}$. However, the communication complexity of the protocol (which is $O(n^t)$ bits) is *far away* from the *optimal* communication complexity. It is well known that *any* BB protocol where the input of the sender is a single-bit needs to communicate $\Omega(n^2)$ bits [45] and there exists BB protocol whose communication complexity is $O(n^2)$ bits [23].

Finally, we note that protocol $\Pi_{\mathsf{EIG}}^{(n,t)}$ achieves *perfect* security. Moreover, it is a *deterministic* protocol, where the parties compute their next-round messages and the final output *deterministically*. Later we will see that if we allow a small (but *negligible*) error in the security guarantees, then one can *improve* the resilience of the protocol $\Pi_{\mathsf{EIG}}^{(n,t)}$. Moreover, if we go for *randomized* protocols, then one can achieve the properties of BB *probabilistically* in a *constant* expected number of rounds. Furthermore, if one settles for *cryptographic security* (where the adversary

[8] As mentioned earlier, in the subsequent chapters, we will see that $t < \frac{n}{3}$ is the *optimal* resilience for *any* BB protocol in the model $\mathcal{M}_{\mathsf{auth}}$, *irrespective* of the type of security. Hence protocol $\Pi_{\mathsf{EIG}}^{(n,t)}$ offers *optimal* resilience.

[9] As mentioned earlier, in the subsequent chapters, we will see that $t+1$ rounds is the *minimum* number of rounds required by *any deterministic* BB protocol, *irrespective* of the model. Hence protocol $\Pi_{\mathsf{EIG}}^{(n,t)}$ offers *optimal* round complexity.

is *computationally bounded*), then one can deploy various cryptographic tools and tremendously improve the round and communication complexity of the protocol.

EIG Protocol for L-bit input.

In protocol $\Pi_{\mathsf{EIG}}^{(n,t)}$, we assumed that the input m of the sender is a *single* bit. What if instead $m \in \{0, 1\}^L$? Then there are two options.

Let $m = (m_1, \ldots, m_L) \in \{0, 1\}^L$ be the input of the sender, where $L \geq 1$. The *first* option is to let the sender invoke L instances of the protocol $\Pi_{\mathsf{EIG}}^{(n,t)}$, where the ℓth instance is invoked with input m_ℓ, for $\ell = 1, \ldots, L$ and the parties participate in these instances. From the *t-consistency* property of $\Pi_{\mathsf{EIG}}^{(n,t)}$, all honest parties will have a *common* output bit, say m'_ℓ, at the end of the ℓth instance $\Pi_{\mathsf{EIG}}^{(n,t)}$. Moreover, $m'_\ell = m_\ell$ will hold, if the sender is *honest*, which follows from the *t-validity* property of $\Pi_{\mathsf{EIG}}^{(n,t)}$. Consequently, the parties can output $m' = (m'_1, \ldots, m'_L)$. The resultant protocol will satisfy the properties of BB with *perfect* security. The protocol will require $t + 1$ communication rounds and incur a communication complexity of $\mathcal{BC}(L)$ bits where $\mathcal{BC}(L) = \mathcal{O}(n^t L)$.

The *second option* would be to run a *single* instance of the protocol $\Pi_{\mathsf{EIG}}^{(n,t)}$, where at each step the parties exchange L-bit values. A careful investigation of the protocol $\Pi_{\mathsf{EIG}}^{(n,t)}$ will reveal that the protocol will work even if, at each step, the parties exchange L-bit values. For instance, during the first round, the sender sends its L-bit input to all, which is assigned to the root node of the respective parties' EIG-trees. And during each subsequent round, the parties exchange the values of the most recently filled nodes in their respective EIG-trees, where each node value is an L-bit value. The protocol will require $t + 1$ communication rounds. The communication complexity $\mathcal{BC}(L)$ will be the same as in the first approach, since at each step, the parties exchange L-bit node values. Hence $\mathcal{BC}(L) = \mathcal{O}(n^t L)$. To avoid repetition, we do not provide the formal details.

EIG Protocol for Byzantine Agreement.

Protocol $\Pi_{\mathsf{EIG}}^{(n,t)}$ is a BB protocol. One can even design a protocol for *Byzantine agreement* (BA), based on EIG-tree. For this, we can rely on the generic *equivalence* between the BB and BA, which comes from Theorem 2.3.[10] The resultant protocol will be perfectly-secure, require $t+1$ communication rounds (*same* number of rounds as required for $\Pi_{\mathsf{EIG}}^{(n,t)}$) and incur a communication complexity of $\mathcal{BA}(L)$ bits where $\mathcal{BA}(L) = \mathcal{O}(n^{t+1} L)$ (as there will be n instances of $\Pi_{\mathsf{EIG}}^{(n,t)}$ invoked).

[10] Since $t < \frac{n}{3}$, one can trigger Theorem 2.3 and get a BA protocol with $t < \frac{n}{3}$.

Chapter 4
Efficient Phase-King Protocols for Distributed Consensus

The EIG protocol presented in the previous chapter has a huge communication complexity, which is *exponentially* large. In this chapter, we discuss consensus protocols with *polynomial* communication (and computation) complexity and *perfect* security. We focus on the agreement variant of consensus; namely, we discuss protocols for Byzantine agreement (BA). We will present two protocols, one with *non-optimal* resilience of $t < \frac{n}{4}$, followed by the protocol with *optimal* resilience of $t < \frac{n}{3}$. The former protocol is simpler and requires a smaller number of communication rounds than the latter protocol. Both the protocols are based on what is called the *phase-king* paradigm and attributed to [23, 22]. The description of the protocols in this chapter is due to [1], which builds the protocols on top of the graded agreement (GA) primitive. This greatly *simplifies* the description of the protocols and the proof of its properties.

The network model and the adversarial setting considered in this chapter are the same as those of the previous chapter. Namely, we work in the pairwise-authentic channel model $\mathcal{M}_{\mathsf{auth}}$, where the adversary Adv is *computationally-unbounded* and can control any subset of *at most t* parties in a Byzantine fashion.

4.1 The Generic Phase-King BA Protocol from GA

In this section, we present a generic phase-king BA protocol for L-bit inputs, assuming an instantiation of GA for L-bit inputs. In the subsequent sections, we will see two instantiations of the GA, one with $t < \frac{n}{4}$ and the other with $t < \frac{n}{3}$. While the former requires 1 rounds, the latter requires 2 rounds. When fitted in the generic phase-king BA protocol, we will get two instantiations of BA, one with $t < \frac{n}{4}$ and the other with $t < \frac{n}{3}$. Both the instantiations of GA (and hence BA) are *perfectly-secure*.

The protocol proceeds in *phases*, wherein in each phase, a *distinct* party from $\mathcal{P}$ is publicly designated as the *king*. The protocol consists of $t + 1$ phases, and hence it will be guaranteed that there will be at least one phase where the designated king is *honest*. The general idea behind the protocol is very simple. In each phase, the parties

A. Choudhury and A. Patra, *Fault-Tolerant Distributed Consensus in Synchronous Networks*, Information Security and Cryptography,
https://doi.org/10.1007/978-3-031-80460-1_4

attempt to check if all the *honest* parties have the same input. Then, depending upon the outcome, the parties do one of the following.

- If all honest parties are found to hold a common input, then the parties "stick" to that input for all subsequent phases, *irrespective* of the king parties.
- Else, the parties take the "help" of the king-party of the phase so that if the king-party is *honest*, then, at the end of the phase, all *honest* parties have the same input.

If all *honest* parties start the protocol with a *common* input, say u, then throughout the protocol, the parties *retain* the input u (due to the first property), and finally output u, thus ensuring *validity*. On the other hand, *consistency* is guaranteed even if the honest parties start the protocol with *different* inputs. This is because there will be at least one phase where the corresponding king-party is guaranteed to be *honest*. And hence, at the end of that phase, all honest parties will have a *common* input (due to the second property), which they retain till the end of the protocol.

To achieve the above goals, each phase k consists of *two* sub-phases. During the *first* sub-phase, the parties run an instance of a GA protocol with their current preferred inputs (at the beginning of the protocol, the preferred input of every party is initialized to its input for the BA). If a party obtains an output with the *highest* grade at the end of the GA instance, then it updates its preferred input to that output. However, there might be parties who may *not* obtain any output with the highest grade. To take care of this scenario, the designated king-party comes into the picture during the *second* sub-phase. Namely, the king sends its output from the GA instance to all the parties (irrespective of its grade), who update their preferred input to this value, provided they have *not* received an output with the highest grade from the GA instance.

The idea behind the protocol is as follows: if all *honest* parties start the protocol with the *same* input u, then they will output u. This is because, in each phase, the instance of GA will output u with the *highest* grade, due to the *validity* of GA. Consequently, the value sent by the king will be *never* considered throughout the protocol. On the other hand, if the honest parties start the protocol with *different* inputs, then we consider the *first* phase where the designated king is *honest* (note that such a phase exists). At the end of that phase, all honest parties will have the *same* preferred input, which they will retain for the rest of the protocol. This is because at the end of the phase, either *all* honest parties update their preferred input to the one received from the king (implying that the instance of GA *did not* output any value with the highest grade) or there might be an honest party who obtains an output with the highest grade from the GA instance, which it sets as its updated preferred input. In the latter case, the *knowledge-of-agreement* of GA guarantees that every other honest party (*including* the king) will output the same value during the GA instance, either with the highest grade or medium grade. So irrespective of the case, the updated preferred input of every other honest party will be the *same*.

The generic phase-king BA protocol $\Pi^{(n,t)}_{\mathsf{PhaseKingBA}}$ is formally presented in Fig 4.1. In the protocol, we assume that $\Pi^{(n,t)}_{\mathsf{GA}}$ is a *t-secure* GA protocol in the model $\mathcal{M} \in \{\mathcal{M}_{\mathsf{auth}}, \mathcal{M}_{\mathsf{secure}}, \mathcal{M}^{\mathsf{pki}}_{\mathsf{auth}}, \mathcal{M}^{\mathsf{pki}}_{\mathsf{secure}}\}$ with security level $\mathsf{Sec} \in$

{PerSec, StatSec, CryptoSec}, requiring r rounds of communication and incurring a communication of $\mathcal{GA}(L)$ bits, where L is the size of the inputs of the parties in bits, such that $L \geq 1$ and known publicly.

Protocol $\Pi^{(n,t)}_{\text{PhaseKingBA}}$

Public Knowledge: A t-*secure* GA protocol $\Pi^{(n,t)}_{\text{GA}}$ in the model $\mathcal{M} \in \{\mathcal{M}_{\text{auth}}, \mathcal{M}_{\text{secure}}, \mathcal{M}^{\text{pki}}_{\text{auth}}, \mathcal{M}^{\text{pki}}_{\text{secure}}\}$ with security level Sec $\in$ {PerSec, StatSec, CryptoSec}, requiring r rounds of communication.

Initialization: do the following.

- On having the input $u_i \in \{0,1\}^L$, set $\text{pref}_i^{(0)} = u_i$.
- For $k = 1, \ldots, t+1$, designate the party P_k as the *king* for phase k.
- For $k = 1, \ldots, t+1$, do the following during phase k.
  - **Sub-phase I (executing an instance of GA)**: Participate in the instance $\Pi^{(k)}_{\text{GA}}$ of $\Pi^{(n,t)}_{\text{GA}}$ with input $\text{pref}_i^{(k-1)}$. Let $(c_i^{(k)}, g_i^{(k)})$ be the output from the instance $\Pi^{(k)}_{\text{GA}}$, where $c_i^{(k)} \in \{0,1\}^L$ and $g_i^{(k)} \in \{0,1,2\}$.
  - **Sub-phase II (communication from the king)**: If $P_i = P_k$, then send $c_k^{(k)}$ to all the parties in $\mathcal{P}$ (including itself).
  - **(Updating the preferred input)**: Compute the updated preferred input $\text{pref}_i^{(k)}$ as follows.
    - If $g_i^{(k)} = 2$, then set $\text{pref}_i^{(k)} := c_i^{(k)}$;
    - Else set $\text{pref}_i^{(k)} := c_k^{(k)}$, where $c_k^{(k)}$ is received from the king P_k during the sub-phase II.[a]
- **(Output Computation)**: Output $\text{pref}_i^{(t+1)}$ and terminate.

[a] If no $c_k^{(k)}$ is received from P_k then set $c_k^{(k)}$ to 0^L.

Fig. 4.1: The generic phase-king BA protocol from any GA protocol. The above code is executed by every P_i

We now proceed to prove the properties of the protocol $\Pi^{(n,t)}_{\text{PhaseKingBA}}$, based on the properties of $\Pi^{(n,t)}_{\text{GA}}$.

Lemma 4.1 *Protocol* $\Pi^{(n,t)}_{\text{PhaseKingBA}}$ *achieves t-validity.*

Proof Let $\mathcal{H}$ be the set of *honest* parties and let all the parties in $\mathcal{H}$ have input u. It then follows from the t-*validity* of $\Pi^{(n,t)}_{\text{GA}}$ that each $P_i \in \mathcal{H}$ will output $(u, 2)$ during the instance $\Pi^{(k)}_{\text{GA}}$, for $k = 1, \ldots, t+1$. Consequently, at the end of phase $t+1$, each $P_i \in \mathcal{H}$ will have $\text{pref}_i^{(t+1)} = u$ and hence each $P_i \in \mathcal{H}$ will output u, thus proving the t-*validity* of $\Pi^{(n,t)}_{\text{PhaseKingBA}}$. □

Lemma 4.2 *If $t < n$, then protocol* $\Pi^{(n,t)}_{\text{PhaseKingBA}}$ *achieves t-consistency.*

Proof Let $\mathcal{H}$ be the set of *honest* parties. As there can be at most t corrupt parties and each phase has a *distinct* king-party, there exists at least one phase where the designated king is *honest*. Let k be the *first* such phase where $P_k \in \mathcal{H}$. We first show that each $P_i \in \mathcal{H}$ will have the *same* preferred input $\text{pref}_i^{(k)}$ at the end of the phase

k. For this, we note that there are *two* possible cases with respect to the grade of the output of the parties in $\mathcal{H}$, obtained during the instance $\Pi_{\mathsf{GA}}^{(k)}$.

- **Case I —** $g_i^{(k)} < 2$ **for every** $P_i \in \mathcal{H}$: In this case, each $P_i \in \mathcal{H}$ sets $\mathsf{pref}_i^{(k)} = c_k^{(k)}$, where $c_k^{(k)}$ is received from the king P_k during the second sub-phase of phase k. Moreover, since P_k is assumed to be *honest*, it will send the *same* $c_k^{(k)}$ to all the parties. Hence, $\mathsf{pref}_i^{(k)} = \mathsf{pref}_j^{(k)}$ holds for every $P_i, P_j \in \mathcal{H}$.
- **Case I —** $g_i^{(k)} = 2$ **for at least one** $P_i \in \mathcal{H}$: Let $P_i \in \mathcal{H}$ be an *arbitrary* party such that P_i obtains the output $(c, g_i^{(k)})$ during the instance $\Pi_{\mathsf{GA}}^{(k)}$, where $g_i^{(k)} = 2$. From the *t-knowledge-of-agreement* property of $\Pi_{\mathsf{GA}}^{(n,t)}$, it follows that each $P_j \in \mathcal{H}$ where $P_j \neq P_i$ will output $(c_j^{(k)}, g_j^{(k)})$ during the instance $\Pi_{\mathsf{GA}}^{(k)}$, where $g_j^{(k)} \in \{1, 2\}$ and $c_j^{(k)} = c$. Since $P_k \in \mathcal{H}$, it implies that $c_k^{(k)} = c$. Now there are two possibilities for the updated preferred input $\mathsf{pref}_j^{(k)}$ of P_j.
  - P_j *sets* $\mathsf{pref}_j^{(k)} := c_j^{(k)}$ — Since $c_j^{(k)} = c$, it follows that $\mathsf{pref}_i^{(k)} = \mathsf{pref}_j^{(k)}$ holds.
  - P_j *sets* $\mathsf{pref}_j^{(k)} := c_k^{(k)}$ — Since $c_k^{(k)} = c$, it follows that $\mathsf{pref}_i^{(k)} = \mathsf{pref}_j^{(k)}$ holds even in this case.

Now similar to the proof of Lemma 4.1, it can be shown that each $P_i \in \mathcal{H}$ will have c as their updated preferred input at the end of phases $k+1, \ldots, t+1$. As a result, $p_i^{(t+1)} = c$ holds for each $P_i \in \mathcal{H}$ and hence each $P_i \in \mathcal{H}$ outputs c. □

Theorem 4.1 *Let* $\Pi_{\mathsf{GA}}^{(n,t)}$ *be a t-secure GA protocol in the model* $\mathcal{M} \in \{\mathcal{M}_{\mathsf{auth}}, \mathcal{M}_{\mathsf{secure}}, \mathcal{M}_{\mathsf{auth}}^{\mathsf{pki}}, \mathcal{M}_{\mathsf{secure}}^{\mathsf{pki}}\}$ *with security level* $\mathsf{Sec} \in \{\mathsf{PerSec}, \mathsf{StatSec}, \mathsf{CryptoSec}\}$. *Moreover, let* $\Pi_{\mathsf{GA}}^{(n,t)}$ *require r rounds of communication over the point-to-point channels and incur a communication of* $\mathcal{GA}(L)$ *bits, where L is the size of the inputs of the parties in bits, such that* $L \geq 1$. *If* $t < n$, *then protocol* $\Pi_{\mathsf{PhaseKingBA}}^{(n,t)}$ *is a t-secure BA protocol in the model* $\mathcal{M} \in \{\mathcal{M}_{\mathsf{auth}}, \mathcal{M}_{\mathsf{secure}}, \mathcal{M}_{\mathsf{auth}}^{\mathsf{pki}}, \mathcal{M}_{\mathsf{secure}}^{\mathsf{pki}}\}$ *with security level* $\mathsf{Sec} \in \{\mathsf{PerSec}, \mathsf{StatSec}, \mathsf{CryptoSec}\}$. *The protocol requires* $(t+1)(r+1)$ *rounds of communication over the point-to-point channels and incurs a communication complexity of* $\mathcal{BA}(L)$ *bits where* $\mathcal{BA}(L) = (t+1)(\mathcal{GA}(L) + L)$.

Proof Each phase involves an instance of GA that requires r rounds of communication, followed by the king sending its GA outcome to all, which requires one round. As there are $t+1$ phases, the protocol requires $(t+1)(r+1)$ rounds of communication, after which the parties terminate the protocol, thus proving *t-liveness*. Each phase incurs a communication complexity of $\mathcal{GA}(L) + L$ bits, and so the overall communication complexity is $(t+1)(\mathcal{GA}(L)+L)$ bits. The proof now follows from Lemma 4.1 and Lemma 4.2. □

On the importance of $t + 1$ phases in the protocol $\Pi^{(n,t)}_{\mathsf{PhaseKingBA}}$.

What happens if we run the protocol $\Pi^{(n,t)}_{\mathsf{PhaseKingBA}}$ *only* for t phases? One can verify that the t-validity *still* holds since Lemma 4.1 will still hold. Unfortunately, the t-consistency is *not* guaranteed. This is because in the worst case, *all* the t phases may have king-parties who are *corrupt*. Consequently, Lemma 4.2 may *no* longer hold.

We now present two different instantiations of GA, both with *perfect security*. The first instantiation is with $t < \frac{n}{4}$.

4.2 Perfectly Secure GA with $t < \frac{n}{4}$

In this section, we present a perfectly-secure GA protocol with $t < \frac{n}{4}$. The protocol is very simple and consists of just a single round of communication, where each party sends its input to others. Each party then computes its output as follows: if there exists some value which has been reported as the input by *more than* $\frac{n}{2} + t$ parties, then it is taken as the output with grade 2. Otherwise, if there exists some value which has been reported as the input by *more than* $\frac{n}{2}$ parties, then it is taken as the output with grade 1. Otherwise, the party outputs its input with grade 0.

The idea here is the following: if all *honest* parties have the same input say u, then all honest parties will output u with grade 2. This is because more than $\frac{n}{2} + t$ parties (namely the honest parties) will report u as their input. This ensures the *validity*. On the other hand, consider the case when some honest party outputs a value, say v, with grade 2. It implies that *more* than $\frac{n}{2} + t$ parties reported v as their input. Among these parties, more than $\frac{n}{2}$ are *honest*, who will report v as their input to everyone. As a result, every other honest party will output v, either with grade 2 or 1. The formal details of the protocol are presented in Fig 4.2.

Protocol $\Pi^{(n,t)}_{\mathsf{PerSecGAOneFourth}}$

- **Round 1 (exchanging inputs)**
  - On having the input $u_i \in \{0,1\}^L$, send u_i to all the parties in $\mathcal{P}$ (including itself).
  - For $j = 1, \ldots, n$, let $u_{j,i} \in \{0,1\}^L$ be the input received from P_j during this round.[a]
- **Output computation**
  - If there exists some value from $\{0,1\}^L$ which occurs more than $\frac{n}{2} + t$ times in the vector of inputs $(u_{1,i}, \ldots, u_{n,i})$, then output that value with grade 2 and terminate.
  - Else if there exists some value from $\{0,1\}^L$ which occurs more than $\frac{n}{2}$ times in the vector of inputs $(u_{1,i}, \ldots, u_{n,i})$, then output that value with grade 1 and terminate.
  - Else output u_i with grade 0 and terminate.

[a] If no input is received from P_j by the end of this round then set $u_{j,i} = 0^L$.

Fig. 4.2: A perfectly-secure GA protocol tolerating $t < \frac{n}{4}$ corruptions. The above code is executed by every party P_i

We now proceed to prove the properties of the protocol. We first prove a helping fact that if $t < \frac{n}{4}$, then the set of honest parties is always greater than $\frac{n}{2} + t$.

Claim 4.1 If $t < \frac{n}{4}$ then $n - t > \frac{n}{2} + t$ holds.

Proof Let $n > 4t$. Then the following holds.

$$\frac{n}{2} > 2t.$$

Adding $\frac{n}{2}$ on both the sides we get

$$\frac{n}{2} + \frac{n}{2} > \frac{n}{2} + 2t.$$

From the above, we get that

$$n > \frac{n}{2} + 2t.$$

Consequently, the following holds

$$n - t > \frac{n}{2} + t.$$

We next show that if all honest parties start the protocol with the *same* input, then they all output that value with the highest grade, thus guaranteeing *validity*.

Lemma 4.3 *If* $t < \frac{n}{4}$, *then protocol* $\Pi^{(n,t)}_{\mathsf{PerSecGAOneFourth}}$ *achieves* t*-validity.*

Proof Let $\mathcal{H}$ be the set of *honest* parties, where $|\mathcal{H}| \geq n - t$. Then, as per the lemma's hypothesis, all the parties in $\mathcal{H}$ start the protocol with the *same* input, say $u \in \{0, 1\}^L$. Every $P_j \in \mathcal{H}$ will send u as its input to all the parties. Hence, each party $P_i \in \mathcal{H}$ will receive u as the input from all the parties in $\mathcal{H}$ during the protocol. From Claim 4.1, the condition $|\mathcal{H}| > \frac{n}{2} + t$ will also hold. Hence, at the end of the protocol, every party in $\mathcal{H}$ will output $(u, 2)$, thus proving the t*-validity*. □

We next prove the *knowledge-of-agreement.*

Lemma 4.4 *Protocol* $\Pi^{(n,t)}_{\mathsf{PerSecGAOneFourth}}$ *achieves* t*-knowledge-of-agreement.*

Proof Let $\mathcal{H}$ be the set of honest parties and consider an *arbitrary* $P_i \in \mathcal{H}$, who outputs $(v, 2)$. We wish to show that every party $P_j \in \mathcal{H}$ where $P_j \neq P_i$ will output either $(v, 2)$ or $(v, 1)$. Since P_i outputs $(v, 2)$, it implies that during the protocol, party P_i has received v as the input from *more* than $\frac{n}{2} + t$ parites. Let $\mathcal{S}_i$ be the set of parties who sent v as their input to P_i. Hence $|\mathcal{S}_i| \geq \frac{n}{2} + t + 1$. Let $\mathcal{S}_{\mathcal{H},i}$ be the set of *honest* parties in $\mathcal{S}_i$. It follows that $|\mathcal{S}_{\mathcal{H},i}| \geq \frac{n}{2} + 1$. Moreover, the parties in $\mathcal{S}_{\mathcal{H},i}$ will send v as their input to P_j *as well* during the protocol. Hence, P_j would receive v as the input from more than $\frac{n}{2}$ parties. This also implies that there exists no other value $v' \neq v$ such that P_j receives v' as the input from more than $\frac{n}{2}$ parties. Consequently, P_j will output either $(v, 2)$ or $(v, 1)$, thus proving the t*-knowledge-of-agreement.* For a pictorial illustration of the above argument, see Fig 4.3.

The proof of Theorem 4.2 now follows easily from the above discussion.

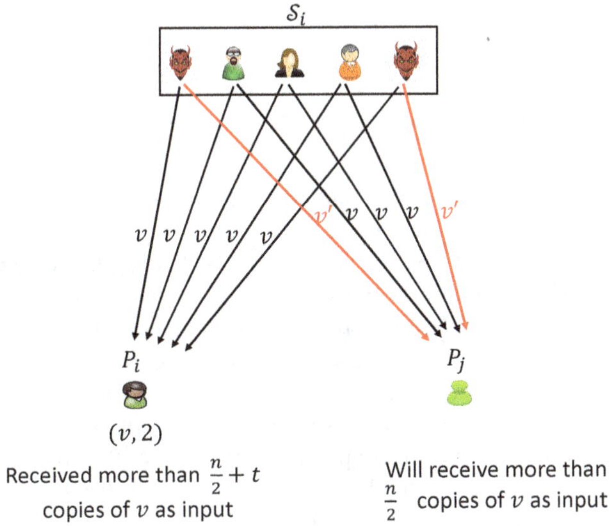

Fig. 4.3: Pictorial illustration of the proof of Lemma 4.4. Party P_i is an honest party who outputs $(v, 2)$ in the protocol. This implies that P_i has received v as the input from a set of parties $\mathcal{S}_i$ where $|\mathcal{S}_i| \geq \frac{n}{2} + t + 1$. There might be up to t corrupt parties in $\mathcal{S}_i$, who may report a different input $v' \neq v$ to another honest party P_j. However, there will still be $\frac{n}{2} + 1$ honest parties in $\mathcal{S}_i$ who will send v as their input to P_j. As a result, P_j will set its output to either $(v, 2)$ or $(v, 1)$

Theorem 4.2 *If $t < \frac{n}{4}$ then protocol $\Pi^{(n,t)}_{\mathsf{PerSecGAOneFourth}}$ is a t-secure GA protocol with perfect security in the model $\mathcal{M}_{\mathsf{auth}}$. The protocol needs a 1 round of communication over the point-to-point channels and incurs a communication of $\mathcal{GA}(L)$ bits where $\mathcal{GA}(L) = O(n^2 L)$ and L is the size of the inputs of the parties.*

Proof The round and communication complexity follows from the protocol inspection. The *t-liveness* follows from the fact that the honest parties terminate the protocol after one round. The *t-validity* and *t-knowledge-of-agreement* follows from Lemma 4.3 and Lemma 4.4 respectively. □

On the importance of the condition $t < \frac{n}{4}$.

Protocol $\Pi^{(n,t)}_{\mathsf{PerSecGAOneFourth}}$ can tolerate up to $t < \frac{n}{4}$ corrupt parties. What happens if the adversary corrupts t parties where $t \geq \frac{n}{4}$. It then follows that Claim 4.1 may *no* longer hold. As a result, Lemma 4.3 may *no* longer hold and hence *t-validity* is not guaranteed.

4.3 Perfectly Secure GA with $t < \frac{n}{3}$

In this section, we present another instantiation of GA with perfect security but with resilience $t < \frac{n}{3}$. The protocol requires 2 rounds of communication. During the *first* round, the parties exchange their respective inputs. During the *second* round, the parties do "voting", based on the reported inputs. Namely, a party sends a vote for some value, if it has seen *more than* $\frac{2n}{3}$ parties reporting that value as their input. Note that it is *not* necessary that a party sees more than $\frac{2n}{3}$ parties reporting a particular value as their input, and consequently, it is *not* necessary that each party votes during the second round. However, as it will be shown later, two different *honest* parties will *never* vote for *different* values; this property is at the crux of the protocol and is often called the *quorum argument* in the literature. At the end of the second round, each party computes its output as follows: if the party sees *more than* $\frac{2n}{3}$ parties voting for the same value, then the party outputs that value with grade 2. Else if the party sees more than $\frac{n}{3}$ parties voting for the same value, then the party outputs that value with grade 1. Otherwise, the party outputs its input with grade 0.

If all honest parties start the protocol with the same input, say u, then all honest parties will output $(u, 2)$, thus ensuring *validity*. This is because during the second round, each *honest* party will vote for u, since all honest parties would report u as their input during the first round and *more than* $\frac{2n}{3}$ parties are *honest*. For *knowledge-of-agreement*, if any honest party outputs $(v, 2)$, then it implies that it has seen *more than* $\frac{2n}{3}$ parties voting for v during the second round. Among these parties, more than $\frac{n}{3}$ are honest and will vote for v to every other honest party. Moreover, from the *quorum argument* (which will be proved later), *no* other honest party will ever vote for a value, different from v. Consequently, every other honest party will output the value v, either with grade 2 or 1. The formal details of the protocol are presented in Fig 4.4.

Protocol $\Pi^{(n,t)}_{\mathsf{PerSecGAOneThird}}$

- **Round 1 (exchanging inputs)**
  - On having the input $u_i \in \{0, 1\}^L$, send u_i to all the parties including itself. If no input is received from a party by the end of this round, then set 0^L as the input for such parties.
  - **(Computing the vote)**: Let $\mathcal{A}_i$ denote the set of parties of the *maximum* size, who have sent the same input, say u. If $|\mathcal{A}_i| > \frac{2n}{3}$, then set $\mathsf{vote}_i = u$, else set $\mathsf{vote}_i = \perp$.
- **Round 2 (exchanging votes)**
  - **(Sending the vote (optional))**: If $\mathsf{vote}_i \neq \perp$, then send vote_i to all the parties including itself.
  - **(Computing the maximum vote)**: Let $\mathcal{B}_i$ denote the set of parties of the *maximum* size, who have sent the same vote, say v.
- **Output computation and termination**
  - If $|\mathcal{B}_i| > \frac{2n}{3}$, then output $(v, 2)$ and terminate;

- Else if $|\mathcal{B}_i| > \frac{n}{3}$, then output $(v, 1)$ and terminate;
- Else output $(u_i, 0)$ and terminate.

Fig. 4.4: A perfectly-secure GA protocol tolerating $t < \frac{n}{3}$ corruptions. The above code is executed by every party P_i

We now proceed to prove the properties of the protocol $\Pi^{(n,t)}_{\mathsf{PerSecGAOneThird}}$. We start with the *validity* property.

Lemma 4.5 *If $t < \frac{n}{3}$ then protocol $\Pi^{(n,t)}_{\mathsf{PerSecGAOneThird}}$ achieves t-validity.*

Proof Let $\mathcal{H}$ be the set of *honest* parties, where $|\mathcal{H}| \geq n - t > \frac{2n}{3}$. For validity, we need to consider the case when all the parties in $\mathcal{H}$ start the protocol with the *same* input, say $u \in \{0, 1\}^L$. We wish to show that all the parties in $\mathcal{H}$ will output $(u, 2)$.

During the first round, every party in $\mathcal{H}$ will send u as its input to all the parties, while the corrupt parties may send $u' \neq u$ as their input. Since $\frac{2n}{3} > \frac{n}{3}$, it follows that $\mathcal{H} \subseteq \mathcal{A}_i$ will hold for each $P_i \in \mathcal{H}$, who will set vote_i to u. Hence, during the second round, each $P_i \in \mathcal{H}$ will send u as its vote to all the parties, while the corrupt parties may send $u' \neq u$ as their vote. Again, since $\frac{2n}{3} > \frac{n}{3}$, it follows that $\mathcal{H} \subseteq \mathcal{B}_i$ will hold for each $P_i \in \mathcal{H}$. Moreover, since $|\mathcal{B}_i| > \frac{2n}{3}$ will hold, P_i will output $(u, 2)$. □

We now proceed to prove the *knowledge-of-agreement* property. For this, we first show that in the protocol, honest parties will *never* vote for *different* values. The proof for this is based on what is often referred to as *quorum argument* and which will be repeatedly used in the rest of the monogram.

Claim 4.2 If $t < \frac{n}{3}$ and if P_i and P_j are distinct honest parties who sets vote_i and vote_j to values a and b respectively where $a, b \in \{0, 1\}^L$, then $a = b$ holds.

Proof The proof is by contradiction. Let $\mathcal{H}$ and C be the set of *honest* and *corrupt* parties respectively, where $|\mathcal{H}| \geq n - t > \frac{2n}{3}$ and $|C| \leq t < \frac{n}{3}$. Let $P_i, P_j \in \mathcal{H}$ and $a \neq b$. Now consider the sets $\mathcal{A}_i$ and $\mathcal{A}_j$. From the protocol steps, it follows that $|\mathcal{A}_i| > \frac{2n}{3}$ and $|\mathcal{A}_j| > \frac{2n}{3}$. Moreover, P_i has received a as the input from all the parties in $\mathcal{A}_i$, while P_j has received b as the input from all the parties in $\mathcal{A}_j$ during the first round. Then consider the set $\mathcal{A}_i \cap \mathcal{A}_j$. It follows that $|\mathcal{A}_i \cap \mathcal{A}_j| > \frac{n}{3}$. Since $|C| < \frac{n}{3}$, it follows that $|\mathcal{H} \cap \mathcal{A}_i \cap \mathcal{A}_j| \neq \emptyset$ and hence there exists at least one *honest* party, say P_m, present in *both* $\mathcal{A}_i$ as well as $\mathcal{A}_j$. This implies that during the first round of the protocol, party P_m has sent the values a and b as its input to P_i and P_j respectively, where $a \neq b$. However, this is a contradiction, since P_m being *honest* will send the *same* input to all the parties. For a pictorial depiction of the above argument, see Fig 4.5.[1]

Now, using the help of Claim 4.2, we next prove the *knowledge-of-agreement*.

Lemma 4.6 *If $t < \frac{n}{3}$ then protocol $\Pi^{(n,t)}_{\mathsf{PerSecGAOneThird}}$ achieves t-knowledge-of-agreement.*

[1] The reason that the above argument is referred to as the quorum argument is that we finally derive the existence of at least one *common* honest party in the quorum of parties $\mathcal{A}_i$ and $\mathcal{A}_j$.

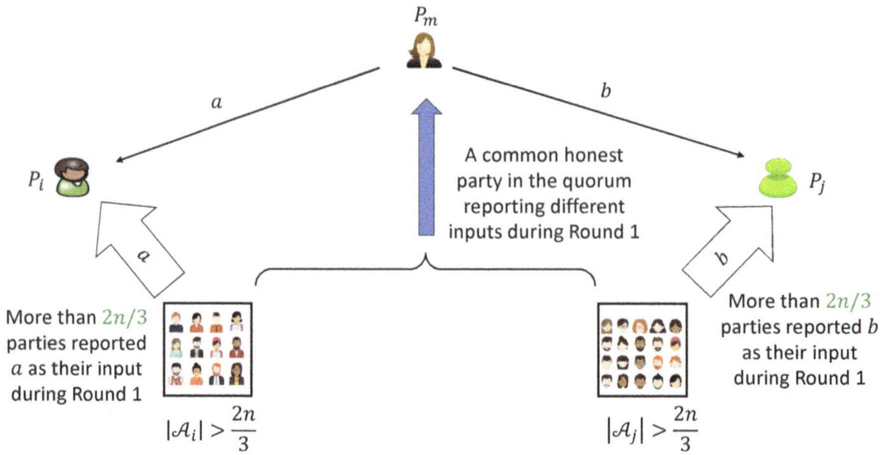

Fig. 4.5: Pictorial illustration of the quorum argument

Proof Let $\mathcal{H}$ be the set of *honest* parties. Consider an *arbitrary* $P_i \in \mathcal{H}$ such that P_i outputs $(v, 2)$. We wish to show that every other party $P_j \in \mathcal{H}$ outputs $(v, 2)$ or $(v, 1)$. Since P_i outputs $(v, 2)$ it implies there exists a set of parties $\mathcal{B}_i$, where $|\mathcal{B}_i| > \frac{2n}{3}$, such that P_i has received the value v as the vote from all the parties in $\mathcal{B}_i$ during the second round of the protocol. Let $\mathcal{B}_{i,\mathcal{H}}$ be the set of *honest* parties in $\mathcal{B}_i$; i.e. $\mathcal{B}_{i,\mathcal{H}} = \mathcal{H} \cap \mathcal{B}_i$. It then follows that $|\mathcal{B}_{i,\mathcal{H}}| > \frac{n}{3}$, since there can be at most t corrupt parties in the set $\mathcal{B}_i$ and $t < \frac{n}{3}$. Since the parties in $\mathcal{B}_{i,\mathcal{H}}$ are *honest*, they will send v as their vote to P_j during the second round. Moreover, from Claim 4.2 *no* party in $\mathcal{H} \setminus \mathcal{B}_{i,\mathcal{H}}$ will ever send v' as their vote to P_j where $v' \neq v$. Hence, $\mathcal{B}_{i,\mathcal{H}} \subseteq \mathcal{B}_j$ will hold and as a result $|\mathcal{B}_j| > \frac{n}{3}$ will also hold. Consequently, P_j will output either $(v, 2)$ or $(v, 1)$.

For a pictorial illustration illustration of the above argument, see Fig 4.6.

The proof of Theorem 4.3 now follows easily from the above discussion.

Theorem 4.3 *If* $t < \frac{n}{3}$ *then protocol* $\Pi^{(n,t)}_{\mathsf{PerSecGAOneThird}}$ *is a* t*-secure GA protocol in the model* $\mathcal{M}_{\mathsf{auth}}$ *with perfect security. The protocol needs* 2 *rounds of communication over the point-to-point channels and incurs a communication of* $\mathcal{GA}(L)$ *bits where* $\mathcal{GA}(L) = O(n^2 L)$ *and where* L *is the size of the inputs of the parties, such that* $L \geq 1$.

Proof The round and communication complexity follows from the protocol description. The *t-liveness* follows from the fact that the honest parties terminate the protocol after 2 rounds. The *t-validity* and *t-knowledge-of-agreement* follows from Lemma 4.5 and Lemma 4.6 respectively. □

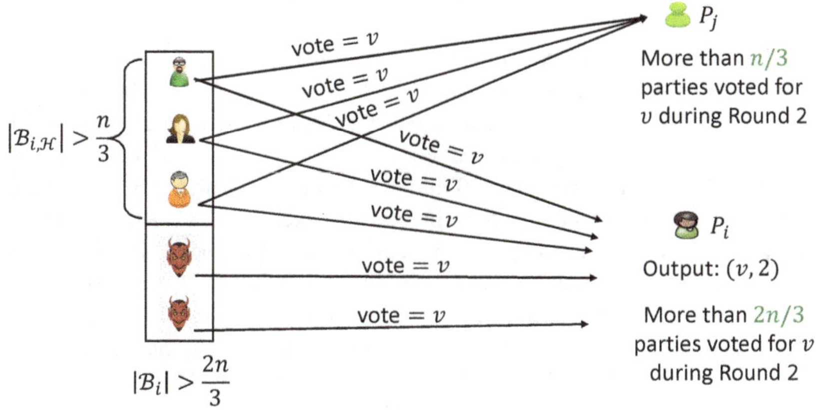

Fig. 4.6: Pictorial illustration of the proof of Lemma 4.6. Party P_i is an honest party who outputs $(v, 2)$ because there exists a subset of parties $\mathcal{B}_i$ of size more than $\frac{2n}{3}$ who voted for v to P_i. Among $\mathcal{B}_i$ there will exist a subset of honest parties $\mathcal{B}_{i,\mathcal{H}}$ of size more than $\frac{n}{3}$ who will vote for v to every other honest party P_j. Moreover, from the quorum argument (Claim 4.2), no honest party outside $\mathcal{B}_i$ will ever vote for a value different from v. So, the conditions for outputting a value different from v will be never satisfied for P_j. Hence P_j will output either $(v, 2)$ or $(v, 1)$

On the importance of the condition $t < \frac{n}{3}$.

Protocol $\Pi^{(n,t)}_{\mathsf{PerSecGAOneThird}}$ can tolerate up to $t < \frac{n}{3}$ corrupt parties. What happens if the adversary corrupts t parties where $t \geq \frac{n}{3}$. It then follows that the quorum argument may *no* longer be applicable and hence Claim 4.2 may *no* longer hold. As a result, Lemma 4.6 may *no* longer hold, which may further *affect* the *t-knowledge-of-agreement* property.

On the importance of 2 rounds.

What happens if we *do not* have the second round in the protocol $\Pi^{(n,t)}_{\mathsf{PerSecGAOneThird}}$? Then we *may not* be able to achieve *t-knowledge-of-agreement*. For instance, it may happen that some *honest* party P_i receives a value v from *more than* $\frac{2n}{3}$ parties during the first round, while another *honest* party P_j receives the v from more than $\frac{n}{3}$ parties *as well as* another value $v' \neq v$ from another set of more than $\frac{n}{3}$ parties. This can happen if the honest parties have *different* inputs and the corrupt parties report *different* inputs to different honest parties. Consequently, P_j will *not* be able to decide its output.

To make it more concrete, consider the case when $L = 1$, the number of parties $n = 3t + 3$, the set of *honest* parties $\mathcal{H} = \{P_1, \ldots, P_{2t+3}\}$ and the set of *corrupt* parties $C = \{P_{2t+4}, \ldots, P_{3t+3}\}$. Moreover, let $\mathcal{H}_0$ and $\mathcal{H}_1$ be a partition of the set $\mathcal{H}$, where $\mathcal{H}_0 = \{P_1, \ldots, P_{t+3}\}$ and $\mathcal{H}_1 = \{P_{t+4}, \ldots, P_{2t+3}\}$. Furthermore, let the parties in $\mathcal{H}_0$ and $\mathcal{H}_1$ have inputs 0 and 1 respectively. During the first round, the parties in $\mathcal{H}$ correctly exchange their inputs with each other. However, the parties in C send 0 as their input to the parties in $\mathcal{H}_0$, while to the parties in $\mathcal{H}_1$, they report 1 as their input. Consequently, the parties in $\mathcal{H}_0$ receive $t + 3 + t = 2t + 3$ number of 0's and t number of 1's and and hence will output the bit 0 with grade 2, since $2t + 3 > \frac{2n}{3}$; i.e. their output will be $(0, 2)$. On the other hand, the parties in $\mathcal{H}_1$ will receive $t + t = 2t$ number of 1's and $t + 3$ number of 0's. Since the number of 0's as well as the number of 1's are both *greater* than $\frac{n}{3}$, the parties in $\mathcal{H}_1$ will *not* be sure whether to output the bit 0 with grade 1 or the bit 1 with grade 1.

4.4 The Phase-King BA Protocols

By instantiating the abstract GA protocol in the abstract phase-king BA protocol $\Pi^{(n,t)}_{\mathsf{PhaseKingBA}}$ (Fig 4.1) with the *perfectly-secure* instantiations $\Pi^{(n,t)}_{\mathsf{PerSecGAOneFourth}}$ (Fig 4.2) and $\Pi^{(n,t)}_{\mathsf{PerSecGAOneThird}}$ (Fig 4.4) respectively, we get two phase-king BA protocols with $t < \frac{n}{4}$ and $t < \frac{n}{3}$ respectively. We call these protocols as $\Pi^{(n,t)}_{\mathsf{PKNO}}$ and $\Pi^{(n,t)}_{\mathsf{PKO}}$ respectively, standing for phase-king BA protocol with *non-optimal* and *optimal* resilience respectively.[2] Since the number of rounds r is 1 and 2 respectively for $\Pi^{(n,t)}_{\mathsf{PerSecGAOneFourth}}$ and $\Pi^{(n,t)}_{\mathsf{PerSecGAOneThird}}$, from Theorem 4.1, the round complexity of $\Pi^{(n,t)}_{\mathsf{PKNO}}$ and $\Pi^{(n,t)}_{\mathsf{PKO}}$ turns out to be $2(t + 1)$ and $3(t + 1)$ respectively. Since $\mathcal{GA}(L) = O(n^2L)$ bits for *both* $\Pi^{(n,t)}_{\mathsf{PerSecGAOneFourth}}$ and $\Pi^{(n,t)}_{\mathsf{PerSecGAOneThird}}$, from Theorem 4.1, the communication complexity of $\Pi^{(n,t)}_{\mathsf{PKNO}}$ and $\Pi^{(n,t)}_{\mathsf{PKO}}$ turns out to be $\mathcal{BA}(L)$ where $\mathcal{BA}(L) = O(n^3L)$. We summarize the above discussion in Theorem 4.4.

Theorem 4.4 – *If $t < \frac{n}{4}$, then there exists a t-secure BA protocol $\Pi^{(n,t)}_{\mathsf{PKNO}}$ with perfect security in the model $\mathcal{M}_{\mathsf{auth}}$ for L-bit inputs where $L \geq 1$. The protocol requires $2(t + 1)$ rounds of communication over the point-to-point channels and incurs a communication complexity of $\mathcal{BA}(L)$ bits where $\mathcal{BA}(L) = O(n^3L)$.*

– *If $t < \frac{n}{3}$, then there exists a t-secure BA protocol $\Pi^{(n,t)}_{\mathsf{PKO}}$ with perfect security in the model $\mathcal{M}_{\mathsf{auth}}$ for L-bit inputs where $L \geq 1$. The protocol requires $3(t+1)$ rounds*

[2] Looking ahead, $t < \frac{n}{3}$ is the *optimal* resilience for *any* BA protocol in the model $\mathcal{M}_{\mathsf{auth}}$.

of communication over the point-to-point channels and incurs a communication complexity of $\mathcal{BA}(L)$ bits where $\mathcal{BA}(L) = O(n^3 L)$.

Finally, comparing protocol $\Pi_{\text{EIG}}^{(n,t)}$ (Fig 3.11) and protocol $\Pi_{\text{PKO}}^{(n,t)}$, we find that there is a trade-off between the round and communication (and computation) complexity of BA protocols. While the former requires a *lesser* number of communication rounds, efficiency-wise it performs poorly and requires an *exponential* amount of computation and communication. By letting *more* interaction among the parties (from $t + 1$ rounds to $3t + 3$ rounds), we could *bring* down the communication (and computation) complexity from *exponential* to *polynomial*. In fact, by *decreasing* the resilience from $t < \frac{n}{3}$ to $t < \frac{n}{4}$, one can further *improve* the number of communication rounds from $3t + 3$ to $2t + 2$. Hence, depending on whether one would like to minimize the computation and communication complexity at the expense of *non-optimal* resilience and round-complexity, one can decide the choice of the protocol.

4.5 Phase-King BA with Optimal Resilience and Optimal Communication Complexity

Protocol $\Pi_{\text{PKO}}^{(n,t)}$ has the *optimal* resilience of $t < \frac{n}{3}$. Moreover, its communication complexity is *polynomial*. In [45], it is shown that *any* BA protocol where the parties have a *single* bit input necessarily needs to communicate $\Omega(n^2)$ bits, irrespective of the level of the security and the communication model; i.e. $\mathcal{BA}(1) = \Omega(n^2)$ holds. Hence, the communication complexity of the protocol $\Pi_{\text{PKO}}^{(n,t)}$ for single-bit inputs is *not* optimal, since $\mathcal{BA}(1) = O(n^3)$ for protocol $\Pi_{\text{PKO}}^{(n,t)}$. The reason that protocol $\Pi_{\text{PKO}}^{(n,t)}$ incurs a communication of $O(n^3)$ bits is that it requires each party to communicate with every other party $t + 1$ times, to ensure that we have a phase with an *honest* king. Interestingly, the authors in [23] have presented another perfectly-secure protocol with $t < \frac{n}{3}$, which achieves the *optimal* communication complexity of $\mathcal{BA}(1) = O(n^2)$ bits. The key insight is to ensure that we encounter an honest king "quickly". For this, the protocol calls itself twice on roughly half of the parties, replacing the king by running a consensus protocol on each subset. Since $t < \frac{n}{3}$, the adversary *will not* have the capacity to corrupt sufficiently many parties to fail *both* the instances. Moreover, in the recursive calls, fewer parties are involved in exchanging messages. Since the protocol is slightly involved, we avoid discussing it here.

Chapter 5
Lower Bound on the Resilience of Consensus Protocols Without Any Set-Up

All the protocols discussed till now are *without* any set-up. Namely, all the protocols are designed in the *pairwise-authentic* channel model $\mathcal{M}_{\mathsf{auth}}$, where the *only* assumption is that the parties are connected by pairwise-authentic channels. All the protocols presented in this model have a resilience of $t < \frac{n}{3}$.[1] A natural question is, what is the resilience of *any* distributed consensus protocol in this model? Towards this, we show that the *optimal* resilience for *any* consensus protocol (*both* for BA as well as BB) in this model is $t < \frac{n}{3}$. This fundamental lower bound, attributed to Fischer, Lynch and Merritt [49], is also known as the FLM lower bound. To prove the lower bound, we will introduce several powerful proof mechanisms, like *indistinguishability* (where honest parties may not be able to distinguish between two potential worlds), *hybridization* (where we build intermediate worlds between two contradicting worlds and use a chain of indistinguishability arguments for a contradiction) and *player-partioning* (where we show the *impossibility* of a distributed protocol for a "larger" number of parties, based on the *impossibility* of the same protocol for a "smaller" number of parties). We will also show that the FLM lower bound holds *both* for deterministic as well as randomized consensus protocols, where security properties are guaranteed *probabilistically*. This is based on the lower bound due to Karlin and Yao [63].

We remark that our proof of the FLM lower bound is significantly borrowed from [1], and to make the proof simpler, we do skip certain formal details and refer to [74] for a more formal and comprehensive treatment.

5.1 Impossibility of Distributed Consensus with Three Parties and One Corruption

To begin with, we will first show that it is *impossible* to design *any* distributed consensus protocol in a system with *three* parties, where *one* of the parties may get

[1] The resilience of the protocol $\Pi_{\mathsf{PKNO}}^{(n,t)}$ is $t < \frac{n}{4}$.

A. Choudhury and A. Patra, *Fault-Tolerant Distributed Consensus in Synchronous Networks*, Information Security and Cryptography,
https://doi.org/10.1007/978-3-031-80460-1_5

Byzantine corrupt. For simplicity, we will consider the BA variant of the consensus and the proof is applicable even for the BB variant of consensus.

5.1.1 The Underlying Intuition

Consider a system of *three* parties, say A, B and C, connected by pairwise authentic channels, such that the adversary can corrupt *at most one* among the three parties. Consider an execution scenario for any BA protocol, where B and C "blame" each other for "lying" and provide no proof-of-malice to A. Then A has no way to decide who is corrupt between B and C and hence A has *no* way of knowing whom to trust and agree with.

In more detail, let $\Pi_{\mathsf{BA}}^{(3,1)}$ be an *arbitrary* BA protocol which is 1-*secure*, tolerating up to *one* corruption. Then, consider an execution of $\Pi_{\mathsf{BA}}^{(3,1)}$, where A and B are *honest* and have inputs 0 and 1 respectively, while C is *corrupt*. The strategy for party C in the execution is as follows: to party A, it reports its input as 0, while to party B, it reports its input as 1. Hence, the *corrupt* C caused the honest parties A and B to *conflict* with each other. Note that further interaction between B and C will *not* help to "improve" the situation. Consequently, from the point of view of A, it has *no* way to find out whether B is cheating or C. Similarly, from the point of view of B, it has *no* way to find out whether A is cheating or B. Hence, there is *no* way for A and B to compute the *same* output, thus resulting in a *violation* of the 1-*consistency* property. Note that the above strategy by a *corrupt* C is *possible*, since adversary *will* be *knowing* the steps of the protocol $\Pi_{\mathsf{BA}}^{(3,1)}$. Hence, it can run *two* instances of the protocol in *parallel* in its mind, where in one instance, it executes the steps of C, considering its input being 0 and sends those messages to A, while in the other instance, it executes the steps of C, considering its input being 1 and sends those messages to B. The above strategy by the adversary is also called adversary *simulating* the behaviour of C with different inputs.

For a pictorial illustration of the above argument, see Fig 5.1.

Remark 5.1 Note that the above argument *may fail*, if the parties are provided with some set-up, say for example, a setup for *public-key infrastructure* (PKI); i.e. if the protocol is designed in the model $\mathcal{M}_{\mathsf{auth}}^{\mathsf{pki}}$. For instance, suppose we *modify* the steps of $\Pi_{\mathsf{BA}}^{(3,1)}$ where *instead* of simply sending its input to all the parties, each party sends a signed version of its input. And later in the subsequent rounds, the parties exchange the signed version of the inputs received from each other. If the signature scheme is *unforgeable*, then both A and B will be able to identify the *corrupt* behaviour of C. For instance, B will now report to A that C has reported its input as 1 to B, *along* with C's signature. And A would have received the input 0 on the behalf of C, along with C's signature. Now the presence of C's *signature* on *two different* inputs will

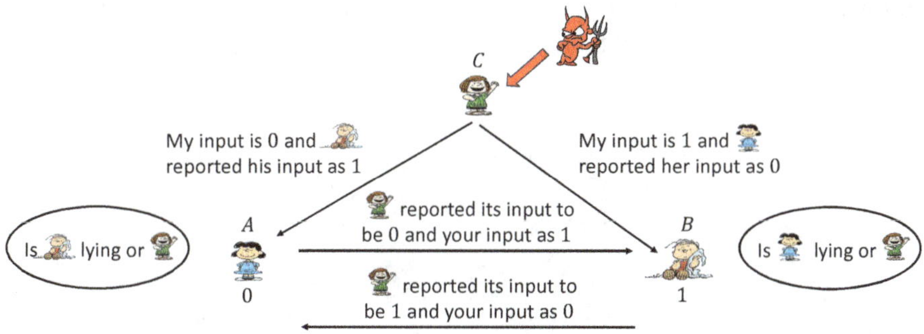

Fig. 5.1: Pictorial illustration of the intuition that why BA among three parties tolerating one corrupt party is not possible in the absence of any set-up. The strategy of the adversary here is to simulate the behaviour of C with conflicting inputs towards A and B. This leads to a situation where A cannot decide who is corrupt between B and C and B cannot decide who is corrupt between A and B

serve as a witness for the *corrupt* behaviour of C, which is possible only if a PKI set-up is available.[2]

5.1.2 The Formal Security Proof

In this section, we formalize the intuition discussed in the previous section.

Theorem 5.1 *There exists no* 1*-secure BA protocol for* 3 *parties in the model* $\mathcal{M}_{\mathsf{auth}}$ *or* $\mathcal{M}_{\mathsf{secure}}$ *with security level* Sec ∈ {PerSec, StatSec, CryptoSec}.

Proof The proof is by contradiction. Let there exist a 1-*secure* BA protocol among 3 parties in the model $\mathcal{M}_{\mathsf{auth}}$ or $\mathcal{M}_{\mathsf{secure}}$ with security level Sec. Moreover, let A, B and C denote the steps of $\Pi_{\mathsf{BA}}^{(3,1)}$, for the three parties respectively.[3] Then consider a synchronous system of *six* parties $P_1, \ldots, P_6$, connected in a ring system as shown in part (a) in Fig 5.2, where P_1 and P_4 run steps A, party P_2 and P_5 run steps B and party P_3 and P_6 run steps C. Note that any *three* consecutive parties in the ring are running the steps A, B and C in some order. Then consider an execution β of this ring system, where there is *no* corruption and where P_1, P_2, P_3 participate with input 1, while P_4, P_5, P_6 participate with input 0. This execution has some

[2] Looking ahead, we will see a concrete BA protocol for 3 parties tolerating 1 corruption based on the above idea, in the model $\mathcal{M}_{\mathsf{auth}}^{\mathsf{pki}}$.

[3] The steps A, B and C will be *publicly* known, and in any execution of $\Pi_{\mathsf{BA}}^{(3,1)}$, it will be known which of the three parties is designated to execute steps A, B and C.

well-defined behaviour, especially given that there are *no* corruptions during this execution. The execution β will be now used to define few *adversarial* strategies during some execution of $\Pi_{\text{BA}}^{(3,1)}$ involving three parties connected in a triangle. In more detail, consider the following three executions α_1, α_2 and α_3 of $\Pi_{\text{BA}}^{(3,1)}$.

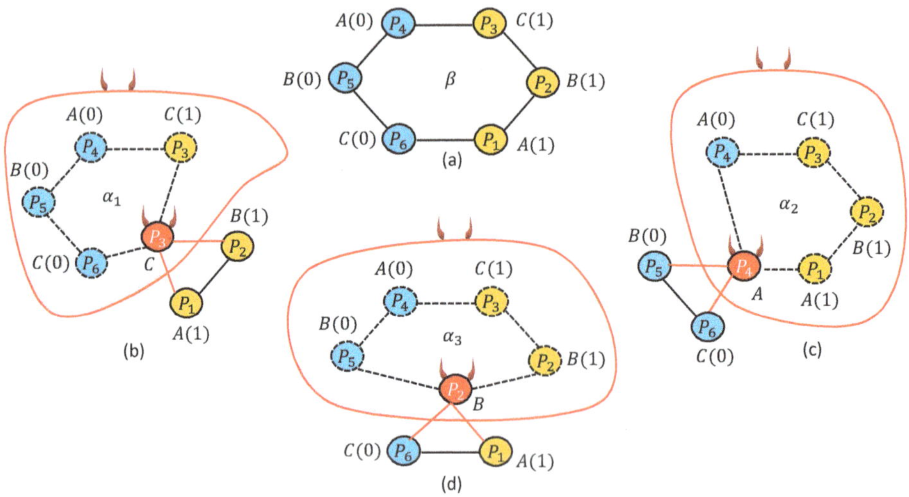

Fig. 5.2: Pictorial illustration of the various executions considered in the proof of Theorem 5.1. During execution β, there is *no* corruption. Executions α_1, α_2 and α_3 are three possible executions of $\Pi_{\text{BA}}^{(3,1)}$, wherein in each of these executions, the adversary corrupts one of the protocol participants. The goal of the corrupt party in each of these executions is to simulate the same sequence of messages as the remaining two honest parties would have seen during the execution β in the hexagonal ring system. To achieve this goal, the corrupt party has to simulate four parties as per the execution β. For instance, in execution α_1, party P_3 is corrupt and simulates the role of P_3, P_4, P_5 and P_6 as per β and sends the corresponding messages to P_2 and P_1. Whatever messages P_6 would have sent to P_1 in β, they are now sent by P_3 to P_1 in α_1, while whatever messages P_3 would have sent to P_2 in β, those messages are now sent by P_3 to P_2.

- **Execution** α_1: in this execution, parties P_1, P_2 and P_3 participate, such that P_1 and P_2 are *honest* and have input 1, while P_3 is under the control of the adversary. Moreover, P_1, P_2 and P_3 are designated to run steps A, B and C respectively. The strategy of the adversary in this execution is as follows: the adversary let P_3 send the same messages to P_2 as in execution β, while it let P_3 send the same messages sent by P_6 to P_1 in β. For this, the adversary has to *simulate* the role of parties P_3, P_4, P_5 and P_6, running steps C, A, B and C, with inputs $1, 0, 0$ and 0 respectively and connected with P_1 and P_2 as per the ring system. Note that the above strategy is possible for the adversary since it knows the protocol steps and hence can simulate the execution β and send the required messages to P_1 and P_2. Intuitively, by sending the messages as above, based on what it receives from P_4 in execution β, party P_3 is trying to *frame* P_1 as if P_1 started the protocol with input 0 (which is *not* the case). Similarly, by sending the messages as above, based on what P_6 receives from P_5 in execution β, party P_3 is trying to *frame* P_2 as if P_2 started the protocol with input 0 (which is *not* the case). Note that the way parties $P_1, \ldots, P_6$ are connected in the execution β, it is possible for the adversary to simulate the parties as described above and send the appropriate messages to P_1 and P_2.

Since protocol $\Pi_{\mathsf{BA}}^{(3,1)}$ satisfies the 1-*validity* condition and since the *honest* parties P_1 and P_2 have the *same* input 1 during the execution α_1, it follows that *both* P_1 and P_2 will output 1 during the execution α_1, irrespective of the above behaviour of the *corrupt* P_3. The execution α_1 is pictorially illustrated in part (b) of Fig 5.2.

- **Execution** α_2: in this execution, shown in part (c) of Fig 5.2 parties P_4, P_5 and P_6 participate, running steps A, B and C respectively. Party P_5 and P_6 are *honest* and have input 0, while P_4 is under the control of the adversary. The strategy of the adversary in this execution is as follows: the adversary let P_4 send the same messages to P_5 as in execution β, while it let P_4 send the same messages sent by P_1 to P_6 in β. For this, the adversary has to *simulate* the role of parties P_1, P_2, P_3 and P_4, running steps A, B, C and A, with inputs $1, 1, 1$ and 0 respectively and connected with P_5 and P_6 as per the ring system. Note that the above strategy is possible for the adversary since it knows the protocol steps and hence can simulate the execution β and send the required messages to P_5 and P_6.

  Intuitively, by sending the messages as above, based on what it receives from P_3 in execution β, party P_4 is trying to *frame* P_6 as if P_6 started the protocol with input 1 (which is *not* the case). Similarly, by sending the messages as above, based on what P_1 receives from P_2 in execution β, party P_4 is trying to *frame* P_5 as if P_5 started the protocol with input 1 (which is *not* the case). Note that the way parties $P_1, \ldots, P_6$ are connected in the execution β, it is possible for the adversary to simulate the parties as described above and send the appropriate messages to P_5 and P_6.

  Since protocol $\Pi_{\mathsf{BA}}^{(3,1)}$ satisfies the 1-*validity* condition and since the *honest* parties P_5 and P_6 have the *same* input 0 during the execution α_2, it follows that *both* P_5 and P_6 will output 1 during the execution α_2, irrespective of the above behaviour of the *corrupt* P_4.
- **Execution** α_3: in this execution, shown in part (d) of Fig 5.2 parties P_1, P_2 and P_6 participate, running steps A, B and C respectively. Party P_1 and P_6 are *honest* and have input 1 and 0 respectively, while P_2 is under the control of the adversary. The strategy of the adversary in this execution is as follows: the adversary let P_2 send the same messages to P_1 as in execution β, while it let P_2 send the same messages sent by P_5 to P_6 in β. For this, the adversary has to *simulate* the role of parties P_2, P_3, P_4 and P_5, running steps B, C, A and B, with inputs $1, 1, 0$ and 0 respectively and connected with P_1 and P_6 as per the ring

system. Note that the above strategy is possible for the adversary since it knows the protocol steps and hence can simulate the execution β and send the required messages to P_1 and P_6.

Intuitively, by sending the messages as above, based on what it receives from P_3 in execution β, party P_2 is trying to *frame* P_6 as if P_6 started the protocol with input 1 (which is *not* the case). Similarly, by sending the messages as above, based on what P_5 receives from P_4 in execution β, party P_2 is trying to *frame* P_1 as if P_1 started the protocol with input 0 (which is *not* the case). Note that the way parties $P_1, \ldots, P_6$ are connected in the execution β, it is possible for the adversary to simulate the parties as described above and send the appropriate messages to P_1 and P_6.

What will be the output of the *honest* parties P_1 and P_6 in the execution α_3? Let us first consider the party P_1. From the point of view of P_1, the executions α_1 and α_3 are *indistinguishable*, since the messages which it sends and receives in both the executions are the *same* as that in β. Note that the *exact* identity of the parties which participate in the executions α_1 and α_3 *does not* matter for this indistinguishability argument. This is because *both* α_1 and α_3 can be visualized as if there are three parties running steps A, B and C, wherein in both the executions, the party running steps A has the input 1. Moreover, in both executions, from the point of view of the party running the steps A, the party running the steps B has input 1. Furthermore, in both executions, from the point of view of the party running the steps A, the party running the steps C has input 0. Now, since the output of party P_1 in execution α_1 is 1, the output of the party P_1 will be 1 even in the execution α_3.

Let us next consider party P_6. From the point of view of P_6, the executions α_2 and α_3 are *indistinguishable*, since the messages which it sends and receives in both the executions are the *same* as that in β. Note that the *exact* identity of the parties which participate in the executions α_2 and α_3 *does not* matter for this indistinguishability argument. This is because *both* α_2 and α_3 can be visualized as if there are three parties running steps A, B and C, wherein in both the executions, the party running steps C has the input 0. Moreover, in both executions, from the point of view of the party running the steps C, the party running the steps B has input 0. Furthermore, in both executions, from the point of view of the party running the steps C, the party running the steps A has input 1. Now, since the output of party P_6 in execution α_2 is 0, the output of the party P_6 will be 0 even in the execution α_3.

However, we now get a *contradiction*. This is because *both* P_1 and P_6 are *honest* parties. And from the above argument, they have *different* outputs in the execution α_3, which is a *violation* of the 1-*consistency* property. Hence protocol $\Pi_{\mathsf{BA}}^{(3,1)}$ *does not* exist. □

The main thing to note in the proof of Theorem 5.1 is the *ability* of the adversary to *simulate* the behaviour of other parties. Specifically, in the proof, the adversary needs to simulate the behaviour of *four* parties. Theorem 5.1 *does not* hold, if the adversary is *unable* to simulate other parties. Some of the scenarios where adversary *cannot* simulate other parties are as follows:

- **Trusted Setup**: If there is *no* setup, apart from the pairwise channels, then Theorem 5.1 *holds*, *even* if the adversary is a *polynomial time* adversary. However, Theorem 5.1 *no* longer holds if there is a PKI setup available to the parties. Intuitively, this is because the adversary will *not* know the corresponding *private* keys of the honest parties, in the absence of which the adversary will *not* be able to *forge* signed messages on behalf of honest parties.
- **Computationally Bounded Adversaries**: Under more fine-grained assumptions where the adversaries' power to solve certain *computational puzzles* is restricted, it is in fact, possible to circumvent the lower bound of Theorem 5.1 and that too *without* any trusted setup; see for instance [68, 8, 56].

We finally note that Theorem 5.1 holds even for the BB variant of consensus. Moreover, the lower bound holds even for *randomized* protocols, *disallowing* protocols that reach agreement with a small *constant* probability of error. We discuss this in the next section.

5.1.3 FLM Lower Bound for Randomized Consensus Protocols

The FLM lower bound (Theorem 5.1) states that in a synchronous system, it is *impossible* to design any consensus protocol for *three* parties tolerating one corruption. In this section, we show that bound is "strong" in the following sense:

- **Randomization**: We show that randomization *does not* help in circumventing the FLM lower bound. Namely, we show that even if we allow an *error probability* of up to $\frac{1}{3}$ in the security properties, it is *not* possible to circumvent the lower bound. This result is due to [63].
- **Weaker form of agreement**: We show that even if we "weaken" the consistency property, the FLM lower bound still *holds*. This result is based on Dolev's work on crusader agreement [43].

We next define the *crusader agreement* (CA) and probabilistic crusader agreement. Informally, CA is the same as BA, except that the consistency property is slightly *weakened*.

Definition 5.1 (Crusader Agreement (CA)) Let Π be a synchronous protocol for n parties, where each party has a private input $b_i \in \{0, 1\}$ and an output from the set $\{0, 1\} \cup \{\perp\}$. Protocol Π is then a *t-secure* CA if it achieves the following properties in the presence of an adversary, who can control up to t parties in a Byzantine fashion.

- **t-liveness**: We say that Π has *t-liveness* if every honest party terminates the protocol.
- **t-validity**: We say that Π has *t-validity* if the following holds.
  - If all honest parties have the same input bit $b \in \{0, 1\}$, then all honest parties output b.

- **t-weak consistency**: We say that Π has *t-weak consistency* if it is never the case that two different honest parties output different bits.[4]

We next define probabilistic CA, where the above security properties are achieved except with some error probability.

Definition 5.2 (CA with ϵ Error) Let Π be a synchronous protocol for n parties, where each party has a private input $b_i \in \{0, 1\}$ and an output from the set $\{0, 1\} \cup \{\perp\}$. Moreover, let ϵ be a given error parameter where $0 < \epsilon < 1$. Then protocol Π is a *t-secure* CA with *ϵ error*, if it achieves the following properties in the presence of an adversary who can control up to t parties in a Byzantine fashion, where the probability is over the random coins of the honest parties in the protocol.

- **t-liveness with ϵ error**: except with probability ϵ, every honest party computes an output.
- **t-validity with ϵ error**: if all honest parties have the same input bit $b \in \{0, 1\}$, then except with probability ϵ, all honest parties output b.
- **t-weak consistency with ϵ error**: the probability that two different honest parties output different bits is at most ϵ.

We next show that the FLM lower bound stated in Theorem 5.1 *holds* even for CA with ϵ error, for *any* $\epsilon < \frac{1}{3}$.

Theorem 5.2 *There exists no* 1*-secure CA protocol for* 3 *parties with* ϵ *error for any* $\epsilon < \frac{1}{3}$ *in the model* $\mathcal{M}_{\mathsf{auth}}$ *or* $\mathcal{M}_{\mathsf{secure}}$.

Proof The proof of the theorem is similar to that of Theorem 5.1. Let there exist a 1-*secure* CA protocol $\Pi_{\mathsf{CA}}^{(3,1)}$ with ϵ error for *three* parties in the model $\mathcal{M}_{\mathsf{auth}}$ or $\mathcal{M}_{\mathsf{secure}}$, where $\epsilon < \frac{1}{3}$. Moreover, let A, B and C be the steps of $\Pi_{\mathsf{CA}}^{(3,1)}$, for the three parties respectively.[5] Then consider a synchronous system of *six* parties $P_1, \ldots, P_6$, connected in a ring system and the execution β, as shown in part (a) in Fig 5.2. Moreover, consider the executions α_1, α_2 and α_3 as defined in the proof of Theorem 5.1 (shown in parts (b), (c) and (d) of Fig 5.2).

Since in execution α_1, party P_1 and P_2 are *honest* and have the *same* input 1, from 1-*validity* with ϵ error, it follows that P_1 and P_2 will output 1 with probability *more* than $\frac{2}{3}$, since $\epsilon < \frac{1}{3}$. Similarly, since in execution α_2, party P_5 and P_6 are *honest* and have the *same* input 0, from 1-*validity* with ϵ error, it follows that P_5 and P_6 will output 0 with probability *more* than $\frac{2}{3}$, since $\epsilon < \frac{1}{3}$.

Now consider the execution α_3. As shown in the proof of Theorem 5.1, from the point of view of P_1, executions α_1 and α_2 are *indistinguishable* and hence P_1 will output 1 in the execution α_3 with probability *more* than $\frac{2}{3}$. On the other hand, from the point of view of P_6, executions α_1 and α_3 are *indistinguishable* and hence P_6 will output 0 in the execution α_3, with probability *more* than $\frac{2}{3}$. Consequently, the *honest* parties P_1 and P_6 output *different* bits 0 and 1, with probability *more than* $\frac{2}{3}$,

---

[4] It may be possible that some honest party outputs a bit b while another honest party outputs $\perp$.

[5] The steps A, B and C will be publicly known, and in any execution of $\Pi_{\mathsf{CA}}^{(3,1)}$, it will be known which of the three parties is designated to execute steps A, B and C.

where $\frac{2}{3} > \epsilon$, since as per the theorem statement $\epsilon < \frac{1}{3}$. This is a *violation* of the 1-*weak consistency* with ϵ *error* property. Hence, protocol $\Pi_{\mathsf{CA}}^{(3,1)}$ *does not* exist. □

5.2 Impossibility of Distributed Consensus with $t \geq \frac{n}{3}$

In this section, we generalize the FLM lower bound given in Theorem 5.1 for any $t \geq \frac{n}{3}$. Specifically, we show that with *no* setup, it is impossible to design any *t-secure* BA protocol for n parties, where $t \geq \frac{n}{3}$.[6] To prove the result, we will show that if there exists any *t-secure* BA protocol for n parties, where $t \geq \frac{n}{3}$, then there also exists a 1-*secure* BA protocol for *three* parties tolerating one corruption, which according to Theorem 5.1 is *not* possible.

Theorem 5.3 *There exists no t-secure BA protocol for n parties where $t \geq \frac{n}{3}$ in the model $\mathcal{M}_{\mathsf{auth}}$ or $\mathcal{M}_{\mathsf{secure}}$ with with security level* Sec ∈ {PerSec, StatSec, CryptoSec}.

Proof The proof is by contradiction. Let $\Pi_{\mathsf{BA}}^{(n,t)}$ be a *t-secure* BA protocol for n parties $\{P_1, \ldots, P_n\}$ in the model $\mathcal{M}_{\mathsf{auth}}$ or $\mathcal{M}_{\mathsf{secure}}$ with security level Sec, tolerating t corruptions where $t \geq \frac{n}{3}$. For simplicity and without loss of generality, let $t = \frac{n}{3}$. We next show that protocol $\Pi_{\mathsf{BA}}^{(n,t)}$ can be used to get a 1-*secure* BA protocol $\Pi_{\mathsf{BA}}^{(3,1)}$ in the model $\mathcal{M}_{\mathsf{auth}}$ or $\mathcal{M}_{\mathsf{secure}}$ for *three* parties P_A, P_B and P_C, with security level Sec. However, from Theorem 5.1 we know that there exists no such protocol $\Pi_{\mathsf{BA}}^{(3,1)}$, which nullifies the existence of $\Pi_{\mathsf{BA}}^{(n,t)}$ as well. The derivation of $\Pi_{\mathsf{BA}}^{(3,1)}$ from $\Pi_{\mathsf{BA}}^{(n,t)}$ is through a technique called *player-partitioning* (see Fig 5.3 for a pictorial depiction).

The steps of the protocol $\Pi_{\mathsf{BA}}^{(3,1)}$ are as follows:

- Party P_A with input $a \in \{0, 1\}$ plays the role of the parties $P_1, \ldots, P_t$ as per the protocol $\Pi_{\mathsf{BA}}^{(n,t)}$ with inputs $b_1, \ldots, b_t$ respectively, where $b_1 = \ldots = b_t = a$. Party P_B with input $b \in \{0, 1\}$ plays the role of the parties $P_{t+1}, \ldots, P_{2t}$ as per the protocol $\Pi_{\mathsf{BA}}^{(n,t)}$ with inputs $b_{t+1}, \ldots, b_{2t}$ respectively, where $b_{t+1} = \ldots = b_{2t} = b$. Party P_C with input $c \in \{0, 1\}$ plays the role of the parties $P_{2t+1}, \ldots, P_{3t}$ as per the protocol $\Pi_{\mathsf{BA}}^{(n,t)}$ with inputs $b_{2t+1}, \ldots, b_{3t}$ respectively, where $b_{2t+1} = \ldots = b_{3t} = c$.
- Let $\mathcal{P}_1 \stackrel{def}{=} \{P_1, \ldots, P_t\}, \mathcal{P}_2 \stackrel{def}{=} \{P_{t+1}, \ldots, P_{2t}\}$ and $\mathcal{P}_3 \stackrel{def}{=} \{P_{2t+1}, \ldots, P_{3t}\}$. In the protocol $\Pi_{\mathsf{BA}}^{(n,t)}$, whenever any party $P_i \in \mathcal{P}_1$ needs to send any message m to any party in $\mathcal{P}_2$ or $\mathcal{P}_3$, then in the protocol $\Pi_{\mathsf{BA}}^{(3,1)}$, party P_A sends m to P_B or P_C respectively. Similarly, in the protocol $\Pi_{\mathsf{BA}}^{(n,t)}$, whenever any party $P_i \in \mathcal{P}_2$ needs to send any message m to any party in $\mathcal{P}_1$ or $\mathcal{P}_3$, then in the protocol $\Pi_{\mathsf{BA}}^{(3,1)}$, party P_B sends m to P_A or P_C respectively. Similarly, in the protocol $\Pi_{\mathsf{BA}}^{(n,t)}$, whenever any party $P_i \in \mathcal{P}_3$ needs to send any message m to any party in $\mathcal{P}_1$ or $\mathcal{P}_2$, then in the protocol $\Pi_{\mathsf{BA}}^{(3,1)}$, party P_C sends m to P_A or P_B respectively.

[6] The result holds even for the BB variant of consensus.

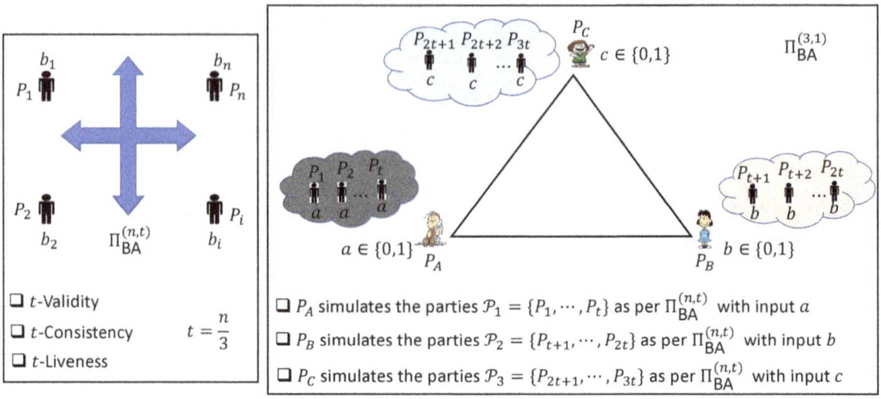

Fig. 5.3: Pictorial depiction of the transformation of $\Pi_{\text{BA}}^{(n,t)}$ into $\Pi_{\text{BA}}^{(3,1)}$

- In the protocol $\Pi_{\text{BA}}^{(n,t)}$, whenever any party $P_i \in \mathcal{P}_1$ needs to send any message m to any party in $\mathcal{P}_1$, then in the protocol $\Pi_{\text{BA}}^{(3,1)}$, party P_A sends m to itself. Similarly, in the protocol $\Pi_{\text{BA}}^{(n,t)}$, whenever any party $P_i \in \mathcal{P}_2$ needs to send any message m to any party in $\mathcal{P}_2$, then in the protocol $\Pi_{\text{BA}}^{(3,1)}$, party P_B sends m to itself. And finally, in the protocol $\Pi_{\text{BA}}^{(n,t)}$, whenever any party $P_i \in \mathcal{P}_3$ needs to send any message m to any party in $\mathcal{P}_3$, then in the protocol $\Pi_{\text{BA}}^{(3,1)}$, party P_C sends m to itself.
- P_A, P_B and P_C output whatever P_1, P_{t+1} and P_{2t+1} output respectively in protocol $\Pi_{\text{BA}}^{(n,t)}$.

In protocol $\Pi_{\text{BA}}^{(3,1)}$, if P_A is *corrupt*, then its view will be the *same* as the view of the parties $P_1, \ldots, P_t$ in the protocol $\Pi_{\text{BA}}^{(n,t)}$.[7] Similarly, if P_B is *corrupt*, then its view will be the *same* as the view of the parties $P_{t+1}, \ldots, P_{2t}$ in the protocol $\Pi_{\text{BA}}^{(n,t)}$. And finally, if P_C is *corrupt*, then its view will be the *same* as the view of the parties $P_{2t+1}, \ldots, P_{3t}$ in the protocol $\Pi_{\text{BA}}^{(n,t)}$. We next show that if $\Pi_{\text{BA}}^{(n,t)}$ is a *t-secure* BA with $t = \frac{n}{3}$, then protocol $\Pi_{\text{BA}}^{(3,1)}$ is a 1-*secure* BA protocol.

We start with showing that protocol $\Pi_{\text{BA}}^{(3,1)}$ has 1-*liveness*. This follows from the *t-liveness* of $\Pi_{\text{BA}}^{(n,t)}$. Namely, in protocol $\Pi_{\text{BA}}^{(3,1)}$ *at most* one of the three parties may be corrupt. For simplicity and without loss of generality, let it be the party P_A, implying that party P_B and P_C are *honest*. Since P_A, P_B and P_C simulates the roles of the parties in $\mathcal{P}_1, \mathcal{P}_2$ and $\mathcal{P}_3$ respectively as per $\Pi_{\text{BA}}^{(n,t)}$, it implies that any execution of

[7] Here view of a party denotes its input and the messages sent and received by the party during the protocol execution.

$\Pi_{\mathsf{BA}}^{(3,1)}$ with a *corrupt* P_A and *honest* P_B, P_C corresponds to an execution of $\Pi_{\mathsf{BA}}^{(n,t)}$ where the parties in $\mathcal{P}_1$ are *corrupt* and the parties in $\mathcal{P}_2$ and $\mathcal{P}_3$ are *honest*. Since the protocol $\Pi_{\mathsf{BA}}^{(n,t)}$ has *t-liveness*, it implies that irrespective of the strategy of the corrupt parties in $\mathcal{P}_1$, the parties in $\mathcal{P}_2$ and $\mathcal{P}_3$ will terminate the protocol $\Pi_{\mathsf{BA}}^{(n,t)}$. This automatically implies that the parties P_B and P_C will terminate the protocol $\Pi_{\mathsf{BA}}^{(3,1)}$. Hence *t-liveness* of $\Pi_{\mathsf{BA}}^{(n,t)}$ implies 1-*liveness* of $\Pi_{\mathsf{BA}}^{(3,1)}$.

We next show that protocol $\Pi_{\mathsf{BA}}^{(3,1)}$ has 1-*validity*, which follows from the *t-validity* of $\Pi_{\mathsf{BA}}^{(n,t)}$. For simplicity and without loss of generality, let party P_A be corrupt in the protocol $\Pi_{\mathsf{BA}}^{(3,1)}$, implying that party P_B and P_C are *honest*. Moreover, let P_B and P_C have the *same* input bit $b \in \{0, 1\}$ for $\Pi_{\mathsf{BA}}^{(3,1)}$. As argued above, any execution of $\Pi_{\mathsf{BA}}^{(3,1)}$ with a *corrupt* P_A and *honest* P_B, P_C corresponds to an execution of $\Pi_{\mathsf{BA}}^{(n,t)}$ where the parties in $\mathcal{P}_1$ are *corrupt* and the parties in $\mathcal{P}_2$ and $\mathcal{P}_3$ are *honest*. Moreover, since we are considering the case when P_B and P_C have the same input, it implies that in the corresponding execution of $\Pi_{\mathsf{BA}}^{(n,t)}$, the parties in $\mathcal{P}_2$ and $\mathcal{P}_3$ have the same input bit b. This is because in this case both P_B and P_C will simulate the role of the parties in $\mathcal{P}_2$ and $\mathcal{P}_3$ respectively, with input b. Since the protocol $\Pi_{\mathsf{BA}}^{(n,t)}$ has *t-validity*, it implies that irrespective of the strategy of the corrupt parties in $\mathcal{P}_1$, the parties in $\mathcal{P}_2$ and $\mathcal{P}_3$ will output b. This automatically implies that the parties P_B and P_C will output b during the execution of $\Pi_{\mathsf{BA}}^{(3,1)}$. Hence *t-validity* of $\Pi_{\mathsf{BA}}^{(n,t)}$ implies 1-*validity* of $\Pi_{\mathsf{BA}}^{(3,1)}$.

We finally show that protocol $\Pi_{\mathsf{BA}}^{(3,1)}$ has 1-*consistency*, which follows from the *t-consistency* of $\Pi_{\mathsf{BA}}^{(n,t)}$. For simplicity and without loss of generality, let party P_A be corrupt in the protocol $\Pi_{\mathsf{BA}}^{(3,1)}$, implying that party P_B and P_C are *honest*. As argued above, any execution of $\Pi_{\mathsf{BA}}^{(3,1)}$ with a *corrupt* P_A and *honest* P_B, P_C corresponds to an execution of $\Pi_{\mathsf{BA}}^{(n,t)}$ where the parties in $\mathcal{P}_1$ are *corrupt* and the parties in $\mathcal{P}_2$ and $\mathcal{P}_3$ are *honest*. Since the protocol $\Pi_{\mathsf{BA}}^{(n,t)}$ has *t-consistency*, it implies that irrespective of the strategy of the corrupt parties in $\mathcal{P}_1$, the parties in $\mathcal{P}_2$ and $\mathcal{P}_3$ will have a *common* output bit, say b. This automatically implies that the parties P_B and P_C will output b during the execution of $\Pi_{\mathsf{BA}}^{(3,1)}$. Hence *t-consistency* of $\Pi_{\mathsf{BA}}^{(n,t)}$ implies 1-*consistency* of $\Pi_{\mathsf{BA}}^{(3,1)}$. □

5.2.1 Impossibility of Randomized Distributed Consensus with $t \geq \frac{n}{3}$

We can use the player partitioning argument used in the proof of Theorem 5.3 and extend it to show the *impossibility* of randomized distributed consensus protocols for any $t \geq \frac{n}{3}$, *without* any setup. In fact, we can claim a *stronger* result and show that in the *absence* of any setup, it is *not* possible to design any *t-secure* CA protocol with ϵ *error* for n parties where $\epsilon < \frac{1}{3}$, for any $t \geq \frac{n}{3}$. The proof will be the same as that of Theorem 5.3, except that we now depend upon Theorem 5.2, *instead* of Theorem 5.1.

The idea will be to show that if there exists any t-*secure* CA protocol $\Pi_{\mathsf{CA}}^{(n,t)}$ with ϵ *error* for n parties where $\epsilon < \frac{1}{3}$, for any $t \geq \frac{n}{3}$, then using $\Pi_{\mathsf{CA}}^{(n,t)}$, one can design a 1-*secure* CA protocol $\Pi_{\mathsf{CA}}^{(3,1)}$ with ϵ *error* for three parties tolerating one corruption. However, from Theorem 5.2 we know that there exists *no* such protocol $\Pi_{\mathsf{CA}}^{(3,1)}$ which automatically *nullifies* the existence of the protocol $\Pi_{\mathsf{CA}}^{(n,t)}$ as well.

The way we get the protocol $\Pi_{\mathsf{CA}}^{(3,1)}$ from $\Pi_{\mathsf{CA}}^{(n,t)}$ is similar as in the proof of Theorem 5.1. Namely, we assume that $t = \frac{n}{3}$ and consider *three disjoint* subsets of parties $\mathcal{P}_1, \mathcal{P}_2$ and $\mathcal{P}_3$, each of size *exactly* t. To get the protocol $\Pi_{\mathsf{CA}}^{(3,1)}$ involving *three* parties P_A, P_B and P_C with input bits a, b and c respectively, we let P_A, P_B and P_C *simulate* and play the role of the parties in $\mathcal{P}_1, \mathcal{P}_2$ and $\mathcal{P}_3$ respectively as per the steps of $\Pi_{\mathsf{CA}}^{(n,t)}$, with input bits a, b and c respectively. The simulation and the communication among the parties P_A, P_B and P_C is handled in exactly the *same* way as in the proof of Theorem 5.3 (we leave the details as an exercise for the readers).

Chapter 6
Domain Extension for Distributed Consensus with Perfect Security

Typically, BA and BB protocols are designed for the case when the input of the parties is a *single* bit and such protocols are called bit-BB and bit-BA protocols. However, there might be scenarios where this need *not* be the case and instead, the parties' inputs consist of *several* bits. In many distributed computing applications, like reaching an agreement on a large file in a fault-tolerant distributed storage system, distributed voting where ballots containing gigabytes of data are to be handled, secure *multiparty computation* (MPC) protocols [88, 59, 21, 30, 81, 35] where "multiple" instances of BB and BA are invoked, there is an inherent need for dealing with long messages for BB and BA protocols.

In this chapter, we discuss the *domain extension* for consensus protocols, where we present efficient protocols to handle the case where the inputs of the parties consist of several bits, *instead* of a single bit. Our treatment will be for protocols with *perfect security* and we will focus on *both* the BA as well as BB variant of the consensus problem.[1] We will first present the classic domain extension for BA due to Turpin and Coan [85], followed by the more efficient state-of-the-art extension protocols based on the properties of error-correcting codes over a finite field due to [55].

6.1 The Goal of Domain Extension

Let $\mathcal{BA}(1)$ denote the *communication complexity* of any *given* bit-BA protocol, say $\Pi_{\mathsf{BA}}^{(n,t)}$, where the inputs of the parties consist of a *single* bit. Then consider a scenario where the inputs of the parties are from the set $\{0,1\}^L$, where $L \geq 1$ and known *publicly*. To design a BA protocol for this scenario, one can always use the following *naive* approach: run L instances of the protocol $\Pi_{\mathsf{BA}}^{(n,t)}$ in parallel, say $\Pi_{\mathsf{BA},1}^{(n,t)}, \ldots, \Pi_{\mathsf{BA},L}^{(n,t)}$, where the during the ℓth instance, the parties participate with the

[1] Later, in the second part of the monogram, we will present domain extension protocols with statistical and cryptographic security.

A. Choudhury and A. Patra, *Fault-Tolerant Distributed Consensus in Synchronous Networks*, Information Security and Cryptography,
https://doi.org/10.1007/978-3-031-80460-1_6

ℓ^{th} bit of their input. The output of each party then consists of the concatenation of the output bits obtained during the instances $\Pi_{\mathsf{BA},1}^{(n,t)}, \ldots, \Pi_{\mathsf{BA},L}^{(n,t)}$. Let us call this naive protocol as $\Pi_{\mathsf{MI}}^{(n,t)}$, where MI signifies *multi-bit input*. If protocol $\Pi_{\mathsf{BA}}^{(n,t)}$ is resilient against t corruptions, then it is easy to see that the *t-consistency* and *t-validity* of $\Pi_{\mathsf{BA}}^{(n,t)}$ translates to the *t-consistency* and *t-validity* of $\Pi_{\mathsf{MI}}^{(n,t)}$ respectively. What will be the *communication complexity* $\mathcal{BA}(L)$ of the protocol $\Pi_{\mathsf{MI}}^{(n,t)}$? As per our notation, $\mathcal{BA}(L) = L \cdot \mathcal{BA}(1)$. For instance, if we instantiate $\Pi_{\mathsf{BA}}^{(n,t)}$ with the protocol $\Pi_{\mathsf{EIG}}^{(n,t)}, \Pi_{\mathsf{PKNO}}^{(n,t)}$ and $\Pi_{\mathsf{PKO}}^{(n,t)}$ respectively, then the communication complexity of the resultant protocol will be $\mathcal{O}(n^{t+1}L), \mathcal{O}(n^3L)$ and $\mathcal{O}(n^3L)$ bits respectively.[2]

Instead of invoking L instances of $\Pi_{\mathsf{BA}}^{(n,t)}$, a domain extension protocol for BA invokes the bit-BA protocol protocol $\Pi_{\mathsf{BA}}^{(n,t)}$ a number of times which is *independent* of L and aims to achieve a communication complexity of $\mathcal{O}(\text{poly}(n, L) + x \cdot \mathcal{BA}(1))$ bits. Here x is some value which is *independent* of L and $\text{poly}(n, L)$ denotes some *polynomial* function of n and L. Note that one *cannot* hope to solve the BA problem for L-bit inputs *without* invoking any instance of the bit-BA protocol $\Pi_{\mathsf{BA}}^{(n,t)}$. There are several advantages of such a (domain extension) protocol.

- The number of instances of the bit-BA protocol $\Pi_{\mathsf{BA}}^{(n,t)}$ is *independent* of the input size L of the parties.
- For a sufficiently large L, if the term $x \cdot \mathcal{BA}(1)$ is "subsumed" by $\mathcal{O}(\text{poly}(n, L)$, then *asymptotically*, the *amortized* communication complexity of the protocol will be $\mathcal{O}(\text{poly}(n, L)$.

In fact, we will present domain extension protocol with an *asymptotic* communication complexity of $\mathcal{O}(nL)$ bits, which can be shown to be provably *optimal* for *any* BA/BB protocol, *irrespective* of the type of security and *irrespective* of the communication model. Note that the $\mathcal{O}(nL)$ bits of communication is *asymptotic* and is achieved only for "sufficiently large" values of L.

In the above discussion, we focussed on the BA variant of consensus. One can think of domain extension even for the BB variant of consensus, where the input for the designated sender party is from the set $\{0, 1\}^L$ where $L \geq 1$. The goal is then to design a BB protocol, where the parties invoke *any given* bit-BB protocol (where the input of the designated sender party is a *single* bit) a number of times which is *independent* of L.

Remark 6.1 (**On the Term Domain Extension**) We note that domain extension protocols are also referred to by *different* names, such as *multi-bit* consensus protocols and *multi-valued* consensus protocols. We prefer to use the name domain extension to signify that such protocols help to *extend* the input domain of consensus protocols from $\{0, 1\}$ to $\{0, 1\}^L$, by using *any given* bit-consensus protocol (where the input domain is $\{0, 1\}$) as an *oracle*.

[2] Recall that even though the communication complexity of $\Pi_{\mathsf{PKO}}^{(n,t)}$ and $\Pi_{\mathsf{PKNO}}^{(n,t)}$ is the *same*, the protocols have *different* resilience, namely $t < \frac{n}{3}$ and $t < \frac{n}{4}$ respectively.

6.2 Round Complexity, Seed-Round Complexity and Seed-Communication Complexity of any Extension Protocol

Note that a *concrete* consensus protocol is obtained from an extension protocol by *replacing* the oracle-access to the underlying bit-BA/bit-BB with a *concrete* bit-BA/bit-BB protocol. The number of *sequential* and *parallel* instances of bit-BB and bit-BA protocol inherently dictate the complexities of such a concrete protocol. As noted in [55], to control the inflation in the round and communication complexity due to composition issues in the concrete protocols, *two* more complexity measures for extension protocols are considered.

- *Seed-round complexity*: it refers to the number of rounds in the extension protocol in which a bit-BA/bib-BB oracle is invoked.
- *Seed-communication complexity*: it refers to the total number of bits for which the bit-BA/bit-BB oracle is invoked in the extension protocol.

For ease of presentation, in any extension protocol, it is assumed that apart from the point-to-point channels, the parties also have an *oracle* access to some bit-BB/BA protocol. Consequently, in any round of the extension protocol, the parties may perform *both* point-to-point communication as well as call bit-BA/BB via oracle calls. In this model, the *round* complexity of any extension protocol is simply defined to be the number of rounds in the protocol. The parties can call the BB/BA oracle with their respective input(s) in a round and get the required output during that round. For instance, if any party P_i wants to broadcast some bit b during any round, then it can invoke the BB oracle with input b, and all the parties will get the output b from the oracle in that round. Similarly, if the parties want to run an instance of a bit-BA, then they can call the underlying BA oracle with their respective inputs. The oracle will then check the input bits provided by the honest parties.[3] If all these input bits are the same, then it is provided as the output by the oracle to all the parties (thus ensuring t-*validity*); else it provides some default bit, say 0, as the output to everyone (thus ensuring the t-*consistency*). We also stress that in any round, the underlying oracles can be invoked multiple times in parallel if the underlying inputs for the respective calls are *independent*.

6.3 Turpin-Coan Domain Extension Protocol for BA

This section presents the domain extension protocol $\Pi_{\mathsf{TC}}^{(n,t)}$ for BA due to Turpin and Coan [85]. The protocol assumes the existence of a t-*secure* GA protocol $\Pi_{\mathsf{GA}}^{(n,t)}$ for L-bit inputs and an oracle access to a bit-BA protocol.

In the protocol, the parties first run an instance of GA with their respective inputs for the BA. Then, based on the grade of the output obtained from the GA, the parties prepare a *binary* vote and call the bit-BA oracle with their respective votes. The vote is computed as follows: if a party has got the *highest* grade, namely 2 from the GA,

[3] We assume that the oracle will *know* the identity of the honest parties.

then the vote is set to 1 else the vote is set to 0. Finally, based on the outcome from the bit-BA, the parties decide their output as follows: if the output from the BA is 0, then the parties output some *default* L-bit string. Otherwise, the parties take the L-bit output from the GA as the output.

The idea behind the protocol is as follows: if *all honest* parties have the *same* L-bit input, say v, then every *honest* party will get the output v with grade 2 from the GA (follows from the *t-validity* of GA) and hence will call the bit-BA with the vote being 1. Consequently, all honest parties get the output 1 from the bit-BA (follows from the *t-validity* of BA) and hence all honest parties output v. On the other hand, consider the case when the honest parties have *different* L-bit inputs. Then there are *two* possibilities. If the output from the bit-BA is 0, then all honest parties have the *same* output. On the other hand, if the output from the bit-BA is 1, then at least one *honest* party, say P_h, called the BA with the vote being 1. This implies that the output P_h got from GA is obtained with the *highest* grade, namely 2. Let w_h be the output that P_h obtained from the GA. Consequently, every other honest party will get the output w_h from GA, either with the grade 2 or grade 1 (follows from the *t-knowledge-of-agreement* of GA). As a result, all honest parties take w_h as the output for the BA. Protocol $\Pi_{\mathsf{TC}}^{(n,t)}$ is formally presented in Fig 6.1.

Protocol $\Pi_{\mathsf{TC}}^{(n,t)}$

Public knowledge: the description of a *t-secure* GA protocol for L-bit inputs in the model $\mathcal{M} \in \{\mathcal{M}_{\mathsf{auth}}, \mathcal{M}_{\mathsf{secure}}, \mathcal{M}_{\mathsf{auth}}^{\mathsf{pki}}, \mathcal{M}_{\mathsf{secure}}^{\mathsf{pki}}\}$ and security level $\mathsf{Sec} \in \{\mathsf{PerSec}, \mathsf{StatSec}, \mathsf{CryptoSec}\}$, requiring r rounds of communication. Additionally, the parties have oracle access to a bit-BA oracle.

- **Round 1 to r (executing GA with respective inputs)**
  - On having the input $v_i \in \{0, 1\}^L$, participate in an instance of $\Pi_{\mathsf{GA}}^{(n,t)}$ with input v_i.
  - Let (w_i, g_i) be the output from $\Pi_{\mathsf{GA}}^{(n,t)}$, where $w_i \in \{0, 1\}^L$ and $g_i \in \{0, 1, 2\}$.
- **Round $r + 1$ (agreeing on the output grade of GA)**
  - If $g_i = 2$ then set $\mathsf{vote}_i := 1$, else set $\mathsf{vote}_i := 0$.
  - Call the BA oracle with input vote_i and let c_i be the output obtained, where $c_i \in \{0, 1\}$.
- **Output computation and termination**
  - If $c_i = 1$, then output w_i and terminate;
  - Else output 0^L and terminate.

Fig. 6.1: The Turpin-Coan domain extension protocol. The above code is executed by every party P_i

We now proceed to prove the properties of the protocol $\Pi_{\mathsf{TC}}^{(n,t)}$. We start with the *validity* property.

Lemma 6.1 *In protocol $\Pi_{\mathsf{TC}}^{(n,t)}$, if all honest parties have the same input $v \in \{0, 1\}^L$, then all honest parties output v.*

Proof Let $\mathcal{H}$ be the set of *honest* parties and let all the parties in $\mathcal{H}$ have input $v \in \{0, 1\}^L$. The *t-validity* of $\Pi_{\mathsf{GA}}^{(n,t)}$ implies that all the parties in $\mathcal{H}$ get the output $(v, 2)$ from the instance of $\Pi_{\mathsf{GA}}^{(n,t)}$. Consequently, every $P_i \in \mathcal{H}$ sets $\mathsf{vote}_i = 1$ and calls the BA oracle with input 1. The *t-validity* of BA implies that all the parties in $\mathcal{H}$ get the output 1 from the BA oracle. Consequently, every party in $\mathcal{H}$ outputs v. □

We next proceed to prove the *consistency* property.

Lemma 6.2 *In protocol* $\Pi_{\mathsf{TC}}^{(n,t)}$*, all honest parties have a common output.*

Proof Let $\mathcal{H}$ be the set of *honest* parties. From the *t-consistency* of the BA, every party in $\mathcal{H}$ will have a *common* output bit c from the BA oracle. Now there are *two* possibilities for c.

- $c = 0$: In this case, every party in $\mathcal{H}$ outputs 0^L and so the lemma is true.
- $c = 1$: In this case, there exists at least one party in $\mathcal{H}$, say P_h, who called the BA oracle with input $\mathsf{vote}_h = 1$. If this is *not* the case and if *every* party in $\mathcal{H}$ called the BA oracle with $\mathsf{vote} = 0$, then from the *t-validity* of BA it follows that every party in $\mathcal{H}$ should get the output $c = 0$ from the BA oracle, which is a *contradiction*.
  Since P_h sets $\mathsf{vote}_h = 1$, it follows that it gets an output $(w_h, 2)$ from the instance of $\Pi_{\mathsf{GA}}^{(n,t)}$ and outputs w_h in $\Pi_{\mathsf{TC}}^{(n,t)}$. Let $P_i \in \mathcal{H}$ be an *arbitrary* party, *different* from P_h. To prove the lemma, we want to show that P_i also outputs w_h. Let (w_i, g_i) be the output for P_i from the instance of $\Pi_{\mathsf{GA}}^{(n,t)}$. From the protocol steps, P_i outputs w_i. However, $w_i = w_h$, which follows from the *t-knowledge-of-agreement* of $\Pi_{\mathsf{GA}}^{(n,t)}$. □

Theorem 6.1 now follows from the above discussion.

Theorem 6.1 *Let* $\Pi_{\mathsf{GA}}^{(n,t)}$ *be a t-secure GA protocol for L-bit inputs in the model* $\mathcal{M} \in \{\mathcal{M}_{\mathsf{auth}}, \mathcal{M}_{\mathsf{secure}}, \mathcal{M}_{\mathsf{auth}}^{\mathsf{pki}}, \mathcal{M}_{\mathsf{secure}}^{\mathsf{pki}}\}$ *with security level* Sec ∈ {PerSec, StatSec, CryptoSec}*, requiring r rounds of communication. Moreover, let the parties have access to a bit-BA oracle. Then protocol* $\Pi_{\mathsf{TC}}^{(n,t)}$ *is a t-secure BA protocol for L-bit inputs in the model* $\mathcal{M}$ *with security level* Sec *and following complexities.*

- *The protocol requires* $r + 1$ *rounds.*
- *The seed-round complexity of the protocol is* 1.
- *The communication complexity of the protocol is* $\mathcal{GA}(L) + \mathcal{BA}(1)$ *bits. Here* $\mathcal{GA}(L)$ *denotes the communication complexity of* $\Pi_{\mathsf{GA}}^{(n,t)}$ *and* $\mathcal{BA}(1)$ *denotes the communication complexity of emulating one invocation of the bit-BA oracle.*
- *The seed-communication complexity of the protocol is* $\mathcal{O}(1)$.

Proof The *t-validity* and *t-consistency* follows from Lemma 6.1 and Lemma 6.2 respectively. The round complexity follows from the protocol description. During the first r rounds, the parties call $\Pi_{\mathsf{GA}}^{(n,t)}$ with L-bit inputs, incurring a communication of $\mathcal{GA}(L)$ bits. During the round $r+1$, the parties call the BA oracle with a 1-bit input, incurring a communication of $\mathcal{BA}(1)$ bits. Hence, the seed-round complexity of the protocol is 1 since the BA oracle is invoked only during the $(r+1)^{th}$ round. Moreover, the seed-communication complexity of the protocol is $\mathcal{O}(1)$ since the parties invoke the BA oracle with a single-bit input. The *t-liveness* of $\Pi_{\mathsf{GA}}^{(n,t)}$ guarantees that the honest parties terminate after round $r + 1$, thus guaranteeing *t-liveness* for $\Pi_{\mathsf{TC}}^{(n,t)}$. □

Notice that in Theorem 6.1, we *did not* claim anything about the exact *resilience* of the protocol $\Pi_{\mathsf{TC}}^{(n,t)}$. This is determined by the underlying building blocks, namely the instantiation of bit-BA and $\Pi_{\mathsf{GA}}^{(n,t)}$. For instance, if the instantiations of bit-BA and $\Pi_{\mathsf{GA}}^{(n,t)}$ can tolerate up to $t < \frac{n}{3}$ corruptions, then so will the resultant protocol $\Pi_{\mathsf{TC}}^{(n,t)}$.

6.3.1 On the Exact Complexity of the Turpin-Coan Domain Extension

In this section, we present the "exact" round and communication complexity of the protocol $\Pi_{\mathsf{TC}}^{(n,t)}$, by considering various instantiations of the GA and bit-BA discussed till now. The figures are presented in Table 6.1. We consider *two* instantiations for the bit-BA, namely the two phase-king protocols presented in the previous chapter. Similarly, we consider *two* instantiations of the GA presented in the previous chapter. Since all the instantiations of bit-BA and GA enjoy *perfect security*, the resultant $\Pi_{\mathsf{TC}}^{(n,t)}$ protocol obtained also enjoys *perfect security*.

Instantiation of the bit-BA				Instantiation of $\Pi_{\mathsf{GA}}^{(n,t)}$				Instantiation of $\Pi_{\mathsf{TC}}^{(n,t)}$			
Protocol	Resilience	Rounds	$\mathcal{BA}(1)$	Protocol	Resilience	Rounds	$\mathcal{GA}(L)$	Security	Resilience	Rounds	$\mathcal{BA}(L)$
$\Pi_{\mathsf{PKNO}}^{(n,t)}$	$t < \frac{n}{4}$	$2t + 2$	$O(n^3)$	$\Pi_{\mathsf{PerSecGAOneFourth}}^{(n,t)}$	$t < \frac{n}{4}$	1	$O(n^2L)$	Perfect	$t < \frac{n}{4}$	$2t + 3$	$O(n^2L + n^3)$
$\Pi_{\mathsf{PKO}}^{(n,t)}$	$t < \frac{n}{3}$	$3t + 3$	$O(n^3)$	$\Pi_{\mathsf{PerSecGAOneThird}}^{(n,t)}$	$t < \frac{n}{3}$	2	$O(n^2L)$	Perfect	$t < \frac{n}{3}$	$3t + 5$	$O(n^2L + n^3)$

Table 6.1: Complexity of the various instantiations of protocol $\Pi_{\mathsf{TC}}^{(n,t)}$ by plugging in different instantiations of $\Pi_{\mathsf{GA}}^{(n,t)}$ and bit-BA oracle

Advantage of the Protocol $\Pi_{\mathsf{TC}}^{(n,t)}$

From Table 6.1 it follows that the communication complexity of each instantiation of $\Pi_{\mathsf{TC}}^{(n,t)}$ is $O(n^2L+n^3)$ bits. If the value of L is "sufficiently large", namely if $L = \Omega(n)$, then *asymptotically* the communication complexity of each instantiation of $\Pi_{\mathsf{TC}}^{(n,t)}$ becomes $O(n^2L)$ bits. Now compare this with the communication complexity of the phase-king protocols $\Pi_{\mathsf{PKNO}}^{(n,t)}$ and $\Pi_{\mathsf{PKO}}^{(n,t)}$ with L-bit inputs. From Theorem 4.4, the communication complexity $\mathcal{BA}(L)$ for *both* these protocols will be $O(n^3L)$ bits, *irrespective* of the value of L. We find that clearly, the communication complexity of the protocol $\Pi_{\mathsf{TC}}^{(n,t)}$ *outperforms* the existing BA protocols for L-bit inputs, thus demonstrating the merit of doing domain extension for BA to handle *large* sized inputs.

We end our discussion on the Turpin-Coan protocol by discussing how to get a variant of the protocol $\Pi_{\mathsf{TC}}^{(n,t)}$ for BB.

Remark 6.2 (**Turpin-Coan Domain Extension Protocol for BB**) One can easily adapt the protocol $\Pi_{\mathsf{TC}}^{(n,t)}$ to get a domain extension protocol for BB. The idea will be to use the "equivalence" between the BB and BA variants of the consensus problem. In more detail, let the sender S have input $m \in \{0, 1\}^L$. Then consider the following BB protocol: during the *first* round, S sends m to all the parties. This is followed by the parties running an instance of the BA protocol $\Pi_{\mathsf{TC}}^{(n,t)}$, where the input of each party is the L-bit string which it receives from S during the first round. Each party then outputs whatever it gets as the output from the instance of $\Pi_{\mathsf{TC}}^{(n,t)}$. It is easy to see that the resultant protocol constitutes a t-secure BB protocol incurring a communication of $\mathcal{O}(nL) + \mathcal{BA}(L)$ bits, where $\mathcal{BA}(L)$ denotes the communication complexity of $\Pi_{\mathsf{TC}}^{(n,t)}$.

6.4 Perfectly-Secure Domain Extension Based on Reed-Solomon (RS) Error-Correcting Codes

In this section, we discuss domain extension with perfect security based on the properties of Reed-Solomon (RS) error-correcting codes [75]. Since we will be considering RS codes over a finite field, we first quickly discuss the properties of a field. We will keep the discussion brief, touching upon only the properties required for domain extension and refer to any standard text on abstract algebra, such as [24], for a more comprehensive and detailed treatment of finite fields.

6.4.1 Fields and Polynomials Over a Field

Definition 6.1 ((Field)) A set $\mathbb{F}$ with abstract binary operations + and $\cdot$ over the elements in $\mathbb{F}$, is called a field if all the following properties (also known as *field-axioms*) are satisfied:

- F_1: The set $\mathbb{F}$ along with the operation + constitutes an Abelian group. That is, all the following properties are satisfied:
  - **Closure**: for every $a, b \in \mathbb{F}$, the element $a + b \in \mathbb{F}$.
  - **Associativity**: for every $a, b, c \in \mathbb{F}$, the condition $(a + b) + c = a + (b + c)$ holds.
  - **Existence of identity**: there exists a unique *additive identity* element in $\mathbb{F}$, denoted by 0, such that for every $a \in \mathbb{F}$, the condition $(a + 0) = (0 + a) = a$ holds.
  - **Existence of inverse**: for every $a \in \mathbb{F}$, there exists a unique *additive inverse* element in $\mathbb{F}$ denoted by $-a$, such that the condition $(a + -a) = (-a + a) = 0$ holds.
  - **Commutativity**: for every $a, b \in \mathbb{F}$, the condition $a + b = b + a$ holds.
- F_2: The set $\mathbb{F} - \{0\}$ along with the operation $\cdot$ constitutes an Abelian group, where the element $0 \in \mathbb{F}$ and denotes the *additive identity*. That is, all the following properties are satisfied:
  - **Closure**: for every $a, b \in \mathbb{F} - \{0\}$, the element $a \cdot b \in \mathbb{F} - \{0\}$.

  - **Associativity**: for every $a, b, c \in \mathbb{F} - \{0\}$, the condition $(a \cdot b) \cdot c = a \cdot (b \cdot c)$ holds.
  - **Existence of identity**: there exists a unique *multiplicative identity* element in $\mathbb{F} - \{0\}$, denoted by 1, such that for every $a \in \mathbb{F} - \{0\}$, the condition $(a \cdot 1) = (1 \cdot a) = a$ holds.
  - **Existence of inverse**: for every $a \in \mathbb{F} - \{0\}$, there exists a unique *multiplicative inverse* element in $\mathbb{F}$ denoted by a^{-1}, such that the condition $(a \cdot a^{-1}) = (a^{-1} \cdot a) = 1$ holds.
  - **Commutativity**: for every $a, b \in \mathbb{F} - \{0\}$, the condition $a \cdot b = b \cdot a$ holds.
- F_3: For all $a, b, c \in \mathbb{F}$, the following distributive laws hold:
  - $a \cdot (b + c) = (a \cdot b) + (a \cdot c)$.
  - $(a + b) \cdot c = (a \cdot c) + (b \cdot c)$.

We next define polynomials over a field. Informally, they are similar to polynomials with integer/real-number coefficients, except that the coefficients are elements of a field and the underlying addition and multiplication operations are performed over the field.

Definition 6.2 (d-degree Polynomial Over a Field) Let $(\mathbb{F}, +, \cdot)$ be a field. Then a d-degree polynomial in variable X over $\mathbb{F}$ is of the form

$$f(X) = a_0 + a_1 \cdot X + \ldots + a_d \cdot X^d,$$

where all the + and $\cdot$ operations are performed over $\mathbb{F}$ and where $a_0, \ldots, a_d \in \mathbb{F}$ are called the *coefficients* of the polynomial. Note that, as per the definition, the coefficient a_d of a d-degree polynomial *can* be 0.

We next define the root of a polynomial over a field.

Definition 6.3 (Root of a Polynomial) Let $f(X)$ be a polynomial over some field $\mathbb{F}$. Then an element $v \in \mathbb{F}$ is called a *root* of $f(X)$ if $f(v) = 0$ holds, where 0 is the additive identity in $\mathbb{F}$.

We now state some standard properties of polynomials over a field.

Theorem 6.2 ([24]) *Let $\mathbb{F}$ be a field. Then the following properties hold.*

- *Let $(x_1, y_1), \ldots, (x_{d+1}, y_{d+1})$ be pairs of elements from $\mathbb{F}$, where $x_1, \ldots, x_{d+1}$ are distinct. Then there exists a unique d-degree polynomial over $\mathbb{F}$, say $f(X)$, such that $f(x_i) = y_i$ holds for $i = 1, \ldots, d + 1$.*
- *Two different d-degree polynomials over $\mathbb{F}$ can have at most d common values.*
- *Any d-degree polynomial over $\mathbb{F}$ has at most d roots.*

6.4.2 Error-Correcting Codes Over a Field

Informally, error-correcting codes are used for reliable communication over "noisy" channels. Let $\mathbb{F}$ be a *finite* field. In the setting of (N, K, T)-error-correcting code, there exists a *sender* S and a *receiver* R, connected by a noisy or unreliable channel. The sender S has an input message $m \in \mathbb{F}^K$, consisting of K elements from $\mathbb{F}$. The goal of S is to reliably send m to R even if up to T *errors* occur during the transmission; i.e. even if up to T elements get changed arbitrarily during the transmission. To achieve this goal, S introduces some "redundancy" in m, which is incorporated by "transforming" the message m into some *codeword* $C \in \mathbb{F}^N$, where $N \geq K$. This is achieved by a *publicly* known *deterministic encoding function* Encode. We use the notation $\mathsf{Encode}(m) := C$ to denote the invocation of Encode over input m.

Instead of sending m over the channel, S sends the codeword C to R. Let $C' \in \mathbb{F}^N$ denote the vector received by R and let $\mathsf{dist}(C, C')$ denote the number of components, which are *different* in C and C'. As per the assumption on the number of errors which can be introduced over the channel, it follows that $\mathsf{dist}(C, C') \leq T$. Note that R *will not* know C and hence will have *no* apriori information about the exact components of C' which are *different* from C. The goal for R is to recover back the message m from C'. Towards this, R applies a publicly known *deterministic decoding function*, denoted as $\mathsf{Decode}(C')$ and gets an output $m' \in \mathbb{F}^K$. We use the notation $\mathsf{Decode}(C') := m'$ to denote the invocation of Decode over the input C'. According to coding theory, the output m' of the decoding function will be the same as m, provided the following holds:

$$N - K \geq 2T.$$

6.4.3 Reed-Solomon (RS) Error-Correcting Code

One popular instantiation of error-correcting codes is RS codes. The code's encoding function is very simple. It interprets the message elements as the coefficients of a polynomial. The codeword components then consist of distinct points on the polynomial. Formally, the encoding function is presented in Fig 6.2. In the function, $\alpha_1, \ldots, \alpha_N$ denotes *distinct, non-zero* elements from $\mathbb{F}$, which are known *publicly*.[4] These elements serve as the "evaluation points", for evaluating the underlying polynomial constituted from the coefficients of sender's message. All instances of the encoding (and the decoding) use the *same* $\alpha_1, \ldots, \alpha_N$.

Protocol $\mathsf{RSEncode}(m, N, K, T)$

Public input: parameters N, K, T and distinct, non-zero evaluation points $\alpha_1, \ldots, \alpha_N \in \mathbb{F}$.

- Let $m = (m_0, \ldots, m_{k-1})$. Set $f_m(X) \stackrel{def}{=} m_0 + m_1 \cdot X + \ldots + m_{k-1} \cdot X^{k-1}$.
- Output $C = (C_1, \ldots, C_N)$, where $C_i \stackrel{def}{=} f_m(\alpha_i)$ for $i = 1, \ldots, N$.

Fig. 6.2: The encoding function for (N, K, T) RS error-correcting code

We will use the notation $\mathsf{RSEncode}(m, N, K, T) := C$ to denote the invocation of RSEncode over input m.

[4] Consequently, we need $|\mathbb{F}| > N$.

RS Decoding Function.

Let $\mathsf{RSEncode}(m, N, K, T) := C$, where $C = (C_1, \ldots, C_N)$, $m \in \mathbb{F}^K$ and $C_i = f_m(\alpha_i)$, for $i = 1, \ldots, N$. Here $f_m(X)$ denotes the $(k-1)$-degree polynomial $m_0 + m_1 \cdot X + \ldots + m_{k-1} \cdot X^{k-1}$. Let $C' = (C'_1, \ldots, C'_N) \in \mathbb{F}^N$ denote the vector received by R over the noisy channel, such that $\mathsf{dist}(C, C') \leq T$. The goal of the RS decoding function $\mathsf{RSDecode}(C', N, K, T)$ is to get back the message m. Towards this, the algorithm tries to compute the polynomial $f_m(X)$ using the points $(\alpha_1, C'_1), \ldots, (\alpha_N, C'_N)$. Note that N, K and T satisfy the following condition, as imposed by the coding theory:

$$N - K \geq 2T.$$

Algorithm $\mathsf{RSDecode}$ works as follows: let $R(X)$ denote the polynomial, passing through the components of C'. That is, the following holds, for $i = 1, \ldots, N$:

$$R(\alpha_i) = C'_i$$

From Theorem 6.2, polynomial $R(X)$ is an $(N-1)$-degree polynomial. Next, let $E(X)$ denote the *error polynomial*, whose *roots* are the α components, corresponding to which errors have been introduced in the codeword C during the transmission. Formally, for every $i \in \{1, \ldots, N\}$ where $C'_i \neq C_i$, the element α_i constitutes a root of the polynomial $E(X)$. Since $\mathsf{dist}(C, C') = T$, it follows that the polynomial $E(X)$ has T roots and consequently, the degree of $E(X)$ can be T. For simplicity and without loss of generality, let $\mathsf{dist}(C, C') = T$ and hence $E(X)$ has *exactly* T roots. Let $e_1, \ldots, e_T$ denote the roots of the polynomial $E(X)$, where $e_1, \ldots, e_T \in \{\alpha_1, \ldots, \alpha_N\}$. Hence,

$$E(X) = (X - e_1) \cdot \ldots \cdot (X - e_T).$$

Note that *exact identity* of the roots $e_1, \ldots, e_T$ are *not* known. Next, we note that the following relation holds, for $X = \alpha_1, \ldots, \alpha_N$:

$$\begin{aligned} f(X) \cdot E(X) &= R(X) \cdot E(X) \\ Q(X) &= R(X) \cdot E(X), \end{aligned}$$

where $Q(X) \stackrel{def}{=} f(X) \cdot E(X)$. This is because for every $i \in \{1, \ldots, N\}$, there are *two* possible cases:

- $C'_i = C_i$: In this case, the above relationship holds because $f(\alpha_i) = C_i = C'_i = R(\alpha_i)$ holds.
- $C'_i \neq C_i$: in this case, the above relationship still holds, since $E(\alpha_i) = 0$ and hence both the sides of the above equation will be 0.

Now in the above equation, $Q(X)$ is an *unknown* $(k-1+T)$-degree polynomial, with $k+T$ *unknown* coefficients since it is the product of a $(k-1)$-degree and a T-degree polynomial. On the other hand, $E(X)$ is an *unknown* T-degree polynomial, with T *unknown* variables. Hence, the *total* number of *unknown* variables is $k+2T$.

Note that the polynomial $R(X)$ is *known*, since it can be computed by interpolating the points $(\alpha_1, C'_1), \ldots, (\alpha_N, C'_N)$. Since the elements $\alpha_1, \ldots, \alpha_N$ are *distinct* and $N \geq k+2T$, by substituting $X = \alpha_1, \ldots, \alpha_N$ in the above equation, we get a system of *at least* $k+2T$ *independent* equations over $k+2T$ unknown variables. Consequently, by solving these equations, we can compute the error polynomial $E(X)$ and hence its roots. Now once the roots of $E(X)$ are identified, we *know* the exact components C'_i in C', such that $C'_i \neq C_i$ and hence which components of C' are the *same* as in C. Note that there will be *at least* $N - T > K$ such *correct* components. Consequently, by interpolating the points $\{(\alpha_i, C'_i)\}_{C'_i = C_i}$, we can compute the polynomial $f_m(X)$ and hence the message m.

6.4.3.1 RS Codes: More Properties

We now discuss some more properties of RS codes, which will be useful in the context of domain extension. The first property is that any subset of an RS codeword consisting of "sufficiently many" components uniquely determines the remaining components of the codeword. Hence, to find out the *entire* codeword, it is sufficient to have *those many* (correct) components of the codeword.

Lemma 6.3 *For every* $m \in \mathbb{F}^K$ *where* $\mathsf{RSEncode}(m, N, K, T) := C$ *and where* $C \in \mathbb{F}^N$, *any* K *components of* C *uniquely determine the remaining components of* C.

Proof Let $m = (m_0, \ldots, m_{K-1})$ and let $C = (C_1, \ldots, C_N)$, where $C_i = f_m(\alpha_i)$, for $i = 1, \ldots, N$. Here $f_m(X)$ denotes the $(K-1)$-degree polynomial $f_m(X) = m_0 + m_1 \cdot X + \ldots + m_{K-1} \cdot X^{K-1}$. Then consider a subset of indices $\mathcal{K} \subset \{1, \ldots, N\}$, such that $|\mathcal{K}| = K$. Let $f_{m'}(X)$ be the $(K-1)$-degree polynomial passing through the points $\{(\alpha_i, C_i)\}_{i \in \mathcal{K}}$. From Theorem 6.2, the condition $f_{m'}(X) = f_m(X)$ holds.

Let $C'_i = f_{m'}(\alpha_i)$, for *each* $i \in \{1, \ldots, N\} \setminus \mathcal{K}$. To prove the lemma, we wish to show that $C'_i = C_i$ holds for *each* $i \in \{1, \ldots, N\} \setminus \mathcal{K}$. However, this simply follows from the fact that $f_{m'}(X) = f_m(X)$ holds. □

A consequence of the above property is that if two RS codewords have "sufficiently many" *common* components, then they correspond to the same message.

Lemma 6.4 *For every* $m_1, m_2 \in \mathbb{F}^K$ *where* $\mathsf{RSEncode}(m_1, N, K, T) := C_1$ *and* $\mathsf{RSEncode}(m_2, N, K, T) := C_2$ *with* $C_1, C_2 \in \mathbb{F}^N$, *if* C_1 *and* C_2 *have* K *common components, then* $m_1 = m_2$.

Proof For $i = 1, 2$, let $m_i = (m_{i,0}, \ldots, m_{i,k-1})$ and let $C_i = (C_{i,1}, \ldots, C_{i,N})$ such that $C_{i,j} = f_{m_i}(\alpha_j)$, for $j = 1, \ldots, N$. Here $f_{m_i}(X)$ is the $(K-1)$-degree polynomial $f_{m_i}(X) = m_{i,0} + m_{i,1} \cdot X + \ldots + m_{i,k-1} \cdot X^{k-1}$. Consider a subset of indices $\mathcal{K} \subset \{1, \ldots, N\}$, where $|\mathcal{K}| = K$, such that $C_{1,j} = C_{2,j}$, for each $j \in \mathcal{K}$. From Theorem 6.2, it follows that $f_{m_1}(X) = f_{m_2}(X)$ holds because both $f_{m_1}(X)$ and $f_{m_2}(X)$ are $(K-1)$-degree polynomials. Consequently, from Lemma 6.3, $C_1 = C_2$ holds and hence $m_1 = m_2$ holds as well. □

6.4.4 Domain Extension for Byzantine Broadcast with Exponential Computation Complexity

In this section, we present a domain extension for Byzantine broadcast (BB) with *perfect security*, based on the properties of RS error-correcting codes.[5] For simplicity, we first present a protocol which requires the parties to perform *exponential* (in n) amount of computation. Looking ahead, this is because there will be a step in the protocol where the parties need to find a *clique* (a complete subgraph) of a certain size in an undirected graph. In the next section, we will show how to improve the computation complexity to *polynomial* (in n) by modifying this step and instead looking for a *different* structure in the graph.

In this section, we will explicitly work in the pairwise-authentic channel model $\mathcal{M}_{\mathsf{auth}}$ and assume that $t < \frac{n}{3}$.[6] All computations in the protocol will now be performed over some finite field $\mathbb{F}$, where $|\mathbb{F}| > n$. There exists a designated *sender* party $\mathsf{S} \in \mathcal{P}$ with input $m \in \{0,1\}^L$, where $L \geq (t+1)\log|\mathbb{F}|$ bits.[7] Since we aim for *perfect security*, we assume that the adversary is computationally-unbounded and can corrupt up to t parties, where $t < \frac{n}{3}$. For simplicity, we consider the case when $n = 3t + 1$, which is the *minimum* value of n, satisfying the condition $t < \frac{n}{3}$. Since $n = 3t + 1$, it follows that asymptotically, $t = \Theta(n)$ holds. We also assume the existence of a bit-BB oracle available to the parties using which the parties can reliably broadcast bit(s).

6.4.4.1 A Warm-Up Protocol

As a warm-up, we first present a protocol $\Pi^{(n,t)}_{\mathsf{WarmUp}}$, where $L = (t+1)\log|\mathbb{F}|$. The communication complexity of the protocol will be $O(n^2 \log|\mathbb{F}|) + n^2 \cdot \mathcal{BC}(1)$ bits; here, $\mathcal{BC}(1)$ denotes the communication complexity of emulating one instance of the bit-BB oracle where the input of the designated sender party is a single bit. Later, we will see a simple modification of the protocol to handle the case when $L \geq (t+1)\log|\mathbb{F}|$, such that the resultant communication complexity becomes $O(nL) + n^2 \cdot \mathcal{BC}(1)$ bits. Hence, for a sufficiently large value of L, the *asymptotic* communication complexity of the protocol becomes $O(nL)$ bits.

The high level idea behind the protocol $\Pi^{(n,t)}_{\mathsf{WarmUp}}$ is as follows: S encodes its input m into an RS codeword using an $(n, t+1, t)$-RS error-correcting code. For this, it divides m into $t+1$ blocks of $\log|\mathbb{F}|$ bits each, which are then considered elements of $\mathbb{F}$. Hence m is mapped to $t+1$ elements of $\mathbb{F}$. Then an n-length RS codeword $C = (C_1, \ldots, C_n)$ is computed corresponding to m. The sender then sends m to all the parties by sending the codeword C to all the parties. If S is *honest*, then

[5] Considering the BB variant of consensus is just for simple presentation of the protocol. Later we will see how to even get a BA variant of the protocol.

[6] Recall that $t < \frac{n}{3}$ is the *optimal* resilience for *any* BA/BB protocol in the model $\mathcal{M}_{\mathsf{auth}}$.

[7] Looking ahead, the requirement on the minimum size of L is to ensure that we get an amortized communication complexity of $O(nL)$ bits for the domain extension protocol.

it will send a *common* codeword to all the parties. However, a potentially *corrupt* S *may not* do the same. To "verify" this, the rest of the protocol involves *publicly* verifying whether S has sent some *common* RS codeword to the parties. Since the potentially *corrupt* parties may always *deny* receiving a common codeword and try to *falsely* "accuse" an *honest* sender, the parties publicly check whether a set CORE of at least $n - t$ parties have received some common codeword from S. Note that if S is potentially *corrupt*, then CORE *may not* have all honest parties. Hence, once the existence of CORE is confirmed, the parties ensure that even the (honest) parties *outside* CORE get the common codeword, which is received by the *honest* parties in CORE. Throughout the verification process, the parties *do not* exchange their entire codeword vector received from the sender with each other. Instead, each party exchanges only a *constant* number of components from its received codeword with every other party. And the bit-BB oracle is used to only publicly broadcast the status of *pairwise consistency* of the supposedly common components of the codewords received by every pair of parties.

In more detail, let $C^{(i)} = (C_1^{(i)}, \ldots, C_n^{(i)})$ denote the RS codeword received by party P_i from S. Then *every* pair of parties (P_i, P_j) check the pairwise consistency of the supposedly common i^{th} and j^{th} components of their respective codewords $C^{(i)}$ and $C^{(j)}$. That is, party P_i sends the components $C_i^{(i)}$ and $C_j^{(i)}$ to party P_j. Then upon receiving the components $C_j^{(j)}$ and $C_i^{(j)}$ from the party P_j, party P_i *publicly* confirms whether the components of P_j's codeword are the *same* as that of P_i's codeword. For this, P_i calls the bit-BB oracle. Since the confirmations of the pairwise consistency checks happen through calls to the bit-BB oracle, all (honest) parties see the *same* responses on behalf of each party. Once all the responses are publicly available, the parties check if there exists a subset of at least $n - t$ parties who have "positively" confirmed the pairwise consistency of the components of their respective codewords. Such a subset, if it exists, is designated as the CORE set.

If S is *honest*, then a CORE set as described above always *exists*, since the set of honest parties always constitute a candidate CORE set. Hence if *no* CORE set is identified, then clearly S is *corrupt* and consequently, the parties exit the protocol by *discarding* S and taking a *default* output on the behalf of S. If a CORE set is identified, then it implies that there exists at least $|\text{CORE}| - t \geq t + 1$ *honest* parties in CORE, who received some *common* RS codeword, say $\mathsf{C} = (\mathsf{C}_1, \ldots, \mathsf{C}_n)$ from S, where $\mathsf{C} = C$ if S is *honest*. To complete the protocol, we need to ensure that *all* honest parties have the codeword C, after which they can *decode* C and get back the message encoded in C.

The above final goal is achieved in two steps. We first ensure that *each* party P_i has the ith component C_i of the codeword C. This step *does not* require any new communication among the parties. This is because as part of the pairwise consistency checks, P_i would have received the ith component of the codewords of *all* the parties in CORE. Since *majority* of the parties in CORE will be *honest*, P_i takes the majority of these i^{th} components to get the desired component C_i. Note that if S is *honest*, then C_i will be the *same* as C_i, since *all* honest parties in CORE would have sent C_i to P_i during the pairwise consistency test. Once P_i computes C_i, it sends it to all the parties. As the *corrupt* parties P_j may send an *incorrect* C_j, the parties apply the RS error-correction procedure to error-correct the *incorrect* C_j components and recover back the message corresponding to the codeword C. The error-correction will work correctly because of the choice of the parameters of the RS code and due to the fact that there can be, at most t errors which need to be error-corrected.

To summarize, protocol $\Pi^{(n,t)}_{\mathsf{WarmUp}}$ consists of the following stages, each having a different purpose. Noticeably, the bit-BB oracle is invoked in *only one* stage.

- **Codeword distribution**: in this stage, S distributes the RS codeword corresponding to its input.
- **Pairwise consistency check**: in this stage, the parties check the pairwise consistency of the supposedly common components of their respective received codewords.
- **Public announcement of status of pairwise consistency checks**: this stage involves making oracle calls to the bit-BB oracle for *publicly* announcing the statuses of pairwise consistency checks.
- **Checking for the existence of** CORE **set**: based on the *publicly* known results of the pairwise consistency tests, the parties check for the presence of a CORE set of parties.
- **Obtaining the common codeword held by the honest parties in** CORE: Once the existence of a CORE set is confirmed, in this stage, it is ensured that *all* honest parties have the common codeword, held by the honest parties in CORE.

Protocol $\Pi^{(n,t)}_{\mathsf{WarmUp}}$ is formally presented in Fig 6.3.

Protocol $\Pi^{(n,t)}_{\mathsf{WarmUp}}(m, L)$

Public knowledge: the description of $(n, t+1, t)$-RS error-correcting code over $\mathbb{F}$ with encoding and decoding algorithms RSEncode and RSDecode respectively. Additionally, the parties have oracle access to a bit-BB oracle.

- **Round 1 (codeword distribution)**: S on having the input $m \in \{0,1\}^L$ where $L = (t+1)\log|\mathbb{F}|$, does the following.
  - Divide m into blocks $m_0, \ldots, m_t$ consisting of $\log|\mathbb{F}|$ bits. Let $M_0, \ldots, M_t \in \mathbb{F}$ be the elements from $\mathbb{F}$, represented by the bit-string $m_0, \ldots, m_t$ respectively.
  - Let $M \stackrel{def}{=} (M_0, \ldots, M_t)$. Compute $\mathsf{RSEncode}(M, n, t+1, t) := C$, where $C = (C_1, \ldots, C_n) \in \mathbb{F}^n$.
  - For $i = 1, \ldots, n$, send C to party P_i.
- **Round 2 (pairwise consistency check)**: Every party $P_i \in \mathcal{P}$ (including S) does the following.
  - Let $C^{(i)} = (C^{(i)}_1, \ldots, C^{(i)}_n) \in \mathbb{F}^n$ denote the RS codeword received by P_i from S during the previous round. If $C^{(i)}$ is *not* a valid RS codeword, then set $C^{(i)} = (0, \ldots, 0(n \text{ times}))$.[a]
  - For $j = 1, \ldots, n$, send $(C^{(i)}_i, C^{(i)}_j)$ to party P_j.
- **Round 3 (public announcement of the status of pairwise consistency checks)**: Every party $P_i \in \mathcal{P}$ (including S) does the following.
  - For $j = 1, \ldots, n$, upon receiving $(C^{(j)}_j, C^{(j)}_i)$ from party P_j, set the bit $V_{i,j}$ to 1, if and only if the following holds.[b]

$$(C^{(j)}_j = C^{(i)}_j) \wedge (C^{(j)}_i = C^{(i)}_i)$$

- Let $V_i \stackrel{def}{=} (V_{i,1}, \ldots, V_{i,n}) \in \{0,1\}^n$ denote the Boolean *response vector* of P_i.
- Publicly broadcast the vector V_i. For this, act as a sender and call the bit-BB oracle n times, where the input for the jth call is the bit $V_{i,j}$.

• **(Checking for the existence of** CORE **set)**: Every party $P_i \in \mathcal{P}$ (including S) does the following.
  - For $j, k = 1, \ldots, n$, let $V'_{j,k} \in \{0,1\}$ be the output from the kth call to the bit-BB oracle invoked by P_j as a sender and let $V'_j \stackrel{def}{=} (V'_{j,1}, \ldots, V'_{j,n})$.
  - Construct an undirected *consistency graph* $G^{(i)}$ over the set of vertices $\{P_1, \ldots, P_n\}$, where the edge (P_j, P_k) is added to $G^{(i)}$ if and only if $V'_{j,k} = V'_{k,j} = 1$
  - Check if there exists a complete subgraph (clique) of size at least $n-t$ in the graph $G^{(i)}$.
    - If there is *no* clique of size $n-t$, then *discard* S, output 0^L and terminate.
    - Else set CORE to be the set of parties which constitute a clique in the graph $G^{(i)}$. In case there are multiple cliques of size $n-t$, then consider the one with the *largest* size.

• **Round 4 (obtaining the common codeword held by the honest parties in** CORE**)**: Every party $P_i \in \mathcal{P}$ (including S) does the following.
  - Let $\mathsf{C}_i \stackrel{def}{=} \mathsf{Majority}(\{C_i^{(j)}\}_{P_j \in \mathsf{CORE}})$, where $\mathsf{Majority}(\cdot)$ denotes the *majority* function and where $C_i^{(j)}$ has been received from P_j during **Round 2**.[c]
  - For $j = 1, \ldots, n$, send C_i to every party P_j.

• **(Output computation and termination)**: Every party $P_i \in \mathcal{P}$ (including S) does the following.
  - Let $C^\star \stackrel{def}{=} (C_1^\star, \ldots, C_n^\star)$, where $C_j^\star$ is received from P_j during **Round 4**, for $j = 1, \ldots, n$.[d]
  - Let $\mathsf{RSDecode}(C^\star, n, t+1, t) := M^\star = (M_0^\star, \ldots, M_t^\star) \in \mathbb{F}^{t+1}$. Let $m_0^\star, \ldots, m_t^\star$ be the bit-string representing the elements $M_0^\star, \ldots, M_t^\star$ respectively.
  - Output $m^\star \stackrel{def}{=} m_0^\star || \ldots || m_t^\star$ and terminate, where $||$ denotes the concatenation operation.

---

[a] To check if $(C_1^{(i)}, \ldots, C_n^{(i)})$ is a valid codeword, P_i can check if the points $\{(\alpha_j, C_j^{(i)})\}_{j=1,\ldots,n}$ lie on a t-degree polynomial.
[b] If P_i does not receive any $(C_j^{(j)}, C_i^{(j)})$ from party P_j then it sets $V_{i,j}$ to 0.
[c] If no $C_i^{(j)}$ has been received from P_j during **Round 2** then set $C_i^{(j)}$ to 0.
[d] If no $C_j^\star$ is received from P_j during **Round 4** then set $C_j^\star$ to 0.

Fig. 6.3: The warmup protocol for domain extension where $L = (t+1)\log|\mathbb{F}|$ bits

For a pictorial depiction of the various stages of the protocol $\Pi_{\mathsf{WarmUp}}^{(n,t)}$, see Fig 6.4-6.7.

We now proceed to prove the properties of the protocol $\Pi_{\mathsf{WarmUp}}^{(n,t)}$. While proving the properties, we denote by $\mathcal{H}$ the set of *honest* parties. Note that $|\mathcal{H}| \geq n-t$. We first start with the case when S is *honest*. We begin by showing that if S is *honest* then it is *not* discarded.

Claim 6.1 In protocol $\Pi_{\mathsf{WarmUp}}^{(n,t)}$, if S is honest, then all honest parties will find a common set CORE where $|\mathsf{CORE}| \geq n-t$.

Proof Let S be *honest*. During **Round 1**, it sends the codeword C to all the parties. Consequently, $C^{(i)} = C$ holds for *every* $P_i \in \mathcal{H}$. During **Round 2**, *every* $P_i \in \mathcal{H}$

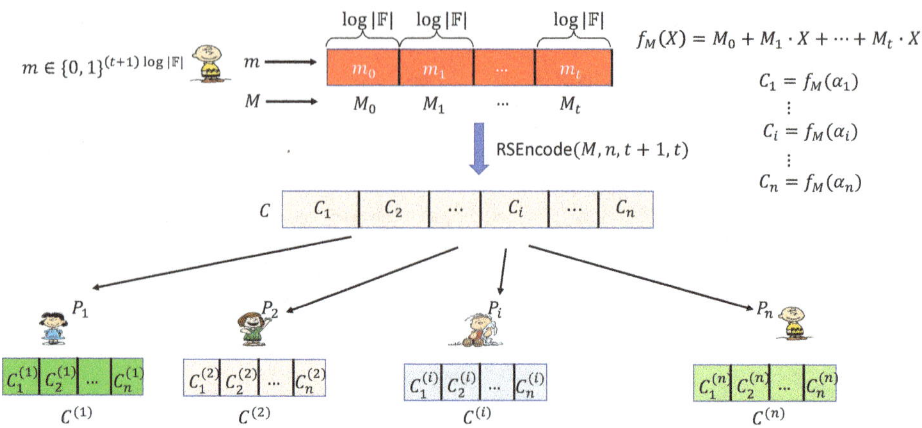

Fig. 6.4: The first stage of the protocol $\Pi_{\mathsf{WarmUp}}^{(n,t)}$ where S distributes its input m to all the parties by sending the corresponding RS codeword C. If S is *honest* then $C^{(i)} = C^{(j)} = C$ for every pair of honest parties P_i and P_j

sends $(C_i^{(i)}, C_j^{(i)})$ to every party. Consequently, for *every pair* of parties $P_j, P_k \in \mathcal{H}$, the conditions $C_k^{(k)} = C_k^{(j)}$ and $C_j^{(k)} = C_j^{(j)}$ hold. Hence P_j sets $V_{j,k} = 1$ and P_k sets $V_{k,j} = 1$. Since *every* $P_j \in \mathcal{H}$ broadcasts the vector response vector V_j through calls to bit-BB oracle, it follows that $V'_{j,k} = V_{j,k}$ holds for $k = 1, \ldots, n$ and hence $V'_j = V_j$ holds. Now consider an *arbitrary* $P_i \in \mathcal{H}$. Then in the graph $G^{(i)}$, the edge (P_j, P_k) will be present for every $P_j, P_k \in \mathcal{H}$. Since $|\mathcal{H}| \geq n - t$, it follows that P_i will *not* discard S since the set of parties in $\mathcal{H}$ will constitute a clique of size at least $n - t$ in the graph $G^{(i)}$. Hence, P_i will find a CORE set.

To complete the proof, we need to show that *all* the parties in $\mathcal{H}$ will have the *same* CORE set. For this, it is enough to show that all the parties in $\mathcal{H}$ will have the *same* consistency graph since CORE is set to the set of parties which constitute the *largest* clique in the consistency graph. However, this follows from the fact that the response vectors are broadcasted through calls to the bit-BB oracle. In more detail, consider an *arbitrary* party P_j and consider the calls to the bit-BB oracle invoked by P_j as a sender. Then it follows that for $k = 1, \ldots, n$, *all* the parties in $\mathcal{H}$ will have a common output $V'_{j,k}$ from the kth call of the bit-BB oracle invoked by P_j. □

We next show that if S is *honest*, then all honest parties in CORE will have a common codeword.

Claim 6.2 Let $m \in \{0,1\}^{(t+1)\log|\mathbb{F}|}$ be the input of S for $\Pi_{\mathsf{WarmUp}}^{(n,t)}$ and let $m_0, \ldots, m_t$ be the blocks of m consisting of $\log|\mathbb{F}|$ bits each. Moreover, let $M_0, \ldots, M_t$ be the elements of $\mathbb{F}$, represented by the bit-string $m_0, \ldots, m_t$ respectively. Furthermore,

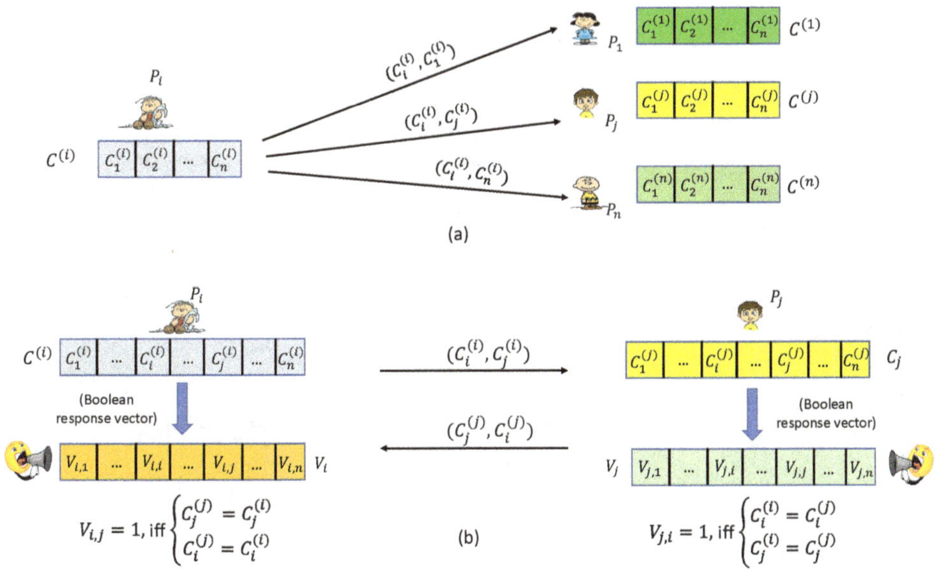

Fig. 6.5: The second and the third stage of the protocol $\Pi^{(n,t)}_{\mathsf{WarmUp}}$. Fig (a) denotes the components of the codeword C_i that party P_i sends to every other party. Fig (b) denotes parties making public their Boolean response vectors by making oracle calls to the bit-BB oracle

let $M \stackrel{def}{=} (M_0, \ldots, M_t)$ and let $\mathsf{RSEncode}(M, n, t+1, t) := C$. Then every honest party in CORE will have the codeword C, received from S during **Round 1**.

Proof The proof follows from the fact if S is *honest*, then it sends the RS codeword C to *all* the parties. □

We finally show that if S is *honest*, then all honest parties output m, thus proving the *t-validity* of the protocol

Lemma 6.5 *If* S *is honest then all honest parties output* m*, where* $m \in \{0,1\}^{(t+1)\log|\mathbb{F}|}$ *is the input of* S *for the protocol* $\Pi^{(n,t)}_{\mathsf{WarmUp}}$.

Proof Let S be *honest*. Then from Claim 6.1 and Claim 6.2, all parties in $\mathcal{H}$ will have a *common* core set CORE where $|\mathsf{CORE}| \geq n - t$, such that all the parties in $(\mathcal{H} \cap \mathsf{CORE})$ have the RS codeword C received from S during **Round 1**, where $C = (C_1, \ldots, C_n)$. Since there can be *at most t corrupt* parties in CORE and $n - t \geq 2t + 1$, it follows that the *majority* of the parties in CORE are *honest*.

Consider an *arbitrary* $P_i \in \mathcal{H}$. Then during **Round 4**, party P_i sets $C_i^{\star} = C_i$. This is because $C_i^{(j)} = C_i$ for *every* party $P_j \in (\mathcal{H} \cap \mathsf{CORE})$ and as shown above, the majority of the parties in CORE are *honest*. During this round, *every* party $P_j \in \mathcal{H}$ sends $C_j^{\star}$ to all the parties. However, the *corrupt* parties P_j may send an *incorrect* $C_j^{\star}$

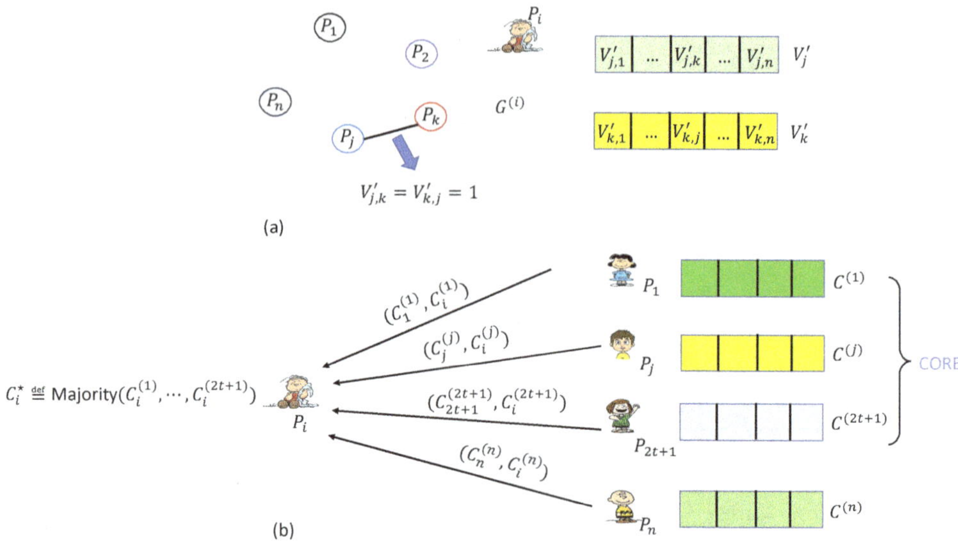

Fig. 6.6: The fourth stage of the protocol $\Pi_{\text{WarmUp}}^{(n,t)}$. Fig (a) denotes the process of constructing the consistency graph $G^{(i)}$ by party P_i, based on the response vectors available with P_i. Fig (b) denotes the process of P_i computing the ith component of the common codeword held by the honest parties in CORE, assuming CORE $= \{P_1, \ldots, P_{2t+1}\}$

to the parties. Then consider the vector $C^\star = (C_1^\star, \ldots, C_n^\star)$ available with P_i where $C_j^\star$ is received from P_j. From the above arguments, $C_j^\star = C_j$, for every $P_j \in \mathcal{H}$. Since the parameters of RS code is set to $N = n, K = t + 1$ and $T = t$, it follows that $N - K \geq 2T$ holds, since $n > 3t$ holds. Consequently, the output $M^\star$ obtained from the RSDecode algorithm will be the *same* as M. This implies that $m_j^\star = m_j$ holds for $j = 0, \ldots, t$ and hence P_i outputs $m^\star = m$. □

We next focus on the case when S is *corrupt*. We wish to show that all *honest* parties will have a *common* output. We first claim that all *honest* parties will have the *same* consistency graph.

Claim 6.3 In protocol $\Pi_{\text{WarmUp}}^{(n,t)}$, even if S is *corrupt*, all honest parties will have the same consistency graph.

Proof In the protocol, the consistency graphs are constructed based on the response vectors broadcasted by the individual parties through oracle calls to the bit-BB oracle. Consider an *arbitrary* party P_j and consider the calls to the bit-BB oracle invoked by P_j. It follows that for $k = 1, \ldots, n$, *all* the parties in $\mathcal{H}$ will have a common output $V'_{j,k}$ from the kth call to the bit-BB oracle invoked by P_j. Hence,

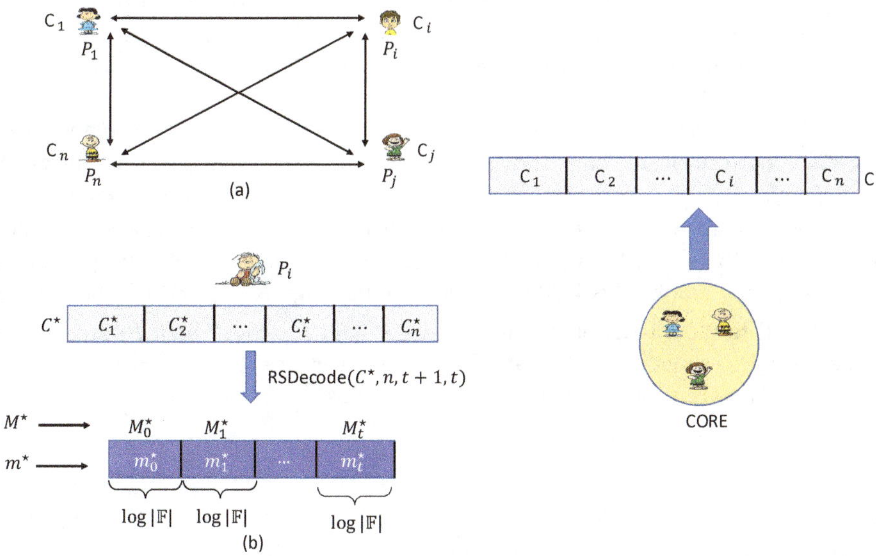

Fig. 6.7: The last stage of the protocol $\Pi^{(n,t)}_{\mathsf{WarmUp}}$. C denotes the common codeword held by the honest parties in CORE. Fig (a) denotes the process of parties exchanging among themselves only their respective component of C. Fig (b) denotes the process of P_i applying the RS decoding process to get back the message encoded in the codeword C

every party in $\mathcal{H}$ will have the *same* vector V_j' and consequently, all the parties in $\mathcal{H}$ will have the same consistency graph. □

Now, based on the above claim, we can claim that if a *corrupt* S is *not* discarded, then all honest parties will have a *common* core set.

Claim 6.4 In protocol $\Pi^{(n,t)}_{\mathsf{WarmUp}}$, if S is *corrupt* and S is not discarded, then all honest parties will have a common set CORE.

Proof From Claim 6.3, all parties in $\mathcal{H}$ will have a *common* consistency graph. Let S be *not* discarded. This implies that all parties in $\mathcal{H}$ find a clique of size at least $n-t$ in their consistency graphs, which is set as the CORE set of parties. Moreover, the set CORE will be the *same* for all the parties in $\mathcal{H}$, since it is set to the *largest* clique in the consistency graph. □

We next show that if S is *not* discarded, then all *honest* parties in CORE received a common RS codeword from the sender.

Claim 6.5 In protocol $\Pi^{(n,t)}_{\mathsf{WarmUp}}$, if S is *corrupt* and S is not discarded, then all honest parties in CORE received a common RS codeword from S during **Round 1**.

Proof If S is *not* discarded then from Claim 6.4, it follows that all parties in $\mathcal{H}$ find a *common* core set of parties CORE, where $|\mathsf{CORE}| \geq n - t$. Let $\mathcal{H}_{\mathsf{CORE}}$ be the set of *honest* parties in CORE; i.e. $\mathcal{H}_{\mathsf{CORE}} = (\mathcal{H} \cap \mathsf{CORE})$. Hence $|\mathcal{H}_{\mathsf{CORE}}| \geq |\mathsf{CORE}| - t \geq t + 1$.

Consider an *arbitrary* $P_k \in \mathcal{H}_{\mathsf{CORE}}$. We next show that the kth component of the RS codeword of all the parties in $\mathcal{H}_{\mathsf{CORE}}$ will be the *same*. That is, for every $P_i, P_j \in \mathcal{H}_{\mathsf{CORE}}$, the condition $C_k^{(i)} = C_k^{(j)}$ holds, where $C^{(i)}$ and $C^{(j)}$ denotes the RS codewords received by P_i and P_j respectively from S during **Round 1**. Since $P_i, P_j, P_k \in \mathcal{H}_{\mathsf{CORE}}$, it follows that the edges (P_i, P_k) and (P_j, P_k) are present in the consistency graph. This further implies that the outputs $V'_{i,k}$ and $V'_{j,k}$ are 1 from the kth call to the bit-BB oracle invoked by P_i and P_j. Since both P_i and P_j are *honest*, it follows that $V'_{i,k} = V_{i,k}$ and $V'_{j,k} = V_{j,k}$. Hence $V_{i,k} = V_{j,k} = 1$.

Since $V_{i,k} = 1$, it follows that the following holds:

$$C_k^{(k)} = C_k^{(i)},$$

where $C^{(k)}$ denotes the RS codeword received by P_k from S during **Round 1**. Similarly, since $V_{j,k} = 1$, it follows that the following holds as well:

$$C_k^{(k)} = C_k^{(j)}.$$

Now, based on the above two conditions, it follows that $C_k^{(i)} = C_k^{(j)}$ holds. Since P_k above is an *arbitrary* party from the set $\mathcal{H}_{\mathsf{CORE}}$ and $|\mathcal{H}_{\mathsf{CORE}}| \geq t + 1$ and since the parameter K for the RS code is set to $t + 1$, from Lemma 6.3 and Lemma 6.4 it follows that *all* the parties in $\mathcal{H}_{\mathsf{CORE}}$ have received the *same* RS codeword from S during **Round 1**. That is, $C^{(i)} = C^{(j)}$ holds for every $P_i, P_j \in \mathcal{H}_{\mathsf{CORE}}$. □

We next show that if a *corrupt* sender is *not* discarded, then all *honest* parties will have a *common* output.

Claim 6.6 In protocol $\Pi_{\mathsf{WarmUp}}^{(n,t)}$, if S is *corrupt* and S is not discarded, then all honest parties will have a common output.

Proof If S is *not* discarded then from Claim 6.4, it follows that all parties in $\mathcal{H}$ find a *common* core set of parties CORE, where $|\mathsf{CORE}| \geq n - t$. Moreover, from Claim 6.5 all *honest* parties in CORE received the *same* RS codeword from S during **Round 1**.

Let $\mathsf{C} = (\mathsf{C}_1, \ldots, \mathsf{C}_n)$ denote the RS codeword received by the *honest* parties in CORE from S. Moreover, let $\mathsf{M} = (\mathsf{M}_0, \ldots, \mathsf{M}_t) \in \mathbb{F}^{t+1}$ be the message such that $\mathsf{RSEncode}(\mathsf{M}, n, t + 1, t) := \mathsf{C}$. We wish to show that at the end of **Round 4**, the output of $\mathsf{RSDecode}$ will be M for every party in $\mathcal{H}$. However, the proof for this is exactly the *same* as that of Lemma 6.5 except that C is now replaced with C and M is replaced with M. Once the parties in $\mathcal{H}$ have M, they output the message represented by the elements $\mathsf{M}_0, \ldots, \mathsf{M}_t$. □

We finally show that all honest parties will have a *common* output even if the sender is *corrupt*, thus proving the *t-consistency* of the protocol.

Lemma 6.6 *In protocol* $\Pi^{(n,t)}_{\mathsf{WarmUp}}$*, if* S *is corrupt, then all honest parties have a common output.*

Proof Let S be *corrupt*. From Claim 6.3, all the parties in $\mathcal{H}$ will have a *common* consistency graph. Now there are *two* possible cases, based on whether the parties in $\mathcal{H}$ find a set of core parties CORE in the consistency graph.

- **No CORE set is found**: In this case, all the parties in $\mathcal{H}$ discard S and output $0^{(t+1)\log|\mathbb{F}|}$. Hence the lemma holds in this case.
- **A CORE set is found**: In this case, from Claim 6.6, all the parties in $\mathcal{H}$ have a common output from $\{0,1\}^{(t+1)\log|\mathbb{F}|}$ and hence the lemma holds. □

Theorem 6.3 now follows easily from the above discussion.

Theorem 6.3 *Let* $t < \frac{n}{3}$ *and let the parties have oracle access to a bit-BB oracle. Moreover let* S *has an input* $m \in \{0,1\}^L$ *for protocol* $\Pi^{(n,t)}_{\mathsf{WarmUp}}$ *where* $L = (t+1)\log|\mathbb{F}|$*. Then protocol* $\Pi^{(n,t)}_{\mathsf{WarmUp}}$ *is a t-secure BB protocol with perfect security in the model* $\mathcal{M}_{\mathsf{auth}}$ *with the following complexities.*

- *The protocol requires* 4 *rounds.*
- *The seed-round complexity of the protocol is* 1.
- *The protocol incurs a communication of* $O(n^2\log|\mathbb{F}|) + n^2\cdot\mathcal{BC}(1)$ *bits, where* $\mathcal{BC}(1)$ *denotes the communication complexity of emulating one instance of the bit-BB oracle with a single-bit input.*
- *The seed-communication complexity of the protocol is* $O(n^2)$ *bits.*

Proof The *t-validity* and *t-consistency* follows from Lemma 6.5 and Lemma 6.6 respectively. The round complexity follows from the protocol description. During **Round 1**, S needs to send an RS codeword consisting of n elements from $\mathbb{F}$ to all the parties. This incurs a communication of $O(n^2\log|\mathbb{F}|)$ bits. During **Round 2**, every party needs to send 2 components from its codeword to every other party. This requires 1 round and a communication of $O(n^2\log|\mathbb{F}|)$ bits. During **Round 3**, every party calls the bit-BB oracle as a sender n times to broadcast a bit. This requires a communication of $n^2\cdot\mathcal{BC}(1)$ bits. Finally, during **Round 4**, every party needs to send one field element to all the parties, which requires communication of $O(n^2\log|\mathbb{F}|)$ bits. Hence, the seed-round complexity of the protocol is 1, since bit-BB oracle is invoked during the third round. Moreover, the seed-communication complexity of the protocol is $O(n^2)$ bits since $O(n^2)$ bits are broadcasted through oracle calls to the bit-BB oracle. All honest parties terminate after the fourth round, thus guaranteeing *t-liveness* for $\Pi^{(n,t)}_{\mathsf{WarmUp}}$. □

6.4.4.2 Protocol $\Pi^{(n,t)}_{\mathsf{WarmUp}}$ for Any $L \geq (t+1)\log|\mathbb{F}|$

Let us now consider the case when the input m of the sender in the protocol $\Pi^{(n,t)}_{\mathsf{WarmUp}}$ is from the set $\{0,1\}^L$ where $L \geq (t+1)\log|\mathbb{F}|$. As a starting idea, let S divide m into blocks of length $(t+1)\log|\mathbb{F}|$ bits and run an instance of $\Pi^{(n,t)}_{\mathsf{WarmUp}}$ for each block of size $(t+1)\log|\mathbb{F}|$ bits. A default *padding* can be used if the last block is *not* of size $(t+1)\log|\mathbb{F}|$ bits, which can be then later *removed* from the final output. Let B denote the number of blocks of size $(t+1)\log|\mathbb{F}|$ bits in m, where $B \stackrel{def}{=} \frac{L}{(t+1)\log|\mathbb{F}|}$. For simplicity and without loss of generality, let L be a multiple of $(t+1)\log|\mathbb{F}|$. Then what will be the communication complexity of the protocol? From Theorem 6.3, it turns out to be $O(Bn^2\log|\mathbb{F}|) + Bn^2 \cdot \mathcal{BC}(1)$ bits, which will be the same as

$$O\left(n^2 \log|\mathbb{F}| \cdot \frac{L}{(t+1)\log|\mathbb{F}|}\right) + n^2 \cdot \frac{L}{(t+1)\log|\mathbb{F}|} \cdot \mathcal{BC}(1).$$

By substituting $t = \Theta(n)$, the above communication complexity turns out to be the following:

$$O(nL) + \frac{nL}{\log|\mathbb{F}|} \cdot \mathcal{BC}(1).$$

Clearly, the seed-communication complexity of the protocol is $O\left(\frac{nL}{\log|\mathbb{F}|}\right)$, which is *not* independent of L and hence the resultant protocol *cannot* be considered as a domain extension protocol.[8]

To make the number of calls to the bit-BB oracle *independent* of L, we take a closer look into the protocol $\Pi^{(n,t)}_{\mathsf{WarmUp}}$ and find that the calls to the bit-BB oracle are made in $\Pi^{(n,t)}_{\mathsf{WarmUp}}$ *only* during **Round 3** to make public the Boolean response vectors. Since the response vector of each party has n bits, each party needs to call the bit-BB oracle n times, leading to a *total* of n^2 bits being broadcasted. Since we are now running B instances of $\Pi^{(n,t)}_{\mathsf{WarmUp}}$, *each* party will have B number of Boolean response vectors and hence Bn bits to broadcast, leading to a total of Bn^2 calls to the bit-BB oracle. Instead, we let each party compute and broadcast a *single* response vector across *all* the B instances of $\Pi^{(n,t)}_{\mathsf{WarmUp}}$, which will incur *only* n^2 calls to the bit-BB oracle. Namely, party P_i sets the bit $V_{i,j}$ in its response vector to 1 provided the supposedly common components of P_i's and P_j's codewords are the *same* across *all* the B instances of $\Pi^{(n,t)}_{\mathsf{WarmUp}}$, which *should* be the case if S, P_i and P_j are *honest*. Consequently, each party will construct a *single* consistency graph on behalf of *all* the B instances of $\Pi^{(n,t)}_{\mathsf{WarmUp}}$ and computes a *single* CORE set. With this modification, the resultant protocol turns out to be a candidate domain extension protocol. We call the resultant protocol as $\Pi^{(n,t)}_{\mathsf{GenWarmUp}}$ and present it in Fig 6.8.

Protocol $\Pi^{(n,t)}_{\mathsf{GenWarmUp}}(m, L)$

Public knowledge: the description of $(n, t+1, t)$-RS error-correcting code over $\mathbb{F}$ with encoding and decoding algorithms $\mathsf{RSEncode}$ and $\mathsf{RSDecode}$ respectively. Additionally, the parties have oracle access to a bit-BB oracle.

- **Round 1 (codeword distribution)**: S on having the input $m \in \{0,1\}^L$, does the following.

[8] Recall that the goal of the domain extension is to ensure that the number of bits broadcasted through the broadcast oracle is *independent* of L.

- Divide m into blocks $m^{(1)}, \ldots, m^{(B)}$ each of size $(t+1)\log|\mathbb{F}|$ bits, where $B \stackrel{def}{=} \frac{L}{(t+1)\log|\mathbb{F}|}$.[a]
- For $\ell = 1, \ldots, B$, further divide the block $m^{(\ell)}$ into sub-blocks $m_0^{(\ell)}, \ldots, m_t^{(\ell)}$ consisting of $\log|\mathbb{F}|$ bits each. Let $M_0^{(\ell)}, \ldots, M_t^{(\ell)} \in \mathbb{F}$ be the elements from $\mathbb{F}$, represented by the bit-string $m_0^{(\ell)}, \ldots, m_t^{(\ell)}$ respectively.
- For $\ell = 1, \ldots, B$, let $M^{(\ell)} \stackrel{def}{=} (M_0^{(\ell)}, \ldots, M_t^{(\ell)})$. Compute $\mathsf{RSEncode}(M^{(\ell)}, n, t+1, t) := C^{(\ell)}$, where $C^{(\ell)} = (C_1^{(\ell)}, \ldots, C_n^{(\ell)}) \in \mathbb{F}^n$.
- For $\ell = 1, \ldots, B$ and $i = 1, \ldots, n$, send $C^{(\ell)}$ to party P_i.

• **Round 2 (pairwise consistency check)**: Every party $P_i \in \mathcal{P}$ (including S) does the following.
  - For $\ell = 1, \ldots, B$, let $C^{(\ell,i)} = (C_1^{(\ell,i)}, \ldots, C_n^{(\ell,i)}) \in \mathbb{F}^n$ denote the RS codeword received by P_i from S. If no codeword is received from S by the end of the previous round or if $C^{(\ell,i)}$ is *not* a valid RS codeword, then set $C^{(\ell,i)} := (0, \ldots, 0(n \text{ times}))$.[b]
  - For $\ell = 1, \ldots, B$ and $j = 1, \ldots, n$, send $(C_i^{(\ell,i)}, C_j^{(\ell,i)})$ to party P_j.

• **Round 3 (public announcement of the status of pairwise consistency checks)**: Every party $P_i \in \mathcal{P}$ (including S) does the following.
  - For $\ell = 1, \ldots, B$ and $j = 1, \ldots, n$, upon receiving $(C_j^{(\ell,j)}, C_i^{(\ell,j)})$ from party P_j, set the bit $V_{i,j}$ to 1, if and only if the following holds for *each* $\ell \in \{1, \ldots, B\}$:

$$(C_j^{(\ell,j)} = C_j^{(\ell,i)}) \wedge (C_i^{(\ell,j)} = C_i^{(\ell,i)}).$$

    If no $(C_j^{(\ell,j)}, C_i^{(\ell,j)})$ has been received from P_j then set $V_{i,j} := 0$.
  - Let $V_i \stackrel{def}{=} (V_{i,1}, \ldots, V_{i,n}) \in \{0,1\}^n$ denote the Boolean *response vector* of P_i.
  - Publicly broadcast the vector V_i. For this, act as a sender and make n calls to the bit-BB oracle, where the input for the jth call is the bit $V_{i,j}$.

• **(Checking for the existence of** CORE **set)**: Every party $P_i \in \mathcal{P}$ (including S) does the following.
  - For $j, k = 1, \ldots, n$, let $V'_{j,k} \in \{0,1\}$ be the output from the kth calls to the bit-BB oracle invoked by P_j as a sender.
  - Construct an undirected *consistency graph* $G^{(i)}$ over the set of vertices $\{P_1, \ldots, P_n\}$, where the edge (P_j, P_k) is added to $G^{(i)}$ if and only if $V'_{j,k} = V'_{k,j} = 1$
  - Check if there exists a complete subgraph (clique) of size at least $n-t$ in the graph $G^{(i)}$.
    - If there is *no* clique of size $n-t$, then *discard* S, output 0^L and terminate.
    - Else set CORE to be the set of parties which constitute a clique in the graph $G^{(i)}$. In case there are multiple cliques of size $n-t$, then consider the one with the *largest* size.

• **Round 4 (obtaining the common codeword held by the honest parties in** CORE**)**: Every party $P_i \in \mathcal{P}$ (including S) does the following.
  - For $\ell = 1, \ldots, B$, let $\mathsf{C}_i^{(\ell)} \stackrel{def}{=} \mathsf{Majority}(\{C_i^{(\ell,j)}\}_{P_j \in \mathsf{CORE}})$, where $\mathsf{Majority}(\cdot)$ denotes the *majority* function and where $C_i^{(\ell,j)}$ has been received from P_j during **Round 2.**[c]
  - For $\ell = 1, \ldots, B$ and $j = 1, \ldots, n$, send $\mathsf{C}_i^{(\ell)}$ to every party P_j.

• **(Output computation and termination)**: Every party $P_i \in \mathcal{P}$ (including S) does the following.
  - For $\ell = 1, \ldots, B$, let $\mathsf{C}^{(\ell)} \stackrel{def}{=} (\mathsf{C}_1^{(\ell)}, \ldots, \mathsf{C}_n^{(\ell)})$, where $\mathsf{C}_j^{(\ell)}$ is received from P_j during the previous round, for $j = 1, \ldots, n$.[d]
  - For $\ell = 1, \ldots, B$, let $\mathsf{RSDecode}(\mathsf{C}^{(\ell)}, n, t+1, t) := \mathsf{M}^{(\ell)} = (\mathsf{M}_0^{(\ell)}, \ldots, \mathsf{M}_t^{(\ell)}) \in \mathbb{F}^{t+1}$. Let $\mathsf{m}_0^{(\ell)}, \ldots, \mathsf{m}_t^{(\ell)}$ be the bit-string representing the elements $\mathsf{M}_0^{(\ell)}, \ldots, \mathsf{M}_t^{(\ell)}$

respectively and let $\mathsf{m}^{(\ell)} = \mathsf{m}_0^{(\ell)} || \ldots || \mathsf{m}_t^{(\ell)}$, where $||$ denotes the string concatenation operation.

– Output $\mathsf{m}^{(1)} || \ldots || \mathsf{m}^{(B)}$ and terminate.

---

[a] For simplicity and without loss of generality, let $L = c \cdot (t+1) \log |\mathbb{F}|$ for some integer $c \geq 1$. Hence $B = c$.

[b] To check if $(C_1^{(\ell,i)}, \ldots, C_n^{(\ell,i)})$ is a valid codeword, P_i can check if the points $\{(\alpha_j, C_j^{(\ell,i)})\}_{j=1,\ldots,n}$ lie on a t-degree polynomial.

[c] If no $C_i^{(\ell,j)}$ has been received from P_j then set $C_i^{(\ell,j)} := 0$.

[d] If no $\mathsf{C}_j^{(\ell)}$ is received from P_j then set $\mathsf{C}_j^{(\ell)} := 0$.

Fig. 6.8: The warmup protocol for domain extension where $L \geq (t+1) \log |\mathbb{F}|$ bits

The security properties of protocol $\Pi_{\mathsf{GenWarmUp}}^{(n,t)}$ follow from the properties of the protocol $\Pi_{\mathsf{WarmUp}}^{(n,t)}$ and so we do not provide the formal proofs to avoid repetition. However, we do derive the various complexities of the protocol $\Pi_{\mathsf{GenWarmUp}}^{(n,t)}$.

Lemma 6.7 *Protocol* $\Pi_{\mathsf{GenWarmUp}}^{(n,t)}$ *has the following complexities.*

– *The protocol requires* 4 *rounds.*
– *The seed-round complexity of the protocol is* 1.
– *The protocol incurs a communication of* $O(nL) + n^2 \cdot \mathcal{BC}(1)$ *bits, where* $\mathcal{BC}(1)$ *denotes the communication complexity of emulating one call to the bit-BB oracle with a single-bit input.*
– *The seed-communication complexity of the protocol is* $O(n^2)$ *bits.*

Proof The round complexity follows from the protocol inspection. Let $B \stackrel{def}{=} \frac{L}{(t+1)\log|\mathbb{F}|}$. During **Round 1**, S needs to send B number of RS codewords, each consisting of n elements from $\mathbb{F}$ to all the parties. This incurs a communication of $O(Bn^2 \log |\mathbb{F}|)$ bits. During **Round 2**, every party needs to send $2B$ components from its codewords to every other party. This requires a communication of $O(Bn^2 \log |\mathbb{F}|)$ bits. During **Round 3**, every party makes n calls to the bit-BB oracle as a sender to broadcast a bit. This incurs a communication of $n^2 \cdot \mathcal{BC}(1)$ bits. Finally, during **Round 4**, every party needs to send B field element to all the parties, which requires communication of $O(Bn^2 \log |\mathbb{F}|)$ bits. Hence the total communication complexity is $O(Bn^2 \log |\mathbb{F}|) + n^2 \cdot \mathcal{BC}(1)$ bits. Now, substituting the value of B and using the fact that $t = \Theta(n)$, the total communication complexity turns out to be $O(nL) + n^2 \cdot \mathcal{BC}(1)$ bits. □

We finally end this section with a discussion on the *computation complexity* of the protocol $\Pi_{\mathsf{GenWarmUp}}^{(n,t)}$ (and $\Pi_{\mathsf{WarmUp}}^{(n,t)}$).

On the Computation Complexity of the Protocol $\Pi_{\mathsf{GenWarmUp}}^{(n,t)}$.

The most computationally expensive step in the protocol $\Pi_{\mathsf{GenWarmUp}}^{(n,t)}$ is where the parties need to check if there is a *clique* of size at least $n-t$ in their consistency graph.

One way to check this will be to do a *brute force* and exhaustively search all possible subsets of size $n - t$ in the graph and see if any of these subsets constitute a clique. However, this will require a running time of $\Omega(n^{n-t})$, which is clearly *exponential* in n. In fact, it is well-known that finding the maximum-sized clique in a graph is an NP-complete problem [37, 64]. Hence, even though the asymptotic communication complexity of the protocol $\Pi^{(n,t)}_{\mathsf{GenWarmUp}}$ is $O(nL)$ bits, it is computationally efficient only for *smaller* values of n.

Motivated by the above shortcomings, we next try to improve the computation complexity of the protocol $\Pi^{(n,t)}_{\mathsf{GenWarmUp}}$ to *polynomial* (in n). The idea will be to look for an *alternate* structure in the *consistency graph* to find a candidate CORE set, such that finding the alternate structure requires only a *polynomial* amount of computation.

6.4.5 Domain Extension for Byzantine Broadcast with Polynomial Computation Complexity

We start this section with the discussion on $(n,t)-$star, an alternate structure in a graph which is used to check for the presence of a CORE set of parties in the protocol $\Pi^{(n,t)}_{\mathsf{WarmUp}}$ and $\Pi^{(n,t)}_{\mathsf{GenWarmUp}}$.

6.4.5.1 $(n,t)-$star

An $(n,t)-$star is formally defined as follows.

Definition 6.4 ($(n,t)-$star **[20]**) Let $G = (V, E)$ be an *undirected* graph where $V = \{1, \ldots, n\}$. Then a pair $(C, \mathcal{D})$ where $C, \mathcal{D} \subseteq V$ is called an $(n,t)-$star in G, if all the following holds:

- $|C| \geq n - 2t$;
- $|\mathcal{D}| \geq n - t$;
- $C \subseteq \mathcal{D}$;
- For every $i \in C$ and every $j \in \mathcal{D}$, the edge $(i, j) \in E$.[9]

Note that Definition 6.4 *does not* imply that the nodes in $\mathcal{D}$ constitute a clique in G. For an illustration of an $(n,t)-$star, see Fig 6.9.

The next question is how do we check whether a given graph has an $(n,t)-$star and that too in *polynomial* (in n) time? For this, we present an algorithm AlgStar from [20]. The algorithm takes *input* an *arbitrary* graph G of n nodes. The *output* of the algorithm is either an $(n,t)-$star or the message "*star not present*". If G has a *clique* of size at least $n - t$, then the algorithm will *always* output an $(n,t)-$star. However, if the output of the algorithm is "*star not found*" then it is *not* necessary that there is no $(n,t)-$star in the graph. The algorithm actually operates over the

[9] This implies that the nodes in C constitute a *clique* in G.

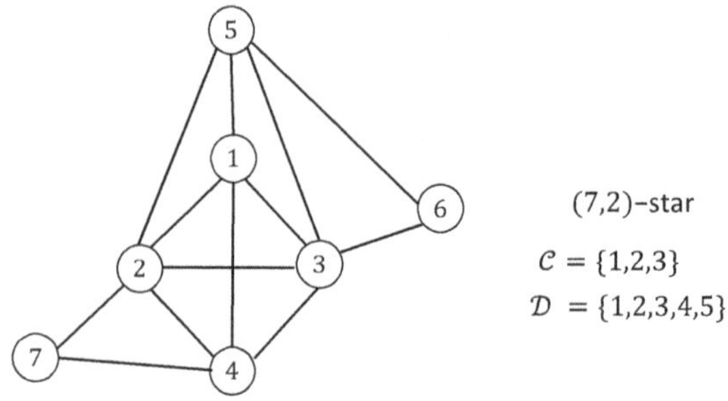

Fig. 6.9: An example of an $(n,t)-$star. The set of nodes $C = \{1,2,3\}$ and $\mathcal{D} = \{1,2,3,4,5\}$ constitute a $(7,2)-$star in the graph where $V = \{1,\ldots,7\}$

complementary graph $\overline{G}$ and instead tries to find an $(n,t)-\overline{\text{star}}$ in $\overline{G}$, which we define next.

Definition 6.5 (((n,t)$-\overline{\text{star}}$ **[20]**)) Let $H = (V', E')$ be an *undirected* graph where $V' = \{1,\ldots,n\}$. Then a pair $(C,\mathcal{D})$ where $C,\mathcal{D} \subseteq V'$ is called an $(n,t)-\overline{\text{star}}$ in H, if all the following holds:

- $|C| \geq n - 2t$;
- $|\mathcal{D}| \geq n - t$;
- $C \subseteq \mathcal{D}$;
- For every $i \in C$ and every $j \in \mathcal{D}$, the edge $(i,j) \notin E'$.[10]

Consider the graph in Fig 6.10 where $V = \{1,\ldots,7\}$. Then consider the set of nodes $C = \{1,2,3\}$ and $\mathcal{D} = \{1,2,3,4,5\}$. The pair of sets $(C,\mathcal{D})$ constitute a $(7,2)-\overline{\text{star}}$ in the graph.

From Definition 6.4 and Definition 6.5 it follows that if a graph G has an $(n,t)-$star $(C,\mathcal{D})$, then $(C,\mathcal{D})$ also constitutes an $(n,t)-\overline{\text{star}}$ in the *complementary* graph $\overline{G}$.[11] For a demonstration of this, see Fig 6.11.

We next define the notion of *matching* in a graph, which will be used in the star-finding algorithm. Informally, a collection of edges in a graph is called a *matching* if *no* two edges in the collection are incident with a *common* vertex.

Definition 6.6 (Matching in a Graph [87]) Let $G = (V,E)$ be an undirected graph and let $M \subseteq E$. Then M is called a matching in G if the following holds.

$$\forall e_i, e_j \in M \text{ such that } e_i \neq e_j : \text{ if } e_i = (v_{i_1}, v_{i_2}) \text{ and } e_j = (v_{j_1}, v_{j_2}) \\ \Rightarrow v_{i_1} \neq v_{i_2} \neq v_{j_1} \neq v_{j_2}.$$

[10] This implies that the nodes in C constitute an *independent set* in H.

[11] If $G = (V,E)$, then $\overline{G} = (V,\overline{E})$ where $(i,j) \in E$ if and only if $(i,j) \notin \overline{E}$.

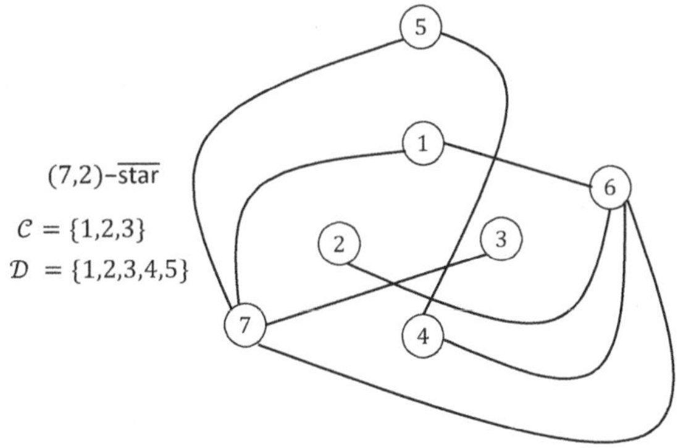

Fig. 6.10: An example of an $(n,t)-\overline{\text{star}}$. The set of nodes $C = \{1,2,3\}$ and $\mathcal{D} = \{1,2,3,4,5\}$ constitute a $(7,2)-\overline{\text{star}}$ in the graph

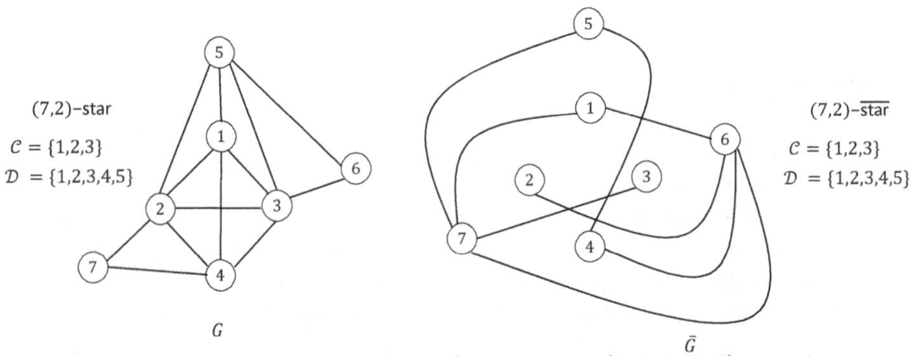

Fig. 6.11: The set of nodes $C = \{1,2,3\}$ and $\mathcal{D} = \{1,2,3,4,5\}$ constitute a $(7,2)-$star in the graph G. The same set of nodes C and $\mathcal{D}$ constitute a $(7,2)-\overline{\text{star}}$ in the graph $\overline{G}$

A vertex $v \in V$ is called *matched* with respect to M, if v is the end point of some edge in M. That is, the following holds:

$$\exists e, u : (e \in M \ \wedge \ e = (u, v)).$$

A matching M in G is called a *maximum* matching if it has the largest cardinality. That is, there *does not* exist any other matching $M' \neq M$ in G, such that $|M'| > |M|$.

For a demonstration of matching and maximum matching, see Fig 6.12.

There are well-known algorithms available to find the maximum matching in a given arbitrary graph $G = (V, E)$, which takes time poly$(|V|, |E|)$. We refer to [87] for such algorithms. For our discussion, we will use MaxMatching to denote

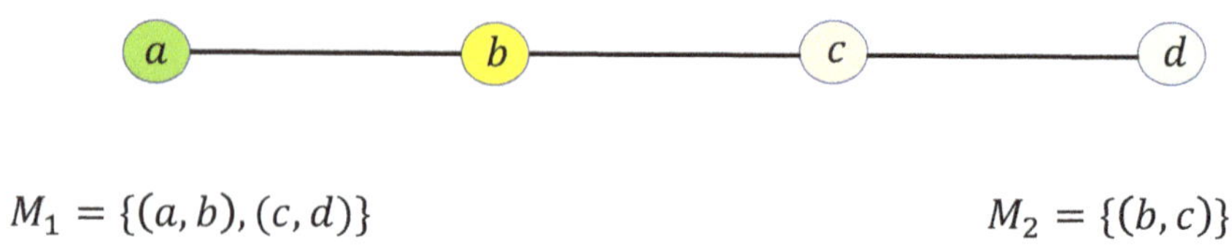

Fig. 6.12: Both M_1 and M_2 are matching in the above graph. However, M_1 *is* a maximum matching, while M_2 is *not* a maximum matching

a *polynomial* time algorithm which takes input a graph G and outputs a *maximum* matching $M_{\max}$ in G.

Algorithm AlgStar.

We are now ready to present the algorithm AlgStar. The algorithm takes input a graph G with n nodes and outputs either an $(n,t)-\text{star}$ $(C, \mathcal{D})$ or the message "*star not found*". If there exists a *clique* of size at least $n - t$, then the algorithm is *guaranteed* to output an $(n,t)-\text{star}$ $(C, \mathcal{D})$. The algorithm internally operates over the *complementary* graph $\overline{G}$ and tries to search for an $(n,t)-\overline{\text{star}}$ $(C, \mathcal{D})$. As discussed earlier, an $(n,t)-\overline{\text{star}}$ $(C, \mathcal{D})$ in $\overline{G}$ actually constitutes an $(n,t)-\text{star}$ in G. If there is an *independent set* of size at least $n - t$ in $\overline{G}$ (implying that there is a *clique* of size at least $n - t$ in G), then the algorithm will indeed find an $(n,t)-\overline{\text{star}}$ $(C, \mathcal{D})$.[12]

The high-level idea behind the algorithm is as follows. We first find a *maximum matching* M in the graph $\overline{G}$. Let V_M be the set of *matched* nodes. If $\overline{G}$ has an *independent set* $\mathcal{I}$ of size at least $n - t$, then clearly $|M| \leq t$ and hence $|V_M| \leq 2t$. This is because each edge in the matching M will have at least one vertex from the set $\overline{\mathcal{I}}$, where $\overline{\mathcal{I}} = V - \mathcal{I}$ (if this is *not* the case and M has an edge with both its vertices in $\mathcal{I}$ then $\mathcal{I}$ *does not* constitute an independent set). Consequently, there will be *at least* $n - 2t$ *unmatched* nodes. That is, the set of unmatched nodes $V - V_M$ will have a cardinality of at least $n - 2t$. Moreover, the set $V - V_M$ will constitute an independent set in $\overline{G}$ (if this is *not* the case and if there is an edge between any two *unmatched* nodes, then it implies that the matching M is *not* maximum). This further implies that the set of nodes $V - V_M$ would constitute a *clique* in the graph G of size

[12] An independent set is a set of vertices in a graph, *no* two of which are *adjacent*. That is, a set of vertices S is called an independent set if, for every two vertices in S, there is *no* edge connecting the two.

at least $n - 2t$. Hence if the cardinality of the set $V - V_M$ of unmatched nodes turns out to be *at least* $n - 2t$, then one can assign the set $V - V_M$ as a *candidate* C. Next, to find the corresponding *candidate* $\mathcal{D}$, one can simply take the set C along with all the *matched* nodes, which *do not* have any edge with any node in C and set it as the candidate $\mathcal{D}$ set. Stated differently, one can find the set of all the *matched* nodes B, which *has* an edge with any unmatched node in the graph $\overline{G}$ and assign $V - B$ as the candidate $\mathcal{D}$. This is because for an $(n, t)-\overline{\text{star}}$ in $\overline{G}$, we *do not* want to have an edge between any node in the candidate C and the candidate $\mathcal{D}$.

Note that the way sets C and $\mathcal{D}$ are computed, it is guaranteed that $C \subseteq \mathcal{D}$. This is because the set C consists of unmatched nodes and B will *not* consist of any unmatched node, since B is selected from the set of matched nodes. Hence, every node in C *will be* included in $\mathcal{D}$. We also note that there will be *no* edge between any node $v_i \in C$ and any node $v_j \in \mathcal{D}$. If this is *not* the case, then the matching M is *not* a maximum matching. This is because $v_j \in \mathcal{D}$ means $v_j \notin B$ and consequently v_j has to be an *unmatched* node (if v_j is a matched node and the edge (v_i, v_j) is present in $\overline{G}$, then $v_j \in B$ and hence $v_j \notin \mathcal{D}$). Consequently, we have two unmatched nodes v_i, v_j and the edge (v_i, v_j) in $\overline{G}$, implying that M is *not* a maximum matching.

Unfortunately, the above ideas alone *may not* lead to finding an $(n, t)-\overline{\text{star}}$ in $\overline{G}$, even if there is an independent set $\mathcal{I}$ in $\overline{G}$ of size at least $n - t$. The reason is that is it *not* guaranteed that the candidate $\mathcal{D}$ computed above has the cardinality at least $n - t$, which is one of the requirements of an $(n, t)-\text{star}$, even if the candidate C computed above has size at least $n - 2t$. This is because in order to ensure that the candidate $\mathcal{D}$ has size *at least* $n - t$, we need to ensure that the set B above has *at most* t nodes. And this will be guaranteed provided for *each* edge $(v_j, v_k) \in M$, *at most* one of the endpoints v_j and v_k gets *included* in B and *does not* make it to the set $\mathcal{D}$. Unfortunately, this *need not* be the case always. For instance, it *might* be possible that there is some node v_i in the candidate C computed above, such that the edges (v_i, v_j) as well as (v_i, v_k) are *both present* in $\overline{G}$ and where $(v_j, v_k) \in M$. This will then lead to *both* v_j as well as v_k being *included* in B and hence *both* v_j as well as v_k getting *discarded* from the candidate $\mathcal{D}$.

To deal with the above problem, *instead* of simply setting the set of unmatched nodes $V - V_M$ as a candidate C, we further *remove* the "triangle heads" from the set $V - V_M$. Here an *unmatched* node v_i is called a *triangle head*, provided it is adjacent to nodes v_j and v_k such that the edge (v_j, v_k) is present in the maximum matching M. Consequently, *at most* one of the nodes among v_j and v_k will be included B and *barred* from making it to the $\mathcal{D}$. One can show that even *after* removing the triangle heads from the set $V - V_M$ of unmatched nodes, the resultant candidate C will have at least $n - 2t$ nodes, provided $\overline{G}$ has an independent set of size at least $n - t$. Algorithm AlgStar is formally presented in Fig 6.13.

Algorithm AlgStar(G)

- Let $G = (V, E)$. Compute the complementary graph $\overline{G} = (V, \overline{E})$, where the edge $(v_i, v_j) \in \overline{E}$ if and only if $(v_i, v_j) \notin E$.
- Find a maximum matching M in $\overline{G}$ and let V_M denote the set of matched nodes.

- V_T be the set of triangle heads in $\overline{G}$ where

$$V_T = \{v_i \in (V - V_M) | \exists v_j, v_k \text{ such that } (v_i, v_j) \in \overline{E}, (v_i, v_k) \in \overline{E} \text{ and } (v_j, v_k) \in M\}.$$

  Let $C \stackrel{def}{=} (V - V_M) - V_T$.
- Let B be the set of matched nodes that have neighbours in C. That is:

$$B = \{v_j \in V_M\} | \exists v_i \in C \text{ such that } (v_i, v_j) \in \overline{E}.$$

  Let $\mathcal{D} \stackrel{def}{=} V - B$.
- Compute the output as follows:
  - If $|C| \geq n - 2t$ and $|\mathcal{D}| \geq n - t$ then output $(C, \mathcal{D})$;
  - Else output "*star not found*".

Fig. 6.13: Algorithm for finding an (n, t)−star in a graph

Consider the graph in Fig 6.14 where the number of vertices $n = 7$. Let $t = 2$. Then as demonstrated in the figure, algorithm AlgStar outputs a $(7, 2)$−star.

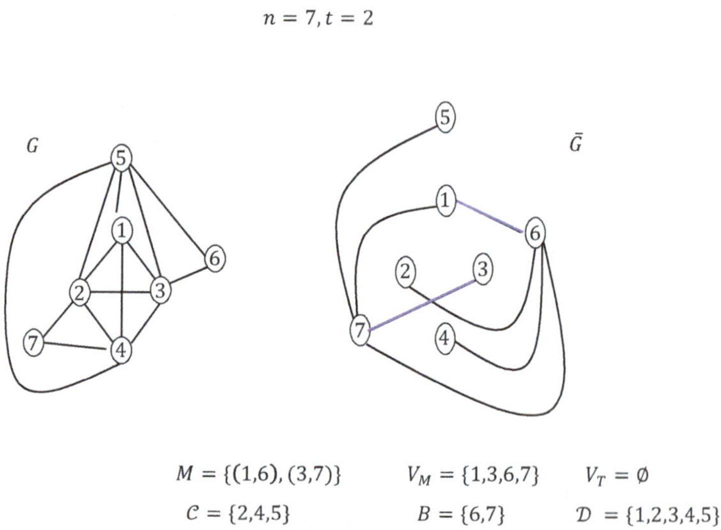

Fig. 6.14: Demonstration of the algorithm AlgStar where $n = 7$ and $t = 2$. The blue-coloured edges denote the maximum matching in the graph. There are no triangle heads with respect to the maximum matching. The nodes 6 and 7 are barred from making it to $\mathcal{D}$. Since the candidate C and $\mathcal{D}$ have the desired cardinalities, the output of the algorithm is the $(7, 2)$−star $C = \{2, 4, 5\}$ and $\mathcal{D} = \{1, 2, 3, 4, 5\}$

The properties of the algorithm AlgStar are stated in the following lemmas, whose proofs are available in [20]. For the sake of completeness, we present them here.

Looking ahead, the *second* property constitutes the crux of the *polynomial* time domain extension protocol, based on finding star in the consistency graph.

Lemma 6.8 ([20]) *Let* $G = (V, E)$ *be an undirected graph where* $|V| = n$. *If the algorithm outputs* $(C, \mathcal{D})$, *then* $(C, \mathcal{D})$ *constitutes an* $(n, t)-\mathsf{star}$ *in the graph* $\overline{G}$ *and hence* $(C, \mathcal{D})$ *constitutes an* $(n, t)-\mathsf{star}$ *in the graph* G.

Proof Let the algorithm output $(C, \mathcal{D})$. We wish to show that it constitutes an $(n, t)-\mathsf{star}$ in the graph $\overline{G}$. It is easy to see that $|C| \geq n - 2t$ and $|\mathcal{D}| \geq n - t$ hold. Moreover, $C \subseteq \mathcal{D}$ holds as well. This is because the set B *only* consists of nodes from the set V_M and hence the set $\mathcal{D}$ *excludes* nodes only from the set V_M. As a result, $V - V_M \subseteq \mathcal{D}$. Since $C \subseteq V - V_M$, it follows that $C \subseteq \mathcal{D}$ holds. Finally, we show that for every $v_i \in C$ and every $v_j \in \mathcal{D}$, the edge (v_i, v_j) is *not* present in $\overline{G}$.

On contrary, let the edge (v_i, v_j) be present in $\overline{G}$. From the construction of C, it follows that $v_i \in V - V_M$. Similarly, from the construction of $\mathcal{D}$, it follows that $v_j \notin B$. If $(v_i, v_j) \in \overline{E}$ and $v_j \notin B$, then it implies that $v_j \in V - V_M$ (otherwise, if $v_j \in V_M$ and if $(v_i, v_j) \in \overline{E}$ then $v_j \in B$ and hence $v_j \notin \mathcal{D}$, which is a contradiction). Now if both $v_i, v_j \in V - V_M$, then one can add the edge (v_i, v_j) to the matching M and get a larger matching, implying that the matching M is *not* the maximum matching, which is a contradiction. Hence the edge (v_i, v_j) is *not* present in $\overline{G}$, completing the proof. □

Lemma 6.9 ([20]) *Let* $G = (V, E)$ *be an undirected graph where* $|V| = n$. *If there exists a clique* $\mathcal{K}$ *of size at least* $n - t$ *in* G, *then the algorithm outputs an* $(n, t)-\mathsf{star}$ $(C, \mathcal{D})$, *such that* $|C \cap \mathcal{K}| \geq n - 2t$.

Proof Let $\mathcal{K}$ be a clique of size at least $n - t$ in the graph. This implies that the vertices in $\mathcal{K}$ constitute an *independent set*, say $\mathcal{I}$, in the graph $\overline{G}$, where $\mathcal{I} = \mathcal{K}$. We show that the sets C and $\mathcal{D}$ computed in the algorithm will have size at least $n - 2t$ and $n - t$ respectively. Consequently, the algorithm will output $(C, \mathcal{D})$, which from Lemma 6.8 will constitute an $(n, t)-\mathsf{star}$ in the graph G. While proving that $|C| \geq n - 2t$, we will also show that there will be *at most* t nodes from $\mathcal{I}$, which *may not* belong to C; i.e. $|\mathcal{I} - C| \leq t$. This will imply that $|C \cap \mathcal{I}| \geq n - 2t$, which further implies that $|C \cap \mathcal{K}| \geq n - 2t$.

We first show that $|C| \geq n - 2t$. Let $\overline{\mathcal{I}} \stackrel{def}{=} V - \mathcal{I}$. Since $|\mathcal{I}| \geq n - t$, it follows that $|\overline{\mathcal{I}}| \leq t$. Let F be the set of nodes from $\mathcal{I}$, which "fail" to make it to the set C. That is, $F \stackrel{def}{=} \mathcal{I} - C$. We will now show that $|F| \leq |\overline{\mathcal{I}}|$. Since $|\overline{\mathcal{I}}| \leq t$, it follows that the following will hold:

$$|C| \geq |\mathcal{I}| - |F| \geq n - 2t.$$

Moreover, the above will imply that in $\overline{G}$, the condition $|C \cap \mathcal{I}| \geq n - 2t$ holds, which further implies that $|C \cap \mathcal{K}| \geq n - 2t$ holds.

In order to show that $|F| \leq |\overline{\mathcal{I}}|$, we will show an *injective* mapping $\phi : F \rightarrow \overline{\mathcal{I}}$ from the set F to the set $\overline{\mathcal{I}}$. The mapping ϕ is defined as follows: consider an *arbitrary* node $v_i \in F$, implying that $v_i \in \mathcal{I}$, but $v_i \notin C$. Since $v_i \notin C$, this further implies that there are *two* possible cases, depending upon whether $v_i \in V_M$ or $v_i \in V_T$.[13] The image $\phi(v_i)$ is defined as follows, depending upon these two cases as follows.

- **Case I** — $v_i \in V_M$: in this case, we define $\phi(v_i)$ to be the node which is matched to v_i with respect to M. That is, let $(v_i, v_j) \in M$. Then we define $\phi(v_i) = v_j$. It is easy to see that indeed $v_j \in \overline{\mathcal{I}}$. On *contrary*, if $v_j \in \mathcal{I}$, then it implies that we have the edge (v_i, v_j) present in the graph $\overline{G}$ where *both* $v_i, v_j \in \mathcal{I}$, which is a *contradiction*, since $\mathcal{I}$ constitutes an *independent set* in $\overline{G}$.
- **Case II** — $v_i \in V_T$: in this case, as per the definition of V_T, there exist nodes v_j, v_k, such that the edges (v_i, v_j), (v_i, v_k) and (v_j, v_k) are present in the graph $\overline{G}$, with the edge $(v_j, v_k) \in M$. In this case, we arbitrarily define $\phi(v_i) = v_j$. It is easy to see that even in this case, $v_j \in \overline{\mathcal{I}}$, due to the same reason as for the previous case.

We next proceed to show that the mapping ϕ is an *injective* mapping. For this, consider a pair of *arbitrary, distinct* nodes $v_l, v_m \in F$, implying that $v_l, v_m \in (V_M \cup V_T)$. We wish to show that $\phi(v_l) \neq \phi(v_m)$. For this, we consider the following *three* possible cases.

- **Case i** — $v_l, v_m \in V_M$: In this case, as per the definition of ϕ, the edges $(v_l, \phi(v_l)), (v_m, \phi(v_m)) \in M$. So clearly $\phi(v_l) \neq \phi(v_m)$, since M constitutes a *matching*.
- **Case ii** — $v_l \in V_M$ **and** $v_m \in V_T$: In this case, from the definition of V_T, there exists an edge between v_m and the node matched to $\phi(v_m)$ with respect to M. Let $\phi(v_l) = \phi(v_m)$. Since $v_l \in V_M$, as per the definition of ϕ, the node matched to $\phi(v_l)$ with respect to M is the node v_l. This implies that the node $\phi(v_m)$ (which is assumed to be the same as $\phi(v_l)$) is matched to the node v_l with respect to M. Now since there exists an edge between v_m and the node matched to $\phi(v_m)$ (which turned out to be v_l), it follows that the edge (v_l, v_m) is present in $\overline{G}$. However, this is a *contradiction*, since both $v_l, v_m \in F$, implying $v_l, v_m \in \mathcal{I}$ and hence the edge (v_l, v_m) *does not* in $\overline{G}$.
- **Case iii** — $v_l, v_m \in V_T$: Let $\phi(v_l) = \phi(v_m)$. Let v_a be the node matched to $\phi(v_m)$ with respect to M. That is, the edge $(v_a, \phi(v_m)) \in M$. Then as per the definition of V_T, *both* v_l and v_m are neighbours of *both* $\phi(m)$ and v_a. That is, the edges $(v_l, \phi(v_m)), (v_l, v_a), (v_m, \phi(v_m))$ and (v_m, v_a) are all present in $\overline{G}$. However, in this case the matching M is *not* a maximum matching, since the matching $M - \{(\phi(v_m), v_a)\} \cup \{(\phi(v_m), v_l), (v_a, v_m)\}$ constitutes a larger matching, which is a contradiction. □

The above three cases with respect to v_l and v_m are demonstrated in Fig 6.15.

To complete the proof, it remains to show that $|\mathcal{D}| \geq n-t$. Recall that $\mathcal{D} = V - B$. We show that $|B| \leq |M|$. Since $\overline{G}$ contains an independent set $\mathcal{I}$ of size at least $n-t$, it follows that $|M| \leq t$. Consequently, $|\mathcal{D}| = |V| - |B| \geq n - |M| \geq n - t$.

Recall that B is the set of all matched nodes, which have neighbours in C in the graph $\overline{G}$. To show that $|B| \leq |M|$, we show that *at most* one of the end-points of every edge $(v_a, v_b) \in M$ will be in B. On *contrary*, let *both* v_a and v_b are in B, implying that *both* v_a and v_b have neighbours in C. Let v_c and v_d be the neighbours

[13] Recall that $C \stackrel{def}{=} (V - V_M) - V_T$.

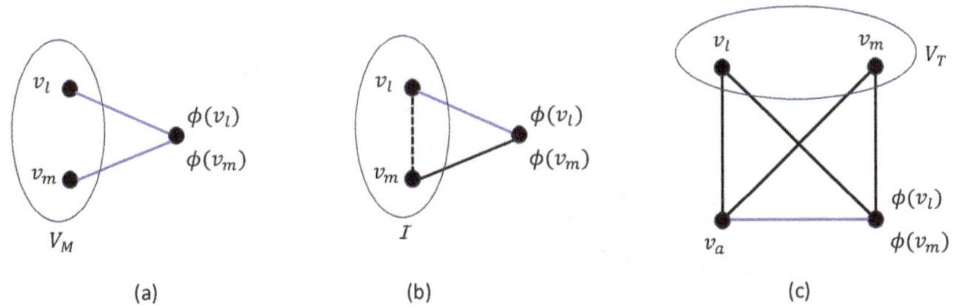

Fig. 6.15: Demonstration of the proof that the mapping ϕ defined in the proof of Lemma 6.9 indeed constitutes an injective mapping for all three cases. Figure (a) denotes the case when *both* v_l and v_m are from the set V_M, implying that the edges $(v_l, \phi(v_l))$ and $(v_m, \phi(v_m))$ are part of the matching M, as indicated by blue colour. Then if $\phi(v_l) = \phi(v_m)$ we get a contradiction since the end-points of all the edges in a matching are distinct. Figure (b) denotes the case when $v_l \in V_M$ and $v_m \in V_T$. In this case the node $\phi(v_l)$ is matched to the node v_l and the edge $(v_l, \phi(v_l))$ is a part of the matching M as indicated in blue colour. Since v_m is a triangle head, the edge $(v_m, \phi(v_m))$ is present in $\overline{G}$ and v_m will *also* be adjacent to the node matched to $\phi(v_m)$ with respect to M. Then if $\phi(v_l) = \phi(v_m)$, it implies that the edge (v_l, v_m) is present in $\overline{G}$, which is a contradiction since *both* v_l and v_m are part of the independent set I. Figure (c) denotes the case when both v_l and v_m are triangle heads. In this case, the edges $(v_l, \phi(v_l))$ and (v_l, v_a) are present in $\overline{G}$, where the node $\phi(v_l)$ is matched to v_a with respect to M and hence the edge $(v_a, \phi(v_l))$ is part of the matching M as indicated in blue colour. Since v_m is a triangle head, the edge $(v_m, \phi(v_m))$ is present in $\overline{G}$. And if $\phi(v_l) = \phi(v_m)$, then we also have the edge (v_m, v_a) present in $\overline{G}$. But this leads to a contradiction that M is the maximum matching, since the matching $M - \{(\phi(v_m), v_a)\} \cup \{(\phi(v_m), v_l), (v_a, v_m)\}$ constitutes a *larger* matching

of v_a and v_b respectively in C. Note that $v_c \neq v_d$. On the contrary, if $v_c = v_d$, then v_c constitutes a triangle head, which is a *contradiction*, since $v_c \in C$ and hence $v_c \notin V_T$. However, if $v_c \neq v_d$, then the matching M is *not* a maximum matching, since the matching $M - \{(v_a, v_b)\} \cup \{(v_a, v_c), (v_b, v_d)\}$ constitutes a *larger* matching in $\overline{G}$ which is a *contradiction*. For a pictorial depiction of the above argument, see Fig 6.16.

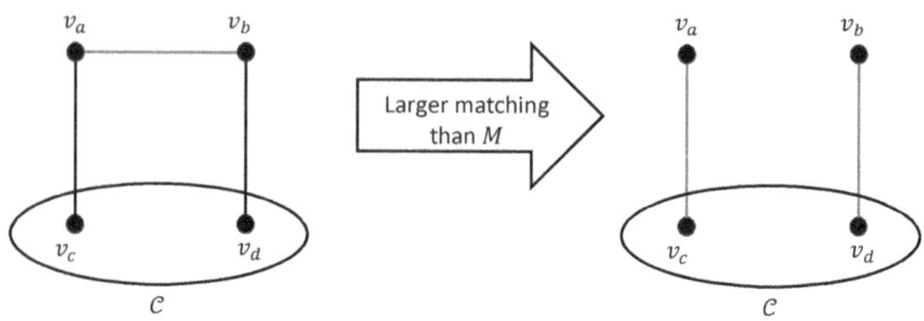

Fig. 6.16: Demonstration of the proof that for every edge $(v_a, v_b) \in M$ (shown in blue colour), *at most* one of the end-points will have a neighbour in C in $\overline{G}$. On the contrary, if both v_a and v_b have neighbours in C, say v_c and v_d respectively, then the matching M is not a maximum matching. This is because $v_c \neq v_d$ (otherwise, v_c is a triangle head, which is *not* possible) and hence the matching $M - \{(v_a, v_b)\} \cup \{(v_a, v_c), (v_b, v_d)\}$ constitutes a *larger* matching, as shown in blue colour

6.4.5.2 Protocol $\Pi^{(n,t)}_{\mathsf{WarmUp}}$ with Polynomial Computation Complexity Using (n, t)−star

In this section, we will now see how to modify the protocol $\Pi^{(n,t)}_{\mathsf{WarmUp}}$ (see Fig 6.3) so that it requires only a *polynomial* amount of computation.[14] Recall that the main bottleneck in the protocol $\Pi^{(n,t)}_{\mathsf{WarmUp}}$ is that the parties *may* need to perform an *exponential* amount of computation to check for the presence of a *clique* of size at least $n-t$ to find a candidate CORE set. Instead, we now look for an (n, t)−star in the *consistency graph* by using the algorithm AlgStar, which requires only a *polynomial* amount of computation. If *no* (n, t)−star is found then clearly the sender S is *corrupt*, and the parties can discard the sender. This is because for an *honest* S, the set of *honest* parties will constitute a *clique* of size at least $n - t$ in the consistency graph and consequently, *some* (n, t)−star will be obtained and hence an *honest* sender will be *never* discarded.

Now suppose an (n, t)−star $(C, \mathcal{D})$ is *found* in the consistency graph. Then, how do we compute the set of CORE parties from C and $\mathcal{D}$? We observe that since $(C, \mathcal{D})$ constitutes an (n, t)−star, we can claim that *all honest* parties in C have received the *same* codeword from the sender. This is because the codeword of each *honest* party in C is pair-wise consistent with the codewords of each *honest* party in

[14] Once this is achieved, then we can always use the idea used in the protocol $\Pi^{(n,t)}_{\mathsf{GenWarmUp}}$ to get a full-fledged domain extension protocol with polynomial computation cost.

$\mathcal{D}$ and there are at least $|\mathcal{D}| - t \geq t + 1$ *honest* parties in $\mathcal{D}$, since $|\mathcal{D}| \geq n - t$. Let $\mathsf{C} = (\mathsf{C}_1, \ldots, \mathsf{C}_n)$ be the *common* codeword received by the *honest* parties in C from the sender. Unfortunately, the set C *may not* be sufficiently large to be considered as a candidate CORE. This is because we *require* the set CORE to *have at least* $n - t$ parties, which *need not* be the case since $|C| \geq n - 2t$.

What about the set $\mathcal{D}$? Can it be considered as a candidate CORE set, given that it has size *at least* $n - t$? Unfortunately, the answer is *no*. This is because it is *not* guaranteed that *all honest* parties in $\mathcal{D}$ have received the same codeword from S, which is the central requirement of the CORE set. The above shortcoming is because as per the properties of an (n, t)−star, it is *not* guaranteed that the parties in $\mathcal{D}$ constitute a clique.

To hunt for a candidate CORE from an (n, t)−star $(C, \mathcal{D})$, we look for *additional* (honest) parties who have also received the codeword C from the sender and keep adding those parties in C and check if the "expanded" C achieves a size of at least $n - t$, in which case it can be set as the candidate CORE set. The idea here is that if the sender is *honest*, then *all honest* parties would have received the *same* codeword from the sender, and there are at least $n - t$ such parties. So if we look for additional parties as above, then every honest party who *could not* make it to the set C initially will be finally included in the *expanded* C, which will take up a cardinality of at least $n - t$. The next question is how do we look for those "additional" parties and how do we "expand" the set C?

To *expand* the star (n, t)−star $(C, \mathcal{D})$, we follow a somewhat non-intuitive approach, which requires *two* stages. In the *first* stage, we expand the set $\mathcal{D}$ by computing a set $\mathcal{F}$, which includes all those parties which are adjacent to at least $t + 1$ parties from the set C in the consistency graph. Notice that all the parties in $\mathcal{D}$ will *satisfy* the above condition and get included in the set $\mathcal{F}$. What can we claim about the codeword of the *honest* parties in $\mathcal{F}$, received from the sender? We can claim that for *any honest* party $P_k \in \mathcal{F}$, the kth component of its codeword is the same as C_k. Why? This is because P_k is guaranteed to have an edge with *at least* one *honest* party P_i in C, implying a pairwise consistency between the kth component of P_i's and P_k's respective codewords. And the kth component of P_i's codeword is C_k.

Once the set $\mathcal{F}$ is computed, we next compute a set $\mathcal{E}$, which includes all those parties which are adjacent to at least $2t + 1$ parties from the set $\mathcal{F}$ in the consistency graph. Notice that all the parties in C will *satisfy* the above condition and get included in the set $\mathcal{E}$, since the parties in $\mathcal{D}$ are *guaranteed* to be present in $\mathcal{F}$. What can we claim about the codeword of the *honest* parties in $\mathcal{E}$, received from the sender? We can claim that for *any honest* party $P_k \in \mathcal{E}$, the codeword it received from the sender is the *same* as C. While this is *obviously true* if P_k makes its way to $\mathcal{E}$ from C, why it is true even for the "new" parties who were *not* present in C but are *present* in $\mathcal{E}$? This is because P_k is adjacent to at least $t + 1$ *honest* parties in $\mathcal{F}$, implying pairwise consistency of P_k's codeword components with the respective components of those $t + 1$ *honest* parties. However, the respective components of those $t + 1$ honest parties define C, implying that P_k's codeword is also C.

One may wonder what goes *wrong* if we proceed to "directly" expand the set C to set $\mathcal{E}$, *without* computing the "intermediate" set $\mathcal{F}$ (which can be considered as the "expanded" version of $\mathcal{D}$)? That is, we include those parties in $\mathcal{E}$, which are adjacent to at least $2t + 1$ parties in $\mathcal{D}$. The problem is, in that case, it is *not* guaranteed that any *new* party "qualifies" to be included in $\mathcal{E}$ and *only* the parties in C may end up making it to $\mathcal{E}$, resulting in $\mathcal{E} = C$. And this *can* happen even if the sender is *honest*, since it is *not* guaranteed that *all honest* parties will be present in $\mathcal{D}$. We leave proving this claim as an exercise for the readers. However, by first expanding the set $\mathcal{D}$ to $\mathcal{F}$, we are ensuring that *all honest* parties make it to $\mathcal{F}$, provided sender has behaved *honestly*. This central idea constitutes the *crux* of the protocol and is based on subtle observations related to the working of the algorithm AlgStar.

In more detail, if the sender behaves *honestly*, then the algorithm AlgStar will output an (n, t)−star $(C, \mathcal{D})$ such that the set C will have at least $t + 1$ *honest* parties, *irrespective* of the edges between the corrupt and honest parties in the *consistency graph*. This is because the set of *honest* parties will constitute a clique of size at least $n - t$ in the consistency graph of the honest parties. Hence, from Lemma 6.9, there will be at least $n - 2t \geq t + 1$ parties from this clique of *honest* parties, which will *make* it to the set C during the algorithm AlgStar. Now, since the set of honest parties forms a clique, it follows that every *honest* party who could *not* make it to $\mathcal{D}$ will now make it to $\mathcal{F}$, since they will be adjacent to at least $t + 1$ (honest) parties in C. And once *all* honest parties make it to $\mathcal{F}$, it will be guaranteed that all honest parties who *could not* make it to C, make it to $\mathcal{E}$, provided sender has behaved *honestly*.

After computing the set $\mathcal{E}$ if its size turns out to be at least $n - t$ (which we show will happen if the sender behaves *honestly*), then it is taken as the CORE set, and after that, the rest of the protocol steps remain the same. Otherwise, the sender is *corrupt*, in which case the parties publicly *discard* the sender and take a default output on behalf of the sender. The modified protocol called $\Pi_{\mathsf{ModWarmUp}}^{(n,t)}$ (where Mod stands for modified) is presented in Fig 6.17.

Protocol $\Pi_{\mathsf{ModWarmUp}}^{(n,t)}(m, L)$

Public input: the description of $(n, t+1, t)$-RS error-correcting code over $\mathbb{F}$ with encoding and decoding algorithms RSEncode and RSDecode respectively and the description of the algorithm AlgStar. Additionally, the parties have oracle access to a bit-BB oracle.

- **Round 1(codeword distribution)**: S on having the input $m \in \{0, 1\}^L$, does the following.
  - Divide m into blocks $m_0, \ldots, m_t$ consisting of $\log |\mathbb{F}|$ bits. Let $M_0, \ldots, M_t \in \mathbb{F}$ be the elements from $\mathbb{F}$, represented by the bit-string $m_0, \ldots, m_t$ respectively.
  - Let $M \stackrel{def}{=} (M_0, \ldots, M_t)$. Compute $\mathsf{RSEncode}(M, n, t + 1, t) := C$, where $C = (C_1, \ldots, C_n) \in \mathbb{F}^n$.
  - For $i = 1, \ldots, n$, send C to party P_i.
- **Round 2 (pairwise consistency check)**: Every party $P_i \in \mathcal{P}$ (including S) does the following.
  - Let $C^{(i)} = (C_1^{(i)}, \ldots, C_n^{(i)}) \in \mathbb{F}^n$ denote the RS codeword received by P_i from S. If no codeword is received from S by the end of the previous round or if $C^{(i)}$ is *not* a valid RS codeword, then set $C^{(i)} := (0, \ldots, 0(n \text{ times}))$.[a]
  - For $j = 1, \ldots, n$, send $(C_i^{(i)}, C_j^{(i)})$ to party P_j.
- **Round 3 (public announcement of the status of pairwise consistency checks)**: Every party $P_i \in \mathcal{P}$ (including S) does the following.
  - For $j = 1, \ldots, n$, upon receiving $(C_j^{(j)}, C_i^{(j)})$ from party P_j, set the bit $V_{i,j}$ to 1, if and only if the following holds.

$$(C_j^{(j)} = C_j^{(i)}) \wedge (C_i^{(j)} = C_i^{(i)})$$

If no $(C_j^{(j)}, C_i^{(j)})$ is received from P_j then set $V_{i,j} := 0$.

- Let $V_i \stackrel{def}{=} (V_{i,1}, \ldots, V_{i,n}) \in \{0,1\}^n$ denote the Boolean *response vector* of P_i.
- Publicly broadcast the vector V_i. For this, act as a sender and make n calls to the bit-BB oracle, where the input for the jth call is the bit $V_{i,j}$.

- **(checking for the existence of CORE set)**: Every party $P_i \in \mathcal{P}$ (including S) does the following.
  - For $j, k = 1, \ldots, n$, let $V'_{j,k} \in \{0,1\}$ be the output from the kth calls to the bit-BB oracle made by P_j as a sender and let $V'_j \stackrel{def}{=} (V'_{j,1}, \ldots, V'_{j,n})$.
  - Construct an undirected *consistency graph* $G^{(i)}$ over the set of vertices $\{P_1, \ldots, P_n\}$, where the edge (P_j, P_k) is added to $G^{(i)}$ if and only if $V'_{j,k} = V'_{k,j} = 1$
  - Run the algorithm AlgStar$(G^{(i)})$. If AlgStar$(G^{(i)})$ outputs "*star not found*", then discard S, output 0^L and terminate, else continue as follows.
    - Let $(C, \mathcal{D})$ be the (n,t)−star obtained from the algorithm AlgStar$(G^{(i)})$.
    - Let $\mathcal{F}$ be the parties which are adjacent to at least $t+1$ parties in C. That is:

$$\mathcal{F} \stackrel{def}{=} \{P_k \mid \text{there exist at least } t{+}1 \text{ parties } P_j \in C, \text{ such that } (P_j, P_k) \in G^{(i)}\}$$

    - Let $\mathcal{E}$ be the parties which are adjacent to at least $2t+1$ parties in $\mathcal{F}$. That is:

$$\mathcal{E} \stackrel{def}{=} \{P_k \mid \text{there exist at least } 2t{+}1 \text{ parties } P_j \in \mathcal{F}, \text{ where } (P_j, P_k) \in G^{(i)}\}$$

    - If $|\mathcal{E}| < n - t$, then discard S, output 0^L and terminate, else set CORE = $\mathcal{E}$.

- **Round 4 (obtaining the common codeword held by the honest parties in CORE)**: Every party $P_i \in \mathcal{P}$ (including S) does the following.
  - Let $\mathsf{C}_i \stackrel{def}{=}$ Majority$(\{C_i^{(j)}\}_{P_j \in \text{CORE}})$, where Majority$(\cdot)$ denotes the *majority* function and where $C_i^{(j)}$ has been received from P_j during **Round 2**.[b]
  - For $j = 1, \ldots, n$, send C_i to every party P_j.
- **(Output computation and termination)**
  - Let $C^\star \stackrel{def}{=} (C_1^\star, \ldots, C_n^\star)$, where $C_j^\star$ is received from P_j, for $j = 1, \ldots, n$.[c]
  - Let RSDecode$(C^\star, n, t+1, t) := M^\star = (M_0^\star, \ldots, M_t^\star) \in \mathbb{F}^{t+1}$. Let $m_0^\star, \ldots, m_t^\star$ be the bit-string representing the elements $M_0^\star, \ldots, M_t^\star$ respectively.
  - Output $m^\star \stackrel{def}{=} m_0^\star || \ldots || m_t^\star$ where $||$ denotes the concatenation operation and terminate.

[a] To check if $(C_1^{(i)}, \ldots, C_n^{(i)})$ is a valid codeword, P_i can check if the points $\{(\alpha_j, C_j^{(i)})\}_{j=1,\ldots,n}$ lie on a t-degree polynomial.

[b] If no $C_i^{(j)}$ has been received from P_j then set $C_i^{(j)} := 0$.

[c] If no $C_j^\star$ is received from P_j then set $C_j^\star := 0$.

Fig. 6.17: The modified warmup protocol for domain extension where $L = (t+1)\log|\mathbb{F}|$ bits

For a demonstration of protocol $\Pi_{\mathsf{ModWarmUp}}^{(n,t)}$, see Fig 6.18, where we consider the case when S is *honest* and show that an $\mathcal{E}$ set satisfying the requirements of CORE will be indeed computed.

Most of the properties of the protocol $\Pi_{\mathsf{ModWarmUp}}^{(n,t)}$ follow from the properties of the protocol $\Pi_{\mathsf{WarmUp}}^{(n,t)}$, provided the set $\mathcal{E}$ computed in the protocol indeed constitutes

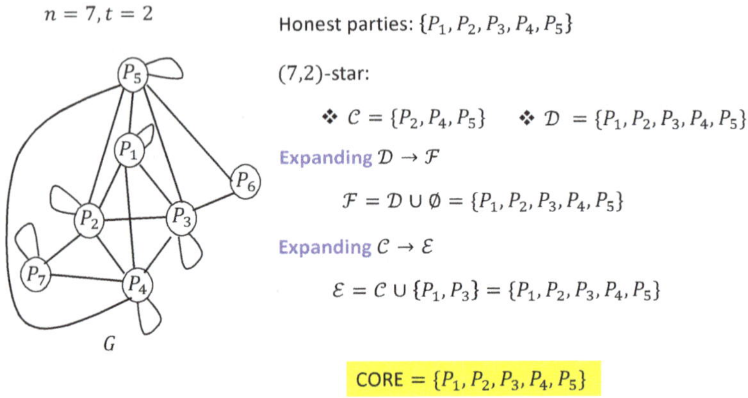

Fig. 6.18: Demonstration of the expansion of an (n, t)−star $(C, \mathcal{D})$ to sets $\mathcal{F}$ and $\mathcal{E}$. We consider the case when $n = 7$ and $t = 2$ and the honest parties being $\{P_1, \ldots, P_5\}$ and the set $\{P_6, P_7\}$ being the corrupt set of parties, with P_1 being the sender S. The algorithm AlgStar outputs the (n, t)−star $(C, \mathcal{D})$ where $C = \{P_2, P_4, P_5\}$ and $\mathcal{D} = \{P_1, P_2, P_3, P_4, P_5\}$. Clearly, all honest parties are *not* in C. The set $\mathcal{F}$ is the same as $\mathcal{D}$ and the set $\mathcal{E} = \{P_1, P_2, P_3, P_4, P_5\}$, with P_1 and P_3 now getting newly added to $\mathcal{E}$

a candidate CORE, so we proceed to prove the same. We first show that if S is *honest*, then all honest parties will compute a CORE set.

Lemma 6.10 *In protocol* $\Pi^{(n,t)}_{\mathsf{ModWarmUp}}$, *if* S *is honest, then all honest parties will compute a* CORE *set, where* $|\mathsf{CORE}| \geq n - t$, *such that all honest parties in* CORE *receive the same codeword from* S *during* **Round 1**.

Proof Let $\mathcal{H}$ be the set of *honest* parties. Let $\mathsf{S} \in \mathcal{H}$. Then from the proof of Claim 6.1, the set of parties $\mathcal{H}$ constitute a clique in the consistency graph $G^{(i)}$ of every party $P_i \in \mathcal{H}$. Moreover, the consistency graph $G^{(i)}$ will be the *same* for every party $P_i \in \mathcal{H}$. Let us denote this *common* consistency graph as G. Since $|\mathcal{H}| \geq n - t$, from Lemma 6.9 by substituting $\mathcal{K} = \mathcal{H}$, algorithm AlgStar will output an (n, t)−star $(C, \mathcal{D})$ for every party in $\mathcal{H}$, such that $|C \cap \mathcal{H}| \geq n - 2t \geq t + 1$. Let $\mathcal{H}_C$ be the set of *honest* parties in C; i.e. $\mathcal{H}_C \overset{def}{=} (C \cap \mathcal{H})$. As shown above, we have $|\mathcal{H}_C| \geq t + 1$. We also note that since S is *honest*, every party in $\mathcal{H}$ and hence $\mathcal{H}_C$ have received the codeword $C = (C_1, \ldots, C_n)$ from S during **Round 1**.

We next claim that *all* parties in $\mathcal{H}$ will be present in $\mathcal{F}$. So consider an *arbitrary* $P_k \in \mathcal{H}$. Then, there are two possible cases for P_k.

- **Case I** — $P_k \in \mathcal{D}$: In this case, from the definition of (n, t)−star, the edge (P_j, P_k) is present in the consistency graph G, for *every* $P_j \in C$. Now since

$|C| \geq n - 2t \geq t + 1$, from the definition of $\mathcal{F}$ it follows that P_k will be included in the set $\mathcal{F}$.

- **Case II** — $P_k \notin \mathcal{D}$: Since the parties in $\mathcal{H}$ constitute a clique in the consistency graph G, it follows that the edge (P_j, P_k) is present in the consistency graph G, for *every* $P_j \in C_{\mathcal{H}}$. Now since $|C_{\mathcal{H}}| \geq t + 1$, from the definition of $\mathcal{F}$ it follows that P_k will be included in the set $\mathcal{F}$ in this case as well.

We next show that *all* parties in $\mathcal{H}$ will be present in $\mathcal{E}$, which will complete the proof since $|\mathcal{H}| \geq n - t$ and since the parties in $\mathcal{H}$ set $\mathcal{E}$ as the set CORE. So consider an *arbitrary* $P_k \in \mathcal{H}$. Since the parties in $\mathcal{H}$ constitute a clique in the graph G and since we have shown that $\mathcal{H} \subseteq \mathcal{F}$, it follows that there are at least $n - t \geq 2t + 1$ parties P_j in $\mathcal{F}$, such that the edge (P_j, P_k) is present in the consistency graph G. Consequently, from the definition of $\mathcal{E}$, party P_k will be included in $\mathcal{E}$. □

We next show that if a *corrupt* S is *not* discarded, then the *honest* parties compute a CORE set of size at least $n - t$, such that *all honest* parties in CORE receive a common RS codeword from S during **Round 1**.

Lemma 6.11 *In protocol* $\Pi^{(n,t)}_{\mathsf{ModWarmUp}}$, *if* S *is corrupt and not discarded, then all honest parties compute a* CORE *set, where all honest parties in* CORE *receive a common RS codeword from* S *during* **Round 1**.

Proof Let S be *corrupt* and let $\mathcal{H}$ be the set of *honest* parties where $|\mathcal{H}| \geq n - t$. From Claim 6.3, all the parties in $\mathcal{H}$ will have the *same* consistency graph, say G. Consequently, *all* the parties in $\mathcal{H}$ will compute the *same* (n, t)−star, say $(C, \mathcal{D})$ and the corresponding sets $\mathcal{F}$ and $\mathcal{E}$. If S is *not* discarded then it implies that $|\mathcal{E}| \geq n - t$ and the parties in $\mathcal{H}$ set $\mathcal{E}$ as CORE. Let $\mathcal{H}_{\mathcal{E}}$ be the set of *honest* parties in $\mathcal{E}$; i.e. $\mathcal{H}_{\mathcal{E}} = (\mathcal{E} \cap \mathcal{H})$. We wish to show that all the parties in $\mathcal{H}_{\mathcal{E}}$ received a *common* RS codeword from S during **Round 1**.

Let $\mathcal{H}_C = (C \cap \mathcal{H})$ be the set of *honest* parties in C and $\mathcal{H}_{\mathcal{D}} = (\mathcal{D} \cap \mathcal{H})$ be the set of *honest* parties in $\mathcal{D}$. Note that $|\mathcal{H}_{\mathcal{D}}| \geq |\mathcal{D}| - t \geq t + 1$. This is because $(C, \mathcal{D})$ constitutes an (n, t)−star and hence $|\mathcal{D}| \geq n - t$. We first claim that *all* the parties in $\mathcal{H}_C$ received a *common* RS codeword from S during **Round 1**. So consider an *arbitrary* pair of *distinct* parties $P_i, P_j \in \mathcal{H}_C$ and an *arbitrary* party $P_k \in \mathcal{H}_{\mathcal{D}}$. Since $(C, \mathcal{D})$ constitute an (n, t)−star, it follows that the edges (P_i, P_k) and (P_j, P_k) are present in the graph G. This further implies that the outputs $V'_{i,k}$ and $V'_{j,k}$ received as output from the respective calls to the bit-BB oracle are 1. Since both P_i and P_j are *honest*, it follows that $V'_{i,k} = V_{i,k}$ and $V'_{j,k} = V_{j,k}$. Hence $V_{i,k} = V_{j,k} = 1$.

Since $V_{i,k} = 1$, it follows that the following holds.

$$C^{(k)}_k = C^{(i)}_k,$$

where $C^{(k)}$ denotes the RS codeword received by P_k from S during **Round 1**. Similarly, since $V_{j,k} = 1$, it follows that the following holds as well.

$$C^{(k)}_k = C^{(j)}_k$$

Now, based on the above two conditions, it follows that $C_k^{(i)} = C_k^{(j)}$ holds. Since P_k above is an *arbitrary* party from the set $\mathcal{H}_\mathcal{D}$ and $|\mathcal{H}_\mathcal{D}| \geq t+1$ and since the parameter K for the RS code is set to $t+1$, from Lemma 6.3 and Lemma 6.4 it follows that *all* the parties in $\mathcal{H}_C$ have received the *same* RS codeword from S during **Round 1**. That is, $C^{(i)} = C^{(j)}$ holds for every $P_i, P_j \in \mathcal{H}_C$. Let $\mathsf{C} = (\mathsf{C}_1, \ldots, \mathsf{C}_n)$ be the *common* RS codeword received by the parties in $\mathcal{H}_C$ from S. That is, $C^{(i)} = C^{(j)} = \mathsf{C}$ for *every* $P_i, P_j \in \mathcal{H}_C$.

Let $\mathcal{H}_\mathcal{F} = (\mathcal{F} \cap \mathcal{H})$ be the set of *honest* parties in $\mathcal{F}$. We next claim that for *every* $P_k \in \mathcal{H}_\mathcal{F}$, the kth component $C_k^{(k)}$ of the RS codeword $C^{(k)}$ received by P_k from S during **Round 1** is the *same* as C_k. So consider an *arbitrary* party $P_k \in \mathcal{H}_\mathcal{F}$. Let V_k be the set of parties from C, such that the edge (P_j, P_k) is present in the graph G for *every* $P_j \in V_k$. Then from the definition of $\mathcal{F}$, it follows that $|V_k| \geq t+1$. This further implies that $|(\mathcal{H}_C \cap V_k)| \geq 1$. Let $P_j \in (\mathcal{H}_C \cap V_k)$, implying that the edge (P_j, P_k) is present in the graph G. This further implies that the output $V'_{j,k}$ received from the respective call to the bit-BB oracle is 1. Since P_j is *honest*, it follows that $V'_{j,k} = V_{j,k} = 1$. Since $V_{j,k} = 1$, it follows that the following holds.

$$C_k^{(k)} = C_k^{(j)} = \mathsf{C}_k.$$

Let $\mathcal{H}_\mathcal{E} = (\mathcal{E} \cap \mathcal{H})$ be the set of *honest* parties in $\mathcal{E}$. We next claim that *all* the parties in $\mathcal{E}$ received the RS codeword C from S during **Round 1**, which will complete the proof of the lemma. So consider an *arbitrary* party $P_k \in \mathcal{E}_\mathcal{H}$. Let $\mathcal{V}_k$ be the set of parties from $\mathcal{F}$, such that the edge (P_j, P_k) is present in the graph G for *every* $P_j \in \mathcal{V}_k$. Then from from the definition of $\mathcal{E}$, it follows that $|\mathcal{V}_k| \geq 2t+1$. This further implies that $|(\mathcal{H}_\mathcal{F} \cap \mathcal{V}_k)| \geq t+1$. Now consider an *arbitrary* $P_j \in (\mathcal{H}_\mathcal{F} \cap \mathcal{V}_k)$, implying that the edge (P_j, P_k) is present in the graph G. This further implies that the output $V'_{j,k}$ received from the corresponding call to the bit-BB oracle is 1. Since P_j is *honest*, it follows that $V'_{j,k} = V_{j,k} = 1$. Since $V_{j,k} = 1$, it follows that the following holds.

$$C_k^{(k)} = C_k^{(j)}.$$

However, we have already shown above that $C_k^{(j)} = \mathsf{C}_k$. Consequently, the following holds.

$$C_k^{(k)} = \mathsf{C}_k.$$

Since P_j is an *arbitrary* party from $(\mathcal{H}_\mathcal{F} \cap \mathcal{V}_k)$ and $|(\mathcal{H}_\mathcal{F} \cap \mathcal{V}_k)| \geq t+1$, from Lemma 6.3 and Lemma 6.4 it follows that the codeword $C^{(k)}$ received by P_k from S during **Round 1** is the same as C. □

The proof of Theorem 6.4 is exactly the same as that of Theorem 6.3, except that we now rely on Lemma 6.10 and Lemma 6.11 to argue about the properties of CORE set for an *honest* and *corrupt* S respectively.

Theorem 6.4 *Let $t < \frac{n}{3}$ and let the parties have oracle access to a bit-BB oracle. Moreover let S has an input $m \in \{0,1\}^L$ for protocol $\Pi_{\mathsf{WarmUp}}^{(n,t)}$ where $L = (t +$*

1) $\log |\mathbb{F}|$. *Then protocol* $\Pi^{(n,t)}_{\mathsf{ModWarmUp}}$ *is a t-secure BB protocol with perfect security in the model* $\mathcal{M}_{\mathsf{auth}}$ *with the following complexities.*

- *The protocol requires* 4 *rounds.*
- *The seed-round complexity of the protocol is* 1.
- *The protocol incurs a communication of* $O(n^2 \log |\mathbb{F}|) + n^2 \cdot \mathcal{BC}(1)$ *bits, where* $\mathcal{BC}(1)$ *denotes the communication complexity of emulating one call to the bit-BB oracle with a single-bit input.*
- *The seed-communication complexity of the protocol is* $O(n^2)$ *bits.*
- *The computation complexity of the protocol is poly*(n, L).

On the Computation Complexity of the Protocol $\Pi^{(n,t)}_{\mathsf{ModWarmUp}}$.

What will be the computational complexity of the protocol $\Pi^{(n,t)}_{\mathsf{ModWarmUp}}$? Unlike protocol $\Pi^{(n,t)}_{\mathsf{WarmUp}}$, the parties *do not* need to check for a *clique* of size at least $n-t$ for finding a candidate CORE set. Instead, the parties need to run the algorithm AlgStar to check for the existence of a candidate CORE set. It is easy to see that the rest of the steps of the protocol $\Pi^{(n,t)}_{\mathsf{ModWarmUp}}$ also need a *polynomial* amount of computation. Hence, *unlike* the protocol $\Pi^{(n,t)}_{\mathsf{WarmUp}}$, the computation complexity of the protocol $\Pi^{(n,t)}_{\mathsf{ModWarmUp}}$ is polynomial in n and L.

6.4.5.3 The Final Domain Extension Protocol with Polynomial Computation Complexity

We now present the final domain extension protocol $\Pi^{(n,t)}_{\mathsf{PerDomExt}}$ (standing for domain extension with *perfect security*), with polynomial computation cost. In the protocol S has an input $m \in \{0,1\}^L$, where $L \geq (t+1)\log|\mathbb{F}|$. The idea behind the protocol is the same as $\Pi^{(n,t)}_{\mathsf{GenWarmUp}}$, where we now run B instances of $\Pi^{(n,t)}_{\mathsf{ModWarmUp}}$ in parallel, where $B \stackrel{def}{=} \frac{L}{(t+1)\log|\mathbb{F}|}$. Moreover, as done in the protocol $\Pi^{(n,t)}_{\mathsf{GenWarmUp}}$, each party constructs a *single* binary response vector of size n bits and makes *only* n calls to the bit-BB oracle to make public its response vector, based on which the parties construct a *single* consistency graph. The protocol is presented in Fig 6.19.

Protocol $\Pi^{(n,t)}_{\mathsf{PerDomExt}}(m, L)$

Public input: the parameter L, the description of $(n, t+1, t)$-RS error-correcting code over $\mathbb{F}$ with encoding and decoding algorithms RSEncode and RSDecode respectively and the description of the algorithm AlgStar. Additionally, the parties have oracle access to a bit-BB oracle.

- **Round 1 (codeword distribution)**: S on having the input $m \in \{0,1\}^L$, does the following.
  - Divide m into blocks $m^{(1)}, \ldots, m^{(B)}$ each of size $(t+1)\log|\mathbb{F}|$ bits, where $B \stackrel{def}{=} \frac{L}{(t+1)\log|\mathbb{F}|}$.[a]

- For $\ell = 1, \ldots, B$, further divide the block $m^{(\ell)}$ into sub-blocks $m_0^{(\ell)}, \ldots, m_t^{(\ell)}$ consisting of $\log |\mathbb{F}|$ bits each. Let $M_0^{(\ell)}, \ldots, M_t^{(\ell)} \in \mathbb{F}$ be the elements from $\mathbb{F}$, represented by the bit-string $m_0^{(\ell)}, \ldots, m_t^{(\ell)}$ respectively.
- For $\ell = 1, \ldots, B$, let $M^{(\ell)} \stackrel{def}{=} (M_0^{(\ell)}, \ldots, M_t^{(\ell)})$. Compute $\mathsf{RSEncode}(M^{(\ell)}, n, t+1, t) := C^{(\ell)}$, where $C^{(\ell)} = (C_1^{(\ell)}, \ldots, C_n^{(\ell)}) \in \mathbb{F}^n$.
- For $\ell = 1, \ldots, B$ and $i = 1, \ldots, n$, send $C^{(\ell)}$ to party P_i.

• **Round 2 (pairwise consistency check)**: Every party $P_i \in \mathcal{P}$ (including S) does the following.
  - For $\ell = 1, \ldots, B$, let $C^{(\ell,i)} = (C_1^{(\ell,i)}, \ldots, C_n^{(\ell,i)}) \in \mathbb{F}^n$ denote the RS codeword received by P_i from S. If no codeword is received from S by the end of the previous round or if $C^{(\ell,i)}$ is *not* a valid RS codeword, then set $C^{(\ell,i)} := (0, \ldots, 0(n \text{ times}))$.[b]
  - For $\ell = 1, \ldots, B$ and $j = 1, \ldots, n$, send $(C_i^{(\ell,i)}, C_j^{(\ell,i)})$ to party P_j.

• **Round 3 (public announcement of the status of pairwise consistency checks)**: Every party $P_i \in \mathcal{P}$ (including S) does the following.
  - For $\ell = 1, \ldots, B$ and $j = 1, \ldots, n$, upon receiving $(C_j^{(\ell,j)}, C_i^{(\ell,j)})$ from party P_j, set the bit $V_{i,j}$ to 1, if and only if the following holds for *each* $\ell \in \{1, \ldots, B\}$.

$$(C_j^{(\ell,j)} = C_j^{(\ell,i)}) \wedge (C_i^{(\ell,j)} = C_i^{(\ell,i)})$$

    If no $(C_j^{(\ell,j)}, C_i^{(\ell,j)})$ is received from party P_j then set $V_{i,j} := 0$.
  - Let $V_i \stackrel{def}{=} (V_{i,1}, \ldots, V_{i,n}) \in \{0,1\}^n$ denote the Boolean *response vector* of P_i.
  - Publicly broadcast the vector V_i. For this, act as a sender and make n calls to the bit-BB oracle, where the input for the jth call is the bit $V_{i,j}$.

• **(checking for the existence of CORE set)**: Every party $P_i \in \mathcal{P}$ (including S) does the following.
  - For $j, k = 1, \ldots, n$, let $V'_{j,k} \in \{0,1\}$ be the output from the kth calls to the bit-BB oracle invoked by P_j as a sender and let $V'_j \stackrel{def}{=} (V'_{j,1}, \ldots, V'_{j,n})$.
  - Construct an undirected *consistency graph* $G^{(i)}$ over the set of vertices $\{P_1, \ldots, P_n\}$, where the edge (P_j, P_k) is added to $G^{(i)}$ if and only if $V'_{j,k} = V'_{k,j} = 1$
  - Run the algorithm $\mathsf{AlgStar}(G^{(i)})$. If $\mathsf{AlgStar}(G^{(i)})$ outputs "*star not found*", then discard S, output 0^L and terminate. Else continue as follows.
    - Let $(C, \mathcal{D})$ be the (n,t)−star obtained from the algorithm $\mathsf{AlgStar}(G^{(i)})$.
    - Let $\mathcal{F}$ be the parties which are adjacent to at least $t+1$ parties in C. That is:

$$\mathcal{F} \stackrel{def}{=} \{P_k \mid \text{there exist at least } t{+}1 \text{ parties } P_j \in C, \text{ such that } (P_j, P_k) \in G^{(i)}\}$$

    - Let $\mathcal{E}$ be the parties which are adjacent to at least $2t+1$ parties in $\mathcal{F}$. That is:

$$\mathcal{E} \stackrel{def}{=} \{P_k \mid \text{there exist at least } 2t{+}1 \text{ parties } P_j \in \mathcal{F}, \text{ where } (P_j, P_k) \in G^{(i)}\}$$

    - If $|\mathcal{E}| < n - t$, then discard S, output 0^L and terminate, else set CORE $= \mathcal{E}$.

• **Round 4 (obtaining the common codeword held by the honest parties in CORE)**: Every party $P_i \in \mathcal{P}$ (including S) does the following.
  - For $\ell = 1, \ldots, B$, let $\mathsf{C}_i^{(\ell)} \stackrel{def}{=} \mathsf{Majority}(\{C_i^{(\ell,j)}\}_{P_j \in \mathsf{CORE}})$, where $\mathsf{Majority}(\cdot)$ denotes the *majority* function and where $C_i^{(\ell,j)}$ has been received from P_j during **Round 2**.[c]
  - For $\ell = 1, \ldots, B$ and $j = 1, \ldots, n$, send $\mathsf{C}_i^{(\ell)}$ to every party P_j.

• **(Output computation and termination)**: Every party $P_i \in \mathcal{P}$ (including S) does the following.

- For $\ell = 1, \ldots, B$, let $\mathsf{C}^{(\ell)} \stackrel{def}{=} (\mathsf{C}_1^{(\ell)}, \ldots, \mathsf{C}_n^{(\ell)})$, where $\mathsf{C}_j^{(\ell)}$ is received from P_j during the previous round, for $j = 1, \ldots, n$.[d]
- For $\ell = 1, \ldots, B$, let $\mathsf{RSDecode}(\mathsf{C}^{(\ell)}, n, t+1, t) := \mathsf{M}^{(\ell)} = (\mathsf{M}_0^{(\ell)}, \ldots, \mathsf{M}_t^{(\ell)}) \in \mathbb{F}^{t+1}$. Let $\mathsf{m}_0^{(\ell)}, \ldots, \mathsf{m}_t^{(\ell)}$ be the bit-string representing the elements $\mathsf{M}_0^{(\ell)}, \ldots, \mathsf{M}_t^{(\ell)}$ respectively and let $\mathsf{m}^{(\ell)} = \mathsf{m}_0^{(\ell)} || \ldots || \mathsf{m}_t^{(\ell)}$, where $||$ denotes the string concatenation operation.
- Output $\mathsf{m}^{(1)} || \ldots || \mathsf{m}^{(B)}$ and terminate.

---

[a] For simplicity and without loss of generality, let $L = c \cdot (t+1) \log |\mathbb{F}|$ for some integer $c \geq 1$. Hence $B = c$.

[b] To check if $(C_1^{(\ell,i)}, \ldots, C_n^{(\ell,i)})$ is a valid codeword, P_i can check if the points $\{(\alpha_j, C_j^{(\ell,i)})\}_{j=1,\ldots,n}$ lie on a t-degree polynomial.

[c] If no $C_i^{(\ell,j)}$ is received from P_j then set $C_i^{(\ell,j)} := 0$.

[d] If no $\mathsf{C}_j^{(\ell)}$ is received from P_j then set $\mathsf{C}_j^{(\ell)} := 0$.

Fig. 6.19: Perfectly secure protocol for domain extension where $L \geq (t+1) \log |\mathbb{F}|$ bits with polynomial computation complexity

The properties of the protocol $\Pi_{\mathsf{PerDomExt}}^{(n,t)}$ follow from the properties of the protocol $\Pi_{\mathsf{ModWarmUp}}^{(n,t)}$. The round and communication complexity of $\Pi_{\mathsf{PerDomExt}}^{(n,t)}$ is derived in the same way as done for $\Pi_{\mathsf{GenWarmUp}}^{(n,t)}$. We do not provide the formal proofs to avoid repetition.

Theorem 6.5 *Let $t < \frac{n}{3}$ and let the parties have oracle access to a bit-BB oracle. Moreover let S has an input $m \in \{0,1\}^L$ for protocol $\Pi_{\mathsf{WarmUp}}^{(n,t)}$ where $L \geq (t+1) \log |\mathbb{F}|$. Then protocol $\Pi_{\mathsf{PerDomExt}}^{(n,t)}$ is a t-secure BB protocol with perfect security in the model $\mathcal{M}_{\mathsf{auth}}$ with the following complexities.*
- *The protocol requires* 4 *rounds.*
- *The seed-round complexity of the protocol is* 1.
- *The protocol incurs a communication of $O(nL) + n^2 \cdot \mathcal{BC}(1)$ bits, where $\mathcal{BC}(1)$ denotes the communication complexity of emulating one instance of the bit-BB oracle with a single-bit input.*
- *The seed-communication complexity of the protocol is $O(n^2)$ bits.*
- *The computation complexity of the protocol is poly(n, L).*

Advantage of Protocol $\Pi_{\mathsf{PerDomExt}}^{(n,t)}$.

From Theorem 6.5 it follows that the communication complexity of the protocol $\Pi_{\mathsf{PerDomExt}}^{(n,t)}$ is $O(nL) + n^2 \cdot \mathcal{BC}(1)$ bits, where $\mathcal{BC}(1)$ denotes the communication complexity of emulating one call to the underlying bit-BB protocol with a single-bit input. If we instantiate the oracle with the BB variant of the phase-king protocol $\Pi_{\mathsf{PKO}}^{(n,t)}$ for which $\mathcal{BC}(1) = O(n^3)$ bits, then the communication complexity of the resultant protocol $\Pi_{\mathsf{PerDomExt}}^{(n,t)}$ becomes $O(nL + n^5)$ bits. Hence, if $L = \Omega(n^4)$, then the *asymptotic* communication complexity of protocol $\Pi_{\mathsf{PerDomExt}}^{(n,t)}$ becomes $O(nL)$

bits. On the other hand, the communication complexity of *none* of the BA protocols with $t < \frac{n}{3}$ discussed till now is $O(nL)$ bits for any value of L. This demonstrates the merit of doing domain extension for BA to handle *large* sized inputs.

6.4.6 Domain Extension for Byzantine Agreement from Error-Correcting Codes

Protocol $\Pi^{(n,t)}_{\mathsf{PerDomExt}}$ is a domain extension protocol for BB. How can we adapt the protocol to get a domain extension for BA? Since $t < \frac{n}{3}$, one may be tempted to use the "equivalence" between the BB and BA variants of the consensus problem. However, the communication complexity of the resultant protocol will *no* longer be $O(nL)$ bits.

In more detail, let each party P_i has an input $m_i \in \{0,1\}^L$, where $L \geq (t+1)\log|\mathbb{F}|$. Then consider the following BA protocol: each party P_i acts as S and invokes an instance of $\Pi^{(n,t)}_{\mathsf{PerDomExt}}$ with input m_i to broadcast m_i. Let $m'_1, \ldots, m'_n \in \{0,1\}^L$ be the outputs from the instances of $\Pi^{(n,t)}_{\mathsf{PerDomExt}}$ invoked by $P_1, \ldots, P_n$ respectively. Note that if P_i is *honest*, then $m'_i = m_i$ holds, which follows from the *t-validity* of $\Pi^{(n,t)}_{\mathsf{PerDomExt}}$. Moreover, each (honest) party will have the outputs $m'_1, \ldots, m'_n$ from the instances of $\Pi^{(n,t)}_{\mathsf{PerDomExt}}$, which follows from the *t-consistency* of $\Pi^{(n,t)}_{\mathsf{PerDomExt}}$. The final output is computed as follows: if any $m' \in \{0,1\}^L$ occurs as an output at least $n-t$ times among $m'_1, \ldots, m'_n$, then m' is set as the output, else the default 0^L is set as the output. It is easy to see that the above protocol satisfies the requirements of a *t-secure* BA. However, the *asymptotic* communication complexity of the protocol is $O(n^2L)$ bits, since n instances of $\Pi^{(n,t)}_{\mathsf{PerDomExt}}$ are executed.

One can *instead* modify the above protocol as follows to get an *asymptotic* communication complexity of $O(nL)$ bits. Each party P_i encodes its input m_i into an RS codeword as done in the protocol $\Pi^{(n,t)}_{\mathsf{PerDomExt}}$. The parties then start executing the steps of $\Pi^{(n,t)}_{\mathsf{PerDomExt}}$ from the *second* phase onward, "pretending" as if the codewords are supplied by some "external" sender party. It is easy to see that the final output of all honest parties will be the *same*, thus guaranteeing *t-consistency*. Moreover, *t-validity* is also achieved. This is because if all *honest* parties have the *same* input (implying that they have the *same* RS codewords), then it corresponds to the external sender behaving *honestly* and sending a common RS codeword to all the parties. Since the parties *do not* exchange complete RS codewords, but rather a fraction of their respective codewords, the overall asymptotic communication complexity of the protocol becomes $O(nL)$ bits. For the sake of completeness, we provide the formal details in Fig 6.20.

Protocol $\Pi^{(n,t)}_{\mathsf{PerDomExt}}(L)$

Public input: the parameter L, the description of $(n, t+1, t)$-RS error-correcting code over $\mathbb{F}$ with encoding and decoding algorithms RSEncode and RSDecode respectively and the description of the algorithm AlgStar. Additionally, the parties have oracle access to a bit-BB oracle.

- **(Codeword computation)**: For $i = 1, \ldots, n$, party P_i on having the input $m_i \in \{0,1\}^L$, does the following.
  - Divide m_i into blocks $m^{(i,1)}, \ldots, m^{(i,B)}$ each of size $(t+1)\log|\mathbb{F}|$ bits, where $B \stackrel{def}{=} \frac{L}{(t+1)\log|\mathbb{F}|}$.[a]
  - For $\ell = 1, \ldots, B$, further divide the block $m^{(i,\ell)}$ into sub-blocks $m_0^{(i,\ell)}, \ldots, m_t^{(i,\ell)}$ consisting of $\log|\mathbb{F}|$ bits each. Let $M_0^{(i,\ell)}, \ldots, M_t^{(i,\ell)} \in \mathbb{F}$ be the elements from $\mathbb{F}$, represented by the bit-string $m_0^{(i,\ell)}, \ldots, m_t^{(i,\ell)}$ respectively.
  - For $\ell = 1, \ldots, B$, let $M^{(i,\ell)} \stackrel{def}{=} (M_0^{(i,\ell)}, \ldots, M_t^{(i,\ell)})$. Compute $\mathsf{RSEncode}(M^{(i,\ell)}, n, t+1, t) := C^{(i,\ell)}$, where $C^{(i,\ell)} = (C_1^{(i,\ell)}, \ldots, C_n^{(i,\ell)}) \in \mathbb{F}^n$.
- **Round 1 (pairwise consistency check)**: Every party $P_i \in \mathcal{P}$ does the following.
  - For $\ell = 1, \ldots, B$ and $j = 1, \ldots, n$, send $(C_i^{(\ell,i)}, C_j^{(\ell,i)})$ to party P_j.
- **Round 2 (public announcement of the status of pairwise consistency checks)**: Every party $P_i \in \mathcal{P}$ does the following.
  - For $\ell = 1, \ldots, B$ and $j = 1, \ldots, n$, upon receiving $(C_j^{(\ell,j)}, C_i^{(\ell,j)})$ from party P_j, set the bit $V_{i,j}$ to 1, if and only if the following holds for *each* $\ell \in \{1, \ldots, B\}$.

$$(C_j^{(\ell,j)} = C_j^{(\ell,i)}) \wedge (C_i^{(\ell,j)} = C_i^{(\ell,i)})$$

    If no $(C_j^{(\ell,j)}, C_i^{(\ell,j)})$ is received from P_j during the previous round, then set $V_{i,j} := 0$.
  - Let $V_i \stackrel{def}{=} (V_{i,1}, \ldots, V_{i,n}) \in \{0,1\}^n$ denote the Boolean *response vector* of P_i.
  - Publicly broadcast the vector V_i. For this, act as a sender and make n calls to the bit-BB oracle, where the input for the jth instance is the bit $V_{i,j}$.
- **(Checking for the existence of CORE set)**: Every party $P_i \in \mathcal{P}$ does the following.
  - For $j, k = 1, \ldots, n$, let $V'_{j,k} \in \{0,1\}$ be the output from k^{th} call to the bit-BB oracle invoked by P_j as a sender and let $V'_j \stackrel{def}{=} (V'_{j,1}, \ldots, V'_{j,n})$.
  - Construct an undirected *consistency graph* $G^{(i)}$ over the set of vertices $\{P_1, \ldots, P_n\}$, where the edge (P_j, P_k) is added to $G^{(i)}$ if and only if $V'_{j,k} = V'_{k,j} = 1$
  - Run the algorithm $\mathsf{AlgStar}(G^{(i)})$. If $\mathsf{AlgStar}(G^{(i)})$ outputs "*star not found*", then output 0^L and terminate, else continue as follows.
    - Let $(\mathcal{C}, \mathcal{D})$ be the (n,t)–star obtained from the algorithm $\mathsf{AlgStar}(G^{(i)})$.
    - Let $\mathcal{F}$ be the parties which are adjacent to at least $t+1$ parties in $\mathcal{C}$. That is:

$$\mathcal{F} \stackrel{def}{=} \{P_k \mid \text{there exist at least } t{+}1 \text{ parties } P_j \in \mathcal{C}, \text{ such that } (P_j, P_k) \in G^{(i)}\}$$

    - Let $\mathcal{E}$ be the parties which are adjacent to at least $2t+1$ parties in $\mathcal{F}$. That is:

$$\mathcal{E} \stackrel{def}{=} \{P_k \mid \text{there exist at least } 2t{+}1 \text{ parties } P_j \in \mathcal{F}, \text{ where } (P_j, P_k) \in G^{(i)}\}$$

    - If $|\mathcal{E}| < n - t$, then output 0^L and terminate, else set CORE $= \mathcal{E}$.
- **Round 3 (obtaining the common codeword held by the honest parties in CORE)**: Every party $P_i \in \mathcal{P}$ does the following.
  - For $\ell = 1, \ldots, B$, let $\mathsf{C}_i^{(\ell)} \stackrel{def}{=} \mathsf{Majority}(\{C_i^{(\ell,j)}\}_{P_j \in \mathsf{CORE}})$, where $\mathsf{Majority}(\cdot)$ denotes the *majority* function and where $C_i^{(\ell,j)}$ has been received from P_j during **Round 1**.[b]
  - For $\ell = 1, \ldots, B$ and $j = 1, \ldots, n$, send $\mathsf{C}_i^{(\ell)}$ to every party P_j.

- **(Output computation and termination)**: Every party $P_i \in \mathcal{P}$ does the following.
  - For $\ell = 1, \ldots, B$, let $\mathsf{C}^{(\ell)} \stackrel{def}{=} (\mathsf{C}_1^{(\ell)}, \ldots, \mathsf{C}_n^{(\ell)})$, where $\mathsf{C}_j^{(\ell)}$ is received from P_j during the previous round, for $j = 1, \ldots, n$.[c]
  - For $\ell = 1, \ldots, B$, let $\mathsf{RSDecode}(\mathsf{C}^{(\ell)}, n, t+1, t) := \mathsf{M}^{(\ell)} = (\mathsf{M}_0^{(\ell)}, \ldots, \mathsf{M}_t^{(\ell)}) \in \mathbb{F}^{t+1}$. Let $\mathsf{m}_0^{(\ell)}, \ldots, \mathsf{m}_t^{(\ell)}$ be the bit-string representing the elements $\mathsf{M}_0^{(\ell)}, \ldots, \mathsf{M}_t^{(\ell)}$ respectively and let $\mathsf{m}^{(\ell)} = \mathsf{m}_0^{(\ell)} || \ldots || \mathsf{m}_t^{(\ell)}$, where $||$ denotes the string concatenation operation.
  - Output $\mathsf{m}^{(1)} || \ldots || \mathsf{m}^{(B)}$ and terminate.

[a] For simplicity and without loss of generality, let $L = c \cdot (t+1) \log |\mathbb{F}|$ for some integer $c \geq 1$. Hence $B = c$.
[b] If no $C_i^{(\ell,j)}$ is received from P_j then set $C_i^{(\ell,j)} := 0$.
[c] If no value is received from P_j then set $\mathsf{C}_j^{(\ell)} := 0$.

Fig. 6.20: Protocol $\Pi_{\mathsf{PerDomExt}}^{(n,t)}$ adapted for domain extension for BA where each party has an L-bit input such that $L \geq (t+1) \log |\mathbb{F}|$

6.5 Lower Bounds on the Communication Complexity of Deterministic Domain Extension Protocols

In this section, we derive the lower bound on the communication complexity of *deterministic* domain extension protocols for BB and BA. The lower bound is due to [53]. The lower bound says that in *any deterministic* domain extension protocol for BB and BA where the inputs are over the domain $\{0,1\}^L$, the parties need to communicate $\Omega(nL)$ bits. This automatically implies that the communication complexity of the protocol $\Pi_{\mathsf{PerDomExt}}^{(n,t)}$ is *asymptotically optimal.*

6.5.1 The Case of Byzantine Broadcast

We start with the case of Byzantine Broadcast (BB). We show that *any deterministic* domain extension protocol for BB which tolerates a *constant* fraction of corrupt parties (i.e. $t \in \Omega(n)$) incurs a communication of $\Omega(nL)$ bits.

Theorem 6.6 *Let $\Pi_{\mathsf{BB}}^{(n,t)}$ be a deterministic t-secure BB protocol for L-bit input in the model $\mathcal{M} \in \{\mathcal{M}_{\mathsf{auth}}, \mathcal{M}_{\mathsf{secure}}, \mathcal{M}_{\mathsf{auth}}^{\mathsf{pki}}, \mathcal{M}_{\mathsf{secure}}^{\mathsf{pki}}\}$ with security level* $\mathsf{Sec} \in \{\mathsf{PerSec}, \mathsf{StatSec}, \mathsf{CryptoSec}\}$. *If $t \in \Omega(n)$, then protocol $\Pi_{\mathsf{BB}}^{(n,t)}$ requires a communication of $\Omega(nL)$ bits.*

Proof The proof simply follows from the fact that if S is *honest*, then to guarantee *t-validity*, *every* honest party needs to learn the input m of S. Hence in $\Pi_{\mathsf{BB}}^{(n,t)}$, every bit of m needs to be communicated to *every* honest party. Since the number of honest parties is at least $n - t$ which is $\Omega(n)$ for $t \in \Omega(n)$, this trivially incurs a communication of $\Omega(nL)$ bits because $m \in \{0, 1\}^L$. □

We stress that the above proof *does not* hold for *randomized* BB protocols since in a randomized protocol, the output of a party is computed as a *probabilistic* function of the messages seen by the party throughout the protocol. For instance, a protocol which involves *no* communication among the parties and where the parties randomly output an L-bit string also constitutes a randomized BB protocol, where *t-validity* and *t-consistency* are achieved *probabilistically* (with a negligible probability).

6.5.2 The Case of Byzantine Agreement

We next consider the case of BA and prove a similar result as for BB.

Theorem 6.7 *Let* $\Pi_{\mathsf{BA}}^{(n,t)}$ *be a deterministic t-secure BA protocol for L-bit inputs in the model* $\mathcal{M} \in \{\mathcal{M}_{\mathsf{auth}}, \mathcal{M}_{\mathsf{secure}}, \mathcal{M}_{\mathsf{auth}}^{\mathsf{pki}}, \mathcal{M}_{\mathsf{secure}}^{\mathsf{pki}}\}$ *with security level* $\mathsf{Sec} \in \{\mathsf{PerSec}, \mathsf{StatSec}, \mathsf{CryptoSec}\}$. *If* $t \in \Omega(n)$, *then protocol* $\Pi_{\mathsf{BA}}^{(n,t)}$ *requires a communication of* $\Omega(nL)$ *bits.*

Proof Let A and B be two *disjoint* sets of parties where $|A| = n - t$ and $|B| = t$. Then consider the following two executions E_1 and E_2 of $\Pi_{\mathsf{BA}}^{(n,t)}$.

- **Execution** E_1: In this execution, *all* the parties in A are *honest* and participates with input m. The parties in B are under the control of the *adversary*. However, the parties in B behave *honestly* as per the steps of the protocol Π_{BA}, with input being $m' \neq m$. Then due to the *t-validity* condition of $\Pi_{\mathsf{BA}}^{(n,t)}$, the parties in A output m in this execution.
- **Execution** E_2: In this execution, the parties in B are *honest* and participate with input m', while the *honest* parties in A participate with input m where $m' \neq m$. Moreover, the parties under the control of the *adversary* in the set A behave *honestly* as per the steps of the protocol $\Pi_{\mathsf{BA}}^{(n,t)}$, with input being m. Now, from the point of view of the *honest* parties in A, execution E_2 is the *same* as E_1 and *indistinguishable*. That is the messages sent and received by the *honest* parties in A in this execution are the *same* as in E_1. This is because protocol $\Pi_{\mathsf{BA}}^{(n,t)}$ is a *deterministic* protocol and hence the messages sent by any (honest) party in the protocol during *any* round r is a *deterministic* function of the input of the party and the messages sent and received by the party till round $r - 1$.
  Since the *honest* parties in A output m during the execution E_1, it follows that even in execution E_2, the *honest* parties in A output m. Since protocol $\Pi_{\mathsf{BA}}^{(n,t)}$ is a *t-secure* BA protocol, to ensure *t-consistency*, even the parties in B should output m during the execution E_2. However, to output m, *every* party in B must learn the message m, for which they need to receive *every* bit of m. Since $|B| = t$ and $t \in \Omega(n)$, it follows that in order for the parties in B to learn m, $\Omega(nL)$ bits need to be communicated since $m \in \{0, 1\}^L$.

For a pictorial depiction of executions E_1 and E_2, see Fig 6.21. □

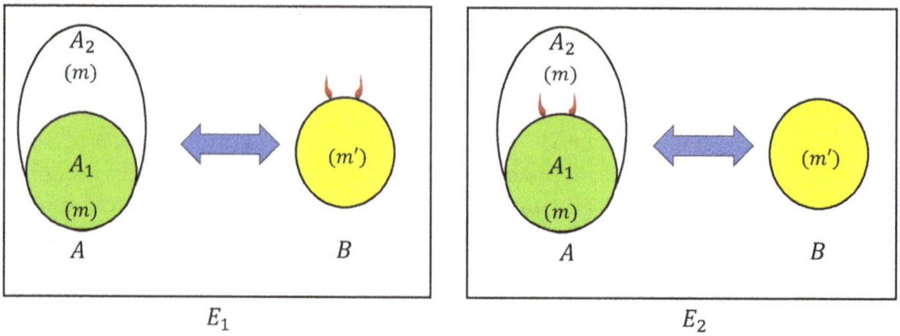

Fig. 6.21: Pictorial illustration of the executions E_1 and E_2 in the proof of Theorem 6.7. In execution E_1, the parties in A are honest and participate with input m, while the parties in B are under the control of the adversary but behave honestly with input m'. Due to *t-validity*, the parties in A, consisting of the subsets A_1 and A_2 output m. In execution E_2, the parties in B are honest and participate with input m'. The parties in A_2 are honest and participate with input m. The parties in A_1 are under the control of the adversary but behave honestly with input m. The view of the parties in A_2 will be the same in both executions

As it was the case for Theorem 6.6, Theorem 6.7 holds *only* for *deterministic* BA protocols. For instance, if protocol $\Pi_{\mathsf{BA}}^{(n,t)}$ is a *randomized* BA protocol, then during the execution E_2, the parties in B *may* have a strategy to *probabilistically* compute the output m, *without* even learning m.

We finally end this section by "reinterpreting" the proof of Theorem 6.7 in the context of the protocol $\Pi_{\mathsf{PerDomExt}}^{(n,t)}$ presented in Fig 6.20. In the protocol, the parties first check for the existence of a set of parties CORE of size at least $n - t$, who have the *same* input. Then, once the existence of a CORE set is guaranteed, the next step is to ensure that even the (honest) parties *outside* CORE get the common input, held by the *honest* parties *inside* CORE. This happens during the last round of the protocol, which incurs a communication of $O(nL)$ bits. Note that the parties *cannot* afford to end the protocol immediately after finding a CORE set, since it is *not* known whether all the honest parties are in CORE and whether the parties *outside* CORE consists of *only* corrupt parties. In the *absence* of the last round, the potential *honest* parties *outside* CORE may end up computing an output which is *different* from the output of the *honest* parties *inside* CORE, which will be a *violation* of the *t-consistency* property. This is precisely the argument used in the execution E_2 for the abstract BA protocol $\Pi_{\mathsf{BA}}^{(n,t)}$. In the proof, one can interpret the set CORE as the set A, while the set B corresponds to the parties outside CORE.

6.6 Concluding Remarks

The topic of domain extension for consensus protocols is a very active area of research. In this chapter, we focussed only on *perfectly-secure* extension protocols. Subsequent chapters will discuss extension protocols with statistical and cryptographic security, with *better* resilience.

The seed-round and seed-communication complexity of the protocol $\Pi^{(n,t)}_{\mathsf{PerDomExt}}$ (both for the BB as well as BA variant) is *one* and $O(n^2)$ respectively. The seed-round complexity of the protocol is *optimal*. This is because in *any* extension protocol, the parties need to call bit-BB/bit-BA in *at least* one round. Prior to [55], the *only known* extension protocol for BA with *perfect security*, resilience $t < \frac{n}{3}$ and *asymptotic* communication complexity of $O(nL)$ bits was due to [71]. The seed-round and seed-communication complexity of the protocol is $O(\sqrt{L} + n^2)$ and $O(n^2 \cdot \sqrt{L} + n^4)$ respectively. So clearly the protocol of [55] outperforms the protocol of [71] in terms of both seed-round and seed-communication complexity.

The round complexity of the protocol $\Pi^{(n,t)}_{\mathsf{PerDomExt}}$ for BA (Fig 6.20) is *three*. The round complexity of the protocol $\Pi^{(n,t)}_{\mathsf{PerDomExt}}$ for BB (Fig 6.19) is *four*. Hence, the round complexity of both the protocols is a *constant*, which is provably *optimal* as per the lower bound proved in [53]. The round complexity of the protocol in [71] is $O(\sqrt{L} + n^2)$. This implies that the protocol $\Pi^{(n,t)}_{\mathsf{PerDomExt}}$ outperforms the protocol of [71] *even* in terms of round complexity.

Even though the round complexity of the protocol $\Pi^{(n,t)}_{\mathsf{PerDomExt}}$ is *asymptotically optimal*, it is *not* known whether one can further *reduce* the underlying constants; i.e. further reduce the number of rounds from 3 and 4 for the BA and BB variants of the protocol $\Pi^{(n,t)}_{\mathsf{PerDomExt}}$. Similarly, it is *not* known whether the *seed-communication* complexity of the protocol $\Pi^{(n,t)}_{\mathsf{PerDomExt}}$ is *optimal*.

Chapter 7
Lower Bound on the Number of Rounds for Deterministic Consensus Protocols

All the protocols discussed till now are *deterministic* and require *at least* $t + 1$ rounds of communication, *irrespective* of the value of n and t. One may wonder whether this is an artefact of these protocols or it is inherently the case for *any* consensus protocol. In this chapter, we show that it is *indeed* the case for *any deterministic* consensus protocol, *irrespective* of whether any setup is available or not. Moreover, the lower bound is applicable, *irrespective* of the type of security achieved by the protocol and *irrespective* of the value of n and t. The lower bound is due to Lamport and Fischer [69]. While proving the bound, we will use techniques from [50] and [7].

Surprisingly, the lower bound of $t + 1$ rounds holds for *crash* failures, where the strategy of the adversary is to *only* crash the parties under its control, where the corrupt parties *do not* deviate from the instructions of the protocol as long as they are functioning. Obviously, the lower bound will hold even for a more *stronger* Byzantine corruption model, which *subsumes* crash failures. The idea behind the proof of the lower bound is to show the existence of an adversarial strategy leading to a "bad" execution for *any deterministic* consensus protocol where the honest parties will *not* be able to compute an output after t rounds of communication, otherwise it will *violate* the *t-consistency* property. We stress that the lower bound holds only for *deterministic* protocols. In subsequent chapters, we will see how to design consensus protocols with a *constant expected* number of communication rounds. Note that incorporating randomness *does not* circumvent the lower bound of $t + 1$ rounds. Instead, it just "reduces" the probability of "bad events" implied by the lower bound. We stress that the lower bound of $t + 1$ rounds is for *both* the BB as well as BA variant of consensus. For simplicity, our treatment in this chapter will be for the BA variant of the consensus problem.

A. Choudhury and A. Patra, *Fault-Tolerant Distributed Consensus in Synchronous Networks*, Information Security and Cryptography,
https://doi.org/10.1007/978-3-031-80460-1_7

7.1 The Underlying Intuition

Before going into the formal proof, let us try to understand the underlying intuition behind the proof. Consider a system of n parties where $n \geq t+2$, of which up to t parties may get *crashed*. Then consider an arbitrary *deterministic* BA protocol $\Pi_{\mathsf{BA}}^{(n,t)}$, consisting of *only* t rounds. For the ease of understanding, let $n = t+2$ and let $P_1, \ldots, P_t$ be under the control of the adversary, implying P_{t+1} and P_{t+2} are honest. Moreover, let the input of the party be from domain $\mathcal{D}$, where $|\mathcal{D}| \geq 2$. Then consider the following execution of the protocol $\Pi_{\mathsf{BA}}^{(n,t)}$: party P_{t+2} has input b. Moreover, let P_1 have input a and let *no* party have input a. The adversary strategy is as follows: during the *first* round, it let P_1 send its input a *only* to party P_2 and then crashes P_1. Hence, P_1 is *not* able to send its input a to everyone, but *only* to P_2. Then in the *second* round, the adversary let P_2 send the value a received from P_1 in the previous round *only* to party P_3 and then crashes P_2. Hence, P_2 is *not* able to relay a to everyone, but *only* to P_3. In general, during the rth round, the adversary let P_r send the value a received from P_{r-1} in the *previous* round *only* to party P_{r+1} and then crashes P_r. Hence, P_r is *not* able to relay a to everyone, but *only* to P_{r+1}. For a pictorial illustration of the above strategy, see Fig 7.1.

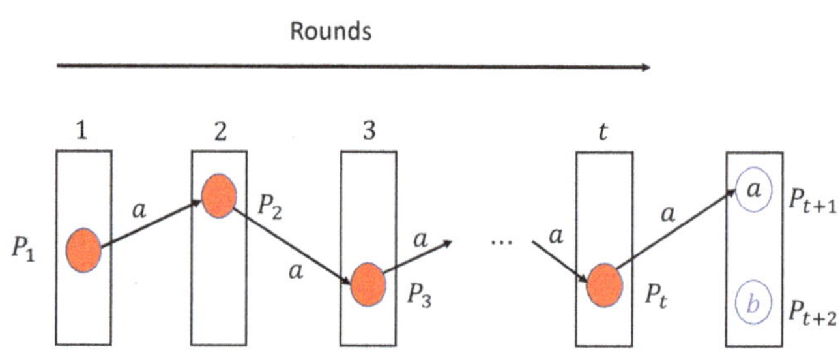

Fig. 7.1: Pictorial depiction of the adversarial strategy explaining why at least $t+1$ rounds are required for any deterministic consensus protocol

If the adversary behaves as above, then after t rounds, party P_{t+1} will *have* a in its view, while a will be *absent* from the view of P_{t+2}. Since there are *no* further rounds in the protocol and since a is *not* present in the view of *both* honest parties P_{t+1} and P_{t+2}, parties P_{t+1} and P_{t+2} will end up computing *different* outputs. This is because since $\Pi_{\mathsf{BA}}^{(n,t)}$ is a *deterministic* protocol, the final output of every (honest) party is computed as a *deterministic* function of its view. However, if P_{t+1} and P_{t+2} compute *different* outputs, then it is a *violation* of the *t-consistency* property.

If we observe the adversary strategy, then it crashes only a *single* party in each round. Moreover, it crashes the corrupt party for the rth round in such a way that the crashed party is able to relay its "state" to *only one* party before crashing, resulting in a *difference* in the states of the honest parties after the end of the rth round. So if only t rounds are available in the protocol, then the final state of the honest parties after t rounds will be *different*. The lower bound discussed in the next section precisely formalizes this intuition. Note that if there is one *more* round in the protocol, then the honest parties could exchange their states during that round and hence the above adversarial strategy *no* longer leads to a violation of the *t-consistency* property.

7.2 Few Definitions

In this section, we present a few definitions from [1], which will be later used in the lower bound proof. We first begin with an abstraction of a distributed protocol for n parties.

Parties as interactive state machines.

How do we abstract parties in any *deterministic* distributed protocol? The standard approach is to model each party as a *deterministic* state machine. Each state machine has access to an *input* register, a read-only *incoming-messages* queue, and a write-only *outgoing-messages* queue. At any given moment, the *local state* of a party is completely determined by the state of its state machine, the content of its input register, incoming-messages queue and outgoing-messages queue. A distributed protocol for n parties is then a set of n state machines.

Message passing.

Whenever any party P_i wishes to send some message m to any party P_j, it writes (m, P_j) on its outgoing-messages queue. Consequently, the system then adds an *event* $e = (m, P_j)$ to a *global* set of *pending messages*. Once an event makes it to the pending messages set, the adversary can decide when to deliver the event with the following constraint: any event $e = (m, P_j)$ which is added *during* round r, needs to be delivered to the intended recipient party P_j by the *end* of round r. This models the fact that in a *synchronous* protocol, every message being sent during round r gets delivered by the end of round r. Whenever an event $e = (m, P_j)$ is delivered, the system adds the message m to the *local* incoming-messages queue of party P_j.

Configuration.

Given a protocol Π, a *configuration* of a system consists of the state of all the parties and the set of all pending, undelivered messages. More formally, a configuration C is a vector of local states and a set C_{PM} of *pending messages*. Given any event $e = (m, P_j)$, we say that $e \in C_{\mathsf{PM}}$, if the configuration C has some pending message m intended for the recipient P_j, which is *not* yet received by P_j.

Next, we define two special types of configurations.

Definition 7.1 (Initial Configuration and Deciding Configuration) Given any protocol Π, the *initial* configuration of the system is the vector of inputs of the *honest* parties.

A configuration C is called a *deciding* configuration, if all *honest* parties compute an output in C. Configuration C is called a *b-deciding* configuration, if *all* honest parties output b in the configuration C.

Transition from one configuration to another.

Let C be a configuration with a corresponding set of *pending messages* C_{PM} and let $e = (m, P_j)$ be an event such that $e \in C_{\mathsf{PM}}$. We use the notation $C \xrightarrow{e} C'$ to denote that the configuration C changes to configuration C', once the event e is delivered and message m is received by party P_j. The *difference* between the configurations C and C' will be as follows:

- The incoming-messages queue of party P_j will *have* the message m in configuration C'.
- The set of *pending messages* C'_{PM} in configuration C' will be *different* from C_{PM}, since $e \notin C'_{\mathsf{PM}}$.

Note that if $C \xrightarrow{e} C'$ and $e = (m, P_j)$, then for *every* party P_k where $P_k \neq P_j$, the *local state* of party P_k remains the *same* as it was in C. If we *do not* want to *explicitly* mention the event e which leads to the transition of the configuration C to C', then we simply use the notation $C \rightarrow C'$.

We use the notation $C \rightsquigarrow C'$ to denote that there exists a sequence of configurations $C_1, \ldots, C_k$, such that the following holds:

$$C = C_1 \rightarrow C_2 \rightarrow \ldots \rightarrow C_k = C'.$$

Hence, $\rightsquigarrow$ denotes the *transitive closure* of the relation $\rightarrow$.

Based on the above definitions, we next define *committed* and *uncommitted* configurations, which are central to the proof of the lower bound.

Committed and uncommitted configuration.

The goal of *any* consensus protocol is for the system to finally reach a *deciding configuration*, *irrespective* of the behaviour of the adversary. To achieve this goal, the system tries to reach a *special* configuration, called *committed configuration.* Informally, this is a configuration where *irrespective* of the adversarial behaviour from this point onwards, the eventual final output value is already *fixed.* A configuration which is *not* a committed configuration is called an *uncommitted* configuration.

In more detail, let C be a configuration. Then C is called an *uncommitted configuration*, if it has a future 0*-deciding* configuration, as well as a future 1*-deciding* configuration. That is, there exists 0-deciding and 1-deciding configurations D_0 and D_1 respectively, such that *both* $C \rightsquigarrow D_0$ as well as $C \rightsquigarrow D_1$ holds. Intuitively, an uncommitted configuration is a configuration where the adversary still has "control" over the final output value in the sense that there are some adversarial strategies (for example, crash events, message delivery orders, sending incorrect messages, etc.) that will cause the honest parties to finally output 0 and some other adversarial strategies that will cause the honest parties to finally output 1.[1]

A configuration C is called a *committed* configuration, if *every* future *deciding* configuration D where $C \rightsquigarrow D$ is b-deciding, for some value b. In other words, a committed configuration is a configuration where the adversary has *no more* any control over the final output value of the honest parties. We will say that C is a 0*-committed* configuration if all future deciding configurations are 0-deciding. On the other hand, C is called a 1*-committed* configuration if all future deciding configurations are 1-deciding.[2]

Using the definition of various types of configurations, one can restate the requirements of a synchronous bit-BA protocol as follows.

Definition 7.2 (Bit-BA in Terms of Configurations) Let Π be a synchronous protocol for n parties in the model $\mathcal{M} \in \{\mathcal{M}_{\mathsf{auth}}, \mathcal{M}_{\mathsf{secure}}, \mathcal{M}^{\mathsf{pki}}_{\mathsf{auth}}, \mathcal{M}^{\mathsf{pki}}_{\mathsf{secure}}\}$, where each party P_i has input a private bit $b_i \in \{0, 1\}$ and an output bit. Then protocol Π is called a t*-secure* BA protocol in the model $\mathcal{M}$, if it achieves the following properties in the presence of an adversary who can corrupt up to t parties in a Byzantine fashion.

- t**-liveness**: all honest parties reach a deciding configuration.
- t**-validity**: if all honest parties have input b, then the initial configuration is a b-committed configuration.
- t**-consistency**: all honest parties reach a b-committed configuration, for some $b \in \{0, 1\}$.

Note that the protocol's security level Sec could be PerSec, $\mathsf{StatSec}$ or $\mathsf{CryptoSec}$. We are now well equipped to prove the lower bound. The proof will be done in *three* parts, each part proving one of the remarkable properties of any consensus protocol. We first show that in any consensus protocol, there *always exists* an *initial* configuration, which is *uncommitted.* Moreover, this holds even if the adversary is allowed to just *crash* at least one party during the protocol execution.

[1] The classical name for an *uncommitted* configuration is *bivalent* configuration, signifying that the current configuration can lead to *two* possible future candidate output values. As in [1], we prefer to use the name *uncommitted* configuration, to signify that there could be *multiple* future candidate output values obtained from the current configuration if the domain of output values is of size *more than* 2.

[2] The classical name for a *committed* configuration is *univalent* configuration, signifying that the current configuration can lead to *exactly one* possible future candidate output value.

7.3 The Existence of an Initial Uncommitted Configuration

In this section, we show that in *any* bit-BA protocol, there exists at least one initial configuration, which is *uncommitted*, provided the adversary is allowed to *crash* at least one party. This automatically implies that it is *not* the case that *all* initial configurations are either 1-committed or 0-committed and hence, the parties need to communicate *at least* for one round to achieve consensus. The result is due to [50]. Note that the proof is *non-constructive*, where we *do not* show a *concrete* uncommitted initial configuration, but rather logically argue about the existence of such a configuration.

Theorem 7.1 *Let* Π *be a t-secure deterministic bit-BA protocol for n parties in the model* $\mathcal{M} \in \{\mathcal{M}_{\mathsf{auth}}, \mathcal{M}_{\mathsf{secure}}, \mathcal{M}^{\mathsf{pki}}_{\mathsf{auth}}, \mathcal{M}^{\mathsf{pki}}_{\mathsf{secure}}\}$ *with security level* $\mathsf{Sec} \in \{\mathsf{PerSec}, \mathsf{StatSec}, \mathsf{CryptoSec}\}$. *Then* Π *has an initial uncommitted configuration.*

Proof The proof is by contradiction. So let *each* initial configuration of Π be either 1-committed or 0-committed. We call two initial configurations as *i-adjacent*, if the inputs of all the parties are the *same* in both the configurations, *except* the input of party P_i. Then consider the following $(n + 1)$ *initial* configurations:

$$
\begin{aligned}
C_0 &= (0, 0, \ldots, 0(n \text{ times}))\\
C_1 &= (1, 0, \ldots, 0(n-1 \text{ times}))\\
C_2 &= (1, 1, 0, \ldots, 0(n-2 \text{ times}))\\
&\vdots\\
C_{i-1} &= (1, 1, \ldots, 1(i-1 \text{ times}), 0, \ldots, 0(n-i+1 \text{ times}))\\
C_i &= (1, 1, \ldots, 1(i \text{ times}), 0, \ldots, 0(n-i \text{ times}))\\
&\vdots\\
C_n &= (1, \ldots, 1(n \text{ times}))
\end{aligned}
$$

It is easy to see that for $i = 1, \ldots, n$, the initial configurations C_{i-1} and C_i are *i-adjacent*. As per our assumption, *each* of the above $n + 1$ initial configurations is either 0-committed or 1-committed. Moreover, since Π is a *t-secure* protocol, it satisfies the *t-validity* property. Consequently, the configurations C_0 and C_n are 0-*committed* and 1-*committed* respectively. It then follows that there *exists* some i and initial configurations $C, C' \in \{C_0, \ldots, C_{n+1}\}$, such that all the following holds:

- C is 0-*committed* and C' is 1-*committed*.
- C and C' are *i-adjacent*.

Next, consider the following adversarial strategy during the execution of Π with respect to the initial configurations C and C'.

- The initial configuration is C and adversary *crashes* party P_i, right at the *start* of the protocol Π, *without* letting P_i send any message to any party. Let $\hat{C}$ be the resulting configuration of the system, hence $C \rightarrow \hat{C}$. Since C is a 0-*committed* configuration, it follows that $\hat{C}$ is also a 0-*committed* configuration. Hence *every* future deciding configuration of $\hat{C}$ is a 0-*deciding* configuration.

- The initial configuration is C' and adversary *crashes* party P_i, right at the *start* of the protocol Π, *without* letting P_i send any message to any party. Let $\hat{C}'$ be the resulting configuration of the system, hence $C' \longrightarrow \hat{C}'$. Since C' is a 1-*committed* configuration, it follows that $\hat{C}'$ is also a 1-*committed* configuration. Hence *every* future deciding configuration of $\hat{C}'$ is a 1-*deciding* configuration. □

Now what can we say about the configurations $\hat{C}$ and $\hat{C}'$? They are *indistinguishable* from the point of view of *all* honest parties. This is because in *none* of the configurations $\hat{C}$ and $\hat{C}'$, the honest parties receive any message from the *crashed* party P_i. Moreover, the inputs of the remaining parties are the *same* in both $\hat{C}$ and $\hat{C}'$ and the protocol Π is a *deterministic* protocol. Consequently, *every* future deciding configuration of $\hat{C}$ and $\hat{C}'$ should be the *same*. However, this is a contradiction since every future deciding configuration of $\hat{C}$ is a 0-*deciding* configuration, while every future deciding configuration of $\hat{C}'$ is a 1-*deciding* configuration. Hence at least one of the initial configurations $C_0, \ldots, C_n$ is an *uncommitted* configuration.

For a pictorial illustration of the above argument for $n = 4$ parties, see Fig 7.2.

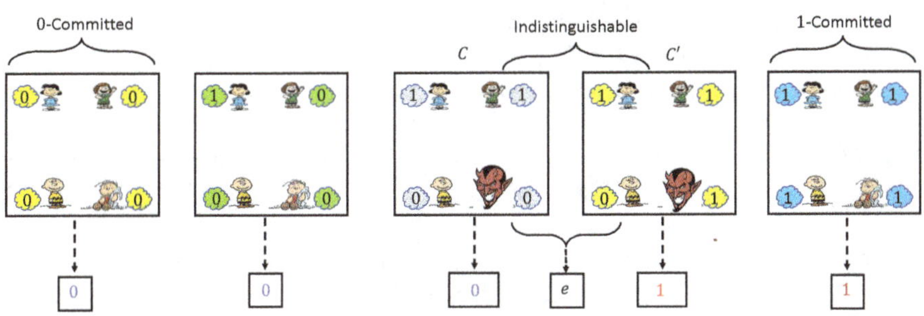

Fig. 7.2: Pictorial depiction of the proof of why an initial uncommitted configuration exists for $n = 4$. Configurations C and C' are *i-adjacent*, where C and C' are 0-*committed* and 1-*committed* respectively. If the adversary just crashes party P_i at the beginning of the protocol execution in C and C', then the view of the honest parties will be *indistinguishable*, leading to the *same* future deciding configuration, which is *not* possible

In the next section, we show the existence of an *uncommitted* configuration even after $t - 1$ rounds. This will imply that the parties *cannot* hope to achieve consensus after $t - 1$ rounds of communication.

7.4 Uncommitted Configuration Exists Even after $t - 1$ Rounds

In this section, we show that in any synchronous deterministic agreement protocol, an *uncommitted* configuration exists even after $t - 1$ rounds of communication. Consequently, the protocol needs to run for at least *one more* round to satisfy the desired security properties. To prove the statement, we use the proof strategy from [7] and consider a *special* adversarial strategy, where the adversary can *crash at most one* party in every round of the protocol execution, for $t - 1$ rounds. Note that this is allowed as per the corruption model since the adversary has the "quota" to corrupt up to t parties.

Theorem 7.2 *Let* Π *be a t-secure deterministic bit-BA protocol for n parties in the model* $\mathcal{M} \in \{\mathcal{M}_{\mathsf{auth}}, \mathcal{M}_{\mathsf{secure}}, \mathcal{M}^{\mathsf{pki}}_{\mathsf{auth}}, \mathcal{M}^{\mathsf{pki}}_{\mathsf{secure}}\}$ *with security level* $\mathsf{Sec} \in \{\mathsf{PerSec}, \mathsf{StatSec}, \mathsf{CryptoSec}\}$. *If the adversary can crash at most one party every round, then there must exist an uncommitted configuration at the end of* $t - 1$ *rounds.*

Proof We show the existence of a sequence of configurations $C_0, \ldots, C_{t-1}$, such that the following holds:

- For $k = 0, \ldots, t-1$, the configuration C_k is the configuration at the end of round k of an execution of protocol Π;
- For $k = 0, \ldots, t-1$, the configuration C_k is *uncommitted*;
- $C_0 \rightarrow C_1 \rightarrow C_2 \rightarrow \ldots \rightarrow C_{t-1}$ holds.

We prove the above properties through *induction* on k.

Base Case. The base case is when $k = 0$. Then the existence of an *initial uncommitted* configuration C_0 has been already shown in Theorem 7.2.

Inductive Hypothesis. Let the statement be true for $k - 1$. That is, if the adversary crashes *at most one* party in each of the rounds $1, \ldots, k-1$ during the execution of Π, then there exist configurations $C_0, \ldots, C_{k-1}$ satisfying the above properties.

Inductive Step. We now want to prove the statement for k. For this take the *uncommitted* configuration C_{k-1} which is bound to exist at the end of round $k - 1$ during an execution of Π, as per the induction hypothesis. Then consider *all* one-round extensions of configuration C_{k-1} as per the steps of Π, where adversary *crashes* at most *one* party during round k of Π. We claim that *at least one* of these new configurations is *uncommitted*, thus confirming the existence of the required configuration C_k. We claim the proof through contradiction. So let *all* one-round extensions of the configuration C_{k-1} with at most one crash happening during round k, be either 0-*committed* or 1-*committed.*

Let β_k denote the one-round *failure-free* extension of the configuration C_{k-1}, where *no* crash occurs during round k of the protocol Π. Hence, the following holds:

$$C_{k-1} \rightarrow \beta_k.$$

As per our assumption, β_k is a *committed* configuration. For simplicity and without loss of generality, let β_k be 1-*committed*. Since C_{k-1} is an *uncommitted* configuration, there exists some party, say P_i and a one-round extension γ_k of the configuration C_k, such that *all* the following holds:

- $C_{k-1} \rightarrow \gamma_k$;
- In configuration γ_k, party P_i *crashes* during round k of the protocol Π;
- The configuration γ_k is 0-*committed*.

If the above is *not* true and if *all* one-round extensions γ_k of C_{k-1} where *exactly one* party crashes during round k is 1-*committed*, then it implies that the configuration C_{k-1} is also a 1-*committed* configuration, since we have assumed that the *failure-free* extension β_k of C_{k-1} is *also* 1-*committed*. However, C_{k-1} is an *uncommitted* configuration. Hence, a configuration γ_k exists, satisfying all the above properties. We next focus on party P_i, which crashes during round k of Π in configuration γ_k.

Let $P_{q_1}, \ldots, P_{q_m}$ be the set of m parties to which P_i *fails* to send any message during round k of the protocol Π in configuration γ_k; here $1 \leq m \leq n$. Then for $j = 0, \ldots, m$, we define a one-round extension $\alpha_k^{(j)}$ of the configuration C_{k-1}, satisfying the following conditions:

- $C_{k-1} \rightarrow \alpha_k^{(j)}$;
- Party P_i crashes during round k of the protocol Π;
- Party P_i fails to send any message to the parties $P_{q_1}, \ldots, P_{q_j}$ during round k.

Now notice that the configuration $\alpha_k^{(0)}$ is the same as the *failure-free* one-round extension β_k of C_{k-1}. This is because as per the definition of $\alpha_k^{(j)}$, execution $\alpha_k^{(0)}$ refers to the one-round extension of C_{k-1}, where the supposedly crashed party P_i for round k fails to send message to *no body*; i.e. P_i *does not* crash and hence $\alpha_k^{(0)}$ is a failure-free one-round extension of C_{k-1}. On the other hand, the configuration $\alpha_k^{(m)}$ is the *same* as the configuration γ_k. We also note that since each of the configurations $\alpha_k^{(0)}, \ldots, \alpha_k^{(m)}$ is a one-round extension of C_{k-1} with at most one crash happening during round k, as per our assumption, each of these configurations $\alpha_k^{(0)}, \ldots, \alpha_k^{(m)}$ is a *committed* configuration. We also note that, as per our assumption, the configurations $\alpha_k^{(0)}$ and $\alpha_k^{(m)}$ are 1-*committed* and 0-*committed* respectively because $\alpha_k^{(0)} = \beta_k$ and $\alpha_k^{(m)} = \gamma_k$. Consequently, somewhere in the sequence of configurations $\alpha_k^{(0)}, \ldots, \alpha_k^{(m)}$, there is a switch from 1-*committed* configuration to a 0-*committed* configuration. That is, there exist *adjacent* configurations $\alpha_k^{(j)}$ and $\alpha_k^{(j+1)}$, such that $\alpha_k^{(j)}$ is 1-*committed* and $\alpha_k^{(j+1)}$ is 0-*committed*. To prove the inductive step, we next focus on the configurations $\alpha_k^{(j)}$ and $\alpha_k^{(j+1)}$ and arrive at a contradiction.

What is the difference between configurations $\alpha_k^{(j)}$ and $\alpha_k^{(j+1)}$? The only difference is that in $\alpha_k^{(j)}$, party $P_{q_{j+1}}$ *receives* messages from P_i during round k, while in $\alpha_k^{(j+1)}$, party $P_{q_{j+1}}$ *does not receive* messages from P_i during round k. We also note that the total number of crashed parties in *both* $\alpha_k^{(j)}$ as well as $\alpha_k^{(j+1)}$ is *at most* k, where $k \leq t-1$. This is because *at most* $k-1$ parties could crash in C_{k-1} and party P_i crashes during round k in both $\alpha_k^{(j)}$ as well as $\alpha_k^{(j+1)}$. Since $k \leq t-1$, it implies that the adversary has the capability to crash *one more* party, *without* violating the bound t on the maximum number of corruptions. Then consider a one-round extension $\gamma_k^{(j)}$ as well as $\gamma_k^{(j+1)}$ of $\alpha_k^{(j)}$ and $\alpha_k^{(j+1)}$ respectively, where the following holds:

- $\alpha_k^{(j)} \to \gamma_k^{(j)}$ and $\alpha_k^{(j+1)} \to \gamma_k^{(j+1)}$;
- In both $\gamma_k^{(j)}$ as well as $\gamma_k^{(j+1)}$, party $P_{q_{j+1}}$ crashes at the *beginning* of round $k+1$, *without* sending any message to any other party. Hence in both configurations, during round $k+1$, party $P_{q_{j+1}}$ *fails* to reveal whether it received any message from P_i in the previous round or not. □

Note that $\gamma_k^{(j)}$ and $\gamma_k^{(j+1)}$ is 1-*committed* and 0-*committed* respectively, since $\alpha_k^{(j)}$ is 1-*committed* and $\alpha_k^{(j+1)}$ is 0-*committed*. What can we say about the configurations $\gamma_k^{(j)}$ and $\gamma_k^{(j+1)}$ from the point of view of the *honest* parties? Well, they are *indistinguishable*. This is because the only difference between them is that P_i sends messages to $P_{q_{j+1}}$ during round k in $\gamma_k^{(j)}$ but not in $\gamma_k^{(j+1)}$, yet $P_{q_{j+1}}$ crashes during round $k+1$ before revealing this information. Moreover protocol Π is a *deterministic* protocol. This implies that *both* $\gamma_k^{(j)}$ as well as $\gamma_k^{(j+1)}$ must be b-*committed*, for some *common* $b \in \{0, 1\}$. But this is a contradiction since we know that $\gamma_k^{(j)}$ and $\gamma_k^{(j+1)}$ is 1-*committed* and 0-*committed* respectively. This further implies that there exists some one-round extension of the configuration C_{k-1} with at most one crash occurring during round k, which is *uncommitted*, proving the inductive step.

For a pictorial illustration of the above argument, see Fig 7.3 and Fig 7.4.

Till now, we have shown that $t-1$ rounds are *not* sufficient since there will be *uncommitted* configurations at the end of each of the first $t-1$ rounds. What if we let the parties communicate for *one more* round? It turns out that we *may not* be able to now show the existence of an *uncommitted* configuration after t rounds; indeed, the proof of Theorem 7.2 may *no* longer hold, since we need round number $t+1$ to show the existence of configurations $\gamma_k^{(j)}$ and $\gamma_k^{(j+1)}$. However, we will next show that there will be a configuration after t rounds, where *honest* parties will *not* be able to decide the final output, because if they try to do so, then it *will* lead to a violation of t-*consistency* property. This will imply that the parties need to communicate at least for one more round, after t rounds, to achieve consensus.

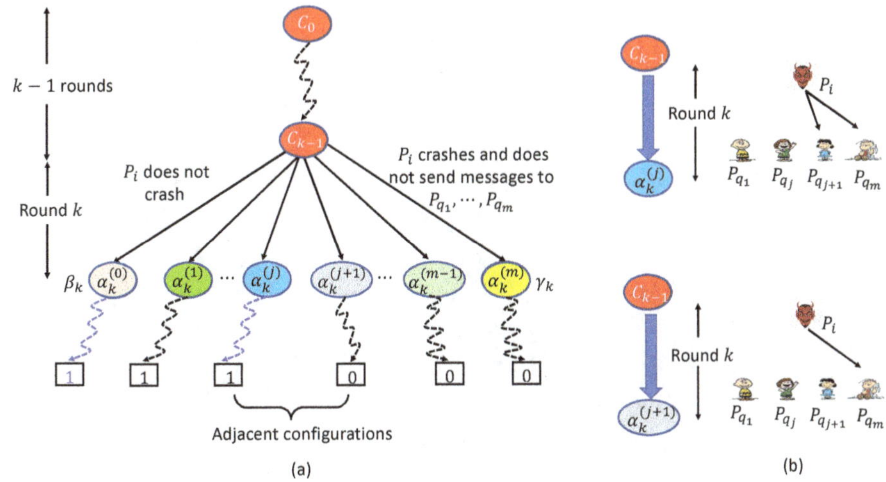

Fig. 7.3: Pictorial illustration of the proof of Theorem 7.2. Part (a) shows the uncommitted configurations $C_0, \ldots, C_{k-1}$, which exist after the first $k - 1$ rounds. Configurations $\alpha_k^{(0)}, \ldots, \alpha_k^{(m)}$ are all one-round extensions of the configuration C_{k-1}. Configuration $\alpha_k^{(0)}$ is 1-*committed* and is the *same* as β_k, which is a *fault-free* extension of C_{k-1}, where *no* party crashes during round k. Configuration $\alpha_k^{(m)}$ is 1-*committed* and is the *same* as γ_k, which is a one-round extension of C_{k-1}, where party P_i crashes during round k and *does not* send messages to parties $P_{q_1}, \ldots, P_{q_m}$. Configurations $\alpha_k^{(j)}$ and $\alpha_k^{(j+1)}$ are *adjacent* configurations, which are 1-*committed* and 0-*committed* respectively. Part (b) illustrates the configurations $\alpha_k^{(j)}$ and $\alpha_k^{(j+1)}$. The difference between the configurations $\alpha_k^{(j)}$ and $\alpha_k^{(j+1)}$ is that in $\alpha_k^{(j)}$, party $P_{q_{j+1}}$ *does receive* messages from the crashed party P_i, while in $\alpha_k^{(j+1)}$, party $P_{q_{j+1}}$ *does not receive* messages from the crashed party P_i

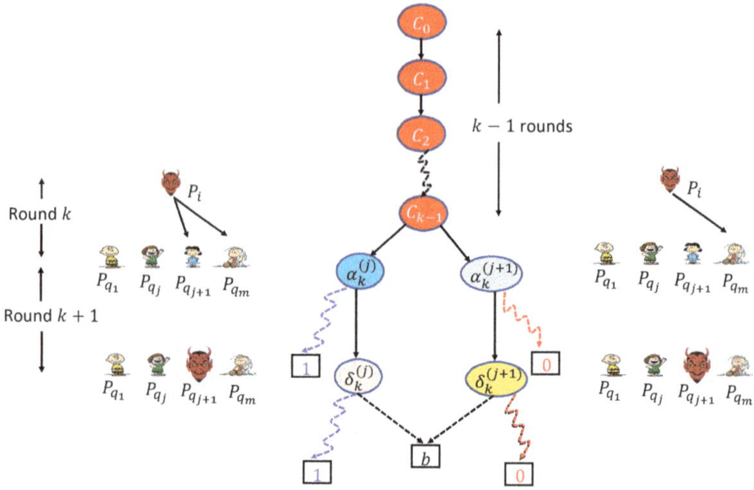

Fig. 7.4: Configurations $\delta_k^{(j)}$ and $\delta_k^{(j+1)}$ in the proof of Theorem 7.2. These are one-round extensions of the configurations $\alpha_k^{(j)}$ and $\alpha_k^{(j+1)}$ respectively. Configuration $\delta_k^{(j)}$ is 1-*committed*, while $\delta_k^{(j+1)}$ is 0-*committed*. In both configurations, the party $P_{q_{j+1}}$ crashes at the beginning of round $k+1$. From the point of view of the honest parties, these configurations are indistinguishable and must be b-*committed*, for some $b \in \{0, 1\}$, which is a contradiction

7.5 Parties Cannot Always Decide After t Rounds

In this section, we show that in any synchronous deterministic agreement protocol, there always exists a configuration after t rounds, where parties cannot decide the output value without violating the consistency property. To prove the statement, we again use techniques from [7] and consider a *special* adversarial strategy, where the adversary can *crash at most one* party in every round of the protocol execution.

Theorem 7.3 *Let* Π *be a* t*-secure deterministic bit-BA protocol for* n *parties in the model* $\mathcal{M} \in \{\mathcal{M}_{\mathsf{auth}}, \mathcal{M}_{\mathsf{secure}}, \mathcal{M}^{\mathsf{pki}}_{\mathsf{auth}}, \mathcal{M}^{\mathsf{pki}}_{\mathsf{secure}}\}$ *with security level* $\mathsf{Sec} \in \{\mathsf{PerSec}, \mathsf{StatSec}, \mathsf{CryptoSec}\}$ *such that* $n \geq t + 2$*. If* Π *has an execution where the adversary crashes at most one party every round for* t *rounds which leads to an uncommitted configuration at the end of round* $t - 1$*, then, in that execution, there always exists at least one honest party which cannot decide its output at the end of round* t*.*

Proof From Theorem 7.2, the premise of the theorem is indeed true since we have shown the existence of an *uncommitted* configuration C_{t-1} at the end of round $t - 1$, if the adversary crashes at most one party in every round. We prove the theorem using a contradiction. So let *all* one-round extension of C_{t-1} where adversary can crash at most one party during round t, is either 0-*deciding* or 1-*deciding*.

Let (β_t, γ_t) be a pair of one-round extensions of the configuration C_{t-1}, where at most one party can crash during round t. We say (β_t, γ_t) is j, i*-adjacent*, if there exists a *corrupt* party P_i and an *honest* party P_j, such that the only *difference* between β_t and γ_t is that in β_t, party P_i crashes *after* sending messages to P_j during round t, while in γ_t, party P_i crashes *before* sending any messages to P_j during round t.

Since C_{t-1} is an *uncommitted* configuration, it implies that there exist a pair of j, i*-adjacent* configurations (β_t, γ_t), such that β_t is 1-*deciding* and γ_t is 0-*deciding*. If this is *not* the case and if *all* j, i*-adjacent* configurations (β_t, γ_t) are b*-deciding* for some $b \in \{0, 1\}$, then it would imply that C_{t-1} was a *committed* configuration, which is *not* the case. Hence, in β_t, the *honest* party P_j decides the output 1, while in γ_t, it decides the output 0. Since $n \geq f + 2$ and at most t parties could crash by the end of round t, it implies that there exists *another honest* party P_k, where $P_j \neq P_k$.

Now consider another one-round extension δ_t of C_{t-1} where party P_i crashes during round t and behaves as follows: it crashes *after sending* messages to P_k while it crashes *before sending* any messages to P_j. Moreover, let in β_t, party P_i crash *after* sending messages to P_k; it *doesn't* matter whether in γ_t party P_i crashes before or after sending messages to P_k (see Fig 7.5 for a pictorial illustration).

Note that as per our assumption, configuration δ_t should be b*-deciding* for some $b \in \{0, 1\}$. However, we will now show that it is *not* the case. For this we compare the views of *honest* parties P_j and P_k in δ_t.

- From the point of view of P_k, configurations β_t and δ_t are indistinguishable. Hence, P_k should decide the output 1 in configuration δ_t, since β_t is assumed to be 1-*deciding*.

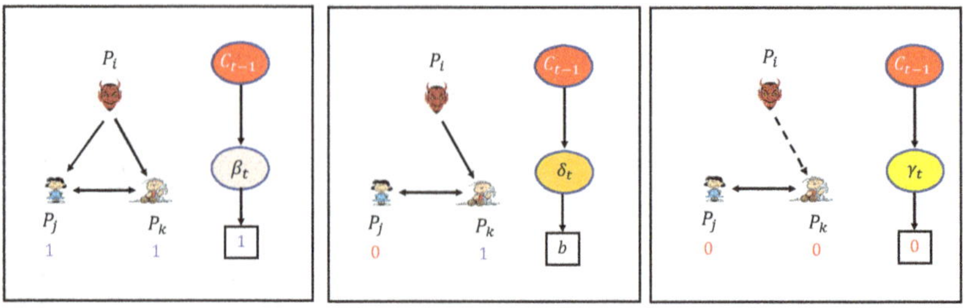

Fig. 7.5: Various configurations in the proof of Theorem 7.3. Configuration C_{t-1} is an *uncommitted* configuration after $t-1$ rounds. Configurations β_t and γ_t are one-round extensions of C_{t-1}, which are j,i-adjacent and which are 1-*deciding* and 0-*deciding* respectively. The only difference between these two configurations is that the party P_i crashes *after* and *before* sending any messages to P_j. Configuration δ_t is another one-round extension of C_{t-1}, which is b-*deciding* and where P_i crashes *before* sending anything to P_j and crashes *after* sending messages to P_k. For P_j, configurations δ_t and γ_t are indistinguishable, while for P_k, configurations δ_t and β_t are indistinguishable

- From the point of view of P_j, configurations γ_t and δ_t are indistinguishable. Hence, P_j should decide the output 0 in configuration δ_t, since γ_t is assumed to be 0-*deciding*.

Since P_j and P_k decides on *different* outputs in δ_t, it is a *violation* of t-*consistency*. Hence, *every* one-round extension of C_{t-1} is *not* a deciding configuration, proving the theorem. □

7.6 Putting Everything Together

Finally, based on Theorem 7.1-7.3, we can conclude the following theorem, stating the lower bound on the number of rounds of any *deterministic* bit-BA protocol in the *synchronous* communication model.

Theorem 7.4 *Let* Π *be a* t-*secure deterministic bit-BA protocol for* n *parties where* $n \geq t+2$ *in the model* $\mathcal{M} \in \{\mathcal{M}_{\mathsf{auth}}, \mathcal{M}_{\mathsf{secure}}, \mathcal{M}^{\mathsf{pki}}_{\mathsf{auth}}, \mathcal{M}^{\mathsf{pki}}_{\mathsf{secure}}\}$ *with security level* $\mathsf{Sec} \in \{\mathsf{PerSec}, \mathsf{StatSec}, \mathsf{CryptoSec}\}$. *Then protocol* Π *requires at least* $t+1$ *rounds of communication.*

Further discussion.

To summarize, to prove the above theorem, we first showed the existence of an initial *uncommitted* configuration (Theorem 7.1). We then showed through induction that if we continue for $t - 1$ rounds, then at the end of $t - 1$ rounds, we will still have an *uncommitted* configuration, if the adversary crashes exactly one party in every round (Theorem 7.2). Finally, we showed that if one more crash occurs during round t, then we still have an *undeciding* configuration (Theorem 7.3). Note that the proof of each of the Theorems 7.1, 7.2 and 7.3 is *non-constructive*. A crucial observation here is that in order to create a "long" execution (of at least $t + 1$ rounds), the adversary must corrupt parties *gradually* at the rate of one corrupt party per round; in fact, this was precisely the underlying intuition behind the lower bound, as discussed in Section 7.1 and illustrated in Fig 7.1.

Chapter 8
Distributed Consensus with a Constant Expected Number of Rounds

All the protocols discussed till now require $\Theta(t)$ number of communication rounds. The round complexity of a consensus protocol is an important parameter, and one would prefer a protocol with fewer communication rounds. This would be preferred in networks with *high* latency and where the round-trip delay is significantly high. Hence, a natural question is whether we can design consensus protocols with a *constant* number of rounds. Unfortunately, as shown in the previous chapter, we *cannot* hope to get a *deterministic* protocol with a constant number of rounds since any such protocol *necessarily* requires *at least* $t + 1$ rounds of communication. Consequently, we have to follow a different approach altogether. A prevalent approach is to embrace *randomness* and design *randomized* consensus protocols, an approach pioneered by the works of Rabin [80] and Ben-Or [19]. Such protocols require a *constant* number of rounds in *expectation* and provide what is called as *almost-surely termination*, meaning that the honest parties terminate the protocol *asymptotically* with probability 1. We stress that the termination guarantee of these protocols is probabilistic and the number of rounds is a constant *only* in *expectation* and there is always a chance that the honest parties keep running the protocol *forever*, *without* obtaining any output. The good news is that the probability of the latter event is *asymptotically* 0.

In this chapter, we will discuss the framework of Rabin and Ben-Or to get consensus protocols with a *constant* expected number of rounds. We will consider the case when *no* setup is available and hence the condition $t < \frac{n}{3}$ will be satisfied.[1] Our treatment will be for the BA variant of the consensus. Since the condition $t < \frac{n}{3}$ holds, a BB protocol with a constant expected number of rounds follows automatically due to the equivalence between the BB and BA variants of the consensus problem.

---

[1] Recall that $t < \frac{t}{3}$ is the *lower bound* on the resilience of any consensus protocol *without* any setup, as proved in Chapter 5.

A. Choudhury and A. Patra, *Fault-Tolerant Distributed Consensus in Synchronous Networks*, Information Security and Cryptography,
https://doi.org/10.1007/978-3-031-80460-1_8

8.1 Ingredients Required for Randomized BA

To get a randomized BA, we need *two* primitives. The first primitive is a *t-secure* graded agreement (GA) protocol, which has already been defined in Chapter 2 (see Definition 2.5). We also note that we have an instantiation $\Pi^{(n,t)}_{\mathsf{PerSecGAOneThird}}$ of a *t-secure* GA with $t < \frac{n}{3}$ (see Fig 4.4), which requires *two* rounds of communication. Note that the protocol is a *deterministic* protocol.

The randomness in the randomized BA is incorporated through the *second* primitive, a *t-secure common-coin* (CC), also known as collective coin-flipping. Informally, the primitive allows the (honest) parties to jointly "flip" a *common random* bit with a certain *non-zero* probability, which is also called the *success* probability of CC.

Definition 8.1 (Common Coin (CC)) Let Π be a protocol for the parties in $\mathcal{P}$ in the model $\mathcal{M} \in \{\mathcal{M}_{\mathsf{auth}}, \mathcal{M}_{\mathsf{secure}}, \mathcal{M}^{\mathsf{pki}}_{\mathsf{auth}}, \mathcal{M}^{\mathsf{pki}}_{\mathsf{secure}}\}$, where each party has some local random input and a binary output. Then Π is a *t-secure* p-CC protocol where $0 < p < 1$, if all the following holds for every possible adversary corrupting up to t parties in a Byzantine fashion.

- t-**liveness**: If all honest parties participate in Π, then every honest party terminates the protocol.
- (t, p)-**Correctness**: For every $\sigma \in \{0, 1\}$, all honest parties output σ with probability at least p.

We stress that Definition 8.1 *does not* require the honest parties to *always* output the same bit, and the honest parties may have different outputs. The "favourable" output desired from the primitive is that *all* honest parties have the same output bit and we require this event to occur with a probability of at least p. We also note that a CC protocol can be either *unconditionally* secure or *conditionally* (*cryptographically*) secure, depending upon if the underlying adversary is computationally unbounded or bounded, respectively.

8.2 A Generic Framework for Randomized BA with a Fixed Number of Iterations

Let $\Pi^{(n,t)}_{\mathsf{CC}}$ be a *t-secure* p-CC protocol and let $\Pi^{(n,t)}_{\mathsf{GA}}$ be a *t-secure* GA protocol in the model $\mathcal{M} \in \{\mathcal{M}_{\mathsf{auth}}, \mathcal{M}_{\mathsf{secure}}, \mathcal{M}^{\mathsf{pki}}_{\mathsf{auth}}, \mathcal{M}^{\mathsf{pki}}_{\mathsf{secure}}\}$. We next show how to combine these two primitives generically and get a *randomized* BA protocol, using the framework of [80, 19] in the model $\mathcal{M}$. Note that the framework is *generic* and uses the GA and CC primitives as a *black-box*. We also note that the resultant BA protocol is a *bit*-BA protocol where the parties' inputs is a *single* bit.

The randomized BA protocol consists of a *fixed* number of iterations k, where k is a parameter which determines the *error probability* of the protocol. Each iteration further consists of *two* instances of GA and *one* instance of CC, which are carefully "stitched" together. During the first instance of GA, the parties participate with their "current input", which is *initialized* to their respective input bits for BA in the *first* iteration. Then, independent of the output received from the GA instance, the parties next participate in an CC instance. Next, the parties decide their respective inputs for the second instance of GA, *based* on the output they received from the first. If a party has received the *highest* grade (namely 2) during the first instance of GA, then the party *continues* with the output bit of the first instance of GA for the second instance of GA. Otherwise, the party *switches* to the output received from CC. The output from the second GA instance is then set as the *modified* input for the *next* iteration, *provided* it is obtained with a grade higher than 0, else the input of the second instance of GA is taken as the modified input for the next iteration. Finally, after k iterations, the parties output their modified input bit.

The intuition behind the protocol is the following. In the protocol, there can be two cases. The *first* case is when all honest parties start with the *same* input bit, say b. Then, they will obtain the output b from all the instances of GA protocol in all the iterations and the outputs from CC will be *never* considered. Consequently, each honest party outputs b after k iterations.

The *second* case is when the honest parties start the protocol with *different* input bits. In this case, the protocol tries to take the help of CC to ensure that all honest parties reach an iteration with a *common* modified input bit for that iteration. Once such an iteration is reached, this *second* case gets "transformed" to the *first* case; hence, all honest parties will output that common bit.

In more detail, in each iteration r, it will be ensured that *every* honest party have the same input bit for the second instance of GA with a probability at least $p \cdot \frac{1}{2} = \frac{p}{2}$. This is because the input for the second instance of GA is either the output bit of the first instance of GA or the output of CC, both of which are *independent* of each other. Hence if the output of CC is the *same* for all honest parties with probability p, then with probability $p \cdot \frac{1}{2}$, this bit will be the same as the output bit from the first instance of GA. If in any iteration r, it is *guaranteed* that all honest parties have the same inputs for the second instance of GA, then the parties will obtain a common output with the highest grade from the second instance of GA. And then from the next iteration onward, all honest parties will stick to that common bit and finally output that common bit. Consequently, the probability that consistency *is* achieved after k iterations is $1 - (1 - \frac{p}{2})^k$. To ensure that this probability becomes closer to 1, one can appropriately select the value of k. The resultant BA protocol called $\Pi_{\text{RandBA}}^{(n,t)}$ is presented in Fig 8.1.

Protocol $\Pi_{\text{RandBA}}^{(n,t)}(k)$

Input: Party P_i has the bit b_i as input for the BA protocol.

– **Initialization**: Set $b = b_i$. Then for $r = 1, \ldots, k$, do the following.

1. Participate in an instance of $\Pi_{\text{GA}}^{(n,t)}$ protocol with input b. Let (c, g) be the output from the instance of $\Pi_{\text{GA}}^{(n,t)}$, where $c \in \{0, 1\}$ and $g \in \{0, 1, 2\}$.

2. Participate in an instance of $\Pi_{\mathsf{CC}}^{(n,t)}$ and let $\mathsf{Coin} \in \{0, 1\}$ be the output from the instance of $\Pi_{\mathsf{CC}}^{(n,t)}$.
3. If $g < 2$, then set $b = \mathsf{Coin}$.
4. Participate in an instance of $\Pi_{\mathsf{GA}}^{(n,t)}$ protocol with input b and let (d, g') be the output obtained, where $d \in \{0, 1\}$ and $g' \in \{0, 1, 2\}$.
5. If $g' > 0$, then set $b = d$.

– **Output Computation**: Output b and terminate.

Fig. 8.1: The generic randomized bit-BA protocol from any GA and CC protocol. The above code is executed by every $P_i \in \mathcal{P}$

We next proceed to prove the properties of the protocol $\Pi_{\mathsf{RandBA}}^{(n,t)}$. We start by proving that if all the honest parties start any iteration with a *common* bit, then they stick to that bit at the end of that iteration. This would automatically imply the *validity* property.

Claim 8.1 In protocol $\Pi_{\mathsf{RandBA}}^{(n,t)}$, if all honest parties have the same input bit at the beginning of any iteration, then their modified bit remains the same at the end of that iteration.

Proof Consider an *arbitrary* iteration $r \in \{1, \ldots, k\}$, such that all the honest parties have the *same* input bit b at the beginning of the iteration r. Consequently, all honest parties participate with input b during the first instance of $\Pi_{\mathsf{GA}}^{(n,t)}$. Then from the *t-validity* of $\Pi_{\mathsf{GA}}^{(n,t)}$, it follows that all honest parties will get the output (c, g) from the first instance of $\Pi_{\mathsf{GA}}^{(n,t)}$ during iteration r, where $c = b$ and $g = 2$ holds. Hence, all honest parties participate with input b during the second instance of $\Pi_{\mathsf{GA}}^{(n,t)}$. Again, from the *t-validity* of $\Pi_{\mathsf{GA}}^{(n,t)}$, it follows that all honest parties will get the output (d, g') from the second instance of $\Pi_{\mathsf{GA}}^{(n,t)}$ during iteration r, such that $d = b$ and $g' = 2$ holds. Consequently, the honest parties will update their input bit to d, the same as b. □

We next show that in each iteration, with probability at least $\frac{p}{2}$, all honest parties will have the same input bit for the second instance of GA.

Claim 8.2 In protocol $\Pi_{\mathsf{RandBA}}^{(n,t)}$, in each iteration, all honest parties participate with the same input bit during the second instance of $\Pi_{\mathsf{GA}}^{(n,t)}$ with probability at least $\frac{p}{2}$.

Proof Consider an *arbitrary* iteration $r \in \{1, \ldots, k\}$. We first note that with a probability at least p, all honest parties will have a *common* random output $\mathsf{Coin} \in \{0, 1\}$ from the instance of $\Pi_{\mathsf{CC}}^{(n,t)}$ during iteration r. This follows from the (t, p)-*correctness* of $\Pi_{\mathsf{CC}}^{(n,t)}$. Moreover, the bit Coin will be *independent* of the output obtained from the first instance of $\Pi_{\mathsf{GA}}^{(n,t)}$ during iteration r. The latter property follows from the fact that the honest parties invoke the instance of $\Pi_{\mathsf{CC}}^{(n,t)}$ *only* after getting their output from the first instance of $\Pi_{\mathsf{GA}}^{(n,t)}$ during iteration r.

Now, two cases are possible with respect to the inputs of the honest parties for the second instance of $\Pi_{\mathsf{GA}}^{(n,t)}$ during iteration r.

- **Case I: All honest parties set the output from the instance of $\Pi_{\mathsf{CC}}^{(n,t)}$ as their input for the second instance of $\Pi_{\mathsf{GA}}^{(n,t)}$**: In this case, with probability at least $p > \frac{p}{2}$, *all* honest parties will have the same input bit for the second instance of $\Pi_{\mathsf{GA}}^{(n,t)}$ during iteration r and hence the claim statement is true.
- **Case II: Some honest parties set their input for the second instance of $\Pi_{\mathsf{GA}}^{(n,t)}$ to the output from the instance of $\Pi_{\mathsf{CC}}^{(n,t)}$ while others set it to the output from the first instance of $\Pi_{\mathsf{GA}}^{(n,t)}$**: Let $\mathcal{H}_1$ be the set of honest parties who set their input for the second instance of $\Pi_{\mathsf{GA}}^{(n,t)}$ to the output obtained from the instance of $\Pi_{\mathsf{CC}}^{(n,t)}$. Moreover, let $\mathcal{H}_2$ be the set of honest parties who set their input for the second instance of $\Pi_{\mathsf{GA}}^{(n,t)}$ to the output obtained from the first instance of $\Pi_{\mathsf{GA}}^{(n,t)}$. From the (t, p)-*correctness* of $\Pi_{\mathsf{CC}}^{(n,t)}$, all the parties in $\mathcal{H}_1$ will have a common output bit $\mathsf{Coin} \in \{0, 1\}$, which will be random. Hence with probability at least p, all the parties in $\mathcal{H}_1$ have input Coin for the second instance of $\Pi_{\mathsf{GA}}^{(n,t)}$.
  Next, consider an *arbitrary* $P_i \in \mathcal{H}_2$. From the definition of $\mathcal{H}_2$, it follows that P_i obtains the output (c, g) from the first instance of $\Pi_{\mathsf{GA}}^{(n,t)}$ during iteration r where $c \in \{0, 1\}$ and $g = 2$. Moreover, P_i's input for the second instance of $\Pi_{\mathsf{GA}}^{(n,t)}$ during iteration r is c. We also note that *every* party in $\mathcal{H}_2$ will have the input c for the second instance of $\Pi_{\mathsf{GA}}^{(n,t)}$ during iteration r. This follows from the t-*knowledge-of-agreement* property of $\Pi_{\mathsf{GA}}^{(n,t)}$ which ensures that every honest party with an output with grade 2 have the same output bit from the first instance of $\Pi_{\mathsf{GA}}^{(n,t)}$ during iteration r. What is the probability that $c = \mathsf{Coin}$? Conditioned on the event that all parties in $\mathcal{H}_1$ output the *same* Coin from the instance of $\Pi_{\mathsf{CC}}^{(n,t)}$, the probability that $c = \mathsf{Coin}$ is $\frac{1}{2}$. Hence the probability that the parties in $\mathcal{H}_1 \cup \mathcal{H}_2$ have the *same* input bit for the second instance of $\Pi_{\mathsf{GA}}^{(n,t)}$ is at least $p \cdot \frac{1}{2}$. □

An immediate consequence of Claim 8.2 is that if the honest parties start any iteration with *different* bits, then with probability at least $\frac{p}{2}$, they will have a *common* modified bit at the end of the iteration.

Claim 8.3 In protocol $\Pi_{\mathsf{RandBA}}^{(n,t)}$, if all honest parties have different input bits at the beginning of any iteration, then with probability at least $\frac{p}{2}$, they will have a common modified input bit at the end of that iteration.

Proof Consider an arbitrary iteration $r \in \{1, \ldots, k\}$. From Claim 8.2, *all* honest parties will have the *same* input for the second instance of $\Pi_{\mathsf{GA}}^{(n,t)}$ during iteration r with probability at least $\frac{p}{2}$. Moreover, if all honest parties have the *same* input for the second instance of $\Pi_{\mathsf{GA}}^{(n,t)}$ during iteration r, then all honest parties will have a common output (d, g') from the second instance of $\Pi_{\mathsf{GA}}^{(n,t)}$ where $d \in \{0, 1\}$ and $g' = 2$, which follows from the t-*validity* of $\Pi_{\mathsf{GA}}^{(n,t)}$. Furthermore, if $g' = 2$, then all honest parties would update their input bit to d at the end of iteration r. Hence, conditioned on the event that *all* honest parties have the *same* input for the second instance of $\Pi_{\mathsf{GA}}^{(n,t)}$ during iteration r, which occurs with probability at least $\frac{p}{2}$, all honest parties will have a common modified input bit at the end of iteration r. □

Now, using the help of the previous claims, we prove that protocol $\Pi_{\mathsf{RandBA}}^{(n,t)}$ satisfies the properties of BA *probabilistically*.

Theorem 8.1 *Let $\Pi_{\mathsf{GA}}^{(n,t)}$ be a t-secure GA protocol for L-bit inputs and let $\Pi_{\mathsf{CC}}^{(n,t)}$ be a t-secure p-CC protocol in the model $\mathcal{M} \in \{\mathcal{M}_{\mathsf{auth}}, \mathcal{M}_{\mathsf{secure}}, \mathcal{M}_{\mathsf{auth}}^{\mathsf{pki}}, \mathcal{M}_{\mathsf{secure}}^{\mathsf{pki}}\}$, for any given p where $0 < p < 1$. Moreover, let $\Pi_{\mathsf{GA}}^{(n,t)}$ and $\Pi_{\mathsf{CC}}^{(n,t)}$ require r_1 and r_2 rounds of communication. Furthermore, let $\mathcal{GA}(L)$ and $\mathcal{CC}(1)$ denote the communication complexity in bits for $\Pi_{\mathsf{GA}}^{(n,t)}$ and $\Pi_{\mathsf{CC}}^{(n,t)}$ respectively. Then protocol $\Pi_{\mathsf{RandBA}}^{(n,t)}(k)$ is a t-secure bit-BA protocol in the model $\mathcal{M}$, with probability at least $1 - (1 - \frac{p}{2})^k$. The protocol requires $k \cdot (2r_1 + r_2)$ rounds of communication, and the communication complexity of the protocol is $\mathcal{BA}(1)$ bits where $\mathcal{BA}(1) = k \cdot (2\mathcal{GA}(1) + \mathcal{CC}(1))$.*

The protocol is unconditionally-secure if $\Pi_{\mathsf{GA}}^{(n,t)}$ and $\Pi_{\mathsf{CC}}^{(n,t)}$ are unconditionally-secure. If $\Pi_{\mathsf{GA}}^{(n,t)}$ and $\Pi_{\mathsf{CC}}^{(n,t)}$ are conditionally (cryptographically) secure, then the protocol is conditionally (cryptographically) secure.

Proof The *t-liveness* follows from the fact that the honest parties terminate the protocol after k iterations, where each iteration invokes *two* instances of $\Pi_{\mathsf{GA}}^{(n,t)}$ and *one* instance of $\Pi_{\mathsf{CC}}^{(n,t)}$. This automatically implies the number of rounds and communication complexity, as the theorem states.

The *t-validity* follows from Claim 8.1. Namely, if *all* honest parties start the protocol with the *same* input bit b, then their updated input bit remains b after the end of each iteration, and hence, all honest parties output b after k iterations.

For *t-consistency*, let all honest parties start the protocol with *different* input bits. Then from Claim 8.3, at the end of *any* iteration $r \in \{1, \ldots, k-1\}$, all honest parties will have the *same* updated bit with probability at least $\frac{p}{2}$. Hence, with probability at least $\frac{p}{2}$, all honest parties will start the iteration $r+1$ with the *same* input bit, say b. Consequently, from Claim 8.1, all honest parties will set b as their updated input bit at the end of iterations $r+1, \ldots, k$ and finally output b, which will imply *t-consistency*. Hence the probability that *t-consistency* is *not* achieved after k iterations is the *same* as the probability that the honest parties *do not* have a common updated input bit at the end of any of the iterations $1, \ldots, k$, which is at most $(1 - \frac{p}{2})^k$. This implies that the probability that *t-consistency* is achieved after k iterations is at least $1 - (1 - \frac{p}{2})^k$. □

8.2.1 On the Number of Iterations Required in the Protocol $\Pi_{\mathsf{RandBA}}^{(n,t)}$

From the discussion on the protocol $\Pi_{\mathsf{RandBA}}^{(n,t)}$, a natural question is what should be the appropriate value of k, namely the number of iterations if we want to implement the protocol. As we will show, it is inversely proportional to the success probability p of the common coin protocol. From the proof of Theorem 8.1, it follows that once all honest parties have the same updated bit at the end of an iteration, consistency will be achieved from the next iteration. We next derive the expected number of iterations when this "magical event" happens. So let τ be the random variable, which denotes the number of iterations after which all honest parties have the same updated bit. We want to derive the expected value of τ. The probability that $\tau = r$ for any $r \in \mathbb{N}$ is given by

$$\begin{aligned}\Pr(\tau = r) = \Pr(\tau \neq 1) \cdot \Pr(\tau \neq 2|\tau \neq 1) \cdot \ldots \cdot \Pr(\tau \neq (r-1)|\tau \neq 1 \cap \ldots \\ \cap \tau \neq (r-2)) \cdot \Pr(\tau = r|\tau \neq 1 \cap \ldots \cap \tau \neq (r-1)).\end{aligned}$$

Now, from Theorem 8.1, each multiplicand on the right-hand side of the above equation, except the last one, is upper bounded by $(1 - \frac{p}{2})$. And the last multiplicand is lower bounded by $\frac{p}{2}$. This is because with probability at least $\frac{p}{2}$, all honest parties will have the same updated bit at the end of any iteration and hence, with probability at most $1 - \frac{p}{2}$, they may have different updated bits at the end of any iteration. Hence, we get that

$$\Pr(\tau = r) \leq (1 - \frac{p}{2})^{r-1} \cdot (\frac{p}{2}).$$

Now the expected value $E(\tau)$ of τ is computed as follows:

$$\begin{aligned}E(\tau) &= \sum_{r=1}^{\infty} r \Pr(\tau = r) \\ &\leq \sum_{r=1}^{\infty} r(1 - \frac{p}{2})^{r-1}(\frac{p}{2}) \\ &\leq \frac{p}{2} \cdot \sum_{r=1}^{\infty} r(1 - \frac{p}{2})^{r-1} = \frac{p}{2} \cdot \left(\frac{1}{1 - (1 - \frac{p}{2})} + \frac{(1)(1 - \frac{p}{2})}{(1 - (1 - \frac{p}{2}))^2}\right) = \frac{2}{p}.\end{aligned}$$

The expression for $E(\tau)$ is a sum of AGP up to infinite terms, which is given by $\frac{a}{1-R} + \frac{DR}{(1-R)^2}$, where $a = 1$, $R = 1 - \frac{p}{2}$ and $D = 1$. Hence, we have that $E(\tau) \leq \frac{2}{p}$.

As evident from the above derivation, the expected number of iterations required in the protocol $\Pi_{\mathsf{RandBA}}^{(n,t)}$ is inversely proportional to the success probability p of the CC protocol. One can set k to the smallest positive integer greater than or equal to $\frac{2}{p}$. This implies that if p is a *constant* (which will be the case in our instantiation of CC), then it will take a constant number of iterations in expectation to achieve consistency. While one could indeed set k to a *fixed* value using the above approach, it is *not* a practically good approach since consensus may be achieved way before k iterations, resulting in a tremendous "wastage" of iterations. For instance, suppose depending upon p we set $k = 1000$, but after 10 iterations, the honest parties have the same updated bit, thus unnecessarily resulting in a wastage of 990 iterations!! Instead, a *better* approach would be to let somehow the honest parties "detect" that they have the same updated bit at the end of an iteration, after which they can safely exit the protocol, *without* running the protocol till k iterations. Note that this will require a very careful design approach since the exit of one honest party may affect the "progress" of other honest parties who may *not* have exited the protocol yet. For the moment, we *do not* go into the details of this alternate approach and keep it pending for a later stage of this chapter. Instead, we next focus on the possible instantiation of the CC primitive *without* any setup.

8.3 Instantiating the Common Coin Primitive Without Any Setup

In this section, we show how to instantiate the CC primitive *without* any setup in the *pairwise-secure* channel model $\mathcal{M}_{\mathsf{secure}}$.[2] A simple idea would be to let each party P_i output a uniformly random bit b_i. Then the probability p that all honest parties have a *common* output bit is $\frac{1}{2^{n-t}}$, since there are at least $n-t$ honest parties. Looking ahead, we would like to have an instantiation of CC where the success probability p is a *constant*. This is because, as discussed in the previous section, such an instantiation will lead to a BA protocol with a *constant* expected number of rounds since the expected number of rounds required is *inversely* proportional to the success probability p of the common coin protocol.

Instead of the above approach, one can use techniques from [48] and [65]. The central idea here is associating a uniformly random value c_i with every party P_i. Then, if the random value associated with *any* party is 0, the parties output 0 as the coin; else, the parties output 1. It can be then shown that if each associated value c_i is selected from the set $\{0, \ldots, u-1\}$ for some *parameter* u, then the *success probability* p of the resultant CC protocol will be $\min(1-(1-\frac{1}{u})^{n-t}, (1-\frac{1}{u})^n)$. Hence, the parties can select an appropriate value of u to set the success probability p to a desired value.

To materialize the above idea, we *cannot* let the parties P_i pick the value c_i itself. This is because a potentially *corrupt* P_i can *always* select $c_i = 0$, hence resulting in the coin to be *always* 0. Instead, every party "contribute" for the random value to be associated with each party P_i. That is, each party P_j picks a uniformly random value $c_{j \rightarrow i}$ for party P_i and then the parties define $c_i = \sum_{j=1}^{n} c_{j \rightarrow i} \mod u$ as the value associated with P_i. This guarantees that the value c_i is uniformly distributed over $\{0, \ldots, u-1\}$ *irrespective* of P_i, since the values $c_{j \rightarrow i}$ selected by the *honest* parties P_j will be indeed *random*.

Unfortunately, the above idea *does not* work as it is since the parties *cannot* afford to *publicly* announce their random choices $c_{j \rightarrow i}$ in the presence of a *rushing* adversary. Informally, in the *rushing* adversarial model, the adversary is allowed to see all the messages sent to the corrupt parties in any round r before it must decide what to send in its round r messages. Now coming back to the above idea, clearly, a rushing adversary *can* "control" the value c_i associated with any party P_i by selecting its contributions $c_{j \rightarrow i}$ as a function of the $c_{j \rightarrow i}$ values selected and

[2] Note that this is the *first* time any protocol is designed in this model in the monogram, since all the protocols designed till now consider the pairwise-authentic channel model $\mathcal{M}_{\mathsf{auth}}$.

announced by the honest parties. In more detail, let $\mathcal{H}$ and C be the set of *honest* and *corrupt* parties respectively. Then a rushing adversary can use the following strategy to ensure that c_i associated with P_i takes the value X, for any $X \in \{0, \ldots, u-1\}$ of the adversary's choice: the adversary first waits to learn the values $\{c_{j \to i}\}_{P_j \in \mathcal{H}}$. Then the adversary can select and announce the values $\{c_{j \to i}\}_{P_j \in C}$, such that the following holds:

$$\Big(\sum_{P_j \in \mathcal{H}} c_{j \to i} + \sum_{P_j \in C} c_{j \to i}\Big) \mod u = X.$$

A common trick used to prevent the above strategy of a rushing adversary is to use a *verifiable secret sharing* (VSS) [33] scheme. Informally, a VSS scheme consists of *two* phases, a *sharing* phase, followed by a *reconstruction* phase, each implemented by a protocol. During the sharing phase, there exists a *designated* party called *dealer*, who has a private input s, which is also called dealer's *secret*. The sharing phase protocol aims to enable each party to get a *share* of the dealer's secret. During the reconstruction phase, the parties reconstruct back the shared value. The primitive guarantees that if the dealer is *honest* during the sharing phase, then the adversary *does not* learn s (also called the *hiding* property). Later, during the reconstruction phase, the parties reconstruct s, irrespective of the behaviour of the corrupt parties. We stress that the hiding property is required only if the dealer is *honest* and that too till the end of the sharing phase, since the shared value will be reconstructed back by *everyone* during the reconstruction phase. The crucial property achieved by a VSS is that of *binding* (which can also be viewed as some form of distributed commitment), which guarantees that even if the dealer is *corrupt* during the sharing phase, there exists some value $s^\star$, which could be *different* from s, such that $s^\star$ is shared among the parties, and later, during the reconstruction phase, only $s^\star$ is reconstructed back. In other words, at the end of the sharing phase, even a potentially *corrupt* dealer is committed to some well-defined value $s^\star$, which will be reconstructed back later during the reconstruction phase.

Given a VSS scheme, we can get a CC protocol as follows: each party P_j picks a random value $c_{j \to i}$ on behalf of every party P_i. Party P_j then acts as a dealer and verifiably shares $c_{j \to i}$ by invoking an instance of the sharing phase protocol. Once all the parties secret-share their respective $c_{j \to i}$ values, the parties run instances of the reconstruction protocol to get back the contributions and then, compute the values c_i associated with each party P_i and decide the final coin accordingly. Clearly, the rushing strategy by the adversary will *no* longer work because the $c_{j \to i}$ values are now *publicly* available *only* after all these values are secret-shared. Moreover, the adversary will *not* learn the $c_{j \to i}$ values shared by the *honest* dealers P_j, thanks to the *hiding* property of VSS. Furthermore, the values shared by the *honest* dealers will be *independent* of the values shared by the potentially *corrupt* dealers.

A problem: VSS uses Byzantine Broadcast.

A problem with the above approach is that *all* VSS schemes use Byzantine broadcast (BB) instances, at least during the sharing phase. In more detail, *all* VSS protocols are designed in the setting $\mathcal{M}_{\mathsf{secure}}$ or $\mathcal{M}^{\mathsf{pki}}_{\mathsf{secure}}$. Moreover, in all these protocols, apart from the pairwise-secure channels, it is also assumed that the parties have access to a BB oracle for reliably broadcasting values. Hence in each round, the parties can exchange messages over the point-to-point channels *as well as* broadcast values by calling the BB oracle.[3] Intuitively, the broadcast oracle is used during the sharing phase to reach an agreement among the parties on whether the dealer has shared its input "consistently". The presence of the broadcast oracle is only a *simplifying abstraction* to simplify the protocol description, and in reality, each invocation of the broadcast oracle needs to be emulated by running an instance of a *t-secure* BB protocol. Unfortunately, *any* (deterministic) instantiation of BB needs at least $t + 1$ rounds and we want to use VSS to get a BA (BB) protocol with a *constant* (expected) number of rounds; hence, this becomes circular reasoning!!

To deal with the above problem, we instead use a variant of VSS, called *moderated* VSS, introduced in [65], where the idea is to have a designated party who is "responsible" for taking care of all the messages to be broadcasted via the broadcast oracle in the underlying VSS protocol. In the sequel, we first define the VSS primitive and present an instantiation of the VSS assuming a broadcast oracle. This is followed by the definition of moderated VSS and its instantiation in the pairwise-secure channel model. We will then finally see the instantiation of CC based on moderated VSS in the pairwise-secure channel model.

8.4 Verifiable Secret Sharing (VSS)

The current discussion on VSS is adapted from [29]. Following [57], *any* VSS scheme can be structured into two phases. A *sharing phase* executed by a designated protocol $\Pi^{(n,t)}_{\mathsf{Sh}}$, followed by a *reconstruction phase* executed by another designated protocol $\Pi^{(n,t)}_{\mathsf{Rec}}$. The goal of protocol $\Pi^{(n,t)}_{\mathsf{Sh}}$ is to share a secret held by a designated *dealer* $\mathsf{D} \in \mathcal{P}$. On the other hand, the aim of $\Pi^{(n,t)}_{\mathsf{Rec}}$ is to reconstruct the shared secret. In more detail, during $\Pi^{(n,t)}_{\mathsf{Sh}}$, the input of D is some secret $s \in \mathcal{S}$, where $\mathcal{S}$ is some publicly-known *secret-space* which is the set of all possible D's secrets. Additionally, the parties may have random inputs for the protocol. Let view_i denote the view of P_i at the end of $\Pi^{(n,t)}_{\mathsf{Sh}}$. Here the *view* of a party during a protocol execution consists of its inputs, random coins and all the messages received by the party throughout the protocol execution. The *view* of the adversary is the collection of the views of the corrupt parties. Based on view_i, each P_i outputs a *share* s_i, as determined by $\Pi^{(n,t)}_{\mathsf{Sh}}$.

[3] This is *similar* to domain extension protocols where parties have access to *both* point-to-point channels as well as BB/BA oracles.

During $\Pi_{\mathsf{Rec}}^{(n,t)}$, each P_i reveals a subset of view_i, as per $\Pi_{\mathsf{Rec}}^{(n,t)}$. The parties then apply a reconstruction function on the revealed views, as per $\Pi_{\mathsf{Rec}}^{(n,t)}$ and reconstruct some output. We next formally define a VSS scheme.

Definition 8.2 (Verifiable Secret Sharing (VSS)) Let $(\Pi_{\mathsf{Sh}}^{(n,t)}, \Pi_{\mathsf{Rec}}^{(n,t)})$ be a pair of protocols for the parties in $\mathcal{P}$ in the model $\mathcal{M} \in \{\mathcal{M}_{\mathsf{secure}}, \mathcal{M}_{\mathsf{secure}}^{\mathsf{pki}}\}$, where a designated *dealer* $\mathsf{D} \in \mathcal{P}$ has some private input $s \in \mathcal{S}$ for the protocol $\Pi_{\mathsf{Sh}}^{(n,t)}$. Then $(\Pi_{\mathsf{Sh}}^{(n,t)}, \Pi_{\mathsf{Rec}}^{(n,t)})$ is called a *t-secure VSS scheme*, if the following requirements hold, for every possible adversary corrupting up to t parties in $\mathcal{P}$ in a Byzantine fashion, possibly including D.

- t-**liveness**: The following conditions should hold:
  - All honest parties terminate the protocol $\Pi_{\mathsf{Sh}}^{(n,t)}$;
  - All honest parties terminate the protocol $\Pi_{\mathsf{Rec}}^{(n,t)}$.
- t-**hiding**: If D is *honest* during $\Pi_{\mathsf{Sh}}^{(n,t)}$, then the view of the adversary during $\Pi_{\mathsf{Sh}}^{(n,t)}$ is distributed independent of s.
- t-**correctness**: If D is *honest* during $\Pi_{\mathsf{Sh}}^{(n,t)}$, then all honest parties output s at the end of $\Pi_{\mathsf{Rec}}^{(n,t)}$.
- t-**binding**: Even if D is *corrupt*, in any execution of $\Pi_{\mathsf{Sh}}^{(n,t)}$, the joint view of the honest parties defines a unique value $s^\star \in \mathcal{S}$ (which could be different from s), such that all honest parties output $s^\star$ at the end of $\Pi_{\mathsf{Rec}}^{(n,t)}$, irrespective of the behaviour of the adversary.[4]

VSS protocol can be either *unconditionally-secure* if the adversary is *computationally unbounded* or *cryptographically-secure* if the adversary is *computationally bounded*. The former category of protocols can be further classified as *perfectly-secure* where all the guarantees are achieved *without* any error or *statistically-secure* where a *negligible* error is allowed in the protocol outcomes.

We will now give an instantiation of *perfectly-secure* VSS in the model $\mathcal{M}_{\mathsf{secure}}$. For this, we require bivariate polynomials over finite fields, which we discuss next.

8.4.1 Properties of Bivariate Polynomials Over a Field

In Section 6.4.1, we defined fields and discussed the properties of *univariate* polynomials (namely polynomials in a *single* variable) over a field. For VSS, we need *bivariate* polynomials (namely polynomials in *two* variables) over a field.

Let $(\mathbb{F}, +, \cdot)$ be a field. A (t,t)-degree *bivariate polynomial* over $\mathbb{F}$ is of the following form:

$$F(x, y) = \sum_{i,j=0}^{i=t,j=t} r_{ij} x^i y^j, \text{ where } r_{ij} \in \mathbb{F}.$$

[4] The *binding* property is also known as the *strong commitment* property in the literature of VSS. We prefer to call it the *binding* property to avoid terms like strong and weak commitment, etc.

Let $\alpha_1, \ldots, \alpha_n \in \mathbb{F}$ be *distinct* elements from $\mathbb{F}$. The polynomials $f_i(x) \stackrel{def}{=} F(x, \alpha_i)$ and $g_i(y) \stackrel{def}{=} F(\alpha_i, y)$ are called the ith *row* and *column-polynomial* respectively of $F(x, y)$. This is because evaluating $f_i(x)$ and $g_i(y)$ at $x, y = \alpha_1, \ldots, \alpha_n$ respectively results in an $n \times n$ matrix of points on $F(x, y)$ (see Fig 8.2).

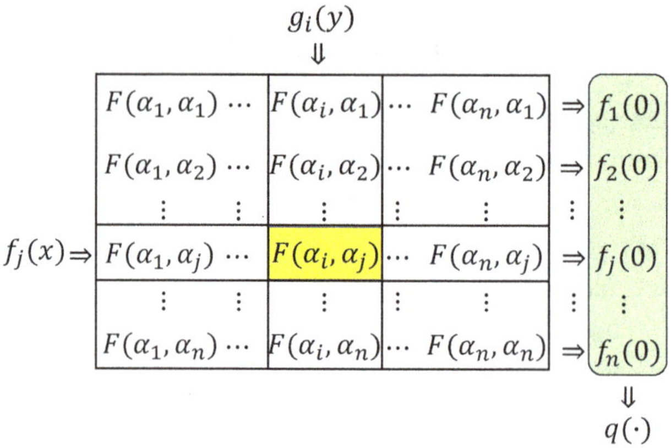

Fig. 8.2: Pictorial representation of the various points lying on a (t, t)-degree bivariate polynomial. The points $\{(\alpha_i, F(\alpha_i, \alpha_j))\}_{i=1,\ldots,n}$ lie on the jth row polynomial $f_j(x)$. The points $\{(\alpha_j, F(\alpha_i, \alpha_j))\}_{j=1,\ldots,n}$ lie on the ith column polynomial $g_i(y)$. The condition $f_j(\alpha_i) = g_i(\alpha_j) = F(\alpha_i, \alpha_j)$ holds, as highlighted in yellow colour

Note that $f_j(\alpha_j) = g_i(\alpha_i) = F(\alpha_i, \alpha_j)$ holds for all α_i, α_j. We say a t-degree univariate polynomial $F_j(x)$ where $j \in \{1, \ldots, n\}$ *lies* on a (t, t)-degree bivariate polynomial $F(x, y)$, if $F(x, \alpha_j) = F_j(x)$ holds. Similarly, we say a t-degree univariate polynomial $G_i(y)$ where $i \in \{1, \ldots, n\}$ *lies* on a (t, t)-degree bivariate polynomial $F(x, y)$, if $F(\alpha_i, y) = G_i(y)$ holds.

It is a well-known fact that there always exists a *unique* t-degree univariate polynomial over $\mathbb{F}$, passing through $t + 1$ *distinct* points. A generalization of this result for bivariate polynomials is that if there are "sufficiently many" univariate polynomials which are "pair-wise consistent", then together they lie on a unique bivariate polynomial. Formally:

Lemma 8.1 (Pair-wise Consistency Lemma [12]) *Let* $\{f_{i_1}(x), \ldots, f_{i_q}(x)\}$ *and* $\{g_{j_1}(y), \ldots, g_{j_r}(y)\}$ *be t-degree polynomials respectively where* $q, r \geq t + 1$ *and where* $i_1, \ldots, i_q, j_1, \ldots, j_r \in \{1, \ldots, n\}$. *Moreover, let for every* $i \in \{i_1, \ldots, i_q\}$

and every $j \in \{j_1, \ldots, j_r\}$, the condition $f_i(\alpha_j) = g_j(\alpha_i)$ holds. Then there exists a unique (t,t)-degree bivariate polynomial $F^\star(x, y)$, such that the polynomials $f_{i_1}(x), \ldots, f_{i_q}(x)$ and $g_{j_1}(y), \ldots, g_{j_r}(y)$ lie on $F^\star(x, y)$.

Looking ahead, in our instantiation of the VSS scheme, D on having input $s \in \mathbb{F}$, embeds s in the constant term of a *random* (t,t)-degree bivariate polynomial $F(x, y)$. Each party P_i then receives the row-polynomial $f_i(x) = F(x, \alpha_i)$ and the column-polynomial $g_i(y) = F(\alpha_i, y)$ from D and the *share* of each party P_i is defined to be $s_i = f_i(0)$, which is the same as $F(0, \alpha_i)$. A natural question here is how much information about s is learnt by the adversary, who may get up to t row and column-polynomials, corresponding to t *corrupt* parties? It can be shown that the adversary *does not* learn anything about s. Intuitively, this is because $(t + 1)^2$ *distinct* points on $F(x, y)$ are required to uniquely determine $F(x, y)$ and hence s, but the adversary learns *at most* $t^2 + 2t$ distinct points through the t row and column-polynomials. Hence there will be *one* "degree-of-freedom" from the point of view of the adversary. In fact, it can be shown that for every two degree-t polynomials $q_1(y), q_2(y)$ such that $q_1(\alpha_i) = q_2(\alpha_i) = f_i(0)$ holds for every $P_i \in C$ (where C is the set of corrupt parties), the distribution of the polynomials $\{f_i(x), g_i(y)\}_{P_i \in C}$ learnt by the adversary will be the same, *irrespective* of whether $F(0, y) = q_1(y)$ or $F(0, y) = q_2(y)$. That is, from the point of view of the adversary, the probability that $F(0, 0) = q_1(0)$ and $F(x, \alpha_i) = f_i(x)$ and $F(\alpha_i, y) = g_i(y)$ hold for every $P_i \in C$ is the *same* as the probability that $F(0, 0) = q_2(0)$ and $F(x, \alpha_i) = f_i(x)$ and $F(\alpha_i, y) = g_i(y)$ hold for every $P_i \in C$. Formally:

Lemma 8.2 ([12]) *Let $C \subset \mathcal{P}$ where $|C| \leq t$, and let $q_1(\cdot) \neq q_2(\cdot)$ be degree-t polynomials where $q_1(\alpha_i) = q_2(\alpha_i)$ holds for all $P_i \in C$. Then the probability distributions $\left\{\{F(x, \alpha_i), F(\alpha_i, y)\}_{P_i \in C}\right\}$ and $\left\{\{F'(x, \alpha_i), F'(\alpha_i, y)\}_{P_i \in C}\right\}$ are identical, where $F(x, y) \neq F'(x, y)$ are different (t,t)-degree bivariate polynomials, chosen at random, under the constraints that $F(0, y) = q_1(\cdot)$ and $F'(0, y) = q_2(\cdot)$ holds.*

8.4.2 Perfectly Secure VSS with $t < \frac{n}{3}$ in the Model $\mathcal{M}_{\mathsf{secure}}$

In this section, we give an instantiation of a VSS scheme due to [21] in the model $\mathcal{M}_{\mathsf{secure}}$, where the parties also have access to a broadcast oracle. The scheme is *perfectly-secure* and achieves all the security properties even in the presence of a *computationally-unbounded* adversary. The scheme can tolerate up to $t < \frac{n}{3}$ corruptions. In fact, one can show that this is the *optimal* resilience for *any* perfectly-secure VSS [44]. As mentioned earlier, as a simplifying abstraction, we assume that apart from the pairwise-secure channels, the parties also have access to a *system-wide* broadcast oracle, which allows any party to send some message identically to all the parties. Instead of presenting the original VSS scheme from [21], we present its simplified version, taken from [60]. In the protocol, all computations are performed over a *finite* field $\mathbb{F}$, where $|\mathbb{F}| > n$.

To share $s \in \mathbb{F}$, the dealer D picks a random degree-t *sharing polynomial* $q(y)$ where $q(0) = s$ and the goal is to ensure that D *verifiably* distributes the *share* $s_i = q(\alpha_i)$ to each party P_i. Later, during the reconstruction phase, the parties exchange the shares and *robustly* reconstruct $q(\cdot)$ by *error-correcting* up to t incorrect shares using the algorithm RSDecode[5]. The *verifiability* in the sharing phase protocol ensures that even if D is *corrupt*, the shares distributed by D to the (honest) parties lie on some t-degree sharing polynomial, say $q^\star(y)$, thus ensuring that $s^\star \stackrel{def}{=} q^\star(0)$ is shared among the honest parties. Moreover, the same $s^\star$ is reconstructed during the reconstruction phase. This ensures the *binding* property desired from the VSS.

To prove that D is sharing its secret using a t-degree sharing polynomial $q(y)$, the dealer embeds $q(y)$ in a random (t,t)-degree bivariate polynomial $F(x, y)$ at $x = 0$ by setting $F(0, y) = q(y)$ (see Fig 8.2). The dealer then distributes distinct row and column-polynomials to respective parties. If D is *honest*, then this distribution of information maintains the privacy of s, which follows from Lemma 8.2. Also, if D is *honest*, then constant term of the individual row-polynomials constitute the shares of s, as they constitute distinct points on $q(y)$, since $f_i(0)$ is the same as $q(\alpha_i)$. However, a potentially *corrupt* D may distribute *arbitrary* polynomials in the name of row and column-polynomials, resulting in the shares of the honest parties to be "inconsistent" and *not* lying on a t-degree polynomial. Hence, after receiving their respective row and column-polynomials, the parties interact further to verify if D has distributed "consistent" row and column-polynomials lying on a *single* (t,t)-degree bivariate polynomial, *without* revealing any additional information about s.

In more detail, every pair of parties P_i, P_j upon receiving their polynomials $f_i(x), g_i(y)$ and $f_j(x), g_j(y)$ respectively from the dealer, interact and check the pairwise consistency of their supposedly common points. That is, if $f_i(\alpha_j) = g_j(\alpha_i)$ and $f_j(\alpha_i) = g_i(\alpha_j)$ holds. If the checks pass for *every* pair of (honest) parties, then from Lemma 8.1, it follows that D has distributed consistent row and column-polynomials to the *honest* parties, since the number of honest parties is at least $n-t \geq t+1$. However, if the checks do not pass, then either D has distributed inconsistent polynomials or the parties have not exchanged the correct common values. In this case, the parties interact *publicly* with D to resolve these inconsistencies. The details follow.

Every P_i upon receiving the supposedly common values on its column polynomial prepares a *complaint-list* L_i, which includes all the parties P_j whose received value is inconsistent with P_i's column-polynomial (this is interpreted as if there is a dispute between P_i and P_j). If there is a dispute between P_i and P_j, then at least one of the three parties D, P_i, P_j is *corrupt*. Each party then broadcasts its complaint-list. In response, for every dispute reported by a party, the dealer D makes public its version of the disputed value, namely the corresponding value on its bivariate polynomial. This is followed by the *first-stage* accusations against the dealer. Namely, a party publicly "accuses" D, if the party is in dispute with more than t parties or if it finds D making public a value, which is not consistent with its column-polynomial. In response, D makes public the row and column-polynomials of such accusing parties.

---

[5] Recall the properties of RS codes and RS decoding from Section 6.4.3.

However, care has to be taken to ensure that these broadcasted polynomials are consistent with the polynomials of the parties who have *not* accused D till now. This is done through the *second-stage* of public accusations against the dealer, where a party (who has not yet accused D) publicly accuses D, if it finds any inconsistency between the row and column-polynomials held by the party and the polynomials which were made public by D.

An *honest* D always responds correctly against any accusation or dispute. Moreover, there will be at most t accusations against an *honest* D. Consequently, if the parties find D *not* responding to any accusation/dispute or if *more* than t parties accuse D, then clearly D is *corrupt* and hence the parties *publicly discard* D and everyone outputs a *default* share on behalf of D. If D is *honest*, then all the values which are made public correspond to corrupt parties (already known to the adversary) and hence *does not* violate *hiding*. On the other hand, if D is *corrupt* but not discarded, then it ensures that the polynomials of all honest parties are consistent, thus guaranteeing *binding*.

The VSS scheme called BGW is formally presented in Fig 8.3. In the protocol, we use the following (implicit) simplifying convention: if during a round a receiver party *does not* receive an expected message from a designated sender party or receives a syntactically incorrect message, then the receiver party substitutes some default value(s) on behalf of the sender party from the underlying domain and continues the protocol. Hence we do not specify separate steps to deal with the cases when syntactically incorrect or no message is received.

Scheme BGW

Sharing Phase: Protocol $\Pi^{(n,t)}_{\mathsf{BGWSh}}$

- **Round 1 (sending polynomials) — the dealer does the following**
  - On having the input $s \in \mathbb{F}$, pick a random t-degree *sharing polynomial* $q(y)$, such that $q(0) = s$ holds. Then pick a random (t, t)-degree bivariate polynomial $F(x, y)$, such that $F(0, y) = q(y)$ holds.
  - For $i = 1, \ldots, n$, send the polynomials $f_i(x) \stackrel{def}{=} F(x, \alpha_i)$ and $g_i(y) \stackrel{def}{=} F(\alpha_i, y)$ to party P_i.
- **Round 2 (pair-wise consistency checks) — each party $P_i \in \mathcal{P}$ does the following**
  - On receiving t-degree polynomials $f_i(x), g_i(y)$ from D, send $f_{ij} \stackrel{def}{=} f_i(\alpha_j)$ to P_j, for $j = 1, \ldots, n$.
- **Round 3 (broadcast complaints) — each party $P_i \in \mathcal{P}$ does the following**
  - Initialize a *complaint-list* L_i to $\emptyset$.
  - For $j = 1, \ldots, n$, include P_j to L_i, if $f_{ji} \neq g_i(\alpha_j)$.
  - Broadcast L_i by acting as a sender and calling the broadcast oracle with input L_i.
- **Round 4 (resolving complaints) — the dealer does the following**
  - For $i = 1, \ldots, n$, if P_i has broadcast $L_i \neq \emptyset$, then for every $P_j \in L_i$, broadcast the value $F(\alpha_i, \alpha_j)$ by acting as a sender and calling the broadcast oracle with input $F(\alpha_i, \alpha_j)$.
- **Round 5 (first-stage accusations) — each party $P_i \in \mathcal{P}$ does the following**
  - Broadcast the message $(P_i, \mathsf{accuse}, \mathsf{D})$ by acting as a sender and calling the broadcast oracle with input $(P_i, \mathsf{accuse}, \mathsf{D})$, if any of the following conditions hold.

    1. $|L_i| > t$ or if $P_i \in L_i$;

2. If $\exists k \in \{1, \dots, n\}$, such that $P_i \in L_k$ and $F(\alpha_k, \alpha_i) \neq f_i(\alpha_k)$, where $F(\alpha_k, \alpha_i)$ is the value broadcasted by the dealer;
3. If for any $P_j \in L_i$, the condition $F(\alpha_i, \alpha_j) \neq g_i(\alpha_j)$ holds, where $F(\alpha_i, \alpha_j)$ is the value broadcasted by the dealer.

- **Round 6 (resolving first-stage accusations) — the dealer does the following**
  - For every P_i who has broadcast $(P_i, \texttt{accuse}, \mathsf{D})$, broadcast the degree-$t$ polynomials $f_i(x)$ and $g_i(y)$ by acting as a sender and calling the broadcast oracle with input $(f_i(x), g_i(y))$.
- **Round 7 (second-stage accusations) — each party $P_i \in \mathcal{P}$ does the following**
  - Broadcast the message $(P_i, \texttt{accuse}, \mathsf{D})$ by acting as a sender and calling the broadcast oracle with input $(P_i, \texttt{accuse}, \mathsf{D})$, if there exists any $j \in \{1, \dots, n\}$ such that D has broadcast degree-t polynomials $f_j(x), g_j(y)$ and either $f_j(\alpha_i) \neq g_i(\alpha_j)$ or $g_j(\alpha_i) \neq f_i(\alpha_j)$ holds.
- **Output computation and termination — each party $P_i \in \mathcal{P}$ does the following**
  - If more than t parties P_j broadcast $(P_j, \texttt{accuse}, \mathsf{D})$ throughout the protocol, then discard D, output the *share* $s_i = 0$ and terminate.
  - Else output the *share* $s_i = f_i(0)$ and terminate.[a]

Reconstruction Phase: Protocol $\Pi^{(n,t)}_{\mathsf{BGWRec}}$

Each party $P_i \in \mathcal{P}$ does the following.
- Send the share s_i to every party $P_j \in \mathcal{P}$.
- Let W_i be the vector of shares received by P_i from the n parties. Party P_i executes $\mathsf{RSDecode}(W_i, n, t+1, t)$ to reconstruct $q(y)$, outputs $q(0)$ and terminate.

[a] If D has broadcast new polynomials $f_i(x), g_i(y)$ for P_i during Round 6, then consider these new polynomials.

Fig. 8.3: The perfectly-secure BGW VSS scheme

We now proceed to prove the properties of the VSS scheme. We first prove the *liveness* property.

Lemma 8.3 *In scheme* BGW, *the following holds for every possible adversary corrupting up to t parties:*
– *All honest parties terminate the protocol* $\Pi^{(n,t)}_{\mathsf{BGWSh}}$.
– *All honest parties terminate the protocol* $\Pi^{(n,t)}_{\mathsf{BGWRec}}$.

Proof The proof simply follows from the fact that both $\Pi^{(n,t)}_{\mathsf{BGWSh}}$ and $\Pi^{(n,t)}_{\mathsf{BGWRec}}$ are round-based and require a *fixed* number of rounds. In more detail, protocol $\Pi^{(n,t)}_{\mathsf{BGWSh}}$ requires *seven* rounds and hence the honest parties will terminate the protocol after seven rounds.[6] Similarly, protocol $\Pi^{(n,t)}_{\mathsf{BGWRec}}$ requires *one* round and hence the honest parties terminate the protocol after one round. □

We next prove the *correctness* and *hiding* properties for an *honest* dealer.

Lemma 8.4 *In scheme* BGW, *if* D *is honest during* $\Pi^{(n,t)}_{\mathsf{BGWSh}}$ *and participate with input s then the following holds for every possible adversary corrupting up to t parties, provided* $t < \frac{n}{3}$*:*

[6] The seven rounds are calculated assuming that broadcasting messages through the broadcast oracle is treated as one round.

– *All honest parties output s at the end of* $\Pi^{(n,t)}_{\mathsf{BGWRec}}$.
– *The view of the adversary during* $\Pi^{(n,t)}_{\mathsf{BGWSh}}$ *is independent of* s.

Proof If D is *honest* during $\Pi^{(n,t)}_{\mathsf{BGWSh}}$, then $f_i(\alpha_j) = g_j(\alpha_i)$ and $f_j(\alpha_i) = g_i(\alpha_j)$ holds for *every* pair of parties (P_i, P_j). Consequently, no honest P_j will be present in the list L_i of any honest P_i. Moreover, D honestly resolves the first-stage accusations as well as the second-stage accusations and consequently, no honest party accuses and discards D. Hence every honest P_i will output the share s_i during $\Pi^{(n,t)}_{\mathsf{BGWSh}}$, where $s_i = q(\alpha_i)$ and where $q(y)$ is the t-degree sharing polynomial selected by D with $q(0) = s$. Consequently, during $\Pi^{(n,t)}_{\mathsf{BGWRec}}$, the honest parties correctly reconstruct $q(y)$ and hence output s. This follows from the properties of $\mathsf{RSDecode}$ and the fact that $q(y)$ is a t-degree polynomial and at most t corrupt parties out of the n parties can send incorrect shares, where $t < \frac{n}{3}$.

Let C be the set of corrupt parties. If D is *honest*, then throughout $\Pi^{(n,t)}_{\mathsf{BGWSh}}$, the view of the adversary consists of $\{f_i(x), g_i(y)\}_{P_i \in C}$. Moreover, no honest party accuses D and hence all the information which D makes public can be derived from $\{f_i(x), g_i(y)\}_{P_i \in C}$. Now, since these polynomials are derived from $F(x, y)$, which is a randomly chosen (t, t)-degree polynomial embedding $q(y)$, it follows from Lemma 8.2 that the view of the adversary is distributed independently of s. □

We next prove the *binding* property for which we must consider a *corrupt* dealer.

Lemma 8.5 *In scheme* BGW, *even if* D *is corrupt during* $\Pi^{(n,t)}_{\mathsf{BGWSh}}$, *the following holds against every possible adversary corrupting up to t parties, provided* $t < \frac{n}{3}$:
– *There exists some* $s^\star \in \mathbb{F}$ *and a corresponding t-degree polynomial* $q^\star(y)$ *where* $s^\star = q^\star(0)$, *such that every honest party outputs a share* s_i *during* $\Pi^{(n,t)}_{\mathsf{BGWSh}}$ *where* $s_i = q^\star(\alpha_i)$.
– *During* $\Pi^{(n,t)}_{\mathsf{BGWRec}}$, *the honest parties output* $s^\star$.

Proof In protocol $\Pi^{(n,t)}_{\mathsf{BGWSh}}$, there are *two* possible cases. If D is *discarded* then $s^\star \overset{def}{=} 0$ and $q^\star(y) \overset{def}{=} 0$, with the share s_i of every honest P_i being 0, satisfying the condition that $s_i = 0 = q^\star(\alpha_i)$. We also note that in the protocol $\Pi^{(n,t)}_{\mathsf{BGWSh}}$, if D is *discarded*, then it is discarded by *all* honest parties. This is because D is discarded only if *more* than t parties accuse the dealer and in the protocol, the parties broadcast the $(\star, \texttt{accuse}, \mathsf{D})$ messages through the broadcast oracle, which guarantees that all honest parties receive these messages *identically*.

The *second* case is when D is *not* discarded. In this case, we claim that the row and column-polynomials of all the *honest* parties lie a single (t, t)-degree bivariate polynomial, say $F^\star(x, y)$, which we call as D's *committed* bivariate polynomial. If this is indeed the case, then we define $s^\star \overset{def}{=} F^\star(0, 0)$ and $q^\star(y) \overset{def}{=} F^\star(0, y)$, implying that the share s_i of every *honest* party P_i satisfies the condition that $s_i = q^\star(\alpha_i)$. This will also imply that during the protocol $\Pi^{(n,t)}_{\mathsf{BGWRec}}$, the honest parties output $s^\star$. This follows from the properties of $\mathsf{RSDecode}$ and the fact that $q^\star(y)$ is a t-degree polynomial and at most t corrupt parties out of the n parties can send incorrect shares, where $t < \frac{n}{3}$.

To prove the claim, we first note that there are at least $n - t \geq 2t + 1$ parties who *do not* broadcast an accuse message against D (as otherwise D is discarded). Let $\mathcal{H}$ be the set of *honest* parties among these $n - t$ parties. It is easy to see that $|\mathcal{H}| \geq n - 2t \geq t + 1$. The parties in $\mathcal{H}$ receive t-degree row and column-polynomials from D during the first round. Moreover, for every $P_i, P_j \in \mathcal{H}$, their row and column-polynomials are pair-wise consistent (as otherwise either P_i or P_j would broadcast an accuse message against D). It then follows from Lemma 8.1 that the row and column-polynomials of *all* the parties in $\mathcal{H}$ lie on a single (t, t)-degree bivariate polynomial, say $F^\star(x, y)$.

Next consider any *honest* party $P_j \notin \mathcal{H}$, who broadcasts an accuse message against D. Hence, corresponding to P_j, the dealer D makes *public* the row and column-polynomials of P_j. To complete the proof of the claim, we need to show that these polynomials *also* lie on $F^\star(x, y)$. We show it for the row-polynomial of P_j, and a similar argument can be used for the column-polynomial. So let $f_j(x)$ be the t-degree row-polynomial broadcasted by D for P_j. It follows that $f_j(\alpha_i) = g_i(\alpha_j)$ holds for *every* $P_i \in \mathcal{H}$, where $g_i(y)$ is the t-degree column polynomial held by P_i (otherwise P_i would have broadcasted an accuse message against D). Now as per the definition of $F^\star(x, y)$, the condition $g_i(y) = F^\star(\alpha_i, y)$ holds. Moreover, since $|\mathcal{H}| \geq t + 1$, the distinct points $\{(\alpha_j, g_i(\alpha_j))\}_{P_i \in \mathcal{H}}$ uniquely determine the t-degree polynomial $F^\star(x, \alpha_j)$. This implies that $f_j(x) = F^\star(x, \alpha_j)$ holds, as two *different* t-degree polynomials can have *at most* t common points. □

Based on the above discussion, we have the following theorem. In the theorem, communication complexity has two components: communication that happens over point-to-point channels and communication that happens through the broadcast oracle. We abuse the notation $\mathcal{BC}()$ and use it to denote the latter type of communication.

Theorem 8.2 *If $t < \frac{n}{3}$, then the pair of protocols $(\Pi^{(n,t)}_{\mathsf{BGWSh}}, \Pi^{(n,t)}_{\mathsf{BGWRec}})$ constitute a t-secure VSS scheme with perfect security in the model $\mathcal{M}_{\mathsf{secure}}$ with the following complexities.*

- *Protocol $\Pi^{(n,t)}_{\mathsf{BGWSh}}$ requires seven rounds and incurs a communication of $\mathcal{O}(n^2 \log|\mathbb{F}|) + \mathcal{BC}(n^2 \log|\mathbb{F}|)$ bits.*
- *Protocol $\Pi^{(n,t)}_{\mathsf{BGWRec}}$ requires one round and incurs a communication of $\mathcal{O}(n^2 \log|\mathbb{F}|)$ bits.*

Proof The *t-liveness* follows from Lemma 8.3, *t-correctness* and *t-privacy* follow from Lemma 8.4 and *t-binding* follows from Lemma 8.5.

The communication complexity follows easily from the protocol inspection. Namely, in the protocol $\Pi^{(n,t)}_{\mathsf{BGWSh}}$, dealer D sends two t-degree polynomials to each party and every pair of parties exchange 2 common values, which require communication of $\mathcal{O}(n^2)$ field elements. There could be at most t parties corresponding to which D makes *public* their polynomials and this requires a broadcast of $\mathcal{O}(n^2)$ field elements using the broadcast oracle. So this step requires a communication of $\mathcal{BC}(n^2 \log|\mathbb{F}|)$ bits. □

8.4.3 Perfect Secure VSS: Further Discussion

We presented the BGW perfectly secure VSS scheme due to its simplicity. A tremendous amount of research effort has been spent on improving the round and communication complexity of perfectly-secure VSS. Discussing and presenting these is simply out of the scope of this monogram and we refer to [29] for an elaborate survey on perfectly-secure VSS. In this section, we briefly discuss the advancements and state-of-the-art in this domain.

As mentioned earlier, in any VSS scheme, the parties use both the point-to-point channels and a broadcast oracle for broadcasting values. The assumption about the presence of a broadcast oracle is just for simplifying the presentation of the VSS schemes and in reality, such an oracle has to be instantiated from scratch by executing a *t-secure* BB protocol over the point-to-point channels. Let $(\Pi_{\mathsf{Sh}}^{(n,t)}, \Pi_{\mathsf{Rec}}^{(n,t)})$ be an arbitrary VSS scheme. Following the convention of [66], we say that the *round complexity* of $\Pi_{\mathsf{Sh}}^{(n,t)}$ is (R, R'), where $R \geq R'$, if the protocol $\Pi_{\mathsf{Sh}}^{(n,t)}$ involves R rounds and among these R rounds, the broadcast oracle is used for R' rounds. Similarly, the *round complexity* of $\Pi_{\mathsf{Rec}}^{(n,t)}$ is $(\mathsf{R}, \mathsf{R}')$, where $\mathsf{R} \geq \mathsf{R}'$, if the protocol $\Pi_{\mathsf{Rec}}^{(n,t)}$ involves R rounds and among these R rounds, the broadcast oracle is used for R' rounds.[7] For instance, for the BGW scheme $(\Pi_{\mathsf{BGWSh}}^{(n,t)}, \Pi_{\mathsf{BGWRec}}^{(n,t)})$, the round complexity of $\Pi_{\mathsf{BGWSh}}^{(n,t)}$ and $\Pi_{\mathsf{BGWRec}}^{(n,t)}$ is $(7, 2)$ and $(1, 0)$ respectively. This is because during $\Pi_{\mathsf{BGWSh}}^{(n,t)}$, the parties communicate for 7 rounds and among these 7 rounds, the broadcast oracle is used for 5 rounds, namely the last 5 rounds. Similarly, $\Pi_{\mathsf{BGWRec}}^{(n,t)}$ involves 1 rounds of communication and the broadcast oracle is *not* utilized. Note that it is *preferred* to have a VSS scheme where the number of broadcast rounds R' and R' is less. This is because, as mentioned above, the broadcast oracle has to be emulated by executing a BB protocol from scratch.

The following lower bounds on the round complexity of perfectly-secure VSS are well-known.[8]

Theorem 8.3 *Let R be a positive integer where $R \geq 1$ and let $R' \leq R$. Moreover, let t be the maximum number of parties out of the n parties which can be corrupted by the adversary in a Byzantine fashion.*

- *If $R = 1$, then there exists no perfectly-secure VSS scheme with (R, R') rounds in the sharing phase if either $t > 1$ (irrespective of the value of n) or if $(t = 1$ and $n \leq 4)$.*
- *If $R = 2$, then perfectly-secure VSS with (R, R') rounds in the sharing phase is possible only if $t < \frac{n}{4}$.*
- *If $R \geq 3$, then perfectly-secure VSS with (R, R') rounds in the sharing phase is possible only if $t < \frac{n}{3}$.*

[7] We stress that in a given round, multiple sender parties can use the broadcast oracle in parallel for broadcasting their respective messages.

[8] For perfectly-secure VSS, the focus is *only* on the round complexity of the sharing phase. This is because the reconstruction phase of *all* the known instantiations of perfectly-secure VSS involves only 1 round of communication over the point-to-point channels.

The communication complexity of any VSS scheme $(\Pi^{(n,t)}_{\mathsf{Sh}}, \Pi^{(n,t)}_{\mathsf{Rec}})$ can be thought of consisting of *two* components: the number of bits sent by the *honest* parties over the point-to-point channels and the number of bits broadcasted by the *honest* parties using the broadcast oracle, denoted by $\mathcal{BC}(\cdot)$. Our focus in this chapter will be on perfectly-secure VSS with $t < \frac{n}{3}$. In Table 8.1, we summarize the properties of known perfectly-secure VSS with $t < \frac{n}{3}$. In the table, we focus *only* on the sharing-phase protocol. This is because the reconstruction-phase protocols of all these schemes have the round complexity $(1, 0)$ and incur a communication of $O(n^2 \log |\mathbb{F}|)$ bits. We name the schemes based on the names of the authors of the scheme. In the table, $\Pi^{(n,t)}_{\mathsf{ModBGWSh}}$ and $\Pi^{(n,t)}_{\mathsf{ModBGWRec}}$ denote a modified version of the original BGW VSS scheme, presented in [57]. As evident from the table, there is a tradeoff between round and communication complexity. The protocols with *lesser* rounds require more communication.

Scheme	Round Complexity	Communication Complexity
$(\Pi^{(n,t)}_{\mathsf{BGWSh}}, \Pi^{(n,t)}_{\mathsf{BGWRec}})$ [21]	$(7, 5)$	$O(n^2 \log |\mathbb{F}|) + \mathcal{BC}(n^2 \log |\mathbb{F}|)$
$(\Pi^{(n,t)}_{\mathsf{ModBGWSh}}, \Pi^{(n,t)}_{\mathsf{ModBGWRec}})$ [57]	$(5, 3)$	$O(n^2 \log |\mathbb{F}|) + \mathcal{BC}(n^2 \log |\mathbb{F}|)$
$(\Pi^{(n,t)}_{\mathsf{GIKRSh}}, \Pi^{(n,t)}_{\mathsf{GIKRRec}})$ [57]	$(4, 3)$	$O(n^2 \log |\mathbb{F}|) + \mathcal{BC}(n^2 \log |\mathbb{F}|)$
$(\Pi^{(n,t)}_{\mathsf{FGGRSSh}}, \Pi^{(n,t)}_{\mathsf{FGGRSRec}})$ [52]	$(3, 2)$	$O(n^3 \log |\mathbb{F}|) + \mathcal{BC}(n^3 \log |\mathbb{F}|)$
$(\Pi^{(n,t)}_{\mathsf{KKKSh}}, \Pi^{(n,t)}_{\mathsf{KKKRec}})$ [66]	$(3, 1)$	$O(n^3 \log |\mathbb{F}|) + \mathcal{BC}(n^3 \log |\mathbb{F}|)$
$(\Pi^{(n,t)}_{\mathsf{AKPSh}}, \Pi^{(n,t)}_{\mathsf{AKPRec}})$ [14]	$(3, 2)$	$O(n^3 \log |\mathbb{F}|) + \mathcal{BC}(n^3 \log |\mathbb{F}|)$

Table 8.1: Summary of the sharing phase of the known perfectly-secure VSS schemes with $t < \frac{n}{3}$, with $\mathcal{BC}$ denoting communication happening using the broadcast oracle. In all the schemes, computations are performed over a finite field $\mathbb{F}$ where $|\mathbb{F}| > n$

8.5 Moderated Verifiable Secret Sharing (MVSS)

In this section, we discuss *moderated* VSS (MVSS), a variant of VSS introduced in [65]. In the primitive, *apart* from the dealer D, we have an *additional* designated party called the *moderator* M.[9] Intuitively, the goal of the moderator is to "emulate" a broadcast oracle for the parties. Like VSS, an MVSS scheme also has a sharing phase protocol and a reconstruction phase protocol. At the end of the sharing phase protocol, apart from outputting their shares, each party P_i also outputs a boolean flag f_i, which indicates whether the parties "trust" the moderator or not. While different parties *may* set the flag to *different* values, it will be guaranteed that if the moderator is *honest*, then all honest parties set this flag to 1. Moreover, if any honest party sets this flag to 1, then it would be ensured that all the properties of VSS (namely

[9] It could be *possible* that D and M are the *same*.

correctness, hiding and binding) are achieved. More formally, we have the following definition.

Definition 8.3 (Moderated Verifiable Secret Sharing (MVSS)) Let $(\Pi^{(n,t)}_{\mathsf{ModSh}}, \Pi^{(n,t)}_{\mathsf{ModRec}})$ be a pair of protocols for the parties in $\mathcal{P}$ in the model $\mathcal{M} \in \{\mathcal{M}_{\mathsf{secure}}, \mathcal{M}^{\mathsf{pki}}_{\mathsf{secure}}\}$, where there is a designated *dealer* $\mathsf{D} \in \mathcal{P}$ with some private input $s \in \mathcal{S}$ for the protocol $\Pi^{(n,t)}_{\mathsf{Sh}}$ and a designated *moderator* $\mathsf{M} \in \mathcal{P}$. Then $(\Pi^{(n,t)}_{\mathsf{ModSh}}, \Pi^{(n,t)}_{\mathsf{ModRec}})$ is called a *t-secure* MVSS scheme in the model $\mathcal{M}$, if the following requirements hold, for every possible adversary corrupting up to t parties among $\mathcal{P}$ in a Byzantine fashion, possibly including D and M.

- t-**liveness**: The following conditions should hold:
  - All honest parties terminate the protocol $\Pi^{(n,t)}_{\mathsf{ModSh}}$ and output a bit $f_i \in \{0, 1\}$.
  - All honest parties terminate the protocol $\Pi^{(n,t)}_{\mathsf{ModRec}}$ and output a value from $\mathcal{S}$.
- t-**Correctness**: If M is *honest* during $\Pi^{(n,t)}_{\mathsf{ModSh}}$, then all honest parties output $f_i = 1$ at the end of $\Pi^{(n,t)}_{\mathsf{ModSh}}$.
- t-**VSS-Emulation**: If there exists an *honest* party P_i, who outputs $f_i = 1$ during $\Pi^{(n,t)}_{\mathsf{ModSh}}$, then $(\Pi^{(n,t)}_{\mathsf{ModSh}}, \Pi^{(n,t)}_{\mathsf{ModRec}})$ constitute a VSS scheme. That is, all the following properties are achieved:
  - If D is *honest* during $\Pi^{(n,t)}_{\mathsf{ModSh}}$, then the view of the adversary during $\Pi^{(n,t)}_{\mathsf{ModSh}}$ is independent of s and all honest parties output s at the end of $\Pi^{(n,t)}_{\mathsf{ModRec}}$.
  - If D is *corrupt*, then the joint view of the honest parties during $\Pi^{(n,t)}_{\mathsf{ModSh}}$ defines a unique value $s^\star \in \mathcal{S}$ (which could be different from s), such that all honest parties output $s^\star$ at the end of $\Pi^{(n,t)}_{\mathsf{ModRec}}$.

We stress that if *none* of the honest parties P_i output $f_i = 1$ at the end of $\Pi^{(n,t)}_{\mathsf{ModSh}}$, then *no* guarantees are provided. For instance, honest parties may output *different* values from $\mathcal{S}$ during $\Pi^{(n,t)}_{\mathsf{ModRec}}$ or the adversary may learn an honest dealer's input s during $\Pi^{(n,t)}_{\mathsf{ModSh}}$. Similar to VSS, the security of any MVSS scheme could be perfect, statistical or cryptographic, depending upon the computational power of the adversary and whether the properties are achieved with or without error.

Next, we show how to "compile" any VSS scheme that uses a broadcast oracle into an MVSS scheme, where *no* broadcast oracle is required. The compiler is due to [65] and uses *gradecast* (GC) as a primitive (see Definition 2.4 for the definition of GC), which is the broadcast analogue of GA. Also, recall that we have shown that GC and GA are "equivalent" *irrespective* of the model and security level, as long as we are in the *honest-majority* setting; i.e. as long as $t < \frac{n}{2}$ (see Theorem 2.5 and Theorem 2.4).

8.5.1 From VSS to MVSS: A Generic Compiler

We are now ready to present the generic compiler of [65], which takes input *any* VSS scheme using a broadcast oracle and outputs an MVSS scheme which *does not* use any broadcast oracle.

Theorem 8.4 *Let* $(\Pi_{\mathsf{Sh}}^{(n,t)}, \Pi_{\mathsf{Rec}}^{(n,t)})$ *be a t-secure VSS scheme in the model* $\mathcal{M} \in \{\mathcal{M}_{\mathsf{secure}}, \mathcal{M}_{\mathsf{secure}}^{\mathsf{pki}}\}$ *with security level* $\mathsf{Sec} \in \{\mathsf{PerSec}, \mathsf{StatSec}, \mathsf{CryptoSec}\}$, *which has the following properties:*

- *Both* $\Pi_{\mathsf{Sh}}^{(n,t)}$ *and* $\Pi_{\mathsf{Rec}}^{(n,t)}$ *require a constant number of rounds;*
- *A broadcast oracle is used only during* $\Pi_{\mathsf{Sh}}^{(n,t)}$;
- *Protocol* $\Pi_{\mathsf{Sh}}^{(n,t)}$ *and* $\Pi_{\mathsf{Rec}}^{(n,t)}$ *incur a total communication of* $\mathcal{O}(C_1) + \mathcal{BC}(C_2)$ *bits.*

Moreover, let $\Pi_{\mathsf{GC}}^{(n,t)}$ *be a constant round, t-secure GC protocol for L-bit input in the model* $\mathcal{M}$ *with security level* Sec, *incurring a communication of* $\mathcal{GC}(L)$ *bits. Then there exists a t-secure MVSS scheme* $(\Pi_{\mathsf{ModSh}}^{(n,t)}, \Pi_{\mathsf{ModRec}}^{(n,t)})$ *in the model* $\mathcal{M}$ *with security level* Sec, *which has the following properties:*

- *Both* $\Pi_{\mathsf{ModSh}}^{(n,t)}$ *and* $\Pi_{\mathsf{ModRec}}^{(n,t)}$ *require a constant number of rounds;*
- *No broadcast oracle is used during* $\Pi_{\mathsf{ModSh}}^{(n,t)}$ *or* $\Pi_{\mathsf{ModRec}}^{(n,t)}$;
- *Protocol* $\Pi_{\mathsf{ModSh}}^{(n,t)}$ *and* $\Pi_{\mathsf{ModRec}}^{(n,t)}$ *incur a total communication of* $\mathcal{O}(C_1) + \mathcal{GC}(C_2)$ *bits.*

Proof Let $(\Pi_{\mathsf{Sh}}^{(n,t)}, \Pi_{\mathsf{Rec}}^{(n,t)})$ be a *t-secure* VSS scheme with the properties as stated in the theorem. We show how to transform the VSS scheme into an MVSS scheme $(\Pi_{\mathsf{ModSh}}^{(n,t)}, \Pi_{\mathsf{ModRec}}^{(n,t)})$, which *does not* require any broadcast oracle. The protocol $\Pi_{\mathsf{ModRec}}^{(n,t)}$ is the *same* as $\Pi_{\mathsf{Rec}}^{(n,t)}$, since as per the theorem conditions, protocol $\Pi_{\mathsf{Rec}}^{(n,t)}$ *does not* use any broadcast oracle. We now show how to transform the sharing phase protocol $\Pi_{\mathsf{Sh}}^{(n,t)}$ into protocol $\Pi_{\mathsf{ModSh}}^{(n,t)}$. The idea is to *emulate* each instance of communication using the broadcast oracle in $\Pi_{\mathsf{Sh}}^{(n,t)}$ via *two* instances of the GC protocol $\Pi_{\mathsf{GC}}^{(n,t)}$: in the *first* instance, the party that is supposed to broadcast the message acts as the sender and in the *second* instance, the moderator acts as the sender. In the first instance, the message to be broadcast using the broadcast oracle serves as the input of the designated sender party. On the other hand, the message obtained as the *output* from the first instance of GC serves as the *input* for the designated sender party during the second instance. The output received from the second instance then serves as the message "delivered" via the broadcast oracle.

After each emulation of the broadcast oracle through the above procedure, the parties set their boolean flag depending on whether they trust the moderator or not. For instance, if during the *second* instance of GC the output is *not* received with the highest grade (namely grade 2), then clearly the moderator is *corrupt* and hence the flag can be set to 0. Similarly, if the output from the *first* instance of GC is received with the highest grade but *mismatches* with the output received from the second GC instance, then also the moderator is *corrupt*, since the moderator is supposed to use the *output* obtained from the first GC instance as its *input* for the second GC instance.

Hence, the flag can be set as 0 even in this case. In more detail, protocol $\Pi_{\mathsf{ModSh}}^{(n,t)}$ is defined as follows where M is the *moderator* for $\Pi_{\mathsf{ModSh}}^{(n,t)}$:

- At the beginning of $\Pi_{\mathsf{ModSh}}^{(n,t)}$, each party P_i initializes $f_i = 1$. The parties then run the steps of $\Pi_{\mathsf{Sh}}^{(n,t)}$ as follows.
- In $\Pi_{\mathsf{Sh}}^{(n,t)}$, if any party P_i is directed to send some message m to some party P_j over the point-to-point channel, then in $\Pi_{\mathsf{ModSh}}^{(n,t)}$, party P_i sends m to P_j;
- In $\Pi_{\mathsf{Sh}}^{(n,t)}$, if any party P_i is directed to broadcast some message m as a sender using the broadcast oracle, then in $\Pi_{\mathsf{ModSh}}^{(n,t)}$, the parties run the following *emulated broadcast* routine:
  1. The parties run an instance of $\Pi_{\mathsf{GC}}^{(n,t)}$ with P_i playing the role of the sender S with input m. For $j = 1, \ldots, n$, let (m_j, g_j) be the output obtained by P_j from the instance of $\Pi_{\mathsf{GC}}^{(n,t)}$.
  2. Next, the parties run an instance of $\Pi_{\mathsf{GC}}^{(n,t)}$ with M playing the role of the sender S, where the input of M is the output message received from the instance of $\Pi_{\mathsf{GC}}^{(n,t)}$ in the previous step. For $j = 1, \ldots, n$, let (m'_j, g'_j) be the output obtained by P_j from this instance of $\Pi_{\mathsf{GC}}^{(n,t)}$.
  3. For $j = 1, \ldots, n$, party P_j treats m'_j as the message broadcasted by P_i using the broadcast oracle.
  4. For $j = 1, \ldots, n$, party P_j sets $f_j = 0$, if any of the following conditions holds:
     - $g'_j \neq 2$;
     - $g'_j = g_j = 2$ and $m_j \neq m'_j$.
- After executing all the steps of $\Pi_{\mathsf{Sh}}^{(n,t)}$ as above, each party $P_j \in \mathcal{P}$ outputs f_j (along with its share) and terminate.

It is easy to see that protocol $\Pi_{\mathsf{ModSh}}^{(n,t)}$ *does not* involve any broadcast oracle and all communication happens over point-to-point channels. Since the number of rounds in $\Pi_{\mathsf{Sh}}^{(n,t)}$ and $\Pi_{\mathsf{Rec}}^{(n,t)}$ is a constant and the number of rounds in $\Pi_{\mathsf{GC}}^{(n,t)}$ is also a constant, it follows that the number of rounds in $\Pi_{\mathsf{ModSh}}^{(n,t)}$ and $\Pi_{\mathsf{ModRec}}^{(n,t)}$ is also a constant. This is because if in $\Pi_{\mathsf{Sh}}^{(n,t)}$, the broadcast oracle is used in the *same* round by *different* sender parties, then the corresponding emulation of the broadcast oracle via instances of $\Pi_{\mathsf{GC}}^{(n,t)}$ can be executed in parallel. The communication complexity of $\Pi_{\mathsf{ModSh}}^{(n,t)}$ and $\Pi_{\mathsf{ModRec}}^{(n,t)}$ follows from the fact that the communication which happens using the broadcast oracle in $\Pi_{\mathsf{Sh}}^{(n,t)}$ now happens via instances of $\Pi_{\mathsf{GC}}^{(n,t)}$. We now proceed to show that $(\Pi_{\mathsf{ModSh}}^{(n,t)}, \Pi_{\mathsf{ModRec}}^{(n,t)})$ indeed constitutes a *t-secure* MVSS scheme.

The *t-liveness* follows from the *t-liveness* of $\Pi_{\mathsf{Sh}}^{(n,t)}, \Pi_{\mathsf{Rec}}^{(n,t)}$ and $\Pi_{\mathsf{GC}}^{(n,t)}$ and from the steps of the emulated broadcast.

For *t-correctness*, we have to consider an *honest* M. We wish to show that if M is *honest*, then all honest parties set $f = 1$ at the end of $\Pi_{\mathsf{ModSh}}^{(n,t)}$. So consider an *arbitrary* honest party P_j and an *arbitrary* instance of the emulated broadcast routine in the protocol $\Pi_{\mathsf{ModSh}}^{(n,t)}$. From the *t-validity* of $\Pi_{\mathsf{GC}}^{(n,t)}$, it follows that P_j will output

$g'_j = 2$ during step 2 of the routine, since M is the sender for the second instance of $\Pi_{\mathsf{GC}}^{(n,t)}$ and as per our assumption, M is *honest*. Moreover, if P_j outputs $(m_j, 2)$ during step 1 of the routine, then from the *t-knowledge-of-agreement* property of $\Pi_{\mathsf{GC}}^{(n,t)}$, the moderator M will output either $(m_j, 2)$ or $(m_j, 1)$ during step 1 of the routine. Consequently, the input for M during the instance of $\Pi_{\mathsf{GC}}^{(n,t)}$ during the step 2 of the routine will be m_j. Then from the *t-validity* of $\Pi_{\mathsf{GC}}^{(n,t)}$, it follows that $m'_j = m_j$ will hold and hence f_j will remain 1 at the end of the emulated broadcast routine. Since the emulated broadcast routine considered above is *arbitrary*, it follows that at the end of $\Pi_{\mathsf{ModSh}}^{(n,t)}$, party P_j will output $f_j = 1$.

For *t-VSS-Emulation*, we consider the case when some *honest* party P_j outputs $f_j = 1$ during $\Pi_{\mathsf{ModSh}}^{(n,t)}$. This further implies that f_j remained 1 at the end of *each* emulated broadcast routine, throughout the protocol $\Pi_{\mathsf{ModSh}}^{(n,t)}$. We consider any *arbitrary* emulated broadcast routine during $\Pi_{\mathsf{ModSh}}^{(n,t)}$, such that the corresponding sender party in $\Pi_{\mathsf{Sh}}^{(n,t)}$ is party P_i, who wants to broadcast some message through the broadcast oracle during $\Pi_{\mathsf{Sh}}^{(n,t)}$. We wish to show that the emulated broadcast routine will achieve the desired functionality of the broadcast oracle. That is, at the end of the emulated broadcast routine, all honest parties will consider the same message as received from the broadcast oracle and this message will be the message which P_i would like to send using the broadcast oracle during $\Pi_{\mathsf{Sh}}^{(n,t)}$, in case if P_i is *honest*. This will establish that in $\Pi_{\mathsf{ModSh}}^{(n,t)}$, all invocations of the broadcast oracle during $\Pi_{\mathsf{Sh}}^{(n,t)}$ are emulated correctly and hence $\Pi_{\mathsf{ModSh}}^{(n,t)}$ achieves the same functionality as $\Pi_{\mathsf{Sh}}^{(n,t)}$. Now since protocol $\Pi_{\mathsf{ModRec}}^{(n,t)}$ is the *same* as $\Pi_{\mathsf{Rec}}^{(n,t)}$, this will imply that $(\Pi_{\mathsf{ModSh}}^{(n,t)}, \Pi_{\mathsf{ModRec}}^{(n,t)})$ satisfies all the requirements of a VSS scheme.

Since $f_j = 1$ at the end of the emulated broadcast routine, it follows that the output (m'_j, g'_j) obtained by P_j during step 2 of the emulated broadcast routine as part of the second instance of $\Pi_{\mathsf{GC}}^{(n,t)}$ satisfies the condition $g'_j = 2$. Then from the *t-knowledge-of-agreement* property of $\Pi_{\mathsf{GC}}^{(n,t)}$, it follows that every other honest party gets either the output $(m'_j, 2)$ or $(m'_j, 1)$ during step 2 of the emulated broadcast routine, through the second instance of $\Pi_{\mathsf{GC}}^{(n,t)}$. Since the parties consider their respective output message from the second instance of $\Pi_{\mathsf{GC}}^{(n,t)}$ as the message received from the broadcast oracle, it follows that all honest parties agree on the message sent through the broadcast oracle. Next, consider the case when the designated sender P_i is *honest* and let m be the message which it wants to send using the broadcast oracle during $\Pi_{\mathsf{Sh}}^{(n,t)}$. Then from the *t-validity* of $\Pi_{\mathsf{GC}}^{(n,t)}$, it follows that during step 1 of the emulated broadcast routine, every honest party P_k will output $(m_k, 2)$ during step 1 of the routine as part of the first instance of $\Pi_{\mathsf{GC}}^{(n,t)}$, where $m_k = m$. Moreover, since $f_j = 1$ for P_j, the condition $m_j = m'_j$ holds as well. But since $m_j = m$ and since m'_j is taken as the output of the emulated broadcast routine, it follows that all honest parties take m as the message being sent by the broadcast oracle at the end of the emulated broadcast routine in $\Pi_{\mathsf{ModSh}}^{(n,t)}$. □

Recall that in Section 4.3, we provided an instantiation $\Pi^{(n,t)}_{\mathsf{PerSecGAOneThird}}$ for a *t-secure* GA for L-bit inputs with *perfect security*, in the model $\mathcal{M}_{\mathsf{auth}}$ where $t < \frac{n}{3}$ (see Fig 4.4). The protocol requires *two* rounds and incurs a communication of $\mathcal{GA}(L) = \mathcal{O}(n^2 L)$ bits. By using $\Pi^{(n,t)}_{\mathsf{PerSecGAOneThird}}$ as an instantiation of the abstract GA protocol in Theorem 2.4, we get an instantiation of a *t-secure* GC for L-bit inputs with *perfect security*, in the model $\mathcal{M}_{\mathsf{auth}}$ where $t < \frac{n}{3}$. The protocol will require *three* rounds of communication; in the first round, the sender will distribute its input to all and in the next two rounds the parties will execute an instance of $\Pi^{(n,t)}_{\mathsf{PerSecGAOneThird}}$. The communication complexity of the protocol will be $\mathcal{GC}(L) = \mathcal{O}(n^2 L)$ bits. We call the resultant protocol $\Pi^{(n,t)}_{\mathsf{PerSecGCOneThird}}$.

Let us now instantiate the generic VSS scheme $(\Pi^{(n,t)}_{\mathsf{Sh}}, \Pi^{(n,t)}_{\mathsf{Rec}})$ in Theorem 8.4 with the perfectly-secure BGW scheme $(\Pi^{(n,t)}_{\mathsf{BGWSh}}, \Pi^{(n,t)}_{\mathsf{BGWRec}})$. Moreover, let us instantiate the generic GC protocol $\Pi^{(n,t)}_{\mathsf{GC}}$ in Theorem 8.4 with the 3-round perfectly-secure GC protocol $\Pi^{(n,t)}_{\mathsf{PerSecGCOneThird}}$ outlined above. We then get a *constant* round perfectly-secure MVSS scheme in the pairwise-secure channel model, *without* any setup, tolerating $t < \frac{n}{3}$ corrupt parties. We call the resultant MVSS scheme the BGW MVSS scheme (since it is derived from the BGW VSS scheme), whose properties are summarized in Corollary 8.1.

Corollary 8.1 *Protocols* $(\Pi^{(n,t)}_{\mathsf{BGWMSh}}, \Pi^{(n,t)}_{\mathsf{BGWMRec}})$ *constitute a t-secure MVSS scheme with perfect security in the model* $\mathcal{M}_{\mathsf{secure}}$, *tolerating* $t < \frac{n}{3}$ *corruptions. The protocols have the following complexities.*

- *Protocol* $\Pi^{(n,t)}_{\mathsf{BGWMSh}}$ *requires* 32 *rounds while* $\Pi^{(n,t)}_{\mathsf{BGWMRec}}$ *requires* 1 *round.*
- *Protocol* $\Pi^{(n,t)}_{\mathsf{BGWMSh}}$ *incurs a communication of* $\mathcal{O}(n^4 \log |\mathbb{F}|)$ *bits, while* $\Pi^{(n,t)}_{\mathsf{BGWMRec}}$ *incurs a communication of* $\mathcal{O}(n^2 \log |\mathbb{F}|)$ *bits.*

Proof The proof that $(\Pi^{(n,t)}_{\mathsf{BGWMSh}}, \Pi^{(n,t)}_{\mathsf{BGWMRec}})$ constitute a *t-secure* MVSS scheme with perfect security follows from the proof of Theorem 8.4 and the fact that $(\Pi^{(n,t)}_{\mathsf{BGWSh}}, \Pi^{(n,t)}_{\mathsf{BGWRec}})$ constitute a *t-secure* VSS scheme with perfect security, while $\Pi^{(n,t)}_{\mathsf{PerSecGCOneThird}}$ constitute a *t-secure* GC protocol with perfect security.

Let us derive the number of rounds for the MVSS scheme. Since protocol $\Pi^{(n,t)}_{\mathsf{BGWMRec}}$ is the *same* as $\Pi^{(n,t)}_{\mathsf{BGWRec}}$, protocol $\Pi^{(n,t)}_{\mathsf{BGWMRec}}$ requires *one* round. On the other hand, protocol $\Pi^{(n,t)}_{\mathsf{BGWMSh}}$ is the same as $\Pi^{(n,t)}_{\mathsf{BGWSh}}$, with every message broadcasted using the broadcast oracle in $\Pi^{(n,t)}_{\mathsf{BGWSh}}$ being now instead communicated through the emulated broadcast routine, specified in the proof of Theorem 8.4. Each instance of the emulated broadcast routine when instantiated with the GC protocol $\Pi^{(n,t)}_{\mathsf{PerSecGCOneThird}}$ will require 6 rounds. This is because there are two invocations of the GC protocol in *sequence* in the emulated broadcast routine and each instance of the GC protocol $\Pi^{(n,t)}_{\mathsf{PerSecGCOneThird}}$ requires 3 rounds. In protocol $\Pi^{(n,t)}_{\mathsf{BGWSh}}$, the first *two* rounds involve communication over the point-to-point channels, while the next *five* rounds are broadcast rounds, utilizing the broadcast oracle. Consequently, the number of rounds in $\Pi^{(n,t)}_{\mathsf{BGWMSh}}$ will be $2 + 5 \times 6 = 32$.

Let us now derive the communication complexity of the MVSS scheme. The communication complexity of $\Pi^{(n,t)}_{\mathsf{BGWMRec}}$ is the *same* as $\Pi^{(n,t)}_{\mathsf{BGWRec}}$, which is $O(n^2 \log |\mathbb{F}|)$ bits. The communication complexity of $\Pi^{(n,t)}_{\mathsf{BGWMSh}}$ follows from the fact that $O(n^2 \log |\mathbb{F}|)$ bits need to be broadcasted using the broadcast oracle in the protocol $\Pi^{(n,t)}_{\mathsf{BGWSh}}$. In the protocol $\Pi^{(n,t)}_{\mathsf{BGWMSh}}$, each instance of the usage of the broadcast oracle in $\Pi^{(n,t)}_{\mathsf{BGWSh}}$ is emulated by the emulated broadcast routine. Consequently, the communication complexity of $\Pi^{(n,t)}_{\mathsf{BGWMSh}}$ is dominated by the cost of communicating $O(n^2 \log |\mathbb{F}|)$ bits through instances of $\Pi^{(n,t)}_{\mathsf{PerSecGCOneThird}}$. By substituting $L = n^2 \log |\mathbb{F}|$ in the communication cost of $\Pi^{(n,t)}_{\mathsf{PerSecGCOneThird}}$, the communication complexity of $\Pi^{(n,t)}_{\mathsf{BGWMSh}}$ turns out to be $O(n^4 \log |\mathbb{F}|)$ bits over the point-to-point channels. □

Recall that in Table 8.1 we summarized several other instantiations of perfectly-secure VSS with $t < \frac{n}{3}$, apart from the BGW VSS scheme. By instantiating the generic VSS scheme $(\Pi^{(n,t)}_{\mathsf{Sh}}, \Pi^{(n,t)}_{\mathsf{Rec}})$ in Theorem 8.4 with these perfectly-secure VSS schemes and the generic GC protocol $\Pi^{(n,t)}_{\mathsf{GC}}$ with the 3-round perfectly-secure GC protocol $\Pi^{(n,t)}_{\mathsf{PerSecGCOneThird}}$, we get various *constant* round *t-secure* MVSS schemes in the model $\mathcal{M}_{\mathsf{secure}}$ with perfect security, tolerating $t < \frac{n}{3}$ corrupt parties. These MVSS schemes are summarized in Table 8.2.

The round complexity of the various MVSS schemes in Table 8.2 is derived as follows: let (R, R') be the round complexity of the sharing phase protocol of the corresponding VSS scheme. Hence, the number of rounds where the parties perform communication *only* over the point-to-point channels is $R - R'$. Emulating the broadcast rounds (where broadcast oracle is invoked) through the compiler presented in Theorem 8.4 by using instances of GC, the number of rounds in the sharing phase of the compiled MVSS scheme turns out to be $(R - R') + 6R'$. Note that the round complexity of the reconstruction phase of the MVSS schemes will be one, since the reconstruction phase of all the VSS schemes in Table 8.1 is one.

The communication complexity of the MVSS schemes in Table 8.2 is derived by finding the amount of communication L happening via the broadcast oracle in the sharing phase of the corresponding VSS scheme, since it dominates the communication complexity of the sharing phase of the VSS. The communication complexity of the sharing phase of the MVSS is then calculated by finding how much communication happens over the point-to-point channels to communicate L bits through instances of the 3-round perfectly-secure GC protocol $\Pi^{(n,t)}_{\mathsf{PerSecGCOneThird}}$, as done in the compiler presented in Theorem 8.4. Note that the communication complexity of the reconstruction phase of all the MVSS schemes is fixed, namely $O(n^2 \log |\mathbb{F}|)$ bits. This is because the communication complexity of the reconstruction phase of all the MVSS schemes is the same as the reconstruction phase of the corresponding VSS scheme. And the communication complexity of the reconstruction phase of all the VSS schemes in Table 8.1 is $O(n^2 \log |\mathbb{F}|)$ bits. As evident from the table, there is a tradeoff between the round and communication complexity of the various MVSS schemes. The good news is that all the MVSS schemes require a *constant* number of rounds.

Sharing Phase	Round Complexity	Communication Complexity	Reconstruction Phase	Round Complexity	Communication Complexity
$\Pi^{(n,t)}_{\mathsf{BGWMSh}}$	32	$\mathcal{O}(n^4 \log \lvert\mathbb{F}\rvert)$	$\Pi^{(n,t)}_{\mathsf{BGWMRec}}$	1	$\mathcal{O}(n^2 \log \lvert\mathbb{F}\rvert)$
$\Pi^{(n,t)}_{\mathsf{ModBGWMSh}}$	20	$\mathcal{O}(n^4 \log \lvert\mathbb{F}\rvert)$	$\Pi^{(n,t)}_{\mathsf{ModBGWMRec}}$	1	$\mathcal{O}(n^2 \log \lvert\mathbb{F}\rvert)$
$\Pi^{(n,t)}_{\mathsf{GIKRMSh}}$	19	$\mathcal{O}(n^4 \log \lvert\mathbb{F}\rvert)$	$\Pi^{(n,t)}_{\mathsf{GIKRMRec}}$	1	$\mathcal{O}(n^2 \log \lvert\mathbb{F}\rvert)$
$\Pi^{(n,t)}_{\mathsf{FGGRMSh}}$	13	$\mathcal{O}(n^5 \log \lvert\mathbb{F}\rvert)$	$\Pi^{(n,t)}_{\mathsf{FGGRMRec}}$	1	$\mathcal{O}(n^2 \log \lvert\mathbb{F}\rvert)$
$\Pi^{(n,t)}_{\mathsf{KKKMSh}}$	8	$\mathcal{O}(n^5 \log \lvert\mathbb{F}\rvert)$	$\Pi^{(n,t)}_{\mathsf{KKKMRec}}$	1	$\mathcal{O}(n^2 \log \lvert\mathbb{F}\rvert)$
$\Pi^{(n,t)}_{\mathsf{AKPMSh}}$	13	$\mathcal{O}(n^5 \log \lvert\mathbb{F}\rvert)$	$\Pi^{(n,t)}_{\mathsf{AKPMRec}}$	1	$\mathcal{O}(n^2 \log \lvert\mathbb{F}\rvert)$

Table 8.2: Summary of the various *t-secure* MVSS schemes with perfect security and $t < \frac{n}{3}$ in the model $\mathcal{M}_{\mathsf{secure}}$, obtained by instantiating the generic VSS scheme $(\Pi^{(n,t)}_{\mathsf{Sh}}, \Pi^{(n,t)}_{\mathsf{Rec}})$ in Theorem 8.4 with the various perfectly-secure VSS schemes summarized in Table 8.1 and the generic GC protocol $\Pi^{(n,t)}_{\mathsf{GC}}$ with the 3-round perfectly-secure GC protocol $\Pi^{(n,t)}_{\mathsf{PerSecGCOneThird}}$. In all the schemes, computations are performed over a finite field $\mathbb{F}$ where $|\mathbb{F}| > n$

8.6 A Generic Common Coin from Any Generic MVSS

In this section, we discuss how to get an instantiation of CC from any given MVSS scheme. The construction is *generic* and is *independent* of the underlying MVSS. The high-level idea behind the instantiation has been discussed in Section 8.3. The idea is to associate a uniformly random value $c_i \in \{0, \ldots, u-1\}$ with every party P_i for some given parameter u and then based on the values associated with the parties, the parties decide their respective output for CC.[10] To associate a random value c_i with party P_i, each party P_j picks uniformly random value $c_{j\to i}$ and verifiably secret-shares it and then c_i is set to be the sum of the values $c_{j\to i}$ modulo u. However, a problem with the above approach is that the sharing-phase protocol of *any* VSS scheme requires a broadcast oracle (which can be emulated by a BB protocol) and we want to design a CC protocol to get a BA (BB) protocol. To get around this circular reasoning, *instead* of using VSS, we will use an MVSS scheme. The details follow.

Let $(\Pi^{(n,t)}_{\mathsf{ModSh}}, \Pi^{(n,t)}_{\mathsf{ModRec}})$ be a *t-secure* MVSS scheme in the model $\mathcal{M} \in \{\mathcal{M}_{\mathsf{secure}}, \mathcal{M}^{\mathsf{pki}}_{\mathsf{secure}}\}$ with security level $\mathsf{Sec} \in \{\mathsf{PerSec}, \mathsf{StatSec}, \mathsf{CryptoSec}\}$, where all computations are performed over a finite field $\mathbb{F}$. The CC protocol $\Pi^{(n,t)}_{\mathsf{CC}}$ consists of two *phases*. During the first phase, each party P_j picks a uniformly random value $c_{j\to i}$ from $\mathbb{F}$ on behalf of P_i and secret-shares it by invoking an instance of $\Pi^{(n,t)}_{\mathsf{ModSh}}$ as a

[10] The parameter u "controls" the success probability p for the resultant CC protocol.

dealer with input $c_{j \to i}$ where P_i plays the role of the *moderator*. After all the values are secret-shared (ensuring that even the *corrupt* dealers P_j are committed to some value $c_{j \to i}$ in their respective $\Pi^{(n,t)}_{\mathsf{ModSh}}$ instances), the parties start the second phase where they reconstruct the values being shared in the respective $\Pi^{(n,t)}_{\mathsf{ModSh}}$ instances, by participating in the corresponding instances of $\Pi^{(n,t)}_{\mathsf{ModRec}}$. Then once all the values are reconstructed, each party P_k decides the value *associated* with P_i as follows: if there is any $\Pi^{(n,t)}_{\mathsf{ModSh}}$ instance with P_i playing the role of the moderator where P_k graded P_i with grade 0, then P_k associates the value $\perp$ with P_i. Otherwise, the value associated with P_i is set to the sum of the values reconstructed by P_k in the corresponding $\Pi^{(n,t)}_{\mathsf{ModRec}}$ instances modulo u. Finally, P_k considers all the associated values which are *not* $\perp$: if any of these associated values is 0, then the coin for P_k is 0, else it is 1.

The idea here is the following: if the moderator P_i is *honest*, then *irrespective* of the dealers, all honest parties will give the grade 1 in all the instances of $\Pi^{(n,t)}_{\mathsf{ModSh}}$ where P_i plays the role of the moderator. Hence, these $\Pi^{(n,t)}_{\mathsf{ModSh}}$ instances, along with the corresponding $\Pi^{(n,t)}_{\mathsf{ModRec}}$ instances, will achieve all the properties of a VSS (namely binding and hiding). Consequently, all honest parties will associate a *common* value with P_i, which will be randomly distributed over $\{0, \ldots, u-1\}$ since the honest parties share random values on behalf of P_i. As a result, each honest party will consider the values associated with the honest parties when deciding its final coin. If any of these associated values turn out to be 0, then all honest parties will output 0 as the final coin. The probability of this event is at least $1 - (1 - \frac{1}{u})^{n-t}$, since there are at least $n - t$ honest parties and the probability that the associated value of an honest party is 0 is $\frac{1}{u}$. Thus with a probability of at least $1 - (1 - \frac{1}{u})^{n-t}$, all honest parties will output 0 as the coin value.

If the moderator P_i is *corrupt* and if every honest party has graded P_i with grade 0 in at least one of the $\Pi^{(n,t)}_{\mathsf{ModSh}}$ instances where P_i served as the moderator, then clearly every honest party will associate $\perp$ with P_i, which will *not* be considered to determine the final coin of the honest parties.

The tricky case is when the moderator P_i is *corrupt* but some honest party has graded 1 in all the n instances of $\Pi^{(n,t)}_{\mathsf{ModSh}}$ where P_i served as the moderator. In this case, these $\Pi^{(n,t)}_{\mathsf{ModSh}}$ instances along with the corresponding $\Pi^{(n,t)}_{\mathsf{ModRec}}$ instances will achieve all the properties of a VSS. As a result, all honest parties who graded P_i with 1 will associate a common random value with P_i. However, there might be *disagreement* with respect to the value associated with P_i, if some set of honest parties, say $\mathcal{H}_1$, give the grade 1 for the moderator P_i, while other honest parties, say $\mathcal{H}_2$, give the grade 0. This is because the parties in $\mathcal{H}_2$ will associate $\perp$ with P_i, while the parties in $\mathcal{H}_1$ will associate a random yet common value from $\{0, \ldots, u-1\}$ with P_i. Consequently, the value associated with P_i is *not* considered by the parties in $\mathcal{H}_2$ while determining their coin value, while the value associated with P_i *is* considered by the parties in $\mathcal{H}_1$ while determining their coin value. Even though there is a possibility of honest parties getting *different* coin outputs, the way parties determine the associated values and the final coin based on these associated values, the probability that all honest parties output 1 is at least $(1 - \frac{1}{u})^n$. This is because for every potential *corrupt* moderator P_i whose resultant associated value is considered while determining the final coin, it turns out that the associated value is distributed *randomly* over $\{0, \ldots, u-1\}$ and hence can take the value 0 with probability $\frac{1}{u}$. Consequently, if *none* of the associated values (different from $\perp$) which are considered for determining the final coin turns out to be 0, then all honest parties will output 1 as the final coin. Since in the worst case, all the n associated values may turn out to be different from $\perp$ and might be considered for determining the final coin, the probability of $(1 - \frac{1}{u})^n$ follows. Protocol $\Pi_{\mathsf{CC}}^{(n,t)}$ is formally presented in Fig 8.4.

Protocol $\Pi_{\mathsf{CC}}^{(n,t)}$

Public knowledge: the description of a *t-secure* MVSS scheme $(\Pi_{\mathsf{ModSh}}^{(n,t)}, \Pi_{\mathsf{ModRec}}^{(n,t)})$ in the model $\mathcal{M} \in \{\mathcal{M}_{\mathsf{secure}}, \mathcal{M}_{\mathsf{secure}}^{\mathsf{pki}}\}$ with security level $\mathsf{Sec} \in \{\mathsf{PerSec}, \mathsf{StatSec}, \mathsf{CryptoSec}\}$.

- **Phase I — Secret-Sharing Values on Behalf of the Parties**:
  - Each party $P_j \in \mathcal{P}$ picks a uniformly value $c_{j \to i} \in \mathbb{F}$ on behalf of every party $P_i \in \mathcal{P}$. Moreover, each party $P_k \in \mathcal{P}$ initializes $\mathsf{trust}_{k,i} := 1$, for $i = 1, \ldots, n$.
  - For every *ordered* pair $(j, i) \in \{1, \ldots, n\} \times \{1, \ldots, n\}$, the parties in $\mathcal{P}$ participate in an instance of $\Pi_{\mathsf{ModSh}}^{(n,t)}$ where P_j plays the role of the *dealer* D with input $c_{j \to i}$ and P_i plays the role of the *moderator* M. If any party $P_k \in \mathcal{P}$ outputs $f_k = 0$ at the end of this instance of $\Pi_{\mathsf{ModSh}}^{(n,t)}$, then P_k sets $\mathsf{trust}_{k,i} := 0$.
  - For $k = 1, \ldots, n$, party P_k sets $\mathsf{trust}_k := \{P_i : \mathsf{trust}_{k,i} = 1\}$.
- **Phase II — Reconstructing the Secret-Shared Values**:
  - For every *ordered* pair $(j, i) \in \{1, \ldots, n\} \times \{1, \ldots, n\}$, the parties in $\mathcal{P}$ participate in an instance of $\Pi_{\mathsf{ModRec}}^{(n,t)}$ to reconstruct the value shared in the instance of $\Pi_{\mathsf{ModSh}}^{(n,t)}$ where P_j and P_i played the role of D and M respectively. For $k = 1, \ldots, n$, let $c_{j \to i}^{(k)}$ be the value reconstructed by P_k in this instance of $\Pi_{\mathsf{ModRec}}^{(n,t)}$.
  - For $i = 1, \ldots, n$, every party $P_k \in \mathcal{P}$ computes the value $c_i^{(k)}$ *associated* with P_i as follows:
    - If $P_i \notin \mathsf{trust}_k$, then set $c_i^{(k)} = \perp$;
    - Else set

$$c_i^{(k)} = \sum_{j=1}^{n} c_{j \to i}^{(k)} \mod u.$$

- **Output Computation**: Every party $P_k \in \mathcal{P}$ computes its output as follows and terminate.
  - If there is any party $P_i \in \mathsf{trust}_k$ such that $c_i^{(k)} = 0$, then output 0;
  - Else output 1.

Fig. 8.4: A generic CC from any given *t-secure* MVSS scheme $(\Pi_{\mathsf{ModSh}}^{(n,t)}, \Pi_{\mathsf{ModRec}}^{(n,t)})$. In the protocol, u is a parameter to control the success probability of the protocol

We now start proving the properties of the protocol $\Pi_{\mathsf{CC}}^{(n,t)}$. We start with the termination property and derive the round and communication complexity.

Claim 8.4 Let $(\Pi_{\mathsf{ModSh}}^{(n,t)}, \Pi_{\mathsf{ModRec}}^{(n,t)})$ be a *t-secure* MVSS scheme where $\Pi_{\mathsf{ModSh}}^{(n,t)}$ and $\Pi_{\mathsf{ModRec}}^{(n,t)}$ require R_1 and R_2 rounds respectively. Then all the following holds in the protocol $\Pi_{\mathsf{CC}}^{(n,t)}$.

- ***t*-liveness**: All honest parties terminate the protocol after $R_1 + R_2$ rounds.

- The communication complexity of the protocol is n^2 times the communication complexity of one instance of $\Pi_{\mathsf{ModSh}}^{(n,t)}$ and one instance of $\Pi_{\mathsf{ModRec}}^{(n,t)}$.

Proof In the protocol, the parties participate in n^2 instances of $\Pi_{\mathsf{ModSh}}^{(n,t)}$, all of which can be executed in parallel. This will require R_1 rounds and the communication complexity will be n^2 times that of one instance of $\Pi_{\mathsf{ModSh}}^{(n,t)}$. Once all the instances of $\Pi_{\mathsf{ModSh}}^{(n,t)}$ are over, the parties participate in n^2 instances of $\Pi_{\mathsf{ModRec}}^{(n,t)}$, again all of which can be executed in parallel. This will further require R_2 rounds and the communication complexity will be n^2 times that of one instance of $\Pi_{\mathsf{ModRec}}^{(n,t)}$. Once all the instances of $\Pi_{\mathsf{ModRec}}^{(n,t)}$ are over, all honest parties terminate the protocol, proving the *t-liveness*. □

We next show that every *honest* moderator will be present in the trust vector of every *honest* party and *all* the instances of the MVSS with respect to an honest moderator will satisfy the properties of VSS, *irrespective* of the corresponding dealer. Moreover, all honest parties will associate a common value with the moderator, which will be distributed uniformly over $\{0, \ldots, u-1\}$.

Claim 8.5 Let $(\Pi_{\mathsf{ModSh}}^{(n,t)}, \Pi_{\mathsf{ModRec}}^{(n,t)})$ be a *t-secure* MVSS scheme. Then in protocol $\Pi_{\mathsf{CC}}^{(n,t)}$, all the following holds for every honest party P_i:

- $P_i \in \mathsf{trust}_k$, for every honest party P_k.
- All honest parties will associate a common value c_i with P_i, where c_i will be a uniformly random value from the set $\{0, \ldots, u-1\}$.

Proof Let $\mathcal{H}$ be the set of *honest* parties and let $P_i \in \mathcal{H}$ be an *arbitrary* party. Then from the *t-correctness* of $\Pi_{\mathsf{ModSh}}^{(n,t)}$, it follows that every party $P_k \in \mathcal{H}$ will output $f_k = 1$ at the end of *all* the n instances of $\Pi_{\mathsf{ModSh}}^{(n,t)}$, where P_i played the role of the moderator M. Consequently, the condition $\mathsf{trust}_{k,i} = 1$ holds at the end of phase I and hence $P_i \in \mathsf{trust}_k$.

Now consider an *arbitrary* instance of $\Pi_{\mathsf{ModSh}}^{(n,t)}$ with P_j playing the role of the dealer and P_i playing the role of moderator. Since $P_i \in \mathsf{trust}_k$, from the *t-VSS-Emulation* property of the MVSS it follows that $(\Pi_{\mathsf{ModSh}}^{(n,t)}, \Pi_{\mathsf{ModRec}}^{(n,t)})$ satisfy the properties of a *t-secure VSS*. Namely, if $P_j \in \mathcal{H}$, then the value $c_{j\to i}$ remains private from the point of view of the adversary during phase I and every party in $\mathcal{H}$ reconstruct $c_{j\to i}$ from the instance of $\Pi_{\mathsf{ModRec}}^{(n,t)}$ during phase II; this follows from the *t-hiding* and *t-correctness* properties of VSS. Moreover, even if $P_j \notin \mathcal{H}$, there exists some well-defined value $c_{j\to i} \in \mathbb{F}$, such that every party in $\mathcal{H}$ reconstruct $c_{j\to i}$ from the instance of $\Pi_{\mathsf{ModRec}}^{(n,t)}$ during phase II; this follows from the *t-binding* property of VSS. We also note that the values $c_{j\to i}$ picked and shared by the dealers $P_j \in \mathcal{H}$ are randomly chosen from $\mathbb{F}$ and *independent* of the values $c_{j\to i}$ picked and shared by the dealers $P_j \notin \mathcal{H}$. This follows from the fact that due to *t-hiding* of VSS, the dealers $P_j \notin \mathcal{H}$ will *not* know the values picked and shared by the dealers $P_j \in \mathcal{H}$. Now consider the value c_i where

$$c_i \stackrel{def}{=} \sum_{j=1}^{n} c_{j\to i} \mod u.$$

From the above arguments, it follows that every party in $\mathcal{H}$ will associate the value c_i with P_i during phase II. Moreover, c_i will a random value from the set $\{0, \ldots, u-1\}$, since $\sum_{j=1}^{n} c_{j\to i}$ will be a random value, as the $c_{j\to i}$ values corresponding to the dealers $P_j \in \mathcal{H}$ are random. □

We next focus on a *corrupt* moderator and prove the properties which hold with respect to such moderators.

Claim 8.6 Let $(\Pi_{\mathsf{ModSh}}^{(n,t)}, \Pi_{\mathsf{ModRec}}^{(n,t)})$ be a *t-secure* MVSS scheme and let P_i be a corrupt party in the protocol $\Pi_{\mathsf{CC}}^{(n,t)}$. Moreover, let $\mathcal{H}_i$ be the set of honest parties such that $P_i \in \mathsf{trust}_k$ for every $P_k \in \mathcal{H}_i$ during phase I. If $\mathcal{H}_i \neq \emptyset$, then all the following holds:

- There exists a uniformly random value c_i from the set $\{0, \ldots, u-1\}$.
- Every party in $\mathcal{H}_i$ associates the value c_i with P_i during phase II, while every honest party not present in $\mathcal{H}_i$ associates $\perp$ with P_i.

Proof Let P_i be an arbitrary corrupt party and let $\mathcal{H}_i \neq \emptyset$. Then consider an arbitrary $P_k \in \mathcal{H}_i$. This implies that $P_i \in \mathsf{trust}_k$, which further implies that $\mathsf{trust}_{k,i} = 1$ holds at the end of phase I. This is possible only if P_k outputs $f_k = 1$ at the end of all the $\Pi_{\mathsf{ModSh}}^{(n,t)}$ instances where P_i played the role of moderator.

Now consider an *arbitrary* instance of $\Pi_{\mathsf{ModSh}}^{(n,t)}$ with P_j playing the role of the dealer and P_i playing the role of moderator. Since $P_i \in \mathsf{trust}_k$, from the *t-VSS-Emulation* property of the MVSS it follows that $(\Pi_{\mathsf{ModSh}}^{(n,t)}, \Pi_{\mathsf{ModRec}}^{(n,t)})$ satisfy the properties of a *t-secure VSS*. Namely, if P_j is *honest*, then the value $c_{j\to i}$ remains private from the point of view of the adversary during phase I and every party in $\mathcal{H}$ reconstruct $c_{j\to i}$ from the instance of $\Pi_{\mathsf{ModRec}}^{(n,t)}$ during phase II; this follows from the *t-hiding* and *t-correctness* properties of VSS. Moreover, even if P_j is *corrupt*, there exists some well-defined value $c_{j\to i} \in \mathbb{F}$, such that every party in $\mathcal{H}$ reconstructs $c_{j\to i}$ from the instance of $\Pi_{\mathsf{ModRec}}^{(n,t)}$ during phase II; this follows from the *t-binding* property of VSS. We also note that the values $c_{j\to i}$ picked and shared by the honest dealers P_j are randomly chosen from $\mathbb{F}$ and *independent* of the values $c_{j\to i}$ picked and shared by the corrupt dealers P_j. This follows from the fact that due to *t-hiding* of VSS, the corrupt dealers P_j will *not* know the values picked and shared by the honest dealers P_j. Now consider the value c_i where

$$c_i \stackrel{def}{=} \sum_{j=1}^{n} c_{j\to i} \mod u.$$

From the above arguments, it follows that every party in $\mathcal{H}_i$ will associate the value c_i with P_i during phase II. On the other hand, every honest party which is *not* present in $\mathcal{H}_i$ will associate $\perp$ with P_i. This is because for every such honest party P_k which is not in $\mathcal{H}_i$, the condition $\mathsf{trust}_{k,i} = 0$ holds and hence $P_i \notin \mathsf{trust}_k$. We also note that c_i will a random value from the set $\{0, \ldots, u-1\}$, since $\sum_{j=1}^{n} c_{j\to i}$ will be a random value, as the $c_{j\to i}$ values corresponding to the honest dealers P_j are random. □

We next derive the success probability of the protocol $\Pi_{\mathsf{CC}}^{(n,t)}$.

Lemma 8.6 *Let* $p \stackrel{def}{=} \min\left(1-(1-\frac{1}{u})^{n-t}, (1-\frac{1}{u})^{n}\right)$. *Then in protocol* $\Pi_{\mathsf{CC}}^{(n,t)}$, *for every* $\sigma \in \{0,1\}$, *all honest parties output* σ *with probability at least* p.

Proof Let $\mathcal{H}$ be the set of honest parties where $|\mathcal{H}| \geq n-t$. We first compute the probability of all honest parties computing the output 0. From Claim 8.5, the set $\mathcal{H} \subseteq \mathsf{trust}_k$, for every $P_k \in \mathcal{H}$. Moreover, for every $P_i \in \mathcal{H}$, every $P_k \in \mathcal{H}$ associates a uniformly random value $c_i \in \{0,\ldots,u-1\}$ with P_i. The probability that $c_i = 0$ is $\frac{1}{u}$. If the condition $c_i = 0$ holds for *any* $P_i \in \mathcal{H}$, then clearly every party in $\mathcal{H}$ will output 0. The probability that $c_i = 0$ *does not* hold for any $P_i \in \mathcal{H}$ is $(1-\frac{1}{u})^{|\mathcal{H}|}$. Consequently, the probability that every party in $\mathcal{H}$ outputs 0 is at least $1-(1-\frac{1}{u})^{|\mathcal{H}|}$, which is the same as $1-(1-\frac{1}{u})^{n-t}$.

Next, we compute the probability of honest parties computing the output of 1. Consider the set trust where

$$\mathsf{trust} \stackrel{def}{=} \bigcup_{P_k \in \mathcal{H}} \mathsf{trust}_k.$$

It is easy to see that $|\mathsf{trust}| \leq n$, since $\mathsf{trust} \subseteq \mathcal{P}$. From Claim 8.5 and Claim 8.6, for *any* $P_i \in \mathsf{trust}$, the corresponding associated value $c_i^{(k)}$ computed by any $P_k \in \mathcal{H}$ will be either $\perp$ or a uniformly random value from the set $\{0,\ldots,u-1\}$. Hence if $c_i^{(k)} \neq \perp$, then the probability that $c_i^{(k)} \neq 0$ is $(1-\frac{1}{u})$. From the protocol steps, if the associated value of none of the parties in trust turns out to be 0, then the parties in $\mathcal{H}$ will output 1. The probability of this event is $(1-\frac{1}{u})^{|\mathsf{trust}|}$. Now since $(1-\frac{1}{u})^{|\mathsf{trust}|} \geq (1-\frac{1}{u})^{n}$, it follows that with probability at least $(1-\frac{1}{u})^{n}$, all the parties in $\mathcal{H}$ will output 1. □

Finally, based on the above discussion, we have the following theorem.

Theorem 8.5 *Let* $(\Pi_{\mathsf{ModSh}}^{(n,t)}, \Pi_{\mathsf{ModRec}}^{(n,t)})$ *be a* t*-secure MVSS scheme in the model* $\mathcal{M} \in \{\mathcal{M}_{\mathsf{secure}}, \mathcal{M}_{\mathsf{secure}}^{\mathsf{pki}}\}$. *Moreover, let* $\Pi_{\mathsf{ModSh}}^{(n,t)}$ *and* $\Pi_{\mathsf{ModRec}}^{(n,t)}$ *require* R_1 *and* R_2 *rounds respectively. Then protocol* $\Pi_{\mathsf{CC}}^{(n,t)}$ *is a* t*-secure* p*-CC protocol in the model* $\mathcal{M}$, *where* $p \stackrel{def}{=} \min\left(1-(1-\frac{1}{u})^{n-t}, (1-\frac{1}{u})^{n}\right)$. *The protocol requires* $R_1 + R_2$ *rounds of communication. The communication complexity of the protocol is* n^2 *times the communication complexity of one instance of* $\Pi_{\mathsf{ModSh}}^{(n,t)}$ *and one instance of* $\Pi_{\mathsf{ModRec}}^{(n,t)}$.

If the MVSS scheme is unconditionally-secure then $\Pi_{\mathsf{CC}}^{(n,t)}$ *is also unconditionally-secure. Protocol* $\Pi_{\mathsf{CC}}^{(n,t)}$ *is conditionally (cryptographically) secure, if the MVSS scheme is conditionally (cryptographically) secure.*

By instantiating the generic MVSS scheme $(\Pi_{\mathsf{ModSh}}^{(n,t)}, \Pi_{\mathsf{ModRec}}^{(n,t)})$ in protocol $\Pi_{\mathsf{CC}}^{(n,t)}$ with the BGW MVSS scheme $(\Pi_{\mathsf{BGWMSh}}^{(n,t)}, \Pi_{\mathsf{BGWMRec}}^{(n,t)})$, we get the following corollary of Theorem 8.5.

Corollary 8.2 *Let $\Pi^{(n,t)}_{\mathsf{BGWCC}}$ be the protocol obtained after instantiating the generic MVSS scheme $(\Pi^{(n,t)}_{\mathsf{ModSh}}, \Pi^{(n,t)}_{\mathsf{ModRec}})$ in protocol $\Pi^{(n,t)}_{\mathsf{CC}}$ with the BGW MVSS scheme $(\Pi^{(n,t)}_{\mathsf{BGWMSh}}, \Pi^{(n,t)}_{\mathsf{BGWMRec}})$. If $t < \frac{n}{3}$, then the protocol $\Pi^{(n,t)}_{\mathsf{BGWCC}}$ is a t-secure p-CC protocol in the model $\mathcal{M}_{\mathsf{secure}}$ with unconditional security, where $p \stackrel{def}{=} \min\Big(1 - (1-\frac{1}{u})^{n-t}, (1-\frac{1}{u})^{n}\Big)$. The protocol requires* 33 *rounds of communication and incurs a communication of $O(n^6 \log|\mathbb{F}|)$ bits, where $\mathbb{F}$ is a finite field with $|\mathbb{F}| > n$ over which all computations are performed in the BGW MVSS scheme.*

Proof The corollary follows from Corollary 8.1. In more detail, protocol $\Pi^{(n,t)}_{\mathsf{BGWMSh}}$ requires 32 rounds, while $\Pi^{(n,t)}_{\mathsf{BGWMRec}}$ requires 1 round. Moreover, $\Pi^{(n,t)}_{\mathsf{BGWMSh}}$ and $\Pi^{(n,t)}_{\mathsf{BGWMRec}}$ incurs a communication complexity of $O(n^4 \log|\mathbb{F}|)$ and $O(n^2 \log|\mathbb{F}|)$ bits respectively. Furthermore, $(\Pi^{(n,t)}_{\mathsf{BGWMSh}}, \Pi^{(n,t)}_{\mathsf{BGWMRec}})$ constitute a *t-secure* MVSS scheme for any $t < \frac{n}{3}$ in the model $\mathcal{M}_{\mathsf{secure}}$ with perfect (unconditional) security. The corollary now follows by substituting $R_1 = 32$ and $R_2 = 1$ in Theorem 8.5. □

In Table 8.3, we summarize the various possible CC protocol obtained after instantiating the generic MVSS scheme $(\Pi^{(n,t)}_{\mathsf{ModSh}}, \Pi^{(n,t)}_{\mathsf{ModRec}})$ in protocol $\Pi^{(n,t)}_{\mathsf{CC}}$ with the various MVSS schemes summarized in Table 8.2. The success probability of all the protocols is the same, namely $p \stackrel{def}{=} \min(1 - (1 - \frac{1}{u})^{n-t}, (1 - \frac{1}{u})^{n})$. In all the protocols, computations are performed over a field $\mathbb{F}$ where $|\mathbb{F}| > n$.

Protocol Name	Round Complexity	Communication Complexity
$\Pi^{(n,t)}_{\mathsf{BGWCC}}$	33	$O(n^6 \log|\mathbb{F}|)$
$\Pi^{(n,t)}_{\mathsf{ModBGWCC}}$	21	$O(n^6 \log|\mathbb{F}|)$
$\Pi^{(n,t)}_{\mathsf{GIKRCC}}$	20	$O(n^6 \log|\mathbb{F}|)$
$\Pi^{(n,t)}_{\mathsf{FGGRCC}}$	14	$O(n^7 \log|\mathbb{F}|)$
$\Pi^{(n,t)}_{\mathsf{KKKCC}}$	9	$O(n^7 \log|\mathbb{F}|)$
$\Pi^{(n,t)}_{\mathsf{AKPCC}}$	14	$O(n^7 \log|\mathbb{F}|)$

Table 8.3: Summary of the various unconditionally-secure CC protocols with $t < \frac{n}{3}$, obtained by instantiating the generic MVSS scheme $(\Pi^{(n,t)}_{\mathsf{ModSh}}, \Pi^{(n,t)}_{\mathsf{ModRec}})$ in protocol $\Pi^{(n,t)}_{\mathsf{CC}}$ with the various MVSS schemes summarized in Table 8.2. In all these protocols, computations are performed over a finite field $\mathbb{F}$ where $|\mathbb{F}| > n$. Moreover, the success probability p of all these protocols is $p \stackrel{def}{=} \min\Big(1 - (1 - \frac{1}{u})^{n-t}, (1 - \frac{1}{u})^{n}\Big)$

8.6.1 Common Coin with a Constant Success Probability

In this section, we will discuss how to select the parameter u in the CC protocol $\Pi_{\mathsf{BGWCC}}^{(n,t)}$ to achieve a *constant* success probability.[11] From Corollary 8.2, the success probability p of the protocol $\Pi_{\mathsf{BGWCC}}^{(n,t)}$ is $\min\left(1-(1-\frac{1}{u})^{n-t}, (1-\frac{1}{u})^{n}\right)$, where $t < \frac{n}{3}$. Since $t < \frac{n}{3}$, it follows that $n - t > \frac{2n}{3}$ holds. Consequently, if we set $u = n$, then the following holds:

$$1-(1-\frac{1}{u})^{n-t} \geq 1-e^{-\frac{n-t}{u}} \geq 1-e^{-\frac{2n}{3u}} \geq 1-e^{-\frac{2}{3}} \geq 0.46.$$

Similarly, the following holds:

$$(1-\frac{1}{u})^{n} \geq e^{-\frac{n}{u}} \geq e^{-1} \geq 0.36.$$

Consequently, the success probability of the protocol $\Pi_{\mathsf{BGWCC}}^{(n,t)}$ will be 0.36. In the above calculations, we selected $u = n$ just for simplicity and one could instead set u to a different function of n to get an appropriate constant success probability.

8.7 Randomized BA with a Non-Fixed Number of Iterations

Recall the generic randomized BA protocol $\Pi_{\mathsf{RandBA}}^{(n,t)}$, presented in Fig 8.1, with a *fixed* number of iterations k (and hence a fixed number of rounds). A natural question that is still *unanswered* is what should be the ideal value of k, if we want to implement the protocol in practice? As discussed in Section 8.2.1, one option would be to set k as one more than the expected number of iterations required in the protocol to achieve *consistency*. That is, set k to $\lceil 1+\frac{2}{p} \rceil$, where p is the success probability of the underlying CC protocol.[12] However, fixing k like this will have *two* potential problems:

- There is no *guarantee* that consistency will be achieved after $\lceil 1+\frac{2}{p} \rceil$ many number of iterations. Namely, with probability at most $(1-\frac{p}{2})^{\lceil 1+\frac{2}{p} \rceil}$, which is *non-zero*, consistency *may not* be achieved. This is because from Theorem 8.1, the probability that consistency *is* achieved after k iterations is at least $1-(1-\frac{p}{2})^{k}$.
- There is a possibility that consistency is achieved *before* $\lceil 1+\frac{2}{p} \rceil$ iterations, leading to the parties unnecessarily running the subsequent iterations.

[11] Recall from our discussion in Section 8.2.1, we sought a CC protocol with a constant success probability to get a BA protocol with a constant expected number of rounds.

[12] Recall that in Section 8.2.1, we derived the expected number of iterations required in the protocol $\Pi_{\mathsf{RandBA}}^{(n,t)}$ to achieve consistency to be $\frac{2}{p}$.

The way to deal with both the above problems is to let the parties decide at run time when to stop the protocol as soon as they are sure that consistency is achieved. We will now discuss how to materialize this approach. The idea will be to let the parties terminate the protocol as soon as they obtain a bit with the *highest* grade in any of the two instances of GA in an iteration.[13] Note that this requires a careful design approach because if an *honest* party P_i obtains a bit b with the highest grade in an instance of GA and terminates immediately, it might affect the termination of other honest parties. The trouble stems from the fact that it is *not* necessary that every other honest party P_j will also achieve the bit b with the highest grade from the GA instance. Consequently, P_i will leave the protocol while P_j might still be running the subsequent iterations of the protocol. But then the participation of P_i in the subsequent instances of GA will be *required* so that these instances achieve the outcomes desired from GA (namely validity and knowledge-of-agreement), which in turn will determine how long the remaining honest parties will take to terminate.

To deal with the above challenges, we have to make modifications in the GA as well as the CC protocol, so that even if all honest parties *do not* participate in these protocols, it *does not* hamper the security properties for the "surviving" honest parties. And then we have to tie these modified primitives to get a randomized carefully BA protocol with a *non-fixed* number of iterations. In the sequel, we discuss these modifications followed by the process of tying together these modified primitives.

8.7.1 GA with Virtual Participation by the Parties

We first discuss how to modify the perfectly-secure GA protocol $\Pi^{(n,t)}_{\mathsf{PerSecGAOneThird}}$ with $t < \frac{n}{3}$, presented in Fig 4.4, to handle "virtual" participation by the parties. We now envision a scenario where there will be *multiple* instances of GA executed in *sequence*. Each instance of the GA will be associated with a publicly known *session identifier* $\mathsf{sid} \in \mathbb{N}$, which will be known to all the (honest) parties participating in the corresponding instance of GA. The parties participate in the instance of GA with id sid *only* after terminating the instance of GA with id $\mathsf{sid} - 1$. Each party participating in an instance of the modified GA participate with input from $\{0, 1\}^L$ and the output of every party will be from $\{0, 1\}^L$ with a grade 0, 1 or 2, with 2 denoting the *highest* grade. Moreover, once any *honest* party P_i from $\mathcal{P}$ gets an output with the highest grade from any instance of GA, then it *stops* participating in the *subsequent* instances of GA. To signal about its *non-participation* in the subsequent instances, P_i will now issue a special *halting message* in the last instance of GA where P_i participated. The halting message will also have the *highest* graded output, which P_i obtained in that instance. The interpretation of the halting message is that in all the subsequent instances of GA, *instead* of using an *arbitrary* default input on behalf of P_i (due

[13] Recall that each iteration of $\Pi^{(n,t)}_{\mathsf{RandBA}}$ invokes two instances of GA, one before and one after the instance of $\Pi^{(n,t)}_{\mathsf{CC}}$.

to the non-participation of P_i), the parties should use this highest graded output on behalf of P_i.

We call the modified protocol $\Pi_{\mathsf{PerGAVirOneThird}}^{(n,t)}$ and present it in Fig 8.5. As mentioned earlier, the protocol is a modification of the earlier GA protocol $\Pi_{\mathsf{PerSecGAOneThird}}^{(n,t)}$, where the modifications are highlighted in blue color. Instead of two rounds, the protocol requires three rounds, where the additional round is used for sending the halting messages by the parties who get an output with the highest grade. Since different parties may obtain the highest graded output bit in *different* instances of the modified GA, each party P_i maintains two *dynamic* and *disjoint* sets of parties across various instances of the modified GA protocol, the set of "live" parties $\mathcal{P}_{\mathsf{Live}}^{(i)}$ and the set of "virtual" parties $\mathcal{P}_{\mathsf{Virtual}}^{(i)}$. The sets will get updated after each instance of the modified GA. The interpretation here is that from the point of view of P_i, the parties in $\mathcal{P}_{\mathsf{Live}}^{(i)}$ will *continue* participating in the subsequent instances of the GA, while the parties in $\mathcal{P}_{\mathsf{Virtual}}^{(i)}$ will *no longer* participate in the subsequent instances. Any party from $\mathcal{P}_{\mathsf{Live}}^{(i)}$ who sends a halting message in the current instance of GA will be *removed* by P_i from $\mathcal{P}_{\mathsf{Live}}^{(i)}$ and *moved* to $\mathcal{P}_{\mathsf{Virtual}}^{(i)}$. The sets $\mathcal{P}_{\mathsf{Live}}^{(i)}$ and $\mathcal{P}_{\mathsf{Virtual}}^{(i)}$ are initialized to $\mathcal{P}$ and $\emptyset$ respectively, during the *first* instance of the GA. For every "virtually-participating" party P_j in the set $\mathcal{P}_{\mathsf{Virtual}}^{(i)}$, party P_i will maintain a "default input" $\mathsf{Def}_j^{(i)}$, which should be used on behalf of P_j during the subsequent instances of GA. The default input is set to the one indicated by P_j in its halting message during the instance of GA where P_j participated last. Note that the way the set of live and virtual parties are maintained, the honest parties *may not* have agreement on these sets. This is because a potentially *corrupt* party may send *different* halting status to different honest parties. Similarly, a potentially *corrupt* party may indicate *different* default inputs to be used on its behalf to different parties, as part of its halting message. However, the subset of *honest* virtual parties will be the *same* across the $\mathcal{P}_{\mathsf{Virtual}}^{(i)}$ sets of all the honest parties P_i. This is because if during any instance of the GA, an honest party decides to send a halting message, then it will send the message *identically* to all the honest parties in that instance and would also indicate the *same* default input to be used on its behalf in the future instance of the GA to everyone.

Protocol $\Pi_{\mathsf{PerGAVirOneThird}}^{(n,t)}$ is similar to the protocol $\Pi_{\mathsf{PerSecGAOneThird}}^{(n,t)}$, except that "special" default inputs are used on behalf of the parties who have indicated their virtual participation and default inputs to be used on their behalf through halting messages in *earlier* instances of the protocol. In more detail, during the first round, every "live" party sends its input to every party. On behalf of the "virtual" parties, their prescribed default inputs (from previous instances) are used as their inputs. Then, based on the inputs received from the live and virtual parties, each participating party computes its *optional* vote, depending upon if more than $\frac{2n}{3}$ parties (including live and virtual parties) reported that input. During the second round, the live parties exchange their votes with each other, where on behalf of the "virtual" parties, their prescribed default inputs (from previous instances) are used as their votes. During the third round, each live party checks if more than $\frac{2n}{3}$ parties (including live and virtual parties) reported the same vote. If this is indeed the case, then the party sends the halting message to everyone and reports the vote received from more than $\frac{2n}{3}$ parties to be used as its default input and vote for subsequent instances of GA. Depending on the halting messages received from various live parties, each live party updates its set of live parties and virtual parties and also the default inputs for various virtual parties. Finally, at the end of the third round, each live party computes its output in the same way as done in $\Pi^{(n,t)}_{\mathsf{PerSecGAOneThird}}$. Namely, if a live party sees more than $\frac{2n}{3}$ parties voted for the same value during the second round, then that value is taken as the output with the highest grade. Additionally, the party decides to *not* participate in the subsequent instances of the GA. If more than $\frac{n}{3}$ parties voted for the same value during the second round, then it is taken as the output by the live party with the medium grade (namely grade 1) and the live party *continues* participating in any subsequent instance of the GA. If none of the above conditions is satisfied for the votes, then the live party outputs its input with grade 0 and *continues* participating in any subsequent instance of the GA.

Protocol $\Pi^{(n,t)}_{\mathsf{PerGAVirOneThird}}$ achieves the following properties, which are sufficient for our randomized BA with a variable number of iterations:

- If the inputs of all live and virtual *honest* parties is the same, then every live party outputs that value with the highest grade. This is equivalent to the *t-validity* property of $\Pi^{(n,t)}_{\mathsf{PerSecGAOneThird}}$.
- Once the *first* live honest party terminates any instance of $\Pi^{(n,t)}_{\mathsf{PerGAVirOneThird}}$ with the highest-graded output, then all the live honest parties will also terminate that instance with the *same* output, either with the highest or with the medium grade. This is equivalent to the *t-knowledge-of-agreement* property of $\Pi^{(n,t)}_{\mathsf{PerSecGAOneThird}}$. We stress that the modified GA protocol $\Pi^{(n,t)}_{\mathsf{PerGAVirOneThird}}$ achieves this property *only* for the *first* instance of $\Pi^{(n,t)}_{\mathsf{PerGAVirOneThird}}$ when a live honest party gets an output with the highest grade, implying that *no* honest party is participating virtually during that instance. The property *may not* hold for the subsequent instances of $\Pi^{(n,t)}_{\mathsf{PerGAVirOneThird}}$ and in fact, is *not* needed when used in our randomized BA protocol.

Protocol $\Pi^{(n,t)}_{\mathsf{PerGAVirOneThird}}(\mathsf{sid})$

Input: the input for P_i is its input $u_i \in \{0,1\}^L$. In addition, P_i has two dynamic sets of parties, the set of *live* parties $\mathcal{P}^{(i)}_{\mathsf{Live}}$ and the set of *virtual* parties $\mathcal{P}^{(i)}_{\mathsf{Virtual}}$, where $\mathcal{P} = (\mathcal{P}^{(i)}_{\mathsf{Live}} \cup \mathcal{P}^{(i)}_{\mathsf{Virtual}})$ and where $(\mathcal{P}^{(i)}_{\mathsf{Live}} \cap \mathcal{P}^{(i)}_{\mathsf{Virtual}}) = \emptyset$. The set $\mathcal{P}^{(i)}_{\mathsf{Virtual}}$ includes every party P_j from which P_i has received a halting message $(\mathtt{halt}, P_j, \star)$ in some previous instance $\Pi^{(n,t)}_{\mathsf{PerGAVirOneThird}}(\mathsf{sid}')$ of $\Pi^{(n,t)}_{\mathsf{PerGAVirOneThird}}$, where $\mathsf{sid}' < \mathsf{sid}$, while $\mathcal{P}^{(i)}_{\mathsf{Live}} = \mathcal{P} \setminus \mathcal{P}^{(i)}_{\mathsf{Virtual}}$. Moreover, for every $P_j \in \mathcal{P}^{(i)}_{\mathsf{Virtual}}$, party P_i has some value $\mathsf{Def}^{(i)}_j \in \{0,1\}^L$, which P_i received from P_j along with the halting message. From the point of view of P_i, the parties in $\mathcal{P}^{(i)}_{\mathsf{Live}}$ will be participating in the current instance $\Pi^{(n,t)}_{\mathsf{PerGAVirOneThird}}(\mathsf{sid})$, while for the the parties $P_j \in \mathcal{P}^{(i)}_{\mathsf{Virtual}}$, the value $\mathsf{Def}^{(i)}_j$ will be considered in the current instance $\Pi^{(n,t)}_{\mathsf{PerGAVirOneThird}}(\mathsf{sid})$. If $\mathsf{sid} = 1$, then the sets $\mathcal{P}^{(i)}_{\mathsf{Live}}$ and $\mathcal{P}^{(i)}_{\mathsf{Virtual}}$ are initialized to $\mathcal{P}$ and $\emptyset$ respectively.

- **Round 1**: Do the following.

- **(exchanging inputs)**: On having the input $u_i \in \{0,1\}^L$, send u_i to all the parties in $\mathcal{P}$ including itself.
- **(computing the vote)**:
  - For every party $P_j \in \mathcal{P}^{(i)}_{\mathsf{Virtual}}$, consider the input $\mathsf{Def}^{(i)}_j$ to be received from P_j during this round. If no input is received from a party in $\mathcal{P}^{(i)}_{\mathsf{Live}}$ during this round, then set 0^L as the input for such parties.
  - Let $\mathcal{A}_i$ denote the set of parties of the *maximum* size, who have sent the same input, say u, during this round. If $|\mathcal{A}_i| > \frac{2n}{3}$, then set $\mathsf{vote}_i = u$, else set $\mathsf{vote}_i = \perp$.[a]
- **Round** 2: Do the following.
  - **(Sending the vote (optional))**: If $\mathsf{vote}_i \neq \perp$, then send vote_i to all the parties including itself.
  - **(Computing the maximum vote)**:
    - For every party $P_j \in \mathcal{P}^{(i)}_{\mathsf{Virtual}}$, consider the value $\mathsf{Def}^{(i)}_j$ to be the vote received from P_j during this round.
    - Let $\mathcal{B}_i$ denote the set of parties of the *maximum* size, who have sent the same vote, say v, during this round.[b]
- **Round** 3: Do the following.
  - **(Sending instruction for virtual participation for future instances)**: If $|\mathcal{B}_i| > \frac{2n}{3}$, then send the message $(\mathtt{halt}, P_i, v)$ to all the parties in $\mathcal{P}$.
  - **(Setting the default input for virtual participation of parties for future instances)**: For every $P_j \in \mathcal{P}^{(i)}_{\mathsf{Live}}$, if a message $(\mathtt{halt}, P_j, w)$ is received from P_j where $w \in \{0,1\}^L$, then do the following:
    - Set $\mathcal{P}^{(i)}_{\mathsf{Live}} = \mathcal{P}^{(i)}_{\mathsf{Live}} \setminus \{P_j\}$ and $\mathcal{P}^{(i)}_{\mathsf{Virtual}} = \mathcal{P}^{(i)}_{\mathsf{Virtual}} \cup \{P_j\}$.
    - Set $\mathsf{Def}^{(i)}_j = w$.
- **Output computation and termination**: Compute the output as follows and then terminate.
  - If $|\mathcal{B}_i| > \frac{2n}{3}$, then set $(v, 2)$ as the output and do not participate in any instance $\Pi^{(n,t)}_{\mathsf{PerGAVirOneThird}}(\mathsf{sid}')$ of $\Pi^{(n,t)}_{\mathsf{PerGAVirOneThird}}$ where $\mathsf{sid}' > \mathsf{sid}$.
  - Else if $|\mathcal{B}_i| > \frac{n}{3}$, then output $(v, 1)$;
  - Else output $(u_i, 0)$.

[a] While determining $\mathcal{A}_i$ and computing u, consider $\mathsf{Def}^{(i)}_j$ to be received from $P_j \in \mathcal{P}^{(i)}_{\mathsf{Virtual}}$.

[b] While determining $\mathcal{B}_i$ and computing v, consider $\mathsf{Def}^{(i)}_j$ to be the vote received from $P_j \in \mathcal{P}^{(i)}_{\mathsf{Virtual}}$.

Fig. 8.5: Perfectly-secure GA protocol with virtual participation from the parties tolerating $t < \frac{n}{3}$ corruptions for session id sid. The above code is executed by every party P_i who is participating in the protocol instance

We next proceed to prove the properties of the protocol $\Pi^{(n,t)}_{\mathsf{PerGAVirOneThird}}$. We start with the *liveness* property and derive the communication complexity of the protocol.

Lemma 8.7 *For every* $\mathsf{sid} \in \mathbb{N}$, *all honest parties participating in the protocol instance* $\Pi^{(n,t)}_{\mathsf{PerGAVirOneThird}}(\mathsf{sid})$ *will terminate after three rounds. Moreover, the protocol incurs a communication of* $O(n^2L)$ *bits.*

Proof The proof follows from the fact that the protocol is round-based and it takes two rounds for the *honest* parties participating in the protocol instance to exchange their inputs and their votes. In addition, any participating *honest* party who obtains an output with the highest grade will send a halting instruction during the third round.

The communication complexity follows from the fact that in every round, every party may send an L-bit value to every other party. □

Before proving the validity and knowledge-of-agreement properties, we introduce certain sets that will be useful in proving these properties.

Definition 8.4 Let $\mathsf{sid} \in \mathbb{N}$ and consider an instance $\Pi^{(n,t)}_{\mathsf{PerGAVirOneThird}}(\mathsf{sid})$ of $\Pi^{(n,t)}_{\mathsf{PerGAVirOneThird}}$. Then:

- $\mathcal{H}^{(\mathsf{sid})}_{\mathsf{Live}}$: denotes the set of *honest* parties who participate in the instance $\Pi^{(n,t)}_{\mathsf{PerGAVirOneThird}}(\mathsf{sid})$.
- $\mathcal{H}^{(\mathsf{sid})}_{\mathsf{Virtual}}$: denotes the set of *honest* parties who participate virtually in the instance $\Pi^{(n,t)}_{\mathsf{PerGAVirOneThird}}(\mathsf{sid})$. That is, for every $P_j \in \mathcal{H}^{(\mathsf{sid})}_{\mathsf{Virtual}}$, every party $P_i \in \mathcal{H}^{(\mathsf{sid})}_{\mathsf{Live}}$ uses the default value $\mathsf{Def}^{(i)}_j$ in the instance.

From the definition of the sets $\mathcal{H}^{(\mathsf{sid})}_{\mathsf{Live}}$ and $\mathcal{H}^{(\mathsf{sid})}_{\mathsf{Virtual}}$, it follows that all the following holds:

- $\mathcal{H}^{(\mathsf{sid})}_{\mathsf{Live}} \cap \mathcal{H}^{(\mathsf{sid})}_{\mathsf{Virtual}} = \emptyset$;
- $\mathcal{H}^{(\mathsf{sid})}_{\mathsf{Live}} \cup \mathcal{H}^{(\mathsf{sid})}_{\mathsf{Virtual}} = \mathcal{H}$, where $\mathcal{H}$ is the set of *honest* parties among $\mathcal{P}$.
- If $t < \frac{n}{3}$ then $\mathcal{H}^{(\mathsf{sid})}_{\mathsf{Live}} \cup \mathcal{H}^{(\mathsf{sid})}_{\mathsf{Virtual}} > \frac{2n}{3}$.

We now claim certain properties for the sets defined in Definition 8.4. The first property is that from the point of view of every *live* honest party, the set of *virtual* honest parties will be the same. The second property is that every live honest party will be using the same default input on behalf of each virtual honest party.

Claim 8.7 For every $\mathsf{sid} \in \mathbb{N}$ and every instance $\Pi^{(n,t)}_{\mathsf{PerGAVirOneThird}}(\mathsf{sid})$, all the following holds:

- For every $P_i \in \mathcal{H}^{(\mathsf{sid})}_{\mathsf{Live}}$, the condition $\mathcal{H}^{(\mathsf{sid})}_{\mathsf{Virtual}} \subseteq \mathcal{P}^{(i)}_{\mathsf{Virtual}}$ holds at the beginning of the protocol instance.
- For every $P_i, P_j \in \mathcal{H}^{(\mathsf{sid})}_{\mathsf{Live}}$ and every $P_k \in \mathcal{H}^{(\mathsf{sid})}_{\mathsf{Virtual}}$, the condition $\mathsf{Def}^{(i)}_k = \mathsf{Def}^{(j)}_k$ holds.

Proof We prove both the properties through *induction* on sid. The *base* case is when $\mathsf{sid} = 1$. Since *all* honest parties participate in the instance $\Pi^{(n,t)}_{\mathsf{PerGAVirOneThird}}(\mathsf{sid})$, it follows that $\mathcal{H}^{(1)}_{\mathsf{Virtual}} = \emptyset$ and $\mathcal{H}^{(1)}_{\mathsf{Live}} = \mathcal{H}$. Moreover, for every $P_i \in \mathcal{H}^{(1)}_{\mathsf{Live}}$, the set $\mathcal{P}^{(i)}_{\mathsf{Virtual}}$ is initialized to $\emptyset$. Hence, the condition $\mathcal{H}^{(1)}_{\mathsf{Virtual}} \subseteq \mathcal{P}^{(i)}_{\mathsf{Virtual}}$ holds and so the base case is true. Assume the property is true for $\mathsf{sid} = k$. We now want to prove the property is true for $\mathsf{sid} = k + 1$ as well. If $\mathcal{H}^{(k+1)}_{\mathsf{Live}} = \mathcal{H}^{(k)}_{\mathsf{Live}}$, then the inductive step follows obviously, since in this case $\mathcal{H}^{(k+1)}_{\mathsf{Virtual}} = \mathcal{H}^{(k)}_{\mathsf{Virtual}}$ will also hold as well and hence we can use the inductive hypothesis. So consider the case when $\mathcal{H}^{(k+1)}_{\mathsf{Live}} \neq \mathcal{H}^{(k)}_{\mathsf{Live}}$.

Let $P_k \in \mathcal{H}$ be an *arbitrary* party such that $P_k \in \mathcal{H}^{(k)}_{\mathsf{Live}}$, but $P_k \notin \mathcal{H}^{(k+1)}_{\mathsf{Live}}$. Since P_k *does not* participate during the instance $\Pi^{(n,t)}_{\mathsf{PerGAVirOneThird}}(k+1)$ but participated during the instance $\Pi^{(n,t)}_{\mathsf{PerGAVirOneThird}}(k)$, it follows that during the *third* round of the instance $\Pi^{(n,t)}_{\mathsf{PerGAVirOneThird}}(k)$, party P_k must have sent some halting message $(\texttt{halt}, P_k, w_k)$ for some $w_k \in \{0,1\}^L$, which will be received by *every* party in $\mathcal{H}^{(k)}_{\mathsf{Live}}$ at the end of round three. Now consider an *arbitrary* pair of parties $P_i, P_j \in \mathcal{H}^{(k)}_{\mathsf{Live}}$. Then upon receiving the message $(\texttt{halt}, P_k, w_k)$ from P_k, *both* P_i and P_j will remove P_k from the sets $\mathcal{P}^{(i)}_{\mathsf{Live}}$ and $\mathcal{P}^{(j)}_{\mathsf{Live}}$ and will include P_k to the sets $\mathcal{P}^{(i)}_{\mathsf{Virtual}}$ and $\mathcal{P}^{(j)}_{\mathsf{Virtual}}$ respectively. Moreover, *both* P_i and P_j will set $\mathsf{Def}^{(i)}_k = \mathsf{Def}^{(j)}_k = w_k$. This proves the inductive step and the overall claim. □

We next prove the *validity* property. Namely, we show that if the input of all honest parties is the same then every honest party participating in the protocol will output that value with the highest grade.

Lemma 8.8 *If* $t < \frac{n}{3}$ *then the following holds for every instance* $\Pi^{(n,t)}_{\mathsf{PerGAVirOneThird}}(\mathsf{sid})$ *for every* $\mathsf{sid} \in \mathbb{N}$*: if all the parties in* $\mathcal{H}^{(\mathsf{sid})}_{\mathsf{Live}}$ *participate with input u and if all the parties in* $\mathcal{H}^{(\mathsf{sid})}_{\mathsf{Live}}$ *use u as the default input on behalf of every party in* $\mathcal{H}^{(\mathsf{sid})}_{\mathsf{Virtual}}$*, then every party in* $\mathcal{H}^{(\mathsf{sid})}_{\mathsf{Live}}$ *will output* $(u, 2)$.

Proof Let all the parties in $\mathcal{H}^{(\mathsf{sid})}_{\mathsf{Live}}$ start the protocol instance $\Pi^{(n,t)}_{\mathsf{PerGAVirOneThird}}(\mathsf{sid})$ with the *same* input, say u. Moreover, let for every party $P_k \in \mathcal{H}^{(\mathsf{sid})}_{\mathsf{Virtual}}$, the default input used during the protocol instance is u. Hence from Claim 8.7, the condition $\mathsf{Def}^{(i)}_k = \mathsf{Def}^{(j)}_k = u$ holds for every $P_i, P_j \in \mathcal{H}^{(\mathsf{sid})}_{\mathsf{Live}}$.

During the first round, every party in $\mathcal{H}^{(\mathsf{sid})}_{\mathsf{Live}}$ will send u as their input to all the parties. Moreover, on behalf of every party $P_k \in \mathcal{H}^{(\mathsf{sid})}_{\mathsf{Virtual}}$, the value u will be considered as the input being received from P_k during the first round. Since $\frac{2n}{3} > \frac{n}{3}$, it follows that $(\mathcal{H}^{(\mathsf{sid})}_{\mathsf{Live}} \cup \mathcal{H}^{(\mathsf{sid})}_{\mathsf{Virtual}}) \subseteq \mathcal{A}_i$ will hold for each $P_i \in \mathcal{H}^{(\mathsf{sid})}_{\mathsf{Live}}$ at the end of the first round, who will set $\mathsf{vote}_i = u$. Hence, during the second round, each $P_i \in \mathcal{H}^{(\mathsf{sid})}_{\mathsf{Live}}$ will send the u as their vote to all the parties. Moreover, on behalf of every party $P_k \in \mathcal{H}^{(\mathsf{sid})}_{\mathsf{Virtual}}$, the value u will be considered as the vote being received from P_k during the second round. Again, since $\frac{2n}{3} > \frac{n}{3}$, it follows that $(\mathcal{H}^{(\mathsf{sid})}_{\mathsf{Live}} \cup \mathcal{H}^{(\mathsf{sid})}_{\mathsf{Virtual}}) \subseteq \mathcal{B}_i$ will hold for each $P_i \in \mathcal{H}^{(\mathsf{sid})}_{\mathsf{Live}}$ at the end of the second round. Hence for every *honest* party P_i who participated in the protocol instance, the condition $|\mathcal{B}_i| > \frac{2n}{3}$ will hold and hence P_i will output $(u, 2)$. □

To prove the knowledge-of-agreement, we consider the *first* instance of the protocol where an honest party outputs a value with the *highest* grade and show that in that instance honest parties *do not* vote for different values. The proof for this is exactly the *same* as the quorum argument.[14]

[14] Note that the property is true only for the *first* instance of the protocol when an honest party outputs a value with the highest grade; the property *need not* hold for subsequent instances of the protocol.

Claim 8.8 Let $\Pi_{\mathsf{PerGAVirOneThird}}^{(n,t)}(k)$ be the *first* instance of $\Pi_{\mathsf{PerGAVirOneThird}}^{(n,t)}$ where any honest party outputs a value with grade 2 where $k \in \mathbb{N}$. Moreover, let P_i and P_j be distinct honest parties who sets vote_i and vote_j to some L-bit value during $\Pi_{\mathsf{PerGAVirOneThird}}^{(n,t)}(k)$. Then $\mathsf{vote}_i = \mathsf{vote}_j$ holds.

Proof Since $\Pi_{\mathsf{PerGAVirOneThird}}^{(n,t)}(k)$ is the *first* instance of $\Pi_{\mathsf{PerGAVirOneThird}}^{(n,t)}$ where any honest party outputs a value with the highest grade, it follows that $\mathcal{H}_{\mathsf{Live}}^{(k)} = \mathcal{H}$ and $\mathcal{H}_{\mathsf{Virtual}}^{(k)} = \emptyset$, where $\mathcal{H}$ is the set of honest parties among $\mathcal{P}$. The proof of the statement is by contradiction. Let $P_i, P_j \in \mathcal{H}_{\mathsf{Live}}^{(k)}$ and $\mathsf{vote}_i \neq \mathsf{vote}_j$. Now consider the sets $\mathcal{A}_i$ and $\mathcal{A}_j$. From the protocol steps, it follows that $|\mathcal{A}_i| > \frac{2n}{3}$ and $|\mathcal{A}_j| > \frac{2n}{3}$. Moreover, P_i has received vote_i as the input on behalf of all the parties in $\mathcal{A}_i$ during the first round, while P_j has received vote_j as the input on behalf of all the parties in $\mathcal{A}_j$ during the first round. Then consider the set $\mathcal{A}_i \cap \mathcal{A}_j$. It follows that $|\mathcal{A}_i \cap \mathcal{A}_j| > \frac{n}{3}$. Since there can be at most t corrupt parties where $t < \frac{n}{3}$, it follows that $|\mathcal{H}_{\mathsf{Live}}^{(k)} \cap \mathcal{A}_i \cap \mathcal{A}_j| \neq \emptyset$ and hence there exists at least one *honest* party, say P_m, present in *both* $\mathcal{A}_i$ as well as $\mathcal{A}_j$. Note that $P_m \in \mathcal{H}_{\mathsf{Live}}^{(k)}$ because as per the pre-condition of the claim, $\mathcal{H}_{\mathsf{Live}}^{(k)} = \mathcal{H}$. This implies that during the first round, party P_m has sent vote_i and vote_j as its input to P_i and P_j respectively, where $\mathsf{vote}_i \neq \mathsf{vote}_j$. However, this is a *contradiction*, since P_m being *honest* will send the *same* input to all the parties. □

Now based on Claim 8.8, we prove the knowledge-of-agreement. Namely, we consider the *first* instance of the protocol where an honest party outputs a value with the *highest* grade and show that in that instance, all honest parties will output that value only, where the difference between the grades could be *at most* one.[15]

Lemma 8.9 *Let* $\Pi_{\mathsf{PerGAVirOneThird}}^{(n,t)}(k)$ *be the first instance of* $\Pi_{\mathsf{PerGAVirOneThird}}^{(n,t)}$ *where any honest party outputs a value with grade* 2 *where* $k \in \mathbb{N}$ *and let* $w \in \{0,1\}^L$ *be obtained as the output. If* $t < \frac{n}{3}$ *then every other honest party outputs either* $(w, 2)$ *or* $(w, 1)$ *during* $\Pi_{\mathsf{PerGAVirOneThird}}^{(n,t)}(k)$.

Proof Let P_i be the first honest party, who outputs $(w, 2)$ during the instance $\Pi_{\mathsf{PerGAVirOneThird}}^{(n,t)}(k)$. As per the lemma condition, prior to the instance $\Pi_{\mathsf{PerGAVirOneThird}}^{(n,t)}(k)$, no honest party outputs any value with the grade 2 in any of the instance $\Pi_{\mathsf{PerGAVirOneThird}}^{(n,t)}(\mathsf{sid})$ where $\mathsf{sid} < k$. Hence all honest parties participate during the instance $\Pi_{\mathsf{PerGAVirOneThird}}^{(n,t)}(k)$; i.e.. $\mathcal{H}_{\mathsf{Live}}^{(k)} = \mathcal{H}$ holds where $\mathcal{H}$ is the set of *honest* parties among $\mathcal{P}$. Since P_i outputs $(w, 2)$, it implies that $|\mathcal{B}_i| > \frac{2n}{3}$ and P_i has received the w as vote on behalf of *all* the parties in $\mathcal{B}_i$. Let $\mathcal{B}_{i,\mathcal{H}}$ be the set of *honest* parties in $\mathcal{B}_i$; i.e. $\mathcal{B}_{i,\mathcal{H}} = \mathcal{H}_{\mathsf{Live}}^{(k)} \cap \mathcal{B}_i$. As there can be up to t corrupt parties in $\mathcal{B}_i$, it follows that $|\mathcal{B}_{i,\mathcal{H}}| \geq n - 2t > \frac{n}{3}$. Now consider any *arbitrary* party $P_j \in \mathcal{H}_{\mathsf{Live}}^{(k)}$ where $P_j \neq P_i$. We wish to show that P_j outputs either $(w, 2)$ or $(w, 1)$.

[15] Note that the property is true only for the *first* instance of the protocol when an honest party outputs a value with the highest grade; the property *need not* hold for subsequent instances of the protocol.

Party P_j will receive the w as a vote on behalf of *all* the parties in $\mathcal{B}_{i,\mathcal{H}}$. Moreover, from Claim 8.8, party P_j will *not* receive w' as vote from any party in $\mathcal{H}^{(k)}_{\mathsf{Live}} \setminus \mathcal{B}_{i,\mathcal{H}}$ where $w' \neq w$. Since the corrupt parties may vote for w', party P_j will *not* receive the value w' as vote from more than $\frac{n}{3}$ parties and so P_j will *not* output $(w', 2)$ or $(w', 1)$. Furthermore, as $\mathcal{B}_{i,\mathcal{H}} \subseteq \mathcal{B}_j$ will hold, P_j will output either $(w, 1)$ or $(w, 2)$.□

8.7.2 CC with Virtual Participation by Honest Parties

Looking ahead, in our randomized BA protocol, we may encounter a scenario where *only* a *strict subset* of the honest parties may invoke an instance of the CC protocol $\Pi^{(n,t)}_{\mathsf{CC}}$. In more detail, if $\mathcal{H}$ denotes the set of honest parties among $\mathcal{P}$, then only a subset of parties $\mathcal{H}' \subset \mathcal{H}$ may invoke and participate in an instance of $\Pi^{(n,t)}_{\mathsf{CC}}$. Even if this is the case, we would like the parties in $\mathcal{H}'$ to *terminate* the instance of $\Pi^{(n,t)}_{\mathsf{CC}}$ with *some* output, within the number of rounds designated for the honest parties to terminate the protocol $\Pi^{(n,t)}_{\mathsf{CC}}$. That is, if R is the number of rounds required in the protocol $\Pi^{(n,t)}_{\mathsf{CC}}$ for the parties in $\mathcal{H}$ to terminate in case if *all* the parties in $\mathcal{H}$ would have participated in the protocol $\Pi^{(n,t)}_{\mathsf{CC}}$, then we still require the parties in $\mathcal{H}'$ to terminate after R rounds, even if a subset of the parties in $\mathcal{H}$ are *not* participating in the protocol instance.[16] As it turns out, this property is easily guaranteed if every party in $\mathcal{H}'$ substitutes each "missing" message in the protocol instance with some pre-defined publicly-known message from the appropriate domain. In more detail, protocol $\Pi^{(n,t)}_{\mathsf{CC}}$ involves n^2 instances of the sharing and reconstruction-phase protocols $\Pi^{(n,t)}_{\mathsf{ModSh}}$ and $\Pi^{(n,t)}_{\mathsf{ModRec}}$ respectively of an MVSS scheme. Then if any party P_i in $\mathcal{H}'$ *does not* receive an expected message from any designated sender party during any of the rounds of these instances, then P_i uses some pre-defined default message from the appropriate domain on behalf of the sender party for that round and continues the protocol. Finally, after R rounds, each party P_i will compute some output as per the protocol $\Pi^{(n,t)}_{\mathsf{CC}}$ and hence termination will be guaranteed for all the parties in $\mathcal{H}'$. We capture the above discussion in Claim 8.9, which is just a variation of Claim 8.4.

Claim 8.9 Let $(\Pi^{(n,t)}_{\mathsf{ModSh}}, \Pi^{(n,t)}_{\mathsf{ModRec}})$ be a *t-secure* MVSS scheme where $\Pi^{(n,t)}_{\mathsf{ModSh}}$ and $\Pi^{(n,t)}_{\mathsf{ModRec}}$ require R_1 and R_2 rounds respectively. Moreover, let $\mathcal{H} \subseteq \mathcal{P}$ be the set of honest parties and let $\mathcal{H}' \subseteq \mathcal{H}$ be a subset of the honest parties. Then consider any instance of the protocol $\Pi^{(n,t)}_{\mathsf{CC}}$ (see Fig 8.4), where only the parties in $\mathcal{H}'$ participate in the instance and where each party in $\mathcal{H}'$ substitutes every missing message during any round from any designated sender party with some pre-defined publicly-known default message from the appropriate domain. Then all the following holds for the instance of $\Pi^{(n,t)}_{\mathsf{CC}}$.

16 We stress that we are interested *only* in the termination for the parties in $\mathcal{H}'$ and require *no* other properties with respect to their respective output bits.

- t-**liveness**: All parties in $\mathcal{H}'$ terminate the protocol with some output from $\{0, 1\}$ after $R_1 + R_2$ rounds.
- The communication complexity of the protocol will be n^2 times the communication complexity of one instance of $\Pi_{\mathsf{ModSh}}^{(n,t)}$ and one instance of $\Pi_{\mathsf{ModRec}}^{(n,t)}$.

Before we end this section, we note that Claim 8.9 is *applicable* for all the instantiations of CC summarized in Table 8.3. That is, each of the CC protocols specified in Table 8.3 will terminate after the number of rounds designated for them in the second column of the Table 8.3, even if only a subset of the honest parties participate in these protocols.

8.7.3 An Almost-Surely Terminating Randomized BA Protocol with a Non-Fixed Number of Rounds

We are now well-equipped to present the expected constant-rounds bit-BA protocol, where the number of rounds is *not* fixed apriori. The protocol has a *probabilistic* termination guarantee and achieves what is known as *almost-surely terminating liveness* [6, 16]. Informally, this means that the probability that an honest party terminates the protocol after participating in *infinitely* many rounds approaches 1 *asymptotically*. Formally, an almost-surely terminating BA is defined as follows.

Definition 8.5 (Almost-Surely Terminating Byzantine Agreement (BA)) Let Π be a protocol for the parties in $\mathcal{P}$ in the model $\mathcal{M} \in \{\mathcal{M}_{\mathsf{auth}}, \mathcal{M}_{\mathsf{secure}}, \mathcal{M}_{\mathsf{auth}}^{\mathsf{pki}}, \mathcal{M}_{\mathsf{secure}}^{\mathsf{pki}}\}$, where each party P_i has an input $u_i \in \{0, 1\}^L$ and an output $v_i \in \{0, 1\}^L$, such that $L \geq 1$. Moreover, let t be the maximum number of parties which can get corrupt in a Byzantine fashion during the execution of Π.

- t-**almost-surely liveness**: We say that Π has *t-almost-surely liveness*, if every honest party P_i terminates the protocol Π almost-surely. That is,

$$\lim_{r \to \infty} \Pr[\text{An honest } P_i \text{ terminates after round } r] = 1,$$

  where the probability is over the random coins of the honest parties and the adversary in the protocol.
- t-**validity**: We say that Π has *t-validity*, if the following holds.
  - If all honest parties have input $u \in \{0, 1\}^L$, then every honest party with an output, outputs u.
- t-**consistency**: We say that Π has *t-consistency* if all honest parties with an output, output the same value.

We say that Π is a *t-secure almost-surely terminating* BA protocol in model $\mathcal{M}$, if it has *t-almost-surely liveness*, *t-validity* and *t-consistency*.

We now give an instantiation of a t-secure almost-surely terminating BA protocol called $\Pi_{\mathsf{ConsRandBA}}^{(n,t)}$ and present it in Fig 8.6. The protocol is in the model $\mathcal{M}_{\mathsf{secure}}$ and can tolerate a *computationally-unbounded* adversary, capable of corrupting up to $t < \frac{n}{3}$ corrupt parties. The protocol is a bit-BA where the parties' input is a single bit. The protocol is very similar to the previous (generic) protocol $\Pi^{(n,t)}_{\mathsf{RandBA}}$ (Fig 8.1) and consists of several iterations. However, unlike the protocol $\Pi^{(n,t)}_{\mathsf{RandBA}}$ where the number of iterations is *fixed*, the number of iterations is *no* longer fixed and the parties determine when to exit the protocol, depending upon certain conditions.

In each iteration, the parties invoke an instance of a CC protocol, sandwiched between two instances of the modified GA protocol $\Pi^{(n,t)}_{\mathsf{PerGAVirOneThird}}$. To derive the *exact* expected number of rounds required in the protocol, *instead* of using a generic CC protocol, we use a *concrete* CC protocol, say $\Pi^{(n,t)}_{\mathsf{BGWCC}}$; later we will derive the expected number of rounds, if we instead use other instantiations of the CC protocol from Table 8.3. Similarly, we set the value of the parameter u appropriately in the protocol $\Pi^{(n,t)}_{\mathsf{BGWCC}}$, so that the *success probability* p of the protocol turns out to be at least $\frac{2}{3}$. Again, this is for simplicity and without loss of generality.

In *each* iteration of the protocol $\Pi^{(n,t)}_{\mathsf{ConsRandBA}}$, the parties invoke an instance of the GA protocol $\Pi^{(n,t)}_{\mathsf{PerGAVirOneThird}}$, followed by an instance of the CC protocol $\Pi^{(n,t)}_{\mathsf{BGWCC}}$, followed by another instance of the GA protocol $\Pi^{(n,t)}_{\mathsf{PerGAVirOneThird}}$. The input of the parties for the *first* instance of the GA in an iteration are their *modified* input bits, which is initialized to the input bits of the parties for the BA at the beginning of the protocol. The input of the parties for the *second* instance of the GA in an iteration is either the output from the first instance of GA or the output of CC, which depends upon the grade of the respective output bits of the parties from the *first* instance of the GA: if the grade is *lowest*, then the output of CC is considered, otherwise, the output from the first instance of GA is taken. Finally, at the end of the second instance of the GA, the parties either stick to their current modified input bit or else update it, depending on the grade of the output obtained from the second instance of the GA: if the grade is *medium*, the input bit is modified to the output of the GA, else it is not updated.

The termination criteria are the following: if during any instance of the GA, a party obtains a bit with the *highest* grade, it terminates the protocol with that output, *without* completing the rest of the steps of that iteration. As we will argue next, this will *not* affect the termination of the other (honest) parties and they are *guaranteed* to terminate with the same output bit by the end of the next instance of the GA.

The idea behind the protocol is as follows: either all honest parties start the protocol with the *same* input bit or with *different* input bits. Let us take the former case, when all honest parties start the protocol with the same input bit, say b. Then all honest parties will get the output b with the highest grade from the first instance of the GA during the first iteration and will terminate with output b. This ensures the *t-validity*.

Let us now take the latter case, when the honest parties start the protocol with different input bits. In this case, we can show that once any honest party terminates with an output bit b in some iteration, then all honest parties will also terminate with output b, latest by the next iteration. To see this, let P_i be the *first* honest party to terminate with output b during iteration r. It implies that P_i got the output b

with the highest grade, from one of the instances of the GA, executed during the iteration r. If it is from the *second* instance of the GA during iteration r, then every honest party who has *not* yet terminated, will update its input bit to b (since it will be obtained with the medium grade) and in the next instance of the GA (namely the first instance of the GA during iteration $r + 1$), all the "surviving" honest parties will participate with input b. Moreover, for all honest parties who have terminated during iteration r based on the output b received from the second instance of the GA during iteration r, the bit b will taken as the default input on their behalf and such parties will be considered to participate virtually with input b during the first instance of the GA during iteration $r + 1$. Hence, if at all there are honest parties who have *not yet* terminated at the end of the second instance of the GA during iteration r, they are bound to do so by the end of the first instance of the GA during iteration $r + 1$.

Symmetrically, if the party P_i got the output b with the highest grade from the *first* instance of the GA during the iteration r, then it can be argued that all the surviving honest parties will participate with input b during the second instance of the GA during iteration r. Moreover, on behalf of all honest parties who terminated after the first instance of the GA during iteration r, the surviving honest parties will use the input b on their behalf and such parties will be considered to participate virtually with input b during the second instance of the GA in iteration r. Hence, if at all there are honest parties who have *not yet* terminated at the end of the first instance of the GA during iteration r, they are bound to do so by the end of the second instance of the GA during the same iteration. Note that in this case, there is an instance of the CC protocol in between the two GA instances and some of the honest parties *may not* be participating in the CC protocol (namely the honest parties who got the highest-graded output from the first instance of the GA during iteration r). However, this will *not* affect the termination for the surviving honest parties, since the instance of the CC protocol will terminate for all the surviving honest parties as they will be substituting the "missing" messages in the instance of the CC protocol with pre-defined default messages (see Claim 8.9). Moreover, the output of the CC protocol *does not* affect the input of the surviving honest parties for the second instance of the GA during iteration r.

Hence, to argue about the *t-consistency*, we need to ensure that some honest party terminates the protocol (when honest parties start the protocol with *different* inputs). For this, we show that during each iteration r, if no honest party terminates after the first instance of the GA in iteration r, then with probability at least $p \cdot \frac{1}{2} = \frac{p}{2}$, all honest parties will participate with the same input during the second instance of the GA in iteration r; here p is *success probability* of the underlying CC protocol. Consequently, with probability at least $\frac{p}{2}$, at least one honest party is guaranteed to terminate with an output at the end of the second instance of the GA in each iteration. The argument for this is similar to the one used for protocol $\Pi^{(n,t)}_{\mathsf{RandBA}}$. Namely, the set of honest parties can be partitioned into *two* categories based on the inputs they use for the second instance of the GA. The *first* category is the one who *do not* use their output from the CC protocol and second who *use* the output of the CC protocol. Now conditioned on the event that the output of the CC protocol is common and random for all honest parties (which happens with probability at least p), the probability that the output of the CC protocol is the *same* as the bit used by the first category of the honest parties is $\frac{1}{2}$. Since for concreteness, we are using the BGW CC protocol with success probability $p = \frac{2}{3}$, it implies that with probability at least $\frac{2}{3} \cdot \frac{1}{2} = \frac{1}{3}$, at least one honest party is guaranteed to terminate the protocol with an output.

In protocol $\Pi_{\mathsf{ConsRandBA}}$, the instances of GA are associated with distinct session ids. Specifically, for each iteration r, the first instance of the GA will have a session id $2r - 1$, while the second instance will have a session id $2r$.

Protocol $\Pi^{(n,t)}_{\mathsf{ConsRandBA}}$

Initialization: set $b = b_i$, where $b_i \in \{0, 1\}$ is the input for party P_i. In addition, set $\mathsf{sid} = 0$ and $r = 0$.

Executing the iteration: do the following until termination.

- **Step 0**: Set $r = r + 1$ and $\mathsf{sid} = \mathsf{sid} + 1$.
- **Step 1**: Participate in the instance $\Pi^{(n,t)}_{\mathsf{PerGAVirOneThird}}(\mathsf{sid})$ of $\Pi^{(n,t)}_{\mathsf{PerGAVirOneThird}}$ with input b. Let (c, g) be the output obtained from the instance $\Pi^{(n,t)}_{\mathsf{PerGAVirOneThird}}(\mathsf{sid})$, where $c \in \{0, 1\}$ and $g \in \{0, 1, 2\}$.
  - If $g = 2$, then output c and terminate.
- **Step 2**: Upon computing the output (c, g), participate in an instance of $\Pi^{(n,t)}_{\mathsf{BGWCC}}$, with appropriate value of u, such that the success probability p of the protocol is at least $\frac{2}{3}$. Let $\mathsf{Coin} \in \{0, 1\}$ be the output from the instance.
  - If $g = 0$, then set $b = \mathsf{Coin}$.
- **Step 3**: Set $\mathsf{sid} = \mathsf{sid}+1$ and participate in the instance $\Pi^{(n,t)}_{\mathsf{PerGAVirOneThird}}(\mathsf{sid})$ of $\Pi^{(n,t)}_{\mathsf{PerGAVirOneThird}}$ with input b. Let (d, g') be the output obtained from the instance $\Pi^{(n,t)}_{\mathsf{PerGAVirOneThird}}(\mathsf{sid})$, where $d \in \{0, 1\}$ and $g' \in \{0, 1, 2\}$.
  - If $g' = 2$, then output d and terminate.
  - If $g' = 1$, then set $b = d$.

Fig. 8.6: A randomized almost-surely terminating bit-BA protocol with a constant expected number of rounds without any setup. The above code is executed by every party $P_i \in \mathcal{P}$

We now prove the properties of the protocol $\Pi^{(n,t)}_{\mathsf{ConsRandBA}}$. We first prove the *t-validity* property.

Lemma 8.10 *If $t < \frac{n}{3}$ and if all honest parties participate in the protocol $\Pi^{(n,t)}_{\mathsf{ConsRandBA}}$ with input $v \in \{0, 1\}$, then all the following holds:*

- *All honest parties output v.*
- *The protocol requires three rounds of communication.*
- *The protocol will incur a communication of $O(n^2)$ bits.*

Proof Let $\mathcal{H}$ be the set of *honest* parties and let $C = \mathcal{P} \setminus \mathcal{H}$ be the set of *corrupt* parties. Let every $P_i \in \mathcal{H}$ start the protocol with input $b_i = v$. Then during the *first* iteration, every party in $\mathcal{H}$ will participate with input v in the instance $\Pi^{(n,t)}_{\mathsf{PerGAVirOneThird}}(1)$. As a result, every party in $\mathcal{H}$ computes the output $(v, 2)$ during the instance $\Pi^{(n,t)}_{\mathsf{PerGAVirOneThird}}(1)$, which follows from Lemma 8.8. Consequently, every party in $\mathcal{H}$ will terminate the protocol after step 1 and output v.

Since the parties in $\mathcal{H}$ execute *only* step 1, the round and communication complexity, in this case, will be that of one instance of $\Pi^{(n,t)}_{\mathsf{PerGAVirOneThird}}$, which is three and $O(n^2)$ bits respectively. This follows from Lemma 8.7. □

We next consider the case when the honest parties start the protocol with *different* input bits. We wish to show that in this case, the honest parties will almost-surely terminate with a *common* output bit, in a *constant* expected number of iterations. We establish this result through a series of claims. We first claim that once any honest party terminates the protocol with some bit, all honest parties will terminate the protocol with the *same* bit, either within the same iteration or the latest by the next iteration. Hence, there can be a *gap* of up to one iteration within which the honest parties terminate the protocol.

Claim 8.10 In protocol $\Pi^{(n,t)}_{\mathsf{ConsRandBA}}$, once any honest party terminates the protocol with output $v \in \{0,1\}$, then all honest parties also terminate the protocol with output v, either within the same iteration or during the next iteration.

Proof Let $\mathcal{H}$ be the set of honest parties and $P_i \in \mathcal{H}$ be the *first* party, which terminates the protocol with output $v \in \{0,1\}$. Let $r \in \mathbb{N}$ be the iteration when P_i terminates the protocol. Since P_i terminates with output v, it follows that P_i got the output $(v,2)$ from one of the two instances of $\Pi^{(n,t)}_{\mathsf{PerGAVirOneThird}}$ executed during the iteration r. Now there are *two* possible cases:

- **Case I — P_i got the output $(v,2)$ during the first instance of $\Pi^{(n,t)}_{\mathsf{PerGAVirOneThird}}$ executed during the iteration** r: This implies that P_i got the output $(v,2)$ during the instance $\Pi^{(n,t)}_{\mathsf{PerGAVirOneThird}}(2r-1)$, where $\mathsf{sid} = 2r-1$. Moreover, since P_i is the first party to terminate the protocol, it follows that during the instance $\Pi^{(n,t)}_{\mathsf{PerGAVirOneThird}}(2r-1)$, all honest parties participated in the protocol; i.e. $\mathcal{H}^{(2r-1)}_{\mathsf{Live}} = \mathcal{H}$ and $\mathcal{H}^{(2r-1)}_{\mathsf{Virtual}} = \emptyset$.[17] It then follows from Lemma 8.9, then every party in $\mathcal{H}$ gets the output $(v,2)$ or $(v,1)$ during the instance $\Pi^{(n,t)}_{\mathsf{PerGAVirOneThird}}(2r-1)$. Let $\mathcal{H}_1$ and $\mathcal{H}_2$ be the set of *honest* parties who get the output $(v,1)$ and $(v,2)$ respectively during the instance $\Pi^{(n,t)}_{\mathsf{PerGAVirOneThird}}(2r-1)$. From the protocol steps, it follows that all the parties in $\mathcal{H}_2$ will terminate with output v after getting the output $(v,2)$ from the instance $\Pi^{(n,t)}_{\mathsf{PerGAVirOneThird}}(2r-1)$. We now wish to show that the parties in $\mathcal{H}_1$ will also terminate with output v at the end of iteration r. From Claim 8.9, all the parties in $\mathcal{H}_1$ will terminate the instance of $\Pi^{(n,t)}_{\mathsf{BGWCC}}$ during iteration r with some output. Next, consider the instance $\Pi^{(n,t)}_{\mathsf{PerGAVirOneThird}}(2r)$ of $\Pi^{(n,t)}_{\mathsf{PerGAVirOneThird}}$ with $\mathsf{sid} = 2r$, which is the second instance of $\Pi^{(n,t)}_{\mathsf{PerGAVirOneThird}}$ executed during the iteration r. Note that the parties in $\mathcal{H}_1$ participate in the instance with input v, since these parties got the output v with a grade 1 during the instance $\Pi^{(n,t)}_{\mathsf{PerGAVirOneThird}}(2r-1)$. Hence $\mathcal{H}^{(2r)}_{\mathsf{Live}} = \mathcal{H}_1$. On the other hand, the parties in $\mathcal{H}_2$ will participate *virtually* during the instance $\Pi^{(n,t)}_{\mathsf{PerGAVirOneThird}}(2r)$ and hence $\mathcal{H}^{(2r)}_{\mathsf{Virtual}} = \mathcal{H}_2$. Moreover, on behalf of the parties in $\mathcal{H}^{(2r)}_{\mathsf{Virtual}}$, the parties in $\mathcal{H}^{(2r)}_{\mathsf{Live}}$ will use the *default* input v. This is because every party P_k in $\mathcal{H}_2$ would send the message $(\mathtt{halt}, P_k, v)$ during the *third* round of the instance $\Pi^{(n,t)}_{\mathsf{PerGAVirOneThird}}(2r-1)$. Consequently, every party in $\mathcal{H}_1$ would set v as the default input for the parties in $\mathcal{H}^{(2r)}_{\mathsf{Virtual}}$. It now follows from Lemma 8.8 that all

[17] Recall the definition of the sets $\mathcal{H}^{(\mathsf{sid})}_{\mathsf{Live}}$ and $\mathcal{H}^{(\mathsf{sid})}_{\mathsf{Virtual}}$ given in Definition 8.4.

the parties in $\mathcal{H}_1$ will get the output $(v, 2)$ from the instance $\Pi^{(n,t)}_{\mathsf{PerGAVirOneThird}}(2r)$ and hence will terminate the protocol with output v.

- **Case II — P_i got the output $(v, 2)$ during the second instance of $\Pi^{(n,t)}_{\mathsf{PerGAVirOneThird}}$ executed during the iteration** r: This implies that P_i got the output $(v, 2)$ during the instance $\Pi^{(n,t)}_{\mathsf{PerGAVirOneThird}}(2r)$, where $\mathsf{sid} = 2r$. Moreover, since P_i is the first party to terminate the protocol, it follows that during the instance $\Pi^{(n,t)}_{\mathsf{PerGAVirOneThird}}(2r)$, all honest parties participated in the protocol; i.e. $\mathcal{H}^{(2r)}_{\mathsf{Live}} = \mathcal{H}$ and $\mathcal{H}^{(2r)}_{\mathsf{Virtual}} = \emptyset$. It then follows from Lemma 8.9, then every party in $\mathcal{H}$ gets the output $(v, 2)$ or $(v, 1)$ during the instance $\Pi^{(n,t)}_{\mathsf{PerGAVirOneThird}}(2r)$. Let $\mathcal{H}_1$ and $\mathcal{H}_2$ be the set of *honest* parties who get the output $(v, 1)$ and $(v, 2)$ respectively during the instance $\Pi^{(n,t)}_{\mathsf{PerGAVirOneThird}}(2r)$. From the protocol steps, it follows that all the parties in $\mathcal{H}_2$ will terminate with output v after getting the output $(v, 2)$ from the instance $\Pi^{(n,t)}_{\mathsf{PerGAVirOneThird}}(2r)$. We now wish to show that the parties in $\mathcal{H}_1$ will also terminate with output v during iteration $r + 1$. The proof for this is similar to the previous case.
  Consider the instance $\Pi^{(n,t)}_{\mathsf{PerGAVirOneThird}}(2r+1)$ of $\Pi^{(n,t)}_{\mathsf{PerGAVirOneThird}}$ with $\mathsf{sid} = 2r+1$, which is the *first* instance of $\Pi^{(n,t)}_{\mathsf{PerGAVirOneThird}}$ executed during the iteration $r + 1$. Note that the parties in $\mathcal{H}_1$ participate in the instance with input v, since these parties would modify their input bit to the output bit obtained with grade 1 from the instance $\Pi^{(n,t)}_{\mathsf{PerGAVirOneThird}}(2r)$, which is the bit v. Hence $\mathcal{H}^{(2r+1)}_{\mathsf{Live}} = \mathcal{H}_1$, with the input of every party in $\mathcal{H}^{(2r+1)}_{\mathsf{Live}}$ being v. On the other hand, the parties in $\mathcal{H}_2$ will participate *virtually* during the instance $\Pi^{(n,t)}_{\mathsf{PerGAVirOneThird}}(2r + 1)$ and hence $\mathcal{H}^{(2r+1)}_{\mathsf{Virtual}} = \mathcal{H}_2$. Moreover, on behalf of the parties in $\mathcal{H}^{(2r+1)}_{\mathsf{Virtual}}$, the parties in $\mathcal{H}^{(2r+1)}_{\mathsf{Live}}$ will use the *default* input v. This is because every party P_k in $\mathcal{H}_2$ would send the message $(\mathtt{halt}, P_k, v)$ during the *third* round of the instance $\Pi^{(n,t)}_{\mathsf{PerGAVirOneThird}}(2r)$. Consequently, every party in $\mathcal{H}_1$ would set v as the default input for the parties in $\mathcal{H}^{(2r+1)}_{\mathsf{Virtual}}$. It now follows from Lemma 8.8 that all the parties in $\mathcal{H}_1$ will get the output $(v, 2)$ from the instance $\Pi^{(n,t)}_{\mathsf{PerGAVirOneThird}}(2r + 1)$ and hence will terminate the protocol with output v. □

We next claim that if all honest parties participate in any iteration of the protocol, then with probability at least $\frac{1}{3}$, at least one honest party terminates the protocol with some output during that iteration, assuming that the success probability of the CC protocol $\Pi^{(n,t)}_{\mathsf{BGWCC}}$ is at least $\frac{2}{3}$.

Claim 8.11 If the success probability of the protocol $\Pi^{(n,t)}_{\mathsf{BGWCC}}$ is at least $\frac{2}{3}$, then for any iteration $r \in \mathbb{N}$, if all honest parties participate during the iteration r of the protocol $\Pi^{(n,t)}_{\mathsf{ConsRandBA}}$, then with probability at least $\frac{1}{3}$, some honest party terminates with an output during the iteration r.

Proof Let $\mathcal{H}$ be the set of *honest* parties in $\mathcal{P}$ and consider an *arbitrary* iteration $r \in \mathbb{N}$, such that all the parties in $\mathcal{H}$ participate during the iteration r of the protocol $\Pi^{(n,t)}_{\mathsf{ConsRandBA}}$. Then consider the first instance of $\Pi^{(n,t)}_{\mathsf{PerGAVirOneThird}}$ with $\mathsf{sid} = 2r - 1$, executed during step 1 of the iteration r. Since all the parties in $\mathcal{H}$ are participating in this instance, it follows that $\mathcal{H}_{\text{Live}}^{(2r-1)} = \mathcal{H}$ and $\mathcal{H}_{\text{Virtual}}^{(2r-1)} = \emptyset$. Now there are *two* possible cases with respect to the output obtained by the parties in $\mathcal{H}$ from the instance $\Pi_{\text{PerGAVirOneThird}}^{(n,t)}(2r-1)$:

- **Case I — Some party in $\mathcal{H}$ gets an output with grade 2 from the instance $\Pi_{\text{PerGAVirOneThird}}^{(n,t)}(2r-1)$:** Let $P_i \in \mathcal{H}$ get an output (c, g) from the instance $\Pi_{\text{PerGAVirOneThird}}^{(n,t)}(2r-1)$, where $g = 2$. Then from the protocol steps it follow that P_i terminates the protocol with output c and *does not* participate in the rest of the steps of iteration r. Hence, the claim holds trivially in this case.
- **Case II — No party in $\mathcal{H}$ gets an output with grade 2 from the instance $\Pi_{\text{PerGAVirOneThird}}^{(n,t)}(2r-1)$:** In this case, there are two further sub-cases possible.
  - **Sub-case II.I — All parties in $\mathcal{H}$ get their respective output from the instance $\Pi_{\text{PerGAVirOneThird}}^{(n,t)}(2r-1)$ with grade 0:** In this case, all the parties in $\mathcal{H}$ participate in the instance of $\Pi_{\text{BGWCC}}^{(n,t)}$ during the iteration r. Since the success probability of $\Pi_{\text{BGWCC}}^{(n,t)}$ is assumed to be at least $\frac{2}{3}$, it follows that with probability at least $\frac{2}{3}$, all the parties in $\mathcal{H}$ will get a common output $\text{Coin} \in \{0, 1\}$ from the instance of $\Pi_{\text{BGWCC}}^{(n,t)}$ during step 2 of the iteration r. Moreover, all the parties in $\mathcal{H}$ will modify their input bit to Coin and participate in the second instance of $\Pi_{\text{PerGAVirOneThird}}^{(n,t)}$ with $\text{sid} = 2r$ during step 2 of the iteration r with input Coin. This implies that $\mathcal{H}_{\text{Live}}^{(2r)} = \mathcal{H}$ and $\mathcal{H}_{\text{Virtual}}^{(2r)} = \emptyset$. It now follows from Lemma 8.8 that all the parties in $\mathcal{H}$ will get the output (d, g') from the instance $\Pi_{\text{PerGAVirOneThird}}^{(n,t)}(2r)$ where $d = \text{Coin}$ and $g' = 2$. Consequently, all the parties in $\mathcal{H}$ will terminate with output Coin after executing step 3 of the iteration r. Since $\frac{2}{3} > \frac{1}{3}$, the claim holds in this case as well.
- **Sub-case II.II — Some party in $\mathcal{H}$ gets an output with grade 1 from the instance $\Pi_{\text{PerGAVirOneThird}}^{(n,t)}(2r-1)$ and some party in $\mathcal{H}$ gets an output with grade 0 from the instance $\Pi_{\text{PerGAVirOneThird}}^{(n,t)}(2r-1)$:** In this case, *all* the parties in $\mathcal{H}$ proceed to execute steps 1, 2 and 3 during the iteration r. Let $\mathcal{H}_0$ and $\mathcal{H}_1$ be the set of honest parties, who get their respective outputs from the instance $\Pi_{\text{PerGAVirOneThird}}^{(n,t)}(2r-1)$ with grade 0 and 1 respectively. Moreover, let E be the event that all the parties in $\mathcal{H}$ obtain a common random output bit Coin from the instance of $\Pi_{\text{BGWCC}}^{(n,t)}$ during step 2 of the iteration r. Since the parties in $\mathcal{H}$ start executing step 2 only after finishing step 1, it follows that Coin is *independent* of the output bit obtained by the parties in $\mathcal{H}$ during the instance $\Pi_{\text{PerGAVirOneThird}}^{(n,t)}(2r-1)$. We also note that the event E occurs with probability at least $\frac{2}{3}$, since the success probability of $\Pi_{\text{BGWCC}}^{(n,t)}$ is assumed to be at least $\frac{2}{3}$. From the protocol steps, it follows that all the parties in $\mathcal{H}_0$ participate during the second instance of $\Pi_{\text{PerGAVirOneThird}}^{(n,t)}$ with $\text{sid} = 2r$ with input Coin during step 3 of the iteration r. We next show

that with probability at least $\frac{1}{3}$, all parties in $\mathcal{H}_1$ also participate during the second instance of $\Pi^{(n,t)}_{\mathsf{PerGAVirOneThird}}$ with $\mathsf{sid} = 2r$ with input Coin.
Consider an *arbitrary* $P_i \in \mathcal{H}_1$ and let b be the input of P_i for the instance $\Pi^{(n,t)}_{\mathsf{PerGAVirOneThird}}(2r)$. Since b is *independent* of Coin, then conditioned on the event E, probability that $b = \mathsf{Coin}$ holds is $\frac{1}{2}$. Since the event E occurs with probability at least $\frac{2}{3}$, it follows that the probability that the parties in $\mathcal{H}_1$ have the input Coin for the instance $\Pi^{(n,t)}_{\mathsf{PerGAVirOneThird}}(2r)$ is at least $\frac{2}{3} \cdot \frac{1}{2} = \frac{1}{3}$. Hence with probability at least $\frac{1}{3}$, all the parties in $\mathcal{H}$ participate with the input Coin during the instance $\Pi^{(n,t)}_{\mathsf{PerGAVirOneThird}}(2r)$. It now follows from Lemma 8.8 that all the parties in $\mathcal{H}$ will get the output (d, g') from the instance $\Pi^{(n,t)}_{\mathsf{PerGAVirOneThird}}(2r)$ where $d = \mathsf{Coin}$ and $g' = 2$. Consequently, all the parties in $\mathcal{H}$ will terminate with output Coin after executing step 3 of the iteration r. □

Now based on the previous two claims, we prove the *t-consistency* and derive the expected number of iterations required by the honest parties to terminate the protocol.

Lemma 8.11 *If $t < \frac{n}{3}$ and if all honest parties participate in the protocol $\Pi^{(n,t)}_{\mathsf{ConsRandBA}}$ with different input bits, then all the following holds provided the success probability of $\Pi^{(n,t)}_{\mathsf{BGWCC}}$ is at least $\frac{2}{3}$:*

- *All honest parties will terminate the protocol in an expected 117 rounds.*[18]
- *If the honest parties terminate the protocol, then they do so with a common output bit.*
- *The protocol incurs an expected communication complexity of $O(n^6 \log |\mathbb{F}|)$ bits, where $\mathbb{F}$ is the finite field with $|\mathbb{F}| > n$ over which all computations are performed during the protocol $\Pi^{(n,t)}_{\mathsf{BGWCC}}$.*

Proof Let $\mathcal{H}$ be the set of *honest* parties. We first derive the expected number of iterations required in the protocol for the parties in $\mathcal{H}$ to terminate with some output. From Claim 8.11, if *all* the parties in $\mathcal{H}$ participate during any iteration r of the protocol, then with probability at least $\frac{1}{3}$, some party from $\mathcal{H}$ terminates the protocol with an output by the end of that iteration. Moreover, if any party in $\mathcal{H}$ terminates the protocol with output v during iteration r, then every party in $\mathcal{H}$ terminates the protocol with output v by the end of iteration $r + 1$. So the termination of the protocol depends upon the *first* iteration when any party from $\mathcal{H}$ terminates the protocol, since the termination for all the parties in $\mathcal{H}$ is then guaranteed by the end of the subsequent round. We next derive the expected number of iterations when this "magical event" happens. So let τ be the random variable which denotes the *first* iteration, when any party from $\mathcal{H}$ terminates the protocol. We want to derive the expected value of τ. The probability that $\tau = r$ for any $r \in \mathbb{N}$ is given by

[18] We stress that the number of rounds here is in expectation and there is a possibility that the honest parties never terminate the protocol, though the possibility of it happening is *asymptotically* 0.

$$\Pr(\tau = r) = \Pr(\tau \neq 1) \cdot \Pr(\tau \neq 2|\tau \neq 1) \cdot \ldots \cdot \Pr(\tau \neq (r-1)|\tau \neq 1 \cap \ldots \tau \neq (r-2)) \cdot \Pr(\tau = r|\tau \neq 1 \cap \ldots \cap \tau \neq (r-1)).$$

From Claim 8.11, each multiplicand on the right-hand side of the above equation, except the last one, is upper bounded by $\frac{2}{3}$. And the last multiplicand is upper bounded by $\frac{1}{3}$. This is because, with probability at least $\frac{1}{3}$, at least one party from $\mathcal{H}$ will terminate at the end of any iteration and hence with probability at most $\frac{2}{3}$, no party from $\mathcal{H}$ may terminate at the end of any iteration. Hence we get that

$$\Pr(\tau = r) \leq (\frac{2}{3})^{r-1} \cdot (\frac{1}{3}).$$

Now the expected value $E(\tau)$ of τ is computed as follows:

$$\begin{aligned} E(\tau) &= \sum_{r=1}^{\infty} r \Pr(\tau = r) \\ &\leq \sum_{r=1}^{\infty} r(\frac{2}{3})^{r-1}(\frac{1}{3}) \\ &\leq \frac{1}{3} \cdot \sum_{r=1}^{\infty} r(\frac{2}{3})^{r-1} \leq \frac{1}{3} \cdot 9 \leq 3. \end{aligned}$$

The expression for $E(\tau)$ is a sum of AGP up to infinite terms, which is given by $\frac{a}{1-R} + \frac{DR}{(1-R)^2}$, where $a = 1$, $R = \frac{2}{3}$ and $D = 1$. Hence, we have that $E(\tau) \leq 3$.

Let us now count the number of rounds and communication complexity of each iteration, which will give the expected number of communication rounds and the expected communication complexity of the protocol. In each iteration, two instances of $\Pi^{(n,t)}_{\mathsf{PerGAVirOneThird}}$ and one instance of $\Pi^{(n,t)}_{\mathsf{BGWCC}}$ are executed. From Lemma 8.7, each instance of $\Pi^{(n,t)}_{\mathsf{PerGAVirOneThird}}$ requires 3 rounds and incurs a communication of $O(n^2)$ bits. From Corollary 8.2, each instance of $\Pi^{(n,t)}_{\mathsf{BGWCC}}$ requires 33 rounds and incurs a communication of $O(n^6 \log |\mathbb{F}|)$ bits, where $\mathbb{F}$ is a finite field with $|\mathbb{F}| > n$ over which all the computations are performed in $\Pi^{(n,t)}_{\mathsf{BGWCC}}$. Since it takes 3 iterations in expectation for the parties in $\mathcal{H}$ to terminate the protocol, the expected number of rounds required in the protocol is $3 \cdot (2 \cdot 3 + 33)$ which is 117 rounds. Since the communication complexity of each iteration is $O(n^6 \log |\mathbb{F}|)$ bits and 3 iterations are required in expectation, the expected communication complexity of the protocol is $O(n^6 \log |\mathbb{F}|)$ bits. □

Based on the discussion, we have the following theorem.

Theorem 8.6 *If $t < \frac{n}{3}$, then protocol $\Pi^{(n,t)}_{\mathsf{ConsRandBA}}$ is a t-secure almost-surely terminating BA protocol in the model $\mathcal{M}_{\mathsf{secure}}$ against a computationally-unbounded adversary. The protocol requires 117 rounds in expectation for the honest parties to terminate and incurs an expected communication complexity of $O(n^6 \log |\mathbb{F}|)$ bits, where $\mathbb{F}$ is any finite field with $|\mathbb{F}| > n$.*

8.7.4 Protocol $\Pi^{(n,t)}_{\mathsf{ConsRandBA}}$: Further Discussion

Even though the expected number of rounds required in the protocol $\Pi^{(n,t)}_{\mathsf{ConsRandBA}}$ is a *constant*, namely 117, it is still on a higher end and a natural question is whether one can reduce the expected number of rounds required in the protocol. This can be achieved by doing the following:

1. Reducing the expected number of iterations required in the protocol $\Pi^{(n,t)}_{\mathsf{ConsRandBA}}$ for the honest parties to terminate.
2. Reducing the number of rounds required in the CC protocol.

We now briefly discuss each of the above points. The only way to *reduce* the expected number of iterations required in the protocol $\Pi^{(n,t)}_{\mathsf{ConsRandBA}}$ is to *increase* the success probability of the CC protocol $\Pi^{(n,t)}_{\mathsf{BGWCC}}$. This is because the former is *inversely* proportional to the latter.[19] So the next question is how to increase the success probability of the protocol $\Pi^{(n,t)}_{\mathsf{BGWCC}}$? As shown in Section 8.6.1, the only way to increase the success probability of the protocol $\Pi^{(n,t)}_{\mathsf{BGWCC}}$ will be to adjust the value of the parameter u. For instance, as shown in that section, one can achieve a success probability of $0.36 \approx \frac{9}{25}$ by setting $u = n$. Hence to achieve a success probability closer to 1, one can appropriately select the value of u.

Let us now discuss how to reduce the number of rounds required in the CC protocol. For this, we revisit Table 8.3, where we summarized various possible instantiations of CC tolerating $t < \frac{n}{3}$ corruptions. For uniformity, let us fix the success probability p of all these instantiations to $\frac{2}{3}$. In Table 8.4, we summarize the expected number of rounds and expected communication complexity of the resultant BA protocol, which is obtained by using the various instantiations of CC from Table 8.3 in protocol $\Pi^{(n,t)}_{\mathsf{ConsRandBA}}$. Since we are fixing $p = \frac{2}{3}$ for all CC protocols, as a result, all the BA protocols will require 3 iterations in expectation. However, the number of rounds within each iteration will *vary* for different BA protocols, since each instantiation of the CC requires a different number of rounds.

19 Recall the derivation done in Section 8.2.1.

CC Protocol Used	Expected Round Complexity	Expected Communication Complexity
$\Pi^{(n,t)}_{\mathsf{BGWCC}}$	117	$O(n^6 \log \lvert\mathbb{F}\rvert)$
$\Pi^{(n,t)}_{\mathsf{ModBGWCC}}$	81	$O(n^6 \log \lvert\mathbb{F}\rvert)$
$\Pi^{(n,t)}_{\mathsf{GIKRCC}}$	78	$O(n^6 \log \lvert\mathbb{F}\rvert)$
$\Pi^{(n,t)}_{\mathsf{FGGRCC}}$	60	$O(n^7 \log \lvert\mathbb{F}\rvert)$
$\Pi^{(n,t)}_{\mathsf{KKKCC}}$	45	$O(n^7 \log \lvert\mathbb{F}\rvert)$
$\Pi^{(n,t)}_{\mathsf{AKPCC}}$	60	$O(n^7 \log \lvert\mathbb{F}\rvert)$

Table 8.4: Summary of the various *t-secure* BA protocol with unconditional security and expected constant rounds where $t < \frac{n}{3}$, obtained by using different CC protocols summarized in Table 8.3 in the protocol $\Pi^{(n,t)}_{\mathsf{ConsRandBA}}$. In all these protocols, computations are performed over a finite field $\mathbb{F}$ where $|\mathbb{F}| > n$. Moreover, the success probability p of all the CC protocols is set to $p = \frac{2}{3}$

8.8 Concluding Remarks

This chapter discussed how to design bit-BA protocols with a constant expected number of rounds. We focused on BA protocols with unconditional security, secure against computationally-unbounded adversaries in the model $\mathcal{M}_{\mathsf{secure}}$. A central topic of the discussion was how to instantiate the common-coin (CC) primitive from scratch. Specifically, we discussed how to design CC from scratch *without* any setup and computational hardness assumptions based on verifiable secret sharing (VSS). For the state-of-the-art results related to unconditionally-secure CC, the readers are referred to [2].

As mentioned above, we focused on instantiating CC with unconditional security and without using any set-up. Consequently, the number of rounds required is higher (though it is a *constant*). Later, we will see that if one settles for cryptographic-security, one can design highly efficient and simple CC protocols.

Chapter 9
Dolev-Strong Protocol for Distributed Consensus

In this chapter, we will present the classical BB protocol due to Dolev and Strong [46], which is secure even when the *majority* of the parties are under the adversary's control. That is, the protocol is secure against t Byzantine faults, where $t < n$. The protocol is designed for the *authentic-channel* setting and assumes a PKI set-up already being available to the parties; i.e. the model $\mathcal{M}_{\mathsf{auth}}^{\mathsf{pki}}$. Depending upon whether the PKI is cryptographically or unconditionally-secure, the resultant protocol will be either cryptographically-secure or statistically-secure. The protocol is *deterministic* and requires $t + 1$ rounds of communication, which is provably *optimal*. For the sake of completeness, we will also present the BA variant of Dolev-Strong's protocol in the honest majority setting, i.e. with $t < \frac{n}{2}$.

9.1 The Network Model and Adversarial Setting

We consider the model $\mathcal{M}_{\mathsf{auth}}^{\mathsf{pki}}$ of *pairwise-authentic* channels, where the parties in $\mathcal{P}$ are connected by pairwise-authentic channels. Moreover, we assume the existence of a PKI setup available to the parties, where for each party P_i, there exists a pair of keys $(\mathsf{sk}_i, \mathsf{pk}_i)$ for a signature scheme, with the *signing key* sk_i held by P_i and the *verification key* pk_i being *publicly* available. The distrust among the parties is modelled by a centralized adversary Adv, capable of corrupting up to t parties, where $t < n$. The adversary could be either computationally-bounded (probabilistic polynomial time) or computationally-unbounded. If it is the former, then we assume the PKI setup is for a standard cryptographically-secure *digital signature* scheme. On the other hand, if it is the latter, then we assume that the PKI setup is for an unconditionally-secure signature scheme (namely the *pseudo-signatures*).

A. Choudhury and A. Patra, *Fault-Tolerant Distributed Consensus in Synchronous Networks*, Information Security and Cryptography,
https://doi.org/10.1007/978-3-031-80460-1_9

9.2 The Byzantine Broadcast Protocol

For simplicity and without loss of generality, we assume that party $P_1 \in \mathcal{P}$ is the designated *sender* and has input $b \in \{0, 1\}$. During the protocol, the parties will exchange signed bits. Since there are *two* possible candidates for the sender's input, there will be two types of signed bits exchanged during the protocol, one for bit 0 and another for bit 1. Each party will keep track of how many signed 0-messages and signed 1-messages it has seen during different rounds of the protocol and based on that, decides its final output.

During the *first* round, the sender signs its input b, sends the signed bit to everyone, and terminates with output b. Then in each round r where $r \in \{0, \ldots, t\}$, each party P_i checks whether it should "accumulate" the bit v on behalf of the sender P_1, depending upon whether all the following conditions are satisfied:

- The bit v has *not* been accumulated earlier;[1]
- By the end of round r, party P_i has seen *at least* $r + 1$ parties signing the bit v, *including* the sender P_1.[2]

If all the above conditions are satisfied, P_i accumulates the bit v. Additionally, if there are still rounds left in the protocol, then in the next round, P_i notifies every party that it has accumulated the bit v. For notification, P_i sends all the signatures on bit v that it has seen, along with its signature on the bit v. Notice that if P_i has accumulated the bit v during the *last* round, then it *cannot* notify others about its accumulation, since there is *no* more communication rounds left in the protocol as the protocol has only $t + 1$ rounds. To compute the output, each party checks how many bits it has accumulated after $t + 1$ rounds. If the party has accumulated only one bit, then that is set as the output. Otherwise, the party outputs a predetermined default bit, which is 0.

The idea behind the protocol is as follows: if the sender is *honest*, then all honest parties will accumulate the sender's input bit b at the end of the first round. Moreover, no honest party will accumulate the bit $1-b$, since that will require the corrupt parties to *forge* the sender's signature on the bit $1 - b$.[3] Hence, throughout the protocol, each honest party would accumulate only the bit b and output b, implying the *validity*.

To prove the *consistency*, we can show that even if the sender is *corrupt*, the bits accumulated by the honest parties after $t + 1$ rounds will be the *same*. Specifically, if any honest party P_i accumulates a bit v, then there are *two* possibilities: if the bit v is accumulated by P_i *before* the *last* round, then every other honest party who has yet to accumulate v would do so in the *next* round since P_i will notify everyone about its accumulation of the bit v. On the other hand, if P_i accumulates the bit v during the *last* round, then the above argument no longer holds since there are no more rounds left in the protocol for P_i to notify others that it has accumulated the bit v. However,

---

[1] Hence a bit can be accumulated by a party *at most* once.

[2] Note that it is crucial to check whether among the r signatures, one of the signatures is from the sender P_1.

[3] Recall that one of the conditions to accumulate a bit on behalf of the sender is that sender should have signed that bit.

the accumulation of v by P_i in the last round means that at least $t+1$ parties must have signed the bit v, and among these $t+1$ parties, at least one party is *honest*. That honest party must have signed v to notify others that it has accumulated v, which must have happened in an *earlier* round. Consequently, all honest parties would have accumulated the bit v by the end of the last round. The protocol is formally presented in Fig 9.1.

Protocol $\Pi_{\mathsf{DSBB}}^{(n,t)}$

Setup: A PKI setup where for each $P_j \in \mathcal{P}$, there exists a pair of keys $(\mathsf{sk}_j, \mathsf{pk}_j)$ for a signature scheme $(\mathsf{Sign}, \mathsf{Verify})$, with sk_j held by P_j and pk_j being *publicly* available.

- **Initialization**: Initialize the set of bits accumulated, $\mathsf{ACC}_i := \emptyset$.
- **Round 0**: If $P_i = P_1$, then on having the input bit $b \in \{0,1\}$, do the following:
  - Compute $\sigma_i^{(b)} := \mathsf{Sign}_{\mathsf{sk}_i}(b)$.
  - Set $\mathsf{SET}_i^{(b)} := \{(P_i, \sigma_i^{(b)})\}$ and send $(b, \mathsf{SET}_i^{(b)})$ to every party in $\mathcal{P}$.
- **Round $r = 0$ to t**: On receiving $(v, \mathsf{SET}_j^{(v)})$ from any party $P_j \in \mathcal{P}$ during round r where $v \in \{0,1\}$, check if *all* the following holds.
  - $|\mathsf{SET}_j^{(v)}| \geq r+1$;
  - For every tuple $(P_l, \sigma_l^{(v)}) \in \mathsf{SET}_j^{(v)}$, the condition $\mathsf{Verify}_{\mathsf{pk}_l}(v, \sigma_l^{(v)}) = 1$ holds;
  - A tuple of the form $(P_1, \sigma_1^{(v)}) \in \mathsf{SET}_j^{(v)}$;
  - $v \notin \mathsf{ACC}_i$.

  If all the above holds, then do the following.
  - Set $\mathsf{ACC}_i := \mathsf{ACC}_i \cup \{v\}$.
  - If $r \neq t$, then do the following:
    - Compute $\sigma_i^{(v)} := \mathsf{Sign}_{\mathsf{sk}_i}(v)$.
    - Set $\mathsf{SET}_i^{(v)} := \mathsf{SET}_j^{(v)} \cup \{(P_i, \sigma_i^{(v)})\}$ and send $(v, \mathsf{SET}_i^{(v)})$ to every party in $\mathcal{P}$ during round $r+1$.
- **Output Computation**: After $t+1$ rounds, do the following.
  - If $\mathsf{ACC}_i = \{v\}$ then output v and terminate.
  - Else output 0 and terminate.

Fig. 9.1: The Dolev-Strong bit-BB protocol tolerating $t < n$ corruptions. The above code is executed by every party $P_i \in \mathcal{P}$, where P_1 is the designated sender with input $b \in \{0,1\}$

We now proceed to prove the properties of the protocol. For simplicity, we make the standard convention of treating signatures as *idealized* objects during our protocol analysis. That is, we assume that the signatures are *perfectly unforgeable* and hence adversary will *fail* to forge the signature of an honest party on any message, which the party does not sign. Since there are polynomially (in n) many instances of the signature scheme being invoked in the protocol and since the unforgeability is satisfied in each instance except with a negligible probability by the standard union bound, it follows that the above assumption holds except with a *negligible* probability.

We also assume that the signatures are *transferable* and any party, upon receiving a valid signature from a party, can send and get it verified by any other party. However, *unlike* the standard digital signatures which are *cryptographically-secure* and offer *arbitrary* (polynomial) number of transfers, pseudo-signatures offer a "limited" number of transfers, which is typically bounded as a function of n. We assume that the given PKI setup supports the required number of transfers that the protocol $\Pi_{\mathsf{DSBB}}^{(n,t)}$ demands. During the analysis, we assume that the size of each signature is κ bits where κ is the underlying *security parameter* (see Section 2.1 for details about security parameter and signature schemes) We start with the proof of the *validity* property.

Lemma 9.1 *Protocol* $\Pi_{\mathsf{DSBB}}^{(n,t)}$ *satisfies the following properties, for any* $t < n$.

- *If the PKI is cryptographically-secure then the protocol achieves* t*-validity against a computationally-bounded adversary.*
- *If the PKI is unconditionally-secure then the protocol achieves* t*-validity against a computationally-unbounded adversary.*

Proof Let $\mathcal{H}$ be the set of *honest* parties. To prove the *validity*, we must consider an *honest* sender. Hence $P_1 \in \mathcal{H}$. Let P_1 has input $b \in \{0, 1\}$. We prove that throughout the protocol, every party in $\mathcal{H}$ accumulates *only* the bit b. That is, $\mathsf{ACC}_i = \{b\}$ will hold after $t + 1$ rounds. This will imply that every party in $\mathcal{H}$ outputs b.

During Round 0, party P_1 will sign the bit b and send it to everyone. That is, P_1 will send $(b, \mathsf{SET}_1^{(b)})$ to all the parties where $\mathsf{SET}_1^{(b)} = \{(P_1, \sigma_1^{(b)})\}$ and where $\sigma_1^{(b)} = \mathsf{Sign}_{\mathsf{sk}_1}(b)$. Consequently, all the parties in $\mathcal{H}$ will receive $(b, \mathsf{SET}_1^{(b)})$ from P_1 at the end of Round 0. Moreover, the conditions for accumulating the bit b will be satisfied for all the parties in $\mathcal{H}$. This is because the set ACC_i of every party $P_i \in \mathcal{H}$ will be $\emptyset$ and $|\mathsf{SET}_1^{(b)}| = 1$ will hold. Moreover, the signature of P_1 on bit b will be accepted by every party in $\mathcal{H}$. That is, the condition $\mathsf{Verify}_{\mathsf{pk}_1}(b, \sigma_1^{(b)}) = 1$ will hold for every party $P_i \in \mathcal{H}$. Hence $\mathsf{ACC}_i = \{b\}$ will hold for each $P_i \in \mathcal{H}$ at the end of round 0.

Since $P_1 \in \mathcal{H}$, it will *not* sign and send the bit $1 - b$ to any party. Moreover, since the signature scheme is *unforgeable*, the adversary will *not* be able to forge P_1's signature on the bit $1 - b$ and send it to the parties on behalf of P_1. Consequently, no party P_i in $\mathcal{H}$ will include the bit $1 - b$ in the set ACC_i. □

To prove the *consistency*, we prove a helping property stating that the bits accumulated by the honest parties will be the same after $t + 1$ rounds.

Claim 9.1 In protocol $\Pi_{\mathsf{DSBB}}^{(n,t)}$, the condition $\mathsf{ACC}_i = \mathsf{ACC}_j$ holds at the end of the protocol for every pair of honest parties P_i, P_j, for any $t < n$. If the PKI is cryptographically-secure, then the above property is achieved against a computationally-bounded adversary. If the PKI is unconditionally-secure, then the above property is achieved against a computationally-unbounded adversary.

Proof Let $\mathcal{H}$ be the set of *honest* parties and consider arbitrary parties $P_i, P_j \in \mathcal{H}$. Let ACC_i and ACC_j be the accumulative sets of P_i and P_j at the end of the protocol. Let $v \in \mathsf{ACC}_i$ where $v \in \{0, 1\}$. We wish to show that $v \in \mathsf{ACC}_j$ as well. Let r be the round when P_i adds v to ACC_i. This implies that there exists some party $P_k \in \mathcal{P}$, such that P_i receives $(v, \mathsf{SET}_k^{(v)})$ from P_k during round r where $v \in \{0, 1\}$, such that *all* the following holds.

- $|\mathsf{SET}_k^{(v)}| \geq r + 1$;
- For every tuple $(P_l, \sigma_l^{(v)}) \in \mathsf{SET}_k^{(v)}$, the condition $\mathsf{Verify}_{\mathsf{pk}_l}(v, \sigma_l^{(v)}) = 1$ holds;

– A tuple of the form $(P_1, \sigma_1^{(v)}) \in \mathsf{SET}_k^{(v)}$;
– $v \notin \mathsf{ACC}_i$.

Now there are *two* possible cases with respect to the value of r.

- **Case I** — $r < t$: Since P_i accumulates the bit v for the *first* time and since there is still at least one round left in the protocol, party P_i will itself sign the bit v and send it along with the signatures in the set $\mathsf{SET}_k^{(v)}$ to all the parties during round $r+1$. That is, P_i will compute $\sigma_i^{(v)} := \mathsf{Sign}_{\mathsf{sk}_i}(v)$, set $\mathsf{SET}_i^{(v)} := \mathsf{SET}_k^{(v)} \cup \{(P_i, \sigma_i^{(v)})\}$ and send $(v, \mathsf{SET}_i^{(v)})$ to every party in $\mathcal{P}$ during round $r+1$. Next, consider the party P_j. If v is already present in ACC_j then the proof is done. So consider the case when $v \notin \mathsf{ACC}_j$ and let us consider the round $r+1$ from the point of view of the party P_j. During round $r+1$, party P_j will receive $(v, \mathsf{SET}_i^{(v)})$ from P_i and *all* the following will hold.
  – $|\mathsf{SET}_i^{(v)}| \geq r+2$. This is because $|\mathsf{SET}_k^{(v)}| \geq r+1$ and $\mathsf{SET}_i^{(v)} := \mathsf{SET}_k^{(v)} \cup \{(P_i, \sigma_i^{(v)})\}$, where $(P_i, \sigma_i^{(v)}) \notin \mathsf{SET}_k^{(v)}$.
  – For every tuple $(P_l, \sigma_l^{(v)}) \in \mathsf{SET}_i^{(v)}$, the condition $\mathsf{Verify}_{\mathsf{pk}_l}(v, \sigma_l^{(v)}) = 1$ holds. This is because the signatures are *transferable* and the condition was true for every tuple $(P_l, \sigma_l^{(v)}) \in \mathsf{SET}_k^{(v)}$. Moreover, since P_i is honest, it follows that the condition is true even for the tuple $(P_i, \sigma_i^{(v)})$. Since $\mathsf{SET}_i^{(v)} = \mathsf{SET}_k^{(v)} \cup \{(P_i, \sigma_i^{(v)})\}$, it follows that the condition $\mathsf{Verify}_{\mathsf{pk}_l}(v, \sigma_l^{(v)}) = 1$ holds for every tuple $(P_l, \sigma_l^{(v)}) \in \mathsf{SET}_i^{(v)}$.
  – A tuple of the form $(P_1, \sigma_1^{(v)}) \in \mathsf{SET}_i^{(v)}$. This is because $\mathsf{SET}_i^{(v)} = \mathsf{SET}_k^{(v)} \cup \{(P_i, \sigma_i^{(v)})\}$ and $(P_1, \sigma_1^{(v)}) \in \mathsf{SET}_k^{(v)}$.
  – $v \notin \mathsf{ACC}_j$. This is because we are considering the case when P_j has *not* yet accumulated the bit v in any of the earlier rounds.

  Hence, party P_j will accumulate the bit v during round $r+1$ and include the bit v to the set ACC_j. For a pictorial illustration of this case, see Fig 9.2.
- **Case II** — $r = t$: Since $|\mathsf{SET}_k^{(v)}| \geq r+1$, it implies that in this case, $|\mathsf{SET}_k^{(v)}| \geq t+1$. As there can be at most t corrupt parties, it implies that $\mathcal{H} \cap \mathsf{SET}_k^{(v)} \neq \emptyset$ and hence there exists at least one honest party in the set $\mathsf{SET}_k^{(v)}$, say P_h. This implies that the tuple $(P_h, \sigma_h^{(v)}) \in \mathsf{SET}_k^{(v)}$, such that $\mathsf{Verify}_{\mathsf{pk}_h}(v, \sigma_h^{(v)}) = 1$ holds. Since the signature scheme is *unforgeable*, it follows that the signature $\sigma_h^{(v)}$ has been generated by P_h. Let $r^\star + 1$ be the round during which P_h has computed the signature $\sigma_h^{(v)}$. It follows that $r^\star + 1 < r$, since $(P_h, \sigma_h^{(v)})$ is received by P_i (as part of $\mathsf{SET}_k^{(v)}$) during round r. This also implies that P_h has accumulated the bit v during the round $r^\star$. This further implies that there exists some party $P_m \in \mathcal{P}$, such that P_h receives $(v, \mathsf{SET}_m^{(v)})$ from P_m during round $r^\star$, such that *all* the following holds.
  – $|\mathsf{SET}_m^{(v)}| \geq r^\star + 1$;
  – For every tuple $(P_l, \sigma_l^{(v)}) \in \mathsf{SET}_m^{(v)}$, the condition $\mathsf{Verify}_{\mathsf{pk}_l}(v, \sigma_l^{(v)}) = 1$ holds;

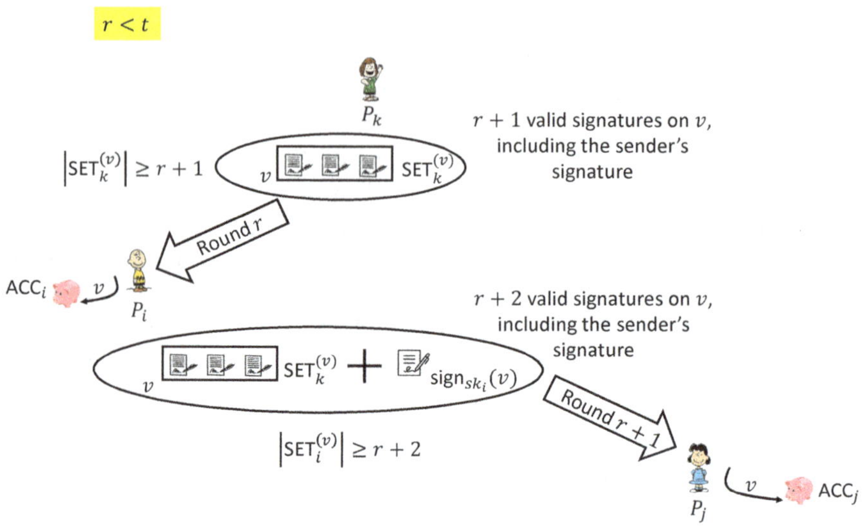

Fig. 9.2: Pictorial illustration of the case I in the proof of Claim 9.1. Party P_i accumulates the bit v during round r where $r < t$, implying that it has received at least $r+1$ valid signatures on the bit v, including the sender's signature. Then, during the round $r + 1$, party P_i will send all those signatures to everyone along with its own signature on the bit v. As a result, whoever has not yet accumulated the bit v will do so during the round $r + 1$ since such parties will now receive at least $r + 2$ valid signatures on the bit v, including the sender's signature

- A tuple of the form $(P_1, \sigma_1^{(v)}) \in \mathsf{SET}_m^{(v)}$;
- $v \notin \mathsf{ACC}_h$. □

It then follows that by the end of round $r^\star + 1$, every party in $\mathcal{H}$ will accumulate the bit v and hence $v \in \mathsf{ACC}_j$. The proof for this is identical to the previous case; hence, the formal details are omitted. Namely, since $r^\star < t$, it follows that during the round $r^\star + 1$, party P_h will itself sign the bit v and send it along with the signatures in the set $\mathsf{SET}_m^{(v)}$ to all the parties. Consequently, any honest party who has *not* yet accumulated the bit v will do so during the rounds $r^\star + 1$.
For a pictorial illustration of this case, see Fig 9.3.

Once we have Claim 9.1, the proof of the *t-consistency* property is straightforward.

Lemma 9.2 *Protocol* $\Pi_{\mathsf{DSBB}}^{(n,t)}$ *satisfies the following properties, for any* $t < n$.
- *If the PKI is cryptographically-secure then the protocol achieves t-consistency against a computationally-bounded adversary.*
- *If the PKI is unconditionally-secure then the protocol achieves t-consistency against a computationally-unbounded adversary.*

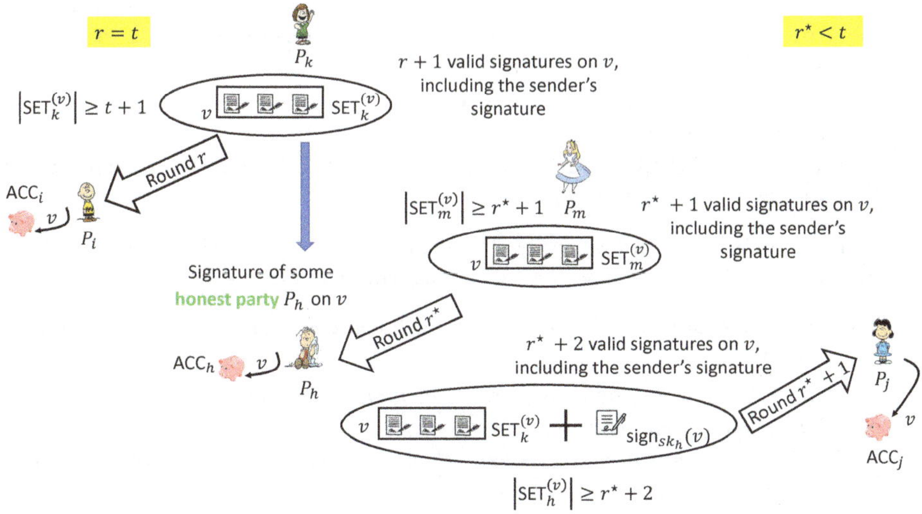

Fig. 9.3: Pictorial illustration of case II in the proof of Claim 9.1. Party P_i accumulates the bit v during round r where $r = t$, implying that it has received at least $t + 1$ valid signatures on the bit v, including the sender's signature. One of these signatures will be from some honest party, say P_h, who would have accumulated the bit v during some round $r^\star$, where $r^\star < t$. Hence, during round $r^\star$, party P_h has received at least $r^\star + 1$ valid signatures on the bit v, including the sender's signature, from some party, say P_m. Then, during the round $r^\star + 1$, party P_h would send all those signatures to everyone along with its signature on the bit v. As a result, whoever has not yet accumulated the bit v will do so during the round $r^\star + 1$, since such parties will now receive at least $r^\star + 2$ valid signatures on the bit v, including the sender's signature

Proof Let $\mathcal{H}$ be the set of *honest* parties. We know that from Claim 9.1, the following holds:

- If the PKI is cryptographically-secure then $\mathsf{ACC}_i = \mathsf{ACC}_j$ holds for every pair of parties $P_i, P_j \in \mathcal{H}$, if the adversary is computationally bounded.
- If the PKI is unconditionally-secure then $\mathsf{ACC}_i = \mathsf{ACC}_j$ holds for every pair of parties $P_i, P_j \in \mathcal{H}$, if the adversary is computationally unbounded.

Since the parties in $\mathcal{H}$ compute their output *deterministically* based on the contents of their respective ACC sets, it follows that every party in $\mathcal{H}$ will have the same output, thus proving the *t-consistency* property. □

Next, we derive the round and communication complexity of the protocol.

Lemma 9.3 *Protocol $\Pi_{\mathsf{DSBB}}^{(n,t)}$ requires $t + 1$ rounds and incurs a communication of $\mathcal{BC}(1) = O(n^3\kappa)$ bits, where κ is the security parameter and represents the size of a signature in bits.*

Proof There are $t + 1$ iterations in the protocol, and each iteration may involve one round of communication, where a party may send signed bits to other parties. Hence, the protocol requires $t + 1$ rounds of communication.

In the protocol, each party P_i can accumulate a bit $v \in \{0, 1\}$ *at most* once and after accumulating v, it may send $\mathsf{SET}_i^{(v)}$ to all the parties, where $|\mathsf{SET}_i^{(v)}| \leq n$ and consists of signatures on the bit v by at most n parties. This results in the communication of $O(n^2\kappa)$ bits for *one* party and hence $O(n^3\kappa)$ bits for the n parties. □

Theorem 9.1 now follows easily from the above discussion. The *t-liveness* follows from the fact that all the honest parties will terminate after $t + 1$ rounds.

Theorem 9.1 *Protocol* $\Pi_{\mathsf{DSBB}}^{(n,t)}$ *satisfies the following properties, for any* $t < n$ *in the model* $\mathcal{M}_{\mathsf{auth}}^{\mathsf{pki}}$.

- *If the PKI is cryptographically-secure then the protocol is a t-secure BB protocol with cryptographic security.*
- *If the PKI is unconditionally-secure then the protocol is a t-secure BB protocol with statistical security.*

The protocol requires $t + 1$ *rounds of communication and incurs a communication of* $\mathcal{BC}(1) = O(n^3\kappa)$ *bits, where* κ *is the security parameter and denotes the size of a signature in bits.*

9.2.1 Dolev-Strong BB Protocol: Further Discussion

Note that protocol $\Pi_{\mathsf{DSBB}}^{(n,t)}$ is a *deterministic* BB protocol since the protocol execution depends *only* on the input of the sender and the behaviour of the adversary. The protocol requires the *optimal* number of communication rounds. This is because from Theorem 7.4 (see Chapter 7), *any* deterministic BB protocol requires *at least* $t + 1$ rounds, *irrespective* of whether any setup is available or not to the parties. The protocol also enjoys the *optimal* resilience since $t < n$ is the *maximum* number of faults that any BB protocol can tolerate.

What goes wrong if protocol $\Pi_{\mathsf{DSBB}}^{(n,t)}$ is executed only for t rounds, *instead* of $t + 1$ rounds? It turns out that the *t-validity* property will be *satisfied*, since the proof of Lemma 9.1 will still work. Unfortunately, the *t-consistency* may *no* longer hold, since Claim 9.1 may *no* longer hold. The problem is that if the protocol lasts for *only* t rounds and if an honest party P_i accumulates a bit v during the *last* round, then it is *not* guaranteed that every other honest party would also accumulate the bit v. This is because there is *no* more round left in the protocol for P_i to notify others that it has accumulated the bit v and hence the argument for *Case I* in the proof of Claim 9.1 fails. On the other hand, since P_i accumulates v during the last round, it might see *at most* t signatures on the bit v while accumulating v and hence it is *no* longer guaranteed that one of these signatures is from an *honest* party, generated in some earlier round. This is because in the worst case, all these t signatures could be from *corrupt* parties. Consequently, the argument for *Case II* in the proof of Claim 9.1 also fails.

Let us take a concrete setting to demonstrate the above arguments. Let $n = t + 2$, with $\mathcal{P} = \{P_1, \ldots, P_{t+2}\}$ and P_1 being the sender. Moreover, let adversary controls the parties $P_1, \ldots, P_t$ and hence $\mathcal{H} = \{P_{t+1}, P_{t+2}\}$. The adversary's strategy is to crash *exactly* one party at the beginning of each round. Let P_1 have the input 1. During round 0, party P_1 signs the bit 1, sends it *only* to P_2 and then crashes. Consequently, party P_2 accumulates the bit 0 and then during round 1, notifies this *only* to P_3 and then crashes.

In general, during round r where $r \in \{0, \ldots, t-2\}$, party P_{r+2} accumulates the bit 1 and during round $r + 1$, notifies it *only* to the party P_{r+3} and then crashes. Note that the above strategy by the adversary is allowed since throughout it corrupts exactly t parties. Now as per the above strategy, during the *last* round $r = t - 1$, party P_{t+1} would accumulate the bit 1, since it would receive t valid signatures on the bit 1 provided by the party P_t and one of these signatures will be from P_1. However, party P_{t+2} would *not* accumulate the bit 1, since P_t crashes after delivering the set of signatures on 1 to P_{t+1}. Consequently, after t rounds, the conditions $\mathsf{ACC}_{t+1} = \{1\}$ and $\mathsf{ACC}_{t+2} = \emptyset$ will hold. As a result, P_{t+1} will output 1, while P_{t+2} will output the default bit 0, thus *violating* the *t-consistency* property. For a pictorial illustration of the above adversarial strategy, see Fig 9.4.

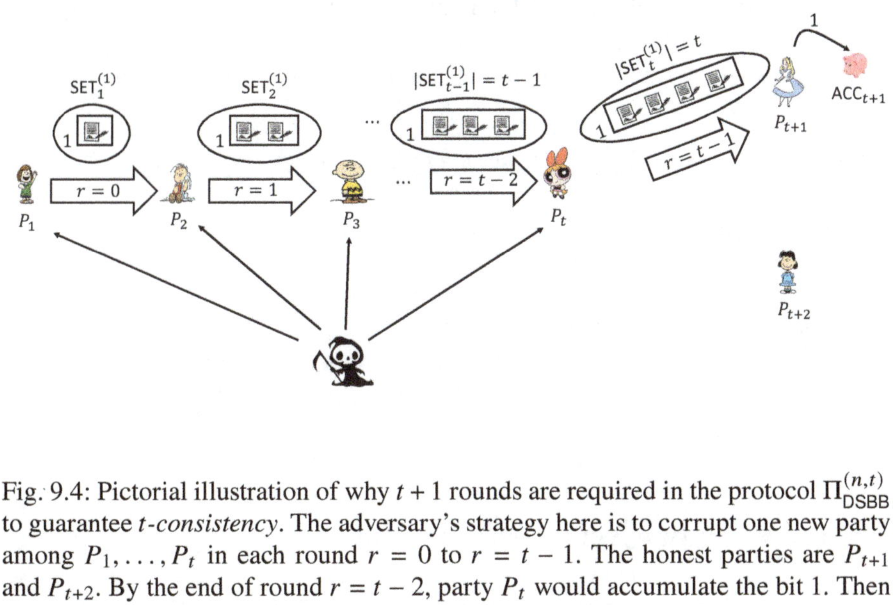

Fig. 9.4: Pictorial illustration of why $t + 1$ rounds are required in the protocol $\Pi_{\mathsf{DSBB}}^{(n,t)}$ to guarantee *t-consistency*. The adversary's strategy here is to corrupt one new party among $P_1, \ldots, P_t$ in each round $r = 0$ to $r = t - 1$. The honest parties are P_{t+1} and P_{t+2}. By the end of round $r = t - 2$, party P_t would accumulate the bit 1. Then during round $r = t - 1$, party P_t notifies about the accumulation of bit 1 *only* to party P_{t+1} and crashes. Consequently, P_{t+1} accumulates the bit 1, while the accumulative set of P_{t+2} remains empty. This would lead to P_{t+1} output 1 and P_{t+2} output 0, thus *violating t-consistency*

A careful observation here reveals that the above strategy by the adversary against a t-round variant of the protocol $\Pi_{\mathsf{DSBB}}^{(n,t)}$ is precisely the one outlined in Fig 7.1 in Section 7.1 against *any* t-round abstract deterministic BB protocol.

9.2.2 Dolev-Strong BB Protocol for L-bit Inputs

For simplicity, protocol $\Pi_{\mathsf{DSBB}}^{(n,t)}$ was presented for the case when the input of the designated sender is a *single* bit. However, a careful observation reveals that the protocol will also work *without* making any modifications to handle the case when the input of the sender consists of L bits, where $L \geq 1$. Namely, during round 0, the sender will send its signed input to everyone. Then in each round $r \in \{0, \ldots, t\}$, a party accumulates a candidate input on behalf of the sender, if the input has *not* been accumulated earlier and if at least $r + 1$ parties have signed that input by the end of that round, *including* the sender. Moreover, after accumulating that candidate input, the party signs that candidate and relays the signatures along with its own signature in the next round. This will ensure that any party who still needs to accumulate that candidate input will do so in the next round. Finally, after $t + 1$ rounds, each party inspects the candidate inputs, which are accumulated on behalf of the sender. If there is exactly one such input (which should be the case for an *honest* sender), then it is taken as the output else a default output of size L bits is taken as the output on behalf of the sender. We abuse the notations and call the protocol as $\Pi_{\mathsf{DSBB}}^{(n,t)}$. To avoid repetition, we do not give the formal steps of the protocol and the proofs and state the following theorem.

Theorem 9.2 *Protocol* $\Pi_{\mathsf{DSBB}}^{(n,t)}$ *satisfies the following properties, for any* $t < n$ *in the model* $\mathcal{M}_{\mathsf{auth}}^{\mathsf{pki}}$

- *If the PKI is cryptographically-secure then the protocol is a* t*-secure BB protocol with cryptographic security for* L*-bit inputs.*
- *If the PKI is unconditionally-secure then the protocol is a* t*-secure BB protocol with statistical security for* L*-bit inputs.*

The protocol requires $t + 1$ *rounds of communication and incurs a communication of* $\mathcal{BC}(L) = \mathcal{O}(n^3 L\kappa)$ *bits, where* κ *is the security parameter and denotes the size of a signature in bits.*

9.3 The Byzantine Agreement Protocol

One can easily obtain a BA variant of Dolev-Strong's BB protocol by using the "equivalence" between the BA and BB variants of distributed consensus (Theorem 2.3), provided $t < \frac{n}{2}$. However, due to its significance and completeness, we present the exact details of the BA variant of Dolev-Strong's protocol. Unlike all the BA protocols discussed till now, which can tolerate up to $t < \frac{n}{3}$ corruptions, Dolev-

Strong's BA protocol can tolerate up to $t < \frac{n}{2}$ Byzantine faults. Note that this *does not* violate the lower bound of $t < \frac{n}{3}$ on the resilience of BA protocols, established in Chapter 5. This is because the bound of $t < \frac{n}{3}$ holds if *no* setup is available to the parties, while the protocol assumes the *existence* of a trusted PKI setup. We also note that with $t < \frac{n}{2}$, the protocol enjoys the merit of having *optimal* resilience, since *any* BA protocol necessarily requires $t < \frac{n}{2}$, irrespective of the underlying model, as established in Theorem 2.1.

The Dolev-Strong's BA protocol is formally presented in Fig 9.5. We present the protocol for simplicity, assuming the parties' inputs are a single bit. However, the protocol will work even if the parties' inputs are from $\{0, 1\}^L$. The high-level idea behind the protocol is as follows: each party acts as a sender and invokes an instance of Dolev-Strong's BB protocol to broadcast its input (for BA) to all the parties. Hence, n instances of the BB protocol are executed in parallel, each for $t + 1$ rounds. Once all the n instances of BB get over, each party checks whether some value has been broadcasted by a *majority* of the parties. If there is any such value, then it is taken as the BA's output, or the party outputs a default value.

Since there are n instances of the BB protocol running in parallel, in the protocol, each party P_i will be maintaining n accumulative sets where $\mathsf{ACC}_{j,i}$ denotes the bit(s) accumulated by P_i on behalf of the party P_j during the instance of the BB protocol where P_j is designated as the sender. Similarly, each signature will have two levels of indexing, the first for denoting the corresponding sender party on behalf of which the signature is generated and the second for denoting the party who has signed the bit. In more detail, the notation $\sigma_{j,i}^{(v)}$ where $j, i \in \{1, \ldots, n\}$ and $v \in \{0, 1\}$ denotes the signature on the bit v generated by P_i on behalf of the party P_j as part of the BB instance where P_j is designated as the sender. Similarly, the notation $\mathsf{SET}_{j,i}^{(v)}$ denotes the set of signatures on the bit v possessed by the party P_i as part of the BB instance where P_j is designated as the sender. Apart from these sets, each party P_i also maintains a final set of bits FIN_i, which is the collection of bits from each instance of the BB protocol.

Protocol $\Pi_{\mathsf{DSBA}}^{(n,t)}$

Setup: A PKI setup where for each $P_j \in \mathcal{P}$, there exists a pair of keys $(\mathsf{sk}_j, \mathsf{pk}_j)$ for a signature scheme (Sign, Verify), with sk_j held by P_j and pk_j being *publicly* available.

- **Initialization**: Initialize the following sets.
  - For $j = 1, \ldots, n$, the set $\mathsf{ACC}_{j,i}$ of bits accumulated on behalf of P_j to $\emptyset$.
  - The final set of bits FIN_i for deciding the output to $\emptyset$.
- **Round 0**: On having the input bit $b_i \in \{0, 1\}$ for BA, do the following:
  - Compute $\sigma_{i,i}^{(b_i)} := \mathsf{Sign}_{\mathsf{sk}_i}(b_i)$.
  - Set $\mathsf{SET}_{i,i}^{(b_i)} := \{(P_i, \sigma_{i,i}^{(b_i)})\}$ and send $(b_i, \mathsf{SET}_{i,i}^{(b_i)})$ to every party in $\mathcal{P}$.
- **Round $r = 0$ to t**: For $k = 1, \ldots, n$, on receiving $(v, \mathsf{SET}_{k,j}^{(v)})$ from any party $P_j \in \mathcal{P}$ during round r where $v \in \{0, 1\}$, check if *all* the following holds.
  - $|\mathsf{SET}_{j,k}^{(v)}| \geq r + 1$;
  - For every tuple $(P_l, \sigma_{k,l}^{(v)}) \in \mathsf{SET}_{k,j}^{(v)}$, the condition $\mathsf{Verify}_{\mathsf{pk}_l}(v, \sigma_{k,l}^{(v)}) = 1$ holds;
  - A tuple of the form $(P_k, \sigma_{k,k}^{(v)}) \in \mathsf{SET}_{k,j}^{(v)}$;
  - $v \notin \mathsf{ACC}_{k,i}$.

If all the above holds, then do the following.
- Set $\mathsf{ACC}_{k,i} := \mathsf{ACC}_{k,i} \cup \{v\}$.
- If $r \neq t$, then do the following:
    - Compute $\sigma_{k,i}^{(v)} := \mathsf{Sign}_{\mathsf{sk}_i}(v)$.
    - Set $\mathsf{SET}_{k,i}^{(v)} := \mathsf{SET}_{k,j}^{(v)} \cup \{(P_i, \sigma_{k,i}^{(v)})\}$ and send $(v, \mathsf{SET}_{k,i}^{(v)})$ to every party in $\mathcal{P}$ during round $r + 1$.
- **Output Computation**: After $t + 1$ rounds, do the following.
    - For $j = 1, \ldots, n$, if $\mathsf{ACC}_{j,i} = \{v\}$ then add (P_j, v) to FIN_i, else add $(P_j, 0)$ to FIN_i.
    - If there exists a bit $v \in \{0, 1\}$ such that there are at least $t + 1$ tuples of the form $(\star, v)$ in FIN_i then output v and terminate; otherwise, output 0 and terminate.

Fig. 9.5: The Dolev-Strong bit-BA protocol tolerating $t < \frac{n}{2}$ corruptions. The above code is executed by every party $P_i \in \mathcal{P}$, where P_i has the input $b_i \in \{0, 1\}$

We now proceed to prove the properties of the BA protocol. We first prove the validity property. For this, we first establish a claim that on behalf of every honest party, only its input (for the BA) will be accumulated by every honest party.

Claim 9.2 In protocol $\Pi_{\mathsf{DSBA}}^{(n,t)}$, for every honest party P_j who participates with input $b_j \in \{0, 1\}$, each honest party P_i adds the tuple (P_j, b_j) to FIN_i. The above property holds against a computationally-bounded adversary if the PKI is cryptographically-secure and against a computationally-unbounded adversary if the PKI is unconditionally-secure.

Proof The proof is similar to the proof of Lemma 9.1. Let $\mathcal{H}$ be the set of *honest* parties and consider an *arbitrary* $P_j \in \mathcal{H}$ who participates with input $b_j \in \{0, 1\}$ in the protocol. Then, during round $r = 0$, party P_j will sign the bit b_j and send it to all the parties. Consequently, at the end of round $r = 0$, every party $P_i \in \mathcal{H}$ will include b_j to the set $\mathsf{ACC}_{j,i}$. Moreover, since P_j is honest, it will *never* sign the bit $1 - b_j$. Furthermore, since the signatures are unforgeable, the adversary cannot forge P_j's signature on the bit $1 - b_j$. Consequently, no party in $\mathcal{H}$ will ever accumulate the bit $1 - b_j$ in the set $\mathsf{ACC}_{j,i}$ and hence $\mathsf{ACC}_{j,i} = \{b_j\}$ will hold after $t + 1$ rounds, for every $P_i \in \mathcal{H}$. As a result, each $P_i \in \mathcal{H}$ will add the tuple (P_j, b_j) to FIN_i. □

Now, based on Claim 9.2, one can easily prove the validity property if *majority* of the parties are honest.

Lemma 9.4 *Protocol* $\Pi_{\mathsf{DSBA}}^{(n,t)}$ *satisfies the following properties, for any* $t < \frac{n}{2}$.
- *If the PKI is cryptographically-secure then the protocol achieves t-validity against a computationally-bounded adversary.*
- *If the PKI is unconditionally-secure then the protocol achieves t-validity against a computationally-unbounded adversary.*

Proof Let $\mathcal{H}$ be the set of *honest* parties and let every party $P_j \in \mathcal{H}$ has the input $b \in \{0, 1\}$ for the protocol $\Pi_{\mathsf{DSBA}}^{(n,t)}$. From Claim 9.2, after $t + 1$ rounds, corresponding to *each* $P_j \in \mathcal{H}$, every $P_i \in \mathcal{H}$ will add the tuple (P_j, b) to the set FIN_i. Since $t < \frac{n}{2}$, it follows that $|\mathcal{H}| \geq n - t \geq t + 1$. Hence there will be at least $t + 1$ tuples of the form $(\star, b)$ in FIN_i for every $P_i \in \mathcal{H}$ and at most t tuples of the form $(\star, 1 - b)$ in FIN_i. Consequently, each $P_i \in \mathcal{H}$ will output b. □

We next prove the consistency property, which is based on the fact that on behalf of each party, the bit(s) accumulated by all honest parties will be the *same*.

Lemma 9.5 *Protocol* $\Pi_{\mathsf{DSBA}}^{(n,t)}$ *satisfies the following properties, for any* $t < n$.[4]

- *If the PKI is cryptographically-secure then the protocol achieves t-consistency against a computationally-bounded adversary.*
- *If the PKI is unconditionally-secure then the protocol achieves t-consistency against a computationally-unbounded adversary.*

Proof Let $\mathcal{H}$ be the set of *honest* parties. Consider any *arbitrary* $P_k \in \mathcal{P}$ and arbitrary pair of distinct parties $P_i, P_j \in \mathcal{H}$. We claim that corresponding to P_k, the condition $\mathsf{ACC}_{k,i} = \mathsf{ACC}_{k,j}$ will hold after $t+1$ rounds. This is identical to the proof of Claim 9.1, so we skip it. This implies that if P_i and P_j adds $(P_k, v_i^{(k)})$ and $(P_k, v_j^{(k)})$ to FIN_i and FIN_j respectively where $v_i^{(k)}, v_j^{(k)} \in \{0,1\}$, then $v_i^{(k)} = v_j^{(k)}$ holds. That is, on behalf of P_k, both P_i and P_j will add the same bit in their respective FIN sets to decide their respective outputs. Since the party P_k is chosen arbitrarily, this further implies that $\mathsf{FIN}_i = \mathsf{FIN}_j$ holds. Now since each party in $\mathcal{H}$ computes its final output *deterministically* as a function of its FIN set, it follows that every party in $\mathcal{H}$ will have the *same* output. □

The round and communication complexity, as stated in the following lemma, follows simply from Lemma 9.3 and the fact that n instances of the BB protocol are executed in parallel.

Lemma 9.6 *Protocol* $\Pi_{\mathsf{DSBA}}^{(n,t)}$ *requires* $t+1$ *rounds and incurs a communication of* $\mathcal{BA}(1) = \mathcal{O}(n^4\kappa)$ *bits, where* κ *represents the size of a signature in bits.*

Theorem 9.3 now follows easily from the above discussion. The *t-liveness* follows from the fact that all the honest parties will terminate after $t+1$ rounds.

Theorem 9.3 *Protocol* $\Pi_{\mathsf{DSBA}}^{(n,t)}$ *satisfies the following properties, for any* $t < \frac{n}{2}$ *in the model* $\mathcal{M}_{\mathsf{auth}}^{\mathsf{pki}}$.

- *If the PKI is cryptographically-secure then the protocol is a t-secure BA protocol with cryptographic security.*
- *If the PKI is unconditionally-secure then the protocol is a t-secure BA protocol with statistical security.*

The protocol requires $t+1$ *rounds of communication and incurs a communication of* $\mathcal{BA}(1) = \mathcal{O}(n^4\kappa)$ *bits, where* κ *is the security parameter and denotes the size of a signature in bits.*

[4] We stress that *unlike* validity, the consistency property holds for *any* $t < n$.

Chapter 10
Domain Extension for BA with Honest Majority and Statistical Security

Once we have distributed consensus protocols with a strict honest majority (i.e. with $t < \frac{n}{2}$), the next obvious question is whether we can have a domain extension protocol with a strict honest majority. This is going to be the focus of this chapter. We first consider the case of *statistical security* in this chapter, assuming a *computationally-unbounded* adversary. In the next chapter, we will focus on *cryptographic security* where we will consider a *computationally-bounded* adversary. We will consider the BA variant of distributed consensus, and a BB variant follows immediately since we will be working with the condition $t < \frac{n}{2}$. The protocol presented in this chapter is from [53] and is the *only known* domain extension protocol with statistical security and a strict honest majority. As a warmup, we will first present a simple domain extension protocol with the *non-optimal* resilience of $t < \frac{n}{3}$, to understand the core ideas. After a clear exposition of the underlying challenges of dealing with the strict honest majority, we will present the actual protocol with $t < \frac{n}{2}$.

10.1 The Setting

The protocols presented in this chapter are in the *pairwise-authentic* channel setting, augmented with an *unconditionally-secure* PKI setup (namely a pseudo-signature setup); i.e. we work in the model $\mathcal{M}_{\mathsf{auth}}^{\mathsf{pki}}$. Hence, the parties are assumed to be connected by pairwise-authentic channels. In addition, each party has a *private* signing key and a *public* verification key for an unconditionally-secure signature scheme. The adversary is assumed to be computationally *unbounded* and can corrupt up to t parties in a Byzantine fashion. As done in the extension protocols presented in the first part of the monogram, we assume the existence of a BB oracle available to the parties, using which any party can send any bit-string identically to everyone. Looking ahead, the unconditional PKI setup is required to emulate the oracle.[1] We

[1] One instantiation of oracle tolerating up to $t < n$ faults with statistical security could be the statistically-secure variant of the Dolev-Strong BB protocol $\Pi_{\mathsf{DSBB}}^{(n,t)}$ presented in Chapter 9.

A. Choudhury and A. Patra, *Fault-Tolerant Distributed Consensus in Synchronous Networks*, Information Security and Cryptography,
https://doi.org/10.1007/978-3-031-80460-1_10

assume the PKI setup supports the total number of *transferability* required in the extension protocols.

In our protocols, we also use the *unconditionally-secure* keyed hash function $U : \mathrm{GF}(2^{\kappa}) \times \{0,1\}^{\ell} \rightarrow \mathrm{GF}(2^{\kappa})$ over $\mathrm{GF}(2^{\kappa})$ [28], where κ denotes the security paramater. Recall that for *any* $m_1, m_2 \in \{0,1\}^{\ell}$ where $m_1 \neq m_2$, the probability that $U_k(m_1) = U_k(m_2)$ holds for a *randomly* chosen key $k \in \mathrm{GF}(2^{\kappa})$ is at most $2^{-\kappa} \cdot \ell$ (see Section 2.1 in Chapter 2 for the details). Looking ahead, the reason for using this specific hash function over $\mathrm{GF}(2^{\kappa})$ is to upper bound the error probability of the extension protocols to $2^{-O(\kappa)}$. We also assume that the input size L of the parties in the extension protocol is some polynomial function of the parameter κ; i.e. $L = \mathrm{poly}(\kappa)$.

10.2 A WarmUp Protocol with $t < \frac{n}{3}$

In this section, we present a warmup domain extension protocol for BA, which achieves the required security properties with a high probability. The protocol has *non-optimal* resilience and can tolerate up to $t < \frac{n}{3}$ Byzantine faults.[2] Nevertheless, the protocol serves as a good warmup to understand how incorporating (a small) error probability helps to simplify domain extension protocols significantly. In the next section, we will see how to enhance the resilience of the protocol further to achieve the *optimal* resilience of $t < \frac{n}{2}$.

The high-level idea behind the protocol is similar to the previous domain extension protocol for BA with $t < \frac{n}{3}$ (see Fig 6.20 in Chapter 6). The protocol consists of two stages: a checking stage and a propagation stage. During the checking stage, the parties check if there is a subset of parties CORE who have the *same* input, such that the *majority* of the parties in CORE are guaranteed to be *honest*. If no such CORE set is identified to exist, then the parties output some default output, *without* executing the second stage. However, if a CORE set is identified to exist, then the parties proceed to the propagation stage, where the goal is to ensure that even the potentially honest parties *outside* CORE also get the same common input held by the honest parties *inside* the CORE. Recall that the protocol in Chapter 6) is *error-free* and uses the properties of Reed-Solomon (RS) error-correcting codes along with the (n,t)–star data structure in a graph to achieve the above properties. We now leverage the incorporation of a negligible error in the security properties and use much *simpler* mechanisms to achieve the above goals. The details follow.

To check for the existence of a CORE set, the parties compute a hash of their inputs and make them public by broadcasting these hash values. For broadcasting the hash values, the parties use the BB oracle. Since the hash size is *independent* of the input size L, the number of bits broadcasted is also *independent* of L. Broadcasting the hash values through BB oracle ensures that the parties have agreement on the hash values. Each party then compares the received hash values with the hash of

---

[2] The reason that the protocol has non-optimal resilience is that with $t < \frac{n}{3}$, one can design consensus protocols with *perfect* security which are *error-free*.

its own input, based on which it can determine its input's equality with the other parties' inputs. The collision-resistance property of the hash function ensures that if the inputs of two parties are *different*, their hash will also be *different* with a high probability. The parties next make public the result of comparing the hash values using calls to the BB oracle. Specifically, each party P_i broadcasts a Boolean response-vector of size n where the jth entry in the vector is 1 if and only if the hash value of P_j's input is the same as that of P_i's input. Using the BB oracle to announce the results of the comparisons guarantees that the parties have an agreement on these response vectors.

Next, to check for the existence of CORE, the parties check if there exists a subset of at least $n-t$ parties who made public the *same* response vector. If such a subset of parties exists, it is set as the CORE set. The idea here is that if all the *honest* parties have the *same* input, then they constitute a candidate CORE set since there are at least $n-t$ honest parties. Moreover, if $t < \frac{n}{3}$, then $n-t > 2t$ and hence the *majority* of the parties in CORE will be honest. Consequently, a CORE set with the desired properties is *always* guaranteed if the honest parties participate with the *same* input. For a pictorial illustration of the checking stage, see Fig 10.1.

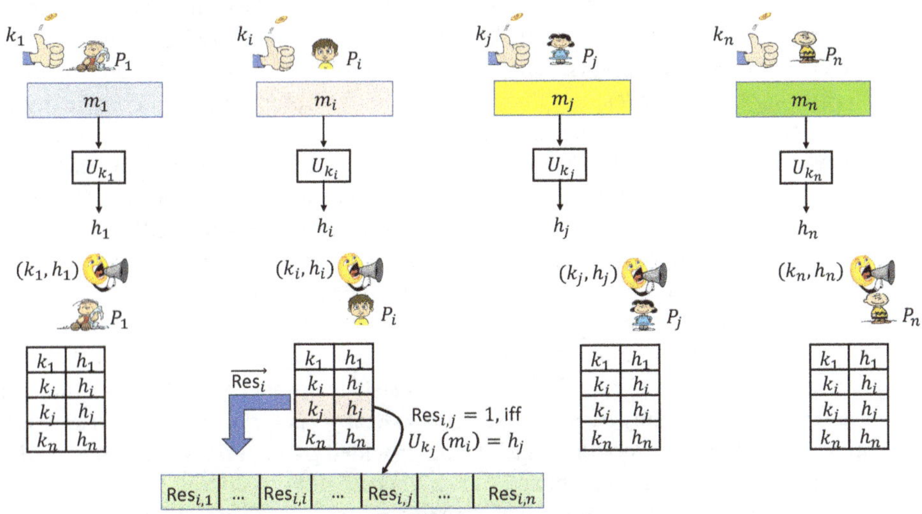

Fig. 10.1: Pictorial illustration of the checking stage of the protocol $\Pi^{(n,t)}_{\text{BAExtHMWarmUp}}$. Each party P_i computes a hash h_i of its input m_i using a random hash key k_i and broadcasts it using the BB oracle. Each party P_i then broadcasts a Boolean response vector of size n where the jth entry is 1 if and only if the hash of P_i's input m_i computed with the key k_j matches the hash value h_j

It might be possible that the honest parties participate with *different* inputs, but still, they find a CORE set of $n-t$ parties who broadcasted the *same* response vector. In this case, the collision-resistance property of the hash function guarantees that the input of every honest party in CORE is the same, say M, with a high probability. Since there might be honest parties *outside* CORE, the next goal will be to ensure that even these honest parties get the input M, which is required for *consistency*. This is achieved through the propagation stage. However, the challenge is ensuring that the propagation stage's communication complexity is $O(nL)$ bits. For this, the protocol uses a very clever trick utilizing the fact that the majority of the parties in CORE are guaranteed to be honest.

In more detail, let $|\mathsf{CORE}| = 2d+1$. Note that this is just for the ease of explanation and without loss of generality. To propagate the input M to the parties outside CORE, the parties in CORE transform M into a d-degree polynomial $f_M(X)$ over the field GF(2^c), where $c \stackrel{def}{=} \frac{L}{d+1}$.[3] The choice of c here is crucial, and looking ahead, this will ensure that the communication of the propagation stage is $O(nL)$ bits. The idea is then to let each (honest) party outside CORE learn $d + 1$ distinct points on the polynomial $f_M(X)$, which will enable it to interpolate the polynomial $f_M(X)$ and get M. For this, each party in CORE sends a distinct point on $f_M(X)$ to every party outside CORE. We stress that each party in CORE sends *only one* point on $f_M(X)$ to the parties outside CORE to keep the communication complexity of the propagation stage within $O(nL)$ bits. Since the potentially *corrupt* parties in CORE may provide *incorrect* points on $f_M(X)$, the parties in CORE also need to supply additional information which will help the parties outside CORE to identify and discard such incorrect points. One solution could be to resort to the properties of RS error-correcting codes, but this would make the communication complexity of the propagation stage to *surpass* the allowed budget of $O(nL)$ bits. Instead, we follow a different approach. Namely, each party, apart from sending a distinct point on the polynomial $f_M(X)$, also supplies the hash of every point on $f_M(X)$, which the parties in CORE are supposed to send to the parties outside CORE. Then, any point on $f_M(X)$ supplied by a party in CORE is verified with respect to its hash value provided by all the parties in CORE. The point is considered valid only if it is found to be consistent with the hash values provided by the majority of the parties in CORE. Notice that the points provided by the *honest* parties in CORE will always *pass* the above sanity check. The collision-resistance property of the hash function would guarantee that any *incorrect* point provided by a *corrupt* party in CORE would *fail* to match the corresponding hash value provided by the honest parties in CORE (with a high probability) and hence such points are not considered for interpolating $f_M(X)$. Since there are at least $d + 1$ honest parties in CORE, every honest party outside CORE will receive sufficient number of correct points on $f_M(X)$ to get back M. For a pictorial illustration of the propagation stage, see Fig 10.2.

We call the protocol $\Pi^{(n,t)}_{\mathsf{BAExtHMWarmUp}}$, which is formally presented in Fig 10.3. In the protocol, we follow a simplifying convention that if, during a round, a receiver party is expecting some message from a designated sender party and if either no message or a syntactically incorrect message is received, then the receiver party

[3] Again for the ease of explanation, we assume that L is a multiple of $d+1$. This is just for simplicity and without loss of generality.

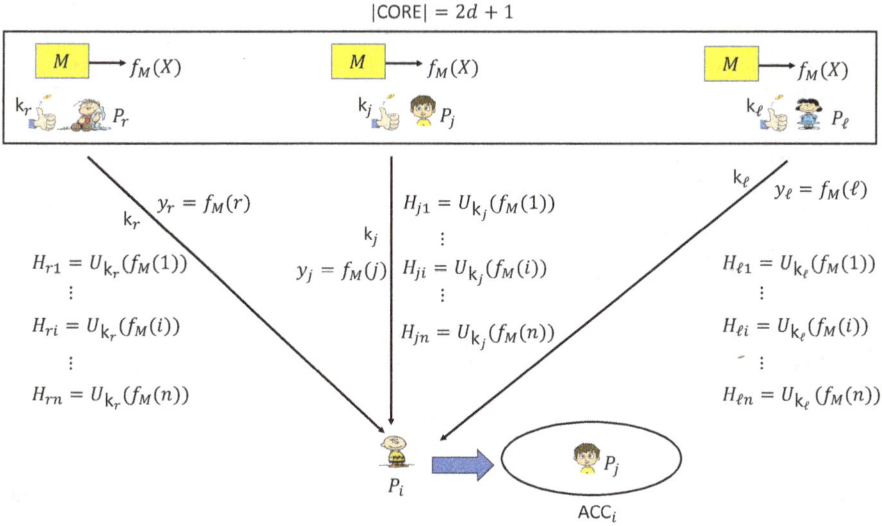

Fig. 10.2: Pictorial illustration of the propagation stage of the protocol $\Pi^{(n,t)}_{\mathsf{BAExtHMWarmUp}}$ which is executed if the parties find a CORE set during the checking stage. It will be guaranteed that the majority of the parties in CORE are honest and all honest parties have the same input, say M. The goal is to let each (honest) party outside CORE also get M. For this, each party in CORE transforms M into a d-degree polynomial $f_M(X)$ over the field GF(2^c), where $c \stackrel{def}{=} \frac{L}{d+1}$ and where $|\mathsf{CORE}| = 2d + 1$. Every party in CORE sends a distinct point on $f_M(X)$ to every party outside CORE. Additionally, each party in CORE authenticates distinct points on $f_M(X)$ by hashing them using a random key and sending the key and the hash values to every party outside CORE. Each party outside CORE identifies the correct points on $f_M(X)$ received from the parties in CORE, by checking their consistency with the corresponding hash values provided by the parties in CORE. Only those points which are consistent with the hash values of the majority of the parties in CORE are accepted for interpolating $f_M(X)$ by the parties outside CORE

substitutes some default value from the underlying domain on behalf of the sender party and continues the protocol.

By comparing protocol $\Pi^{(n,t)}_{\mathsf{BAExtHMWarmUp}}$ with the previous BA domain extension protocol with $t < \frac{n}{3}$ (see Fig 6.20 in Chapter 6), we find that the use of hash function significantly simplifies the protocol. Namely, in the previous protocol, the parties transformed their inputs into RS codewords and compared individual components of their respective codewords over the point-to-point channels to check for the existence of a CORE set, which also requires the usage of (n, t)−star data structure. In contrast, the parties now make public a hash of their respective inputs and then compare these hash values and make the results of the comparisons public. This significantly simplifies the checking of the existence of a CORE set without deploying any (n, t)–star data structure. Similarly, in the previous protocol, the parties deployed the properties of RS error-correction to ensure that all honest parties get the common input held by the honest parties in CORE. In contrast, the parties in CORE again deploy the hash function to authenticate points on the polynomial defined by the common input held by the honest parties in CORE.

Protocol $\Pi^{(n,t)}_{\mathsf{BAExtHMWarmUp}}$

Public knowledge: the description of the unconditionally-secure collision-resistant hash function U over GF(2^κ). Additionally, the parties have oracle access to a bit-BB oracle.

Checking Stage

- **Round 1 (broadcasting the hash of input)**: On having the input $m_i \in \{0, 1\}^L$, do the following.
  - Select a uniformly random key $k_i \in \mathrm{GF}(2^\kappa)$ for the keyed hash function U and compute $h_i := U_{k_i}(m_i)$.
  - Call the BB oracle as a sender with input (k_i, h_i) to broadcast (k_i, h_i).
- **Round 2 (broadcasting response vector)**: For $j = 1, \ldots, n$, let $(k_j, h_j) \in \{0, 1\}^{2\kappa}$ be the output from the BB oracle where P_j is the designated sender. Compute a Boolean response vector $\overrightarrow{\mathsf{Res}_i} \in \{0, 1\}^n$ as follows:
  - If $U_{k_j}(m_i) = h_j$, then set $\overrightarrow{\mathsf{Res}_{ij}} := 1$;[a]
  - Else set $\overrightarrow{\mathsf{Res}_{ij}} := 0$.

  Call the BB oracle as a sender with input $\overrightarrow{\mathsf{Res}_i}$ to broadcast the vector $\overrightarrow{\mathsf{Res}_i}$.
- **Checking for core set and conditional abort**: For $j = 1, \ldots, n$, let $\overrightarrow{\mathsf{Res}_j}$ be the output from the BB oracle where P_j is the designated sender.
  - If there exists a subset of parties $\mathcal{P}' \subseteq \mathcal{P}$, satisfying all the following conditions then set CORE $:= \mathcal{P}'$;[b]
    - $|\mathcal{P}'| \geq n - t$;
    - $\overrightarrow{\mathsf{Res}_j} = \overrightarrow{\mathsf{Res}_k}$ holds for every $P_j, P_k \in \mathcal{P}'$
    - For every $P_j \in \mathcal{P}'$, the condition $\overrightarrow{\mathsf{Res}_{jj}} = 1$ holds.
  - Else output 0^L and terminate.

Propagation Stage

For simplicity and without loss of generality, let $|\mathsf{CORE}| = 2d + 1$ and let L be a multiple of $d + 1$ such that $c \stackrel{def}{=} \frac{L}{d+1}$. Moreover, let GF$(2^c)$ denote the Galois field consisting of c-bit elements.

- **Round 3 (propagating the input)**: If $P_i \in$ CORE, then do the following.
  - Transform the input m_i into a d-degree polynomial $f_i(X)$ over GF(2^c). For this, divide m_i into $d+1$ blocks each of size c-bits and let $f_{i,0}, \ldots, f_{i,d}$ be the resultant elements from GF(2^c) represented by these c-bit blocks. Then set

$$f_i(X) \stackrel{def}{=} f_{i,0} + f_{i,1} \cdot X + \ldots + f_{i,d} \cdot X^d.$$

  - Select a uniformly random key $\mathsf{k}_i \in \mathrm{GF}(2^\kappa)$ for the keyed hash function U and compute the hash values $H_{i1}, \ldots, H_{in}$, where for $j = 1, \ldots, n$, the hash value H_{ij} is defined as follows.

$$H_{ij} \stackrel{def}{=} U_{\mathsf{k}_i}(f_i(j))$$

– Compute $y_i \overset{def}{=} f_i(i)$ and send (y_i, H_i) to every $P_j \notin$ CORE, where $H_i := (\mathsf{k}_i, H_{i1}, \ldots, H_{in})$ denotes the hash-vector.

- **Output computation and termination**: Compute the following output and then terminate.
  – If $P_i \in$ CORE, then output m_i.
  – Else receive (y_j, H_j) from every $P_j \in$ CORE where $H_j = (\mathsf{k}_j, H_{j1}, \ldots, H_{jn})$ and then do the following.
    – For every $P_j \in$ CORE, include P_j to a set ACC_i, initialized to $\emptyset$, if all the following holds.
      - There is a subset of parties $\mathsf{CORE}_j \subseteq$ CORE, where $|\mathsf{CORE}_j| \geq d + 1$;
      - For every $P_r \in \mathsf{CORE}_j$, the following condition is satisfied.

$$H_{rj} = U_{\mathsf{k}_r}(y_j).$$

Here $(y_r, (\mathsf{k}_r, H_{r1}, \ldots, H_{rn}))$ denotes the values received from P_r.

    – Interpolate the points $\{(j, y_j)\}_{P_j \in \mathsf{ACC}_i}$ and compute the d-degree polynomial $f_i(X)$.
    – Let $f_{i,0}, \ldots, f_{i,d} \in \mathrm{GF}(2^c)$ be the coefficients of $f_i(X)$ and let $F_{i,0}, \ldots, F_{i,d}$ be the binary representation of these elements respectively. Then output $(F_{i,0}) || \ldots || F_{i,d}$, where $||$ denotes the concatenation operation.

[a] Note that if P_i is honest then $\mathsf{Res}_{ii} = 1$.

[b] Note that checking for the existence of CORE can be done with poly(n) computational complexity. We leave it as an easy exercise for the reader.

Fig. 10.3: A statistically-secure BA extension protocol with $t < \frac{n}{3}$. The above code is executed by every party $P_i \in \mathcal{P}$

We now proceed to prove the properties of the protocol $\Pi^{(n,t)}_{\mathsf{BAExtHMWarmUp}}$. We first derive the round and communication complexity.

Lemma 10.1 *Protocol* $\Pi^{(n,t)}_{\mathsf{BAExtHMWarmUp}}$ *has the following complexities.*
– *The protocol requires* 3 *rounds.*
– *The seed-round complexity of the protocol is* 2.
– *The protocol incurs a communication of* $n \cdot \mathcal{BC}(2\kappa) + n \cdot \mathcal{BC}(n) + O(nL + n^3\kappa)$ *bits, where* $\mathcal{BC}(\ell)$ *denotes the communication complexity for emulating one call to the BB oracle with an* ℓ*-bit input.*
– *The seed-communication complexity of the protocol is* $O(n\kappa + n^2)$ *bits.*

Proof During the checking stage, *each* party broadcasts a hash key and the hash of its input, both consisting of κ bits, by calling the BB oracle. Since all the calls can be made in parallel, this requires one round and incurs a communication of $n \cdot \mathcal{BC}(2\kappa)$ bits. Next, *each* party broadcasts its response vector, consisting of n bits by calling the BB oracle. Again, all the n calls can be made in parallel. So this step will require one round and incurs a communication complexity of $n \cdot \mathcal{BC}(n)$ bits. Finally, during the propagation stage, *each* party in CORE sends a point on its message-polynomial and hash of n distinct points on its message-polynomial, to *every* party outside CORE. The former information is represented by c bits, since the message-polynomial is computed over $\mathrm{GF}(2^c)$, while the latter consists of $n\kappa$ bits. Hence, every party in CORE sends $(n\kappa + c)$ bits to every party outside CORE. This requires one round and communication of $(n\kappa + c) \cdot (n - |\mathsf{CORE}|) \cdot |\mathsf{CORE}|$ bits. Let us now simplify the term $(n\kappa + c) \cdot (n - |\mathsf{CORE}|) \cdot |\mathsf{CORE}|$.

$$
\begin{aligned}
(n\kappa + c) \cdot (n - |\mathsf{CORE}|) \cdot |\mathsf{CORE}| &\leq (n\kappa + c) \cdot (n|\mathsf{CORE}| - |\mathsf{CORE}|^2) \\
&\leq n^2\kappa|\mathsf{CORE}| + nc|\mathsf{CORE}| \\
&\leq n^3\kappa + nc|\mathsf{CORE}|
\end{aligned}
$$

The last equation follows because $|\mathsf{CORE}| \leq n$. Let us further simplify the term $nc|\mathsf{CORE}|$. By substituting $c = \frac{L}{d+1}$ and $d = \frac{|\mathsf{CORE}|-1}{2}$, we get that $nc|\mathsf{CORE}| = O(nL)$.

The round complexity follows from the protocol description. The seed-round complexity is 2, since the BB oracle is invoked in both rounds of the checking stage. This completes the proof of the lemma. □

We next proceed to prove the *validity* property. For this, we first show that if all honest parties have the *same* input, then all (honest) parties will find a core set of parties during the checking stage.

Claim 10.1 If all honest parties have the same input for the protocol $\Pi^{(n,t)}_{\mathsf{BAExtHMWarmUp}}$, then all honest parties will find a set CORE of size at least $n - t$ during the checking stage. Moreover, all honest parties will be in the set CORE.

Proof Let $\mathcal{H}$ be the set of *honest* parties and let $m_i = m_j = M$ hold for *every* $P_i, P_j \in \mathcal{H}$. We first note that for *every* $P_i \in \mathcal{H}$, the condition $\overrightarrow{\mathsf{Res}}_{ii} = 1$ holds. This is because party P_i will receive (k_i, h_i) from the broadcast of P_i. Moreover, the condition $U_{k_i}(m_i) = h_i$ will hold. Next consider an *arbitrary* pair of parties $P_i, P_j \in \mathcal{H}$. Since both these parties have the same input M, it follows that the condition $\overrightarrow{\mathsf{Res}}_{ii} = \overrightarrow{\mathsf{Res}}_{ji}$ will also hold. This is because party P_j will receive (k_i, h_i) from the broadcast of P_i and the condition $U_{k_i}(m_j) = h_i$ will hold.

Finally, consider any party $P_j \notin \mathcal{H}$. Every party in $\mathcal{H}$ will receive the *same* (k_j, h_j) as output from the broadcast of P_j. Since the input of every $P_i \in \mathcal{H}$ is the same, it follows that the value $\overrightarrow{\mathsf{Res}}_{ij}$ will be the same for every $P_i \in \mathcal{H}$, depending upon whether the hash h_j is consistent with the input M of the parties in $\mathcal{H}$. Namely, if $U_{k_j}(M) = h_j$ holds then $\overrightarrow{\mathsf{Res}}_{ij} = 1$ will hold for every $P_i \in \mathcal{H}$. Otherwise, $\overrightarrow{\mathsf{Res}}_{ij} = 0$ will hold for every $P_i \in \mathcal{H}$.

The above arguments show that each $P_i \in \mathcal{H}$ will broadcast the same response vector through its respective call to the BB oracle. Moreover, these response vectors will be obtained by every party in $\mathcal{H}$. Since $|\mathcal{H}| \geq n - t$, every party in $\mathcal{H}$ will obtain a CORE set during the checking stage. Moreover, $\mathcal{H} \subseteq \mathsf{CORE}$ will also hold. □

Using Claim 10.1, we can directly infer the validity property.

Lemma 10.2 *Protocol* $\Pi^{(n,t)}_{\mathsf{BAExtHMWarmUp}}$ *achieves t-validity for any $t < n$.*[4]

[4] Note that for validity, we *do not* require $t < \frac{n}{3}$.

Proof Let $\mathcal{H}$ be the set of *honest* parties and let every party in $\mathcal{H}$ have the input M for the protocol $\Pi^{(n,t)}_{\mathsf{BAExtHMWarmUp}}$. From Claim 10.1 it follows that every party in $\mathcal{H}$ will find a CORE set during the checking stage and $\mathcal{H} \subseteq$ CORE will also hold. Since the parties in CORE output their respective input in the protocol and since $\mathcal{H} \subseteq$ CORE, it follows that every party in $\mathcal{H}$ outputs M. □

Next, we prove the *consistency* property for which we establish a series of helpful facts about the protocol. We first claim that at the end of the checking stage, all honest parties will agree upon the existence of a CORE set. Moreover, if a CORE set is found, then with a high probability, all honest parties in the CORE participated with the *same* input in the protocol.

Claim 10.2 If U is an unconditionally-secure collision-resistant hash function over GF(2^κ), then all the following holds during the protocol $\Pi^{(n,t)}_{\mathsf{BAExtHMWarmUp}}$.[5]

- All honest parties will agree upon the existence of a CORE set during the checking stage.
- If a CORE set is obtained during the checking stage, then except with a negligible probability, the input of all honest parties in CORE consists of the same L bits.

Proof Let $\mathcal{H}$ be the set of *honest* parties. The first property follows from the fact that the parties broadcast the response vectors. Namely, corresponding to *every* $P_i \in \mathcal{P}$, all the parties in $\mathcal{H}$ will obtain the *same* output $\overrightarrow{\mathsf{Res}_i}$ from the broadcast oracle, invoked by P_i as a sender party for broadcasting its response vector. If the parties in $\mathcal{H}$ find that at least $n - t$ parties have broadcasted the same response vector, these parties are set as the CORE set.

We next prove the second property. For this, consider an *arbitrary* pair of parties $P_i, P_j \in (\mathcal{H} \cap \mathsf{CORE})$, who participate with input m_i and m_j respectively. We wish to show that $m_i = m_j$ holds. As shown in the proof of Claim 10.1, the following conditions hold for P_i and P_j in their respective response vectors $\overrightarrow{\mathsf{Res}_i}$ and $\overrightarrow{\mathsf{Res}_j}$:

$$\overrightarrow{\mathsf{Res}}_{ii} = 1 \quad \text{and} \quad \overrightarrow{\mathsf{Res}}_{jj} = 1$$

Since $P_i, P_j \in$ CORE, it follows that $\overrightarrow{\mathsf{Res}_i} = \overrightarrow{\mathsf{Res}_j}$ holds as well and in particular, the following holds:

$$\overrightarrow{\mathsf{Res}}_{ii} = \overrightarrow{\mathsf{Res}}_{ji} = 1$$

We will now show that if $m_i \neq m_j$, then except with a negligible probability, the condition $\overrightarrow{\mathsf{Res}}_{ii} \neq \overrightarrow{\mathsf{Res}}_{ji}$ will hold, which is a *contradiction*. Then, iterating over all possible pairs of honest parties in CORE and noting that $|\mathsf{CORE}| \leq n$, it follows from the union bound that the inputs of all honest parties in CORE will be the same, except with a negligible probability, thus proving the second property.

Since $P_i \in \mathcal{H}$, it follows that every party in $\mathcal{H}$ will obtain the output (k_i, h_i) from the broadcast oracle invoked by P_i as a sender to broadcast its hash key and the hash of its input m_i, where the following holds.

[5] Again note that the condition $t < \frac{n}{3}$ is *not* required for the claim to be true.

$$h_i = U_{k_i}(m_i).$$

If $m_j \neq m_i$, then $U_{k_i}(m_i) \neq U_{k_i}(m_j)$ will also hold as well, except with a negligible probability, since the key k_i is randomly chosen by P_i. Consequently, P_j upon having (k_i, h_i) will find that $U_{k_i}(m_j) \neq h_i$ holds, except with a negligible probability. This further implies that P_j will set $\overrightarrow{\mathsf{Res}}_{ji} = 0$ and hence $\overrightarrow{\mathsf{Res}}_{ii} \neq \overrightarrow{\mathsf{Res}}_{ji}$ will hold. □

We next proceed to show that if the *majority* of the parties in the CORE set are honest, then the protocol achieves *consistency* with a high probability.

Claim 10.3 In protocol $\Pi^{(n,t)}_{\mathsf{BAExtHMWarmUp}}$ if the honest parties find a CORE set during the checking stage and if the majority of the parties in CORE are honest, then protocol $\Pi^{(n,t)}_{\mathsf{BAExtHMWarmUp}}$ achieves *t-consistency*, except with a negligible probability, provided U is an unconditionally-secure collision-resistant hash function over $\mathrm{GF}(2^\kappa)$.[6]

Proof Let $\mathcal{H}$ be the set of honest parties and let all the parties in $\mathcal{H}$ find a CORE set during the checking stage, such that the majority of the parties in CORE are honest. For simplicity and without loss of generality, let $|\mathsf{CORE}| = 2d + 1$, implying that *at most* d parties in CORE are corrupt. Let E be the event that all the parties in $(\mathsf{CORE} \cap \mathcal{H})$ have the *same* input, say $M \in \{0, 1\}^L$, in the protocol $\Pi^{(n,t)}_{\mathsf{BAExtHMWarmUp}}$. We now show that conditioned on the event E, every party in $\mathcal{H}$ outputs M, except with a negligible probability. From the protocol steps, all the parties in $(\mathsf{CORE} \cap \mathcal{H})$ output M. Now consider an *arbitrary* $P_i \in \mathcal{H}$, such that $P_i \notin \mathsf{CORE}$. We wish to show that P_i outputs M with a high probability. Let $f_M(X)$ be the d-degree polynomial over $\mathrm{GF}(2^c)$, defined by M. Hence $f_j(X) = f_M(X)$ holds for every $P_j \in (\mathsf{CORE} \cap \mathcal{H})$, since we are conditioning on the event E according to which all honest parties in CORE have input M. We will show that P_i will accumulate at least $d + 1$ parties in the set ACC_i and all the parties in ACC_i would have provided correct points on the polynomial $f_M(X)$ during the propagation stage with a high probability.

First, consider the *honest* parties in the set CORE. We will show that *all* honest parties in CORE will be included in ACC_i. During the propagation stage, each $P_j \in (\mathsf{CORE} \cap \mathcal{H})$ will send the point $y_j = f_M(j)$ to party P_i. Moreover, each $P_j \in (\mathsf{CORE} \cap \mathcal{H})$ will also send the hash key k_j and the hash-vector $H_j = (H_{j1}, \ldots, H_{jn})$ to P_i, where $H_{jr} = U_{\mathsf{k}_j}(f_M(r))$, for $r = 1, \ldots, n$. Next consider an *arbitrary* $P_j \in (\mathsf{CORE} \cap \mathcal{H})$. We show that P_j will be included to the set ACC_i. This is because the set $(\mathsf{CORE} \cap \mathcal{H})$ constitutes a candidate CORE_j set. In more detail, $|(\mathsf{CORE} \cap \mathcal{H})| \geq d+1$, since the majority of the parties in CORE are assumed to be honest and $|\mathsf{CORE}| = 2d + 1$. Moreover, for every $P_r \in (\mathsf{CORE} \cap \mathcal{H})$, the condition $H_{rj} = U_{\mathsf{k}_r}(y_j)$ will hold.

Till now, we have shown that $(\mathsf{CORE} \cap \mathcal{H}) \subseteq \mathsf{ACC}_i$ and hence P_i will have at least $d + 1$ correct points on $f_M(X)$ for interpolation. We next show that even if a potentially *corrupt* $P_j \in \mathsf{CORE}$ is included to the set ACC_i, the point y_j received by P_i from P_j during the propagation stage indeed satisfies the condition $y_j = f_M(j)$,

[6] Again note that the condition $t < \frac{n}{3}$ is *not* required for the claim to be true.

except with a negligible probability. For this we note that if $P_j \in \mathsf{ACC}_i$ then it implies that there is a subset $\mathsf{CORE}_j \subseteq \mathsf{CORE}$ of size at least $d+1$, such that y_j is consistent with the jth entry H_{rj} in the hash-vector H_r of *all* the parties in CORE_j. Since $|\mathsf{CORE}_j| \geq d+1$, it implies that $(\mathsf{CORE}_j \cap \mathcal{H}) \neq \emptyset$ and hence CORE_j consists of at least one *honest* party, say P_r. Let k_r be the hash key and $H_r = (H_{r1}, \ldots, H_{rn})$ be the hash-vector received by P_i from P_r during the propagation stage. Then consider the entry H_{rj} where $H_{rj} = U_{\mathsf{k}_r}(f_M(j))$. Now if $y_j \neq f_M(j)$ then the condition $U_{\mathsf{k}_r}(f_M(j)) \neq U_{\mathsf{k}_r}(y_j)$ will also hold, except with a negligible probability. This is because the key k_r is randomly chosen by P_r. Since $|\mathsf{CORE}| \leq n$, it follows from the union bound that if P_j sends an incorrect point $y_j \neq f_M(j)$ to P_i, then except with a negligible probability, the value y_j will be *inconsistent* with respect to the hash key of all the parties in $(\mathsf{CORE} \cap \mathcal{H})$ and hence P_j will *not* be included to ACC_i.

Hence, we have shown that P_i will have at least $d+1$ correct points on $f_M(X)$ received from the *honest* parties in CORE. Moreover, if any *corrupt* party in CORE provides an *incorrect* point on $f_M(X)$, then that party is *not* included by P_i in the set ACC_i, except with a negligible probability. Since the size of CORE is upper bounded by n, from the union bound, all the parties in ACC_i provided correct points on $f_M(X)$ to P_i, except with a negligible probability. Hence, by interpolating the points provided by the parties in ACC_i, party P_i will be able to interpolate $f_M(X)$ and hence output M. Now, as the number of honest parties *outside* CORE is upper bounded by n, it follows from the union bound that conditioned on the event E, all honest parties will output M, except with a negligible probability.

Finally, from Claim 10.2, we know that the event E occurs except with a negligible probability. Consequently, all honest parties will have the output M, except with a negligible probability. □

Now, based on Claim 10.3 and using the fact that $t < \frac{n}{3}$, we prove the *t-consistency*.

Lemma 10.3 *If U is an unconditionally-secure collision-resistant hash function over $GF(2^\kappa)$, then protocol $\Pi^{(n,t)}_{\mathsf{BAExtHMWarmUp}}$ achieves t-consistency except with a negligible probability, provided $t < \frac{n}{3}$.*

Proof From Claim 10.2, during the checking stage, all honest parties agree upon the existence of a CORE set of parties. Now there are two possible cases.

- **Case I — Honest Parties Do Not Find Any CORE Set During the Checking Stage**: In this case the *t-consistency* follows trivially since all honest parties abort the protocol with output 0^L.
- **Case II — Honest Parties Find A CORE Set During the Checking Stage**: In this case, the majority of the parties in CORE will be honest. This is because $|\mathsf{CORE}| \geq n-t$ and $t < \frac{n}{3}$. Hence from Claim 10.3, all honest parties will have a common output from $\{0,1\}^L$, except with a negligible probability. □

Theorem 10.1 now follows easily from the above discussion.

Theorem 10.1 *Let the parties have access to a bit-BB oracle for broadcasting bits and let U be an unconditionally-secure collision-resistant hash function over*

$GF(2^\kappa)$. If $t < \frac{n}{3}$, then protocol $\Pi^{(n,t)}_{\mathsf{BAExtHMWarmUp}}$ is a t-secure BA protocol for L-bit inputs with statistical security in the model $\mathcal{M}_{\mathsf{auth}}$ with the following complexities.[7]

- *The protocol requires 3 rounds.*
- *The seed-round complexity of the protocol is 2.*
- *The protocol incurs a communication of $n \cdot \mathcal{BC}(2\kappa) + n \cdot \mathcal{BC}(n) + O(nL + n^3\kappa)$ bits, where $\mathcal{BC}(\ell)$ denotes the communication complexity for emulating one call to the BB oracle with an ℓ-bit input.*
- *The seed-communication complexity of the protocol is $O(n\kappa + n^2)$ bits.*

10.3 Statistically-Secure Protocol with $t < \frac{n}{2}$

In this section, we show how to modify the protocol $\Pi^{(n,t)}_{\mathsf{BAExtHMWarmUp}}$ to tolerate up to $t < \frac{n}{2}$ corruptions. The propagation stage remains the *same* and what *differs* is the process of finding the CORE set during the checking stage. Recall that in protocol $\Pi^{(n,t)}_{\mathsf{BAExtHMWarmUp}}$, the set CORE is computed by checking if there is a subset of at least $n-t$ parties, who broadcast *identical* response vectors. Since $t < \frac{n}{3}$ holds, $n-t > 2t$ holds as well, implying that the *majority* of the parties in CORE are *honest*, which is the crucial requirement from CORE for the working of the propagation stage. Unfortunately, if $t < \frac{n}{2}$, then computing CORE like this will *not* guarantee an honest majority in the CORE set and hence we have to follow a different approach.

The idea is to compute the CORE set in *two* phases. First, as done in the protocol $\Pi^{(n,t)}_{\mathsf{BAExtHMWarmUp}}$, the parties check if at least $n-t$ parties have made public the same response vectors corresponding to the public hash of the inputs of the respective parties. Such a subset of parties is labelled as *accepting-set* of parties and denoted as $\mathcal{P}_{\mathsf{acc}}$. If the parties *fail* to find a candidate $\mathcal{P}_{\mathsf{acc}}$ subset then clearly it implies that the honest parties have *different* inputs, and hence the parties can safely terminate the protocol pre-maturely with some default output.[8] On the other hand, if the parties find a candidate $\mathcal{P}_{\mathsf{acc}}$ subset, then it is guaranteed that all *honest* parties in $\mathcal{P}_{\mathsf{acc}}$ have the same input, say M (with a high probability). The reason for this is the same as in the protocol $\Pi^{(n,t)}_{\mathsf{BAExtHMWarmUp}}$. However, as discussed above it is *not* guaranteed that $\mathcal{P}_{\mathsf{acc}}$ has an *honest* majority and hence it *cannot* serve as a candidate CORE set. The next goal will be then to build a CORE set of parties which has an honest majority, such that all the honest parties in CORE have an updated input M. Once this is ensured, the parties can execute the propagation stage of the protocol $\Pi^{(n,t)}_{\mathsf{BAExtHMWarmUp}}$ with the CORE set. Creating the CORE set on top of $\mathcal{P}_{\mathsf{acc}}$ is very subtle for two reasons. First, we *may not* have an honest majority within $\mathcal{P}_{\mathsf{acc}}$. Second, we have an allowed budget of only $O(nL)$ bits of communication over the point-to-point channels. The

[7] We stress that the protocol $\Pi^{(n,t)}_{\mathsf{BAExtHMWarmUp}}$ *does not* need any PKI setup, provided the parties have access to a BB oracle.

[8] If all the honest parties start the protocol with the same input, then the parties are bound to get a $\mathcal{P}_{\mathsf{acc}}$ set since the set of honest parties will constitute one such candidate.

computation of the CORE set constitutes the second phase of the checking stage; the details follow.

Once a candidate $\mathcal{P}_{\text{acc}}$ is obtained, the parties in $\mathcal{P}_{\text{acc}}$ try to ensure that the common input M held by the honest parties in $\mathcal{P}_{\text{acc}}$ is also made available to as many (honest) *non-accepting* parties (namely the parties in $\mathcal{P} \setminus \mathcal{P}_{\text{acc}}$) as possible. One could have used the idea used in the propagation stage of the protocol $\Pi^{(n,t)}_{\text{BAExtHMWarmUp}}$ for this. However, that would require $\mathcal{P}_{\text{acc}}$ to have an honest majority, which is *not* guaranteed. Another approach could be to let each party in the accepting-set send its input to every party in the non-accepting set. However, there are two potential problems in following this approach. First, this may incur a communication of $O(n^2L)$ bits. Second, the potentially *corrupt* parties from the accepting-set may send $M' \neq M$, which the honest parties in the non-accepting set will fail to identify. Hence, we follow a different approach.

Instead of letting each party in $\mathcal{P}_{\text{acc}}$ send its input to every party in $(\mathcal{P} \setminus \mathcal{P}_{\text{acc}})$, we let each party in $\mathcal{P}_{\text{acc}}$ send its input to *at most* one party in $(\mathcal{P} \setminus \mathcal{P}_{\text{acc}})$. The choice of the designated sender party in $\mathcal{P}_{\text{acc}}$ and the corresponding receiver party in $(\mathcal{P} \setminus \mathcal{P}_{\text{acc}})$ is made *publicly* available through a publicly-known *injective* mapping $\Phi : (\mathcal{P} \setminus \mathcal{P}_{\text{acc}}) \rightarrow \mathcal{P}_{\text{acc}}$. Since $t < \frac{n}{2}$ and $|\mathcal{P}_{\text{acc}}| \geq n - t$, a simple candidate for Φ could be to map the party with the smallest index in $(\mathcal{P} \setminus \mathcal{P}_{\text{acc}})$ to the party with the smallest index in the set $\mathcal{P}_{\text{acc}}$. For every pair of parties $\{\Phi(P_k), P_k\}$ where $P_k \in (\mathcal{P} \setminus \mathcal{P}_{\text{acc}})$ and $\Phi(P_k) \in \mathcal{P}_{\text{acc}}$, party $\Phi(P_k)$ send its input to the party P_k, which is supposed to be M. Note that this transfer of inputs incurs a *total* communication cost of $O(nL)$ bits. This is because $(\mathcal{P} \setminus \mathcal{P}_{\text{acc}})$ and $\mathcal{P}_{\text{acc}}$ constitute a partition of $\mathcal{P}$ and each party in $(\mathcal{P} \setminus \mathcal{P}_{\text{acc}})$ receives L bits from exactly one party in $\mathcal{P}_{\text{acc}}$. Once the transfer of inputs is over for every pair of parties $\{\Phi(P_k), P_k\}$, the next step is to let P_k *publicly* verify whether it received the supposedly-common input M from $\Phi(P_k)$. The verification is done in such a way that if an *honest* P_k receives $M' \neq M$ from $\Phi(P_k)$ then it is *publicly* detected (with a high probability).

To perform the verification, every $P_k \in (\mathcal{P} \setminus \mathcal{P}_{\text{acc}})$ upon receiving the input of its designated sender party $\Phi(P_k)$, publicly broadcasts a hash of the received input. In response, every party P_j in $\mathcal{P}_{\text{acc}}$ upon getting this hash, publicly declares whether this hash is "consistent" with its input. Now the verification for P_k is considered to be "successful" only if a "positive" declaration is identified from a subset of parties $\mathcal{P}'_{\text{acc}} \subseteq \mathcal{P}_{\text{acc}}$ of size at least $n - t$. The idea here is that if P_k is *honest* and if the verification is found to be successful, then indeed P_k received the supposedly common M from $\Phi(P_k)$ (with a high probability). This is because there will be at least one *honest* party among $\mathcal{P}'_{\text{acc}}$ and if P_k received $M' \neq M$ from $\Phi(P_k)$, then that honest party would find the hash made public by P_k to be inconsistent with its input M. If the verification for P_k is found to be *unsuccessful*, then it implies that either $\Phi(P_k)$ is corrupt and transferred an input different from M to P_k, or P_k is corrupt and made an incorrect hash public. Whatever may be the case, at least one of the parties among $\{\Phi(P_k), P_k\}$ is guaranteed to be corrupt and both P_k as well as $\Phi(P_k)$ are *barred* from the candidate CORE set. On the other hand, if the verification for P_k is found to be successful, then P_k updates its input to the one received from

$\Phi(P_k)$ and both P_k as well as $\Phi(P_k)$ are *included* in the candidate CORE set. For a pictorial depiction of the verification process, see Fig 10.4.

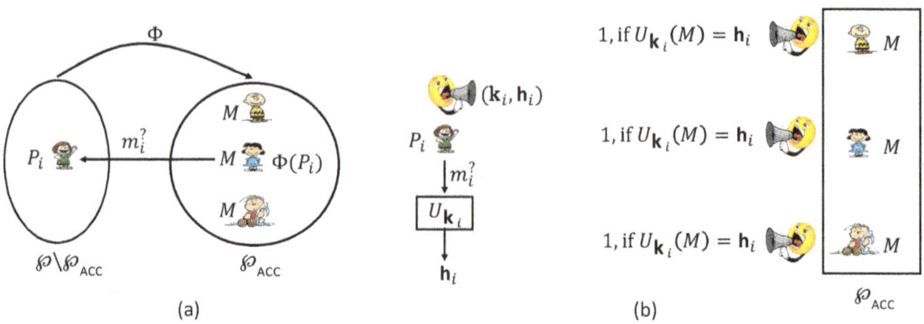

Fig. 10.4: Pictorial illustration of the second phase of the checking stage, once a set of accepting parties $\mathcal{P}_{\text{acc}}$ of size at least $n - t$ is identified. A publicly-known injective mapping Φ is identified from the set $(\mathcal{P} \setminus \mathcal{P}_{\text{acc}})$ to $\mathcal{P}_{\text{acc}}$. All (honest) parties in $\mathcal{P}_{\text{acc}}$ are supposed to have the same input, say M. Fig (a) denotes each party P_i in $(\mathcal{P} \setminus \mathcal{P}_{\text{acc}})$ receiving the supposed input M from the designated party $\Phi(P_i)$ in the set $\mathcal{P}_{\text{acc}}$. Fig (b) denotes the verification process of the received input, where P_i upon receiving $m_i^?$ from $\Phi(P_i)$ would like to verify if $m_i^? = M$ holds. For this, it computes a random hash $\mathbf{h}_i$ of the received $m_i^?$ using a key $\mathbf{k}_i$ and broadcasts the pair $(\mathbf{k}_i, \mathbf{h}_i)$. Every party in $\mathcal{P}_{\text{acc}}$ then verifies the pair with its supposed input M and makes public the response. If at least $n - t$ parties from $\mathcal{P}_{\text{acc}}$ respond positively (by broadcasting 1), then it guarantees that $m_i^? = M$ with a high probability, since there will be at least one *honest* party in that collection of $n - t$ verifiers, who would have performed the verification honestly. If $n - t$ verifiers from $\mathcal{P}_{\text{acc}}$ *do not* respond positively, then either $\Phi(P_i)$ is *corrupt* and sent $m_i^? \neq M$ to P_i or P_i is corrupt and broadcasted an incorrect hash value. Hence, both P_i as well as $\Phi(P_i)$ are barred from entering CORE

It is easy to see that the way the CORE set is computed, it will be guaranteed to have an honest majority. This is because, as discussed above, at least half of the parties who could not make it to the CORE set are guaranteed to be *corrupt* and we have an honest majority among $\mathcal{P}$. Moreover, it is also guaranteed that all honest parties in CORE will have the input M: while this is trivially true for the parties who were already part of $\mathcal{P}_{\text{acc}}$ and are now also part of CORE, it is also true for the new parties from $(\mathcal{P} \setminus \mathcal{P}_{\text{acc}})$ who make their way to CORE. The latter holds because of the public verification which happens after the parties in $\mathcal{P}_{\text{acc}}$ transfer their input to their respective designated receiver parties in $(\mathcal{P} \setminus \mathcal{P}_{\text{acc}})$.

We stress that it is *not* necessary that CORE has all the honest parties, even if all honest parties start the protocol with the same input. For instance, consider a designated pair of sender-receiver parties $(\Phi(P_k), P_k)$, where P_k is *corrupt* and $\Phi(P_k)$ is *honest*. Then P_k, even after receiving M as input from the party $\Phi(P_k)$ may broadcast hash of $M' \neq M$, consequently leading to both P_k as well as $\Phi(P_k)$ being discarded from CORE. However, it is *not* required that CORE should have all honest parties. The existence of an honest majority among CORE, with all honest parties in CORE having the same (updated) input is sufficient for the propagation stage to guarantee that even the honest parties outside CORE outputs this common input. The modified protocol is called $\Pi^{(n,t)}_{\text{BAExtHM}}$, which is presented in Fig 10.5. In the protocol, we follow a simplifying convention that if, during a round, a receiver party is expecting some message from a designated sender party and if either no message or a syntactically incorrect message is received, then the receiver party substitutes some default value from the underlying domain on behalf of the sender party and continues the protocol.

Protocol $\Pi^{(n,t)}_{\text{BAExtHM}}$

Public knowledge: the description of the unconditionally-secure collision-resistant hash function U over $\text{GF}(2^\kappa)$. Additionally, the parties have oracle access to a bit-BB oracle.

Checking Stage

- **Round 1 (broadcasting the hash of the input)**: On having the input $m_i \in \{0,1\}^L$, do the following.
  - Select a uniformly random key $k_i \in \text{GF}(2^\kappa)$ for the keyed hash function U and compute $h_i := U_{k_i}(m_i)$.
  - Call the BB oracle as a sender with input (k_i, h_i) to broadcast (k_i, h_i).
- **Round 2 (broadcasting response vector)**: For $j = 1, \ldots, n$, let $(k_j, h_j) \in \{0,1\}^{2\kappa}$ be the output received from the BB oracle where P_j is the designated sender. Compute a Boolean response vector $\overrightarrow{\text{Res}_i} \in \{0,1\}^n$ as follows:
  - If $U_{k_j}(m_i) = h_j$, then set $\overrightarrow{\text{Res}_{ij}} := 1$;[a]
  - Else set $\overrightarrow{\text{Res}_{ij}} := 0$.

  Call the BB oracle as a sender with input $\overrightarrow{\text{Res}_i}$ to broadcast the vector $\overrightarrow{\text{Res}_i}$.
- **Checking for accepting set and conditional abort**: For $j = 1, \ldots, n$, let $\overrightarrow{\text{Res}_j}$ be the output received from the BB oracle where P_j is the designated sender.
  - If there exists a subset of parties $\mathcal{P}' \subseteq \mathcal{P}$, satisfying all the following conditions then set $\mathcal{P}_{\text{acc}} := \mathcal{P}'$.
    - $|\mathcal{P}'| \geq n - t$;
    - $\overrightarrow{\text{Res}_j} = \overrightarrow{\text{Res}_k}$ holds for every $P_j, P_k \in \mathcal{P}'$
    - For every $P_j \in \mathcal{P}'$, the condition $\overrightarrow{\text{Res}_{jj}} = 1$ holds.
  - Else output 0^L and terminate.

If the checking stage is not terminated, then let $\Phi : (\mathcal{P} \setminus \mathcal{P}_{\text{acc}}) \rightarrow \mathcal{P}_{\text{acc}}$ be the publicly known injective mapping, where the party with the smallest index in $(\mathcal{P} \setminus \mathcal{P}_{\text{acc}})$ is mapped to the party with the smallest index in the set $\mathcal{P}_{\text{acc}}$.

- **Round 3 (transferring the message from accepting set to non-accepting set)**: If $P_i \in \mathcal{P}_{\text{acc}}$, then do the following.
  - Let $P_j \in (\mathcal{P} \setminus \mathcal{P}_{\text{acc}})$ such that $\Phi(P_j) = P_i$.
  - Send M to P_j where $M = m_i$ and let $m_j^?$ denote the message received by P_j from P_i during this round.
- **Round 4 (broadcasting the message hash of transferred message)**: If $P_i \in (\mathcal{P} \setminus \mathcal{P}_{\text{acc}})$, then do the following.
  - Select a uniformly random key $\mathbf{k}_i \in \text{GF}(2^\kappa)$ for the keyed hash function U.
  - Compute $\mathbf{h}_i := U_{\mathbf{k}_i}(m_i^?)$, where $m_i^? \in \{0,1\}^L$ denote the message received from the associated party in $\mathcal{P}_{\text{acc}}$ in the previous round.
  - Call the BB oracle as a sender with input $(\mathbf{k}_i, \mathbf{h}_i)$ to broadcast $(\mathbf{k}_i, \mathbf{h}_i)$.
- **Round 5 (verification of the message transferred from the accepting set to the non-accepting set of parties)**: Corresponding to every $P_j \in (\mathcal{P} \setminus \mathcal{P}_{\text{acc}})$, let $(\mathbf{k}_j, \mathbf{h}_j)$ be the output from the BB oracle where P_j is the sender.
  - If $P_i \in \mathcal{P}_{\text{acc}}$, then do the following.
    - Corresponding to each $P_j \in (\mathcal{P} \setminus \mathcal{P}_{\text{acc}})$, set $v_{ij} := 1$ if $U_{\mathbf{k}_j}(m_i) = \mathbf{h}_j$ holds, else set $v_{ij} := 0$.
    - Let $\vec{V_i} = \{v_{ij}\}_{P_j \in (\mathcal{P} \setminus \mathcal{P}_{\text{acc}})}$. Call the BB oracle as a sender with input $\vec{V}_i$ to broadcast $\vec{V_i}$.
- **Computing the core set**: For every $P_j \in \mathcal{P}_{\text{acc}}$, let $\vec{V_j} = \{v_{jk}\}_{P_k \in (\mathcal{P} \setminus \mathcal{P}_{\text{acc}})}$ be the output from the BB oracle where P_j is the sender. Let $\mathcal{P}'_{\text{acc}} \subseteq \mathcal{P}_{\text{acc}}$ be the subset of parties of maximum size, which broadcasted the same vector $\vec{V}$.
  - If $|\mathcal{P}'_{\text{acc}}| < n - t$, then output 0^L and terminate.
  - Else set $\mathsf{CORE} := \mathcal{P}_{\text{acc}}$ and then update it as per the following criteria.
    - For every $P_k \in (\mathcal{P} \setminus \mathcal{P}_{\text{acc}})$, do the following.
      - If $v_{jk} = 1$ corresponding to each $P_j \in \mathcal{P}'_{\text{acc}}$ then set $\mathsf{CORE} := \mathsf{CORE} \cup \{P_k\}$;
      - Else set $\mathsf{CORE} := \mathsf{CORE} \setminus \{\Phi(P_k)\}$.
- **Updating the input for the propagation stage**: If $P_i \in \mathsf{CORE}$, then update the input for the propagation stage as follows.
  - If $P_i \in (\mathsf{CORE} \cap \mathcal{P}_{\text{acc}})$, then retain m_i as the input for the propagation stage.
  - Else set $m_i := m_i^?$, where $m_i^?$ denotes the message received from the mapped party $\Phi(P_i)$ during Round 3.

Propagation Stage

The protocol code for this stage is the same as in the protocol $\Pi^{(n,t)}_{\mathsf{BAExtHMWarmUp}}$ (Fig 10.3).

[a] Note that if P_i is honest then $\mathsf{Res}_{ii} = 1$.

Fig. 10.5: A statistically-secure BA extension protocol with $t < \frac{n}{2}$. The above code is executed by every party $P_i \in \mathcal{P}$

We now proceed to prove the properties of the protocol $\Pi^{(n,t)}_{\mathsf{BAExtHM}}$. We first derive the round and communication complexity.

Lemma 10.4 *Protocol $\Pi^{(n,t)}_{\mathsf{BAExtHM}}$ has the following complexities.*

- *The protocol requires* 6 *rounds.*
- *The seed-round complexity of the protocol* 4.
- *The protocol incurs a communication of* $2n \cdot \mathcal{BC}(2\kappa) + 2n \cdot \mathcal{BC}(n) + O(nL + n^3\kappa)$ *bits.*
- *The seed-communication complexity of the protocol is* $O(n\kappa + n^2)$ *bits.*

Proof Since protocol $\Pi^{(n,t)}_{\mathsf{BAExtHM}}$ is almost identical to protocol $\Pi^{(n,t)}_{\mathsf{BAExtHMWarmUp}}$ with the additional steps during the checking stage, we only need to focus on the complexity of these additional steps.

Once the parties identify an accepting-set of parties $\mathcal{P}_{\mathsf{acc}}$, then each accepting party in $\mathcal{P}_{\mathsf{acc}}$ sends its input to *at most one* non-accepting party in $\mathcal{P} \setminus \mathcal{P}_{\mathsf{acc}}$. This will require one round of communication and incur a communication of $O(nL)$ bits. Next, each non-accepting party broadcasts a hash key and the hash of the message received from the mapped accepting-party, through BB oracle. Since all these calls can be done in parallel, this requires 1 round and communication of at most $n \cdot \mathcal{BC}(2\kappa)$ bits. This is followed by each accepting-party broadcasting a Boolean response for each non-accepting party through BB oracle. Again all these calls can be executed in parallel, so this step requires 1 round and communication of at most $n \cdot \mathcal{BC}(n)$ bits. The lemma now follows from the communication complexity of the protocol $\Pi^{(n,t)}_{\mathsf{BAExtHMWarmUp}}$ derived in Lemma 10.1. □

We next prove the *validity* property. For this, it is enough to show that if the honest parties start the protocol with the *same* input, then they will compute a CORE set during the checking stage of the protocol, where the *majority* of the parties are guaranteed to be *honest* and these honest parties retain their input as their respective updated inputs for the propagation stage.

Lemma 10.5 *Let U be an unconditionally-secure collision-resistant hash function over $GF(2^\kappa)$. Then protocol $\Pi^{(n,t)}_{\mathsf{BAExtHM}}$ achieves t-validity, except with a negligible probability, provided $t < \frac{n}{2}$.*

Proof Let $\mathcal{H}$ be the set of *honest* parties and let every $P_i \in \mathcal{H}$ have the input $m_i = M \in \{0,1\}^L$. We wish to show that each $P_i \in \mathcal{H}$ outputs M. Since every $P_i \in \mathcal{H}$ have input M, it follows that all the parties in $\mathcal{H}$ will find a common set of accepting-parties $\mathcal{P}_{\mathsf{acc}}$ of size at least $n-t$, such that $\mathcal{H} \subseteq \mathcal{P}_{\mathsf{acc}}$. This follows from Claim 10.2 and the fact that the set $\mathcal{P}_{\mathsf{acc}}$ is computed in exactly the same way as the set CORE in the protocol $\Pi^{(n,t)}_{\mathsf{BAExtHMWarmUp}}$.

We next show that the parties in $\mathcal{H}$ will further find a subset of parties $\mathcal{P}'_{\mathsf{acc}} \subseteq \mathcal{P}_{\mathsf{acc}}$ of size at least $n-t$, who broadcasts the same vector $\overrightarrow{V} \in \{0,1\}^{|\mathcal{P} \setminus \mathcal{P}_{\mathsf{acc}}|}$. This is because the subset $\mathcal{H}$ will constitute a candidate $\mathcal{P}'_{\mathsf{acc}}$ set and $|\mathcal{H}| \geq n-t$. This will further imply that the parties in $\mathcal{H}$ *do not* terminate the protocol pre-maturely with a default output and hence compute a CORE set. So consider an *arbitrary* $P_k \in (\mathcal{P} \setminus \mathcal{P}_{\mathsf{acc}})$, who, upon receiving $m_k^?$ from its mapped party $\Phi(P_k)$, broadcasts its hash key and the hash of the received message, through BB oracle. It follows that all the parties in $\mathcal{H}$ will get $(\mathbf{k}_k, \mathbf{h}_k)$ as the output from the BB oracle. In response to $(\mathbf{k}_k, \mathbf{h}_k)$, all the parties in $\mathcal{H}$ will compute the *same* response. Namely, consider any pair of parties $P_i, P_j \in \mathcal{H}$. Then the following holds:

$$U_{\mathbf{k}_k}(m_i) = \mathbf{h}_k \quad \text{iff} \quad U_{\mathbf{k}_k}(m_j) = \mathbf{h}_k.$$

This is because $m_i = m_j = M$ holds. This further implies that $\overrightarrow{V_i} = \overrightarrow{V_j}$ also holds as well. Since each $P_i \in \mathcal{H}$ broadcasts the vector $\overrightarrow{V_i}$ through the BB oracle, it follows that all the parties in $\mathcal{H}$ will receive $\overrightarrow{V_i}$ from the BB oracle. Now since $\mathcal{H} \subseteq \mathcal{P}_{\mathsf{acc}}$ and $|\mathcal{H}| \geq n - t$, it follows that $\mathcal{H} \subseteq \mathcal{P}'_{\mathsf{acc}}$. This is because $t < \frac{n}{2}$ also holds and hence the vectors broadcasted by the corrupt parties in $\mathcal{P}_{\mathsf{acc}}$, *do not* satisfy the criteria for deciding the set $\mathcal{P}'_{\mathsf{acc}}$.

Till now, we have shown that the parties in $\mathcal{H}$ will compute the sets $\mathcal{P}_{\mathsf{acc}}$ as well as $\mathcal{P}'_{\mathsf{acc}}$. Moreover, these sets will be *common* for all the parties in $\mathcal{H}$, since these sets are computed based on the response vectors of the various parties, which are broadcasted through BB oracle. This implies that the parties in $\mathcal{H}$ will compute a common CORE set. This is because once the sets $\mathcal{P}_{\mathsf{acc}}$ and $\mathcal{P}'_{\mathsf{acc}}$ are decided, the set CORE is *deterministically* computed based on the vectors broadcasted by the parties in $\mathcal{P}'_{\mathsf{acc}}$, corresponding to the parties in $(\mathcal{P} \setminus \mathcal{P}_{\mathsf{acc}})$.

We next show that the majority of the parties in CORE are guaranteed to be *honest*. For this, we first note that all the parties in $(\mathcal{P} \setminus \mathcal{P}_{\mathsf{acc}})$ are guaranteed to be *corrupt*, since $\mathcal{H} \subseteq \mathcal{P}_{\mathsf{acc}}$. Now the set $(\mathcal{P} \setminus \mathsf{CORE})$ consists of pairs of parties $\{P_k, \Phi(P_k)\}$, where $P_k \notin \mathcal{P}_{\mathsf{acc}}$, implying that at least half of the parties in $\mathcal{P} \setminus \mathsf{CORE}$ are *corrupt*. Since $t < \frac{n}{2}$, this further implies that the majority of the parties in CORE are *honest*.

We finally show that the updated input of all the parties in $(\mathcal{H} \cap \mathsf{CORE})$ remains M. However, this trivially follows from the fact that $\mathcal{H} \subseteq \mathcal{P}_{\mathsf{acc}}$ and hence $(\mathcal{H} \cap \mathsf{CORE}) \subseteq (\mathcal{H} \cap \mathcal{P}_{\mathsf{acc}})$. Consequently, each $P_i \in (\mathcal{H} \cap \mathsf{CORE})$ retains m_i as its updated input for the propagation stage, and $m_i = M$ holds.

The lemma now follows from Claim 10.3, which ensures that if the majority of the parties in CORE are honest and have the same input M, then at the end of the propagation stage, all the parties in $\mathcal{H}$ will output M, except with a negligible probability. □

Remark 10.1 Before we proceed, we note a difference between the validity properties of the protocol $\Pi^{(n,t)}_{\mathsf{BAExtHMWarmUp}}$ (Lemma 10.2) and $\Pi^{(n,t)}_{\mathsf{BAExtHM}}$ (Lemma 10.5). For the former protocol, the validity is achieved *without* any error, while for the latter, there is some (non-zero) probability for the validity property being violated. The reason behind this is that for the protocol $\Pi^{(n,t)}_{\mathsf{BAExtHMWarmUp}}$, *all* honest parties are guaranteed to be present in the CORE set at the end of the checking stage, who simply output their respective input during the propagation stage. However, this *need not* be the case for the protocol $\Pi^{(n,t)}_{\mathsf{BAExtHM}}$. More specifically, while all honest parties are guaranteed to be part of the set $\mathcal{P}_{\mathsf{acc}}$, during the computation of the set CORE, some of the parties in $\mathcal{P}_{\mathsf{acc}}$ may be "excluded" from being part of CORE. That is, there may be pair of parties $\{P_k, \Phi(P_k)\}$ with P_k being corrupt and $\Phi(P_k)$ being honest such that both P_k and $\Phi(P_k)$ get excluded from CORE. Consequently, during the propagation stage, there might be some honest parties outside CORE, who will compute their output based on the data propagated by the parties in set CORE. However, since the verification of the propagated data happens probabilistically, there is some (non-zero) probability that the honest parties outside CORE end up computing an incorrect output.

We now prove a series of claims, which will help us to establish the consistency property. Recall that for proving the consistency, we need to consider the case when the honest parties start the protocol with *different* inputs. A trivial claim is that if the parties find an accepting-set of parties, all honest parties in this set are guaranteed to have the same input. This is because the accepting-set is computed in precisely the *same* way as the CORE set in the protocol $\Pi^{(n,t)}_{\mathsf{BAExtHMWarmUp}}$.

Claim 10.4 If U is an unconditionally-secure collision-resistant hash function over $\mathrm{GF}(2^\kappa)$, then all the following holds during the protocol $\Pi^{(n,t)}_{\mathsf{BAExtHM}}$.

- All honest parties will agree upon the existence of a candidate set $\mathcal{P}_{\mathsf{acc}}$ during the checking stage.
- If a set $\mathcal{P}_{\mathsf{acc}}$ is obtained during the checking stage, then except with a negligible probability, the input of all honest parties in $\mathcal{P}_{\mathsf{acc}}$ consists of the same L bits.

Proof The proof simply follows from Claim 10.2 and the fact that set $\mathcal{P}_{\mathsf{acc}}$ in protocol $\Pi^{(n,t)}_{\mathsf{BAExtHM}}$ is computed in exactly the same way as the set CORE in the protocol $\Pi^{(n,t)}_{\mathsf{BAExtHMWarmUp}}$. □

Now, based on the previous claim, we can show that if any honest party from the accepting-set "rejects" the message received by any party in the non-accepting set, then either the receiver party or the corresponding sender party from the accepting-set is *corrupt*.

Claim 10.5 If U is an unconditionally-secure collision-resistant hash function over $\mathrm{GF}(2^\kappa)$, then during the protocol $\Pi^{(n,t)}_{\mathsf{BAExtHM}}$, the following holds for every pair of parties $\{P_k, \Phi(P_k)\}$ except with a negligible probability, where $P_k \in (\mathcal{P} \setminus \mathcal{P}_{\mathsf{acc}})$ and $\Phi(P_k) \in \mathcal{P}_{\mathsf{acc}}$.

- If any honest $P_j \in \mathcal{P}_{\mathsf{acc}}$ sets $v_{jk} = 0$, then either P_k or $\Phi(P_k)$ is corrupt.

Proof Let $\mathcal{H}$ be the set of *honest* parties and consider the event that all the parties in $(\mathcal{H} \cap \mathcal{P}_{\mathsf{acc}})$ have the same input, say $M \in \{0, 1\}^L$. From Claim 10.4, the above event occurs except with a negligible probability. We condition on this event and prove the claim through a contradiction. So consider an *arbitrary* $P_j \in (\mathcal{H} \cap \mathcal{P}_{\mathsf{acc}})$ and an *arbitrary* pair of parties $(P_k, \Phi(P_k))$ where $P_k \in (\mathcal{P} \setminus \mathcal{P}_{\mathsf{acc}})$ and $\Phi(P_k) \in \mathcal{P}_{\mathsf{acc}}$ and let the parties in $\mathcal{H}$ find $v_{jk} = 0$ in the vector $\overrightarrow{V_j}$ broadcasted by P_j. We wish to show that either $P_k \notin \mathcal{H}$ and did not broadcast the correct hash value of the message received from $\Phi(P_k)$ or $\Phi(P_k) \notin \mathcal{H}$ and did not send M to P_k. On *contrary*, let *both* P_k, as well as $\Phi(P_k)$, belong to $\mathcal{H}$ and none of the above holds. If $\Phi(P_k) \in \mathcal{H}$, it will send its input M to the party P_k and hence the following will hold:

$$m_k^? = M.$$

If $P_k \in \mathcal{H}$, it will randomly select the key $\mathbf{k}_k \in \mathrm{GF}(2^\kappa)$ and compute $\mathbf{h}_k$ where the following will hold:

$$\mathbf{h}_k = U_{\mathbf{k}_k}(m_k^?) = U_{\mathbf{k}_k}(M),$$

where the last equality holds since $m_k^? = M$. Since P_k broadcasts $(\mathbf{k}_k, \mathbf{h}_k)$ through BB oracle, it follows that each party in $\mathcal{H}$ will get the output $(\mathbf{k}_k, \mathbf{h}_k)$ from the oracle. Since $P_j \in \mathcal{H}$, it follows that the following will hold for P_j:

$$U_{\mathbf{k}_k}(m_j) = \mathbf{h}_k.$$

This is because as per our assumption, $m_j = M$ holds. Consequently, P_j will set $v_{jk} = 1$ in its vector $\overrightarrow{V_j}$. Since P_j broadcasts $\overrightarrow{V_j}$ through BB oracle, it follows that every party in $\mathcal{H}$ will get the output $\overrightarrow{V_j}$ from the broadcast oracle and find that $v_{jk} = 1$ holds. However, this is a *contradiction* since, as per our assumption, $v_{jk} = 0$. Hence our assumption that both P_k as well as $\Phi(P_k)$ belong to $\mathcal{H}$ is incorrect and either $P_k \notin \mathcal{H}$ or $\Phi(P_k) \notin \mathcal{H}$. □

Using the previous claim, we next show that if the parties compute a CORE set on top of the accepting-set of parties, then the *majority* of the parties in CORE are indeed *honest*, provided $t < \frac{n}{2}$. Intuitively, this is because at least *half* of the parties *outside* CORE set are guaranteed to be *corrupt*. Hence if the majority of the parties *inside* CORE are not honest, then it implies that we *do not* have honest majority among $\mathcal{P}$, since the set of parties inside and outside CORE are *disjoint*.

Claim 10.6 Let U be an unconditionally-secure collision-resistant hash function over $\mathrm{GF}(2^{\kappa})$. Moreover, let the honest parties compute a CORE set during the checking stage of the protocol $\Pi^{(n,t)}_{\mathsf{BAExtHM}}$. Then, the majority of the parties in CORE are honest except with a negligible probability, provided $t < \frac{n}{2}$.

Proof Let $\mathcal{H}$ be the set of *honest* parties and consider the event that all the parties in $(\mathcal{H} \cap \mathcal{P}_{\mathsf{acc}})$ have the same input. We will prove the claim conditioned on the above event, provided $t < \frac{n}{2}$. From Claim 10.4, the above event occurs except with a negligible probability. Consequently, the claim holds except with a negligible probability.

From the protocol steps, the sets CORE and $\overline{\mathsf{CORE}} = \mathcal{P} \setminus \mathsf{CORE}$ are disjoint. This is because the set CORE is initialized to $\mathcal{P}_{\mathsf{acc}}$ and every party $P_k \in \mathcal{P} \setminus \mathcal{P}_{\mathsf{acc}}$ either gets included in CORE or remains outside CORE. We also note that for every party $P_k \in \mathcal{P} \setminus \mathcal{P}_{\mathsf{acc}}$, which *does not* make it to CORE, the corresponding mapped party $\Phi(P_k)$ in $\mathcal{P}_{\mathsf{acc}}$ also gets *excluded* from CORE. Hence $\overline{\mathsf{CORE}}$ consists of pairs of parties $\{P_k, \Phi(P_k)\}$, satisfying all the following conditions:

- $P_k \in \mathcal{P} \setminus \mathcal{P}_{\mathsf{acc}}$;
- $\Phi(P_k) \in \mathcal{P}_{\mathsf{acc}}$;
- For every $P_j \in \mathcal{P}'_{\mathsf{acc}}$, the entry $v_{jk} = 0$ in the vector $\overrightarrow{V_j}$ broadcasted by the party P_j. Here $\mathcal{P}'_{\mathsf{acc}} \subseteq \mathcal{P}_{\mathsf{acc}}$ denotes the *maximum-sized* subset of $\mathcal{P}_{\mathsf{acc}}$ which broadcasted the same vector $\overrightarrow{V}$ such that $|\mathcal{P}'_{\mathsf{acc}}| \geq n - t$.

Since $|\mathcal{P}'_{\mathsf{acc}}| \geq n-t$ and $t < \frac{n}{2}$, it follows that $(\mathcal{P}'_{\mathsf{acc}} \cap \mathcal{H}) \neq \emptyset$ and hence $\mathcal{P}'_{\mathsf{acc}}$ consists of at least one *honest* party, say P_j. Since $v_{jk} = 0$, from Claim 10.5 it follows that either $P_k \notin \mathcal{H}$ or $\Phi(P_k) \notin \mathcal{H}$. Hence for *every* pair of parties $\{P_k, \Phi(P_k)\}$ which *does not* make it to CORE, at least one of the parties in the pair $\{P_k, \Phi(P_k)\}$ is guaranteed to be corrupt, implying that at least half of the parties in $\overline{\mathsf{CORE}}$ are *corrupt*. Since $t < \frac{n}{2}$ and since the sets CORE and $\overline{\mathsf{CORE}}$ are *disjoint*, it then follows that the majority of the parties in CORE are honest. □

Until now, we have shown that if the honest parties compute a CORE set, the majority of the parties in CORE are guaranteed to be *honest*. We next show that all honest parties in CORE will have the same (updated) input at the end of the checking stage. For this, we show that if any honest party *outside* the set of accepting-parties get included to the set CORE, then it is guaranteed to have received the common input held by the honest parties in the accepting-set, from its corresponding mapped party in the accepting set.

Claim 10.7 Let U be an unconditionally-secure collision-resistant hash function over $\text{GF}(2^\kappa)$. Moreover, let the honest parties compute a CORE set during the checking stage of the protocol $\Pi^{(n,t)}_{\mathsf{BAExtHM}}$. Then, all honest parties in CORE will have the same updated input except with a negligible probability, provided $t < \frac{n}{2}$.

Proof Let $\mathcal{H}$ be the set of *honest* parties and let the parties in $\mathcal{H}$ compute a CORE set during the checking stage. This implies that the parties in $\mathcal{H}$ compute an accepting-set of parties $\mathcal{P}_{\mathsf{acc}}$, since CORE is computed on top of $\mathcal{P}_{\mathsf{acc}}$. Moreover, $|\mathcal{P}_{\mathsf{acc}}| \geq n-t$ holds. Let E be the event that all the parties in $(\mathcal{H} \cap \mathcal{P}_{\mathsf{acc}})$ have the same input, say $M \in \{0,1\}^L$. From Claim 10.4, the event E occurs except with a negligible probability. We will condition on the event E and prove the claim. Since the parties compute a CORE set, it implies that there exists a subset of parties $\mathcal{P}'_{\mathsf{acc}} \subseteq \mathcal{P}_{\mathsf{acc}}$ where $|\mathcal{P}'_{\mathsf{acc}}| \geq n-t$, such that all the parties in $\mathcal{P}'_{\mathsf{acc}}$ broadcasted the same vector $\vec{V} \in \{0,1\}^{|\mathcal{P} \setminus \mathcal{P}_{\mathsf{acc}}|}$ in response to the hash values broadcasted by the respective parties in $(\mathcal{P} \setminus \mathcal{P}_{\mathsf{acc}})$.

Now consider an *arbitrary* $P_i \in (\mathcal{H} \cap \text{CORE})$. We wish to show that the updated input of P_i at the end of the checking stage will be M. For this, we have to consider two possible cases, which depend on whether P_i was already a part of the accepting-set of parties or newly added to the set CORE. That is, we have the following cases.

- **Case I** — $P_i \in (\text{CORE} \cap \mathcal{P}_{\mathsf{acc}})$: In this case, P_i retains M as its updated input.
- **Case II** — $P_i \notin \mathcal{P}_{\mathsf{acc}}$: In this case, P_i sets $m_i^?$ as its updated input, where $m_i^?$ denotes the message received by P_i from the party $\Phi(P_i)$, where $\Phi(P_i) \in \mathcal{P}_{\mathsf{acc}}$. Now, here we again have two cases, which depend on whether $\Phi(P_i)$ is honest or corrupt.
  - **Case A** — $\Phi(P_i) \in \mathcal{H}$: In this case, $m_i^? = M$ holds. This is because the input of $\Phi(P_i)$ is M and since $\Phi(P_i)$ is honest, it will send M to P_i.
  - **Case B** — $\Phi(P_i) \notin \mathcal{H}$: Let $M' \in \{0,1\}^L$ be the input, transferred by $\Phi(P_i)$ to P_i. We show that if $M' \neq M$, then P_i *does not* get included to CORE, except with a negligible probability, which is a contradiction. For this, consider an *arbitrary* $P_j \in (\mathcal{H} \cap \mathcal{P}_{\mathsf{acc}})$. If $M' \neq M$, then P_j will set $v_{ji} = 0$ in the vector $\vec{V_j}$, except with a negligible probability. This is because the honest P_i will pick the hash key $\mathbf{k}_i$ randomly from $\text{GF}(2^\kappa)$ and compute $\mathbf{h}_i$, where the following holds:

$$\mathbf{h}_i = U_{\mathbf{k}_i}(m_i^?) = U_{\mathbf{k}_i}(M').$$

Since P_i broadcasts $(\mathbf{k}_i, \mathbf{h}_i)$ through BB oracle, it follows that P_j will get the output $(\mathbf{k}_i, \mathbf{h}_i)$ from the oracle. Moreover if $M' \neq M$, then the following will hold for P_j, except with a negligible probability:

$$\mathbf{h}_i \neq U_{\mathbf{k}_i}(M).$$

Hence P_j will set $v_{ji} = 0$ in the vector $\overrightarrow{V_j}$. Since P_j broadcasts $\overrightarrow{V_j}$ through BB oracle, it follows that all the parties in $\mathcal{H}$ will get the output $\overrightarrow{V_j}$ from the oracle and find $v_{ji} = 0$. Since there can be up to n honest parties in $\mathcal{P}_{\mathsf{acc}}$, from the union bound it follows that if $M' \neq M$, then except with a negligible probability, no party in $\mathcal{H}$ will ever set $v_{ji} = 1$. If $P_i \in \mathsf{CORE}$, then it implies that $v_{ji} = 1$ in the vector $\overrightarrow{V_j}$ of all the parties $P_j \in \mathcal{P}'_{\mathsf{acc}}$. Since $t < \frac{n}{2}$ and $|\mathcal{P}'_{\mathsf{acc}}| \geq n - t$, it implies that $(\mathcal{H} \cap \mathcal{P}'_{\mathsf{acc}}) \neq \emptyset$ and hence consists of at least one honest party P_j, who sets $v_{ji} = 1$. However, as argued above, this implies that $M' = M$, except with a negligible probability.

As there can be $\mathcal{O}(n)$ honest parties outside $\mathcal{P}_{\mathsf{acc}}$ who may get transferred to CORE, from the union bound it follows that all honest parties in CORE will have the same updated input at the end of the checking stage, except with a negligible probability. Since we have conditioned on the event E, which occurs except with a negligible probability, it now follows that the claim holds except with a negligible probability. □

We are now well-equipped to prove the consistency property.

Lemma 10.6 *Let U be an unconditionally-secure collision-resistant hash function over $GF(2^\kappa)$. Then protocol $\Pi^{(n,t)}_{\mathsf{BAExtHM}}$ achieves t-consistency except with a negligible probability, provided $t < \frac{n}{2}$.*

Proof Let $\mathcal{H}$ be the set of honest parties and let the parties in $\mathcal{H}$ participate in the protocol with *different* inputs. Then there are the following *two* possible cases, depending on whether the honest parties find a CORE set during the checking stage.

- **Case I — The Parties in $\mathcal{H}$ Do Not Find a CORE Set**: In this case, all the parties in $\mathcal{H}$ terminate with the same output 0^L, and hence consistency holds.
- **Case II — The Parties in $\mathcal{H}$ Find a CORE Set**: Let E be the event that the majority of the parties in CORE are *honest* and have the same updated input at the end of the checking stage. Now conditioned on the event E, it follows from Claim 10.3 that all the parties in $\mathcal{H}$ will have a common output at the end of the propagation phase, except with a negligible probability. From Claim 10.7, the event E occurs except with a negligible probability. Hence, all the parties in $\mathcal{H}$ will have a common output, except with a negligible probability. □

Theorem 10.2 now follows easily from the above discussion.

Theorem 10.2 *Let U be an unconditionally-secure collision-resistant hash function over $GF(2^\kappa)$ and let the parties have access to a bit-BB oracle for broadcasting bits. If $t < \frac{n}{2}$, then protocol $\Pi^{(n,t)}_{\mathsf{BAExtHM}}$ is a t-secure BA protocol with statistical security for L-bit inputs in the model $\mathcal{M}_{\mathsf{auth}}$ where $L \geq 1$. The protocol has the following complexities.*[9]

---

[9] We stress that the protocol $\Pi^{(n,t)}_{\mathsf{BAExtHM}}$ *does not* need any PKI setup. The setup will be required only to emulate the BB oracle with statistical security and $t < \frac{n}{2}$ (see the next section).

– *The protocol requires* 6 *rounds.*
– *The seed-round complexity of the protocol* 4.
– *The protocol incurs a communication of* $2n \cdot \mathcal{BC}(2\kappa) + 2n \cdot \mathcal{BC}(n) + O(nL + n^3\kappa)$ *bits, where* $\mathcal{BC}(\ell)$ *denotes the communication complexity for emulating one call to the BB oracle with an* ℓ*-bit input such that* $\ell \geq 1$.
– *The seed-communication complexity of the protocol is* $O(n\kappa + n^2)$ *bits.*

10.4 Protocol $\Pi^{(n,t)}_{\mathsf{BAExtHM}}$: Further Discussion

Let us now try to derive the "concrete" communication complexity of the protocol $\Pi^{(n,t)}_{\mathsf{BAExtHM}}$, by instantiating the BB oracle with a concrete *t-secure* BB protocol with *statistical* security. One option would be to use the statistically-secure variant of the Dolev-Strong BB protocol $\Pi^{(n,t)}_{\mathsf{DSBB}}$ (see Section 9.2.2), assuming a trusted setup for unconditionally-secure PKI (i.e. in the model $\mathcal{M}^{\mathsf{pki}}_{\mathsf{auth}}$). From Theorem 9.2, the protocol needs a communication of $\mathcal{BC}(\ell) = O(n^3\ell\kappa)$ bits, where ℓ is the size of the input of the designated sender in bits and where κ is the security parameter and denotes the size of a signature in bits. Consequently, by substituting $\mathcal{BC}(\ell) = O(n^3\ell\kappa)$ in Theorem 10.2 and using protocol $\Pi^{(n,t)}_{\mathsf{DSBB}}$ as an instantiation of the BB oracle, we get the following corollary of Theorem 10.2.

Corollary 10.1 *Let U be an unconditionally-secure collision-resistant hash function over* $GF(2^\kappa)$*. If* $t < \frac{n}{2}$*, then protocol* $\Pi^{(n,t)}_{\mathsf{BAExtHM}}$ *is a t-secure BA protocol with statistical security for L-bit inputs in the model* $\mathcal{M}^{\mathsf{pki}}_{\mathsf{auth}}$*, where* $L \geq 1$*. The protocol incurs a communication of* $O(nL + n^4\kappa^2 + n^5\kappa)$ *bits, where* κ *is the security parameter and denotes the size of a signature as well as the size of a hash value in bits.*

Minimum Message Size in $\Pi^{(n,t)}_{\mathsf{BAExtHM}}$ for Optimal Communication Complexity.

From Corollary 10.1, it follows that if $L = \Omega(n^3\kappa^2 + n^4\kappa)$, then protocol $\Pi^{(n,t)}_{\mathsf{BAExtHM}}$ will incur an *asymptotic* communication of $O(nL)$ bits. This will be *optimal*, since from Theorem 6.7, *any* t-secure BA protocol must incur a communication of $\Omega(nL)$ bits.

10.5 Open Problems

As mentioned earlier, protocol $\Pi^{(n,t)}_{\mathsf{BAExtHM}}$ (due to [53]) is the *only* known domain extension protocol with *statistical* security and the *optimal* resilience of $t < \frac{n}{2}$. Even though the seed-round complexity of the protocol is a *constant* (namely 4), it is still high and *not* optimal. Recall that the *optimal* seed-round complexity of any domain extension protocol is 1. Moreover, if we consider the domain extension protocol with *perfect security* and resilience $t < \frac{n}{3}$, presented in Chapter 6 (namely protocol $\Pi^{(n,t)}_{\mathsf{PerDomExt}}$ presented in Fig 6.19), then it enjoys both *optimal resilience* as well as *optimal* seed-round complexity of 1. It is an open problem to further improve the seed-round complexity of the protocol $\Pi^{(n,t)}_{\mathsf{BAExtHM}}$. Similarly, compared to protocol $\Pi^{(n,t)}_{\mathsf{PerDomExt}}$ whose seed-communication complexity is $\mathcal{O}(n^2)$ bits, the seed-communication complexity of the protocol $\Pi^{(n,t)}_{\mathsf{BAExtHM}}$ is $\mathcal{O}(n^2+n\kappa)$ bits. Further improving the seed-communication complexity of the protocol $\Pi^{(n,t)}_{\mathsf{BAExtHM}}$ is also an interesting open research question. It is also an interesting research problem to reduce further the size of L for which one can design an extension protocol with statistical security, incurring an asymptotic communication complexity of $\mathcal{O}(nL)$ bits and having optimal resilience.

Chapter 11
Domain Extension for BA with Honest Majority and Cryptographic Security

In this chapter, we continue our discussion on domain extension protocols with a strict honest majority (i.e. with $t < \frac{n}{2}$). However, *instead* of statistical security, we will focus on cryptographic security, where the adversary is assumed to be computationally bounded. We show that by replacing the unconditionally-secure collision-resistant hash function in the protocol $\Pi^{(n,t)}_{\mathsf{BAExtHM}}$ (Fig 10.5) with a cryptographically-secure collision-resistant hash function, one can significantly simplify the protocol design and improve the protocol's seed-round complexity and communication complexity. This shows a trade-off between the level of security achieved and the complexity of the resultant protocols.

11.1 The Setting

The setting considered in this chapter is almost the same as that in the previous chapter, except with the following *differences*:

- Instead of considering a computationally-unbounded adversary, we consider a computationally-bounded adversary, who can corrupt up to t parties in a Byzantine fashion.
- Since we will be dealing with computationally-bounded adversaries, instead of assuming the setup of an unconditionally-secure PKI, we will assume the setup for a cryptographically-secure PKI.

The protocol presented in this chapter will be in the model $\mathcal{M}^{\mathsf{pki}}_{\mathsf{auth}}$. We also assume that the parties have oracle access to a bit-BB oracle that allows them to broadcast bits. Looking ahead, the cryptographically-secure PKI setup is required to emulate the BB oracle.[1]

In our protocol, we also use a *cryptographically-secure collision-resistant* hash function $H : \{0,1\}^{\ell} \rightarrow \{0,1\}^{\kappa}$. Recall that the collision-resistance guarantees that

[1] One instantiation of the BB oracle with cryptographic security could be the cryptographically-secure variant of the Dolev-Strong BB protocol $\Pi^{(n,t)}_{\mathsf{DSBB}}$ presented in Chapter 9.

A. Choudhury and A. Patra, *Fault-Tolerant Distributed Consensus in Synchronous Networks*, Information Security and Cryptography,
https://doi.org/10.1007/978-3-031-80460-1_11

it is infeasible for any PPT algorithm to output a pair of *distinct* messages (m, m'), such that $H(m) = H(m')$ holds, except with some negligible probability in κ. We also assume that the input size L of the parties' input for the extension protocol is some polynomial function in κ; i.e. $L = \text{poly}(\kappa)$.

11.2 The Domain Extension Protocol with $t < \frac{n}{2}$

In this section, we present a *cryptographically-secure* domain extension protocol for BA, tolerating $t < \frac{n}{2}$ Byzantine corruptions. The protocol is almost the same as the unconditionally-secure extension protocol $\Pi^{(n,t)}_{\mathsf{BAExtHM}}$ (Fig 10.5), except that we now use a cryptographically-secure collision-resistant hash function. As it turns out, this makes the protocol remarkably simpler and improves its seed-round and seed-communication complexity. The protocol consists of two stages: a checking stage and a propagation stage. In the checking stage, the parties look for a CORE set of parties, where the majority of the parties are guaranteed to be honest and who have the same updated input, which is later propagated to all the parties outside CORE during the propagation stage, provided the existence of a CORE set is confirmed.

The search for a candidate CORE set during the checking stage proceeds as in the protocol $\Pi^{(n,t)}_{\mathsf{BAExtHM}}$, where each party first tries to search for a candidate set of accepting-parties $\mathcal{P}_{\mathsf{acc}}$ of size at least $n - t$, who have the same input. For this, each party broadcasts a (cryptographic) hash of its input using the BB oracle. Note that, *unlike* the protocol $\Pi^{(n,t)}_{\mathsf{BAExtHM}}$, the parties broadcast just the hash of their respective inputs, and *no* keys are used and broadcasted since the hash function H is unkeyed. Consequently, the parties *need not* have to broadcast any response vector $\overrightarrow{\mathsf{Res}_i}$ in response to the hash values broadcasted by the respective parties. As a result, to look for a candidate $\mathcal{P}_{\mathsf{acc}}$ set, the parties just need to check if at least $n - t$ parties have broadcasted the *same* hash value, say h. Hence, searching for a candidate $\mathcal{P}_{\mathsf{acc}}$ set requires *just* one seed-round, *instead* of two seed-rounds. Moreover, the seed-communication complexity is just $n \cdot \mathcal{BC}(\kappa)$ bits instead of $n \cdot \mathcal{BC}(2\kappa) + n \cdot \mathcal{BC}(n)$ bits. If no candidate $\mathcal{P}_{\mathsf{acc}}$ set is identified, then the parties can safely terminate the protocol prematurely with some default output.

If a candidate $\mathcal{P}_{\mathsf{acc}}$ set is identified, then it implies that all (honest) parties in the set have the same input, say M, whose hash value h is *publicly available*. The next goal is to find a candidate CORE set where the updated input of all the (honest) parties in CORE is M. Towards this, a publicly-known *injective* mapping is identified from the set of non-accepting parties $(\mathcal{P} \setminus \mathcal{P}_{\mathsf{acc}})$ to the set of accepting parties $\mathcal{P}_{\mathsf{acc}}$ and each party $P_i \in (\mathcal{P} \setminus \mathcal{P}_{\mathsf{acc}})$ receives the supposed input M from its designated sender party $\Phi(P_i)$ belonging to the set $\mathcal{P}_{\mathsf{acc}}$. The next task is to let P_i verify whether it received the input M. However, *unlike* protocol $\Pi^{(n,t)}_{\mathsf{BAExtHM}}$, this *does not* require any "help" from the parties in $\mathcal{P}_{\mathsf{acc}}$. Namely, party P_i can simply verify the received input against the public hash h available and announces its response *publicly*, using the BB oracle. If the response is *positive*, then both P_i as well as $\Phi(P_i)$ are moved to the set CORE, with P_i updating its input to the one received from $\Phi(P_i)$. On the other hand, if the response is *negative*, then it implies that either P_i received an incorrect M or broadcasted an incorrect response and *both* P_i, as well as $\Phi(P_i)$, are barred from getting included in the set CORE.

Again notice that compared to the protocol $\Pi^{(n,t)}_{\mathsf{BAExtHM}}$, the number of seed-rounds required for the parties in $(\mathcal{P} \setminus \mathcal{P}_{\mathsf{acc}})$ to verify the inputs received from their designated sender parties is *one*. This is because of the availability of the public hash h of the supposedly common input M held by the (honest) parties in $\mathcal{P}_{\mathsf{acc}}$. Moreover, the whole process involves a seed-communication complexity of $n \cdot \mathcal{BC}(1)$ bits, instead of $n \cdot \mathcal{BC}(2\kappa) + n \cdot \mathcal{BC}(n)$ bits.

If a CORE set is computed, the propagation stage remains similar as in the protocol $\Pi^{(n,t)}_{\mathsf{BAExtHM}}$, except that each party in CORE now authenticates the points on its polynomial using the hash function H, instead of an unconditionally-secure hash function. This leads to a saving in communication, since the parties in CORE *need not* have to send any key for the hash function. We call the resultant protocol $\Pi^{(n,t)}_{\mathsf{CryBAExtHM}}$, which is formally presented in Fig 11.1. In the protocol, we follow a simplifying convention that if, during a round, a receiver party is expecting some message from a designated sender party and if either no message or a syntactically incorrect message is received, then the receiver party substitutes some default value from the underlying domain on behalf of the sender party and continues the protocol.

Protocol $\Pi^{(n,t)}_{\mathsf{CryBAExtHM}}$

Public knowledge: the description of a cryptographically-secure collision-resistant hash function H. Additionally, the parties have oracle access to a bit-BB oracle.

Checking Stage

- **Round 1 (broadcasting message hash)**: On having the input $m_i \in \{0,1\}^L$, do the following.
  - Compute $h_i := H(m_i)$.
  - Call the BB oracle as a sender with input h_i to broadcast h_i.
- **Checking for accepting set and conditional abort**: For $j = 1, \ldots, n$, let h_j be the output from the BB oracle where P_j is the designated sender.
  - If there exists a subset of parties $\mathcal{P}' \subseteq \mathcal{P}$, satisfying all the following conditions then set $\mathcal{P}_{\mathsf{acc}} := \mathcal{P}'$.
    - $|\mathcal{P}'| \geq n - t$;
    - $h_j = h_k$ holds for every $P_j, P_k \in \mathcal{P}'$

    Let $h \in \{0,1\}^\kappa$ be the common hash value, broadcasted by all the parties in $\mathcal{P}_{\mathsf{acc}}$.
  - Else output 0^L and terminate.

If the checking stage is not terminated, then let $\Phi : (\mathcal{P} \setminus \mathcal{P}_{\mathsf{acc}}) \rightarrow \mathcal{P}_{\mathsf{acc}}$ be the publicly known injective mapping, where the party with the smallest index in $(\mathcal{P} \setminus \mathcal{P}_{\mathsf{acc}})$ is mapped to the party with the smallest index in the set $\mathcal{P}_{\mathsf{acc}}$.

- **Round 2 (transferring the message from accepting set to non-accepting Set)**: If $P_i \in \mathcal{P}_{\mathsf{acc}}$, then do the following.
  - Let $P_j \in (\mathcal{P} \setminus \mathcal{P}_{\mathsf{acc}})$ such that $\Phi(P_j) = P_i$.
  - Send M to P_j where $M = m_i$ and let $m^?_j$ denote the message received by P_j from P_i during this round.

- **Round 3 (verification of the message transferred from accepting set to non-accepting set of parties)**: If $P_i \in (\mathcal{P} \setminus \mathcal{P}_{\mathsf{acc}})$, then do the following.
  - Upon receiving $m_i^?$ from the party $\Phi(P_i)$ in the previous round, set $\mathsf{happy}_i := 1$, if $H(m_i^?) = h$, else set $\mathsf{happy}_i := 0$.
  - Call the BB oracle as a sender with input happy_i to broadcast the bit happy_i.
- **Computing the core set**: For every $P_j \in (\mathcal{P} \setminus \mathcal{P}_{\mathsf{acc}})$, let $\mathsf{happy}_j \in \{0, 1\}$ be the output from the BB oracle where P_j is the sender.
  - Set $\mathsf{CORE} := \mathcal{P}_{\mathsf{acc}}$ and then update it as per the following criteria.
    - For every $P_j \in (\mathcal{P} \setminus \mathcal{P}_{\mathsf{acc}})$, do the following.
      - If $\mathsf{happy}_j = 1$ then set $\mathsf{CORE} := \mathsf{CORE} \cup \{P_j\}$;
      - Else set $\mathsf{CORE} := \mathsf{CORE} \setminus \{\Phi(P_j)\}$.
- **Updating the input for the propagation stage**: If $P_i \in \mathsf{CORE}$, then update the input for the propagation stage as follows.
  - If $P_i \in (\mathsf{CORE} \cap \mathcal{P}_{\mathsf{acc}})$, then retain m_i as the input for the propagation stage.
  - Else set $m_i := m_i^?$, where $m_i^?$ denotes the message received from the mapped party $\Phi(P_i)$ during Round 2.

Propagation Stage[a]

For simplicity and without loss of generality, let $|\mathsf{CORE}| = 2d + 1$ and let L be a multiple of $d + 1$ such that $c \stackrel{def}{=} \frac{L}{d+1}$. Moreover, let $\mathrm{GF}(2^c)$ denote the Galois field consisting of c-bit elements.

- **Round 4 (propagation stage)**: If $P_i \in \mathsf{CORE}$, then do the following.
  - Transform the input m_i into a d-degree polynomial $f_i(X)$ over $\mathrm{GF}(2^c)$. For this, divide m_i into $d+1$ blocks each of size c-bits and let $f_{i,0}, \ldots, f_{i,d}$ be the resultant elements from $\mathrm{GF}(2^c)$ represented by these c-bit blocks. Then set
  $$f_i(X) \stackrel{def}{=} f_{i,0} + f_{i,1} \cdot X + \ldots + f_{i,d} \cdot X^d.$$
  - Compute the hash values $H_{i1}, \ldots, H_{in}$, where for $j = 1, \ldots, n$, the hash value H_{ij} is defined as follows:
  $$H_{ij} \stackrel{def}{=} H(f_i(j))$$
  - Compute $y_i \stackrel{def}{=} f_i(i)$ and send (y_i, H_i) to every $P_j \notin \mathsf{CORE}$, where $H_i = (H_{i1}, \ldots, H_{in})$ denotes the hash-vector.
- **Output Stage**: Compute the following output and terminate.
  - If $P_i \in \mathsf{CORE}$, then output m_i.
  - Else receive (y_j, H_j) from every $P_j \in \mathsf{CORE}$ where $H_j = (H_{j1}, \ldots, H_{jn})$ and then do the following.
    - For every $P_j \in \mathsf{CORE}$, include P_j to a set ACC_i, initialized to $\emptyset$, if all the following holds:
      - There is a subset of parties $\mathsf{CORE}'_j \subseteq \mathsf{CORE}$, where $|\mathsf{CORE}'_j| \geq d + 1$;
      - For every $P_r \in \mathsf{CORE}'_j$, the following condition is satisfied:
      $$H_{rj} = H(y_j).$$
      Here $(y_r, (H_{r1}, \ldots, H_{rn}))$ denotes the values received from P_r.
    - Interpolate the points $\{(j, y_j)\}_{P_j \in \mathsf{ACC}_i}$ and compute the d-degree polynomial $f_i(X)$.
    - Let $f_{i,0}, \ldots, f_{i,d} \in \mathrm{GF}(2^c)$ be the coefficients of $f_i(X)$ and let $F_{i,0}, \ldots, F_{i,d}$ be the binary representation of these elements respectively. Then output $(F_{i,0}) || \ldots || F_{i,d}$.

[a] Note that the steps of the propagation stage here are almost the same as in the protocol $\Pi^{(n,t)}_{\mathsf{BAExtHMWarmUp}}$, except that the parties in CORE now use the cryptographically-secure collision-resistant hash function H to authenticate points on its polynomial, *instead* of an unconditionally-secure collision-resistant hash function.

Fig. 11.1: A cryptographically-secure BA extension protocol with $t < \frac{n}{2}$. The above code is executed by every party $P_i \in \mathcal{P}$

We now proceed to prove the properties of the protocol $\Pi^{(n,t)}_{\mathsf{CryBAExtHM}}$. We start with the derivation of various complexity figures associated with the protocol.

Lemma 11.1 *Let the parties have oracle access to a BB oracle. Then protocol $\Pi^{(n,t)}_{\mathsf{CryBAExtHM}}$ have the following complexities.*

- *The protocol requires* 4 *rounds.*
- *The seed-round complexity of the protocol is* 2*.*
- *The protocol incurs a communication of $O(nL + n^3\kappa) + n \cdot \mathcal{BC}(\kappa) + n \cdot \mathcal{BC}(1)$ bits, where the $\mathcal{BC}(\ell)$ denotes the communication complexity for emulating one call to the BB oracle with an ℓ-bit input.*
- *The seed-communication complexity of the protocol is $O(n\kappa)$ bits.*

Proof During the checking stage, the parties first broadcast the hash of their respective inputs through the BB oracle. This requires 1 round and incurs a communication of $n \cdot \mathcal{BC}(\kappa)$ bits, since each hash value is of size κ bits. This step contributes 1 to the seed-round complexity of the protocol and incurs a seed-communication complexity of $O(n\kappa)$ bits. Finding a candidate $\mathcal{P}_{\mathsf{acc}}$ set requires only local computation and does not require any interaction among the parties.

Next, each party in $(\mathcal{P} \setminus \mathcal{P}_{\mathsf{acc}})$ receives the input of the designated sender party from the set $\mathcal{P}_{\mathsf{acc}}$. This requires one round and incurs a communication of $O(nL)$ bits, since each party in $\mathcal{P}_{\mathsf{acc}}$ sends its input of size L bits to *at most* one party in the set $(\mathcal{P} \setminus \mathcal{P}_{\mathsf{acc}})$. This is followed by each party in $(\mathcal{P} \setminus \mathcal{P}_{\mathsf{acc}})$ broadcasting its happy bit through the BB oracle. This requires 1 round and incurs a communication of $n \cdot \mathcal{BC}(1)$ bits. This step contributes 1 to the seed-round complexity of the protocol and incurs a seed-communication complexity of $O(n)$ bits.

The propagation stage requires one round and incurs a communication of $O(nL + n^3\kappa)$ bits, which follows from Lemma 10.1. This completes the proof of the lemma. □

We next prove the *validity* property, whose proof is almost the same as the proof of the validity property for the protocol $\Pi^{(n,t)}_{\mathsf{BAExtHM}}$ (Lemma 10.5).

Lemma 11.2 *Let H be a cryptographically-secure collision-resistant hash function. Then protocol $\Pi^{(n,t)}_{\mathsf{CryBAExtHM}}$ achieves t-validity, except with a negligible probability, provided $t < \frac{n}{2}$.*

Proof Let $\mathcal{H}$ be the set of *honest* parties and let every $P_i \in \mathcal{H}$ have the input $m_i = M \in \{0,1\}^L$. We wish to show that each $P_i \in \mathcal{H}$ outputs M. Since every $P_i \in \mathcal{H}$ have input M, it follows that all the parties in $\mathcal{H}$ will find a common set of accepting-parties $\mathcal{P}_{\mathsf{acc}}$ of size at least $n - t$, such that $\mathcal{H} \subseteq \mathcal{P}_{\mathsf{acc}}$. This is because each $P_i \in \mathcal{H}$ will broadcast the hash value $h \in \{0, 1\}^\kappa$ using the BB oracle where $h = H(m)$, and all the parties in $\mathcal{H}$ will receive h as the output from the BB oracle, corresponding to the sender parties in $\mathcal{H}$. Hence, all the parties in $\mathcal{H}$ will find at least $n-t$ parties broadcasting a common hash value during the first round of the checking stage. Consequently, the parties in $\mathcal{H}$ do not terminate the protocol prematurely. The condition $\mathcal{H} \subseteq \mathcal{P}_{\mathsf{acc}}$ will be satisfied since the set of *corrupt* parties $\mathcal{P} \setminus \mathcal{H}$ do not satisfy the conditions for a candidate $\mathcal{P}_{\mathsf{acc}}$ set, as $|\mathcal{P} \setminus \mathcal{H}| \leq t$ and $n - t > t$ holds.

Since the parties in $\mathcal{H}$ *do not* terminate the protocol prematurely, it implies they will also find a candidate CORE set. We next show that the majority of the parties in CORE are guaranteed to be *honest*. For this, we first note that all the parties in $(\mathcal{P} \setminus \mathcal{P}_{\mathsf{acc}})$ are guaranteed to be *corrupt*, since $\mathcal{H} \subseteq \mathcal{P}_{\mathsf{acc}}$. Now the set $(\mathcal{P} \setminus \mathsf{CORE})$ consists of pairs of parties $\{P_k, \Phi(P_k)\}$, where $P_k \notin \mathcal{P}_{\mathsf{acc}}$, implying that at least half of the parties in $\mathcal{P} \setminus \mathsf{CORE}$ are *corrupt*. Since $t < \frac{n}{2}$, this further implies that the majority of the parties in CORE are *honest*.

We finally show that the updated input of all the parties in $(\mathcal{H} \cap \mathsf{CORE})$ remains M. However, this trivially follows from the fact that $\mathcal{H} \subseteq \mathcal{P}_{\mathsf{acc}}$ and hence $(\mathcal{H} \cap \mathsf{CORE}) \subseteq (\mathcal{H} \cap \mathcal{P}_{\mathsf{acc}})$. Consequently, each $P_i \in (\mathcal{H} \cap \mathsf{CORE})$ retains m_i as its updated input for the propagation stage, and $m_i = M$ holds.

Now, once it is guaranteed that the majority of the parties in CORE are honest and have the same input M, then it follows that at the end of the propagation stage, all the parties in $\mathcal{H}$ will output M, except with a negligible probability. The proof for this is the same as Claim 10.3, except that we now rely on the collision-resistance property of the hash function H. □

We next prove the *consistency* property by establishing a series of claims. We first claim that if the (honest) parties find a candidate set of accepting parties, then all honest parties in the set have the same input (with a high probability).

Claim 11.1 If H is a cryptographically-secure collision-resistant hash function, then all the following holds during the protocol $\Pi^{(n,t)}_{\mathsf{CryBAExtHM}}$.

- All honest parties will agree upon the existence of the set $\mathcal{P}_{\mathsf{acc}}$ during the checking stage.
- If a set $\mathcal{P}_{\mathsf{acc}}$ is identified during the checking stage, then except with a negligible probability, the input of all honest parties in $\mathcal{P}_{\mathsf{acc}}$ consists of the same L bits.

Proof From the protocol steps, the set $\mathcal{P}_{\mathsf{acc}}$ is determined deterministically based on the hash values h_i broadcasted by the different parties P_i during the checking stage. Since each P_i broadcasts h_i using the BB oracle, all honest parties will get the h_i as output from the BB oracle invoked by P_i. Consequently, if a candidate set $\mathcal{P}_{\mathsf{acc}}$ is computed during the checking stage, then all honest parties will have the same $\mathcal{P}_{\mathsf{acc}}$, proving the first property.

The second property follows from the collision-resistance property of the hash function H. Namely, consider an arbitrary pair of *honest* parties $P_i, P_j \in \mathcal{P}_{\mathsf{acc}}$, implying that $h_i = h_j$ holds, where $h_i = H(m_i)$ and $h_j = H(m_j)$. If $m_i \neq m_j$, except with a negligible probability, the condition $h_i \neq h_j$ will also hold, which is a contradiction. □

Next, we show that if any party from the non-accepting set "rejects" the message received from its designated sender party in the accepting-set, then at least one of these two parties is *corrupt*.

Claim 11.2 If H is a cryptographically-secure collision-resistant hash function, then during the protocol $\Pi^{(n,t)}_{\mathsf{CryBAExtHM}}$, the following holds for every pair of parties $\{P_k, \Phi(P_k)\}$, where $P_k \in (\mathcal{P} \setminus \mathcal{P}_{\mathsf{acc}})$ and $\Phi(P_k) \in \mathcal{P}_{\mathsf{acc}}$.

- If P_k broadcasts $\mathsf{happy}_k = 0$, then either P_k or $\Phi(P_k)$ is corrupt.

Proof Let $\mathcal{H}$ be the set of *honest* parties and let the parties in $\mathcal{H}$ compute a candidate set $\mathcal{P}_{\mathsf{acc}}$. This implies that all the parties in $\mathcal{P}_{\mathsf{acc}}$ broadcasted a common hash value, say h, during the checking stage such that $H(m_i) = H(m_j) = h$ holds for every $P_i, P_j \in \mathcal{H}$. Now consider an *arbitrary* pair of parties $\{P_k, \Phi(P_k)\}$ where $P_k \in (\mathcal{P} \setminus \mathcal{P}_{\mathsf{acc}})$ and $\Phi(P_k) \in \mathcal{P}_{\mathsf{acc}}$, such that P_k broadcasts $\mathsf{happy}_k = 0$. We wish to show that either P_k or $\Phi(P_k)$ is *corrupt*. On the contrary, let $P_k, \Phi(P_k) \in \mathcal{H}$.

If $\Phi(P_k) \in \mathcal{H}$, then it will send its input m_k to P_k and hence $m_k^? = m_k$ holds for P_k. Consequently, $H(m_k^?) = h$ will also hold as well, since $H(m_k^?) = H(m_k)$ and $H(m_k) = h$ holds. So if $P_k \in \mathcal{H}$ as well then P_k will set $\mathsf{happy}_k = 1$ and broadcast $\mathsf{happy}_k = 1$, which is a *contradiction*. □

An immediate implication of the previous claim is that if a CORE set is computed, then the majority of the parties in CORE are guaranteed to be honest, provided honest majority holds in $\mathcal{P}$.

Claim 11.3 Let H be a cryptographically-secure collision-resistant hash function. Moreover, let the honest parties compute a CORE set during the checking stage of the protocol $\Pi^{(n,t)}_{\mathsf{CryBAExtHM}}$. Then, the majority of the parties in CORE are honest, provided $t < \frac{n}{2}$.

Proof From the protocol steps, the sets CORE and $\overline{\mathsf{CORE}} = \mathcal{P} \setminus \mathsf{CORE}$ are disjoint. This is because the set CORE is initialized to $\mathcal{P}_{\mathsf{acc}}$ and every party $P_k \in \mathcal{P} \setminus \mathcal{P}_{\mathsf{acc}}$ either gets included in CORE or remains outside CORE. We also note that for every party $P_k \in \mathcal{P} \setminus \mathcal{P}_{\mathsf{acc}}$, which *does not* make it to CORE, the corresponding mapped party $\Phi(P_k)$ in $\mathcal{P}_{\mathsf{acc}}$ also gets *excluded* from CORE. Moreover, for such pair of parties $(P_k, \Phi(P_k))$, party P_k broadcasts $\mathsf{happy}_k = 0$. Furthermore, from Claim 11.2, for every such pair of parties $(P_k, \Phi(P_k))$, either P_k or $\Phi(P_k)$ is guaranteed to be corrupt. This implies that at least half of the parties in $\overline{\mathsf{CORE}}$ are *corrupt*. Since $t < \frac{n}{2}$ and since the sets CORE and $\overline{\mathsf{CORE}}$ are *disjoint*, it then follows that the majority of the parties in CORE are honest. □

We next show that all honest parties in CORE will have the same (updated) input at the end of the checking stage.

Claim 11.4 Let H be a cryptographically-secure collision-resistant hash function. Moreover, let the honest parties compute a CORE set during the checking stage of the protocol $\Pi^{(n,t)}_{\mathsf{CryBAExtHM}}$. Then all honest parties in CORE will have the same updated input except with a negligible probability, provided $t < \frac{n}{2}$.

Proof Let $\mathcal{H}$ be the set of *honest* parties and let the parties in $\mathcal{H}$ compute a CORE set during the checking stage. This implies that the parties in $\mathcal{H}$ compute an accepting-set of parties $\mathcal{P}_{\mathsf{acc}}$, since CORE is computed on top of $\mathcal{P}_{\mathsf{acc}}$. Moreover, $|\mathcal{P}_{\mathsf{acc}}| \geq n-t$ holds. From Claim 11.1, all the parties in $(\mathcal{H} \cap \mathcal{P}_{\mathsf{acc}})$ have the same input, say $M \in \{0,1\}^L$, except with a negligible probability. Moreover, from the protocol steps, all the parties in $\mathcal{P}_{\mathsf{acc}}$ broadcasted a common hash value h, where $h = H(m)$ holds.

Now consider an *arbitrary* $P_i \in (\mathcal{H} \cap \mathsf{CORE})$. We wish to show that the updated input of P_i at the end of the checking stage will be M. For this, we have to consider two possible cases, which depend on whether P_i was already a part of the accepting-set of parties or newly added to the set CORE. That is, we have the following cases.

- **Case I —** $P_i \in (\mathsf{CORE} \cap \mathcal{P}_{\mathsf{acc}})$: In this case, P_i retains M as its updated input.
- **Case II —** $P_i \notin \mathcal{P}_{\mathsf{acc}}$: In this case, P_i sets $m_i^?$ as its updated input, where $m_i^?$ denotes the message received by P_i from the party $\Phi(P_i)$, where $\Phi(P_i) \in \mathcal{P}_{\mathsf{acc}}$. Now, here we again have two cases, which depend on whether $\Phi(P_i)$ is honest or corrupt.
  - **Case A —** $\Phi(P_i) \in \mathcal{H}$: In this case, $m_i^? = M$ holds. This is because the input of $\Phi(P_i)$ is M and since $\Phi(P_i)$ is honest, it will send M to P_i.
  - **Case B —** $\Phi(P_i) \notin \mathcal{H}$: Let $M' \in \{0,1\}^L$ be the input, transferred by $\Phi(P_i)$ to P_i. We show that if $M' \neq M$, then P_i *does not* get included to CORE, except with a negligible probability, which is a contradiction. Since $P_i \in \mathsf{CORE}$, from the protocol steps it follows that P_i broadcasts $\mathsf{happy}_i = 1$. This implies that $H(M') = h$ holds for P_i. Since $h = H(M)$, this implies that $M = M'$ holds as well, except with a negligible probability, which follows from the collision-resistance of the hash function H. □

We finally prove the *consistency* property.

Lemma 11.3 *Let H be a cryptographically-secure collision-resistant hash function. Then protocol $\Pi^{(n,t)}_{\mathsf{CryBAExtHM}}$ achieves t-consistency except with a negligible probability, provided $t < \frac{n}{2}$.*

Proof Let $\mathcal{H}$ be the set of honest parties and let the parties in $\mathcal{H}$ participate in the protocol with *different* inputs. Then there are the following *two* possible cases, depending on whether the honest parties find a CORE set during the checking stage.

- **Case I — The Parties in $\mathcal{H}$ Do Not Find a CORE Set**: In this case, all the parties in $\mathcal{H}$ terminate with the same output 0^L, and hence consistency holds.
- **Case II — The Parties in $\mathcal{H}$ Find a CORE Set**: Let E be the event that the majority of the parties in CORE are *honest* and have the same updated input at the end of the checking stage, say m. Now, conditioned on the event E, all the parties in $\mathcal{H}$ will have a common output at the end of the propagation phase, except with a negligible probability. The proof for this is similar to Claim 10.3, except that we depend upon the collision-resistance property of the hash function H. From Claim 11.4, the event E occurs except with a negligible probability. Hence all the parties in $\mathcal{H}$ will have a common output, except with a negligible probability. □

Theorem 11.1 now follows easily from the above discussion.

Theorem 11.1 *Let the parties have oracle access to a bit-BB oracle for broadcasting bits. Moreover, let H be a cryptographically-secure collision-resistant hash function. If* $t < \frac{n}{2}$*, then protocol* $\Pi^{(n,t)}_{\mathsf{CryBAExtHM}}$ *is a t-secure BA protocol for L-bit messages with cryptographic security in the model* $\mathcal{M}_{\mathsf{auth}}$ *with the following complexities.*[2]

- *The protocol requires* 4 *rounds.*
- *The seed-round complexity of the protocol is* 2.
- *The protocol incurs a communication of* $O(nL+n^3\kappa)+n\cdot\mathcal{BC}(\kappa)+n\cdot\mathcal{BC}(1)$ *bits, where* $\mathcal{BC}(\ell)$ *denotes the communication complexity for emulating one call to the BB oracle with an* ℓ*-bit input.*
- *The seed-communication complexity of the protocol is* $O(n\kappa)$ *bits.*

Minimum Message Size for Optimal Communication Complexity.

By emulating the BB oracle with the cryptographically-secure variant of the Dolev-Strong BB protocol $\Pi^{(n,t)}_{\mathsf{DSBB}}$ in the model $\mathcal{M}^{\mathsf{pki}}_{\mathsf{auth}}$ (see Section 9.2.2), we find that protocol $\Pi^{(n,t)}_{\mathsf{CryBAExtHM}}$ (in the model $\mathcal{M}^{\mathsf{pki}}_{\mathsf{auth}}$) will incur a total communication of $O(nL+n^4\kappa^2)$ bits over the point-to-point channels. This is because $\mathcal{BC}(\ell) = O(n^3\ell\kappa)$ for the protocol $\Pi^{(n,t)}_{\mathsf{DSBB}}$, where κ is the size of a signature in bits. By comparing this with Corollary 10.1, we find that protocol $\Pi^{(n,t)}_{\mathsf{CryBAExtHM}}$ outperforms the statistically-secure domain extension protocol $\Pi^{(n,t)}_{\mathsf{BAExtHM}}$ (Fig 10.5), both in terms of the number of rounds as well as communication complexity.[3]

Since the communication complexity of $\Pi^{(n,t)}_{\mathsf{CryBAExtHM}}$ is $O(nL + n^4\kappa^2)$ bits, it follows that if $L = \Omega(n^3\kappa^2)$, then the *asymptotic* communication complexity of the protocol will be $O(nL)$ bits, which is optimal.

11.3 Open Problems

Even though the seed-round complexity of the protocol $\Pi^{(n,t)}_{\mathsf{CryBAExtHM}}$ is a constant (namely 2), it is *not* optimal.[4] Getting a cryptographically-secure domain extension protocol with optimal resilience of $t < \frac{n}{2}$ and having a seed-round complexity of 1 is an open research problem.

Even though the asymptotic communication complexity of the protocol $\Pi^{(n,t)}_{\mathsf{CryBAExtHM}}$ is *optimal* (namely $O(nL)$ bits), it is optimal only if $L = \Omega(n^3\kappa^2)$ bits. In a re-

[2] We stress that the protocol $\Pi^{(n,t)}_{\mathsf{CryBAExtHM}}$ *does not* need any PKI setup. The setup will be required only to emulate the BB oracle with cryptographic security and $t < \frac{n}{2}$.

[3] Recall that protocol $\Pi^{(n,t)}_{\mathsf{BAExtHM}}$ requires 6 rounds, has a seed-round complexity of 4 and incurs a total communication of $O(nL + (n^4\kappa + n^5)\kappa)$ bits after emulating the BB oracle.

[4] Recall that the optimal seed-round complexity of any domain extension protocol is 1.

cent work [77], this bound on L has been further improved. Namely, they present an extension protocol with cryptographic security which achieves an asymptotic communication complexity of $O(nL)$ bits where $L = \Omega(n^2\kappa^2)$ bits. They deploy *additional* cryptographic primitives, such as multisignatures [26] and cryptographic accumulators [17, 41]. It is an interesting research problem to reduce further the size of L for which one can design an extension protocol with cryptographic security, incurring an asymptotic communication complexity of $O(nL)$ bits and having optimal resilience.

Chapter 12
Domain Extension for Byzantine Broadcast with Dishonest Majority and Statistical Security

In the last two chapters, we have discussed domain extension protocols with setup assumptions, but in the *honest-majority* setting, where $t < \frac{n}{2}$. The next natural question is what can be done in the *dishonest-majority* setting, where $t < n$. Note that in this setting, BA is *impossible*, but only BB is possible.[1] The focus of this and the next chapter will be extension protocols for BB tolerating $t < n$ corruptions. We will present both statistically-secure as well as cryptographically-secure variants. We first consider the statistically-secure variant in this chapter, and the cryptographically-secure variant will be discussed in the next chapter. The protocol presented in this chapter is due to [62].

12.1 The Setting

The protocols presented in this chapter are in the model $\mathcal{M}^{\mathsf{pki}}_{\mathsf{auth}}$, where the PKI setup is unconditionally-secure. The adversary is assumed to be computationally *unbounded* and can corrupt up to t parties in a Byzantine fashion. We assume the parties have oracle access to a bit-BB oracle, allowing them to broadcast bits reliably. Looking ahead, the unconditionally-secure PKI setup is required to emulate the BB oracle when $t < n$.[2] We assume the PKI setup supports the total number of *transferability* required in the extension protocol.

In our protocols, we also use the unconditionally-secure collision-resistant keyed hash function $U : \mathrm{GF}(2^{\kappa}) \times \{0, 1\}^{\ell} \rightarrow \mathrm{GF}(2^{\kappa})$ over $\mathrm{GF}(2^{\kappa})$, where κ denotes the security parameter. Recall that for *any* $m_1, m_2 \in \{0, 1\}^{\ell}$ where $m_1 \neq m_2$, the probability that $U_k(m_1) = U_k(m_2)$ holds for a *randomly* chosen key $k \in \mathrm{GF}(2^{\kappa})$ is at most $2^{-\kappa} \cdot \ell$, which is negligible in κ, provided ℓ is some polynomial function of κ. Looking ahead, the reason for using this specific hash function over $\mathrm{GF}(2^{\kappa})$

[1] Recall that the Dolev-Strong BB protocol remains secure even if $t < n$.

[2] One instantiation of the BB oracle could be the statistically-secure variant of the Dolev-Strong BB protocol $\Pi^{(n,t)}_{\mathsf{DSBB}}$ presented in Chapter 9.

A. Choudhury and A. Patra, *Fault-Tolerant Distributed Consensus in Synchronous Networks*, Information Security and Cryptography,
https://doi.org/10.1007/978-3-031-80460-1_12

is to upper bound the error probability of the extension protocol to $2^{-O(\kappa)}$. We also assume that the input size L of the sender's input for the extension protocol is some polynomial function in κ; i.e. $L = \text{poly}(\kappa)$.

12.2 Statistically-Secure Domain Extension with $t < n$

On a high level, the domain extension protocol broadcasts the long message (namely the sender's input) block by block, where a special broadcast protocol is used to broadcast each block, which we call the block-broadcast protocol. The block-broadcast protocol achieves optimal communication complexity in *optimistic* case when *no* corruption occurs (also called "good" execution), while in the "bad" executions (where corruption occurs), more bits need to be communicated. However, in the latter case, a provision is made to *publicly* identify *disputes* between pairs of parties, where it will be guaranteed that at least one of the parties in the disputed pair is corrupt. Moreover, the disputes are managed in such a way that previously occurred disputes *do not* show up again in the future instances of the block-broadcast protocol. Note that the *maximum* number of disputes is upper bounded by $O(n^2)$. The number of blocks is selected so that good executions outnumber bad ones, and the overall communication complexity is asymptotically optimal. This is reminiscent of the *dispute-control* framework [18], which has been used to design communication-efficient *multi-party computation* (MPC) protocols.

Informally, the dispute-control framework works as follows. The parties globally maintain a publicly-known set $\mathsf{Dispute}$ of unordered pairs of parties across various instances of the block-broadcast protocol, where $(P_i, P_j) \in \mathsf{Dispute}$ represents the fact that P_i and P_j "accuse" each other of behaving maliciously. Initially, $\mathsf{Dispute}$ is set to $\emptyset$. Then, during any instance of the block-broadcast protocol, the parties add new disputes to $\mathsf{Dispute}$ when they learn about new accusations. It will be always ensured that if $(P_i, P_j) \in \mathsf{Dispute}$, then at least one of the parties among P_i and P_j has behaved maliciously.

In the next section, we present the block-broadcast protocol for broadcasting shorter messages. Then, we will use this block-broadcast protocol for broadcasting an L-bit message, block by block q times. In each invocation of the block-broadcast protocol, we will use the global set $\mathsf{Dispute}$ of disputes among the parties. This means that if P_i and P_j are in dispute with each other during any instance of the block-broadcast protocol, then they remain in dispute in all the subsequent invocations of the block-broadcast protocol. We will then compute the communication complexity of the resultant extension protocol and then select q, which will lead to optimal communication complexity.

12.2.1 Staitistically-Secure Block-Broadcast Protocol

The statistically-secure block-broadcast protocol $\Pi^{(n,t)}_{\mathsf{BlockBC}}$ takes input a global set of disputes $\mathsf{Dispute}$ and the input V_s of the sender P_s; the exact size of V_s will be determined later. Throughout the protocol, the parties maintain two global disjoint subsets of $\mathcal{P}$, a set of *happy* parties H and the set $\overline{H} = \mathcal{P} \setminus H$ of *unhappy* parties. The set H will consist of all the parties who have already learned the input V_s, while the remaining parties will be in $\overline{H}$. Initially, only P_s will be present in H. The protocol consists of several iterations, where during each iteration, we try to move one party from $\overline{H}$ to H. For this, we identify a designated pair of parties (P_x, P_y), where $P_x \in H$ and $P_y \in \overline{H}$. Then P_x sends the value it holds to P_y. This procedure is meaningless if P_x and P_y are already in dispute with each other, so the pair is chosen so that $(P_x, P_y) \notin \mathsf{Dispute}$. Once P_y receives a value from P_x, then the next goal is to publicly verify if P_y received the right value or not, such that the communication complexity during the verification is *independent* of the size of V_s. Towards this, the parties deploy an unconditionally-secure hash function over $\mathrm{GF}(2^\kappa)$.

To do the verification, party P_y broadcasts a random key k for the hash function, followed by P_s broadcasting the hash h of its input for this key k. Next, each party in the set $H \cup \{P_y\} \setminus \{P_s\}$ computes a hash of the value it holds for the key k and publicly announces whether the hash matches h by broadcasting a bit. Note that the sender P_s is not allowed to broadcast any bit since an *honest* sender should broadcast only 1, since h was computed by P_s only. Consequently, it is *implicitly* assumed that P_s has broadcasted the bit 1. The idea here is that if the honest parties in the set $H \cup \{P_y\}$ hold different values, then with a high probability, their hash values for the key k will be different, since an honest P_y picks k uniformly at random, after getting P_x's value.

If every party in $H \cup \{P_y\} \setminus \{P_s\}$ broadcasts 1, then it implies that all the honest parties in the set $H \cup \{P_y\}$ now have the same value (with a high probability). Consequently, the iteration is considered to be *successful* and P_y is moved to the set H. Otherwise, some of the parties in the set $H \cup \{P_y\}$ *do not* hold the right value and the iteration is considered to be *unsuccessful*. In this case, the protocol proceeds to search for new disputes.

Note that searching for new disputes is tricky since it is *not* necessary that the dispute is between P_x and P_y as it might be possible that both P_x and P_y broadcasts 1. Similarly, it is *not* necessary that the dispute is between P_s and P_y. This is because P_y may *not* have received the value it holds from P_s (i.e. $P_s \neq P_x$ may hold) or it could be the case that both P_s and P_y have broadcasted 1. One needs to track the entire history of how the set H was formed in prior iterations to find the disputes. For this, inside each iteration, the parties maintain a *history* set T, consisting of pairs of parties (P_i, P_j), such that P_j learnt the value it holds from P_i. Then, to find new disputes, the parties track all the pairs in the set T and identify the pairs $(P_i, P_j) \in T$, where P_i broadcasted 1 but P_j broadcasted 0. Note that it will be guaranteed that the parties find at least one such pair of disputed parties (P_i, P_j), in case the iteration is *unsuccessful*. This is because if we track the sequence of pairs of parties in the set T, then we have P_s who (implicitly) broadcasted 1 and some other party in the sequence, say P_z, who broadcasted 0. Such pairs are then added to the set Dispute, followed by parties *restarting* the protocol, with H being again initialized to $\{P_s\}$ and T being reset to $\emptyset$. For a pictorial illustration of this case, see Fig 12.1.

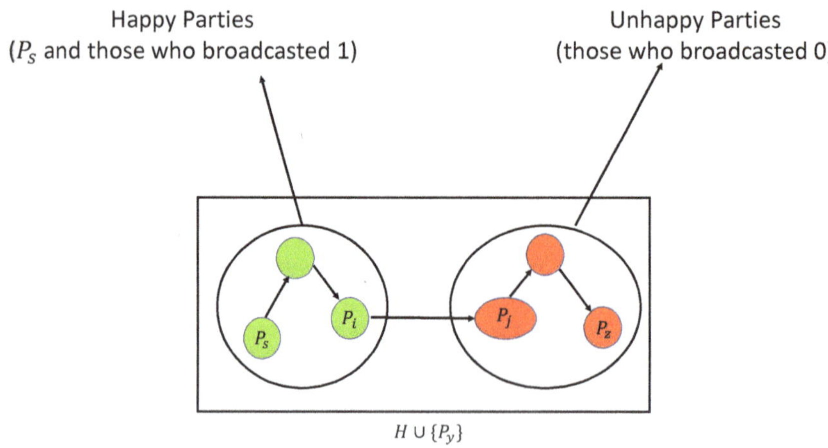

Fig. 12.1: Pictorial illustration of the case when an iteration is unsuccessful in the protocol $\Pi^{(n,t)}_{\mathsf{BlockBC}}$. The parties in $H \cup \{P_y\}$ can be partitioned into two subsets, depending upon whether they broadcasted 1 or 0 in response to the hash value broadcasted by P_s. The subset of parties who are happy and broadcasted 1 are shown in green, and this implicitly includes P_s. The subset of parties who are unhappy and broadcasted 0 are shown in red. The directed arrows show the history of how the set H has been built over the previous iterations, where an arrow from any party P_x to party P_y indicates that $(P_x, P_y) \in T$ and P_y learnt the value it holds from P_x. If an iteration is unsuccessful then it implies that we have P_s remaining happy and some party P_z becoming unhappy. So, if we track the sequence of parties in T, then it is guaranteed that we will find at least one pair of parties $(P_i, P_j) \in T$, such that P_i is happy while P_j is unhappy. Such a pair will be identified and added to the dispute set Dispute

Note that at least one of the parties in every new disputed pair (P_i, P_j) is guaranteed to be *corrupt*. This is because if *both* P_i and P_j are honest, then both of them would have broadcasted the *same* bit (either both of them would broadcast 0 or both of them would broadcast 1), since $(P_i, P_j) \in T$ and P_j learnt the value it holds from P_i. Hence, the response of P_i and P_j for the hash value broadcasted by P_s should be the *same*.

Note that the way set H is computed and maintained, it is *not* necessary to grow monotonically. Some parties may get added or removed from H several times. However, the set Dispute *always* grows monotonically and each unsuccessful iteration will lead to the increase in the size of Dispute set, at least by 1. Once there exists no further candidate pair of non-disputed parties (P_x, P_y) where $P_x \in H$ and $P_y \in \overline{H}$, where P_x could transfer its value to P_y, the protocol gets over. Since the maximum size of Dispute could be $O(n^2)$, it automatically implies that there exists an upper bound on the maximum number of iterations in the protocol. Protocol $\Pi_{\mathsf{BlockBC}}^{(n,t)}$ is formally presented in Fig 12.2. In the protocol, we follow a simplifying convention that if, during a round, a receiver party is expecting some message from a designated sender party and if either no message or a syntactically incorrect message is received, then the receiver party substitutes some default value from the underlying domain on behalf of the sender party and continues the protocol.

Protocol $\Pi_{\mathsf{BlockBC}}^{(n,t)}(V_s)$

Global Input: A publicly-known dispute set Dispute which is a collection of unordered pairs of elements over $\mathcal{P}$.

Public knowledge: the description of the unconditionally-secure collision-resistant hash function U over GF(2^κ). Additionally, the parties have oracle access to a bit-BB oracle.

Initialization: The parties initialize the following sets.
- The set of *happy* parties $H := \{P_s\}$, where $P_s \in \mathcal{P}$ is the designated sender.
- The history set $T := \emptyset$.

Iteration: While $\exists P_x, P_y \in \mathcal{P}$ such that $P_x \in H$ and $P_y \in \overline{H}$ and $(P_x, P_y) \notin$ Dispute, the parties do the following:[a]
- **Round** $(r.1)$: Party P_x sends V_x to P_y and all the parties in $\mathcal{P}$ add (P_x, P_y) to T.
- **Round** $(r.2)$: Let V_y be the value received by P_y from P_x in the previous round. Party P_y picks a uniformly random key $k \in$ GF(2^κ) and calls the BB oracle as a sender with input k to broadcast k. All the parties in $\mathcal{P}$ receive the output k from the BB oracle.
- **Round** $(r.3)$: Sender P_s computes $h := U_k(V_s)$ and calls the BB oracle as a sender with input h to broadcast h. All the parties in $\mathcal{P}$ receive the output h from the BB oracle.
- **Round** $(r.4)$: Every party $P_i \in H \cup \{P_y\} \setminus \{P_s\}$ doe the following.
  - Set $\mathsf{Res}_i := 1$ if $h = U_k(V_i)$ holds, else set $\mathsf{Res}_i := 0$.
  - Call the BB oracle as a sender with input Res_i to broadcast Res_i. All the parties in $\mathcal{P}$ receive the output Res_i from the BB oracle.
- If $\mathsf{Res}_i = 1$ for every party $P_i \in H \cup \{P_y\} \setminus \{P_s\}$, then the parties in $\mathcal{P}$ set $H := H \cup \{P_y\}$, else the parties in $\mathcal{P}$ do the following.
  - For every $(P_i, P_j) \in T$, check if the following holds.
    - $\mathsf{Res}_i = 1$ and $\mathsf{Res}_j = 0$;
    - $P_i = P_s$ and $\mathsf{Res}_j = 0$.

    If any of the above conditions is true, then do the following.
    - Set Dispute := Dispute $\cup \{(P_i, P_j)\}$.
    - Set $H := \{P_s\}$.
    - Set $T := \emptyset$.

(Output computation and termination): Every $P_i \in \mathcal{P}$ computes its output as follows and then terminate.

- If $P_i \in H$, then output V_i;
- Else output $\perp$.

[a] Here $\overline{H} = \mathcal{P} \setminus H$. If there are multiple candidate pairs (P_x, P_y), then parties consider the one where P_x and P_y has the smallest indices.

Fig. 12.2: A statistically-secure broadcast protocol with dispute control for broadcasting a block

We now establish a series of claims which will help to establish the properties of the protocol $\Pi^{(n,t)}_{\mathsf{BlockBC}}$. We first show that if, in any iteration, the set of happy parties H is expanded and if the newly added party is *honest*, then all the honest parties in H are guaranteed to hold a common value, say V, provided all the honest parties in H prior to the expansion held V.

Claim 12.1 Let U be an unconditionally-secure collision-resistant hash function over GF(2^κ). Consider an arbitrary iteration r in the protocol $\Pi^{(n,t)}_{\mathsf{BlockBC}}$, where (P_x, P_y) is the designated pair of parties, where $P_x \in H, P_y \in \overline{H}$ and $(P_x, P_y) \notin \mathsf{Dispute}$ at the beginning of the iteration r. Moreover, let P_y be included in H at the end of the iteration r. Then at the end of iteration r, except with a negligible probability, all honest parties in $H \cup \{P_y\}$ have a common value, say V, provided all the honest parties in H had the value V at the beginning of the iteration r.

Proof Let $\mathcal{H}_H \subseteq H$ be the set of *honest* parties in H and let the premise of the claim be true. This implies that all the parties in $\mathcal{H}_H$ hold the same value, say V, at the beginning of iteration r. Let (P_x, P_y) be the designated pair of parties during the iteration r, where $P_x \in H, P_y \in \overline{H}$ and $(P_x, P_y) \notin \mathsf{Dispute}$. Let at the end of iteration r, party P_y is included in the set H. This implies that every $P_i \in H \cup \{P_y\} \setminus \{P_s\}$ broadcasts $\mathsf{Res}_i = 1$. Now, there are two possible cases, depending upon whether P_y is honest or corrupt.

- **Case I — P_y is Corrupt**: In this case, the claim holds trivially.
- **Case II — P_y is Honest**: In this case, we need to show that $V_y = V$ holds, where V_y denotes the value received by P_y from P_x. If $P_x \in \mathcal{H}_H$, then this is true, since as per our assumption, $V_x = V$ holds and an honest P_x will send V to P_y. On the other hand, consider the case when P_x is *corrupt*. Notice that P_y selects the key k randomly, only *after* receiving V_x from P_x. Since P_y broadcasts $\mathsf{Res}_y = 1$, it implies that P_y verified that $h = U_k(V_y)$ holds, where h is the hash value broadcasted by the sender P_s. On the other hand, since every $P_i \in \mathcal{H}_H$ broadcasts $\mathsf{Res}_i = 1$, it implies that P_i verified that $h = U_k(V_i) = U_k(V)$ holds, where the last equality holds because as per our assumption, $V_i = V$ holds for every $P_i \in \mathcal{H}_H$. This implies that $U_k(V_y) = U_k(V) = h$ holds for a uniformly random key. This further implies that $V_y = V$ holds, except with a negligible probability, which follows from the collision-resistance property of the hash function U. □

We next show that if any iteration in the protocol is "unsuccessful", then at least one *new* conflict is identified.

Claim 12.2 Consider an arbitrary iteration r in the protocol $\Pi^{(n,t)}_{\mathsf{BlockBC}}$, where (P_x, P_y) is the designated pair of parties, where $P_x \in H, P_y \in \overline{H}$ and $(P_x, P_y) \notin \mathsf{Dispute}$ at the beginning of the iteration r. If all the parties $P_i \in H \cup \{P_y\} \setminus \{P_s\}$ do not broadcast $\mathsf{Res}_i = 1$, then at least one new conflict is added to the set $\mathsf{Dispute}$ at the end of iteration r.

Proof Let the premise of the claim be true and let there exist some party $P_i \in H \cup \{P_y\} \setminus \{P_s\}$ who broadcasts $\mathsf{Res}_i = 0$. We consider two cases, depending upon whether all the parties in $H \setminus \{P_s\}$ broadcast 1 or not.

- **Case I — Every $P_i \in H \setminus \{P_s\}$ broadcasts $\mathsf{Res}_i = 1$.** This implies that P_y broadcasted $\mathsf{Res}_y = 0$. Moreover, either $P_x = P_s$ or P_x broadcasted $\mathsf{Res}_x = 1$. Furthermore, $(P_x, P_y) \in T$ holds. Consequently, the dispute (P_x, P_y) will be added to $\mathsf{Dispute}$. We also note that the dispute (P_x, P_y) will *not* be present in the set $\mathsf{Dispute}$ at the beginning of iteration r, as otherwise the parties will *not* be considering the pair of parties (P_x, P_y) during iteration r.
- **Case II — There exists some $P_z \in H \setminus \{P_s\}$ who broadcasts $\mathsf{Res}_z = 0$.** Let P_z be added to the set H during iteration r', where $r' < r$.[3] This implies that during iteration r', there exists a sequence of parties $P_{i_1}, P_{i_2}, \ldots, P_{i_k} \in H$, such that all the following holds:
  - $P_{i_1} = P_s$;
  - $P_{i_k} = P_z$;
  - $(P_{i_j}, P_{i_{j+1}}) \in T$, for $j = 1, \ldots, k-1$.

  Now let us consider the rth iteration, where P_s stayed happy (by default) and P_z became unhappy (since it broadcasted $\mathsf{Res}_z = 0$). Hence in the sequence $P_{i_1}, \ldots, P_{i_k}$, we have both happy and unhappy parties. This further implies that there exist two parties in the sequence, say P_{i_u} and $P_{i_{u+1}}$, where P_{i_u} stays happy and $P_{i_{u+1}}$ becomes unhappy, such that $(P_{i_u}, P_{i_{u+1}}) \in T$. Since $(P_{i_u}, P_{i_{u+1}}) \in T$, it implies that $(P_{i_u}, P_{i_{u+1}}) \notin \mathsf{Dispute}$, as otherwise $(P_{i_u}, P_{i_{u+1}}) \notin T$. Consequently, the pair $(P_{i_u}, P_{i_{u+1}})$ will be identified as a *new* conflict and added to the set $\mathsf{Dispute}$ during iteration r. □

We next prove the "validity" of disputes computed during the protocol by showing that at least one of the disputed parties in every dispute is guaranteed to be corrupt.

Claim 12.3 In protocol $\Pi^{(n,t)}_{\mathsf{BlockBC}}$, if a pair (P_i, P_j) is added to the set $\mathsf{Dispute}$ during any iteration, then either P_i or P_j is corrupt.

Proof From the protocol steps, the pair (P_i, P_j) is added to the set $\mathsf{Dispute}$ only when P_i sends some value V to P_j (implying that $(P_i, P_j) \in T$) and they disagree for some key k whether $U_k(V) = h$ holds or not. However, if *both* P_i as well as P_j are honest, then the disagreement will never happen. Consequently, if (P_i, P_j) is added to the set $\mathsf{Dispute}$, then either P_i or P_j is corrupt. □

[3] The reason $r' < r$ is that in each iteration, at most one new party gets added to the set H and as per our assumption, party P_z is already a part of the set H during iteration r. Hence, it must have been added to the set H earlier.

We finally define the notion of successful and unsuccessful iterations in the protocol $\Pi_{\mathsf{BlockBC}}^{(n,t)}$. Informally, an iteration is considered successful if a new party gets added to the happy set of parties; otherwise, the iteration is considered unsuccessful. More formally, we have the following definition.

Definition 12.1 Consider an arbitrary iteration r in the protocol $\Pi_{\mathsf{BlockBC}}^{(n,t)}$, We say that the iteration r is *successful*, if the set H gets expanded by one, otherwise the iteration is called *unsuccessful*.

From the above definition, it follows that if an iteration succeeds, one new party gets added to the set H. On the other hand, from Claim 12.2, it follows that if an iteration is unsuccessful, all honest parties will identify at least one *new* dispute.

We are now well-equipped to prove the properties of the protocol. We start with the *liveness* property by showing that there is always an upper bound on the maximum number of rounds within which the honest parties will terminate the protocol.

Claim 12.4 Let $\mathsf{Dispute}_{\mathsf{start}}$ and $\mathsf{Dispute}_{\mathsf{end}}$ be the $\mathsf{Dispute}$ set at the beginning and the end of the protocol $\Pi_{\mathsf{BlockBC}}^{(n,t)}$ respectively. Moreover, let the parties have oracle access to a BB oracle. Then in the protocol $\Pi_{\mathsf{BlockBC}}^{(n,t)}$ the honest parties are guaranteed to terminate within $4(n + nd)$ rounds, where $d \stackrel{def}{=} |\mathsf{Dispute}_{\mathsf{end}}| - |\mathsf{Dispute}_{\mathsf{start}}|$.

Proof Let us consider any arbitrary iteration r in the protocol and compute the number of rounds in that iteration. From the protocol description, it is easy to see that there are 4 rounds in each iteration. Next, we find the maximum number of iterations possible in the protocol.

There can be at most $n - 1$ *consecutive* successful iterations, after which the protocol will terminate, since $H = \mathcal{P}$ and $\overline{H} = \emptyset$ will hold after $n - 1$ consecutive successful iterations. On the other hand, as mentioned earlier, after each unsuccessful iteration, the number of disputes increases at least by 1. We also note that the maximum number of disputes that can occur is upper bounds by n^2. This implies that an upper bound exists for the maximum number of iterations. Let us next compute that upper bound.

As per the premise of the claim, there are d unsuccessful iterations in the protocol since d new disputes have been identified. In the worst case, there can be up to $n-2$ consecutive successful iterations, followed by an unsuccessful iteration, which leads to resetting the set H to the singleton set $\{P_s\}$. This can happen for d times, leading to $d(n-2+1) = d(n-1)$ iterations. After this, there can be $n-1$ consecutive successful iterations. Hence, the maximum number of iterations will be $(n-1)+d(n-1) \leq n+nd$. Since each iteration will require 4 rounds, all honest parties will terminate the protocol after $4(n + nd)$ rounds. □

We next derive the round and communication complexity of the protocol, which follows from the proof of the previous claim.

Lemma 12.1 *Let* $\mathsf{Dispute}_{\mathsf{start}}$ *and* $\mathsf{Dispute}_{\mathsf{end}}$ *be the* $\mathsf{Dispute}$ *set at the beginning and at the end of the protocol* $\Pi_{\mathsf{BlockBC}}^{(n,t)}$ *respectively and let* $d \stackrel{def}{=} |\mathsf{Dispute}_{\mathsf{end}}| - |\mathsf{Dispute}_{\mathsf{start}}|$. *Moreover, let the parties have oracle access to a BB oracle for broadcasting bits. Then protocol* $\Pi_{\mathsf{BlockBC}}^{(n,t)}$ *achieves the following.*

– *The protocol requires at most* $4(n + nd)$ *rounds.*
– *The seed-round complexity of the protocol is* $O(nd)$.
– *The protocol incurs a communication of at most* $(n{+}nd)(|V_s|{+}\mathcal{BC}(\kappa){+}n{\cdot}\mathcal{BC}(1))$ *bits. Here* $|V_s|$ *denotes the size of the input* V_s *in bits, and* $\mathcal{BC}(\ell)$ *denotes the communication complexity of emulating one instance of the BB oracle where the input of the designated sender party is of size* ℓ *bits.*
– *The seed-communication complexity of the protocol is* $O(nd\kappa + n^2d)$ *bits.*

Proof The maximum number of rounds $4(n+nd)$ follows directly from the proof of Claim 12.4. From the protocol description, in each iteration, there are *three* rounds where the BB oracle is called. Since the maximum number of iterations could be $n+nd$, it implies that the seed-round complexity of the protocol is at most $3(n+nd)$, which is $O(nd)$.

In each iteration, a designated party P_x from H sends its version of V_s to another designated receiver party P_y in $\overline{H}$. This is followed by party P_y broadcasting a random hash-key of size κ bits, followed by the sender P_s broadcasting the hash of its input V_s of size κ bits, followed by all the parties in $H \cup \{P_y\} \setminus \{P_s\}$ broadcasting their response bit, where all broadcast instances happen by calling the BB oracle. Hence each iteration involves a total communication of at most $(|V_s| + \mathcal{BC}(\kappa) + n \cdot \mathcal{BC}(1))$ bits. Since the maximum number of iterations could be $n + nd$, it implies that the maximum number of bits communicated in the protocol by the honest parties is $(n{+}nd)(|V_s|{+}\mathcal{BC}(\kappa){+}n{\cdot}\mathcal{BC}(1))$. This automatically implies a seed-communication complexity of $O(nd\kappa + n^2d)$ bits. □

To prove the validity and consistency properties, we next show that at the end of the protocol, either all honest parties belong to the happy set H or the unhappy set $\overline{H}$.

Claim 12.5 In protocol $\Pi^{(n,t)}_{\mathsf{BlockBC}}$, one of the following holds at the end of the protocol.
– All honest parties are in the set H. Moreover, they output a common value different from $\perp$, except with a negligible probability.
– All honest parties are in the set $\overline{H}$ and output $\perp$.

Proof We first show that at the end of the protocol, there *does not* exist any pair of *honest* parties (P_x, P_y), where $P_x \in \mathcal{H}$ and $P_y \in \overline{H}$. From Claim 12.3, throughout the protocol, any pair of honest parties *does not* get added to the dispute set $\mathsf{Dispute}$. Hence, if at the end of the protocol, there exists a pair of honest parties (P_x, P_y), where $P_x \in \mathcal{H}$ and $P_y \in \overline{H}$, then it implies that $(P_x, P_y) \notin \mathsf{Dispute}$. This further implies that the while loop *does not* terminate and hence the honest parties *do not* terminate the protocol, which is a contradiction. Hence, at the end of the protocol, all honest parties are in H, or all honest parties are in $\overline{H}$.

Since all the honest parties in $\overline{H}$ output $\perp$, it follows that if all honest parties are in $\overline{H}$, they output $\perp$. On the other hand, the honest parties in H output the value (namely the version of V_s) they hold. From Claim 12.1, the value held by all honest parties in H at the end of the protocol will be *same*, except with a negligible probability. So if all honest parties are in H, they will have a common output, different from $\perp$, except with a negligible probability. This completes the proof of the claim. □

The *validity* property now follows from the previous claim since the set of happy parties is initialized with the sender P_s.

Lemma 12.2 *Protocol* $\Pi^{(n,t)}_{\mathsf{BlockBC}}$ *achieves t-validity, except with a negligible probability.*

Proof Let P_s be *honest*. The set H is initialized to $\{P_s\}$ in the protocol. From Claim 12.5, it follows that at the end of the protocol, all honest parties will be present in the set H. Moreover, all honest parties in H will output a common value, except with a negligible probability. Since $P_s \in H$ and outputs V_s, all honest parties will output V_s, except with a negligible probability, thus proving the lemma. □

The *consistency* property also follows from the previous claim, since at the end of the protocol, all honest parties *together* are either happy or unhappy.

Lemma 12.3 *Protocol* $\Pi^{(n,t)}_{\mathsf{BlockBC}}$ *achieves t-consistency, except with a negligible probability.*

Proof Let $\mathcal{H}$ be the set of *honest* parties. From Claim 12.5, at the end of the protocol, either $\mathcal{H} \subseteq H$ or $\mathcal{H} \subseteq \overline{H}$.

If $\mathcal{H} \subseteq H$, then from Claim 12.5 it follows that all the parties in $\mathcal{H}$ output a common value, different from $\perp$, except with a negligible probability.

On the other hand, from Claim 12.5, it follows that if $\mathcal{H} \subseteq \overline{H}$, then all the parties in $\mathcal{H}$ output $\perp$. Hence, in either case, the consistency property is achieved. □

Theorem 12.1 now follows easily from the above discussion.

Theorem 12.1 *Let* $\mathsf{Dispute}_{\mathsf{start}}$ *and* $\mathsf{Dispute}_{\mathsf{end}}$ *be the* $\mathsf{Dispute}$ *set at the beginning and the end of the protocol* $\Pi^{(n,t)}_{\mathsf{BlockBC}}$ *respectively and let* $d \stackrel{def}{=} |\mathsf{Dispute}_{\mathsf{end}}| - |\mathsf{Dispute}_{\mathsf{start}}|$. *Moreover, let the parties have oracle access to a BB oracle for broadcasting bits. Furthermore, let U be an unconditionally-secure collision-resistant hash function over* $GF(2^{\kappa})$. *Then protocol* $\Pi^{(n,t)}_{\mathsf{BlockBC}}$ *is a t-secure BB protocol with statistical security, for any* $t < n$ *in the model* $\mathcal{M}_{\mathsf{auth}}$.[4] *The protocol has the following complexities.*

- *The protocol requires at most* $4(n + nd)$ *rounds.*
- *The seed-round complexity of the protocol is* $O(nd)$.
- *The protocol incurs a communication of at most* $(n+nd)(|V_s|+\mathcal{BC}(\kappa)+n\cdot\mathcal{BC}(1))$ *bits. Here* $|V_s|$ *denotes the size of the input* V_s *in bits, and* $\mathcal{BC}(\ell)$ *denotes the communication complexity of emulating one instance of the BB oracle where the input of the designated sender party is of size* ℓ *bits.*
- *The seed-communication complexity of the protocol is* $O(nd\kappa + n^2 d)$ *bits.*

12.2.2 The Domain Extension Protocol

The statistically-secure domain extension BC protocol $\Pi^{(n,t)}_{\mathsf{BCExtDM}}$ with a dishonest majority is formally presented in Fig 12.3. In the protocol, the sender divides its

[4] We stress that the protocol $\Pi^{(n,t)}_{\mathsf{BlockBC}}$ *does not* need any PKI setup. The setup will be required only to emulate the BB oracle with statistical security and $t < n$.

input $m \in \{0, 1\}^L$ into q blocks, each of size $\frac{L}{q}$ bits (some default padding can be done if required). It then invokes q instances of the block-broadcast protocol $\Pi^{(n,t)}_{\mathsf{BlockBC}}$, where for $k = 1, \ldots, q$, the kth instance is used to broadcast the kth block of m. Note that the instances of $\Pi^{(n,t)}_{\mathsf{BlockBC}}$ are executed *sequentially*, so that the disputes which occur in the previous instances of $\Pi^{(n,t)}_{\mathsf{BlockBC}}$ carry over to the subsequent instances. Once all the q instances are over, the parties decide their output as follows: if any of the instances of $\Pi^{(n,t)}_{\mathsf{BlockBC}}$ output $\perp$ (implying that P_s is corrupt), then $\perp$ is set as the overall output. Otherwise, the overall output is set as the concatenation of the outputs from the q instances of $\Pi^{(n,t)}_{\mathsf{BlockBC}}$.

The validity of the block-broadcast protocol $\Pi^{(n,t)}_{\mathsf{BlockBC}}$ will ensure that none of the instances of $\Pi^{(n,t)}_{\mathsf{BlockBC}}$ will produce $\perp$ as the output, if P_s is *honest* (with a high probability). Consequently, if P_s is honest, all honest parties will output m (with a high probability), thus guaranteeing validity for the overall protocol. On the other hand, even if P_s is *corrupt*, the consistency of the block-broadcast protocol guarantees that all honest parties will get a common output from each instance of $\Pi^{(n,t)}_{\mathsf{BlockBC}}$ (with a high probability), thus guaranteeing consistency for the overall protocol. Looking ahead, we will show that if we set q to n^2, the protocol achieves the optimal communication complexity of $O(nL)$ bits asymptotically.

Protocol $\Pi^{(n,t)}_{\mathsf{BCExtDM}}(m, q)$

Public knowledge: the description of the unconditionally-secure collision-resistant hash function U over GF(2^κ). Additionally, the parties have oracle access to a bit-BB oracle.

Initialization: The parties in $\mathcal{P}$ initialize the dispute set $\mathsf{Dispute} := \emptyset$. The sender P_s divides its input $m \in \{0, 1\}^L$ into q blocks $m^{(1)}, \ldots, m^{(q)}$, where a padding is added if required.

(Broadcasting individual blocks): For $k = 1, \ldots, q$, the parties in $\mathcal{P}$ do the following.
- The sender P_s invokes an instance $\Pi^{(n,t)}_{\mathsf{BlockBC}}(m^{(k)})$ of the protocol Π_{BlockBC} and the parties in $\mathcal{P}$ participate in this instance.
- For $i = 1, \ldots, n$, let $m_i^{(k)}$ be the output obtained by the party P_i during the instance $\Pi^{(n,t)}_{\mathsf{BlockBC}}(m^{(k)})$.

(Output computation and termination): For $i = 1, \ldots, n$, party P_i computes its output as follows and then terminate.
- If $m_i^{(k)} = \perp$ for any $k \in \{1, \ldots, q\}$, then set 0^L as the output;
- Else set $m_i^{(1)} || \ldots || m_i^{(q)}$ as the output.

Fig. 12.3: A statistically-secure domain extension protocol for broadcast with a dishonest majority

We now prove the properties of the protocol $\Pi^{(n,t)}_{\mathsf{BCExtDM}}$. We start with the derivation of round and communication complexity.

Lemma 12.4 *Let the parties have oracle access to a BB oracle for broadcasting bits. Then protocol* $\Pi^{(n,t)}_{\mathsf{BCExtDM}}$ *have the following complexities.*
- *The protocol requires at most* $4(nq + n^3)$ *rounds.*
- *The seed-round complexity of the protocol is* $O(nq + n^3)$.

– *The protocol incurs a communication of at most* $(nq+n^3)(\frac{L}{q}+\mathcal{BC}(\kappa)+n\cdot\mathcal{BC}(1))$ *bits. Here L is the number of bits in the sender's input, and* $\mathcal{BC}(\ell)$ *denotes the communication complexity of emulating one call to the BB oracle where the input of the sender party is of size* ℓ *bits.*
– *The seed-communication complexity of the protocol is* $O(nq\kappa + n^3\kappa + n^2q + n^4)$ *bits.*

Proof For $k = 1, \ldots, q$, let d_k be the number of disputes occurring during the instance $\Pi^{(n,t)}_{\mathsf{BlockBC}}(m^{(k)})$ of Π_{BlockBC}. We note that the following holds.

$$\sum_{k=1}^{q} d_k \le n^2.$$

This is because the maximum number of disputes which can occur across all instances of $\Pi^{(n,t)}_{\mathsf{BlockBC}}$ is at most $nt \le n^2$. This follows from the fact that there can be at most t corrupt parties and from Claim 12.3, a dispute *never* occurs between two honest parties. Moreover, from Claim 12.2 any dispute which has already occurred during any earlier instance of $\Pi^{(n,t)}_{\mathsf{BlockBC}}$ never occurs during any subsequent instance of $\Pi^{(n,t)}_{\mathsf{BlockBC}}$.

From Lemma 12.1, the instance $\Pi^{(n,t)}_{\mathsf{BlockBC}}(m^{(k)})$ of $\Pi^{(n,t)}_{\mathsf{BlockBC}}$ requires at most $4(n + nd_k)$ rounds. As there are q instances of $\Pi^{(n,t)}_{\mathsf{BlockBC}}$, the total number of rounds is as follows.

$$\sum_{k=1}^{q} 4(n + nd_k) \le 4(nq + n^3),$$

where the last equality follows because, as argued earlier, the summation of the number of disputes d_k across the q instances of Π_{BlockBC} is upper-bounded by n^2.

From Lemma 12.1, the instance $\Pi^{(n,t)}_{\mathsf{BlockBC}}(m^{(k)})$ of $\Pi^{(n,t)}_{\mathsf{BlockBC}}$ will have a seed-round complexity of at most $3(n + nd_k)$. As there are q instances of $\Pi^{(n,t)}_{\mathsf{BlockBC}}$, the total seed-round complexity is as follows.

$$\sum_{k=1}^{q} 3(n + nd_k),$$

which is $O(nq + n^3)$. This is because the summation of the number of disputes d_k across the q instances of Π_{BlockBC} is upper-bounded by n^2.

From Lemma 12.1, the instance $\Pi^{(n,t)}_{\mathsf{BlockBC}}(m^{(k)})$ of $\Pi^{(n,t)}_{\mathsf{BlockBC}}$ will incur a communication of at most $(n+nd_k)(|m^{(k)}|+\mathcal{BC}(\kappa)+n\cdot\mathcal{BC}(1))$ bits, where $|m^{(k)}| = \frac{L}{q}$. As there are q instances of $\Pi^{(n,t)}_{\mathsf{BlockBC}}$, the total communication complexity is as follows.

$$\sum_{k=1}^{q} (n + nd_k)(|m^{(k)}| + \mathcal{BC}(\kappa) + n \cdot \mathcal{BC}(1)),$$

which is $(nq + n^3)(\frac{L}{q} + \mathcal{BC}(\kappa) + n \cdot \mathcal{BC}(1))$. This is because the summation of the number of disputes d_k across the q instances of Π_{BlockBC} is upper-bounded by n^2. Consequently, the seed-communication complexity of the protocol is $O(nq\kappa + n^3\kappa + n^2q + n^4)$ bits. □

We next prove the validity property of the protocol, which follows from the validity property of the block-broadcast protocol.

Lemma 12.5 *Protocol* $\Pi^{(n,t)}_{\text{BCExtDM}}$ *achieves t-validity, except with a negligible probability.*

Proof Let $\mathcal{H}$ be the set of *honest* parties and let $P_s \in \mathcal{H}$, who has input m. Then from the *t-validity* of $\Pi^{(n,t)}_{\text{BlockBC}}$ (Lemma 12.2), it follows that for $k = 1, \ldots, q$, each $P_i \in \mathcal{H}$ will compute the output $m_i^{(k)}$ during the instance $\Pi^{(n,t)}_{\text{BlockBC}}(m^{(k)})$, where $m_i^{(k)} = m^{(k)}$ will hold, except with a negligible probability. Consequently, $m_i^{(1)}||\ldots||m_i^{(q)} = m$ will hold for each $P_i \in \mathcal{H}$, except with a negligible probability and hence each honest party will output m, except with a negligible probability. □

We next prove the protocol's consistency property, which follows from the consistency property of the block-broadcast protocol.

Lemma 12.6 *Protocol* $\Pi^{(n,t)}_{\text{BCExtDM}}$ *achieves t-consistency, except with a negligible probability.*

Proof Let $\mathcal{H}$ be the set of *honest* parties. From the *t-consistency* of $\Pi^{(n,t)}_{\text{BlockBC}}$ (Lemma 12.3), it follows that for $k = 1, \ldots, q$, all the parties in $\mathcal{H}$ will compute a *common* output at the end of the instance $\Pi^{(n,t)}_{\text{BlockBC}}(m^{(k)})$, except with a negligible probability. Now, there are two possible cases, depending upon whether any of these instances of $\Pi^{(n,t)}_{\text{BlockBC}}(m^{(k)})$ produces an output $\perp$ or not.

- **Case I — There exists some $k \in \{1, \ldots, q\}$ where the parties in $\mathcal{H}$ compute the output $\perp$ during the instance $\Pi^{(n,t)}_{\text{BlockBC}}(m^{(k)})$:** In this case, all the parties in $\mathcal{H}$ will output 0^L, hence achieving consistency.
- **Case II — There exists no $k \in \{1, \ldots, q\}$ where the parties in $\mathcal{H}$ compute the output $\perp$ during the instance $\Pi^{(n,t)}_{\text{BlockBC}}(m^{(k)})$:** In this case, from Lemma 12.3, the condition $m_i^{(k)} = m_j^{(k)}$ holds, for every $k \in \{1, \ldots, q\}$ and every $P_i, P_j \in \mathcal{H}$, except with a negligible probability. Consequently, except with a negligible probability, all the parties in $\mathcal{H}$ will have a common output, different from $\perp$, at the end of the protocol. Hence, consistency is achieved in this case as well. □

The following theorem now follows easily from the above discussion.

Theorem 12.2 *Let the parties have oracle access to a bit-BB oracle for broadcasting bits. Moreover, let U be an unconditionally-secure collision-resistant hash function over* $GF(2^\kappa)$. *Then protocol* $\Pi^{(n,t)}_{\text{BCExtDM}}$ *is a t-secure BB protocol with statistical security in the model* $\mathcal{M}_{\text{auth}}$, *for any* $t < n$.[5] *The protocol has the following complexities.*

[5] We stress that the protocol $\Pi^{(n,t)}_{\text{BCExtDM}}$ *does not* need any PKI setup. The setup will be required only to emulate the BB oracle with statistical security and $t < n$.

– *The protocol requires at most* $4(nq + n^3)$ *rounds.*
– *The seed-round complexity of the protocol is* $O(nq + n^3)$.
– *The protocol incurs a communication of at most* $(nq+n^3)(\frac{L}{q}+\mathcal{BC}(\kappa)+n\cdot\mathcal{BC}(1))$ *bits. Here, L is the number of bits in the sender's input, and* $\mathcal{BC}(\ell)$ *denotes the communication complexity of emulating one call to the BB oracle where the input of the sender party is of size* ℓ *bits.*
– *The seed-communication complexity of the protocol is* $O(nq\kappa + n^3\kappa + n^2q + n^4)$ *bits.*

An immediate corollary of Theorem 12.2 is that if we set $q = n^2$, then the protocol achieves the *optimal* communication complexity asymptotically.

Corollary 12.1 *In protocol* $\Pi^{(n,t)}_{\mathsf{BCExtDM}}$, *if* $q = n^2$, *then the protocol achieves the following.*
– *The protocol requires at most* $4n^3$ *rounds.*
– *The seed-round complexity of the protocol is* $O(n^3)$.
– *The protocol incurs a communication of* $O(nL) + n^3 \cdot \mathcal{BC}(\kappa)$ *bits.*
– *The seed-communication complexity of the protocol is* $O(n^3\kappa + n^4)$ *bits.*

Minimum Message Size for Optimal Communication Complexity.

By emulating the BB oracle with the statistically-secure variant of the Dolev-Strong BB protocol $\Pi^{(n,t)}_{\mathsf{DSBB}}$ in the model $\mathcal{M}^{\mathsf{pki}}_{\mathsf{auth}}$ (see Section 9.2.2), we find that protocol $\Pi^{(n,t)}_{\mathsf{BCExtDM}}$ (in the model $\mathcal{M}^{\mathsf{pki}}_{\mathsf{auth}}$) will incur a total communication of $O(nL + n^6\kappa^2)$ bits over the point-to-point channels, where κ is the security parameter and denotes the size of a pseudo-signature in bits. This is because $\mathcal{BC}(\ell) = O(n^3\ell\kappa)$ for the protocol $\Pi^{(n,t)}_{\mathsf{DSBB}}$. It follows that if $L = \Omega(n^5\kappa^2)$, then the communication complexity of the protocol will be $O(nL)$ bits, which is *asymptotically* optimal.

12.3 Open Problems

Unlike the extension protocols presented till now in the *honest-majority* setting, the seed-round complexity of the protocol $\Pi^{(n,t)}_{\mathsf{BCExtDM}}$ is *not* a constant (namely, it is $O(n^3)$). The work of [32] presents a statistically-secure BB extension protocol with $t < n$, where the seed-round complexity is reduced to $O(n^2)$. It is not known whether this can be further improved or not, which is a very interesting open research problem.

Even though the asymptotic communication complexity of the protocol $\Pi^{(n,t)}_{\mathsf{BCExtDM}}$ and the protocol presented in [32] is *optimal* (namely $O(nL)$ bits), the optimality kicks in only if L is significantly large (for instance, $L = \Omega(n^5\kappa^2)$ for the protocol $\Pi^{(n,t)}_{\mathsf{BCExtDM}}$). It is an interesting research problem to reduce further the size of L for which one can design an extension protocol in the dishonest-majority setting with statistical security, incurring an asymptotic communication complexity of $O(nL)$ bits.

Chapter 13
Domain Extension for Byzantine Broadcast with Dishonest Majority and Cryptographic Security

In this chapter, we continue our discussion on domain extension protocols for BB in the *dishonest majority* setting (i.e. with $t < n$). However, *instead* of statistical security, we will focus on cryptographic security, where the adversary is assumed to be *computationally bounded*. We show that by replacing the unconditionally-secure collision-resistant hash function in the protocol $\Pi_{\mathsf{BCExtDM}}^{(n,t)}$ (Fig 12.3) with a cryptographically-secure collision-resistant hash function, one can significantly simplify the protocol design and improve the protocol's seed-round complexity and communication complexity. This shows a trade-off between the level of security achieved and the complexity of the resultant protocols. The protocol presented in this chapter is due to [62].

13.1 The Setting

The setting considered in this chapter is almost the same as that in the previous chapter, except with the following *differences*:

- Instead of considering a computationally-unbounded adversary, we consider a computationally-bounded adversary, who can corrupt up to t parties in a Byzantine fashion.
- Since we will be dealing with computationally-bounded adversaries, instead of assuming the setup of an unconditionally-secure PKI, we will assume the setup for a cryptographically-secure PKI.

The protocol presented in this chapter will be in the model $\mathcal{M}_{\mathsf{auth}}^{\mathsf{pki}}$. We assume the parties have oracle access to a bit-BB oracle for broadcasting bits. Looking ahead, the cryptographically-secure PKI setup is required to instantiate the BB oracle with a *t-secure* BB protocol with cryptographic security and $t < n$.[1]

[1] One instantiation of the oracle with $t < n$ and cryptographic security could be the cryptographically-secure variant of the Dolev-Strong BB protocol $\Pi_{\mathsf{DSBB}}^{(n,t)}$ presented in Chapter 9.

A. Choudhury and A. Patra, *Fault-Tolerant Distributed Consensus in Synchronous Networks*, Information Security and Cryptography,
https://doi.org/10.1007/978-3-031-80460-1_13

In our protocols, we also use a *cryptographically-secure collision-resistant* hash function $\mathsf{H} : \{0,1\}^{\ell} \rightarrow \{0,1\}^{\kappa}$. Recall that the collision-resistance guarantees that it is infeasible for any PPT algorithm to output a pair of *distinct* messages (m, m'), such that $\mathsf{H}(m) = \mathsf{H}(m')$ holds, except with some negligible probability in κ. We also assume that the input size L of the sender's input in the extension protocol is some polynomial function of the security parameter κ; i.e. $L = \text{poly}(\kappa)$.

13.2 Cryptographically-Secure Domain Extension

In this section, we will present a cryptographically-secure variant of the protocol $\Pi^{(n,t)}_{\mathsf{BCExtDM}}$ (Fig 12.3), presented in the previous chapter. The idea behind the protocol is to broadcast the sender's message block-by-block by dividing the sender's message into q blocks and broadcasting each block through a block-broadcast protocol. The block-broadcast protocol will be based on the dispute-control framework and achieves optimal communication if no cheating occurs. However, if any cheating occurs, it will be detected, and the parties will publicly identify at least one new disputed pair of parties who remain in dispute for all the subsequent invocations of the block-broadcast protocol. Identifying new disputes will require more communication. However, as done in the protocol $\Pi^{(n,t)}_{\mathsf{BCExtDM}}$, the number of blocks q will be selected in such a way that the number of "good" executions (where no fault occurs) will outnumber the number of "bad" executions (where faults occur), and overall, the protocol achieves optimal communication complexity (asymptotically). As we will show later, *unlike* the protocol $\Pi^{(n,t)}_{\mathsf{BCExtDM}}$ where q needs to be set to n^2 to achieve optimal communication complexity, setting q to n will suffice now to achieve the optimal communication complexity.

We next present the block-broadcast protocol, which is a cryptographically-secure variant of the block-broadcast protocol $\Pi^{(n,t)}_{\mathsf{BlockBC}}$ (Fig 12.2).

13.2.1 Cryptographically-Secure Block-Broadcast Protocol

The cryptographically-secure block-broadcast protocol $\Pi^{(n,t)}_{\mathsf{CryBlockBC}}$ takes input a block V_s, which is the message which the sender P_s would like to broadcast, along with publicly-known pairs of disputed parties $\mathsf{Dispute}$. During the protocol, the set of parties is divided into two sets: the set of parties H who already have learnt V_s and the remaining parties $\overline{H}$ who are yet to learn V_s. Initially, only P_s is present in H. At the beginning of the protocol, P_s broadcasts a cryptographic-hash of V_s. The protocol consists of several iterations, and during each iteration, we try to move a new party from $\overline{H}$ to H. For this, we select a designated pair of parties (P_x, P_y) who are *not* in dispute with each other, such that $P_x \in H$ and $P_y \in \overline{H}$ and ask P_x to send the value it holds (which is supposed to be V_s) to P_y. Upon receiving the value, the next goal will be to let P_y verify whether it has received the correct value. For this, party P_y compares the hash of the received value with the public-hash which P_s broadcasted at the beginning of the protocol and announces the result of the comparison publicly. If the result is positive, then it implies that P_y received the right value, and so it is moved from $\overline{H}$ to H, and the iteration is considered to be "successful". Otherwise, it implies that either P_x sent an incorrect value to P_y or P_y made an incorrect result public. Consequently, the pair (P_x, P_y) is added to the set of disputed parties Dispute and the iteration is considered to be "unsuccessful". The protocol stops when there are *no* more candidate pairs of non-disputed parties (P_x, P_y) where $P_x \in H$ and $P_y \in \overline{H}$. The parties in H output their value, while those in $\overline{H}$ output $\perp$. Clearly, the protocol has an upper bound on the maximum number of iterations. This is because each successful iteration increases the size of H by one, and the maximum size of H could be n. On the other hand, each unsuccessful iteration will increase the size of Dispute by one, and the maximum size of Dispute could be n^2.

Even though the idea behind the protocol $\Pi^{(n,t)}_{\mathsf{CryBlockBC}}$ is similar to that of the statistically-secure block-broadcast protocol $\Pi^{(n,t)}_{\mathsf{BlockBC}}$, there are several differences, with the key difference being the sender P_s publicly broadcasting a cryptographic-hash of its input V_s at the beginning of the protocol. This significantly simplifies the verification process for each designated receiver party P_y to verify whether it has received the right value from the designated sender party P_x during each iteration. Namely, P_y needs to compute the hash of the value received from P_x and compare it with the public-hash available.[2] Moreover, to find disputes, the parties *need not* have to maintain the history of how the set H is built over the past iterations. This is because if P_y gets unhappy, it is clear that either P_x is corrupt or P_y. As a result, *unlike* the protocol $\Pi^{(n,t)}_{\mathsf{BlockBC}}$, the set H grows monotonically. This further leads to the reduction in the maximum number of iterations in the protocol, which in turn will lead to the reduction in the number of blocks q to be used in the actual domain extension protocol where $\Pi^{(n,t)}_{\mathsf{CryBlockBC}}$ will be used for broadcasting the sub-blocks of P_s's input. Protocol $\Pi^{(n,t)}_{\mathsf{CryBlockBC}}$ is formally presented in Fig 13.1. In the protocol, we follow a simplifying convention that if, during a round, a receiver party is expecting some message from a designated sender party and if either no message or a syntactically incorrect message is received, then the receiver party substitutes some default value from the underlying domain on behalf of the sender party and continues the protocol.

Protocol $\Pi^{(n,t)}_{\mathsf{CryBlockBC}}(V_s)$

Global Input: A publicly-known dispute set Dispute which is a collection of unordered pairs of elements over $\mathcal{P}$.

[2] We stress that this idea will *not* work with an unconditionally-secure hash function since such functions are keyed functions and produce *different* outputs for the same input for different keys. Consequently, the verifying party must first make public the key with which verification needs to be performed, followed by the respective parties computing and making the hash public.

Public knowledge: the description of a cryptographically-secure collision-resistant hash function H. Additionally, the parties have oracle access to a bit-BB oracle.

Initialization: The parties initialize the set of *happy* parties $H := \{P_s\}$, where $P_s \in \mathcal{P}$ is the designated sender.

Round 1 (broadcasting the hash of input): P_s computes $h := \mathsf{H}(V_s)$ and calls the BB oracle as a sender with input h to broadcast h. All the parties in $\mathcal{P}$ receive the output h from the BB oracle.

Iteration: While $\exists P_x, P_y \in \mathcal{P}$ such that $P_x \in H$ and $P_y \in \overline{H}$ and $(P_x, P_y) \notin \mathsf{Dispute}$, the parties do the following:[a]

- **Round** $(r.1)$: Party P_x sends V_x to P_y.
- **Round** $(r.2)$: Let V_y be the value received by P_y from P_x in the previous round. Party P_y acts as a sender and calls the BB oracle with input b to broadcast the bit b, where $b = 1$ if and only if $h = \mathsf{H}(V_y)$ holds. All the parties in $\mathcal{P}$ receive the output b from the BB oracle.
- If $b = 1$, then the parties in $\mathcal{P}$ set $H := H \cup \{P_y\}$, else they set $\mathsf{Dispute} := \mathsf{Dispute} \cup \{(P_x, P_y)\}$.

(output computation and termination): Every $P_i \in \mathcal{P}$ computes its output as follows and then terminate.

- If $P_i \in H$, then output V_i;
- Else output $\perp$.

[a] Here $\overline{H} = \mathcal{P} \setminus H$. If there are multiple candidate pairs (P_x, P_y), then parties consider the one where P_x and P_y has the smallest indices.

Fig. 13.1: A cryptographically-secure broadcast protocol with dispute control for broadcasting a block

The properties of the protocol $\Pi^{(n,t)}_{\mathsf{CryBlockBC}}$ can be established in a similar way as done for the protocol $\Pi^{(n,t)}_{\mathsf{BlockBC}}$, except that we now rely on the collision-resistance of the hash function H. We first show that the parties in H hold a common value throughout the protocol, different from $\perp$ (with a high probability).

Claim 13.1 Consider an arbitrary iteration r in the protocol $\Pi^{(n,t)}_{\mathsf{CryBlockBC}}$, where (P_x, P_y) is the designated pair of parties, where $P_x \in H, P_y \in \overline{H}$ and $(P_x, P_y) \notin \mathsf{Dispute}$ at the beginning of the iteration r. Moreover, let P_y be included in H at the end of the iteration r. Furthermore, let H be a cryptographically-secure collision-resistant hash function. Then at the end of iteration r, except with a negligible probability, all honest parties in $H \cup \{P_y\}$ have a common value, say V, provided all the honest parties in H had the value V at the beginning of the iteration r.

Proof Let $\mathcal{H}_H \subseteq H$ be the set of *honest* parties in H and let the premise of the claim be true. This implies that all the parties in $\mathcal{H}_H$ hold the same value, say V, at the beginning of iteration r. Moreover, $h = \mathsf{H}(V)$ holds, where h is the hash value broadcasted by P_s at the beginning of the protocol. This is because every party $P_i \in \mathcal{H}_H$ would have verified this condition before P_i gets included to the set H. Let (P_x, P_y) be the designated pair of parties during the iteration r, where $P_x \in H, P_y \in \overline{H}$ and $(P_x, P_y) \notin \mathsf{Dispute}$. Moreover, suppose at the end of iteration r, party P_y is included in the set H. This implies that P_y broadcasted the bit $b = 1$

during the iteration r. Now, there are two possible cases, depending upon whether P_y is honest or corrupt.

- **Case I — P_y is Corrupt**: In this case, the claim statement holds trivially.
- **Case II — P_y is Honest**: In this case, we need to show that $V_y = V$ holds, where V_y denotes the value received by P_y from P_x. If $P_x \in \mathcal{H}_H$, then this is true, since as per our assumption, $V_x = V$ holds and an honest P_x will send V to P_y. On the other hand, consider the case when P_x is *corrupt*. In this case, if $V_y \neq V$ holds, then $\mathsf{H}(V_y) \neq h$ will hold as well, except with a negligible probability, which follows from the collision-resistance of the hash function H. Consequently, P_y would broadcast $b = 0$, which is a contradiction. □

We next show that during any protocol iteration, the set $\mathsf{Dispute}$ or H gets expanded by one.

Claim 13.2 In any iteration of the protocol $\Pi^{(n,t)}_{\mathsf{CryBlockBC}}$, exactly one of the following always holds.

- The set H gets expanded by one;
- The set $\mathsf{Dispute}$ gets expanded by one.

Proof Consider an arbitrary iteration r in the protocol $\Pi^{(n,t)}_{\mathsf{CryBlockBC}}$, where (P_x, P_y) is the designated pair of parties, where $P_x \in H, P_y \in \overline{H}$ and $(P_x, P_y) \notin \mathsf{Dispute}$ at the beginning of the iteration r. Then during round $(r.2)$, party P_y broadcasts a bit b. Now, there are two possible cases, depending upon the value of b.

- **Case I** — $b = 1$: In this case, the parties set $H := H \cup \{P_y\}$ and so the set H gets expanded by 1.
- **Case I** — $b = 1$: In this case, the parties set $\mathsf{Dispute} := \mathsf{Dispute} \cup \{(P_x, P_y)\}$ and so the set $\mathsf{Dispute}$ gets expanded by 1. □

We next prove the "validity" of disputes computed during the protocol by showing that at least one of the disputed parties in every dispute is guaranteed to be corrupt.

Claim 13.3 In protocol $\Pi^{(n,t)}_{\mathsf{CryBlockBC}}$, if a pair (P_x, P_y) is added to the set $\mathsf{Dispute}$ during any iteration, then either P_x or P_y is corrupt.

Proof Let r be the iteration when the pair (P_x, P_y) gets added to the set $\mathsf{Dispute}$. This implies that at the beginning of the iteration r, party $P_x \in H$, party $P_y \in \overline{H}$ and $(P_x, P_y) \notin \mathsf{Dispute}$. Moreover, during round $(r.2)$, party P_y broadcasted the bit $b = 0$. This further implies that $h \neq \mathsf{H}(V_y)$ holds for P_y, where V_y is the value received by P_y from P_x during round $(r.1)$ and where h is the hash value broadcasted by P_s at the beginning of the protocol.

We prove the claim through a contradiction. So assume that *both* P_x and P_y are *honest*. Let V_x be the value held by P_x. Hence, $h = \mathsf{H}(V_x)$ holds since this condition is verified by P_x before it is added to the set H. If P_x is honest, then $V_y = V_x$ holds as well, since an honest P_x will send the value it holds to P_y during round $(r.1)$. Consequently, $h = \mathsf{H}(V_y)$ will also hold as well and hence P_y would broadcast $b = 1$ during round $(r.2)$, which is a contradiction. □

We are now well-equipped to prove the properties of the protocol. We start with the *liveness* property by showing that there is always an upper bound on the maximum number of rounds within which the honest parties will terminate the protocol.

Claim 13.4 Let $\mathsf{Dispute}_{\mathsf{start}}$ and $\mathsf{Dispute}_{\mathsf{end}}$ be the $\mathsf{Dispute}$ set at the beginning and the end of the protocol $\Pi^{(n,t)}_{\mathsf{CryBlockBC}}$ respectively.[3] Moreover, let the parties have oracle access to a BB oracle for broadcasting bits. Then in the protocol $\Pi^{(n,t)}_{\mathsf{CryBlockBC}}$ the honest parties are guaranteed to terminate within $2(n + d) + 1$ rounds, where $d \stackrel{def}{=} |\mathsf{Dispute}_{\mathsf{end}}| - |\mathsf{Dispute}_{\mathsf{start}}|$.

Proof Let us consider any arbitrary iteration r in the protocol and compute the number of rounds in that iteration. From the protocol description, it is easy to see that the number of rounds in iteration r is 2. Next, we find the maximum number of iterations possible in the protocol.

From Claim 13.2, at the end of each iteration, either the set H or the set $\mathsf{Dispute}$ gets expanded by one. The set H can attain a maximum cardinality of n. On the other hand, as per the claim conditions, the set $\mathsf{Dispute}$ gets expanded by size d. Consequently, the maximum number of iterations is $(n + d)$. Additionally, P_s needs to broadcast a hash of its input at the beginning of the protocol through the BB oracle. Hence the protocol requires at most $2(n + d) + 1$ rounds. Thus, the honest parties are guaranteed to terminate by $2(n + d) + 1$ rounds. □

We next derive the round and communication complexity of the protocol, which follows from the proof of the previous claim.

Lemma 13.1 *Let* $\mathsf{Dispute}_{\mathsf{start}}$ *and* $\mathsf{Dispute}_{\mathsf{end}}$ *be the* $\mathsf{Dispute}$ *set at the beginning and at the end of the protocol* $\Pi^{(n,t)}_{\mathsf{CryBlockBC}}$ *respectively and let* $d \stackrel{def}{=} |\mathsf{Dispute}_{\mathsf{end}}| - |\mathsf{Dispute}_{\mathsf{start}}|$. *Moreover, let the parties have oracle access to a BB oracle for broadcasting bits. Then protocol* $\Pi^{(n,t)}_{\mathsf{CryBlockBC}}$ *achieves the following complexities.*

- *The protocol requires at most* $2(n + d) + 1$ *rounds.*
- *The seed-round complexity of the protocol is at most* $n + d + 1$.
- *The protocol incurs a communication of at most* $\mathcal{BC}(\kappa) + (n+d)(|V_s| + \mathcal{BC}(1))$ *bits. Here* $|V_s|$ *denotes the size of the input* V_s *in bits, and* $\mathcal{BC}(\ell)$ *denotes the communication complexity of emulating one call to the BB oracle where the input size of the sender party is* ℓ *bits.*
- *The seed-communication complexity of the protocol is* $O(\kappa + n + d)$ *bits.*

Proof The maximum number of rounds $2(n + d) + 1$ follows directly from the proof of Claim 13.4. From the protocol description, there is *one* round where the BB oracle is called in each iteration. Additionally, P_s needs to broadcast a hash of its input at the beginning of the protocol. Since the maximum number of iterations could be $n + d$, it implies that the seed-round complexity of the protocol is at most $n + d + 1$.

In each iteration, a designated party P_x from H sends its version of V_s to another designated receiver party P_y in $\overline{H}$. This is followed by party P_y broadcasting a bit.

[3] Note that there is an upper bound of n^2 on the maximum number of disputes which can occur during the protocol.

Hence, each iteration involves a total communication of at most $(|V_s| + \mathcal{BC}(1))$ bits. Additionally, P_s needs to broadcast a hash of its input at the beginning of the protocol. Since the maximum number of iterations could be $n + d$, it implies that the maximum number of bits communicated in the protocol by the honest parties is $\mathcal{BC}(\kappa) + (n + d)(|V_s| + \mathcal{BC}(1))$. This automatically implies a seed-communication complexity of $O(\kappa + n + d)$ bits. □

To prove the validity and consistency properties, we next show that at the protocol's end, all honest parties belong to the happy set H or the unhappy set $\overline{H}$. The proof for this is the same as the proof of Claim 12.5. For the sake of completeness, we reproduce the proof here.

Claim 13.5 In protocol $\Pi^{(n,t)}_{\mathsf{CryBlockBC}}$, one of the following holds at the end of the protocol.

- All honest parties are in the set H. Moreover, they output a common value different from $\perp$, except with a negligible probability.
- All honest parties are in the set $\overline{H}$ and output $\perp$.

Proof We first show that at the end of the protocol, there *does not* exist any pair of *honest* parties (P_x, P_y), where $P_x \in \mathcal{H}$ and $P_y \in \overline{H}$. From Claim 13.3, throughout the protocol, any pair of honest parties *does not* get added to the dispute set $\mathsf{Dispute}$. Hence, if at the end of the protocol, there exists a pair of honest parties (P_x, P_y), where $P_x \in \mathcal{H}$ and $P_y \in \overline{H}$, then it implies that $(P_x, P_y) \notin \mathsf{Dispute}$. This further implies that the while loop *does not* terminate and hence the honest parties *do not* terminate the protocol, which is a contradiction. Hence, at the end of the protocol, all honest parties are in H or all honest parties are in $\overline{H}$.

Since all the honest parties in $\overline{H}$ output $\perp$, it follows that if all honest parties are in $\overline{H}$, they output $\perp$. On the other hand, the honest parties in H output the value (namely the version of V_s) they hold. From Claim 13.1, the value held by all honest parties in H at the end of the protocol will be *same*, except with a negligible probability. So if all honest parties are in H, they will have a common output, different from $\perp$, except with a negligible probability. This completes the proof of the claim. □

Using the above claim, one can immediately derive the validity and consistency properties, as done for the statistically-secure block-broadcast protocol in the previous chapter. However, for the sake of completeness, we give the complete proofs.

Lemma 13.2 *Protocol* $\Pi^{(n,t)}_{\mathsf{CryBlockBC}}$ *achieves* t*-validity, except with a negligible probability.*

Proof Let P_s be *honest*. The set H is initialized to $\{P_s\}$ in the protocol. From Claim 13.5, it follows that at the end of the protocol, all honest parties will be present in the set H. Moreover, all honest parties in H will output a common value, except with a negligible probability. Since $P_s \in H$ and outputs V_s, all honest parties will output V_s, except with a negligible probability, thus proving the lemma. □

Lemma 13.3 *Protocol* $\Pi^{(n,t)}_{\mathsf{CryBlockBC}}$ *achieves* t*-consistency, except with a negligible probability.*

Proof Let $\mathcal{H}$ be the set of *honest* parties. From Claim 13.5, at the end of the protocol, either $\mathcal{H} \subseteq H$ or $\mathcal{H} \subseteq \overline{H}$.

If $\mathcal{H} \subseteq H$, then from Claim 13.5 it follows that all the parties in $\mathcal{H}$ output a common value, different from $\perp$, except with a negligible probability.

On the other hand, from Claim 13.5 it follows that if $\mathcal{H} \subseteq \overline{H}$, then all the parties in $\mathcal{H}$ output $\perp$. Hence, in either case, the consistency property is achieved. □

Theorem 13.1 now follows easily from the above discussion.

Theorem 13.1 *Let* $\mathsf{Dispute}_{\mathsf{start}}$ *and* $\mathsf{Dispute}_{\mathsf{end}}$ *be the* $\mathsf{Dispute}$ *set at the beginning and the end of the protocol* $\Pi^{(n,t)}_{\mathsf{CryBlockBC}}$ *respectively and let* $d \stackrel{def}{=} |\mathsf{Dispute}_{\mathsf{end}}| - |\mathsf{Dispute}_{\mathsf{start}}|$. *Moreover, let the parties have oracle access to a BB oracle for broadcasting bits. Furthermore, let* $\mathsf{H} : \{0,1\}^{\ell} \rightarrow \{0,1\}^{\kappa}$ *be a cryptographically-secure collision-resistant hash function. Then protocol* $\Pi^{(n,t)}_{\mathsf{CryBlockBC}}$ *is a* t*-secure BB protocol with cryptographic security, for any* $t < n$ *in the model* $\mathcal{M}_{\mathsf{auth}}$.[4] *The protocol has the following complexities.*

- *The protocol requires at most* $2(n + d) + 1$ *rounds.*
- *The seed-round complexity of the protocol is at most* $n + d + 1$.
- *The protocol incurs a communication of at most* $\mathcal{BC}(\kappa) + (n+d)(|V_s| + \mathcal{BC}(1))$ *bits. Here* $|V_s|$ *denotes the size of the input* V_s *in bits, and* $\mathcal{BC}(\ell)$ *denotes the communication complexity of emulating one call to the BB oracle where the input size of the sender party is* ℓ *bits.*
- *The seed-communication complexity of the protocol is* $O(\kappa + n + d)$ *bits.*

13.2.2 The Domain Extension Protocol

The cryptographically-secure domain extension BC protocol $\Pi^{(n,t)}_{\mathsf{CryBCExtDM}}$ with a dishonest majority is formally presented in Fig 13.2. The protocol is identical to the statistically-secure domain extension protocol $\Pi^{(n,t)}_{\mathsf{BCExtDM}}$ (Fig 12.3), presented in the previous chapter, except that we now use the cryptographically-secure block-broadcast protocol $\Pi^{(n,t)}_{\mathsf{CryBlockBC}}$. Looking ahead, we will show that dividing the sender's message into $q = n$ blocks is sufficient to achieve *optimal* communication complexity (asymptotically).

Protocol $\Pi^{(n,t)}_{\mathsf{CryBCExtDM}}(m, q)$

Public knowledge: the description of the cryptographically-secure collision-resistant hash function H. Additionally, the parties have oracle access to a bit-BB oracle.

Initialization: The parties in $\mathcal{P}$ initialize the dispute set $\mathsf{Dispute} := \emptyset$. The sender P_s divides its input $m \in \{0,1\}^L$ into q blocks $m^{(1)}, \ldots, m^{(q)}$, where a padding is added if required.

(broadcasting individual blocks): For $k = 1, \ldots, q$, the parties in $\mathcal{P}$ do the following.

[4] We stress that the protocol $\Pi^{(n,t)}_{\mathsf{CryBlockBC}}$ *does not* need any PKI setup. The setup will be required only to emulate the BB oracle with cryptographic security and $t < n$.

– The sender P_s invokes an instance $\Pi^{(n,t)}_{\text{CryBlockBC}}(m^{(k)})$ of the protocol $\Pi_{\text{CryBlockBC}}$ and the parties in $\mathcal{P}$ participate in this instance.
– For $i = 1, \ldots, n$, let $m_i^{(k)}$ be the output obtained by the party P_i during the instance $\Pi^{(n,t)}_{\text{CryBlockBC}}(m^{(k)})$.

(output computation and termination): For $i = 1, \ldots, n$, party P_i computes its output as follows and then terminate.
– If $m_i^{(k)} = \perp$ for any $k \in \{1, \ldots, q\}$, then set 0^L as the output;
– Else set $m_i^{(1)} || \ldots || m_i^{(q)}$ as the output.

Fig. 13.2: A cryptographically-secure domain extension protocol for broadcast with a dishonest majority

The validity and consistency of the protocol $\Pi^{(n,t)}_{\text{CryBCExtDM}}$ can be proved in the same way as done for the protocol $\Pi^{(n,t)}_{\text{BCExtDM}}$, except that we now depend upon the properties of the block-broadcast protocol $\Pi^{(n,t)}_{\text{CryBlockBC}}$. However, for completeness, we give the complete details here. We start with the derivation of round and communication complexity.

Lemma 13.4 *Let the parties have oracle access to a BB oracle for broadcasting bits. Then protocol $\Pi^{(n,t)}_{\text{CryBCExtDM}}$ has the following complexities.*
– *The protocol requires at most $2(nq + n^2) + q$ rounds.*
– *The seed-round complexity of the protocol is $O(nq + n^2)$.*
– *The protocol incurs a communication of at most $(nq+n^2)(\frac{L}{q}+\mathcal{BC}(1))+q\cdot\mathcal{BC}(\kappa)$ bits. Here L denotes the size of the sender's input m in bits and $\mathcal{BC}(\ell)$ denotes the communication complexity of emulating one instance of the BB oracle with an ℓ-bit input.*
– *The seed-communication complexity of the protocol is $O(nq + n^2 + q\kappa)$ bits.*

Proof For $k = 1, \ldots, q$, let d_k be the number of disputes occurring during the instance $\Pi^{(n,t)}_{\text{CryBlockBC}}(m^{(k)})$ of $\Pi_{\text{CryBlockBC}}$. We note that the following holds.

$$\sum_{k=1}^{q} d_k \leq n^2.$$

This is because the maximum number of disputes which can occur across all instances of $\Pi^{(n,t)}_{\text{BlockBC}}$ is at most $tn \leq n^2$. This follows from the fact that any dispute which has already occurred during any earlier instance of $\Pi^{(n,t)}_{\text{CryBlockBC}}$ never occurs during any subsequent instance of $\Pi^{(n,t)}_{\text{CryBlockBC}}$.

From Lemma 13.1, the instance $\Pi^{(n,t)}_{\text{CryBlockBC}}(m^{(k)})$ of $\Pi^{(n,t)}_{\text{CryBlockBC}}$ requires at most $2(n + d_k) + 1$ rounds. As there are q instances of $\Pi^{(n,t)}_{\text{CryBlockBC}}$, the total number of rounds is as follows.

$$\sum_{k=1}^{q} 2(n + d_k) + 1 \leq 2(nq + n^2) + q,$$

where the last equality follows because, as argued earlier, the summation of the number of disputes d_k across the q instances of $\Pi_{\text{CryBlockBC}}$ is upper-bounded by n^2.

From Lemma 13.1, the instance $\Pi^{(n,t)}_{\text{CryBlockBC}}(m^{(k)})$ of $\Pi^{(n,t)}_{\text{CryBlockBC}}$ will have a seed-round complexity of at most $(n + d_k + 1)$. As there are q instances of $\Pi^{(n,t)}_{\text{CryBlockBC}}$, the seed-round complexity is as follows.

$$\sum_{k=1}^{q}(n + d_k + 1),$$

which is $O(nq + n^2)$. This is because the summation of the number of disputes d_k across the q instances of $\Pi_{\text{CryBlockBC}}$ is upper-bounded by n^2.

From Lemma 13.1, the instance $\Pi^{(n,t)}_{\text{CryBlockBC}}(m^{(k)})$ of $\Pi^{(n,t)}_{\text{CryBlockBC}}$ will incur a communication of at most $(n+d_k)(|m^{(k)}|+\mathcal{BC}(1))+\mathcal{BC}(\kappa)$ bits, where $|m^{(k)}| = \frac{L}{q}$. As there are q instances of $\Pi^{(n,t)}_{\text{CryBlockBC}}$, the total communication complexity is as follows.

$$\sum_{k=1}^{q}(n + d_k)(|m^{(k)}| + \mathcal{BC}(1)) + \mathcal{BC}(\kappa),$$

which is $(nq + n^2)(\frac{L}{q} + \mathcal{BC}(1)) + q \cdot \mathcal{BC}(\kappa)$. This is because the summation of the number of disputes d_k across the q instances of $\Pi_{\text{CryBlockBC}}$ is upper-bounded by n^2. Consequently, the seed-communication complexity of the protocol is $O(nq+n^2+q\kappa)$ bits. □

We next prove the validity property of the protocol, which follows from the validity property of the block-broadcast protocol.

Lemma 13.5 *Protocol* $\Pi^{(n,t)}_{\text{CryBCExtDM}}$ *achieves* t*-validity, except with a negligible probability.*

Proof Let $\mathcal{H}$ be the set of *honest* parties and let $P_s \in \mathcal{H}$, who has input m. Then from the t*-validity* of $\Pi^{(n,t)}_{\text{CryBlockBC}}$ (Lemma 13.2), it follows that for $k = 1, \ldots, q$, each $P_i \in \mathcal{H}$ will compute the output $m_i^{(k)}$ during the instance $\Pi^{(n,t)}_{\text{CryBlockBC}}(m^{(k)})$, where $m_i^{(k)} = m^{(k)}$ will hold, except with a negligible probability. Consequently, $m_i^{(1)}||\ldots||m_i^{(q)} = m$ will hold for each $P_i \in \mathcal{H}$, except with a negligible probability. Hence, each honest party will output m, except with a negligible probability. □

We next prove the protocol's consistency property, which follows from the consistency property of the block-broadcast protocol.

Lemma 13.6 *Protocol* $\Pi^{(n,t)}_{\text{CryBCExtDM}}$ *achieves* t*-consistency, except with a negligible probability.*

Proof Let $\mathcal{H}$ be the set of *honest* parties. From the t*-consistency* of $\Pi^{(n,t)}_{\text{CryBlockBC}}$ (Lemma 13.3), it follows that for $k = 1, \ldots, q$, all the parties in $\mathcal{H}$ will compute a *common* output at the end of the instance $\Pi^{(n,t)}_{\text{CryBlockBC}}(m^{(k)})$, except with a negligible probability. Now, there are two possible cases, depending upon whether any of these instances of $\Pi^{(n,t)}_{\mathsf{CryBlockBC}}(m^{(k)})$ produces an output $\perp$ or not.

- **Case I — There exists some $k \in \{1, \ldots, q\}$ where the parties in $\mathcal{H}$ compute the output $\perp$ during the instance $\Pi^{(n,t)}_{\mathsf{CryBlockBC}}(m^{(k)})$**: In this case, all the parties in $\mathcal{H}$ will output 0^L, hence achieving consistency.
- **Case II — There exists no $k \in \{1, \ldots, q\}$ where the parties in $\mathcal{H}$ compute the output $\perp$ during the instance $\Pi^{(n,t)}_{\mathsf{CryBlockBC}}(m^{(k)})$**: In this case, from Lemma 13.3, the condition $m_i^{(k)} = m_j^{(k)}$ holds, for every $k \in \{1, \ldots, q\}$ and every $P_i, P_j \in \mathcal{H}$, except with a negligible probability. Consequently, except with a negligible probability, all the parties in $\mathcal{H}$ will have a common output, different from $\perp$, at the end of the protocol. Hence, consistency is achieved in this case as well. □

The following theorem now follows easily from the above discussion.

Theorem 13.2 *Let the parties have oracle access to a BB oracle for broadcasting bits. Moreover, let $\mathsf{H} : \{0,1\}^\ell \rightarrow \{0,1\}^\kappa$ be a cryptographically-secure collision-resistant hash function. Then protocol $\Pi^{(n,t)}_{\mathsf{CryBCExtDM}}$ is a t-secure BB protocol with cryptographic security, for any $t < n$ in the model $\mathcal{M}_{\mathsf{auth}}$.*[5] *The protocol has the following complexities.*

- *The protocol requires at most $2(nq + n^2) + q$ rounds.*
- *The seed-round complexity of the protocol is $\mathcal{O}(nq + n^2)$.*
- *The protocol incurs a communication of at most $(nq+n^2)(\frac{L}{q}+\mathcal{BC}(1))+q\cdot\mathcal{BC}(\kappa)$ bits. Here L denotes the size of the sender's input m in bits and $\mathcal{BC}(\ell)$ denotes the communication complexity of emulating one instance of the BB oracle with an ℓ-bit input.*
- *The seed-communication complexity of the protocol is $\mathcal{O}(nq + n^2 + q\kappa)$ bits.*

An immediate corollary of Theorem 13.2 is that if we set $q = n$, then the protocol achieves the *optimal* communication complexity asymptotically.

Corollary 13.1 *In protocol $\Pi^{(n,t)}_{\mathsf{CryBCExtDM}}$, if $q = n$, then the protocol achieves the following.*

- *The protocol requires at most $4n^2 + n$ rounds.*
- *The seed-round complexity of the protocol is $\mathcal{O}(n^2)$.*
- *The protocol incurs a communication of $\mathcal{O}(nL) + 2n^2 \cdot \mathcal{BC}(1) + n \cdot \mathcal{BC}(\kappa)$ bits.*
- *The seed-communication complexity of the protocol is $\mathcal{O}(n^2 + n\kappa)$ bits.*

Minimum Message Size for Optimal Communication Complexity.

By instantiating the BB oracle with the cryptographically-secure variant of Dolev-Strong BB protocol $\Pi^{(n,t)}_{\mathsf{DSBB}}$ in the model $\mathcal{M}^{\mathsf{pki}}_{\mathsf{auth}}$(see Section 9.2.2), we find that

[5] We stress that the protocol $\Pi^{(n,t)}_{\mathsf{CryBCExtDM}}$ *does not* need any PKI setup. The setup will be required only to emulate the BB oracle with cryptographic security and $t < n$.

protocol $\Pi^{(n,t)}_{\mathsf{CryBCExtDM}}$ (in the model $\mathcal{M}^{\mathsf{pki}}_{\mathsf{auth}}$) will incur a total communication of $O(nL + n^5\kappa + n^4\kappa^2)$ bits; here κ is the security parameter and denotes the size of a signature and the size of a hash value in bits. This is because $\mathcal{BC}(\ell) = O(n^3\ell\kappa)$ for the protocol $\Pi^{(n,t)}_{\mathsf{DSBB}}$. It follows that if $L = \Omega(n^3\kappa^2 + n^4\kappa)$, then the communication complexity of the protocol will be $O(nL)$ bits, which is *asymptotically* optimal.

13.3 More Efficient Domain Extension Protocols

In a recent work [55], the authors have further improved the overall round complexity and the seed-round complexity of the protocol $\Pi^{(n,t)}_{\mathsf{CryBCExtDM}}$ to $O(n^2)$ and $O(n)$ respectively. The idea is to introduce overlaps among the instances of the block-broadcast protocol, which are executed sequentially in the protocol $\Pi^{(n,t)}_{\mathsf{CryBCExtDM}}$. Namely, in the protocol $\Pi^{(n,t)}_{\mathsf{CryBCExtDM}}$, *all* the (honest) parties start attempting to get the kth block of the sender's message *only* after all of them have got the $(k-1)^{th}$ block of the sender's message. The protocol of [55] deviates from this idea. The parties still get the sender's message block-by-block sequentially, where each block is broadcasted through an instance of the block-broadcast protocol, which uses the dispute-control. The framework is where once a pair of parties get into a dispute, they remain forever for the rest of the protocol. However, the instances of the block-broadcast protocol are executed in an overlapped fashion, where different honest parties during any given round might be trying to receive different blocks of the sender's message. For instance, it might be possible that an honest party P_i has already received the $(k-1)^{th}$ block and is now trying to get the kth block while another honest party P_j is still attempting to get the $(k-1)^{th}$ block. Since the protocol is slightly involved, we do not provide the complete details here and refer the interested readers to [55].

In another interesting work [77], the authors have presented a cryptographically-secure domain extension protocol with better round and seed-round complexity. Moreover, the protocol improves upon the minimum message size L for which the protocol achieves (asymptotically) optimal communication complexity. However, the protocol is *not* designed in a *strict* dishonest-majority setting. That is, the resilience of the protocol is $t < (1-\epsilon)n$, where $\epsilon > 0$. We refer interested readers to [77] for the complete details.

Chapter 14
Distributed Consensus with a Constant Expected Number of Rounds and a Strict Honest Majority

Recall that any *deterministic* consensus protocol needs at least $t + 1$ rounds of communication (see the lower bound derived in Chapter 7). In Chapter 8, we have seen how one can "bypass" the lower bound of $t + 1$ rounds by embracing randomness. Specifically, we had seen a generic framework for designing a randomized BA protocol from any given GA and a *common coin* (CC) protocol. In Chapter 7 we had instantiated the framework with $t < \frac{n}{3}$ *without* any setup. A natural question is whether we can instantiate the framework in a strict *honest-majority* setting; i.e. with $t < \frac{n}{2}$, provided we are given some setup. In this chapter, we answer this question affirmatively. Specifically, we show that given a PKI setup, one can design a constant expected round protocol with $t < \frac{n}{2}$, which satisfies the property of BA with a high probability. The protocol achieves either unconditional security or cryptographic security, depending upon if the underlying PKI is unconditionally-secure or cryptographically-secure. Note that the protocol achieves the *optimal reseilience*, since from Theorem 2.1, the condition $t < \frac{n}{2}$ is *necessary* for *any* BA protocol.

To design the BA protocol, we further design a *gradecast* (GC) protocol and a *moderated verifiable secret-sharing* (MVSS) scheme with $t < \frac{n}{2}$. The GC protocol can be used to get a GA protocol with $t < \frac{n}{2}$ using Theorem 2.5. On the other hand, the MVSS scheme can be used to build a CC protocol from scratch with $t < \frac{n}{2}$, using the generic framework presented in Chapter 8. The design of the MVSS further boils down to the design of a VSS scheme with $t < \frac{n}{2}$ for which we present the VSS scheme of [38]. The VSS scheme when compiled using the compiler of [65] (presented in Chapter 8) leads to an MVSS scheme with $t < \frac{n}{2}$.

Finally, we show how one can instantiate CC efficiently with cryptographic security in the random oracle model. Informally, a random oracle is an idealized abstraction of a cryptographic hash function.

A. Choudhury and A. Patra, *Fault-Tolerant Distributed Consensus in Synchronous Networks*, Information Security and Cryptography,
https://doi.org/10.1007/978-3-031-80460-1_14

14.1 The Setting

We consider the model $\mathcal{M}^{\mathsf{pki}}_{\mathsf{secure}}$ of *pairwise-secure* channels, where the parties in $\mathcal{P}$ are connected by pairwise-secure channels. Moreover, we assume the existence of a PKI setup available to the parties, where for each party P_i, there exists a pair of keys $(\mathsf{sk}_i, \mathsf{pk}_i)$ for a signature scheme, with the *signing key* sk_i held by P_i and the *verification key* pk_i being *publicly* available. The distrust among the parties is modelled by a centralized adversary Adv, capable of corrupting up to t parties, where $t < \frac{n}{2}$. The adversary could be either computationally-bounded (probabilistic polynomial time) or computationally-unbounded. If it is the former, then we assume that the PKI setup is that for a standard cryptographically-secure *digital signature* scheme. On the other hand, if it is the latter, then we assume that the PKI setup is for an unconditionally-secure signature scheme (namely the *pseudo-signatures*). Moreover, in the latter case, we assume that the set up supports the required number of pseudo-signature transferability, as needed in the BA protocol.

14.2 Gradecast with $t < \frac{n}{2}$

In this section, we provide an instantiation of gradecast (GC) in the model $\mathcal{M}^{\mathsf{pki}}_{\mathsf{auth}}$ tolerating $t < \frac{n}{2}$ corruptions due to [58]. If the PKI setup is unconditionally-secure, then the resultant GC provides *statistical* security tolerating a computationally-unbounded adversary. At the same time, the security level of the GC is cryptographic if the PKI setup is cryptographically secure and the adversary is computationally bounded. The protocol called $\Pi^{(n,t)}_{\mathsf{GCHM}}$ is presented in Fig 14.1 and consists of three rounds.

During the first round, the sender S distributes its signed input to all the parties. During the second round, the parties check if the sender has distributed a common input to all. To this end, each party P_i, after verifying the signed input received from the sender, endorses the received input by signing it and sending it to all. Note that P_i endorses *at most* one input from the sender, since an *honest* sender will distribute its input *exactly once* to every party. The input received by P_i, along with the sender's and P_i's signature, is called a *doubly-endorsed* tuple. During the third round, every party, upon receiving a doubly-endorsed tuple checks whether it is valid. A doubly-endorsed tuple for a value m is considered *valid* if the tuple consists of valid signatures of the sender and the endorser party on m. Every valid doubly-endorsed tuple is then sent to all the parties. This ensures that if others have not yet received the valid doubly-endorsed tuple, then they receive it at the end of the third round.

After the third round, the parties compute their output as follows. Each party P_i checks if there exists at least $n - t$ parties such that during the third round, each of these parties has individually sent at least $n - t$ valid doubly-endorsed tuples for the same value, say m. Moreover, none of these $n - t$ parties should have sent a valid doubly-endorsed tuple for any other value during the third round. Furthermore, P_i should not have received a valid doubly-endorsed tuple for any other value in the previous rounds. If all these conditions are satisfied, P_i outputs m with the highest grade 2.

If the above conditions are not satisfied, then P_i proceeds to check whether the following conditions are true: there is at least one party who, during the third round, has sent at least $n - t$ valid doubly-endorsed tuples for the same value, say m and no valid doubly-endorsed tuples for any other value. Furthermore, P_i should not have received a valid doubly-endorsed tuple for any other value during the second round. If all these conditions are satisfied, P_i outputs m with the grade 1. If the above conditions are unsatisfied, P_i outputs some default value with grade 0.

The high-level idea behind the protocol is as follows: if the sender S is honest, it will sign its input m and distribute it to all the parties. Hence, all honest parties will double-endorse m during the second round and send it to all other parties. Finally, during the third round, each honest party forwards the doubly-endorsed m received from every other honest party to all. Since S is honest, a corrupt party will *fail* to forge the signature of S on any value m' different from m. Consequently, a corrupt party will fail to generate a valid doubly-endorsed tuple for m'. Hence, only valid doubly-endorsed tuples for m will be generated and circulated among the parties during the second and third rounds. Since there are at least $n - t$ honest parties, it follows that all honest parties will output m with the grade 2, thus guaranteeing *t-validity* of GC.

Next, consider the case when S is *corrupt* and let us see how the *t-knowledge-of-agreement* of GC is achieved. Let P_i be an *honest* party who outputs a value m with the grade 2. This implies that there exists at least $n-t$ parties $\mathcal{A}_i$, such that during the third round, each party in $\mathcal{A}_i$ has individually sent at least $n-t$ valid doubly-endorsed tuples for m to P_i. Moreover, P_i has not received a valid doubly-endorsed tuple for any other value from any party (including the parties in $\mathcal{A}_i$) throughout the protocol. Now consider another *honest* party P_j. The set $\mathcal{A}_i$ is guaranteed to have at least one *honest* party, say P_l, whose valid doubly-endorsed tuples for m (which are at least $n - t$ in number) will be delivered to P_j as well during the third round. Moreover, P_j would *not* receive a valid doubly-endorsed tuple for any value m' different from m from any party during the second round, else P_j would have forwarded that tuple to P_i during the third round, preventing P_i to output $(m, 2)$. Similarly, P_j would *not* receive $n - t$ valid doubly-endorsed tuples for m' from any party during the third round. If this is not the case, then among these $n - t$ doubly-endorsed tuples, at least one of the tuples will be from an honest party, generated during the second round, who would have sent it to all, including P_i, thus preventing P_i from outputting $(m, 2)$. Hence, the conditions for P_j to output any value different from m will *not* be satisfied. Moreover, the conditions for P_j to output $(m, 1)$ will be *definitely* satisfied. Since the conditions for P_j to output $(m, 2)$ might be satisfied as well, it follows that P_j will output either $(m, 2)$ or $(m, 1)$.

Protocol $\Pi_{\mathsf{GCHM}}^{(n,t)}$

Setup: A PKI setup where for each $P_j \in \mathcal{P}$, there exists a pair of keys $(\mathsf{sk}_j, \mathsf{pk}_j)$ for a signature scheme (Gen, Sign, Verify), with sk_j held by P_j and pk_j being *publicly* available. The key-pair of the designated sender $\mathsf{S} \in \mathcal{P}$ is denoted by $(\mathsf{sk}_\mathsf{S}, \mathsf{pk}_\mathsf{S})$.

- **Round 1 (sender distributing signed input)**: S on having the input $m \in \{0,1\}^L$ does the following.
  - Compute $\sigma_\mathsf{S}^{(m)} := \mathsf{Sign}_{\mathsf{sk}_\mathsf{S}}(m)$.
  - Send $(m, \sigma_\mathsf{S}^{(m)})$ to every party in $\mathcal{P}$, including S.
- **Round 2 (parties endorsing the sender's input)**: Each party $P_i \in \mathcal{P}$ (including S) upon receiving $(m, \sigma_\mathsf{S}^{(m)})$ from S for some $m \in \{0,1\}^L$ in the previous round, executes the following steps provided $\mathsf{Verify}_{\mathsf{pk}_\mathsf{S}}(m, \sigma_\mathsf{S}^{(m)}) = 1$ holds.
  - Compute $\sigma_i^{(m)} := \mathsf{Sign}_{\mathsf{sk}_i}(m)$.
  - Send the tuple $(m, \sigma_\mathsf{S}^{(m)}, \sigma_i^{(m)})$ to every party in $\mathcal{P}$, including S. We call the tuple $(m, \sigma_\mathsf{S}^{(m)}, \sigma_i^{(m)})$ as *doubly-endorsed* tuple.

  Once P_i executes the above steps for some $m \in \{0,1\}^L$, it *does not* execute the above steps again if it receives $(m', \sigma_\mathsf{S}^{(m')})$ from S for any $m' \in \{0,1\}^L$.
- **Round 3 (parties exchanging doubly-endorsed sender's input)**: Each party $P_i \in \mathcal{P}$ upon receiving any doubly-endorsed tuple $(m, \sigma_\mathsf{S}^{(m)}, \sigma_j^{(m)})$ from any party $P_j \in \mathcal{P}$ for some $m \in \{0,1\}^L$ in the previous round, sends $(m, \sigma_\mathsf{S}^{(m)}, \sigma_j^{(m)})$ to every party in $\mathcal{P}$, provided all the following holds.
  - $\mathsf{Verify}_{\mathsf{pk}_\mathsf{S}}(m, \sigma_\mathsf{S}^{(m)}) = 1$;
  - $\mathsf{Verify}_{\mathsf{pk}_j}(m, \sigma_j^{(m)}) = 1$.

  Once P_i executes the above steps with respect to P_j for some $m \in \{0,1\}^L$, then it *does not* execute the above steps again if P_i receives any doubly-endorsed tuple $(m', \sigma_\mathsf{S}^{(m')}, \sigma_j^{(m')})$ from P_j, where $m' \neq m$.
- **(identifying the set of consistent doubly-endorsed tuples)**: Each party $P_i \in \mathcal{P}$ does the following.
  - Upon receiving a set Σ_j of doubly-endorsed tuples from any party $P_j \in \mathcal{P}$ during Round 3, party P_i checks if all the following holds.
    - $|\Sigma_j| \geq n - t$;
    - There exists some $m \in \{0,1\}^L$ such that *each* tuple in Σ_j is of the form $(m, \sigma_\mathsf{S}^{(m)}, \sigma_k^{(m)})$, corresponding to some $P_k \in \mathcal{P}$.
    - For every tuple $(m, \sigma_\mathsf{S}^{(m)}, \sigma_k^{(m)}) \in \Sigma_j$, all the following conditions holds.
      - $\mathsf{Verify}_{\mathsf{pk}_\mathsf{S}}(m, \sigma_\mathsf{S}^{(m)}) = 1$;
      - $\mathsf{Verify}_{\mathsf{pk}_k}(m, \sigma_k^{(m)}) = 1$.

    If all the above conditions hold, then we say that Σ_j is a *consistent set of doubly-endorsed tuples for m received from* P_j.
- **(output computation and termination)**: Each party $P_i \in \mathcal{P}$ computes its output as follows and then terminate.
  - If all the following holds then set $(m, 2)$ as the output.
    - P_i has received consistent sets of doubly-endorsed tuples for m from at least $n - t$ different parties during Round 3.
    - P_i has *not* received any doubly-endorsed tuple $(m', \sigma_\mathsf{S}^{(m')}, \sigma_j^{(m')})$ from any party P_j during Round 2 or Round 3, satisfying all the following conditions.
      - $m' \in \{0,1\}^L$;
      - $m' \neq m$;
      - $\mathsf{Verify}_{\mathsf{pk}_\mathsf{S}}(m', \sigma_\mathsf{S}^{(m')}) = 1$;
      - $\mathsf{Verify}_{\mathsf{pk}_j}(m', \sigma_j^{(m')}) = 1$.

- Else if all the following holds then set $(m, 1)$ as the output.
  - P_i has received a consistent set of doubly-endorsed tuples for m from at least 1 party during Round 3.
  - P_i has *not* received any doubly-endorsed tuple $(m', \sigma_{\mathsf{S}}^{(m')}, \sigma_j^{(m')})$ from any party P_j during Round 2, satisfying all the following conditions.
    - $m' \in \{0,1\}^L$;
    - $m' \neq m$;
    - $\mathsf{Verify}_{\mathsf{pk_S}}(m', \sigma_{\mathsf{S}}^{(m')}) = 1$;
    - $\mathsf{Verify}_{\mathsf{pk}_j}(m', \sigma_j^{(m')}) = 1$.
- Else set $(0^L, 0)$ as the output.

Fig. 14.1: The gradecast protocol with a strict honest majority

We now proceed to prove the properties of the protocol $\Pi_{\mathsf{GCHM}}^{(n,t)}$. We first derive the round and communication complexities.

Lemma 14.1 *Protocol* $\Pi_{\mathsf{GCHM}}^{(n,t)}$ *requires* 3 *rounds and incurs a communication of* $\mathcal{GC}(L) = O(n^3(L+\kappa))$ *bits where* κ *is the security parameter and denotes the size of a signature in bits.*

Proof The number of rounds follows from the protocol description. The communication complexity is dominated by the third round, where each party needs to send at most n doubly-endorsed tuple to every party. Since each doubly-endorsed tuple consists of an L-bit value and two signatures, this amounts to $O(n^3(L+\kappa))$ bits of communication. □

Before proving the validity and the consistency properties, we introduce *valid* doubly-endorsed tuples. Informally, a doubly-endorsed tuple is called valid if all the associated signatures on the underlying value are valid, with one of the signatures being from the sender.

Definition 14.1 (Valid Doubly-Endorsed Value) Let $m \in \{0,1\}^L$ and let $P_j \in \mathcal{P}$. Then a doubly-endorsed tuple $(m, \sigma_{\mathsf{S}}^{(m)}, \sigma_j^{(m)})$ generated in the protocol $\Pi_{\mathsf{GCHM}}^{(n,t)}$ is called valid, provided all the following holds.
- $\mathsf{Verify}_{\mathsf{pk_S}}(m, \sigma_{\mathsf{S}}^{(m)}) = 1$;
- $\mathsf{Verify}_{\mathsf{pk}_j}(m, \sigma_j^{(m)}) = 1$.

We next prove the validity property for which we must consider an *honest* sender.

Lemma 14.2 *Protocol* $\Pi_{\mathsf{GCHM}}^{(n,t)}$ *satisfies the following properties, for any* $t < n$.
- *If the PKI is cryptographically-secure then the protocol achieves* t*-validity against a computationally-bounded adversary, except with a negligible probability.*
- *If the PKI is unconditionally-secure then the protocol achieves* t*-validity against a computationally-unbounded adversary, except with a negligible probability.*

Proof Let $\mathcal{H}$ be the set of *honest* parties. Note that $|\mathcal{H}| \geq n-t$. We must consider when the sender S is *honest* to prove validity. So let $\mathsf{S} \in \mathcal{H}$ and let S has input $m \in \{0,1\}^L$.

During the first round, S will send the signed m to all the parties, where the signature will pass the verification for all the parties in $\mathcal{H}$. Consequently, during the second round, every party in $\mathcal{H}$ will send a valid doubly-endorsed m to all the parties. During the third round, every party in $\mathcal{H}$ upon receiving and verifying these valid doubly-endorsed m from the parties in $\mathcal{H}$ will send them to every party.

Note that the *corrupt* parties will *not* be able to send a valid doubly-endorsed m' to any party for any value $m' \neq m$ during the second round. This is because the corrupt parties will fail to generate the signature of S on m'. Consequently, no party will send a valid doubly-endorsed m' during the third round. Since $|\mathcal{H}| \geq n - t$, it follows that at the end of the third round, every party in $\mathcal{H}$ would receive consistent sets of doubly-endorsed tuples for m from at least $n - t$ parties. Moreover, there will be *no* valid doubly-endorsed tuple for any value $m' \neq m$. Consequently, all honest parties will output $(m, 2)$, thus proving the *t-validity* property. □

We next prove the *knowledge-of-agreement* property.

Lemma 14.3 *Protocol* $\Pi_{\mathsf{GCHM}}^{(n,t)}$ *satisfies the following properties, for any* $t < \frac{n}{2}$.

- *If the PKI is cryptographically-secure then the protocol achieves t-knowledge-of-agreement against a computationally-bounded adversary, except with a negligible probability.*
- *If the PKI is unconditionally-secure then the protocol achieves t-knowledge-of-agreement against a computationally-unbounded adversary, except with a negligible probability.*

Proof Let $\mathcal{H}$ be the set of *honest* parties and consider an arbitrary $P_i \in \mathcal{H}$ who outputs $(m, 2)$ where $m \in \{0, 1\}^L$. We wish to show that every other party in $\mathcal{H}$ outputs either $(m, 2)$ or $(m, 1)$. Since P_i outputs $(m, 2)$, it implies that *all* the following holds for P_i.

- There exists a set of parties $\mathcal{A}_i$ where $|\mathcal{A}_i| \geq n - t$, such that P_i has received consistent sets of doubly-endorsed tuples for m from all the parties in $\mathcal{A}_i$ during the third round.
- P_i has *not* received any valid doubly-endorsed tuple for any value $m' \neq m$ during the second round or the third round from any party.

The set $\mathcal{A}_i$ consists of at least $n - 2t$ *honest* parties. Since $t < \frac{n}{2}$, it follows that the set $\mathcal{A}_i$ consists of at least *one* honest party, say P_k, who sent a consistent set Σ_k of doubly-endorsed tuples for m to P_i during the third round. As per the protocol steps, P_k would have sent the set Σ_k to all the parties during the third round.

Now consider an arbitrary party $P_j \in \mathcal{H}$ where $P_j \neq P_i$. As discussed above, the set Σ_k will be delivered to P_j during the third round. Party P_j *cannot* receive consistent sets of doubly-endorsed tuples for any value $m' \neq m$ from at least $n - t$ parties. On the contrary, if there exists such a set $\mathcal{A}_j$ of $n - t$ parties, then it implies that there exists at least one *honest* party in $\mathcal{A}_j$ (since $t < \frac{n}{2}$), say P_l, who sent a consistent set Σ_l of doubly-endorsed tuples for m' to P_j during the third round. As per the protocol steps, P_l would have sent the set Σ_l to all the parties during the third round, *including* P_i. Hence, P_i would *not* output $(m, 2)$, which is a contradiction. Hence P_j *cannot* output $(m', 2)$. We next show that P_j *cannot* output $(m', 1)$.

So that P_j outputs $(m', 1)$, it must be the case that P_j receives a set Σ of at least $n - t$ valid doubly-endorsed tuples for m' from some party during the third round. Since $t < \frac{n}{2}$, among these $n - t$ valid doubly-endorsed tuples, at least one tuple $(m', \sigma_{\mathsf{S}}^{(m')}, \sigma_l^{(m')})$ must have been generated by an *honest* party P_l. This is because the adversary *cannot* forge the signature of an honest party P_l on m' and generate the tuple $(m', \sigma_{\mathsf{S}}^{(m')}, \sigma_l^{(m')})$ itself. Moreover, P_l would have generated and sent the tuple $(m', \sigma_{\mathsf{S}}^{(m')}, \sigma_l^{(m')})$ to *all* the parties (including P_i) during the second round. Consequently, P_i *would not* output $(m, 2)$, which is a contradiction.

Till now, we have shown that P_j *cannot* output a value different from m, either with grade 2 or with grade 1. We now show that the conditions for P_j to output $(m, 1)$ are *definitely* satisfied. This is because, as discussed above, the set Σ_k consisting of valid doubly-endorsed tuples for m will be delivered to P_j during the third round. Moreover, P_j will *not* receive any valid doubly-endorsed tuple for any value m' different from m during the second round. On the contrary, let P_j receive a valid doubly-endorsed tuple $(m', \sigma_{\mathsf{S}}^{(m')}, \sigma_l^{(m')})$ from some party P_l during the second round. Then, as per the protocol steps, during the third round, P_j would have sent the tuple $(m', \sigma_{\mathsf{S}}^{(m')}, \sigma_l^{(m')})$ to all the parties. Consequently, P_i *would not* output $(m, 2)$, which is a contradiction. Hence, the conditions for P_j to output $(m, 1)$ are *definitely* satisfied. Moreover, since P_j would not output any other value with grade 2 or 1, it follows that P_j would output either $(m, 2)$ or $(m, 1)$. This proves the *t-knowledge-of-agreement* property. □

The following theorem now follows easily from the above discussion.

Theorem 14.1 *Protocol* $\Pi_{\mathsf{GCHM}}^{(n,t)}$ *satisfies the following properties, for any* $t < \frac{n}{2}$ *in the model* $\mathcal{M}_{\mathsf{auth}}^{\mathsf{pki}}$.

- *If the PKI is cryptographically-secure then the protocol is a t-secure GC protocol for L-bit values with cryptographic security.*
- *If the PKI is unconditionally-secure then the protocol is a t-secure GC protocol for L-bit values with statistical security.*

The protocol requires 3 *rounds of communication and incurs a communication of* $\mathcal{GC}(L) = \mathcal{O}(n^3(L + \kappa))$ *bits where* κ *is the security parameter and denotes the size of a signature in bits.*

14.3 Graded Agreement with $t < \frac{n}{2}$

Once we have a GC protocol with $t < \frac{n}{2}$, then a GA protocol with $t < \frac{n}{2}$ follows automatically due to Theorem 2.5. We call the resultant protocol $\Pi_{\mathsf{GAHM}}^{(n,t)}$. The protocol will be either statistically-secure or cryptographically-secure, depending upon whether the underlying PKI is unconditionally or cryptographically secure. The protocol will run n instances of the protocol $\Pi_{\mathsf{GCHM}}^{(n,t)}$ in parallel and require 3 rounds. The communication complexity of the protocol will be $\mathcal{O}(n^4(L + \kappa))$ bits. We do not provide the formal details of the protocol $\Pi_{\mathsf{GAHM}}^{(n,t)}$ to avoid repetition and simply state the following theorem.

Theorem 14.2 *There exists a GA protocol* $\Pi_{\mathsf{GAHM}}^{(n,t)}$ *for L-bit inputs for any* $t < \frac{n}{2}$ *in the model* $\mathcal{M}_{\mathsf{auth}}^{\mathsf{pki}}$.

- *If the PKI is cryptographically-secure then the protocol is a t-secure GA protocol for L-bit values with cryptographic security.*
- *If the PKI is unconditionally-secure then the protocol is a t-secure GA protocol for L-bit values with statistical security.*
- *The protocol requires 3 rounds of communication over the point-to-point channels and incurs a communication of* $O(n^4(L + \kappa))$ *bits, where* κ *is the security parameter and denotes the size of a signature in bits.*

14.4 VSS with $t < \frac{n}{2}$ in the Model $\mathcal{M}_{\mathsf{secure}}^{\mathsf{pki}}$

In this section, we present a VSS scheme in the model $\mathcal{M}_{\mathsf{secure}}^{\mathsf{pki}}$, tolerating $t < \frac{n}{2}$ corruptions. The scheme achieves either *statistical* security or *cryptographic* security, depending upon whether the underlying PKI setup is unconditionally or cryptographically secure respectively. The scheme is called CDDHR, attributed to the inventors of the scheme [38]. The scheme assumes the existence of a system-wide broadcast oracle available to the parties, apart from the pairwise-secure channels. The broadcast oracle allows any designated sender party to broadcast any value identically to all the parties.[1]

We present a simplified version of the scheme taken from [65], which is sufficient for our discussion. The simplified version makes the following modifications to the original scheme [38] to simplify the overall presentation.

- The *information-checking signatures* (IC-signatures) are replaced by standard signatures. Informally, IC-signatures [81] are used for authenticating data even in the presence of computationally-unbounded adversaries. IC-signatures are generated by running an *information-checking protocol* (ICP) inside the VSS scheme. It turns out that the IC-signatures can be replaced by pseudo-signatures (resp. digital signatures), depending upon if the underlying adversary is computationally-unbounded (resp. computationally-bounded), which in turn depends upon the security level of the underlying PKI.
- The reconstruction-phase protocol in [38] utilizes the broadcast oracle, which we avoid. Looking ahead, this will be useful while compiling the VSS scheme into an MVSS scheme.[2]

The VSS scheme is very similar to the BGW scheme (Fig 8.3) based on the properties of (t, t)-degree bivariate polynomials. However, since a negligible error is now

---

[1] Recall that as explained in Chapter 8, the presence of a broadcast oracle is just for simplicity and such an oracle needs to be instantiated by running a concrete *t-secure* BB protocol.

[2] Recall that the compiler requires the reconstruction-phase protocol of the underlying VSS scheme to *not* use the broadcast oracle.

allowed in the security properties, the scheme becomes much simplified and can tolerate up to $t < \frac{n}{2}$ corruptions, instead of $t < \frac{n}{3}$ corruptions. The scheme operates over a finite field $\mathbb{F}$ where $|\mathbb{F}| > n$ and where $\alpha_1, \ldots, \alpha_n$ are n publicly-known non-zero elements from $\mathbb{F}$, such that α_i is associated with party P_i as the evaluation point.

Let $s \in \mathbb{F}$ be the input of the dealer, which it would like to secret-share. The sharing-phase protocol generates *2D-secret-sharing of s with authentication.* A value $s \in \mathbb{F}$ is said to be 2D-secret-shared with authentication if all the following holds.

- There is some t-degree *sharing-polynomial* $q(y)$ where $q(0) = s$ and each (honest) party P_i have a *primary-share* s_i of s where $s_i = q(\alpha_i)$ holds.
- Each primary-share is further secret-shared among the parties through a t-degree polynomial (hence the name 2D-secret-sharing). That is for each primary-share s_i, there is some t-degree polynomial $f_i(x)$ held by P_i where $f_i(0) = s_i$, such that each (honest) party P_j have the *secondary-share* $s_{i,j}$ where $s_{i,j} = f_i(\alpha_j)$ holds.
- For each secondary-share $s_{i,j}$, either P_i will hold a valid signature from P_j on $s_{i,j}$ or otherwise the value $s_{i,j}$ will be publicly-known.

For a pictorial illustration of 2D-secret-sharing of a value with authentication, see Fig 14.2.

If the dealer is *honest*, then s remains private till the end of the sharing phase. On the other hand, even if the dealer is *corrupt*, it will be guaranteed that at the end of the sharing phase, there exists some value $s^\star \in \mathbb{F}$ (which could be different from s), such that $s^\star$ is 2D-secret-shared with authentication. The reconstruction-phase protocol takes input a value $s^\star$ (where $s^\star = s$ for an *honest* dealer), which is 2D-secret-shared with authentication. The protocol enables the honest parties to robustly reconstruct $s^\star$ (with a high probability).

Let us now discuss the high-level ideas of the sharing-phase protocol. To secret-share the secret s, the dealer hides it in the constant term of a random t-degree sharing polynomial $q(y)$ at $y = 0$ and distributes shares of s lying on $q(y)$ to the respective parties. To prove that it has distributed shares lying on a t-degree polynomial, the dealer actually embeds $q(y)$ in a random (t, t)-degree bivariate polynomial $F(x, y)$ at $x = 0$, which ensures that $F(0, 0) = s$. The dealer then distributes the row and column-polynomials on $F(x, y)$ to the respective parties. Namely, each party P_i receives the vector of values $\vec{f_i} = (f_{i,1}, \ldots, f_{i,n})$ and $\vec{g_i} = (g_{i,1}, \ldots, g_{i,n})$, lying on t-degree *row-polynomial* $f_i(x)$ and t-degree *column-polynomial* $g_i(y)$ respectively, where $f_i(x) = F(x, \alpha_i)$ and $g_i(y) = F(\alpha_i, y)$. Moreover, each of these values is signed by the dealer. Before proceeding, every party P_i verifies if it has received two vectors of n legitimately signed values from the dealer, lying on t-degree polynomials. If this is not the case, then party P_i complaints publicly during the *second* round and in response, during the *third* round, the dealer makes public both the signed vectors on behalf of P_i, which is used by P_i for the rest of the protocol. The parties can verify if the dealer has made public legitimately-signed vectors of values lying on t-degree polynomials for P_i, and if it is *not* the case, then the dealer is publicly discarded, and the parties abort the protocol prematurely. Note that an *honest* dealer never gets

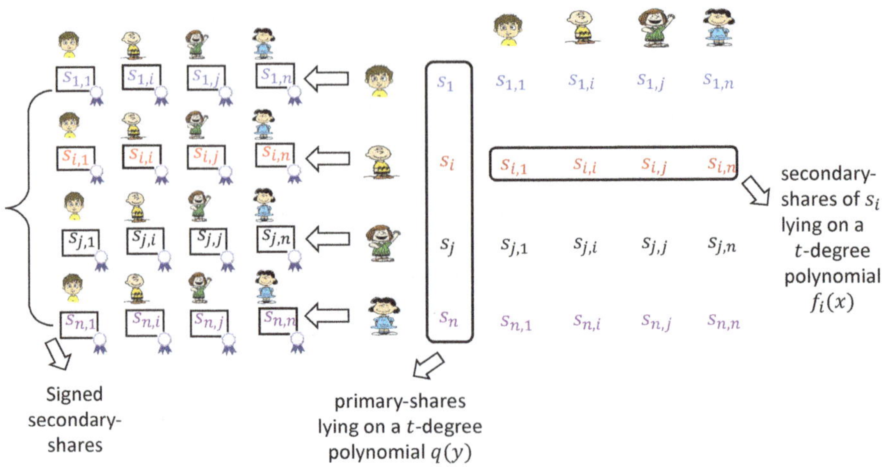

Fig. 14.2: Pictorial representation of $2D$-secret-sharing of s with authentication. The vector of values $(s_1, \ldots, s_n)$ constitutes the *primary-shares*, lying on some t-degree *sharing-polynomial* $q(y)$, with each (honest) P_i having the primary-share s_i where $s_i = q(\alpha_i)$. Each primary-share s_i is further secret-shared through some t-degree polynomial $f_i(x)$, held by P_i, with each (honest) party P_j holding the secondary-share $s_{i,j}$ of s_i where $s_{i,j} = f_i(\alpha_j)$ holds. Moreover, either P_i will have a valid signature from P_j on $s_{i,j}$ or the value $s_{i,j}$ will be known publicly

discarded, and the privacy of s is maintained. This is because if the dealer is honest, then *no* honest party complaints against the dealer and so the values which are made public by the dealer correspond to the corrupt parties and are *already known* to the adversary. Moreover, an honest dealer will always resolve complaints by making public legitimately-signed values, lying on $F(x, y)$.

If the dealer is *not* discarded at the end of the third round, then it is ensured that every party P_i has two vectors $\overrightarrow{f_i} = (f_{i,1}, \ldots, f_{i,n})$ and $\overrightarrow{g_i} = (g_{i,1}, \ldots, g_{i,n})$ of legitimately signed values, lying on t-degree polynomials. We also note that if the dealer is *honest*, then these values lie on t-degree polynomials $f_i(x)$ and $g_i(y)$ respectively, such that $f_i(x) = F(x, \alpha_i)$ and $g_i(y) = F(\alpha_i, y)$. Note that the way an *honest* dealer selects the bivariate polynomial $F(x, y)$, it ensures that $f_i(0) = q(\alpha_i)$ holds. Moreover, $f_{i,j} = g_{j,i} = F(\alpha_j, \alpha_i)$ holds as well. Consequently, one can set $f_i(0)$ as the *primary-share* for P_i and the values $f_{i,1}, \ldots, f_{i,n}$ can be considered as the *secondary-shares* of the primary-share $f_i(0)$, where each party P_j holds the secondary-share $f_{i,j}$ in the form of $g_{j,i}$. However, it is *not known* if the dealer is honest or corrupt. Hence, from the fourth round onward, the parties interact to verify if their vectors of values are "consistent" and lie on a single (t, t)-degree bivariate polynomial, which should be the case if the dealer is *honest*. The details follow.

During the *fourth* round, *every* pair of parties P_i, P_j performs the pair-wise consistency checks of the supposedly common values in their respective vectors. Namely P_i sends the value $g_{i,j}$ to P_j along with its signature and similarly, P_j sends the value $g_{j,i}$ to P_i along with its signature. During the *fifth* round, every party P_i makes public the result of the pair-wise consistency check done with every party P_j. Namely, upon receiving the value $g_{j,i}$ from P_i during the fourth round, P_i checks if the value is legitimately signed and if $g_{j,i}$ is same as $f_{i,j}$ (which should be the case if the dealer and P_j are *honest*). If both these conditions are satisfied then P_i makes public an $\texttt{OK}(P_i, P_j)$ message, else it makes public an $\texttt{NOK}(P_i, P_j)$ message.

If *no* $\texttt{NOK}(\star, \star)$ message is broadcasted during the fifth round, then it implies that the dealer has distributed consistent vectors to the *honest* parties, lying on a unique (t, t)-degree bivariate polynomial. This is because there are at least $n-t \geq t+1$ honest parties whose vectors of values lie on t-degree polynomials, and the components of these vectors corresponding to the honest parties are pair-wise consistent. Hence from Lemma 8.1, the vectors of the honest parties lie on a unique (t, t)-degree bivariate polynomial, say $F^{\star}(x, y)$, even if the dealer is *corrupt* and where $F^{\star}(x, y) = F(x, y)$ if the dealer is *honest*. Moreover, one can see that the value $s^{\star} \stackrel{def}{=} F^{\star}(0, 0)$ is $2D$-secret-shared with authentication, where $s^{\star} = s$ for an *honest* dealer. This is because each *honest* P_i will have the t-degree row polynomial $F^{\star}(x, \alpha_i)$ through the vector of values $\overrightarrow{f_i}$ where $F^{\star}(0, \alpha_i)$ constitutes the *primary-share* of $s^{\star}$ for P_i. And the vector of values $\overrightarrow{f_i} = (f_{i,1}, \ldots, f_{i,n})$ constitutes the *secondary-shares* of $F^{\star}(0, \alpha_i)$, where the secondary-share $f_{i,j}$ is signed by P_j, since P_j signs $g_{j,i}$ and P_i confirms that $f_{i,j}$ and $g_{j,i}$ are the same.

On the other hand, if any $\texttt{NOK}(\star, \star)$ is broadcasted during the fifth round, implying a "dispute" between a pair of parties, then during the *sixth* round, such disputes are publicly resolved. In more detail, if P_i has made public an $\texttt{NOK}(P_i, P_j)$ message during the fifth round then it implies that at least one party among the dealer, P_i and P_j is *corrupt*. Consequently, during the sixth round, all three parties make their respective versions of the disputed value public. Namely, the dealer makes public its version of the disputed value, supposedly lying on its bivariate polynomial, while P_i and P_j make public their respective versions $f_{i,j}$ and $g_{j,i}$, along with the dealer's signature on the respective values. Party P_i or P_j is discarded for the rest of the protocol if the signature they revealed on the disputed value is invalid. On the other hand, if both P_i and P_j reveal valid signatures and if any of the values $f_{i,j}$ or $g_{j,i}$ mismatches the dealer's version of the disputed value, the dealer is discarded, and the parties terminate the protocol. Note that an *honest* dealer will not be discarded (with a high probability), since, in this case, at least one of the parties among P_i and P_j is corrupt. Suppose P_i is *corrupt*. Then, for the dealer to get discarded, P_i has to forge the signature of the dealer on a value *different* from $F(\alpha_j, \alpha_i)$, since an honest dealer will make public the correct disputed value $F(\alpha_j, \alpha_i)$.

If the dealer is not discarded at the end of the sixth round, then it guarantees that the vector of values held by the honest parties are pair-wise consistent and hence lie on a single (t, t)-degree bivariate polynomial, say $F^\star(x, y)$. The value $s^\star \stackrel{def}{=} F^\star(0, 0)$ is then considered the value $2D$-secret-shared with authentication by the dealer. Namely, the polynomial $q^\star(y) \stackrel{def}{=} F^\star(0, y)$ is considered as the *sharing-polynomial* of the dealer and each *honest* party P_i will have the *primary-share* $q^\star(\alpha_i)$. This is because P_i will have the vector of values $\overrightarrow{f_i} = (f_{i,1}, \ldots, f_{i,n})$, lying on polynomial $F^\star(x, \alpha_i)$ and $q^\star(\alpha_i) = F^\star(0, \alpha_i)$ holds. We also note that the vector $\overrightarrow{f_i}$ constitutes the *secondary-shares* of $q^\star(\alpha_i)$, since they lie on the t-degree polynomial $F^\star(x, \alpha_i)$. Moreover, for every party P_j, party P_i will either have a valid signature of P_j on the secondary-share $f_{i,j}$ (if P_i broadcasted an $\mathtt{OK}(P_i, P_j)$ message after the pair-wise consistency check) or the value $f_{i,j}$ along with a valid signature from the dealer will be publicly available (in case P_i broadcasted an $\mathtt{NOK}(P_i, P_j)$ message after the pair-wise consistency check). Finally, we note that the value $s^\star$ will be the same as s, if the dealer is *honest*. This is because the polynomial $F^\star(x, y)$ will be the same as $F(x, y)$ for an honest dealer. This completes the description of the sharing-phase protocol. Let us now discuss the reconstruction phase.

The goal of the reconstruction phase is to reconstruct the value that was $2D$-secret-shared with authentication during the sharing phase. This is achieved by reconstructing the underlying sharing-polynomial for which it suffices to get $t + 1$ *correct* primary-shares, which are always available since $t < \frac{n}{2}$. To achieve this, each party P_i which is *not* discarded during the sharing phase is asked to reveal its primary share. To prevent a potentially *corrupt* P_i from providing an incorrect primary-share, each party P_i is asked to reveal the secondary-shares $f_{i,j}$ signed by the respective parties P_j if they have not been made public during the sharing phase or else the secondary-shares are already available from the sharing phase. These secondary-shares are then further verified if they lie on some t-degree polynomial (which should be true if P_i is *honest*). If any of the verifications fail, then P_i is discarded, and its input is not considered for reconstruction. Note that an *honest* P_i never gets discarded. On the other hand, if a *corrupt* party P_i is not discarded, then it implies that it has revealed secondary shares lying on $F^\star(x, y)$. This is because there are at least $t + 1$ *honest* parties P_j and the secondary-shares $f_{i,j}$ corresponding to these honest parties uniquely defined $F^\star(x, \alpha_i)$. Once the "status" (discarded or not discarded) of every party party is clear, the secondary-shares of the parties which are not discarded are then used to interpolate the underlying (t, t)-degree bivariate polynomial $F^\star(x, y)$ (which will be the same as $F(x, y)$ for an *honest* dealer) and $F^\star(0, 0)$ is taken as the output.

The CDDHR VSS scheme consisting of the protocols $\Pi^{(n,t)}_{\mathsf{CDDHRSh}}$ (for the sharing phase) and $\Pi^{(n,t)}_{\mathsf{CDDHRRec}}$ (for the reconstruction phase) is presented in Fig 14.3.

Scheme CDDHR

Setup: A PKI setup where for each $P_j \in \mathcal{P}$, there exists a pair of keys $(\mathsf{sk}_j, \mathsf{pk}_j)$ for a signature scheme (Sign, Verify), with sk_j held by P_j and pk_j being *publicly* available. Additionally, the parties have oracle access to a BB oracle for broadcasting value(s).

Sharing Phase: Protocol $\Pi^{(n,t)}_{\mathsf{CDDHRSh}}$

- **Round 1 (distributing signed row and column-polynomials)** — the dealer does the following.
  - On having input $s \in \mathbb{F}$, pick a random t-degree *sharing polynomial* $q(y)$ over $\mathbb{F}$, such that $q(0) = s$ holds. Then pick a random (t, t)-degree bivariate polynomial $F(x, y)$ over $\mathbb{F}$ such that $F(0, y) = q(y)$ holds.
  - For $i = 1, \ldots, n$, compute $f_i(x) \stackrel{def}{=} F(x, \alpha_i)$ and $g_i(y) \stackrel{def}{=} F(\alpha_i, y)$.
  - For $i = 1, \ldots, n$, send $\{f_{ij}, g_{ij}\}_{j=1,\ldots,n}$ to party P_i, along with a signature on each of these values, where $f_{ij} \stackrel{def}{=} f_i(\alpha_j)$ and $g_{ij} \stackrel{def}{=} g_i(\alpha_j)$.
- **Round 2 (complaint stage)** — Every party $P_i \in \mathcal{P}$ does the following upon receiving the values $\overrightarrow{f_i} = (f_{i,1}, \ldots, f_{i,n})$ and $\overrightarrow{g_i} = (g_{i,1}, \ldots, g_{i,n})$ from the dealer in the previous round.[a]
  - If the dealer's signature on the values in $\overrightarrow{f_i}$ or $\overrightarrow{g_i}$ are not valid, then P_i broadcasts a complaint against the dealer by acting as a sender and calling the broadcast oracle with input $(\mathsf{complaint}, P_i)$.
  - Else if the values $\{(\alpha_j, f_{i,j})\}_{j=1,\ldots,n}$ or $\{(\alpha_j, g_{i,j})\}_{j=1,\ldots,n}$ do not lie on a t-degree polynomial, then P_i broadcasts those values with the dealer's signature by acting as a sender and calling the broadcast oracle.
- **(local computation at the end of Round 2)** — every party in $\mathcal{P}$ discards the dealer and terminates the protocol if there exists any party $P_i \in \mathcal{P}$, such that all the following conditions are satisfied.
  - P_i broadcasted either the vector of values $\overrightarrow{f_i} = (f_{i,1}, \ldots, f_{i,n})$ or $\overrightarrow{g_i} = (g_{i,1}, \ldots, g_{i,n})$, with valid signature of the dealer on these values.
  - The values $\{(\alpha_j, f_{i,j})\}_{j=1,\ldots,n}$ (resp. $\{(\alpha_j, g_{i,j})\}_{j=1,\ldots,n}$) do not lie on a t-degree polynomial.
- **Round 3 (resolving the complaints of the complaint stage)** — for every $P_i \in \mathcal{P}$ who broadcasts $(\mathsf{complaint}, P_i)$ during Round 2, the dealer does the following.
  - Broadcast the values $\{f_{i,j}\}_{j=1,\ldots,n}$ and $\{g_{i,j}\}_{j=1,\ldots,n}$, along with its signature on these values acting as a sender and calling the broadcast oracle with these values and associated signatures. Party P_i then uses these values for the remainder of the protocol.
- **(local computation at the end of Round 3)** — every party in $\mathcal{P}$ discards the dealer and terminates the protocol if there exists any party $P_i \in \mathcal{P}$, such that all the following conditions are satisfied.
  - P_i broadcasts $(\mathsf{complaint}, P_i)$ during Round 2;
  - In response, the dealer broadcasts either invalid signatures or the values $\{f_{i,j}\}_{j=1,\ldots,n}$ or $\{g_{i,j}\}_{j=1,\ldots,n}$ broadcasted by the dealer during Round 3 do not lie on t-degree polynomials.

  If the dealer is not discarded at the end of the Round 3, then every (honest) party P_i has valid signatures of the dealer on the values $\{f_{ij}\}_{j=1,\ldots,n}$ and $\{g_{ij}\}_{j=1,\ldots,n}$, such that $\{(\alpha_j, f_{i,j})\}_{j=1,\ldots,n}$ and $\{(\alpha_j, g_{i,j})\}_{j=1,\ldots,n}$ lie on t-degree polynomials.
- **Round 4 (pair-wise consistency checks on signed values)** — each party $P_i \in \mathcal{P}$ does the following
  - For $j = 1, \ldots, n$, send the value $g_{i,j}$ to party P_j, along with P_i's signature on the value. Let $\sigma_{i,j}$ denote the signature of P_i on the value $g_{i,j}$.
- **Round 5 (publicly announcing the results of pair-wise consistency checks)** — each party $P_i \in \mathcal{P}$ does the following for every $P_j \in \mathcal{P}$.
  - Broadcast $(\mathtt{OK}, P_i, P_j)$ by acting as a sender and calling the broadcast oracle, if all the following conditions are satisfied.
    - P_i received $g_{j,i}$ and the signature $\sigma_{j,i}$ from P_j during Round 4 such that $\sigma_{j,i}$ is a valid signature of P_j on $g_{j,i}$;
    - $g_{j,i} = f_{i,j}$ holds.
  - If any of the above conditions is not satisfied, then P_i broadcasts $(\mathtt{NOK}, P_i, P_j)$ by acting as a sender and calling the broadcast oracle,

- **Round 6 (resolving pair-wise inconsistencies)** — For every pair of parties P_i, P_j such that P_i broadcasts $(\texttt{NOK}, P_i, P_j)$ during Round 5, the dealer, party P_i and party P_j broadcast the following values respectively by acting as a sender and calling the broadcast oracle with these values as input(s).
  - The dealer broadcasts $F(\alpha_j, \alpha_i)$.
  - Party P_i broadcasts $f_{i,j}$, along with the dealer's signature on the value.
  - Party P_j broadcasts $g_{j,i}$, along with the dealer's signature on the value.
- **(local computation at the end of Round 6 and termination)** — for every pair of parties P_i, P_j such that P_i broadcasts $(\texttt{NOK}, P_i, P_j)$ during Round 5, the parties do the following.
  - If the signature revealed by P_i (resp. P_j) is invalid, then discard P_i (resp. P_j), along with the complaint $(\texttt{NOK}, P_i, P_j)$.
  - Else, if any of the following conditions hold, the parties discard the dealer and terminate the protocol.
    - P_i broadcasted a valid signature on $f_{i,j}$ and $f_{i,j} \neq F(\alpha_j, \alpha_i)$.
    - P_j broadcasted a valid signature on $g_{j,i}$ and $g_{j,i} \neq F(\alpha_j, \alpha_i)$.
  - Else discard the complaint $(\texttt{NOK}, P_i, P_j)$.

  Once the above steps are executed for every candidate pair of parties P_i, P_j, the parties terminate the protocol.

Reconstruction Phase: Protocol $\Pi^{(n,t)}_{\mathsf{CDDHRRec}}$

The parties execute the following steps only if the dealer has not been discarded during the protocol $\Pi^{(n,t)}_{\mathsf{CDDHRSh}}$, else the parties output 0 and terminate.

- **Round 1 (revealing the signed secondary-shares)** — every party $P_i \in \mathcal{P}$ who is not yet discarded does the following.
  - For every party $P_j \in \mathcal{P}$, send $(f_{i,j}, \sigma_{j,i})$ to all the parties who are not yet discarded, provided P_i has not broadcasted $\texttt{NOK}(P_i, P_j)$ during Round 5 of the sharing phase.
- **(output computation and termination)** — every party $P_k \in \mathcal{P}$ who is not yet discarded does the following.
  - For every $P_i \in \mathcal{P}$ who is not yet discarded, party P_k verifies P_i's signatures on the values received from P_i during the previous round. If any of these signatures is found to be invalid, then discard P_i.
  - For every $P_i \in \mathcal{P}$ which is not yet discarded by P_k, party P_k has the values $\overrightarrow{f_i^{(k)}} = (f_{i,1}, \ldots, f_{i,n})$, where each of these values was either received from P_i (along with P_i's signature) in the previous round or was broadcasted by P_i (along with the dealer's signature) during Round 5 of the sharing phase. If the values $\{(\alpha_j, f_{i,j})\}_{j=1,\ldots,n}$ do not lie on a t-degree polynomial, then discard P_i.
  - Let $\mathcal{S}_k$ denote the set of *supportive* parties from the point of view of P_k where $P_i \in \mathcal{S}_k$ if P_i is not yet discarded. For every $P_i \in \mathcal{S}_k$, interpolate the points $\{(\alpha_j, f_{i,j})\}_{j=1,\ldots,n}$ to compute a t-degree polynomial, say $f_i'(x)$.
  - Interpolate the polynomials $\{(\alpha_i, f_i'(x))\}_{P_i \in \mathcal{S}_k}$. If a (t,t)-degree bivariate polynomial, say $F'(x,y)$, is obtained then output $F'(0,0)$ and terminate. Else output 0 and terminate.

[a] If any of these values are not delivered by the end of the first round, then P_i substitutes default values.

Fig. 14.3: The CDDHR VSS scheme with a strict honest majority

We now proceed to prove the properties of the VSS scheme. We first prove the *liveness* property and derive the round and communication complexity.

Lemma 14.4 *In scheme* CDDHR, *the following holds for every possible adversary corrupting up to t parties:*

– *All honest parties terminate the protocol* $\Pi_{\text{CDDHRSh}}^{(n,t)}$ *and* $\Pi_{\text{CDDHRRec}}^{(n,t)}$.
– *Protocol* $\Pi_{\text{CDDHRSh}}^{(n,t)}$ *requires* $(6, 4)$ *rounds and protocol* $\Pi_{\text{CDDHRRec}}^{(n,t)}$ *requires* $(1, 0)$ *round.*
– *Protocol* $\Pi_{\text{CDDHRSh}}^{(n,t)}$ *incurs a communication of* $O(n^2(\log|\mathbb{F}|+\kappa))+\mathcal{BC}(n^2(\log|\mathbb{F}|+\kappa))$ *bits, where* κ *denotes the size of a signature in bits, and* $\mathcal{BC}(\ell)$ *denotes the cost of emulating one call to the BB oracle with an* ℓ*-bit input.*
– *Protocol* $\Pi_{\text{CDDHRRec}}^{(n,t)}$ *incurs a communication of* $O(n^3(\log|\mathbb{F}| + \kappa))$ *bits.*

Proof The round complexity follows from the protocol description. The sharing phase involves 6 rounds, where the broadcast oracle is called during rounds 2, 3, 5 and 6. Hence, the round complexity of $\Pi_{\text{CDDHRSh}}^{(n,t)}$ is $(6, 4)$.[3] During the reconstruction phase, the parties exchange messages only for 1 round and the broadcast oracle is *not* invoked. Hence the round complexity of $\Pi_{\text{CDDHRRec}}^{(n,t)}$ is $(1, 0)$.

The communication complexity of the reconstruction phase follows easily. Each party needs to send at most n signed secondary-shares to every other party. This involves communication of $O(n^3(\log|\mathbb{F}| + \kappa))$ bits. Let us now derive the communication complexity of the sharing phase. During the first round, the dealer distributes n^2 signed secondary-shares, involving communication of $O(n^2(\log|\mathbb{F}| + \kappa))$ bits. During the second round, in the worst case, each party may broadcast $2n$ signed values, which incurs a communication of $\mathcal{BC}(n^2(\log|\mathbb{F}| + \kappa))$ bits. During the third round, the dealer may broadcast $2n$ signed values for each party, which requires communication of $\mathcal{BC}(n^2(\log|\mathbb{F}|+\kappa))$ bits. During the fourth round, every pair of parties exchange 2 signed field elements, incurring a communication of $O(n^2(\log|\mathbb{F}| + \kappa))$ bits. The fifth round involves each party broadcasting either an `OK` or an `NOK` message for every other party, which involves communication of $\mathcal{BC}(n^2)$ bits. Finally, during the sixth round, for every `NOK` message, 2 signed values are broadcasted. As the number of `NOK` messages is upper bounded by n^2, this involves a total communication of $\mathcal{BC}(n^2(\log|\mathbb{F}| + \kappa))$ bits.

The liveness now simply follows from the fact that both $\Pi_{\text{CDDHRSh}}^{(n,t)}$ and $\Pi_{\text{CDDHRRec}}^{(n,t)}$ are round-based and require a *fixed* number of rounds, as derived above. □

We next prove the *hiding* property.

Lemma 14.5 *In scheme* CDDHR, *if the dealer is honest during* $\Pi_{\text{CDDHRSh}}^{(n,t)}$ *and participate with input s, then the view of the adversary during* $\Pi_{\text{CDDHRSh}}^{(n,t)}$ *corrupting up to t parties is independent of s.*

Proof Let C be the set of corrupt parties. We will show that if the dealer is *honest*, then throughout $\Pi_{\text{CDDHRSh}}^{(n,t)}$, the view of the adversary consists of the polynomials $\{f_i(x), g_i(y)\}_{P_i \in C}$ and signature on distinct points on these polynomials. Now since these polynomials are derived from $F(x, y)$, which is a randomly chosen (t, t)-degree polynomial embedding $q(y)$, it follows from Lemma 8.2 that the view of the adversary is distributed independently of s.

[3] Recall that a round complexity of (r, r') where $r' \leq r$ means that the protocol involves r rounds and among these r rounds, the broadcast oracle is invoked in r' rounds.

During the first round, the adversary learns the polynomials $\{f_i(x), g_i(y)\}_{P_i \in C}$ and the dealer's signature on the points on these polynomials. Only the parties in C may broadcast the points on their row and column polynomials during the second round. This is because if $P_i \notin C$, then it will receive valid signatures on $\{f_{i,j}\}_{j=1,\ldots,n}$ and $\{g_{i,j}\}_{j=1,\ldots,n}$ from the dealer during the first round and these values will lie on t-degree polynomials $f_i(x)$ and $g_i(y)$ respectively. Hence, no honest party P_i will complain against the dealer. As a result, the values made public by the dealer during the third round are already known to the adversary. During the fourth round, for every pair of *honest* parties P_i, P_j, the values $g_{i,j}$ and $g_{j,i}$ are exchanged over the point-to-point channels between P_i and P_j and will *not* be learnt by the adversary. Corresponding to every $P_i \in C$, the adversary will learn the values $\{g_{j,i}\}_{P_j \notin C}$. However, these values are already *known* to P_i, since $g_{j,i} = f_{i,j} = F(\alpha_j, \alpha_i) = f_i(\alpha_j)$ and adversary knows the polynomial $f_i(x)$. Since the dealer is honest, the condition $f_{i,j} = g_{j,i}$ will hold for every pair of *honest* parties P_i and P_j. Moreover, P_i and P_j will exchange valid signatures $\sigma_{i,j}$ and $\sigma_{j,i}$. Consequently, P_i and P_j will broadcast $\texttt{OK}(P_i, P_j)$ and $\texttt{OK}(P_j, P_i)$. Hence if any party P_i broadcasts $\texttt{NOK}(P_i, P_j)$ then either P_i or P_j is *corrupt*. Consequently, the values broadcasted during the sixth round are already known to the adversary. Hence, all the information which are made public throughout the protocol can be derived from $\{f_i(x), g_i(y)\}_{P_i \in C}$, thus proving the lemma. □

Next, we show the *correctness* and *binding* properties, for which we prove a series of helping claims. We first claim that an honest dealer never gets discarded during the sharing phase.

Claim 14.1 In scheme CDDHR, if the dealer is honest during $\Pi^{(n,t)}_{\mathsf{CDDHRSh}}$, then except with a negligible probability, the honest parties do not discard the dealer.

Proof Let the dealer be *honest* and let $\mathcal{H}$ be the set of *honest* parties. From the protocol steps, the dealer can get discarded, either at the end of the Round 2 or Round 6. We will show that the conditions for the dealer getting discarded will be *not* satisfied throughout the protocol except with a negligible probability. An honest dealer will distribute valid signatures on the values $\{f_{i,j}, g_{i,j}\}_{j=1,\ldots,n}$ to *every* party $P_i \in \mathcal{P}$, such that the values $\{(\alpha_j, f_{i,j})\}_{j=1,\ldots,n}$ and $\{(\alpha_j, g_{i,j})\}_{j=1,\ldots,n}$ lie on t-degree polynomials. Hence, during the second round, no $P_i \in \mathcal{H}$ will broadcast a complaint against the dealer or broadcast values which will lead to discarding the dealer. So, for an honest dealer to get discarded during the second round, it must be the case that there exists some $P_i \notin \mathcal{H}$, who broadcast values $(f'_{i,1}, \ldots, f'_{i,n})$ and $(g'_{i,1}, \ldots, g'_{i,n})$, along with dealer's valid signature on these values, such that either of the following holds.

- $(f'_{i,1}, \ldots, f'_{i,n}) \neq (f_{i,1}, \ldots, f_{i,n})$ and the values $\{(\alpha_j, f'_{i,j})\}_{j=1,\ldots,n}$ *do not* lie on a t-degree polynomial.
- $(g'_{i,1}, \ldots, g'_{i,n}) \neq (g_{i,1}, \ldots, g_{i,n})$ and the values $\{(\alpha_j, g'_{i,j})\}_{j=1,\ldots,n}$ *do not* lie on a t-degree polynomial.

However, this is possible only if P_i can forge an *honest* dealer's signature on the values $(f'_{i,1}, \ldots, f'_{i,n})$ or $(g'_{i,1}, \ldots, g'_{i,n})$, satisfying the above conditions. Since the signature scheme satisfies the unforgeability property, the above can happen only with a negligible probability.

From the proof of Lemma 14.5, if any party P_i broadcasts the message $\texttt{NOK}(P_i, P_j)$ during Round 5 then either P_i or P_j is *corrupt*. In response to the message $\texttt{NOK}(P_i, P_j)$, the dealer will broadcast the value $F(\alpha_j, \alpha_i)$. If P_i is *corrupt*, then the dealer will get discarded if P_i can broadcast a value $f'_{i,j}$ along with the honest dealer's valid signature on it, such that $F(\alpha_j, \alpha_i) \neq f'_{i,j}$ holds. For this, P_i has to forge the dealer's signature on $f'_{i,j}$, since the dealer gave its signature on $f_{i,j}$ to P_i where $f_{i,j} = F(\alpha_j, \alpha_i)$. Since the signature scheme satisfies the unforgeability property, the above can happen only with a negligible probability. Similarly, if P_j is *corrupt*, then the dealer will get discarded if P_j can broadcast a value $g'_{j,i}$ along with the honest dealer's valid signature on it, such that $F(\alpha_j, \alpha_i) \neq g'_{j,i}$ holds. For this, P_j has to forge the dealer's signature on $g'_{j,i}$, since the dealer gave its signature on $g_{j,i}$ to P_j where $g_{j,i} = F(\alpha_j, \alpha_i)$. Again, this can happen only with a negligible probability.

Hence, throughout the protocol, the conditions for discarding an honest dealer are satisfied only with a negligible probability, thus proving the claim. □

We next claim that if the dealer is not discarded during the sharing phase, then the values held by the honest parties and the values which are public corresponding to the honest parties lie on a unique (t, t)-degree bivariate polynomial.

Claim 14.2 Let $t < \frac{n}{2}$. If the dealer is not discarded during the protocol $\Pi^{(n,t)}_{\text{CDDHRSh}}$, then there exists a unique (t, t)-degree bivariate polynomial, say $F^{\star}(x, y)$, where $F^{\star}(x, y) = F(x, y)$ for an honest dealer, such that all the following holds for every honest party P_i, except with a negligible probability.

- P_i will have the vector of values $(f_{i,1}, \ldots, f_{i,n})$ and $(g_{i,1}, \ldots, g_{i,n})$, where $f_{i,j} = F^{\star}(\alpha_j, \alpha_i)$ and $g_{i,j} = F^{\star}(\alpha_i, \alpha_j)$ holds, for $j = 1, \ldots, n$.
- For $j = 1, \ldots, n$, one of the following holds.
  - P_i has a valid signature $\sigma_{j,i}$ of P_j on the value $f_{i,j}$;
  - The value $f_{i,j}$, along with a valid signature from the dealer, is publicly known.

Proof Let $\mathcal{H}$ be the set of honest parties and the dealer not be discarded during $\Pi^{(n,t)}_{\text{CDDHRSh}}$. From the protocol steps, at the end of Round 3, every $P_i \in \mathcal{H}$ will have a vector of values $(f_{i,1}, \ldots, f_{i,n})$ and $(g_{i,1}, \ldots, g_{i,n})$, along with a valid signature of the dealer on each of these values, such that the points $\{(\alpha_j, f_{i,j})\}_{j=1,\ldots,n}$ and $\{(\alpha_j, g_{i,j})\}_{j=1,\ldots,n}$ lie on t-degree polynomials. While this is true if the dealer is honest, the same holds even if the dealer is corrupt since we assume that the dealer is *not* discarded.

Next, consider an arbitrary pair of parties $P_i, P_j \in \mathcal{H}$. Then $f_{i,j} = g_{j,i}$ holds. This is true if the dealer is honest since $f_{i,j} = g_{j,i} = F(\alpha_j, \alpha_i)$ holds where $F(x, y)$ is the bivariate polynomial used by the dealer. On the other hand, consider the case when the dealer is corrupt. Then if $f_{i,j} \neq g_{j,i}$, then P_i would broadcast an $\texttt{NOK}(P_i, P_j)$ message during Round 5. In response, P_i and P_j would broadcast the values $f_{i,j}$ and $g_{j,i}$ respectively, along with a valid signature of the dealer on these values. From the properties of the signature scheme, these signatures will be accepted by the parties in $\mathcal{H}$. Now, irrespective of the value broadcasted by the dealer during Round 6 in response to the $\texttt{NOK}(P_i, P_j)$ message, the dealer will get discarded, which is a contradiction. Hence $f_{i,j} = g_{j,i}$ holds for every $P_i, P_j \in \mathcal{H}$. Since $|\mathcal{H}| \geq n - t$ and the vector of values $\{(\alpha_j, f_{i,j})\}_{j=1,\ldots,n}$ and $\{(\alpha_j, g_{i,j})\}_{j=1,\ldots,n}$ lie on t-degree polynomials, it follows from Lemma 8.1 that these values lie on a unique (t, t)-degree bivariate polynomial. In more detail, there exists some (t, t)-degree bivariate polynomial, say $F^\star(x, y)$, such that $f_{i,j} = F^\star(\alpha_j, \alpha_i)$ and $g_{i,j} = F^\star(\alpha_i, \alpha_j)$ holds, for $j = 1, \ldots, n$. Note that $F^\star(x, y) = F(x, y)$ for an honest dealer since an honest dealer distributes values lying on $F(x, y)$ to the parties.

Next consider an *arbitrary* $P_i \in \mathcal{H}$ and an *arbitrary* $P_j \in \mathcal{P}$. There are two possible cases, depending upon if P_i broadcasts $\texttt{OK}(P_i, P_j)$ or $\texttt{NOK}(P_i, P_j)$ during Round 5. If P_i broadcasts $\texttt{OK}(P_i, P_j)$ then it implies that P_i received a valid signature $\sigma_{j,i}$ from party P_j on the value $g_{j,i}$ during Round 4 and $f_{i,j} = g_{j,i}$ holds. Hence $\sigma_{j,i}$ is a valid signature from P_j even on the value $f_{j,i}$. On the other hand, if P_i broadcasts $\texttt{NOK}(P_i, P_j)$ during Round 5, then in response, P_i also makes public the value $f_{i,j}$, along with a valid signature from the dealer on $f_{i,j}$. This completes the proof of the claim. □

We next claim that if the dealer is not discarded during the sharing phase, then no honest party gets discarded by any honest party during the reconstruction phase.

Claim 14.3 Let $t < \frac{n}{2}$. In scheme CDDHR, if the dealer is not discarded during $\Pi^{(n,t)}_{\mathsf{CDDHRSh}}$ then the following holds during $\Pi^{(n,t)}_{\mathsf{CDDHRRec}}$ for every *honest* party P_i, except with a negligible probability.

- $P_i \in \mathcal{S}_k$ for every honest party P_k and $f'_i(x) = F^\star(x, \alpha_i)$ holds. Here $f'_i(x)$ is the t-degree polynomial computed by P_k by interpolating the points $\{(\alpha_j, f_{i,j})\}_{j=1,\ldots,n}$. Moreover, $F^\star(x, y)$ is the unique (t, t)-degree bivariate polynomial, defined by the values held by the honest parties, where $F^\star(x, y) = F(x, y)$ for an honest dealer.

Proof Let $\mathcal{H}$ be the set of honest parties and the dealer not be discarded during $\Pi^{(n,t)}_{\mathsf{CDDHRSh}}$. Then from Claim 14.2, at the end of $\Pi^{(n,t)}_{\mathsf{CDDHRSh}}$, there exists some unique (t, t)-degree bivariate polynomial $F^\star(x, y)$, where $F^\star(x, y) = F(x, y)$ for an honest dealer, such that all the following holds for every $P_i \in \mathcal{H}$, except with a negligible probability.

- P_i will have the vector of values $(f_{i,1}, \ldots, f_{i,n})$ and $(g_{i,1}, \ldots, g_{i,n})$, where $f_{i,j} = F^\star(\alpha_j, \alpha_i)$ and $g_{i,j} = F^\star(\alpha_i, \alpha_j)$ holds, for $j = 1, \ldots, n$. This also implies that the values $\{(\alpha_j, f_{i,j})\}_{j=1,\ldots,n}$ lie on a t-degree polynomial, namely $F^\star(x, \alpha_i)$, which is same as $F(x, \alpha_i)$ for an honest dealer.
- For $j = 1, \ldots, n$, one of the following holds.
  - P_i has a valid signature $\sigma_{j,i}$ of P_j on the value $f_{i,j}$;
  - The value $f_{i,j}$, along with a valid signature from the dealer, is publicly known.

Next consider the reconstruction phase protocol $\Pi^{(n,t)}_{\mathsf{CDDHRRec}}$ and consider an arbitrary $P_i \in \mathcal{H}$ and an arbitrary $P_j \in \mathcal{P}$. Then there are two possible cases depending upon if P_i broadcasted $\texttt{OK}(P_i, P_j)$ or $\texttt{NOK}(P_i, P_j)$ during the Round 5 of $\Pi^{(n,t)}_{\mathsf{CDDHRSh}}$.

If P_i has broadcasted $\mathtt{OK}(P_i, P_j)$, then during $\Pi^{(n,t)}_{\mathsf{CDDHRRec}}$, party P_i will send the value $f_{i,j}$ along with the signature $\sigma_{j,i}$ to all the parties. Since the signature is valid, it will be verified and accepted by all the parties in $\mathcal{H}$, except with a negligible probability, which follows from the properties of the signature scheme. On the other hand, if P_i has broadcasted $\mathtt{NOK}(P_i, P_j)$, then during $\Pi^{(n,t)}_{\mathsf{CDDHRRec}}$, the parties in $\mathcal{H}$ will take the value $f_{i,j}$ for P_i on behalf of P_j. Hence each party $P_k \in \mathcal{H}$ will consider the vector of values $\overrightarrow{f_i^{(k)}} = (f_{i,1}, \ldots, f_{i,n})$ for P_i. Moreover, as mentioned above, the the values $\{(\alpha_j, f_{i,j})\}_{j=1,\ldots,n}$ will lie on the t-degree polynomial $F^\star(x, \alpha_i)$. Consequently, P_i will not be discarded and gets included in the set $\mathcal{S}_k$ of every party $P_k \in \mathcal{H}$. Moreover, P_k will interpolate the t-degree polynomial $f_i'(x)$ by interpolating the points $\{(\alpha_j, f_{i,j})\}_{j=1,\ldots,n}$, where $f_i'(x)$ will be the same as $F^\star(x, \alpha_i)$, thus proving the claim. □

We finally claim that if the dealer is not discarded during the sharing phase, then every *corrupt* party which does not get discarded during the reconstruction phase by an honest party, reveals values lying on the dealer's committed bivariate polynomial.[4]

Claim 14.4 Let $t < \frac{n}{2}$. In scheme CDDHR, if the dealer is not discarded during $\Pi^{(n,t)}_{\mathsf{CDDHRSh}}$, then the following holds during $\Pi^{(n,t)}_{\mathsf{CDDHRRec}}$ for every *corrupt* party P_i, except with a negligible probability.

- If $P_i \in \mathcal{S}_k$ of any honest party P_k, then $f_i'(x) = F^\star(x, \alpha_i)$ holds. Here $f_i'(x)$ is the t-degree polynomial computed by P_k by interpolating the points $\{(\alpha_j, f_{i,j})\}_{j=1,\ldots,n}$. Moreover, $F^\star(x, y)$ is the unique (t, t)-degree bivariate polynomial, defined by the values held by the honest parties, where $F^\star(x, y) = F(x, y)$ for an honest dealer.

Proof Let $\mathcal{H}$ be the set of honest parties and the dealer not be discarded during the protocol $\Pi^{(n,t)}_{\mathsf{CDDHRSh}}$. Then from Claim 14.2, at the end of $\Pi^{(n,t)}_{\mathsf{CDDHRSh}}$, there exists some unique (t, t)-degree bivariate polynomial $F^\star(x, y)$, where $F^\star(x, y) = F(x, y)$ for an honest dealer, such that all the following holds for every $P_i \in \mathcal{H}$, except with a negligible probability.

- P_i will have the vector of values $(f_{i,1}, \ldots, f_{i,n})$ and $(g_{i,1}, \ldots, g_{i,n})$, where $f_{i,j} = F^\star(\alpha_j, \alpha_i)$ and $g_{i,j} = F^\star(\alpha_i, \alpha_j)$ holds, for $j = 1, \ldots, n$.

Next consider an *arbitrary* $P_i \notin \mathcal{H}$, such that $P_i \in \mathcal{S}_k$ during $\Pi^{(n,t)}_{\mathsf{CDDHRRec}}$ where $P_k \in \mathcal{H}$. This implies that P_i is not discarded at the end of $\Pi^{(n,t)}_{\mathsf{CDDHRSh}}$ as well as during $\Pi^{(n,t)}_{\mathsf{CDDHRRec}}$. Now consider an *arbitrary* $P_j \in \mathcal{H}$. Then there are two possible cases, depending upon if P_i broadcasted $\mathtt{OK}(P_i, P_j)$ or $\mathtt{NOK}(P_i, P_j)$ for P_j during Round 5 of $\Pi^{(n,t)}_{\mathsf{CDDHRSh}}$.

If P_i has broadcasted $\mathtt{OK}(P_i, P_j)$, then P_i has received a valid signature $\sigma_{j,i}$ from P_j on $g_{j,i}$ during Round 4 of $\Pi^{(n,t)}_{\mathsf{CDDHRSh}}$, where $g_{j,i} = F^\star(\alpha_j, \alpha_i)$. This further implies that the value $f_{j,i}$ revealed by P_i to P_k during $\Pi^{(n,t)}_{\mathsf{CDDHRRec}}$ is the same as

[4] Note that the honest parties always reveal values lying on the dealer's committed bivariate polynomial.

$F^\star(\alpha_j, \alpha_i)$, except with a negligible probability. This is because P_i also reveals the signature $\sigma_{j,i}$ along with $f_{j,i}$. So if $f_{j,i} \neq F^\star(\alpha_j, \alpha_i)$, then except with a negligible probability, the signature $\sigma_{j,i}$ will be invalid, since a *corrupt* P_i *cannot* forge an honest P_j's signature on a value *different* from $F^\star(\alpha_j, \alpha_i)$. Consequently, P_k would discard P_i during $\Pi^{(n,t)}_{\mathsf{CDDHRRec}}$ and hence $P_i \notin \mathcal{S}_k$, which is a contradiction.

Next consider the case if P_i has broadcasted $\mathtt{NOK}(P_i, P_j)$. In this case, P_i produces a valid signature of the dealer on the value $f_{i,j}$ during Round 6, else P_i would have been discarded during $\Pi^{(n,t)}_{\mathsf{CDDHRSh}}$, which is a contradiction. Moreover, P_j would produce a valid signature of the dealer on $g_{j,i}$ during Round 6 where $g_{j,i} = F^\star(\alpha_j, \alpha_i)$. Furthermore, the dealer will make a public value, say c. Since the dealer is *not* discarded, it implies that $f_{i,j} = c = g_{j,i}$ holds. Consequently, every party in $\mathcal{H}$ (including P_k) will have the value $F^\star(\alpha_j, \alpha_i)$ for P_i on behalf of P_j.

Hence, irrespective of whether P_i broadcasted $\mathtt{OK}(P_i, P_j)$ or $\mathtt{NOK}(P_i, P_j)$ for P_j, party P_k will have the values $\{f_{i,j}\}_{P_j \in \mathcal{H}}$ in the vector $\overrightarrow{f_i^{(k)}}$ during $\Pi^{(n,t)}_{\mathsf{CDDHRRec}}$, which will be the same as $\{F^\star(\alpha_j, \alpha_i)\}_{P_j \in \mathcal{H}}$. From the protocol steps, P_k computes a t-degree polynomial $f_i'(x)$ by interpolating the values in $\overrightarrow{f_i^{(k)}}$. On the other hand, the values $\{F^\star(\alpha_j, \alpha_i)\}_{P_j \in \mathcal{H}}$ define the unique t-degree polynomial $F^\star(x, \alpha_i)$. Since $t < \frac{n}{2}$, it implies that $|\mathcal{H}| > t$ and consequently, $f_i'(x) = F^\star(x, \alpha_i)$. This is because two *different* t-degree polynomials can have *at most* t common points. This completes the proof of the claim. □

We are now well-equipped to prove the *correctness* and the *binding* properties. We start with the correctness proof.

Lemma 14.6 *Let* $t < \frac{n}{2}$. *In scheme* CDDHR, *if the dealer is honest during* $\Pi^{(n,t)}_{\mathsf{CDDHRSh}}$ *and participate with input* s, *then except with a negligible probability, the honest parties output* s *during the protocol* $\Pi^{(n,t)}_{\mathsf{CDDHRRec}}$.

Proof Let $\mathcal{H}$ be the set of *honest* parties and let the dealer be *honest*. Then from Claim 14.1, the dealer is not discarded by the parties in $\mathcal{H}$ at the end of $\Pi^{(n,t)}_{\mathsf{CDDHRSh}}$, except with a negligible probability. Moreover, from Claim 14.2, the following will hold for every $P_i \in \mathcal{H}$.

- P_i will have the vector of values $(f_{i,1}, \ldots, f_{i,n})$ and $(g_{i,1}, \ldots, g_{i,n})$, where $f_{i,j} = F(\alpha_j, \alpha_i)$ and $g_{i,j} = F(\alpha_i, \alpha_j)$ holds, for $j = 1, \ldots, n$.

Next consider an *arbitrary* $P_k \in \mathcal{H}$. We wish to show that P_k will interpolate a (t, t)-degree bivariate polynomial $F'(x, y)$ during $\Pi^{(n,t)}_{\mathsf{CDDHRRec}}$ except with a negligible probability, where $F'(x, y) = F(x, y)$ holds. This will imply that P_k outputs s, since as per the protocol steps, P_k outputs $F'(0, 0)$ and $s = F(0, 0)$ holds.

From Claim 14.3, $\mathcal{H} \subseteq \mathcal{S}_k$ will hold, except with a negligible probability, since every party from $\mathcal{H}$ will be present in $\mathcal{S}_k$. Moreover, for every $P_i \in \mathcal{H}$, party P_k will interpolate the t-degree polynomial $f_i'(x)$ during $\Pi^{(n,t)}_{\mathsf{CDDHRRec}}$, which will be the same as $F(x, \alpha_i)$. Since $|\mathcal{H}| > t$ and $F(x, y)$ is a (t, t)-degree bivariate polynomial, it follows that P_k will have sufficiently many number of $f_i'(x)$ polynomials to interpolate back $F(x, y)$. To complete the proof, consider the case when there exists any $P_i \notin \mathcal{H}$ such that $P_i \in \mathcal{S}_k$. Then from Claim 14.4, it follows that P_k will interpolate the t-degree polynomial $f_i'(x)$ during $\Pi^{(n,t)}_{\mathsf{CDDHRRec}}$, which will be the same as $F(x, \alpha_i)$, except with a negligible probability. It now follows that by interpolating the polynomials $\{(\alpha_i, f_i'(x))\}_{P_i \in \mathcal{S}_k}$, party P_k will reconstruct $F(x, y)$, thus proving the lemma. □

We next prove the binding property, similar to the proof of the correctness property.

Lemma 14.7 *Let $t < \frac{n}{2}$. If the dealer is corrupt, then during $\Pi^{(n,t)}_{\mathsf{CDDHRSh}}$, the joint view of the honest parties defines a unique value $s^\star \in \mathbb{F}$ (which could be different from s), such that all honest parties output $s^\star$ during $\Pi^{(n,t)}_{\mathsf{CDDHRRec}}$ except with a negligible probability.*

Proof Let $\mathcal{H}$ be the set of honest parties, where $|\mathcal{H}| \geq n - t > t$, since $t < \frac{n}{2}$. If the parties in $\mathcal{H}$ discard the dealer at the end of $\Pi^{(n,t)}_{\mathsf{CDDHRSh}}$, then the lemma holds trivially. This is because we can define $s^\star \stackrel{def}{=} 0$, since during $\Pi^{(n,t)}_{\mathsf{CDDHRRec}}$, the parties in $\mathcal{H}$ output the default value 0.

Next, consider the case when the dealer is *not* discarded. Then from Claim 14.2, at the end of $\Pi^{(n,t)}_{\mathsf{CDDHRSh}}$, there exists some unique (t, t)-degree bivariate polynomial $F^\star(x, y)$, such that the following will hold for every $P_i \in \mathcal{H}$.

- P_i will have the vector of values $(f_{i,1}, \ldots, f_{i,n})$ and $(g_{i,1}, \ldots, g_{i,n})$, where $f_{i,j} = F^\star(\alpha_j, \alpha_i)$ and $g_{i,j} = F^\star(\alpha_i, \alpha_j)$ holds, for $j = 1, \ldots, n$.

We define $s^\star \stackrel{def}{=} F^\star(0, 0)$ and wish to show that every party in $\mathcal{H}$ will output $s^\star$ at the end of $\Pi^{(n,t)}_{\mathsf{CDDHRRec}}$, except with a negligible probability. For this, we need to show that every honest party will reconstruct $F^\star(x, y)$. So consider an *arbitrary* $P_k \in \mathcal{H}$. From Claim 14.3, $\mathcal{H} \subseteq \mathcal{S}_k$ will hold, except with a negligible probability, since every party from $\mathcal{H}$ will be present in $\mathcal{S}_k$. Moreover, for every $P_i \in \mathcal{H}$, party P_k will interpolate the t-degree polynomial $f_i'(x)$ during $\Pi^{(n,t)}_{\mathsf{CDDHRRec}}$, which will be the same as $F^\star(x, \alpha_i)$. Since $|\mathcal{H}| > t$ and $F^\star(x, y)$ is a (t, t)-degree bivariate polynomial, it follows that P_k will have sufficiently many number of $f_i'(x)$ polynomials to interpolate back $F^\star(x, y)$. To complete the proof, consider the case when there exists any $P_i \notin \mathcal{H}$ such that $P_i \in \mathcal{S}_k$. Then from Claim 14.4, it follows that P_k will interpolate the t-degree polynomial $f_i'(x)$ during $\Pi^{(n,t)}_{\mathsf{CDDHRRec}}$, which will be the same as $F^\star(x, \alpha_i)$, except with a negligible probability. It now follows that by interpolating the polynomials $\{(\alpha_i, f_i'(x))\}_{P_i \in \mathcal{S}_k}$, party P_k will reconstruct $F^\star(x, y)$, thus proving the lemma. □

The following theorem now follows easily from the above discussion.

Theorem 14.3 *If $t < \frac{n}{2}$, then the pair of protocols $(\Pi^{(n,t)}_{\mathsf{CDDHRSh}}, \Pi^{(n,t)}_{\mathsf{CDDHRRec}})$ constitute a t-secure VSS scheme in the model $\mathcal{M}^{\mathsf{pki}}_{\mathsf{secure}}$ with the following complexities, provided the parties have oracle access to a BB oracle.*

- *Protocol $\Pi^{(n,t)}_{\mathsf{CDDHRSh}}$ requires $(6, 4)$ rounds and incurs a communication of $\mathcal{O}(n^2(\log|\mathbb{F}| + \kappa)) + \mathcal{BC}(n^2(\log|\mathbb{F}| + \kappa))$ bits, where κ is the security parameter and denotes the size of a signature in bits and where $\mathcal{BC}(\ell)$ denotes the communication complexity for emulating the BB oracle to broadcast ℓ bits.*

– *Protocol* $\Pi^{(n,t)}_{\mathsf{CDDHRRec}}$ *requires* $(1, 0)$ *round and incurs a communication of* $O(n^3(\log|\mathbb{F}| + \kappa))$ *bits.*
– *If the PKI is unconditionally-secure, then the scheme is statistically-secure. If the PKI is cryptographically-secure, then the scheme is cryptographically-secure.*

14.5 MVSS with $t < \frac{n}{2}$ in the Model $\mathcal{M}^{\mathsf{pki}}_{\mathsf{secure}}$

In this section, we show how to use the compiler of [65] discussed in Theorem 8.4 (see Chapter 8) to get an MVSS scheme with $t < \frac{n}{2}$ in the model $\mathcal{M}^{\mathsf{pki}}_{\mathsf{secure}}$. Recall that the compiler takes input a *t-secure* VSS scheme $(\Pi^{(n,t)}_{\mathsf{Sh}}, \Pi^{(n,t)}_{\mathsf{Rec}})$ in the model $\mathcal{M} \in \{\mathcal{M}_{\mathsf{secure}}, \mathcal{M}^{\mathsf{pki}}_{\mathsf{secure}}\}$ with security level $\mathsf{Sec} \in \{\mathsf{PerSec}, \mathsf{StatSec}, \mathsf{CryptoSec}\}$ and which has the following properties.

– Both $\Pi^{(n,t)}_{\mathsf{Sh}}$ and $\Pi^{(n,t)}_{\mathsf{Rec}}$ require a constant number of rounds;
– The broadcast oracle is used only during $\Pi^{(n,t)}_{\mathsf{Sh}}$;
– Protocol $\Pi^{(n,t)}_{\mathsf{Sh}}$ incurs a total communication of $O(C_1) + \mathcal{BC}(C_2)$ bits and $\Pi^{(n,t)}_{\mathsf{Rec}}$ incurs a communication of $O(C_3)$ bits.

The compiler also takes input a constant round *t-secure* GC protocol $\Pi^{(n,t)}_{\mathsf{GC}}$ for L-bit inputs in the model $\mathcal{M}$ with security level Sec, incurring a communication of $\mathcal{GC}(L)$ bits. The compiler then outputs a *t-secure* MVSS scheme $(\Pi^{(n,t)}_{\mathsf{ModSh}}, \Pi^{(n,t)}_{\mathsf{ModRec}})$ in the model $\mathcal{M}$ with security level Sec, which has the following properties:

– Both $\Pi^{(n,t)}_{\mathsf{ModSh}}$ and $\Pi^{(n,t)}_{\mathsf{ModRec}}$ require a constant number of rounds;
– No broadcast oracle is used during $\Pi^{(n,t)}_{\mathsf{ModSh}}$ or $\Pi^{(n,t)}_{\mathsf{ModRec}}$;
– Protocol $\Pi^{(n,t)}_{\mathsf{ModSh}}$ incurs a communication of $O(C_1) + \mathcal{GC}(C_2)$ bits and $\Pi^{(n,t)}_{\mathsf{ModRec}}$ incurs a communication of $O(C_3)$ bits.

Let us now instantiate the VSS scheme $(\Pi^{(n,t)}_{\mathsf{Sh}}, \Pi^{(n,t)}_{\mathsf{Rec}})$ with the scheme CDDHR (see Fig 14.3) and the GC protocol $\Pi^{(n,t)}_{\mathsf{GC}}$ with the protocol $\Pi^{(n,t)}_{\mathsf{GCHM}}$ (see Fig 14.1). We then get a *t-secure* MVSS scheme with constant rounds during the sharing and reconstruction phase. In more detail, the reconstruction phase of the MVSS scheme will require one round since the round complexity of $\Pi^{(n,t)}_{\mathsf{CDDHRRec}}$ is $(1, 0)$. On the other hand, the sharing phase of the MVSS scheme will require $2 + 6 \cdot 4 = 26$ rounds. This is because the round complexity of $\Pi^{(n,t)}_{\mathsf{CDDHRSh}}$ is $(6, 4)$. Recall that as per the compiler presented in Theorem 8.4, each call to the broadcast oracle is emulated by 2 invocations of the underlying GC protocol, executed *sequentially*. Since $\Pi^{(n,t)}_{\mathsf{GCHM}}$ requires 3 rounds, it follows that each broadcast round (where broadcast oracle is invoked) in the protocol $\Pi^{(n,t)}_{\mathsf{CDDHRSh}}$ will require $3 + 3 = 6$ rounds to be emulated. Hence, the number of rounds in the sharing phase of the MVSS will be 26.

The communication complexity of the reconstruction phase of the MVSS will be the same as that of $\Pi^{(n,t)}_{\mathsf{CDDHRRec}}$, which is $O(n^3(\log|\mathbb{F}| + \kappa))$ bits. Let us now compute the communication complexity of the sharing phase of the MVSS scheme. The communication complexity of the sharing phase is dominated by sending

$O(n^2(\log|\mathbb{F}| + \kappa))$ bits (which were broadcasted through broadcast oracle in the protocol $\Pi^{(n,t)}_{\mathsf{CDDHRSh}}$) through instances of the GC protocol $\Pi^{(n,t)}_{\mathsf{GCHM}}$. From Theorem 14.1, we have $\mathcal{GC}(L) = O(n^3(L + \kappa))$ bits for the protocol $\Pi^{(n,t)}_{\mathsf{GCHM}}$. But substituting $L = n^2(\log|\mathbb{F}| + \kappa)$, it turns out that the communication complexity of the sharing phase of the MVSS will be $O(n^5(\log|\mathbb{F}| + \kappa))$ bits.

We summarize the above discussion in Theorem 14.4.

Theorem 14.4 *If $t < \frac{n}{2}$ then there exists a t-secure MVSS scheme $(\Pi^{(n,t)}_{\mathsf{CDDHRMSh}}, \Pi^{(n,t)}_{\mathsf{CDDHRMRec}})$ in the model $\mathcal{M}^{\mathsf{pki}}_{\mathsf{secure}}$ with the following properties.*

- *Protocol $\Pi^{(n,t)}_{\mathsf{CDDHRMSh}}$ requires 26 rounds and incurs a communication of $O(n^5(\log|\mathbb{F}|+\kappa))$ bits over the point-to-point channels, where κ is the security parameter and denotes the size of a signature in bits.*
- *Protocol $\Pi^{(n,t)}_{\mathsf{CDDHRMRec}}$ requires 1 round and incurs a communication of $O(n^3(\log|\mathbb{F}|+\kappa))$ bits over the point-to-point channels.*
- *If the PKI is unconditionally-secure then the MVSS scheme is statistically-secure.*
- *If the PKI is cryptographically-secure then the MVSS scheme is cryptographically-secure.*

14.6 Common Coin with $t < \frac{n}{2}$ and a Constant Success Probability

Once we have an MVSS scheme with $t < \frac{n}{2}$, a *common coin* (CC) protocol follows automatically using the generic compiler (see Fig 8.4) derived in Theorem 8.5. Recall that the compiler takes input a *t-secure* MVSS scheme $(\Pi^{(n,t)}_{\mathsf{ModSh}}, \Pi^{(n,t)}_{\mathsf{ModRec}})$ in the model $\mathcal{M} \in \{\mathcal{M}_{\mathsf{secure}}, \mathcal{M}^{\mathsf{pki}}_{\mathsf{secure}}\}$, where $\Pi^{(n,t)}_{\mathsf{ModSh}}$ and $\Pi^{(n,t)}_{\mathsf{ModRec}}$ require R_1 and R_2 rounds of communication over the point-to-point channels respectively. The compiler then outputs a *t-secure p-CC* protocol in the model $\mathcal{M}$, which is either unconditionally-secure or cryptographically-secure, depending upon whether the MVSS scheme is unconditionally-secure or cryptographically-secure. The protocol requires $R_1 + R_2$ rounds of communication and its *success probability* p is $\min\left(1 - (1 - \frac{1}{u})^{n-t}, (1 - \frac{1}{u})^n\right)$, where u is a parameter to "control" the success probability p. The communication complexity of the protocol is n^2 times the communication complexity of one instance of $\Pi^{(n,t)}_{\mathsf{ModSh}}$ and one instance of $\Pi^{(n,t)}_{\mathsf{ModRec}}$.

Let us instantiate the MVSS scheme $(\Pi^{(n,t)}_{\mathsf{ModSh}}, \Pi^{(n,t)}_{\mathsf{ModRec}})$ in Fig 8.4 with the CDDHR MVSS scheme and let us set $u = n$. This will give us a *t-secure* CC protocol $\Pi^{(n,t)}_{\mathsf{CDDHRCC}}$ in the model $\mathcal{M}^{\mathsf{pki}}_{\mathsf{secure}}$ with $t < \frac{n}{2}$, which will require $26+1 = 27$ rounds of communication (this is because $R_1 = 26$ and $R_2 = 1$ for $\Pi^{(n,t)}_{\mathsf{CDDHRMSh}}$ and $\Pi^{(n,t)}_{\mathsf{CDDHRMRec}}$ respectively). The protocol will incur a communication complexity of $O(n^7(\log|\mathbb{F}|+\kappa))$ bits. The success probability p of the scheme can be derived as follows. Since $t < \frac{n}{2}$, it follows that $n - t > \frac{n}{2}$ holds. Consequently, the following holds.

$$1-\left(1-\frac{1}{u}\right)^{n-t} \geq 1-e^{-\frac{n-t}{u}} \geq 1-e^{-\frac{n}{2u}} \geq 1-e^{-\frac{1}{2}} \geq 0.39.$$

Similarly, the following holds.

$$\left(1-\frac{1}{u}\right)^{n} \geq e^{-\frac{n}{u}} \geq e^{-1} \geq 0.36.$$

Consequently, the success probability of the protocol $\Pi^{(n,t)}_{\mathsf{CDDHRCC}}$ will be 0.36. In the above calculations, we selected $u = n$ just for simplicity and one could instead set u to a different function of n to get an appropriate constant success probability.

We summarize the above discussion in Theorem 14.5.

Theorem 14.5 *Let $t < \frac{n}{2}$. Then there exists a t-secure 0.36-CC protocol $\Pi^{(n,t)}_{\mathsf{CDDHRCC}}$ in the model $\mathcal{M}^{\mathsf{pki}}_{\mathsf{secure}}$ with the following properties.*

- *The protocol requires 27 rounds of communication over the point-to-point channels.*
- *The protocol incurs a communication complexity of $O(n^7(\log|\mathbb{F}| + \kappa))$ bits.*
- *If the PKI is unconditionally-secure then the protocol is unconditionally-secure.*
- *If the PKI is cryptographically-secure then the protocol is cryptographically-secure.*

14.7 Randomized BA with $t < \frac{n}{2}$ and a Fixed Number of Iterations

Once we have an MVSS scheme and a GA protocol with $t < \frac{n}{2}$, a randomized BA protocol for single-bit input with $t < \frac{n}{2}$ and a *fixed* number of iterations follow immediately, using the generic framework presented in Fig 8.1 and analyzed in Theorem 8.1. Recall that the framework takes input a *t-secure* GA protocol and a *t-secure p-CC* protocol for any given $0 < p < 1$, such that the GA and CC protocol require r_1 and r_2 rounds of communication respectively over the point-to-point channels respectively. The framework then outputs a *t-secure* bit-BA protocol, which satisfies the properties of BA with a probability of at least $1-(1-\frac{p}{2})^k$, where k is the number of iterations in the protocol. The BA protocol is either unconditionally-secure or cryptographically-secure, depending upon the security level of the GA and CC. The protocol requires $k \cdot (2r_1+r_2)$ rounds of communication over the point-to-point channels and incurs a communication complexity of $\mathcal{BA}(1)$ bits where $\mathcal{BA}(1) = k \cdot (2\mathcal{GA}(1) + CC(1))$. Here $\mathcal{GA}(1)$ and $CC(1)$ denote the communication complexity of one instance of the GA and CC protocol, respectively.

We now have all the ingredients to instantiate the above framework with $t < \frac{n}{2}$. For GA, we use the protocol $\Pi^{(n,t)}_{\mathsf{GAHM}}$ (see Theorem 14.2), which requires $r_1 = 3$ rounds of communication and incurs a communication complexity of $\mathcal{GA}(L) = O(n^4(L+\kappa))$ bits for L-bit inputs. The CC protocol is instantiated with the protocol $\Pi^{(n,t)}_{\mathsf{CDDHRCC}}$ (see Theorem 14.5), which has a success probability of $p = 0.36$. The protocol requires

$r_2 = 27$ rounds of communication over the point-to-point channels and incurs a communication communication complexity of $CC(1) = O(n^7(\log|\mathbb{F}| + \kappa))$ bits. We then get a *t-secure* BA protocol with $t < \frac{n}{2}$ in the model $\mathcal{M}^{\mathsf{pki}}_{\mathsf{secure}}$, which satisfies the properties of BA with probability at least $1 - 0.82^k$. One can appropriately select the value of k to make this probability as close as possible to 1. The security of the BA will depend upon the type of security of the underlying PKI. The protocol will require $33k$ rounds of communication over the point-to-point channels and will incur a communication complexity of $O(kn^7(\log|\mathbb{F}| + \kappa))$ bits.

We summarize the above discussion in Theorem 14.6.

Theorem 14.6 *Let $t < \frac{n}{2}$. Then there exists a randomized protocol in the model $\mathcal{M}^{\mathsf{pki}}_{\mathsf{secure}}$ with the following properties.*

- *If the PKI is unconditionally-secure then the protocol is unconditionally-secure.*
- *If the PKI is cryptographically-secure then the protocol is cryptographically-secure.*
- *The protocol satisfies the properties of bit-BA with a probability of at least $1 - 0.82^k$, where k is a parameter to control the error probability.*
- *The protocol requires $33k$ rounds of communication over the point-to-point channels and incurs a communication complexity of $O(kn^7(\log|\mathbb{F}| + \kappa))$ bits where κ denotes the size of a signature in bits.*

14.8 Randomized BA with $t < \frac{n}{2}$ and a Non-fixed Number of Iterations

Note that the BA protocol summarized in Theorem 14.6 requires a *fixed* number of iterations k, even if consensus is achieved *earlier*, leading to wastage of iterations. A better approach would be to let the (honest) parties somehow "detect" that consensus is achieved and immediately exit the protocol without running for k iterations. As discussed in Chapter 8, this requires a very careful design approach since the exit of one (honest) party may affect the "progress" of other (honest) parties who may *not* have exited the protocol yet. For instance, in Chapter 8 we have seen how to make modifications in GA and CC protocols to allow "virtual" participation from the parties. Even if all honest parties do not participate in these protocol instances, it does not hamper the security properties of the "surviving" honest parties. Moreover, these modified primitives (GA and CC with virtual participation) were carefully tied together to get a randomized BA protocol with a *non-fixed* number of iterations. One can make similar modifications along the above line to the GA and CC protocols discussed in this chapter (with $t < \frac{n}{2}$) and tie them together carefully to get a BA protocol with $t < \frac{n}{2}$ and a non-fixed number of iterations. The resultant protocol will be an *almost-surely terminating* BA protocol (see the definition in Chapter 8) with a *constant* expected number of rounds. We leave the details as an exercise for the interested readers.

14.9 More Efficient Cryptographically-Secure Common Coin with $t < \frac{n}{2}$

Even though we have a CC protocol with a *constant* number of rounds and $t < \frac{n}{2}$ (namely protocol $\Pi^{(n,t)}_{\mathsf{CDDHRCC}}$), the constant is large (namely 27), which in turn affects the number of rounds of the resultant BA protocol. This section shows how to get a highly efficient, cryptographically-secure CC protocol, provided the parties have access to a threshold-signature scheme setup. The construction is in the *random oracle model* (ROM) and is attributed to [27]. We first briefly discuss the ROM and threshold signatures scheme in the sequel. We stress that our treatment for ROM and threshold signatures is *not* rigorous, and we only abstract out the key properties needed from them to understand the design of the CC protocol. We will refer interested readers to relevant resources for a more in-depth treatment of these concepts.

14.9.1 Random Oracle Model (ROM)

Real-world cryptographic hash functions such as SHA256 are believed to give random-looking output for each distinct input. For this, cryptographic hash functions are often treated as idealized objects called random oracles. A cryptographic hash function H is modelled as an oracle with the following properties in ROM. The oracle internally keeps a list H for bookkeeping purposes. Each entry in H is initially set to $\perp$. On being queried for input x from the domain of H, the oracle first checks if $\mathsf{H}[x] \neq \perp$. If this is true, it returns $\mathsf{H}[x]$. This ensures that H *does not* give multiple outputs for the same input. On the other hand if $\mathsf{H}[x] = \perp$, then the oracle selects a uniformly random value, say y, from the codomain of H, sets $\mathsf{H}[x] = y$ and returns y. This ensures that the response from the oracle is "consistent" and every time it is queried for an input x, its response will be the same.

The key property of the ROM is that if an input x from the domain of H has not been queried from the oracle, then the value of $\mathsf{H}(x)$ remains random. We refer the interested readers to [67] for a detailed formal description of the ROM. We stress that the real-world cryptographic hash functions are *deterministic* and *cannot* emulate a random oracle. Nevertheless, heuristically, we often pretend and treat them as random oracles. If any protocol is proven to be secure in the ROM, then we often replace the underlying random oracle with a concrete cryptographic hash function in practice and hope it is still secure. If this is not the case, then the flaw is not in the protocol's design but rather in the design of the concrete hash function, which is used to emulate the random oracle. Whether this heuristic is sound or not is debatable. However, it has been widely deployed in several contexts, and we have empirical evidence as to why this could be a good design heuristic.[5]

[5] For instance, one of the key concepts used in modern blockchain protocols is *proof-of-work*, which treats cryptographic hash functions like a random oracle.

14.9.2 Non-interactive Threshold Signatures (NTSIG) with Unique Signatures

Threshold signatures are a special type of digital signature that allows a "sufficiently large" set of signers to create a compact signature on a given message jointly. Typically $t + 1$ signers are required to create a signature, thus guaranteeing that it is computationally infeasible for up to t potentially corrupt signers to generate a signature on a message. The parameter t is often referred to as the threshold for the signature scheme. We are interested in threshold signature schemes with *unique signatures*, where the signature for each message is unique for a given message and a given public key; i.e. it *does not* matter which set of $t + 1$ signers collaborate to generate the signature, the resultant signature for a given message m will be the *same*. We now formally define an NTSIG scheme and the security properties required from the scheme. The current discussion is based on [73].

Definition 14.2 (Non-interactive Threshold Signature (NTSIG)) An NTSIG scheme is a collection of efficient algorithms TSIG.SetUp, TSIG.SignShare, TSIG.VerifyShare, TSIG.Combine and TSIG.VerifySignature with the following properties.

- TSIG.SetUp$(1^\kappa) \rightarrow (mpk, \mathbf{pk}, \mathbf{sk})$: the setup algorithm is a *randomized* algorithm, which outputs a *master public key* mpk, a vector $\mathbf{pk} = (pk_1, \ldots, pk_n)$ of *public-key shares* and a vector of $\mathbf{sk} = (sk_1, \ldots, sk_n)$ of *secret-key shares*, where sk_i is meant for party $P_i \in \mathcal{P}$.
- TSIG.SignShare$(m, sk_i) := \sigma_i$: the signature-share generation algorithm is a *deterministic* algorithm which takes input a message m for signing along with a secret-key share sk_i and outputs a *signature-share* σ_i.[6]
- TSIG.VerifyShare$(m, (P_i, \sigma_i)) := b \in \{0, 1\}$: the signature-share verification algorithm is a *deterministic* algorithm which takes input a message m and a signature-share σ_i (supposedly generated by P_i), along with *implicit* inputs mpk and $\mathbf{pk}$. The algorithm outputs 0 (reject) or 1 (accept).
- TSIG.Combine$(m, \{(P_i, \sigma_i)\}_{P_i \in S}) := \sigma/\perp$: the signature-share combine algorithm is a *deterministic* algorithm which takes input a message m for signature and a set of signature-shares corresponding to the parties in a set S where $|S| = t + 1$, along with implicit inputs mpk and $\mathbf{pk}$. The algorithm either outputs a signature σ on m or $\perp$.[7]
- TSIG.VerifySignature$(m, \sigma) := b \in \{0, 1\}$: the signature-verification algorithm is a *deterministic* algorithm which takes input a message m and an "aggregated" full signature σ, along with implicit inputs mpk and $\mathbf{pk}$. The algorithm outputs 0 (reject) or 1 (accept).

The security properties required from a NTSIG scheme are that of *correctness, unforgeability* and *uniqueness of signature*.

- **Correctness**: There are *two* requirements as part of the correctness property. The first requirement is that any signature-share which is generated "legitimately" when later verified, should always be accepted. The following should hold for

[6] One can interpret σ_i as a "partial signature" on m.

[7] One can interpret σ as the "full" signature on m.

$\forall m$ and $\forall P_i \in \mathcal{P}$, where the probability is over the randomness used inside the algorithm TSIG.SetUp.

$$\Pr\Big(\text{TSIG.VerifyShare}(m, (P_i, \sigma_i)) = 1 | \sigma_i = \text{TSIG.SignShare}(m, sk_i)\Big) = 1.$$

The second requirement of the correctness property is that any full signature that is "legitimately" generated when later verified should always be accepted. That is, the following should hold for $\forall m$ and $\forall S \subset \mathcal{P}$ with $|S| = t + 1$, where the probability is over the randomness used inside the algorithm TSIG.SetUp.

$$\Pr\Big(\text{TSIG.VerifySignature}(m, \sigma) = 1 | \forall P_i \in S, \text{TSIG.SignShare}(m, sk_i) = \sigma_i \text{ and } \sigma = \text{TSIG.Combine}(m, \{(P_i, \sigma_i)\}_{P_i \in S})\Big) = 1.$$

- **Unforgeability**: The property demands that any PPT adversary that corrupts up to f parties and can get signature-shares on any message $m^\star$ from up to f' honest parties where $f + f' \leq t$ can produce a valid full signature on $m^\star$ only with a negligible probability in κ.[8] This property can be formalized using the threshold version of the chosen-message game as formulated in [72].
- **Uniqueness of Signature**: there are two requirements as part of this property. The first requirement is that it *does not* matter which set of $t + 1$ valid signature-shares are used to get a full signature on a message; the resultant full signature will be the *same*.[9] That is, for $\forall m$ and for $\forall A, B \subset \mathcal{P}$ where $|A| = |B| = t + 1$, the condition $\sigma = \sigma'$ holds, where σ and σ' satisfy the following conditions.

$$\forall P_i \in A, \text{TSIG.SignShare}(m, sk_i) = \sigma_i \text{ and } \sigma = \text{TSIG.Combine}(m, \{(P_i, \sigma_i)\}_{P_i \in A}.$$

$$\forall P_j \in B, \text{TSIG.SignShare}(m, sk_j) = \sigma'_j \text{ and } \sigma' = \text{TSIG.Combine}(m, \{(P_j, \sigma'_j)\}_{P_i \in B}.$$

The second requirement of the property is that each message has a unique full signature under any public key. That is, for every mpk, **pk** and every pair of messages m, m' where $m \neq m'$, the following holds.

$$\text{If TSIG.VerifySignature}(m, \sigma) = 1 \text{ and TSIG.VerifySignature}(m', \sigma') = 1 \text{ then } \sigma \neq \sigma'.$$

[8] Hence a full signature on $m^\star$ will be random from the point of view of the adversary if *less than* $t + 1$ signature-shares are available on $m^\star$.

[9] This ensures that the adversary *cannot* "control" the full signature on any message by sending or withholding particular signature-shares.

We will assume the existence of an NTSIG scheme where each signature-share σ_i and each full signature σ is of size $O(\kappa)$ bits. There are several well-known standard instantiations of an NTSIG scheme with the above properties (see, for instance, [27, 72, 15]).

14.9.3 Cryptographically Secure Common Coin in the Random Oracle Model

Given the setup of an NTSIG scheme, the parties can use the following simple approach to generate an unpredictable and unbiased coin $b \in \{0, 1\}$. Each party P_i creates a signature-share σ_i for some predetermined message m and sends σ_i to all the parties.[10] Once a party gets $t + 1$ valid signature-shares for m, it combines them to get a full signature σ on m. Finally once the full signature σ is computed, the parties can set $\mathsf{LSB}(\mathsf{H}(\sigma))$ as the output b, where LSB denotes the least significant bit, and H is a cryptographic hash function modelled as a random oracle.

The *liveness* is guaranteed if $t < \frac{n}{2}$, since there will be at least $t + 1$ *honest* parties who will generate and send valid signature-shares. So even if the corrupt parties do not send any signature-shares or send invalid signature-shares, the honest parties will be able to generate σ and compute the output b. The uniqueness of the signature guarantees that all the honest parties *agree* on the signature σ and hence on the same output b. The uniqueness of the signature also guarantees that an adversary *cannot* bias the outcome b by sending or withholding the particular signature-shares. The bit b remains unpredictable to an adversary controlling up to t parties until the point where the first honest party P_i sends its signature-share σ_i. This is because until any honest party participates in the CC protocol, the signature σ remains random from the adversary's point of view and hence $\mathsf{H}(\sigma)$ also remains random for the adversary. This also implies that the bit b can take value 0 or 1 with probability $\frac{1}{2}$. It is easy to see that the protocol requires 1 round of communication and incurs a communication complexity of $O(n^2\kappa)$ bits.

Even though the protocol is straightforward, for completeness, we present it in Fig 14.4. The protocol is designed in the model $\mathcal{M}_{\mathsf{secure}}$, assuming that a setup for an NTSIG is already available to the protocol participants. This means that some *trusted third party* executes the algorithm TSIG.SetUp and distributes the public and private parameters to the respective parties.

Protocol $\Pi^{(n,t)}_{\mathsf{CryptoCC}}(m)$

Setup assumption: there exists some trusted third party who executes $\mathsf{TSIG.SetUp}(1^\kappa)$ and generates the output $(mpk, \mathbf{pk}, \mathbf{sk})$ where $\mathbf{pk} = (pk_1, \ldots, pk_n)$ and $\mathbf{sk} = (sk_1, \ldots, sk_n)$. The party also makes public mpk and $\mathbf{pk}$ and distributes sk_i to party P_i, for $i = 1, \ldots, n$.

- **Round 1 (exchanging the signature-shares)**: do the following.
  - Compute $\mathsf{TSIG.SignShare}(m, sk_i) := \sigma_i$ and send σ_i to every party in $\mathcal{P}$.

[10] Looking ahead, one can set m to the iteration number when the protocol is used along with a GA protocol to get a randomized BA protocol with a constant number of iterations.

- **(Output computation and termination)**: do the following.
  - Include P_j to a set $\mathcal{S}_i$ (initialized to $\emptyset$), if σ_j is received from P_j and $\mathsf{TSIG.VerifyShare}(m, (P_j, \sigma_j)) := 1$.
  - Compute $\mathsf{TSIG.Combine}(m, \{(P_j, \sigma_j)\}_{P_j \in \mathcal{S}_i}) := \sigma$.[a]
  - Output b where $b := \mathsf{H}(\sigma)$ and terminate.

[a] If $|\mathcal{S}_i| > t + 1$ then take the (P_j, σ_j) tuples of only the first $t + 1$ parties in $\mathcal{S}_i$.

Fig. 14.4: An efficient cryptographically-secure CC protocol using a non-interactive threshold signature scheme in the random oracle model. The above code is executed by every party $P_i \in \mathcal{P}$

The properties of the protocol $\Pi^{(n,t)}_{\mathsf{CryptoCC}}$ are stated in Theorem 14.7, which follows easily from the above discussion.

Theorem 14.7 *Let the parties have access to a trusted setup of an NTSIG scheme and let m be some predetermined public input for the protocol $\Pi^{(n,t)}_{\mathsf{CryptoCC}}$. Moreover, let the parties have access to a cryptographically-secure hash function* H *modelled as a random oracle. If $t < \frac{n}{2}$ and if the underlying adversary is computationally bounded, then the protocol is a t-secure $\frac{1}{2}$-CC protocol in the model $\mathcal{M}_{\mathsf{secure}}$. The protocol requires one round of communication and incurs a communication of $O(n^2\kappa)$ bits.*

14.10 Concluding Remarks

In this chapter, we showed that given a PKI setup, one can design a randomized protocol with a constant number of rounds, which satisfies the properties of BA with a high probability in an honest-majority setting. One can design an almost-surely terminating BA protocol in this setting, which requires a constant expected running time. Designing BA protocols with a strict honest majority and a constant expected running time is a very exciting area of research. We refer the interested readers to [5, 11] for further details.

References

1. Decentralized Thoughts. `https://decentralizedthoughts.github.io/`.
2. I. Abraham, G. Asharov, S. Patil, and A. Patra. Asymptotically Free Broadcast in Constant Expected Time via Packed VSS. In *TCC*, volume 13747 of *Lecture Notes in Computer Science*, pages 384–414. Springer, 2022.
3. I. Abraham, N. Ben-David, and S. Yandamuri. Efficient and Adaptively Secure Asynchronous Binary Agreement via Binding Crusader Agreement. In *PODC*, pages 381–391. ACM, 2022.
4. I. Abraham, T.-H. Hubert Chan, D. Dolev, K. Nayak, R. Pass, L. Ren, and E. Shi. Communication Complexity of Byzantine Agreement, Revisited. *Distributed Comput.*, 36(1):3–28, 2023.
5. I. Abraham, S. Devadas, D. Dolev, K. Nayak, and L. Ren. Synchronous Byzantine Agreement with Expected O(1) Rounds, Expected $O(n^2)$ Communication, and Optimal Resilience. In *Financial Cryptography and Data Security - 23rd International Conference, FC 2019, Frigate Bay, St. Kitts and Nevis, February 18-22, 2019, Revised Selected Papers*, volume 11598 of *Lecture Notes in Computer Science*, pages 320–334. Springer, 2019.
6. I. Abraham, D. Dolev, and J. Y. Halpern. An Almost-Surely Terminating Polynomial Protocol for Asynchronous Byzantine Agreement with Optimal Resilience. In *PODC*, pages 405–414. ACM, 2008.
7. M. K. Aguilera and S. Toueg. A Simple Bivalency Proof that t-Resilient Consensus Requires $t + 1$ Rounds. *Inf. Process. Lett.*, 71(3-4):155–158, 1999.
8. M. Andrychowicz and S. Dziembowski. PoW-Based Distributed Cryptography with No Trusted Setup. In *CRYPTO*, volume 9216 of *Lecture Notes in Computer Science*, pages 379–399. Springer, 2015.
9. A. Appan, A. Chandramouli, and A. Choudhury. Network Agnostic Perfectly Secure MPC Against General Adversaries. In *DISC*, volume 281 of *LIPIcs*, pages 3:1–3:19. Schloss Dagstuhl - Leibniz-Zentrum für Informatik, 2023.
10. A. Appan, A. Chandramouli, and A. Choudhury. Perfectly-Secure Synchronous MPC With Asynchronous Fallback Guarantees. *IEEE Trans. Inf. Theory*, 69(8):5386–5425, 2023.
11. G. Asharov and A. Chandramouli. Perfect (Parallel) Broadcast in Constant Expected Rounds via Statistical VSS. In *EUROCRYPT*, volume 14655 of *Lecture Notes in Computer Science*, pages 310–339. Springer, 2024.
12. G. Asharov and Y. Lindell. A Full Proof of the BGW Protocol for Perfectly Secure Multiparty Computation. *J. Cryptol.*, 30(1):58–151, 2017.
13. H. Attiya and J. L. Welch. *Distributed Computing - Fundamentals, Simulations, and Advanced Topics (2. ed.)*. Wiley series on parallel and distributed computing. Wiley, 2004.
14. b. Applebaum, E. Kachlon, and A. Patra. The Round Complexity of Perfect MPC with Active Security and Optimal Resiliency. In *FOCS*, pages 1277–1284. IEEE, 2020.
15. R. Bacho and J. Loss. On the Adaptive Security of the Threshold BLS Signature Scheme. In *CCS*, pages 193–207. ACM, 2022.
16. L. Bangalore, A. Choudhury, and A. Patra. The Power of Shunning: Efficient Asynchronous Byzantine Agreement Revisited. *J. ACM*, 67(3):14:1–14:59, 2020.
17. N. Baric and B. Pfitzmann. Collision-Free Accumulators and Fail-Stop Signature Schemes Without Trees. In *EUROCRYPT*, volume 1233 of *Lecture Notes in Computer Science*, pages 480–494. Springer, 1997.
18. Z. Beerliová-Trubíniová and M. Hirt. Efficient Multi-party Computation with Dispute Control. In *TCC*, volume 3876 of *Lecture Notes in Computer Science*, pages 305–328. Springer, 2006.
19. M. Ben-Or. Another Advantage of Free Choice: Completely Asynchronous Agreement Protocols (Extended Abstract). In *PODC*, pages 27–30. ACM, 1983.
20. M. Ben-Or, R. Canetti, and O. Goldreich. Asynchronous Secure Computation. In *STOC*, pages 52–61. ACM, 1993.
21. M. Ben-Or, S. Goldwasser, and A. Wigderson. Completeness Theorems for Non-Cryptographic Fault-Tolerant Distributed Computation (Extended Abstract). In *STOC*, pages 1–10. ACM, 1988.

22. P. Berman and J. A. Garay. Cloture Votes: n/4-Resilient Distributed Consensus in $t+1$ Rounds. *Math. Syst. Theory*, 26(1):3–19, 1993.
23. P. Berman, J. A. Garay, and K. J. Perry. Towards Optimal Distributed Consensus (Extended Abstract). In *FOCS*, pages 410–415. IEEE Computer Society, 1989.
24. N. L. Biggs. *Discrete Mathematics*. Oxford University Press, 2002.
25. E. Blum, J. Katz, and J. Loss. Synchronous Consensus with Optimal Asynchronous Fallback Guarantees. In *Theory of Cryptography (TCC)*, volume 11891 of *Lecture Notes in Computer Science*, pages 131–150. Springer, 2019.
26. D. Boneh, C. Gentry, B. Lynn, and H. Shacham. Aggregate and Verifiably Encrypted Signatures from Bilinear Maps. In *EUROCRYPT*, volume 2656 of *Lecture Notes in Computer Science*, pages 416–432. Springer, 2003.
27. C. Cachin, K. Kursawe, and V. Shoup. Random Oracles in Constantinople: Practical Asynchronous Byzantine Agreement Using Cryptography. *J. Cryptol.*, 18(3):219–246, 2005.
28. L. Carter and M. N. Wegman. Universal Classes of Hash Functions. *J. Comput. Syst. Sci.*, 18(2):143–154, 1979.
29. A. Chandramouli, A. Choudhury, and A. Patra. A Survey on Perfectly Secure Verifiable Secret-sharing. *ACM Comput. Surv.*, 54(11s):232:1–232:36, 2022.
30. D. Chaum, C. Crépeau, and I. Damgård. Multiparty Unconditionally Secure Protocols (Extended Abstract). In *STOC*, pages 11–19. ACM, 1988.
31. D. Chaum and S. Roijakkers. Unconditionally Secure Digital Signatures. In *CRYPTO*, volume 537 of *Lecture Notes in Computer Science*, pages 206–214. Springer, 1990.
32. W. Chongchitmate and R. Ostrovsky. Information-Theoretic Broadcast with Dishonest Majority for Long Messages. In *TCC*, volume 11239 of *Lecture Notes in Computer Science*, pages 370–388. Springer, 2018.
33. B. Chor, S. Goldwasser, S. Micali, and B. Awerbuch. Verifiable Secret Sharing and Achieving Simultaneity in the Presence of Faults (Extended Abstract). In *FOCS*, pages 383–395. IEEE Computer Society, 1985.
34. A. Choudhury. Protocols for Reliable and Secure Message Transmission. *IACR Cryptol. ePrint Arch.*, page 281, 2010.
35. A. Choudhury and A. Patra. *Secure Multi-Party Computation Against Passive Adversaries*. Synthesis Lectures on Distributed Computing Theory. Springer Cham, 2023. `https://doi.org/10.1007/978-3-031-12164-7`.
36. Ashish Choudhury. Almost-surely Terminating Asynchronous Byzantine Agreement against General Adversaries with Optimal Resilience. *Theoretical Computer Science*, 995:114492, 2024.
37. S. A. Cook. The Complexity of Theorem-Proving Procedures. In *STOC*, pages 151–158. ACM, 1971.
38. R. Cramer, I. Damgård, S. Dziembowski, M. Hirt, and T. Rabin. Efficient Multiparty Computations Secure Against an Adaptive Adversary. In *EUROCRYPT*, volume 1592 of *Lecture Notes in Computer Science*, pages 311–326. Springer, 1999.
39. G. Deligios and M. Mizrahi Erbes. Closing the Efficiency Gap Between Synchronous and Network-Agnostic Consensus. In *Advances in Cryptology - EUROCRYPT 2024 - 43rd Annual International Conference on the Theory and Applications of Cryptographic Techniques, Zurich, Switzerland, May 26-30, 2024, Proceedings, Part V*, volume 14655 of *Lecture Notes in Computer Science*, pages 432–461. Springer, 2024.
40. G. Deligios, M. Hirt, and C. Liu-Zhang. Round-Efficient Byzantine Agreement and Multi-party Computation with Asynchronous Fallback. In *TCC*, volume 13042 of *Lecture Notes in Computer Science*, pages 623–653. Springer, 2021.
41. D. Derler, C. Hanser, and D. Slamanig. Revisiting Cryptographic Accumulators, Additional Properties and Relations to Other Primitives. In *CT-RSA*, volume 9048 of *Lecture Notes in Computer Science*, pages 127–144. Springer, 2015.
42. W. Diffie and M. E. Hellman. New Directions in Cryptography. *IEEE Trans. Inf. Theory*, 22(6):644–654, 1976.
43. D. Dolev. The Byzantine Generals Strike Again. *J. Algorithms*, 3(1):14–30, 1982.

44. D. Dolev, C. Dwork, O. Waarts, and M. Yung. Perfectly Secure Message Transmission. *J. ACM*, 40(1):17–47, 1993.
45. D. Dolev and R. Reischuk. Bounds on Information Exchange for Byzantine Agreement. *J. ACM*, 32(1):191–204, 1985.
46. D. Dolev and H. R. Strong. Authenticated Algorithms for Byzantine Agreement. *SIAM J. Comput.*, 12(4):656–666, 1983.
47. C. Dwork, N. A. Lynch, and L. J. Stockmeyer. Consensus in the Presence of Partial Synchrony. *J. ACM*, 35(2):288–323, 1988.
48. P. Feldman and S. Micali. An Optimal Probabilistic Protocol for Synchronous Byzantine Agreement. *SIAM J. Comput.*, 26(4):873–933, 1997.
49. M. J. Fischer, N. A. Lynch, and M. Merritt. Easy Impossibility Proofs for Distributed Consensus Problems. In *PODC*, pages 59–70. ACM, 1985.
50. M. J. Fischer, N. A. Lynch, and M. Paterson. Impossibility of Distributed Consensus with One Faulty Process. *J. ACM*, 32(2):374–382, 1985.
51. M. Fitzi. *Generalized communication and security models in Byzantine agreement*. PhD thesis, ETH Zurich, Zürich, Switzerland, 2003.
52. M. Fitzi, J. A. Garay, S. Gollakota, C. Pandu Rangan, and K. Srinathan. Round-Optimal and Efficient Verifiable Secret Sharing. In *TCC*, volume 3876 of *Lecture Notes in Computer Science*, pages 329–342. Springer, 2006.
53. M Fitzi and M. Hirt. Optimally Efficient Multi-Valued Byzantine Agreement. In *PODC*, pages 163–168. ACM, 2006.
54. M. Fitzi and U. M. Maurer. Efficient Byzantine Agreement Secure Against General Adversaries. In *DISC*, volume 1499 of *Lecture Notes in Computer Science*, pages 134–148. Springer, 1998.
55. C. Ganesh and A. Patra. Optimal Extension Protocols for Byzantine Broadcast and Agreement. *Distributed Comput.*, 34(1):59–77, 2021.
56. J. A. Garay, A. Kiayias, N. Leonardos, and G. Panagiotakos. Bootstrapping the Blockchain, with Applications to Consensus and Fast PKI Setup. In *PKC*, volume 10770 of *Lecture Notes in Computer Science*, pages 465–495. Springer, 2018.
57. R. Gennaro, Y. Ishai, E. Kushilevitz, and T. Rabin. The Round Complexity of Verifiable Secret Sharing and Secure Multicast. In *STOC*, pages 580–589. ACM, 2001.
58. D. Ghinea, V. Goyal, and C. Liu-Zhang. Round-Optimal Byzantine Agreement. In *EUROCRYPT*, volume 13275 of *Lecture Notes in Computer Science*, pages 96–119. Springer, 2022.
59. O. Goldreich, S. Micali, and A. Wigderson. How to Play any Mental Game or A Completeness Theorem for Protocols with Honest Majority. In A. V. Aho, editor, *Proceedings of the 19th Annual ACM Symposium on Theory of Computing, 1987, New York, New York, USA*, pages 218–229. ACM, 1987.
60. M. Hirt. *Multi Party Computation: Efficient Protocols, General Adversaries, and Voting*. PhD thesis, ETH Zurich, Zürich, Switzerland, 2001.
61. M. Hirt and U. M. Maurer. Complete Characterization of Adversaries Tolerable in Secure Multi-Party Computation (Extended Abstract). In *PODC*, pages 25–34. ACM, 1997.
62. M. Hirt and P. Raykov. Multi-valued Byzantine Broadcast: The t < n Case. In *ASIACRYPT*, volume 8874 of *Lecture Notes in Computer Science*, pages 448–465. Springer, 2014.
63. A. Karlin and A. C. Yao. Probabilistic Lower Bounds for Byzantine Agreement, 1984. Unpublished manuscript.
64. R. M. Karp. Reducibility Among Combinatorial Problems. In *Complexity of Computer Computations*, The IBM Research Symposia Series, pages 85–103. Plenum Press, New York, 1972.
65. J. Katz and C. Y. Koo. On Expected Constant-Round Protocols for Byzantine Agreement. *J. Comput. Syst. Sci.*, 75(2):91–112, 2009.
66. J. Katz, C. Y. Koo, and R. Kumaresan. Improving the Round Complexity of VSS in Point-to-Point Networks. *Inf. Comput.*, 207(8):889–899, 2009.
67. J. Katz and Y. Lindell. *Introduction to Modern Cryptography, Second Edition*. CRC Press, 2014.
68. J. Katz, A. Miller, and E. Shi. Pseudonymous Secure Computation from Time-Lock Puzzles. *IACR Cryptol. ePrint Arch.*, page 857, 2014.

69. L. Lamport and M. Fischer. Byzantine Generals and Transaction Commit Protocols. 1982.
70. L. Lamport, R. E. Shostak, and M. C. Pease. The Byzantine Generals Problem. *ACM Trans. Program. Lang. Syst.*, 4(3):382–401, 1982.
71. G. Liang and N. H. Vaidya. Error-Free Multi-Valued Consensus with Byzantine Failures. In *PODC*, pages 11–20. ACM, 2011.
72. B. Libert, M. Joye, and M. Yung. Born and Raised Distributively: Fully Distributed Non-Interactive Adaptively-Secure Threshold Signatures with Short Shares. *Theoretical Computer Science*, 645:1–24, Sep 2016.
73. Y. Lu, Z. Lu, Q. Tang, and G. Wang. Dumbo-MVBA: Optimal Multi-Valued Validated Asynchronous Byzantine Agreement, Revisited. In *PODC*, pages 129–138. ACM, 2020.
74. N. A. Lynch. *Distributed Algorithms*. Morgan Kaufmann, 1996.
75. F. J. MacWilliams and N. J. A Sloane. *The Theory of Error-Correcting Codes*. North-holland Publishing Company, 1978.
76. S. Nakamoto. Bitcoin: A Peer-to-Peer Electronic Cash System, 2009.
77. K. Nayak, L. Ren, E. Shi, N. H. Vaidya, and Z. Xiang. Improved Extension Protocols for Byzantine Broadcast and Agreement. In *DISC*, volume 179 of *LIPIcs*, pages 28:1–28:17. Schloss Dagstuhl - Leibniz-Zentrum für Informatik, 2020.
78. M. C. Pease, R. E. Shostak, and L. Lamport. Reaching Agreement in the Presence of Faults. *J. ACM*, 27(2):228–234, 1980.
79. B. Pfitzmann and M. Waidner. Unconditional Byzantine Agreement for any Number of Faulty Processors. In *STACS*, volume 577 of *Lecture Notes in Computer Science*, pages 339–350. Springer, 1992.
80. M. O. Rabin. Randomized Byzantine Generals. In *FOCS*, pages 403–409. IEEE Computer Society, 1983.
81. T. Rabin and M. Ben-Or. Verifiable Secret Sharing and Multiparty Protocols with Honest Majority (Extended Abstract). In *STOC*, pages 73–85. ACM, 1989.
82. R. L. Rivest, A. Shamir, and L. M. Adleman. A Method for Obtaining Digital Signatures and Public-Key Cryptosystems. *Commun. ACM*, 21(2):120–126, 1978.
83. C. Schnorr. Efficient Signature Generation by Smart Cards. *J. Cryptol.*, 4(3):161–174, 1991.
84. E. Shi. Foundations of Distributed Consensus and Blockchains, 2020. Available at `https://www.distributedconsensus.net`.
85. R. Turpin and B. A. Coan. Extending Binary Byzantine Agreement to Multivalued Byzantine Agreement. *Inf. Process. Lett.*, 18(2):73–76, 1984.
86. J. Wan, H. Xiao, S. Devadas, and E. Shi. Round-Efficient Byzantine Broadcast Under Strongly Adaptive and Majority Corruptions. In *TCC*, volume 12550 of *Lecture Notes in Computer Science*, pages 412–456. Springer, 2020.
87. D. B. West. *Introduction to Graph Theory*. Prentice Hall, 2000.
88. A. C. Yao. Protocols for Secure Computations (Extended Abstract). In *FOCS*, pages 160–164. IEEE Computer Society, 1982.

www.ingramcontent.com/pod-product-compliance
Lightning Source LLC
Chambersburg PA
CBHW080610070425
24688CB00002BB/25
* 9 7 8 3 0 3 1 8 0 4 5 9 5 *